♡ P9-APP-996

STRATEGIES FOR TEACHING STUDENTS WITH EMOTIONAL AND BEHAVIORAL DISORDERS

STRATEGIES FOR TEACHING STUDENTS WITH EMOTIONAL AND BEHAVIORAL DISORDERS

Ruth Lyn Meese

Longwood College

Brooks/Cole Publishing Company

I(T)P® An International Thomson Publishing Company

Pacific Grove • Albany • Bonn • Boston • Cincinnati • Detroit • London • Madrid • Melbourne
Mexico City • New York • Paris • San Francisco • Singapore • Tokyo • Toronto • Washington

Sponsoring Editor: *Vicki Knight*
Editorial Associate: *Lauri Banks-Ataide*
Marketing Team: *Carolyn Crockett, Romy Fineroff*
Production Coordinator: *Marjorie Z. Sanders*
Production: *Carol O'Connell,*
    Graphic World Production Services
Permissions Editor: *Catherine Gingras*
Interior Design: *Rita Naughton*

Cover Design: *E. Kelly Shoemaker*
Cover Photo: *Elizabeth Crews*
Art Editor: *Lisa Torri*
Photo Editor: *Robert J. Western*
Typesetting: *Graphic World, Inc.*
Cover Printing: *Lehigh Press Lithographers*
Printing and Binding: *Quebecor Printing/Fairfield*

For more information, contact:

BROOKS/COLE PUBLISHING COMPANY
511 Forest Lodge Road
Pacific Grove, CA 93950
USA

International Thomson Publishing Europe
Berkshire House 168-173
High Holborn
London WC1V 7AA
England

Thomas Nelson Australia
102 Dodds Street
South Melbourne, 3205
Victoria, Australia

Nelson Canada
1120 Birchmount Road
Scarborough, Ontario
Canada M1K 5G4

International Thomson Editores
Campos Eliseos 385, Piso 7
Col. Polanco
11560 México D. F. México

International Thomson Publishing GmbH
Königswinterer Strasse 418
53227 Bonn
Germany

International Thomson Publishing Asia
221 Henderson Road
#05-10 Henderson Building
Singapore 0315

International Thomson Publishing Japan
Hirakawacho Kyowa Building, 3F
2-2-1 Hirakawacho
Chiyoda-ku, Tokyo 102
Japan

Printed in the United States of America

10 9 8 7 6 5 4 3 2 1

Library of Congress Cataloging-in-Publication Data

Meese, Ruth Lyn.
    Strategies for teaching students with emotional and behavioral
disorders / Ruth Lyn Meese.
        p.   cm.
    Includes bibliographical references and indexes.
    ISBN 0-534-24288-X
    1. Problem children—Education—United States.   2. Mentally ill
children—Education—United States.   3. Learning disabled children—
Education—United States.   4. Behavior disorders in children—
United States.   5. Behavior modification—United States.
I. Title.
LC4802.M44 1996
371.93′0973—dc20
                                                    95-42261
                                                    CIP

Ruth Lyn Meese, Ph.D., has taught students with learning disabilities and emotional and behavioral disorders across the grade levels in the public schools. She received her doctorate in special education from the University of Virginia in 1986. She is presently an associate professor of special education and the area coordinator for special education programs at Longwood College where she teaches both undergraduate and graduate courses in special education and serves as a consultant to local school districts. She is the author of *Teaching Learners with Mild Disabilities: Integrating Research and Practice* published by Brooks/Cole in 1994. She resides in Powhatan, Virginia, with her husband Jim, stepsons Tim and Scott, and two cats Shawnee and Ginny.

To my mother, Ruth Morton Meese, and my dad, Billie Getson Meese, who taught me to be responsible and to feel good about myself and, as always, to my husband and best friend, James W. Windle, who is my constant source of encouragement and support.

I began my career as a teacher of students with learning and behavioral problems convinced that the only "true" methods for managing student behavior were those I had learned in my applied behavior analysis class. The methods worked quite well with my younger students, but, needless to say, I became quite dismayed when one of my high schoolers reacted to my praise and point system with "Screw you. I don't give a shit about your points or about what you think." I didn't know how to respond to this student's challenging behavior because I had no other tools at my fingertips.

I am still a firm believer in the techniques of applied behavior analysis. Yet, I believe that other philosophies of classroom management offer many additional effective methods for handling the troubling behaviors of today's children and youth. All too often we teacher educators limit our students by discounting certain theories that hold less appeal for us or by teaching only a few selected behavior management interventions. In addition, textbooks often present only one philosophical orientation regarding behavior management or present many different models without offering teachers a means for choosing strategies from among these models. Contemporary teachers, however, face complex societal problems and more challenging behaviors than ever before. Such complexity dictates multiple approaches to problems and the integration of theories and techniques from differing perspectives. No longer can teachers function with only a limited repertoire of behavior management skills.

This textbook, then, presents a framework for teachers to integrate the major schools of thought regarding student behavior into a unified and personal philosophy of classroom management. No doubt many of my colleagues will find fault with my inclusion of certain theories and techniques; with my categorization of major conceptual models as supportive, directive, or responsibility oriented; or with the similarities I believe exist among seemingly different philosophies in actual practice. The framework is intended only as a starting point for discussion and reflection. I hope professionals will use the integrated framework presented to examine student behavior in new ways. To quote Marcel Proust, "The real voyage of discovery consists not in seeking new landscapes, but in having new eyes."

This text is primarily intended for preservice and inservice teachers of students with mild to moderate emotional and behavioral disorders at either the undergraduate or graduate level. Because many students with learning disabilities also exhibit behavioral problems, however, the text is equally appropriate for teachers of these students. In addition, the regular classroom teacher is being called upon to serve an increasingly diverse student population including children and youth who are "at risk" as well as those with learning and behavioral problems. Too, students with emotional and behavioral disorders are frequently placed into the regular classroom for at least a portion of the school day. The preservice or inservice classroom teacher, therefore, will also benefit from learning a variety of ways to manage student behavior.

The text's 12 chapters are organized into three major sections. Part One, Foundations, contains four chapters, giving the teacher background information for understanding later sections of the textbook. In Chapter 1, teachers explore the major characteristics of students with emotional and behavioral disorders as well as several societal factors related to behavioral disorders among children and adolescents. Chapter 2 presents methods for assessing students with emotional and behavioral disorders. Chapter 3 discusses expectations and interactions of parents, teachers, and others—important factors influencing a teacher's decisions about students and their behaviors. Chapter 4, the final chapter in Part One, presents the integrated framework for decision making used throughout the remainder of the text.

Part Two, Practice, consists of five "methods" chapters. Chapter 5 explores ways to build a positive classroom environment and teach students academic skills. Chapter 6 focuses on the supportive model and offers teachers strategies for respecting the feelings of students and for attending to affective factors in the classroom. Chapters 7 and 8 describe interventions within the directive model for improving behavior and teaching social skills. Chapter 9 contains methods for teaching students responsibility, and Chapter 10 suggests techniques to help teachers collaborate with others in and out of the school setting.

In Part Three, Reflections, teachers are encouraged to think about questions and concerns that arise as they interact with their students. Chapter 11 examines issues affecting teachers in schools today such as violence, gangs, student suicide, suspension and expulsion of students with disabilities, and the provision of services to children and youth under Section 504. Finally, in Chapter 12 the teacher explores ways to lessen stress, prevent burnout, and experience a heightened sense of teaching self-efficacy. Professional responsibility and the development of a personal philosophy of behavior management close this last chapter.

Resources and organizations disseminating additional information, as well as reproducible reinforcers, are contained in the appendices. Throughout the text I have closed each chapter with application exercises, and I have included numerous boxes containing case studies, or "teacher features." These application activities and boxes are designed to foster student in-class discussion and to make connections for students by making what they read in the text relevant to their lives today.

Acknowledgment

I would like to acknowledge the many people who have helped to make this textbook a reality. Several of my colleagues were particularly supportive.

Dr. Frank Howe listened to my many "ravings" and asked numerous thought-provoking questions as I developed my integrated framework for this text. Drs. Patty Whitfield, Bob Gibbons, and Betty Jo Simmons gave me the faith and encouragement needed to pursue a project of this magnitude. My graduate assistants for the last 2 years, Meyon Puent and Christina Galloway, have devoted endless hours to locating references, obtaining permissions, and verifying addresses of organizations and resources. My students, both preservice and inservice teachers of students with emotional and behavioral disorders, also contributed to the development of this text through their many comments and questions during our classes and field work.

Vicki Knight, my sponsoring editor at Brooks/Cole, gave of her precious time to offer her usual good advice and encouraging words. She certainly knows how to give praise as well as effective feedback. Finally, the following reviewers helped significantly to shape this text through their thoughtful comments and suggestions: Ron Alexander, University of Texas at San Antonio; Jerome J. Ammer, University of San Diego; Carol Burdett, University of Vermont; Frances H. Courson, College of Charleston; Donald Doorlag, San Diego State University; Paula M. Gardner; Karen R. Harris, University of Maryland; James T. Jackson, Southern Illinois University; Asha Jitendra, Lehigh University; John Maag, University of Nebraska; and Ellen Marshall, San Antonio College. To each of you, and to the many others who have contributed to the production of this text, I extend a sincere thank you.

Ruth Lyn Meese

PART ONE

FOUNDATIONS

Students with emotional and behavioral disorders can easily challenge the patience of their best teachers. Such constant challenges may contribute to a teacher's feelings of stress and to a reduced sense of joy and competence in the classroom. To prevent these negative outcomes, teachers must understand the nature of children and youth with emotional and behavioral disorders and the many complex factors and interactions that determine both student and teacher behaviors.

In this first section, then, we will develop important understandings about students with behavioral disorders. In Chapter 1, we will explore the major characteristics of students with mild to moderate emotional and behavioral disorders, and we will examine societal factors related to behavioral disorders among today's children and adolescents. In Chapter 2, we will discuss methods for assessing students with emotional and behavioral disorders, and in Chapter 3, we will investigate important expectations and interactions of parents, teachers, and others that may influence decisions about students and their behaviors. Finally, in Chapter 4, we will focus on developing your own philosophy regarding the nature of students with behavior disorders, and we will introduce an integrated framework to facilitate your decisions when selecting intervention strategies.

CHAPTER 1

STUDENTS WITH EMOTIONAL AND BEHAVIORAL DISORDERS

Main Ideas

◆ *How the teacher views the problems of children and youth with emotional and behavioral disorders affects the teacher's responses to these problems.*

◆ *Common characteristics of children and adolescents with emotional and behavioral disorders include attention deficits, poor social skills, school failure, aggression, anxiety and withdrawal, and depression.*

◆ *These characteristics overlap and are also exhibited by many students not in programs for children and youth with emotional and behavioral disorders.*

◆ *Children and youth in today's schools are impacted by many interrelated societal factors, including poverty, abuse and neglect, homelessness, substance abuse and prenatal substance exposure, HIV/AIDS infection, juvenile delinquency, gang membership, and increased acts of violence.*

Teaching in today's schools is a challenging and demanding task. The children in our classrooms are quite diverse, yet all students need to feel safe, secure, and comfortable to learn. All students want to feel liked by their peers and successful at something. Most students will hope that their teachers care about them and that they are treated fairly.

Some students, however, challenge the resourcefulness of their teachers. They display behavioral problems that demand attention and that may easily consume a teacher's time and energy. In your classroom, for example, you may find students like the following:

- Paul is constantly angry and argumentative. He often makes negative comments to his peers or refuses to do the work you assign to him. Paul was abused by his stepfather when he was very young. He is now living in his third foster care home. Paul is easily provoked to fight over minor misunderstandings, and he doesn't trust his teachers, his peers, or his foster parents.
- Keesha is constantly on the move. She fidgets, squirms, and bounces in and out of her seat. Keesha can't seem to finish her work or pay attention to your instructions for more than a minute. She is distractible and distracting to those around her.
- Dante hangs out with members of a gang. He is often absent from school. Today, however, you are told that Dante is absent because he was rushed to the hospital last night with a gunshot wound. He was injured in a fight with a rival gang. Dante performs consistently below his peers on school-work when he does attend classes.
- Shelley has always had the best that her wealthy parents could buy. She is disrespectful to you and to her peers. She could do better work, but she says that everything "bores" her. When you caught her stealing a copy of an upcoming test and called her parents, she denied any wrongdoing. Her parents said the problem was your fault because you shouldn't have left the test in your desk drawer. You suspect that Shelley is under tremendous pressure to be "perfect" at home.
- Fong is painfully shy and withdrawn. When his peers try to draw him into their activities, he retreats by covering his face with his hands. Fong never smiles, and he often cries for no apparent reason. Lately, he has refused to come to school.

This book is about students like Paul, Keesha, Dante, Shelley, and Fong—children and youth with "mild" emotional or behavioral disorders. The problems experienced by these students and the difficulties they create for their teachers, parents, and peers, however, are anything but mild. The term *mild* is used only to differentiate children like Paul from students with more severe behavior disorders such as schizophrenia or other childhood psychoses.

As a teacher, particularly as a teacher of students with emotional and behavioral disorders, you will need to examine your own beliefs about student behavior. You must determine what you expect of your students, what you can tolerate, and whether or not you have cultural biases that predispose you to view certain student behaviors more negatively than others. You will need to be aware of what others expect from your students, and you must become competent with a range of strategies for meeting the social-emotional needs of the children in your care. In short, you must develop a philosophy about student behavior to guide you in making wise decisions in your classroom.

In the following chapters, you will be challenged to develop your own philosophy and to determine how you will respond to your students' problem behaviors. Begin by reading Box 1.1 (pp. 6–7) and reflecting on this teacher's personal viewpoint. You probably noticed when reading Box 1.1 that the students in Mr. Murray's school are considered seriously emotionally disturbed. The youth in this school are aggressive and assaultive. They fight and hurt others and themselves. You may also have noticed that these students were physically or sexually abused, born to substance-abusing parents, or placed in many different foster care homes. Certainly not all students with emotional or behavioral disorders have such traumatic events in their past. Certainly, too, many other students who are not considered to be seriously emotionally disturbed have experienced similar life histories. Are these students, like "Shredder," bad kids who fight all the time? Or, are these students behaving in the only way that makes sense to them because they feel they have no other choice? How you answer this question will, at least in part, determine how you will respond to the behavior of students like Mr. Murray's.

The following important assumptions guided the selection of material in this text:

- ◆ Behaviors occur in complex patterns of interaction. Teachers, parents, and students continuously affect one another's behavior.
- ◆ Behavior is purposeful. Students and teachers have intentions behind their actions, whether these are clearly articulated or not.
- ◆ Students and teachers are all unique individuals; therefore, there is no one "best" or "perfect" way to manage the behaviors of all students.
- ◆ Many students in special education programs for children with learning disabilities or mild mental retardation, and many students not receiving any special education services at all, exhibit behaviors requiring intervention strategies identical to those effective for students with emotional and behavioral disorders.

Let's begin by exploring some of the difficulties your students with emotional and behavioral disorders may experience. First, let's examine the common characteristics of students with emotional and behavioral disorders. Then we will discuss several societal factors that may increase the risk of emotional and behavioral problems and special education placement for children and youth in today's schools.

Common Characteristics of Students with Emotional and Behavioral Disorders

Students are placed in special education programs when they require specially designed instruction to meet their unique or unusual needs. According to recent reports to Congress, just under 1% of students ages 6 to 17 receive special education programs for emotional or behavioral disorders (U.S. Department of

Teacher Feature

I am a teacher. I work at a school. That is what I had always said to my daughter when she wanted to know what my job was. It was simply too difficult to describe to her what my job really is. . . . Perhaps I should try to explain. I work at a residential treatment center for seriously emotionally disturbed, aggressive and assaultive, older adolescents. . . . How do you explain to a five-year-old that there are some kids whose moms and dads don't want them? Or don't even know where they are anymore? That there are some kids who do mean things? Horrible things. They steal things from people. They hurt people. They rape people. They kill people. They hurt themselves. They try to kill themselves. It is so much easier just to tell her that I am a teacher. That I work at a school. But sometimes you have no choice, and you have to give a further explanation.

One afternoon, at school, where I am a teacher, we were walking a large and strong seventeen-year-old man-boy to the time-out room. He went somewhat willingly, or so we thought. Just before we left him there he punched the school director in the eye. Hard. Very hard. I stepped in to intervene. I had no better luck. At this point he was ahead two to nothing. While it is never pleasant to be punched in the face it is an occupational hazard that you accept when you come to work here. My nose hurt, but it wasn't a turning point in my life. I knew I would be back to work the next day. I was recounting this experience a couple of days later to a friend and my daughter overheard me. . . . I explained to her that some kids don't know how to behave right and at the school where I work it is our job to teach them. . . . She wasn't convinced. She asked, ''Are they like ninja turtles?''

Let me digress here for a minute. There may be some of you who are not familiar with Teenage Mutant Ninja Turtles. . . . They are superhero cartoon characters. They are named after renaissance artists. Their biggest foe is the ultimate bad guy, Shredder. Shredder does mean things. Horrible things. . . . In the end the ninja turtles always win, and make the world safe again.

Education, 1993). Authorities estimate, however, that between 6% and 10% of all children and youth in our schools experience significant and persistent emotional and behavioral problems requiring special education (Kauffman, 1993).

These students often exhibit overlapping academic and behavioral characteristics. See Box 1.2 (p. 8) for two current definitions of emotional and behavioral disorders. Among the most common characteristics of students with emotional and behavioral disorders are attentional deficits, poor social skills, school failure, aggression, anxiety and withdrawal, and depression.

Attentional Deficits

Students with emotional and behavioral disorders are often described by their teachers as distractible, hyperactive, or impulsive. Experts believe that focusing and maintaining attention is a significant problem for many children (Shaywitz

I told my daughter, "No, these boys are not like ninja turtles, they are more like Shredder." *Teenage Mutant Ninja Turtles* is a very moralistic show. The good guys always win. The bad guys always lose. . . . You always know who to root for. It is not like real life. I did not want to confuse her with thoughts like "sometimes the people who seem to be bad are really good and sometimes the people who seem to be good are really bad. . . ." Five year olds deserve to know who the good guys are and who the bad guys are. I guess we all do.

I feel bad that I told her the boys are like Shredder. Shredder fights all the time. When he isn't fighting he is making an evil plan. . . . The ninja turtles don't like to fight. But they are very, very good at it. They practice a lot, just in case. . . . But they only fight if they are backed up against the wall and they have no other choice. . . . I should have told her yes, the boys are like ninja turtles. That they only fight when they have no choice, or when they feel that they have no choice. I should have told her that Shredder had been doing mean things to them for many, many years, and that now the boys fight all the time because they think everybody is Shredder. They are confused ninja turtles. Because when Leonardo gets beaten up by his dad when he is only two; when Michelangelo lives in fifteen different foster homes in less than five years; when Donatello was born to a cocaine addicted mother; and when Raphael was raped by his stepfather, then left in an abandoned car by the side of the road, well, what you have is one mixed up bunch of turtles. Turtles that think they have to fight all the time. Turtles that often get mistaken for Shredder. Even by those of us who should know better. . . .

From "Working with Michelangelo" by A. Murray, *Beyond Behavior*, 4(1), 1992, p. 23. Copyright © 1992 by The Council for Exceptional Children. Reprinted with permission.

& Shaywitz, 1988). Students like Keesha, for example, find it difficult to pay attention to their teachers and classwork. Other children, like Paul, have trouble controlling their impulses. These children frequently find themselves at odds with their teachers and peers because they are unable to refrain from behaviors that detract from their learning or that are distracting and distressing to those around them. Children with extreme attention deficits may display obnoxious behaviors that provoke negative reactions from parents, teachers, and peers.

Deficits in attention may manifest through impulsivity and motoric activity beyond that normally expected for a child of a particular age *or* through sluggishness, disorganization, and withdrawal. Attentional deficits include attention deficit hyperactivity disorder predominantly hyperactive-impulsive type, attention deficit hyperactivity disorder predominantly inattentive type, and attention deficit hyperactivity disorder combined type (American Psychological Association, 1994).

BOX 1.2 **Definitions of Emotional and Behavioral Disorders**

In the rules and regulations accompanying IDEA, children with emotional and behavioral disorders are termed "seriously emotionally disturbed." According to the federal definition:

(i) The term means a condition exhibiting one or more of the following characteristics over a long period of time and to a marked extent, which adversely affects educational performance.

(A) An inability to learn that cannot be explained by intellectual, sensory, or health factors;

(B) An inability to build or maintain satisfactory relationships with peers and teachers;

(C) Inappropriate types of behavior or feelings under normal circumstances;

(D) A general pervasive mood of unhappiness or depression; or,

(E) A tendency to develop physical symptoms or fears associated with personal or school problems.

(ii) The term includes children who are schizophrenic. The term does not include children who are socially maladjusted unless it is determined that they are seriously emotionally disturbed. (IDEA, 1990)

For many years, professionals have debated the term "serious emotional disturbance" as well as the exclusion of children who are "socially maladjusted." In 1990, the National Mental Health and Special Education Coalition proposed a new definition for this group of children:

(i) The term emotional or behavioral disorder means a disability characterized by behavioral or emotional responses in school so different from appropriate age, cultural, or ethnic norms that they adversely affect educational performance. Educational performance includes academic, social, vocational, and personal skills. Such a disability

(A) Is more than a temporary, expected response to stressful events in the environment;

(B) Is consistently exhibited in two different settings, at least one of which is school-related; and,

(C) Is unresponsive to direct intervention in general education, or the child's condition is such that general education interventions would be insufficient.

(ii) Emotional and behavioral disorders can co-exist with other disabilities.

(iii) This category may include children or youth with schizophrenic disorders, affective disorders, anxiety disorder, or other sustained disorders of conduct or adjustment when they adversely affect educational performance in accordance with section (i). (Forness & Knitzer, 1992)

Students with attention deficit disorders primarily involving inattention may have trouble following through on instructions or paying attention over time. They appear not to listen, and they may not attend to details. These children may lose things easily, be forgetful or disorganized, and make many careless mistakes. Often, children with attention deficits "daydream," and they may be unmotivated to complete their schoolwork. A key component of this attention deficit hyperactivity disorder, then, is inattention (Barkley, DuPaul, & McMurray, 1990).

For children and youth with attention deficit hyperactivity disorder of the hyperactive-impulsive type, impulsivity and motoric activity are key indicators. These children may have trouble waiting their turn, and they may interrupt others or call out answers, questions, or comments during class time. They may demonstrate their difficulty working or playing quietly by fidgeting, squirming, frequently leaving their seat, or talking excessively. Sometimes teachers and parents describe these children as "driven" to move. Other students considered to have attention deficit hyperactivity disorder of the combined type may exhibit several characteristics of both inattention and hyperactivity-impulsivity.

Children with significant attentional deficits may qualify under the Individuals with Disabilities Education Act of 1990 (IDEA) for special education services for students with emotional and behavioral disorders or for students with learning disabilities or mental retardation. If they do not qualify for services under one of these categories, they may still qualify for special education as children with "other health impairments" if their school performance is adversely affected. Whether or not these students qualify for special education services, however, ADD and ADHD create academic difficulty and significant behavioral and social conflicts placing youngsters at risk for school failure (Moffitt, 1990; Wheeler & Carlson, 1994).

Many authorities now believe that attention deficit hyperactivity disorders present significant and lifelong difficulties for between 3% and 5% of the school-age population (DuPaul, Guevremont, & Barkley, 1991; Lahey & Carlson, 1991). The exact prevalence of attentional deficits among students with emotional and behavioral disorders is difficult to determine (Cohen, Riccio, & Gonzalez, 1994); however, among those students with attention deficit hyperactivity disorders who are receiving special education services, over half are identified as behaviorally disordered (Reid, Maag, Vasa, & Wright, 1994).

Poor Social Skills

Children and adolescents with emotional and behavioral disorders by definition have troublesome interpersonal relationships with peers and adults. Many of these students engage in frequent externalizing behaviors such as hitting, teasing, fighting, bullying, and noncompliance. Such acting-out, aggressive activities rarely endear children like Paul to peers or teachers. Moreover, children who are extremely withdrawn or immature (i.e., those who engage in internalizing behaviors) find themselves alone, like Fong, with few playmates and few social skills for finding and keeping new friends (Kauffman, 1993).

Whether students with emotional and behavioral disorders exhibit externalizing or internalizing behaviors, they are often rejected by peers and treated as social isolates (Sabornie, Kauffman, & Cullinan, 1990). For example, adolescents who cry easily or who make socially inappropriate comments are considered immature, annoying, or "uncool" by peers. Those who constantly lash out at others are avoided. These young people may not perceive the social clues exhibited by their peers through facial expressions or tone of voice regarding behavior considered appropriate, or inappropriate, for the situation. They may not recognize the feelings of others or understand the consequences of their actions. In addition, some students may be unable to take another's point of view or to determine the affect their behavior has on others.

Isolated and rejected children and youth lack the interpersonal behaviors developed naturally by their more socially skilled peers (Asher & Coie, 1990). Kauffman (1993) suggests that students with emotional and behavioral disorders fail to learn these skills through observation of others at home and at school. These students, therefore, require direct instruction in social skills if they are to engage in appropriate interactions with peers and adults.

School Failure

Children and adolescents with emotional and behavioral disorders do experience academic difficulties when compared with their same-age peers (Epstein, Kinder, & Bursuck, 1989; Luebke, Epstein, & Cullinan, 1989). According to Kauffman (1993), few students with emotional and behavioral disorders are academically advanced, and most perform below their same-age peers on standardized tests. Epstein, Kinder, and Bursuck (1989) report that these students often perform 1 year or more below grade level in most academic areas.

As children and youth with emotional and behavioral disorders increasingly fall behind their peers in both academic achievement and appropriate behavior, they may experience a poor self-concept and lowered self-esteem. Although not all students with behavioral disorders will have poor self-esteem, young people like Dante and Shelley who face daily academic and personal failure will not be as likely to form a positive self-concept or positive attachments to school as their more successful and popular peers (Seidel & Vaughn, 1991; Vaughn, 1991). Moreover, low academic achievement and social problems are likely to interact in complex ways (Kauffman, 1993). The student who exhibits numerous inappropriate behaviors is less likely to demonstrate acceptable academic achievement, and the child with low academic achievement is more likely to experience negative social consequences, which may promote additional misbehavior.

Imagine, for example, that day after day other children taunt you on the playground for your "weird" behaviors or call you a "dummy." Imagine, too, that day after day you try as hard as you can to do work that is seemingly easy for others to accomplish but that somehow eludes your understanding. After weeks, months, or years of these frustrating experiences, you might be likely to give up and to decide that school is not worth it. You might come to expect failure and to reduce your efforts to succeed, or you might start to skip school and find your friends "on the streets." You might seek attention and friendship by displaying inappropriate behaviors, or you might become depressed, saddened, and withdrawn. Feelings of academic and personal-social competence are essential to the development of a positive self-concept, a healthy self-esteem, and satisfactory school adjustment (McConaughy, 1986; Seidel & Vaughn, 1991; Whelan, de Saman, & Fortmeyer, 1988).

Adequate academic achievement and social competence are also related to adult outcomes for students with both externalizing and internalizing behavioral disorders. Aggression, anxiety and withdrawal, and depression in children are inextricably linked to the young person's sense of academic and personal success or failure.

Aggression

Low academic achievement alone does not portend adult failure. Many children who struggle to learn in school become adults who are successful in the workplace and in the home. When academic failure is combined with frequent and persistent aggressive and antisocial behaviors, however, the prognosis for successful adult outcomes is seriously reduced, particularly for boys (Loeber, 1982; Robins, 1979, 1986). Unfortunately, students with emotional and behavioral disorders like Paul often exhibit such conduct disorders.

Boys are three times more likely than girls to be identified with aggressive, acting-out conduct disorders (Kauffman, 1993). Conduct disordered boys who, from an early age, engage in numerous acts of overt aggression such as arguing, bullying, fighting, cruelty, and disobedience, both at school and at home, are at grave risk for problems in adulthood (Patterson, Reid, & Dishion, 1992). Those youngsters who are "versatile," engaging in both overt aggression as well as covert antisocial behaviors, such as stealing or lying, are even more likely to drop out of school or to commit criminal acts (Loeber & Schmaling, 1985; Walker, Steiber, Ramsey, & O'Neill, 1990). In fact, extremely aggressive, antisocial behavior is quite stable over time and predictive of later delinquency and adult criminality (Eron & Huesmann, 1990; Loeber, 1982; Loeber, Green, Lahey, Christ, & Frick, 1992; Walker, 1993; Walker, Shinn, O'Neill, & Ramsey, 1987).

Antisocial children are rejected by normal peers and tend to form deviant peer groups by the fourth or fifth grade (Coie & Kupersmidt, 1983; Walker, 1993; Walker, Colvin, & Ramsey, 1995). According to Patterson and his colleagues at the Oregon Social Learning Center, this deviant peer group gives antisocial boys a "support system" for their antisocial acts and teaches them essential skills for additional delinquent acts through modeling and reinforcement. Patterson, Reid, and Dishion (1992) assert that following acceptance into the deviant peer group, approximately 70% of antisocial boys have been arrested for a felony within 2 years.

Walker, Steiber, Ramsey, and O'Neill (1990) followed two groups of boys from the fifth through the tenth grades. Boys who engaged in moderate to high levels of antisocial acts in the fifth grade were more likely to have arrest records by grade ten than were boys from similar neighborhoods with high rates of police contacts but who exhibited only minimal levels of antisocial behavior in grade five. By the seventh grade, 21 of the 40 highly antisocial boys had already been arrested for a total of 68 offenses. Only three boys in the control group had been arrested, for a total of only three arrests. Walker and his colleagues maintain that teacher ratings of social skills, negative playground behaviors, and discipline contacts with the principal's office in the fifth grade are highly pre-

Boys who engage in frequent acts of overt aggression at home and at school are often rejected by peers and at risk for dropping out of school.

dictive of arrest records by tenth grade. Kazdin (1985) further suggests that without intensive and early intervention to change such antisocial behavior patterns before the end of the third grade, these behaviors will become chronic and persist into adulthood.

Patterson (1982, 1986) describes the development of antisocial behavior within families. He suggests that children who engage in irritating and difficult behaviors from birth may provoke increasingly punitive reactions from parents with few coping skills. These parents may demonstrate inconsistent or harsh disciplinary measures, sometimes ignoring the child's misbehavior and other times overreacting to the behavior, while offering only lax supervision and failing to reward the child for appropriate behaviors. Antisocial children tend to increase their inappropriate behaviors in response to punishment, escalating from whining or temper tantrums to physical assaults to avoid unpleasant parental demands or punishment. This behavior, in turn, precipitates ever more punitive, aversive, and controlling actions by parents to reduce the obnoxious behavior of the child. Parent and child are endlessly caught in a battle of negative reinforcement, each attempting to escape or avoid the unpleasant actions of the other.

According to Patterson (1982, 1986) these coercive family patterns increase steadily in number and intensity as the child continually engages the parents in negative, hostile, and counteraggressive interactions. Kauffman (1993) cautions teachers that similar coercive processes can easily develop in schools. Students with emotional and behavioral disorders may be particularly skilled in engaging their teachers ĩn such coercive interaction patterns.

> Among their peers and in interactions with teachers and administrators, students with conduct disorders may be caught in negative reinforcement traps. Educators (like parents) and classroom peers (like siblings) can become entangled in escalating contests of aversiveness, in which the individual who causes greater pain is the winner, obtaining negative reinforcement and digging in for the next round of conflict. (Kauffman, 1993, p. 235)

Anxiety and Withdrawal

Children and adolescents with emotional and behavioral disorders may also exhibit signs of anxiety or withdrawal. They may, for example, experience inappropriate fears and behaviors in circumstances considered normal by their peers and teachers. Others may complain incessantly of aches, pains, and illnesses, or they may demand constant attention. Some students may become painfully shy or withdrawn, like Fong, crying easily and avoiding contact with adults and peers. Still other students develop specific, irrational, and extreme fears called *phobias*. Children with school phobias, for example, display anxiety and physical symptoms such as nausea before going to school.

According to Quay and LaGreca (1986), anxiety and withdrawal affect only about 2% of all children. Moreover, anxiety and withdrawal are the reason for referral for fewer than 30% of all students with behavioral disorders. Although anxiety and withdrawal do not place children at grave risk for later adult problems (Robins, 1966), persistent and extreme anxiety, fears, and social isolation limit a student's positive interactions with others and, therefore, have negative consequences for healthy social and personal growth (Kauffman, 1993).

Depression

Whereas boys experiencing academic failure are more likely to demonstrate aggressive, antisocial acts, girls with poor academic achievement are more likely to demonstrate internalizing, as well as externalizing, behaviors in adulthood (Robins, 1986). That is, while boys may become more aggressive as adolescents, older girls may become more depressed (Harris & Howard, 1987). See Box 1.3 (p. 14) for a list of general symptoms of depression and Box 1.4 (pp. 16–17) for some myths and facts about depression in childhood and adolescence.

Although depression in childhood and adolescence has only recently become a topic of interest, and childhood depression has not yet been well defined, Forness (1988) estimates that up to 60% of the population of children in special education programs may exhibit depression, in addition to other learning difficulties. Maag and Behrens (1989a), for example, found that 21% of the junior and senior high school students with emotional and behavioral disorders and with learning disabilities participating in their study manifested symptoms of severe depression. Interestingly, prevalence did not differ across these two special education categories. Females, however, were at increased risk of dem-

BOX 1.3   Is Your Child or Adolescent Depressed?

The first step in helping children and adolescents with depression is identifying it. The following is a checklist of general symptoms. If four or more symptoms are evident, the need for a professional assessment exists.

Difficulties Experienced

___ Expressed sadness, "emptiness," hopelessness, or pessimism
___ Expressed unnecessary "guilt"
___ Expressed worthlessness
___ Unable to make decisions
___ No interest or pleasure in ordinary activities
___ Increased boredom
___ Dropping hobbies and other activities
___ Increased shouting and screaming
___ Increased intolerance of everyday events
___ May be drinking or taking drugs
___ Talks about death
___ Talks about or attempts suicide

Physical Complaints

___ Loss of energy—seems slowed down
___ Trouble going to sleep, staying asleep, or getting up
___ Appetite problems—losing or gaining weight
___ Headaches, stomachaches, backaches, chronic aches and pains
___ Restless or irritable

Difficulties in School

___ More than usual problems with schoolwork
___ Unable to concentrate or remember
___ Wants to be alone
___ Avoiding social contact with friends
___ Cutting classes

Adapted from "Is Your Child or Adolescent Depressed?" by N. E. Alessi, 1993a, *Journal of Emotional and Behavioral Problems*, 2(2), 21, National Educational Service.

onstrating severe depressive symptomatology (Maag & Behrens, 1989a, 1989b; Maag, Behrens, & DiGangi, 1992).

Kazdin (1987) asserts that many characteristics of depression may vary according to developmental level. Preschoolers, for example, may express depression through motoric behaviors, whereas school-age youngsters may display more overt aggressive and antisocial behaviors. Similarly, Maag and Forness (1991) maintain that children and youth with depression vary widely in associated characteristics. They suggest that depression may be characterized by low self-esteem, deficits in social and problem-solving skills, an inability to self-regulate actions to cope with stress, negative thoughts and viewpoints about the world and self, and learned helplessness, an expectation that what one does will not influence life events (Abramson, Seligman, & Teasdale, 1978).

Other authorities suggest that academic problems and depression may interact, entangling children in a vicious cycle (Patterson & Capaldi, 1990; Stark, 1990). That is, as the student fails, she may feel less confident, less competent, and more depressed. As she feels more depressed, she feels ever decreasing confidence and increasing social and academic failure. Ultimately, the student believes her failure to be due to personal characteristics that she cannot change, contributing to greater feelings of depression.

Depression in children and adolescents, then, is related to poor self-esteem, poor school performance, family variables, and to loneliness and avoidance of social activities (Stark, Kaslow, & Laurent, 1993). Over time, depression may lead to maladjustment in adulthood or even to suicide (Harris & Ammerman, 1986). Teachers, therefore, must recognize the complex symptoms of depression in children and adolescents to provide appropriate interventions (Guetzloe, 1991; Maag & Forness, 1991).

Summary

You have probably noted the interrelated nature of the characteristics of children and youth with emotional and behavioral disorders. Attention deficits, poor social skills, school failure, aggression, anxiety, withdrawal, and depression present significant difficulties for many children and adolescents. You may also have noticed similar behaviors in students not receiving special education, and, as you read Box 1.4, you may have considered the impact of societal forces on our children and youth, whether or not they are students with emotional and behavioral disorders. Let's turn now to an examination of several factors that may place today's children at risk for social-emotional difficulty and behavioral disorders. ◆

Societal Factors Placing Children at Risk

Teachers must be aware of the impact of dramatic societal changes within the past decade on the behaviors of children and youth now in our schools. We must not assume, of course, that stressors in today's society are the primary cause of social-emotional difficulties experienced by children. Teachers who adopt this viewpoint may tend to place blame for a child's behavior on uninvolved or uncaring parents or on the violence in the community. They may believe that nothing they can do will alter the young person's situation, so they may expect little change from the child. A strong, supportive adult role model is, however, a common ingredient in the lives of resilient youth who succeed despite stressful life events, deplorable family histories, or highly crime-ridden neighborhoods (Rutter, 1990; Werner, 1986; Werner & Smith, 1982).

On the other hand, teachers must not underestimate the impact of chaotic family and community environments on developing children. The less functional one's family or community, the more at risk a child is for becoming either victim or victimizer or for engaging in antisocial activities such as gang member- ship, substance abuse, or violent crime (Cantrell, 1992b) (Box 1.5, p. 18). The

Myths about Depressed Children and Adolescents

Childhood and adolescent depression often goes unrecognized. This lack of understanding about depression is related to various myths that determine our perceptions and actions.

Myth	*Fact*
Childhood is a happy time.	Child abuse, poverty, and homelessness are a few factors making childhood today difficult for many children.
Children and adolescents are unable to talk about their feelings.	Children as young as 3 years of age have been shown to understand their feelings. One should assume that children and adolescents can express their feelings.
Prepubertal children are too young to be depressed.	Toddlers as young as 4 years of age have been identified as being depressed.
Depression in children and adolescents is always due to something.	Not all children or adolescents experience depression as a consequence of ''trauma.''
Expressed sadness always accompanies depression.	Depression in children and adolescents often is seen as anxiety, phobias, opposition, aggression, or irritability.
Depressed and sad feelings are short-lived.	Often, children and adolescents experience depression for many years with severe periods and extended times of boredom, poor concentration, and irritability.

two-parent family of yesteryear is rapidly changing, straining the ability of all family members to cope with daily demands. Families in which both parents work outside the home are becoming the norm (Hofferth, 1987), and the number of single-parent families as well as families living below the poverty level has increased dramatically over the last decade (Baumeister, Kupstas, & Klindworth, 1990; Norton & Glick, 1986). Many families with one parent or two parents working outside the home, of course, offer loving and supportive environments for children. Nevertheless, as the level of stress increases, parents may have less energy and fewer resources to assist children displaying academic or behavioral problems (Hallahan, 1992).

Let's examine several of the major societal influences on student behavior in and out of school. These include living in poverty; child abuse and neglect;

Children and adolescents outgrow their depression.	For some children, adolescents, and their families, depression is a way of life, not a passing phase.
Withdrawal is just a part of being an adolescent.	Social withdrawal is an issue of significance, and to mislabel it as a matter of normal adolescent development will have lifelong impact.
Children and adolescents become mad not sad.	Irritability is a frequent symptom, but several disorders co-occur with depression including separation anxiety, phobias, panic attacks, general anxiety, attention deficit hyperactivity disorder, oppositional defiant disorders, and conduct disorders.
All it takes to help a depressed child or adolescent is kindness.	One should not assume that these children will respond to kindness. In fact, being with depressed children can produce within caregivers feelings of pain, lethargy, and fatigue.

Adapted from "Despair at Any Age" by N. E. Alessi, 1993, *Journal of Emotional and Behavioral Problems*, 2(2), 13–17, National Educational Service.

children living in foster care; homeless children; substance abuse and children born substance exposed; HIV infection and children with AIDS; and juvenile delinquency, violence, and gang membership. Obviously, these areas share considerable overlap; however, we will consider them separately paying particular attention to the impact of each factor on children and youth with emotional and behavioral disorders and on their teachers.

Children Living in Poverty

According to recent reports from the Children's Defense Fund (1989), 2.1 million more children were living in poverty in 1989 than in 1982. Of all children in the United States under the age of 18, 20% are presently living in poor homes and,

BOX 1.5   **Violence and Today's Youth**

The following statistics support the contention of many teachers that today's students are experiencing an environment characterized by escalating levels of violence.

According to the Children's Defense Fund (1990), in an average day in the United States:

135,000 children bring a gun to school.

10 children die from gunshots, and 30 are wounded.

211 are arrested for drug abuse.

1295 teenagers give birth, and 2795 get pregnant.

1512 teenagers drop out of school.

1849 children are abused or neglected.

3288 children run away from home.

2989 see their parents divorce.

From "Guest Editorial," by M. L. Cantrell, 1992b, *Journal of Emotional and Behavioral Problems*, *1*(1), 4, National Educational Service.)

In an average year in our schools, according to a survey of 720 affiliated school districts conducted by the National School Boards Association in 1994:

82% of the nation's schools reported increasing violence over the last 5 years.

60% reported weapons incidents.

75% reported their schools had dealt with violent student-on-student attacks last year.

13% reported a knifing or a shooting.

15% of schools reported they are now using metal detectors.

by the year 2000, approximately 25% of *all* children in the United States will be living below the poverty level (Council for Exceptional Children, 1991). Although most poor children are white, children from minority backgrounds are *more likely* to live in poverty than are their white peers. For example, almost 42% of African American children and 35% of Latino children, ages 6 to 17, live below the poverty level (Children's Defense Fund, 1990). Only 14% of white children and youth, however, are living in poor homes.

You may believe that poverty is primarily an urban problem. Most poor children and youth, though, live in rural or suburban settings. In fact 60% of children living in poverty in the United States are in either rural or suburban communities (Council for Exceptional Children, 1991). Just over 25% of children from our nation's urban areas, however, are also living below the poverty level.

Living in a poor home can have a tremendous impact throughout a child's life. The child's mother may, for example, receive little or no prenatal health care, eat poorly, or engage in drug or alcohol abuse while pregnant, predisposing her child to later health and learning problems as well as to emotional and behavioral disorders. Moreover, children and youth from poor homes are more likely than their affluent peers to be exposed to health hazards such as lead poisoning, malnutrition, serious illness, poor medical care, violent crime, drug-related activities, and child abuse and neglect. Each of these hazards may lead to damage to the brain or central nervous system, delayed development, and other causal factors suspected in emotional and behavioral disorders.

Living in substandard conditions also may influence the child's completion of school. Children and youth from poor homes may live with caretakers having few financial and emotional resources. Thus, they may enter school already behind their more affluent peers in important social and academic "readiness" skills. In addition, the schools in crowded urban areas or in small rural communities may lack funding and resouces as well. Children and youth living in poverty, therefore, are more likely than well-to-do peers to be placed into special education programs such as those for children with emotional and behavioral disorders, and they are more likely than their peers to drop out of school (Council for Exceptional Children, 1991). Living in a poor home where one's parents face daily economic or emotional stress may also place a child at risk for abuse and neglect.

Child Abuse and Neglect

The National Center on Child Abuse and Neglect (1988) recently reported over 1 million documented cases of harm to children from maltreatment by caregivers in 1986 alone. Of those children who were abused in 1986, 1100 died. Zirpoli (1986, 1990) suggests that cases of child abuse and neglect often go unreported; therefore, the number of children who are actually abused is probably much greater than that given in the national reports. In addition, children with disabilities and children living in poverty may be at greater risk for abuse and neglect than their peers (Warger, Tewey, & Megivern, 1991; Zirpoli, 1986, 1990). Adolescents with behavioral disorders, for example, report higher rates of both physical and sexual abuse than do their nondisabled peers, with the highest rates of sexual abuse often reported among behaviorally disordered males (Miller, 1993). Abuse and neglect unfortunately may also be one of the causal factors resulting in a child's disability (Mullins, 1986).

Since the passage of The Child Abuse Prevention and Treatment Act (PL 93-247) in 1974, later amended in 1984 as the Child Abuse Prevention, Adoption and Family Services Act (PL 100-294), child abuse and neglect has been defined as physical or mental injury, sexual abuse or exploitation, negligent treatment, or maltreatment of any child under the age of 18 by any person responsible for that child's welfare. Each state has adopted its own definition of abuse and neglect and has passed laws mandating teachers and other professionals who work with children and youth to report all suspected cases of child abuse to the appropriate agency. Because of the possibility of risk to a child or adolescent, teachers may report reasonable suspicion of child abuse and neglect without actual proof, and they may do so with immunity from civil or criminal liability if they make such reports in good faith (Underwood & Mead, 1995). As a teacher of students with emotional and behavioral disorders, then, you must recognize the signs of abuse and neglect, and you must become familiar with the policies

BOX 1.6   Signs of Abuse and Neglect

Zirpoli (1986) suggests that teachers must familiarize themselves with both the physical and behavioral indicators of abuse and neglect. Although certainly not the only symptoms of abuse or neglect, the following signs are among those most commonly observed by teachers. These indicators, of course, do not automatically signal abuse or neglect, but they should prompt the teacher to seek additional information.

Physical Abuse

Physical Signs

Repeated injuries—before old injuries heal

Evidence of frequent bruises, welts, wounds, cuts, burns, and punctures

Frequent abdominal pain

Fractures and bite marks

Behaviors

Wary of physical contact with adults

Afraid to go home or cries when it is time to leave

Becomes apprehensive when others cry

Extremes in behavior not expected at the child's developmental level

Reports injury by parent or caregivers

Sexual Abuse

Physical Signs

Difficulty walking or sitting

Torn, stained, or bloody undergarments

Complains of pain or itching in genital area

Behaviors

Poor peer relationships

Unwilling to change for or participate in P.E.

Commits delinquent acts or runs away

and procedures of your school in reporting suspected abuse. See Box 1.6 for Signs of Child Abuse and Neglect and Box 1.7 (p. 22) for some common Reporting Procedures.

Teachers also must understand that abuse and neglect may be particularly difficult to spot in children with disabilities (Warger, Tewey, & Megivern, 1991). For example, children and youth with poor language skills may be unable to tell their teachers about abusive instances. In addition, some children with disabilities are self-abusive or ''accident prone,'' making detection of actual abuse even more difficult for the teacher. Finally, a child may just be learning daily hygiene and self-help skills; therefore, an unkempt appearance may signal lack of skill rather than neglect by the child's caregivers. The concerned teacher, however, must document observations and gather information as suggested in Box 1.7 before ruling out abuse and neglect.

The teacher also must be sensitive to cultural differences when reporting cases of suspected abuse related to the discipline of children. McIntyre and Silva (1992) suggest that accepted practices for discipline among some ethnic groups

Bruises or bleeding in external genitalia, vaginal or anal areas

Venereal disease, particularly in children under age 13

Pregnancy, particularly in early adolescent years

Appears withdrawn or in an infantile or fantasy state

Demonstrates bizarre, sophisticated, or unusual sexual behaviors or knowledge

Reports sexual assault

Neglect

Physical Signs

Consistently unbathed

Torn, tattered, and unwashed clothing

Clothing inappropriate for the weather

Rejection by others due to body odor

Needs glasses, dental work, or other health care

Listless or lethargic

Lacks proper nourishment

Lacks supervision, especially for extended periods

Behaviors

Begs or steals food

Often falls asleep in class

Comes to school early or leaves late

Habitually absent

Commits delinquent acts such as vandalism or theft

Has alcohol or other drug addictions

States that no one is at home

From *The Educators Role in the Prevention and Treatment of Child Abuse and Neglect,* by the National Center on Child Abuse and Neglect (1984). U.S. Department of Human Services. Reprinted with permission.

may be considered "abusive" by others. For example, the teacher who calls home to discuss with parents the poor behavior of a child at school may be horrified to find the next day that the child received a severe beating for his or her behavior. Caregivers may believe that whippings are necessary for a child's education, and the child may even perceive the beating as a form of care and affection (Hanna, 1988). Again, as a teacher, you must document your observations and seek information from persons familiar with the culture and the family when you suspect abuse or neglect of a child from an ethnic or religious group different from your own (McIntyre & Silva, 1992).

Children and Youth Living in Foster Care

Children are placed with foster care families for many reasons; however, abuse and neglect is one factor often contributing to the placement of children and youth into foster care (White, 1993). Typically, following an investigation by a child protection or law enforcement agency, the child is referred to the juvenile and

BOX 1.7   **Reporting Procedures for Suspected Abuse or Neglect**

The exact procedures and forms for reporting suspected abuse and neglect will vary for each school and locality. Most school districts, however, require that teachers document the behavioral and physical signs of abuse or neglect that they have observed. Also, teachers are usually encouraged to seek additional information from other professionals who might have important insights regarding the child and his or her family. This is particularly important for those children and youth who come from cultural, ethnic, or religious backgrounds different from the teacher's own. Finally, the teacher files a report through the proper channels. Typically, the report contains the following information:

1. Names and addresses for the child and caregivers
2. The child's age, gender, and race
3. The nature and extent of the suspected abuse
4. Any evidence of previous occurrences of abuse
5. The explanation given by the child or youth about observed injuries
6. Name(s) of the person(s) suspected of the abuse
7. Your name, address, telephone number, and relationship to the child or youth
8. Actions taken by you such as notifying medical personnel or detaining the child
9. Any additional relevant information

family court for an emergency protective hearing, during which the judge determines whether or not the child can safely remain in the home. If the determination is an out-of-home placement, the court must quickly plan for the care, custody, control, and conduct of the child (White, 1993).

In the past, children were frequently or unnecessarily removed from their homes and placed with a series of foster care families. Thus, a "temporary solution" became permanent instability in the child's life. Federal and state legislation now encourages the reunification and rehabilitation of families; though, permanent placement outside of the home with an adoptive family or guardian may still be an appropriate alternative for children unable to return home safely. As a matter of fact, approximately 10% of children in the United States now live in a household headed by a grandparent, another relative, a guardian, or foster parents, with no natural parent living in the home (Salend, 1994). Too, children who have been adopted are overrepresented in special education populations, including the category of emotional and behavioral disorders (Brodzinsky & Steiger, 1991).

Not surprisingly, children placed into foster care have many special needs. For example, children and youth in foster care are frequently referred to and placed in special education programs, most often services for students with emotional and behavioral disorders (Goerge, Van Voorhis, Grant, Casey, & Robinson, 1992). Goerge et al. (1992) caution that the teacher, particularly the special education teacher, may find that records are difficult to track down when a child is moved from one foster home to the next and, thus, from one school to another. As a matter of fact, Smucker (1995) reports that 45% of those students with emotional and behavioral disorders who are in foster care experience more than three foster care placements.

Continuing instability in the child or youth's life demands greater effort on the part of teachers and school personnel to provide continuity and stability for the youngster and to promote involvement of caregivers in the school's programs. Hess (1993) maintains that foster care parents are often the best authorities on the needs of the child. They may, however, require training and support to fulfill the often complex responsibilities of caring for a child with emotional and behavioral disorders.

Homeless Children

According to Heflin and Rudy (1991), approximately 4 million people in the United States may be homeless. Families are the most rapidly growing segment of this population; thus, authorities estimate that at least 1.6 million children may be homeless. Financial crises created by the loss of jobs in the last decade or by medical emergencies, the diminishing availability of affordable housing, and an increase in the number of households headed by single and divorced women have each contributed to the escalating number of families with children having no home (Heflin & Rudy, 1991).

In addition, many youth are forced to leave troubled home environments or to run away from homes in which they feel little warmth, care, or support (Schweitzer, Hier, & Terry, 1994). Often called "throwaways" (Stronge & Tenhouse, 1990), some adolescents leave home rather than face continuing sexual or physical abuse or severe maltreatment only to find themselves at increased risk of violence, substance abuse, and HIV infection on the streets.

Unfortunately, children and youth are particularly vulnerable to the effects of homelessness. Poor health care, hunger, inadequate nutrition, and stress place children at risk for physical, cognitive, and emotional and behavioral difficulties (Molnar, Rath, & Klein, 1990; Rafferty, 1990). For example, homeless children and youth experience chronic diseases at a rate twice that of those living in adequate housing (Wright, 1990), and they may be perceived as more aggressive or restless than their peers when they display behaviors such as lying, stealing, or fighting, learned as coping and survival skills on the streets (Stronge & Tenhouse, 1990). Bassuk and Rubin (1987) suggest that young homeless children are also likely to be developmentally delayed or to evidence emotional and behavioral problems requiring psychiatric evaluation.

With the passage of the Stewart B. McKinney Homeless Assistance Act in 1987, homeless children and youth were guaranteed the right to the same free, appropriate education as their nonhomeless peers. In addition, states were mandated to revise laws that create bureaucratic barriers preventing homeless children from attending school (Heflin & Rudy, 1991). Nevertheless, school attendance is significantly lower for homeless children and adolescents than for their peers (Molnar, Rath, & Klein, 1990). Lack of transportation to school and inadequate clothing or school supplies may prevent many children from attending school (First & Cooper, 1990). In addition, school districts often require school records and documentation of immunizations before admission. Homeless students may not have this necessary documentation; therefore, they may be denied or delayed in school attendance (First & Cooper, 1990; Heflin & Rudy, 1991).

Even when admitted to school, however, homeless children have lower attendance rates than nonhomeless peers (Molnar, Rath, & Klein, 1990). Because homeless and other poor children and adolescents often move from school to school or fail to attend school, the academic performance of these youngsters is lower than that of their peers. Although movement from school to school may interfere with determining a student's eligibility for special education, children without homes are more likely than other students to be in special education classes (Bassuk & Rubin, 1987; Molnar, Rath, & Klein, 1990).

Schools must provide a safe and stable environment for those children and youth who are homeless. Teachers, for example, can ensure that the child's basic needs are met by discretely familiarizing caregivers with services available through the school, such as a free breakfast or lunch program. Teachers also can seek assistance to provide the child with necessary school supplies, clothing, or transportation. Finally, teachers can help homeless students feel a sense of identity and of belonging in the classroom group by tutoring them in basic skills, providing them with a "personal space," such as a cubicle for storing books and papers, and directly teaching the rules and social skills critical for success with classmates.

Substance Abuse and Children Born Substance Exposed

As the incidence of alcohol and other substance abuse among youth and adults has increased, so too has the number of infants born prenatally exposed to these drugs. Children born substance exposed are expected to challenge schools and social service agencies with a variety of learning and behavioral problems and complex programmatic needs (Baumeister, Kupstas, & Klindworth, 1990).

The effects of prenatal exposure to alcohol are well documented (Bauer, 1991). Children may be afflicted with either fetal alcohol syndrome or fetal alcohol effect. Children born with fetal alcohol syndrome, a leading cause of mental retardation, typically exhibit retardation in growth and intellectual ability. They may also develop peculiar facial characteristics, including microcephaly (i.e., an abnormally small head with a sloping forehead), a poorly developed groove between the upper lip and the nose, a thin upper lip, and widely spaced eyes. On the other hand, children suffering from fetal alcohol effects possess numerous characteristics that present multiple learning and behavioral challenges to their teachers. Fetal alcohol effects children, for example, may exhibit hyperactivity, distractibility, impulsivity, difficulty with short-term memory and problem solving, and language disorders (Bauer, 1991). Although these signs of fetal alcohol effects appear to be less damaging or dramatic than those of fetal alcohol syndrome, the impact on the child's educational performance may, nevertheless, be quite problematic.

Of grave concern, too, are the increasing numbers of children born prenatally exposed to cocaine. Besharov (1990) estimates that nationally 1% to 2% of all live births, or between 40,000 and 80,000 infants, are "crack babies." Rist (1990) asserts that estimates are even higher for large cities and among minorities. For example, 15% of the newborns in one New York City hospital and 16% of the newborns in a Chicago hospital had traces of cocaine in their urine (Rist, 1990).

Cocaine use by pregnant women results in a host of complications for newborns, including low birth weight, prematurity, and neonatal seizures (Bauer, 1991) as well as physical defects, irritability, and difficulty developing regular sleeping and eating habits (Rist, 1990). Although Griffith (1992) cautions that not all children born prenatally exposed to cocaine will have developmental difficulties, he does report that these youngsters are more likely than those not exposed to cocaine to be overstimulated easily. When overstimulated, cocaine exposed infants may respond by either withdrawing or by uncontrollable tremors and inconsolable crying. In addition, children born cocaine exposed may have difficulty forming attachments from birth onward. Rist (1990) reports that as these children enter school, their teachers indicate they continue to have difficulty forming attachments with peers and adults, and they exhibit distractibility, low frustration tolerance, and a tendency to react with extreme aggression or withdrawal when overstimulated. Griffith (1992) suggests that these children will require a high degree of structure and individual attention as they enter schools, although the impact of prenatal exposure to cocaine on school performance is as yet unknown. Barone (1994), for example, cautions that not all children prenatally exposed to cocaine will require intensive school intervention or reduced environmental stimulation.

The long-term outcomes of exposure to substances such as cocaine, however, are difficult to determine (Vincent Poulsen, Cole, Woodruff, & Griffith, 1991). Mothers who abuse cocaine, for example, may also abuse alcohol or other substances. In addition, substance abusing mothers may live in substandard conditions with poor medical care and poor nutrition, and they may lack the financial or emotional resources to care for themselves and their children during or after pregnancy. As Rist (1990) reports, these children may go home with mothers who are ill-prepared to handle their difficult infants, or worse, they may end up abandoned in the hospital or passed onto various caregivers, further compounding their inability to develop attachments to others. Although certainly not all substance exposed children are born to inner-city or low-income mothers (Barone, 1994), most of these children will, at best, become educationally vulnerable (Vincent, Poulsen, Cole, Woodruff, & Griffith, 1991).

Although some children are born substance exposed, other children and youth expose themselves to these substances. Abuse of illicit drugs such as cocaine is becoming a widespread problem among adolescents and young adults from all economic and ethnic groups in the United States. In one report from the U.S. Department of Education (1989), for example, 54% of high school seniors indicated that they had used an illegal substance at some time before their graduation. In recent surveys, 40% of high school seniors admitted to using marijuana at least once, and 30% reported the use of other illegal drugs such as cocaine or crack, inhalants, or hallucinogens (Johnston, O'Malley, & Bachman, 1992). Alcohol, however, is the drug most often abused by adolescents and young adults, with 90% of youth who responded to a recent poll reporting that they had used alcohol at least once by grade ten (Long, Brendtro, & Johnson, 1993).

Little research exists, however, regarding the extent to which students in special education programs abuse alcohol or other substances. Leone (1991) suggests that the incidence of alcohol and drug abuse among children and youth with disabilities is comparable to that of nondisabled peers but that the impact of substance abuse is more debilitating for children and adolescents with disabilities. On the other hand, students with emotional and behavioral disorders may abuse alcohol and other substances at rates exceeding those of their peers without disabilities (Devlin & Elliott, 1992). In addition, alcohol abuse is related to depression in teenagers (Shedler & Block, 1990). That is, depressed adolescents are more likely to abuse alcohol than are their nondepressed peers, and alcohol abusing youth are also more likely than their peers to be depressed (King, 1993). Substance abuse is also highly correlated with both juvenile delinquency and gang membership (Pollard & Austin, 1990).

Morgan (1993) asserts that effective substance abuse prevention programs must target schools, families, and communities simultaneously. Substance abuse prevention curricula, for example, should emphasize problem solving, decision making, resistance, and coping skills as well as factual and up-to-date information regarding the negative short-term consequences of substance abuse. In addition, teachers must recognize the signs of alcohol or other substance use to identify abusing students accurately and to refer them as quickly as possible for professional assistance. See Box 1.8 for some common indicators of alcohol or other drug use in students.

HIV Infection and Children with AIDS

According to reports from the Centers for Disease Control and Prevention (1993), 315,000 individuals in the United States have acquired immunodeficiency syndrome (AIDS). Over 1 million people may have the human immunodeficiency virus (HIV) that causes AIDS, and by June 1993, AIDS had claimed the lives of 194,000 citizens in the United States alone, including 2500 children under the age of 13 (Centers for Disease Control and Prevention, 1993). AIDS is now the ninth leading cause of death in the United States.

LeRoy, Powell, and Kelker (1994) note that HIV occurs primarily among two groups of children. First, newborns may acquire the infection from their HIV-infected mothers. Most of these infants develop AIDS by age 2, and many die within 1 year after showing the symptoms of AIDS. According to Krasinski, Borkowsky, and Holzman (1989), however, more of these children will survive into the preschool and elementary school age groups as medical advances are made in the treatment of AIDS. Second, adolescents who are sexually active or who engage in intravenous drug use may acquire HIV while they are in school. Unfortunately, students with emotional and behavioral disorders and other disabilities may be particularly vulnerable to these risky activities because they are often impulsive, lack self-esteem, or exhibit poor social perception (Prater, Serna, Sileo, & Katz, 1995). Although these youth may remain asymptomatic while they are in school, teenage mothers may unknowingly pass the virus to their newborns.

Children with AIDS present a variety of symptoms and erratic patterns of neurological deterioration that challenge teachers (Byers, 1989). For example, these children may exhibit attentional or cognitive deficits, visual or hearing problems, central nervous system damage, gross and fine motor difficulties, speech and language delays, emotional and behavioral problems, numerous infections, and extended periods of stability followed by rapidly declining performance (Byers, 1989; LeRoy, Powell, & Kelker, 1994). AIDS is also reportedly becoming the leading cause of mental retardation and brain damage in children (Council for Exceptional Children, 1991; Diamond & Cohen, 1992).

As a teacher, you must possess accurate information regarding HIV transmission and AIDS if you are to assist youngsters with HIV or AIDS in the schools and if you are to teach your students about HIV and AIDS (Foley & Kittleson, 1993; Prater, Serna, Sileo, & Katz, 1995). Children with HIV or AIDS may not be excluded from school or school activities if their health otherwise permits their attendance, and confidentiality regarding the child's condition should be ensured (Underwood & Mead, 1995). Although the risk of school transmission of HIV is very low, teachers should nonetheless use universal precautions, since they may not know if a particular child is HIV infected. These precautions include wearing surgical gloves when changing diapers or providing personal care to students; safely disposing of gloves, diapers, and other items that come in contact with body fluids; wearing gloves when treating injuries and covering wounds so that no one comes in contact with blood; and cleaning surfaces that have absorbed blood from wounds or scratches with a bleach solution (Kelker, Hecimovic, & LeRoy, 1994).

Teachers must also be prepared to provide flexible programing for children with AIDS. As the infection progresses, children with AIDS may require extended stays in the hospital. Lengthy hospitalization may create gaps in the child's educational performance, result in depression and lowered self-esteem, and make the maintenance of normal friendships difficult for the child and his or her peers. In addition, teachers must be prepared to help children with HIV infection cope with the AIDS-related death of their parents, particularly their mothers. Finally, teachers will need to prepare themselves and their other students to face the prolonged sickness and ultimate death of the child with AIDS (Kelker, Hecimovic, & LeRoy, 1994).

Juvenile Delinquency, Violence, and Gang Membership

Schools reflect the society they serve, and increasingly, American neighborhoods and schools have witnessed violent acts. Murder is now the second leading cause of death in the United States among young people ages 15 to 34 (Rosen, 1994), and according to the National Crime Survey, almost 3 million attempted or completed crimes, including assault, rape, robbery, and theft, occurred on school property in 1987 alone (Office of Juvenile Justice and Delinquency Prevention, 1989). As a matter of fact, the President of the National Education Association recently issued a statement indicating that 100,000 children carry guns to school daily and that another 160,000 children miss school every day because of fear of attack or intimidation by other students (NEA, 1993).

Apparently, the problem of children and youth carrying guns or other weapons to school is not limited to large urban areas or certain states only. In one mid-Atlantic state, for example, a total of 20,317 counts of physical battery were recorded during the 1991–92 school year with 949 of these acts committed against school staff (Virginia Department of Education, 1993). Another 196 counts of sexual battery as well as 2016 counts of known weapon possession also occurred during the same school year. Males accounted for more weapon possessions than did females, and weapon possessions occurred most often among students in grades seven through nine.

Authorities attribute this rise in violent crime to several factors, including growing poverty, family disintegration and domestic violence, drugs, the availability of firearms, and the influence of violence in the media (Rosen, 1994). Many studies confirm the relationship between viewing violent acts on television or in movies and antisocial behavior (Pearl, Bouthilet, & Lazar, 1982). Gadow and Sprafkin (1993), following a 10-year study of television violence and aggressive acts, assert that children with emotional and behavioral disorders prefer violent material and aggressive characters on television. Although these students were no more likely than their same-age peers to behave aggressively following television violence, children with emotional and behavioral disorders and learning disabilities viewed more television than did their peers without disabilities, and children with behavioral disorders believed the fictional content to be true. Observing aggressive acts on the screen, then, may not lead directly to acts of violence, but children and youth with emotional and behavioral disorders may be more vulnerable than their less-aggressive peers to the affects of television viewing (Gadow & Sprafkin, 1993). Children who observe aggression, who are reinforced for aggression, and who are the objects of aggression are most likely to learn aggression (Huesmann, 1988).

Certainly, the relationship among aggressive acts, juvenile delinquency, and special education placement is well documented. You might recall from the earlier discussion, for example, Hill Walker's research on the stability of aggressive and antisocial acts over time (Loeber, 1985; Walker, Shinn, O'Neil, & Ramsey, 1987). Teacher ratings of poor social skills, negative playground behaviors, and discipline contacts with the principal's office for antisocial boys in grade five predicted their arrest for criminal behavior by grade ten. Ruhl and Hughes (1985) report that a variety of physically and verbally aggressive acts occur in classrooms for students with behavioral disorders, and, compared with the general population, special education youth are disproportionately represented in juvenile detention centers, state training schools, and adult jails (Leone, Rutherford, & Nelson, 1991; Murphy, 1986). Although special education services are guaranteed to school-age youth with disabilities in juvenile corrections, well-trained teachers and adequate programs to meet the educational needs of these students are still lacking (McIntyre, 1993).

The exact relationship between juvenile delinquency and emotional and behavioral disorders is unknown. Yet, Rutherford, Nelson, and Wolford (1989) estimate that more than 28% of incarcerated youth have disabilities and that approximately 77% of the youth in special education programs within juvenile correction facilities are identified as behaviorally disordered. Factors associated with major offenses committed by incarcerated juveniles with emotional and behavioral disorders include increasing age, sibling incarceration, and running away from home (Bryant, Rivard, Addy, Hinkle, Cowan, & Wright, 1995).

This disproportionate representation of youth with disabilities in the correctional system is attributed to their poorly developed social skills and social comprehension as well as to higher rates of violence, substance abuse, and school disruption for these youth when compared with their nondisabled peers (Leone, Rutherford, & Nelson, 1991; Keilitz & Dunivant, 1986). That is, students with behavioral disorders and learning disabilities may be more sus-

School personnel must work closely with law enforcement agencies to stay current regarding colors, symbols, fashions, vocabulary, and graffiti used by local gang members.

ceptible to arrest because they have poor impulse control or social perception and, thus, they may commit more delinquent acts than their peers. Moreover, following arrest, students with disabilities may be treated more harshly than other juvenile offenders because they lack the social and cognitive skills necessary to conduct themselves appropriately before law enforcement officials and juvenile judges.

Apparently, more juveniles are also committing more violent crimes than ever before as members of gangs. Gangs have existed in the United States for over 150 years, but gang members have become increasingly younger and more violent, and gang membership has become more widespread across the country during the last decade (Jankowski, 1991; National School Safety Center, 1988). According to the National School Safety Center (1988), youth gangs often organize across geographical and ethnic boundaries. Gangs each have their own identifying characteristics such as graffiti, style or color of dress, organizational structure, and activities. Predominant gangs include the Latino gangs; African American gangs (e.g., the Bloods and the Crips); Asian, Chinese, Samoan, and Vietnamese gangs; and the white "Stoner" gangs and Satanic Cults. Although we do not know the percentage of youth with disabilities who join these gangs, we might predict that children and adolescents with emotional and behavioral disorders would be more vulnerable to gang membership than their nondisabled peers. See Box 1.9 for an interview with a gang member identified as a student with a behavioral disorder. In addition, according to some reports (Avery,

BOX 1.9   **The Case of Benz: An Interview with a Gang Member**

The following interview was conducted with a 14-year-old gang member named Benz, a student with a history of assaultive behavior. Benz is in a program for students with severe behavior handicaps.

Why did you join the gang?
One reason was about slobs [derogatory name for members of the Bloods gang]. You know, Crips and Bloods. The goal is to eliminate Bloods. Another reason is I just be fighting all the time and I needed the back-up.

What did you get out of the gang?
Friends and stuff, you know. Then, they started shooting, just driving by and shooting . . . an innocent person just because they had red on.

If you had a younger brother . . .
I do.

What would you tell him would happen if he joined?
He'd end up dead somewhere. He'll get shot. I got into it because all my friends were in it, and they wouldn't let me out. Still, I'm not out.

Why wouldn't they let you out of the gang?
You know where they meet, what's going on, how they do things. If you leave one gang and go in another, they'd try to kill you because you could tell other people how they do things.

Can you make money being in a gang?
Selling drugs there's some places you can't go or you'll get jumped. But, if you're in the gang wouldn't nobody mess with you.

What did you need the money for?
Pocket money. When I was selling drugs I was making more money than he was (pointing).

If your parents could buy you those things, would you have joined the gang anyway?
Really, yes, for the friendship. You could have lots of money, and you'd still join the gang, you know, to be somebody, be popular, give you an identity.

Adapted from ''Voices of Youth: Meet Benz, 14-Year-Old Gang Member,'' by L. A. Monroe and M. A. Felgar, 1992, *Journal of Emotional and Behavioral Problems, 1*(1), 5–8, National Educational Service.

1994), gang members in Florida, New York, and in major cities across the United States are actively soliciting special education students as prospective gang members, and they are also seeking special education status for themselves while still in school as a protection against normal school expulsion policies.

You may have noticed from reading Box 1.9 that Benz joined his gang for income, friendship, and protection. According to experts, gangs are organizations that serve both social and entrepreneurial purposes (Jankowski, 1991;

Gang Identifiers

Although no one sign by itself is enough to indicate a gang member, clusters of signs may indicate gang membership.

Symbols

Stars, crowns, rabbit heads

Physical Signals

Arms or fingers are placed in signals

Graffiti

Symbols and words used to mark territory, anounce activities, or advertise sources and locations for drug sales

Right/Left Rule

One side of the body is adopted by a gang, for example, a belt buckle worn to left or right or a bandana hanging from a pocket, a belt loop, or a leg on that side

Colors

Color combinations are chosen by a gang and worn in friendship beads, clothing, shoes, hair decorations, or earrings

Clothing

Jogging suits in gang colors, sweatshirts with the hood out to show color, or hats tilted in certain directions and identified by color or insignia

National School Safety Center, 1988). Unfortunately, school grounds attract gang members because they serve as meeting grounds and gang territory, as prime targets for producing income for gang members through drug sales, and as potential sources for new gang members (Felgar, 1992).

The National School Safety Center (1988) recommends that school personnel work carefully with law enforcement agencies to become aware of the gangs operating locally and to stay abreast of the rapidly changing symbols designating gang members. For example, gangs often require members to "represent" or show evidence of the gang to which they belong. Colors, symbols, fashions, and vocabulary used by gangs may be signs of local or larger, national groups; however, these identifiers quickly change for gang members to avoid detection by local law enforcement or school officials (Cantrell, 1992a). See Box 1.10 for some common gang identifiers and Box 1.11 (p. 34) for common gang terminology.

Often gang identifiers become "fads" adopted by students not in gangs. School personnel are encouraged to prohibit students like Dante from wearing gang colors, clothing, or other identifiers that might target gang members or other innocent students for attacks by rival gangs. School officials should also

"New Wave Star"—sheets of material worn under the hat and hanging down the back, may have colors or symbols

Glove worn on left or right hand

Color of gym shoes combined with color of laces (colored laces in both or left or right shoe, one colored lace in one shoe only, tongue turned up in one shoe and down in other, one shoe laced only halfway in either right or left shoe

Pockets—insides dyed with gang colors

Pants legs—rolled or cuffed on right or left

Jewelry

Earrings, rings, necklaces, or bracelets worn on the left or right or with specific gang symbols or colors

Rings worn on a specific finger

Jelly Bracelets (plastic loops in colors) worn in certain ways on the body

Buttons and key rings with gangs symbols, slogans, or colors

Hairstyles and Fingernails

Designs cut into the hair, colored beads or barrettes, colored streaks on different sides of the head, rubber bands of different colors

Combs in beard or hair, front or back, left or right

Two nails with gang colors on left or right hand

Adapted from "Gang Identifiers and Terminology," by M. L. Cantrell, 1992, *Journal of Emotional and Behavioral Problems*, 1(1), 13–14, National Educational Service.

immediately erase gang graffiti, which often marks gang territory, claims credit for gang crimes, and challenges rival gangs to fight. Teaching peaceful conflict resolution skills, harnessing the leadership abilities of key gang members, providing adequate job training and up-to-date job skills, and developing after-school programs are additional suggestions for schools confronted with gang activity.

Summary

Schools are no longer the islands of academic activity and safety they once were. As a teacher, you will be increasingly challenged to provide for the many social and emotional needs of your students who come from poor or abusive homes or from shelters for the homeless. Too many students today are affected by substance abuse and exposure to daily violence. Even children from affluent homes may fall victim to drug or alcohol abuse, HIV infection, and the lure of gang membership or juvenile crime. Students with emotional and behavioral disorders may be particularly vulnerable to these societal influences. ◆

Gang members may use specific phrases or words to identify themselves with a particular gang. Common terms used in gang conversations include the following:

Book—run
Check it out—listen to what I have to say
Demonstration—a gang fight
Dis—to do something wrong, disrespect
Drop a dime—tell on someone
Dropping the flag—leaving the gang
Gang banger—gang member
Gang banging—gang activity
Get down—fight
Gun up—ready to fight
Home boy—someone from the same gang, a friend
Hood—neighborhood
Jiving—attempting to fool someone
Packing—has a weapon
Popped a cap—shot at someone
Represent—demand to indicate gang membership
Take him out of the box—to kill someone

Adapted from "Gang Identifiers and Terminology," by M. L. Cantrell, 1992, *Journal of Emotional and Behavioral Problems*, 1(1), 13–14, National Educational Service.

Summary

Students with emotional and behavioral disorders exhibit several overlapping characteristics. These include attention deficits, underachievement in school, poor social skills, aggression, anxiety, withdrawal, and depression. Children and youth in other special education programs and students not in special education programs at all may exhibit very similar behavioral difficulties.

Many societal changes place students at increased risk for emotional and behavioral disorders and for special education placement. Poverty, child abuse and neglect, homelessness, substance abuse, HIV and AIDS, and violence are interrelated factors placing today's children at grave risk. Sensitive teachers must respect the impact of these family and community variables on a child's behavior at school, while still firmly believing that educators can be a positive influence in the child's life. Teachers' beliefs about the nature of their students' behavioral problems implicitly affect how they respond to these behaviors.

Application Exercises

1. Scan the local newspapers for 1 week. Bring to class for discussion those articles covering societal factors in your community that impact children in your local schools.

2. With permission from school officials, interview a teacher from a chosen grade level. What behavioral difficulties are of concern to this teacher? Be sure to protect the identity of the teacher and students by using false names. Try to discern the nature of the home and community life for those students of particular concern to this teacher.

3. Interview a special education teacher of students with emotional and behavioral disorders. What behavioral difficulties are of concern to this teacher? Be sure to protect the identity of the teacher and students by using false names. Try to discern the nature of the home and community life for those students of particular concern to this teacher.

4. Interview a school administrator in your local school division. Is this person aware of gang activity in the local community? If so, what policies and programs are in place to prevent gang violence? How many students in the school or school division are living below the poverty level? Are in foster care or are homeless? What local statistics are available regarding the incidence of child abuse or neglect or substance abuse?

5. Order pamphlets and brochures from the organizations listed in Appendix A. Share this information with your classmates.

References

Abramson, L. Y., Seligman, M. E. P., & Teasdale, J. D. (1978). Learned helplessness in humans: Critique and reformulation. *Journal of Abnormal Psychology, 87*, 49–74.

Alessi, N. E. (1993a). Is your child or adolescent depressed? *The Journal of Emotional and Behavioral Problems, 2*(2), 21.

Alessi, N. E. (1993b). Despair at any age. *The Journal of Emotional and Behavioral Problems, 2*(2), 13–17.

American Psychological Association. (1994). *Diagnostic and Statistical Manual of Mental Disorders* (4th Ed.). Washington, DC: American Psychological Association.

Amundson, K. J. (1994). *Violence in the schools: How America's school boards are safeguarding your children.* Alexandria, VA: National School Boards Association.

Asher, S. R., & Coie, J. D. (Eds.). (1990). *Peer rejection in childhood.* Cambridge, MA: Cambridge University Press.

Avery, G. (1994). *Student discipline in special education: Course workbook.* University Heights, OH: The Law Advisory Group.

Barkley, R. A., DuPaul, G. J., & McMurray, M. B. (1990). A comprehensive evaluation of attention deficit disorder with and without hyperactivity defined by research criteria. *Journal of Consulting and Clinical Psychology, 58*, 580–588.

Barone, D. (1994). Myths about "crack babies." *Educational Leadership, 52*(2), 67–68.

Bassuk, F. & Rubin, L. (1987). Homeless children: A neglected population. *American Journal of Orthopsychiatry, 57*, 279–286.

Bauer, A. M. (1991). Drug and alcohol exposed children: Implications for special education for students identified as behaviorally disordered. *Behavioral Disorders, 17*(1), 72–79.

Baumeister, A., Kupstas, F., & Klindworth, L. M. (1990). New morbidity: Implications for prevention of children's disabilities. *Exceptionality, 1*(1), 1–16.

Besharov, D. J. (1990, July-August). Crack children in foster care. *Children Today*, 21–35.

Brodzinsky, D. M., & Steiger, C. (1991). Prevalence of adoptees among special education populations. *Journal of Learning Disabilities, 24*(8), 484–489.

Bryant, E. S., Rivard, J. C., Addy, C. L., Hinkle, K. T., Cowan, T. M., & Wright, G. (1995). Correlates of major and minor offending among youth with severe emotional disturbance. *Journal of emotional and behavioral disorders, 3*(2), 76–84.

Byers, J. (1989). AIDS in children: Effects on neurological development and implications for the future. *The Journal of Special Education, 23,* 5–16.

Cantrell, M. L. (1992a). Gang identifiers and terminology. *The Journal of Emotional and Behavioral Problems, 1*(1), 13–14.

Cantrell, M. L. (1992b). Guest Editorial. *The Journal of Emotional and Behavioral Problems, 1*(1), 4.

Centers for Disease Control and Prevention (1993). *HIV/AIDS Surveillance Report, 5*(2), Atlanta, GA: U.S. Department of Health and Human Services.

Children's Defense Fund. (1989). *A vision for America's future.* Washington, DC: Author.

Children's Defense Fund. (1990). *Latino youths at a crossroads.* Washington, DC: Author.

Cohen, M. J., Riccio, C. A., & Gonzalez, J. J. (1994). Methodological differences in the diagnosis of attention-deficit hyperactivity disorder: Impact on prevalence. *Journal of Emotional and Behavioral Disorders, 2*(1), 31–38.

Coie, J., & Kupersmidt, J. (1983). A behavioral analysis of emerging social status in boys' groups. *Child Development, 54,* 1400–1416.

Council for Exceptional Children. (1991). Some statistical clues to today's realities and tomorrow's trends. *Teaching Exceptional Children, 24,* 80.

Devlin, S. D., & Elliott, R. N. (1992). Drug use patterns of adolescents with behavioral disorders. *Behavioral Disorders, 17*(4), 264–272.

Diamond, G. W., & Cohen, H. J. (1992). Developmental disabilities in children with HIV infection. In A. Crocker, H. Cohen, & T. Kastner (Eds.), *HIV infection and developmental disabilities: A resource for service providers* (pp. 33–42). Baltimore, MD: Paul H. Brookes.

DuPaul, G. J., Guevremont, D. C., & Barkley, R. A. (1991). Attention-deficit hyperactivity disorder. In T. R. Kratochwill & R. J. Morris (Eds.), *The practice of child therapy* (2nd ed.) (pp. 115–144). New York: Pergamon.

Epstein, M. H., Kinder, D., & Bursuck, B. (1989). The academic status of adolescents with behavioral disorders. *Behavioral Disorders, 14,* 157–165.

Eron, L. D. & Huesmann, L. R. (1990). The stability of aggressive behavior—Even unto the third generation. In M. Lewis & S. M. Miller (Eds.), *Handbook of developmental psychopathology* (pp. 147–156). New York: Plenum Press.

Felgar, M. (1992). Children on the edge: Gangs and youth violence. *The Journal of Emotional and Behavioral Problems, 1*(1), 9–12.

First, P. F., & Cooper, G. R. (1990). Homeless doesn't have to mean hopeless. *The School Administrator,* December 1990, 17–22.

Foley, R. M., & Kittleson, M. J. (1993). Special educators' knowledge of HIV transmission: Implications for teacher education programs. *Teacher Education and Special Education, 16*(4), 342–350.

Forness, S. R. (1988). School characteristics of children and adolescents with depression. In R. B. Rutherford, C. M. Nelson, & S. R. Forness (Eds.), *Bases of severe behavioral disorders of children and youth.* Boston: Little, Brown.

Forness, S. R., & Knitzer, J. (1992). A new proposed definition and terminology to replace "serious emotional disturbance" in Individuals with Disabilities Act. *School Psychology Review, 21,* 12–20.

Gadow, K. D., & Sprafkin, J. (1993). Television "violence" and children with emotional and behavioral disorders. *Journal of Emotional and Behavioral Disorders, 1*(1), 54–63.

Goerge, R. M., Van Voorhis, J., Grant, S., Casey, K., & Robinson, M. (1992). Special-education experiences of foster children: An empirical study. *Child Welfare League of America, 71,* 419–437.

Griffith, D. R. (1992, September). Prenatal exposure to cocaine and other drugs: Developmental and educational prognoses. *Phi Delta Kappa,* 31–34.

Guetzloe, E. C. (1991). *Depression and suicide: Special education students at risk.* Reston, VA: Council for Exceptional Children.

Hallahan, D. P. (1992). Some thoughts on why the prevalence of learning disabilities has increased. *Journal of Learning Disabilities, 25,* 523–528.

Hanna, J. (1988). *Disruptive school behavior: Class, race and culture.* New York: Holmes & Meier.

Harris, F. C., & Ammerman, R. T. (1986). Depression and suicide in children and adolescents. *Education and Treatment of Children, 9,* 334–343.

Harris, I. D., & Howard, K. I. (1987). Correlates of depression and anger in adolescence. *Journal of Child and Adolescent Psychotherapy, 4,* 199–203.

Heflin, L. J., & Rudy, K. (1991). *Homeless and in need of special education.* Reston, VA: Council for Exceptional Children.

Hess, P. M. (1993). Supporting foster families in their support of families. *The Journal of Emotional and Behavioral Problems, 2*(4), 24–27.

Hofferth, S. L. (1987). Implications of family trends for children: A research perspective. *Educational Leadership, 45,* 78–84.

Huesmann, L. R. (1988). An information processing model for the development of aggression. *Aggressive Behavior, 14,* 13–24.

Individuals with Disabilities Education Act. (1990). 20 U.S.C. Chapter 33.

Jankowski, M. S. (1991). *Islands in the street: Gangs and American urban society.* Berkeley, CA: University of California Press.

Johnston, L. D., O'Malley, P. M., & Bachman, J. G. (1992). *Drug use among American seniors, college students and young adults, 1975-1990. Volume I, High school seniors.* Rockville, MD: U.S. Department of Health and Human Services, National Institute on Drug Abuse.

Kauffman, J. M. (1993). *Characteristics of emotional and behavioral disorders in children and youth* (5th ed.). New York: Merrill.

Kazdin, A. (1985). *Treatment of antisocial social behavior.* Homewood, IL: Dorsey Press.

Kazdin, A. E. (1987). Assessment of childhood depression: Current issues and strategies. *Behavioral Assessment, 9,* 291–319.

Keilitz, I., & Dunivant, N. (1986). The relationship between learning disability and juvenile delinquency: Current state of knowledge. *Remedial and Special Education, 7*(3), 18–26.

Kelker, K., Hecimovic, A., & LeRoy, C. H. (1994). Designing a classroom and school environment for students with AIDS: A checklist for teachers. *Teaching Exceptional Children, 26*(4), 52–55.

King, C. A. (1993). Alcohol abuse and depression in teenagers. *The Journal of Emotional and Behavioral Problems, 2*(3), 16–18.

Krasinski, K., Borkowsky, W., & Holzman, R. (1989). Prognosis of human immunodeficiency virus infection in children and adolescents. *Pediatric Infectious Disease Journal, 8,* 216–220.

Lahey, B. B., & Carlson, C. O. (1991). Validity of the diagnostic category of attention deficit disorder without hyperactivity: A review of the literature. *Journal of Learning Disabilities, 24,* 110–120.

Leone, P. (1991). *Alcohol and other drugs: Use, abuse, and disabilities.* Reston, VA: The Council for Exceptional Children.

Leone, P. E., Rutherford, R. B., & Nelson, C. M. (1991). *Special education in juvenile corrections.* Reston, VA: The Council for Exceptional Children.

LeRoy, C. H., Powell, T. H., & Kelker, P. H. (1994). Meeting our responsibilities in special education. *Teaching Exceptional Children, 26*(4), 37–44.

Loeber, R. (1982). The stability of antisocial and delinquent child behavior: A review. *Child Development, 53,* 1431–1446.

Loeber, R. (1985). Patterns and development of antisocial child behavior. *Annals of Child Development, 2*, 77–116.

Loeber, R., Green, S. M., Lahey, B. B., Christ, M. A. G., & Frick, P. J. (1992). Developmental sequences in the age of onset of disruptive child behaviors. *Journal of Child and Family Studies, 1*(1), 21–41.

Loeber, R., & Schmaling, K. B. (1985). The utility of differentiating between mixed and pure forms of antisocial child behavior. *Journal of Abnormal Child Psychology, 13*, 315–336.

Long, N., Brendtro, L., & Johnson, J. (1993). Alcohol and kids: Facing our problem. *The Journal of Emotional and Behavioral Problems, 2*(3), 2–4.

Luebke, J., Epstein, M. H., & Cullinan, D. (1989). Comparison of teacher-rated achievement levels of behaviorally disordered, learning disabled, and nonhandicapped adolescents. *Behavioral Disorders, 15*, 1–8.

Maag, J. W., & Behrens, J. T. (1989a). Depression and cognitive self-statements of learning disabled and seriously emotionally disturbed adolescents. *The Journal of Special Education, 23*(1), 17–27.

Maag, J. W., & Behrens, J. T. (1989b). Epidemiologic data on seriously emotionally disturbed and learning disabled adolescents: Reporting extreme depressive symptomatology. *Behavioral Disorders, 15*(1), 21–27.

Maag, J. W., Behrens, J. T., & DiGangi, S. A. (1992). Dysfunctional cognitions associated with adolescent depression: Findings across special populations. *Exceptionality, 3*(1), 31–47.

Maag, J. W., & Forness, S. R. (1991). Depression in children and adolescents: Identification, Assessment, and Treatment. *Focus on Exceptional Children, 24*(1), 1–19.

McConaughy, S. H. (1986). Social competence and behavioral problems of learning disabled adolescents. *Journal of Learning Disabilities, 19*, 101–106.

McIntyre, T. (1993). Behaviorally disordered youth in correctional settings: Prevalence, programming, and teacher training. *Behavioral Disorders, 18*(3), 167–176.

McIntyre, T., & Silva, P. (1992). Culturally diverse childrearing practices: Abusive or just different? *Beyond Behavior, 4*(1), 8–11.

Miller, D. (1993). Sexual and physical abuse among adolescents with behavioral disorders: Profiles and implications. *Behavioral Disorders, 18*(2), 129–138.

Moffitt, T. E. (1990). Juvenile delinquency and attention deficit disorder: Boys' developmental trajectories from age 3 to 15. *Child Development, 61*, 893–910.

Molnar, J. M., Rath, W. R., & Klein, T. P. (1990). Constantly compromised: The impact of homelessness on children. *Journal of Social Issues, 46*, 109–124.

Monroe, L. A., & Felgar, M. A. (1992). Voices of Youth: Meet Benz, 14-year-old gang member. *The Journal of Emotional and Behavioral Problems, 1*(1), 5–8.

Morgan, D. P. (1993). Substance use prevention and students with behavioral disorders: Guidelines for school professionals. *Journal of Emotional and Behavioral Disorders, 1*(3), 170–178.

Mullins, J. B. (1986). The relationship between child abuse and handicapping conditions. *Journal of School Health, 56*(4), 134–136.

Murphy, D. M. (1986). The prevalence of handicapping conditions among juvenile delinquents. *Remedial and Special Education, 7*(3), 7–17.

Murray, A. (1992). Working with Michelangelo. *Beyond Behavior, 4*(1), 23.

National Center on Child Abuse and Neglect. (1984). *The educator's role in the prevention and treatment of child abuse and neglect.* Washington, DC: U.S. Department of Human Services.

National Center on Child Abuse and Neglect. (1988). *Study findings: Study of national incidence and prevalence of child abuse and neglect, 1988.* Washington, DC: U.S. Department of Human Services.

National Education Association. (1993). National Press Release, January 3. Washington, DC: Author.

National School Safety Center. (1988). *Gangs in schools: Breaking up is hard to do.* Washington, DC: U.S. Department of Justice, Office of Juvenile Justice and Delinquency Prevention.

Norton, A. J., & Glick, P. C. (1986). One parent families: A social and economic profile. *Family Relations, 35*(1), 9–17.

Office of Juvenile Justice and Delinquency Prevention. (1989). *Juvenile Justice Bulletin, October.* Washington, DC: Author.

Patterson, G. R. (1982). *Coercive family process.* Eugene, OR: Castalia Press.

Patterson, G. R. (1986). Performance models for antisocial boys. *American Psychologist, 41*, 432–444.

Patterson, G. R., & Capaldi, D. M. (1990). A mediational model for boys' depressed mood. In J. Rolf, A. S. Masten, D. Cicchetti, K. H. Nuechterlein, & S. Weintraub (Eds.), *Risk and protective factors in the development of psychopathology* (pp. 141–163). Cambridge, MA: Cambridge University Press.

Patterson, G. R., Reid, J., & Dishion, T. (1992). *Antisocial boys.* Eugene, OR: Castalia Press.

Pearl, D., Bouthilet, L., & Lazar, J. (Eds.). (1982). *Television and behavior: Ten years of scientific progress and implications for the eighties (Vol. I)* (DHHS Publication No. ADM 82-1195). Washington, DC: U.S. Government Printing Office.

Pollard, J. A., & Austin, G. (1990). *Substance abuse among juvenile delinquents and gang members* (Prevention Research Update Number 6). Washington, DC: Department of Education Western Center for Drug-Free Schools.

Prater, M. A., Serna, L. A., Sileo, T. W., & Katz, A. R. (1995). HIV disease: Implications for special educators. *Remedial and Special Education, 16*(2), 68–78.

Quay, H. C., & LaGreca, A. M. (1986). Disorders of anxiety, withdrawal, and dysphoria. In H. C. Quay & J. S. Werry (Eds.), *Psychopathological disorders of childhood* (3rd ed.). New York: Wiley.

Rafferty, Y. (1990). *The challenge of educating children who are or have been homeless.* Paper presented at the annual meeting of the American Public Health Association, New York.

Reid, R., Maag, J. W., Vasa, S. F., & Wright, G. (1994). Who are the children with attention deficit-hyperactivity disorder? A school-based survey. *The Journal of Special Education, 28*(2), 117–137.

Rist, M. C. (1990). The shadow children. *American School Board Journal, 177*, 18–24.

Robins, L. N. (1966). *Deviant children grown up.* Baltimore, MD: Williams & Wilkins.

Robins, L. N. (1979). Follow-up studies. In H. C. Quay & J. S. Werry (Eds.), *Psychopathological disorders of childhood* (2nd ed.). New York: Wiley.

Robins, L. N. (1986). The consequences of conduct disorder in girls. In D. Olweus, J. Block, & M. Radke-Yarrow (Eds.), *Development of antisocial and prosocial behavior: Research, theories, and issues.* New York: Academic Press.

Rosen, L. (1994). Violence Prevention: School's newest challenge. *The Journal of Safe Management of Disruptive and Assaultive Behavior, 2*(4), 12–16.

Ruhl, K. L., & Hughes, C. A. (1985). The nature and extent of aggression in special education settings serving behaviorally disordered students. *Behavioral Disorders, 10*(2), 95–104.

Rutherford, R. B., Nelson, C. M., & Wolford, B. I. (1989). Special education in the most restrictive environment: Correctional Special Education. *Journal of Special Education, 19*, 59–71.

Rutter, M. (1990). Psychosocial resilience and protective mechanisms. In J. Rolf, A. S. Masten, D. Cicchetti, K. H. Nuechterlein, & S. Weintraub (Eds.), *Risk and protective factors in the development of psychopathology* (pp. 181–214). Cambridge, MA: Cambridge University Press.

Sabornie, E. J., Kauffman, J. M., & Cullinan, D. A. (1990). Extended sociometric status of adolescents with mild handicaps: A cross-categorical perspective. *Exceptionality, 1*, 197–209.

Salend, S. J. (1994). *Effective mainstreaming: Creating inclusive classrooms* (2nd ed.). New York: Macmillan.

Schweitzer, R. D., Hier, S. J., & Terry, D. (1994). Parental bonding, family systems, and environmental predictors of adolescent homelessness. *Journal of Emotional and Behavioral Disorders, 2*(1), 39–45.

Seidel, J. F., & Vaughn, S. (1991). Social alienation and the learning disabled school dropout. *Learning Disabilities Research and Practice, 6,* 152–157.

Shaywitz, S. E., & Shaywitz, B. A. (1988). Attention deficit disorder: Current perspectives. In J. F. Kavanagh & T. J. Truss, Jr. (Eds.), *Learning disabilities: Proceedings of the National Conference* (pp. 369–523). Parkton, MD: York Press.

Shedler, J., & Block, J. (1990). Adolescent drug use and psychological health: A longitudinal inquiry. *American Psychologist, 45,* 612–630.

Smucker, K. (1995, February 25). *The school related problems and needs of children in foster care and receiving special education services for EBD.* Paper presented at the Virginia Federation Council for Exceptional Children, Charlottesville, VA.

Stark, K. (1990). *Childhood depression: School-based intervention.* New York: Guilford Press.

Stark, K. D., Kaslow, N. J., & Laurent, J. (1993). The assessment of depression in children: Are we assessing depression or the broad-band construct of negative affectivity? *Journal of Emotional and Behavioral Disorders, 1*(3), 149–154.

Stronge, J. H., & Tenhouse, C. (1990). *Educating homeless children: Issues and answers.* Bloomington, IN: Phi Delta Kappa Educational Foundation.

Underwood, J. K., & Mead, J. F. (1995). *Legal aspects of special education and pupil services.* Boston: Allyn & Bacon.

U.S. Department of Education. (1989). *What works: Schools without drugs.* Washington, DC: Author.

U.S. Department of Education. (1993). *The Fifteenth Annual Report to Congress on the Implementation of the Individuals with Disabilities Education Act.* Washington, DC: U.S.D.O.E.

Vaughn, S. (1991). Social skills enhancement in students with learning disabilities. In B. Wong (Ed.), *Learning about learning disabilities* (pp. 409–440). San Diego: Academic Press.

Vincent, L. J., Poulsen, M. K., Cole, C. K., Woodruff, G., & Griffith, D. R. (1991). *Born substance exposed, educationally vulnerable.* Reston, VA: The Council for Exceptional Children.

Virginia Department of Education. (1993). *Report on acts of violence and substance abuse: 1991–92 school year.* Richmond, VA: Author.

Walker, H. M. (1993). Anti-social behavior in school. *Journal of Emotional and Behavioral Problems, 2*(1), 20–24.

Walker, H. M., Colvin, G., & Ramsey, E. (1995). *Antisocial behavior in school: Strategies and best practices.* Pacific Grove, CA: Brooks/Cole.

Walker, H. M., Shinn, M. R., O'Neill, R. E., & Ramsey, E. (1987). A longitudinal assessment of the development of antisocial behavior in boys: Rationale, methodology, and first year results. *Remedial and Special Education, 8*(4), 7–16.

Walker, H. M., Steiber, S., Ramsey, E., & O'Neill, R. E. (1990). Middle school behavioral profiles of antisocial and at-risk control boys: Descriptive and predictive outcomes. *Exceptionality, 1,* 61–77.

Warger, C. L., Tewey, S., & Megivern, M. (1991). *Abuse and neglect of exceptional children.* Reston, VA: Council for Exceptional Children.

Werner, E. E. (1986). The concept of risk from a developmental perspective. In *Advances in special education* (Vol. 5) (pp. 1–23). Greenwich, CT: JAI Press.

Werner, E. E., & Smith, R. S. (1982). *Vulnerable but invincible: A longitudinal study of resilient children and youth.* New York: McGraw-Hill.

Wheeler, J., & Carlson, C. L. (1994). The social functioning of children with ADD with hyperactivity and ADD without hyperactivity: A comparison of their peer relations and social deficits. *Journal of Emotional and Behavioral Disorders, 2*(1), 2–12.

Whelan, R. J., de Saman, L. M., & Fortmeyer, D. J. (1988). The relationship between pupil affect and achievement. In E. L. Meyen, G. A. Vergason, & R. J. Whelan (Eds.), *Effective instructional strategies for exceptional children.* Denver, CO: Love.

White, P. J. (1993). Abused and neglected children in the juvenile and family courts. *The Journal of Emotional and Behavioral Problems, 2*(4), 20–23.

Wright, J. D. (1990). Homelessness is not healthy for children and other living things. In N. A. Boxill (Ed.), *Homeless children: The watchers and the waiters* (pp. 65–88). Binghamton, NY: Haworth.

Zirpoli, T. J. (1986). Child abuse and children with handicaps. *Remedial and Special Education, 7*(2), 39–48.

Zirpoli, T. J. (1990). Physical abuse: Are children with disabilities at greater risk? *Intervention in School and Clinic, 26,* 6–11.

CHAPTER 2

ASSESSING STUDENTS WITH EMOTIONAL AND BEHAVIORAL DISORDERS

Main Ideas:

◆ *Effective assessment may help the teacher address emotional and behavioral difficulties before problems become intractable and to maintain children in the regular classroom whenever possible.*

◆ *Assessment of behavior and social-emotional functioning is used to identify students having difficulty beyond that normally expected for children at a particular age level and to classify students for special education services if appropriate.*

◆ *Standardized assessment instruments include behavior and social skills checklists or rating scales, structured interviews, and self-report measures.*

◆ *Popular and informative informal assessments include sociometric techniques and direct observational recording procedures.*

◆ *Teachers must participate as professionally responsible members of a multidisciplinary team that uses multiple sources of information when making decisions about students with emotional and behavioral disorders.*

Children and youth with emotional and behavioral disorders may experience many difficulties within their lives at home, in the community, and in the classroom. To identify and serve students with behavioral disorders, school personnel must first conduct a careful assessment. Typically, teachers use assessment to screen for students with behavioral problems beyond those normally expected of children or youth at a particular age level, to evaluate a child's eligibility for special education classification, and to determine behavioral and social skills requiring instruction.

In this chapter, we first examine some of the instruments used to screen for children and youth with emotional and behavioral disorders, and we consider some of the issues surrounding this screening. Next, we discuss systems for classifying students with emotional and behavioral disorders. Finally, we explore informal assessment procedures used to determine the performance of students with emotional and behavioral disorders and to help teachers adjust interventions accordingly.

Screening

Screening is required by the Individuals with Disabilities Education Act (IDEA) of 1990 to identify all children in need of special education services. With effective screening, children with emotional and behavioral disorders, hopefully, are given early intervention. Early intervention may assist teachers to maintain the child in the regular classroom and lessen the impact of the problem for the child as well as for his or her family, peers, and teachers. For students presenting particularly troublesome behaviors, effective screening may also assist teachers to make accurate referrals for more comprehensive evaluation for special education services. Screening is often conducted using a variety of behavior and social skills checklists or rating scales, interviews, and direct observations of behavior.

Accurate and effective screening, however, is more difficult than you might think. According to Kauffman (1993), schools often fail to conduct systematic screening efforts *because* these efforts result in identifying students who must then receive costly evaluations for special education services. Further, the special education services, themselves, are costly and potentially stigmatizing for students, thus, only those students most bothersome to their teachers are actually referred for further evaluation (Peacock Hill Working Group, 1991).

Accurate identification of preschoolers or young children with "mild" behavioral problems is also quite difficult because the child's temperament may interact in complex ways with parenting skills and parental tolerance levels (Thomas & Chess, 1984). A child's temperament is his or her typical way of responding to life events. Thomas, Chess, and Birch (1968) report that all infants are born with innate temperamental characteristics such as level of activity, predictability or regularity of bodily functions (e.g., eating, sleeping, or eliminating), adaptability, and so forth. These characteristics are not merely biologically determined, however. Children with "difficult temperaments" such as those often exhibited by children with attention deficit hyperactivity disorders may or may not develop emotional and behavioral disorders depending on circumstances in their environment. For example, skilled parents may mitigate the effects of a "difficult temperament." Conversely, children with "difficult temperaments" may produce negative interactions with adults lacking effective parenting skills.

Of particular concern when conducting screenings is the accurate identification of children from culturally or ethnically diverse groups (Reilly, 1991). Males and children and youth from minority groups are more likely than their peers to be referred and evaluated for special education services (Council for Children with Behavioral Disorders, 1989). Teachers may have a limited picture of the whole child, seeing only the student's "deficits" in school rather than the child's strengths in his or her home, native language, or community (Ruiz, 1989). This limited viewpoint, particularly for children with language or cultural differences, may inadvertently contribute to the teacher overlooking a child's assets and erroneously referring the child for special education evaluation. To minimize the impact of cultural factors when screening or evaluating children and youth for special education programs, the Council for Children with Behavioral Disorders (1989) recommends that professionals adopt the following strategies:

1. Focus attention on classroom and school learning environments (i.e., conduct functional assessments that determine a student's purpose for his or her actions) and on observable student and teacher behaviors as well as the context in which they occur.
2. Attend to the predisposing factors (e.g., culture, expectations, tolerance levels) that characterize the learner, teacher, administrators, and other school personnel.
3. Establish specific, measurable, instructionally based standards for acceptable academic and social behaviors.
4. Develop and implement prereferral intervention procedures that force assessment of the student's current learning environment before referral and certification for special education are considered and that document the results of prereferral attempts.
5. Apply instructional procedures that are known to be the effective and efficient "best practices", and focus evaluation on assessment of the instructional process (e.g., teaching behaviors, instructional organization ans support).
6. Avoid placing the responsibility for learning or performance failure on the student (p. 273).

Obviously, accurate screening requires information from many sources with a focus on how the child functions within particular environments. We will return to this notion of dynamic interactions in Chapter 3. Professionals, however, are currently developing procedures for systematically screening children using multiple sources of information across varying contexts.

One multistep, systematic screening device is Systematic Screening for Behavior Disorders (SSBD) developed by Walker and Severson (1990). The SSBD is a multiple-gate, or three-step, procedure designed to identify elementary-age students at risk for behavioral disorders. The procedure is based on the following three assumptions: (1) Teachers can make valid and reliable judgments about students at risk for behavioral disorders; (2) Students with behavioral disorders must be identified early and accurately to prevent antisocial behaviors from becoming entrenched; (3) Teachers tend to overrefer students with externalizing behavioral problems, while overlooking those with internalizing disorders (Walker, Severson, Nicholson, Kehle, Jenson, & Clark, 1994; Walker, Severson, Stiller, Williams, Haring, Shinn, & Todis, 1988; Walker, Severson, Todis, Block-Pedego, Williams, Haring, & Barckley, 1990).

In the first step, teachers are given behavioral descriptions of students with both externalizing and internalizing disorders, and they are asked to list and rank the order of those students who are most like each of the descriptions. When teachers complete the first step, they have two mutually exclusive rank-ordered lists containing up to ten students each. In the second step, teachers use two checklists to rate the behaviors of the three top students for each list produced in step one. On these checklists, the teacher indicates behaviors exhibited by each student within the last month as well as how often these students exhibit particular behaviors. Students whose scores on these checklists exceed established norms then enter the third gate. During the third step, students are observed both in the classroom and on the playground by a professional other than the regular teacher, such as a school psychologist or guidance counselor. Direct observation determines whether or not students advancing into the third gate are meeting expectations for academic performance in the classroom and for appropriate social behavior with peers on the playground. An adapted version of the SSBD may make the screening of preschoolers at risk for behavioral problems more accurate as well (Feil & Becker, 1993; Sinclair, Del'Homme, & Gonzalez, 1993).

Originally intended as a fourth step within the SSBD, the School Archival Records Search (SARS) may also help teachers make better screening decisions (Walker, Block-Pedego, Todis, & Severson, 1991). The SARS provides teachers with a systematic method for coding information from the files of elementary-level students. Important data such as attendance, retention in grade, disciplinary contacts, referral and placement into special education, and negative comments made in narratives on report cards or other school records are examined to facilitate decision making.

Although the SSBD and SARS provide school personnel with systematic tools for screening children, many other standardized assessment instruments exist to help teachers identify students with behavioral disorders. Most often, these instruments take the form of rating scales or checklists on which teachers, parents, or peers judge the frequency, intensity, or importance of particular behaviors for a targeted student. Other instruments facilitate structured interviews with the parents, peers, or teachers of students, and some instruments allow students themselves to self-report any social-emotional difficulties they are experiencing (Table 2.1).

Checklists and Rating Scales

Checklists and rating scales enable teachers, parents, or peers to record their judgments about a particular child or adolescent's behavior. Typically, checklists give parents and teachers a short behavioral description and ask them to judge

Table 2.1 Instruments for Assessing Students with Emotional and Behavioral Disorders

Name	Author/Date
Checklists and Rating Scales	
Behavior Rating Profile-2	Brown & Hammill, 1990
Social-Emotional Dimension Scale	Hutton & Roberts, 1986
Social Skills Rating System	Gresham & Elliott, 1990
Test of Early Socioemotional Development	Hresko & Brown, 1984
Interviews and Self-Reports	
AAMR Adaptive Behavior Scales—School (2nd edition)	Lambert, Nihira, & Leland, 1993
Child Depression Scale	Reynolds, 1985
Children's Depression Inventory	Kovacs, 1981
Coopersmith Self-Esteem Inventories	Coopersmith, 1981
Culture-Free Self-Esteem Inventories	Battle, 1992
Depression & Anxiety in Youth Scale	Newcomer, Barenbaum, & Bryant, 1994
Multidimensional Self-Concept Scale	Bracken, 1992
Piers-Harris Children's Self-Concept Scale	Piers & Harris, 1984
Self-Esteem Index	Brown & Alexander, 1991
Tennessee Self-Concept Scale	Fitts & Roid, 1988
Vineland Adaptive Behavior Scales	Sparrow, Balla, & Cicchetti, 1984

whether or not the behavior is present for a child. Rating scales, on the other hand, require parents or teachers to evaluate the degree to which a behavior is present or problematic using certain responses, ranging from, for example, "Strongly Agree" to "Strongly Disagree" or from "Always Like" to "Never Like" the child being rated. Because these instruments involve the judgments of others, teachers will need to supplement the use of checklists or rating scales with direct observation of the student in various environments whenever possible. Let's briefly examine several of the often-used checklists and rating scales teachers will need training to use.

Behavior Rating Profile-2 (Brown & Hammill, 1990). An easily completed rating scale, the Behavior Rating Profile-2 actually contains six subtests to assess the behaviors of students in grades 1 through 12 at home, at school, and in interactions with peers. The student completes a 60-item, true-false scale including items for the home (e.g., "My parents bug me a lot."), for the school (e.g., "My teachers give me work I cannot do."), and with peers (e.g., "I seem to get into a lot of fights."). In addition, the parent and teacher rating

Teachers must supplement information obtained from checklists and rating scales with direct observation of a student's behavior at school.

scales contain 30 items each. Parents respond to a four-point scale (e.g., "Very much like my child," "Like my child," "Not very much like my child," and "Not at all like my child") judging their child's behavior in the home. Teachers respond to a similar four-point scale judging behavior to be "Very much like," "Like," "Not very much like," or "Not at all like" the student's behavior in their classroom. Finally, peers are asked to nominate three students in the classroom they would most, or least, like to work with and play with. Using this information, a sociogram is constructed illustrating the social structure of the classroom and the child's social status within the group. (Sociograms are discussed later in this chapter.) The Behavior Rating Profile-2 is helpful for identifying students whose behavior is perceived to be different from that of others, for locating settings in which the child's behavior is perceived to be different, and for determining if some individuals differ markedly in their perceptions of the child's behavior. The normative groups for the Behavior Rating Profile-2 include 2682 students from 26 states, 1948 parents from 19 states, and 1452 teachers from 26 states.

Social-Emotional Dimension Scale (Hutton & Roberts, 1986). The Social-Emotional Dimension Scale is a 32-item rating scale for use by teachers of children ages 5 years, 6 months through 18 years, six months. Teachers rate their students on a three-point scale as "Never or rarely," "Occasionally," or "Frequently" exhibiting listed behaviors. The scale assesses student performance across six subscales including physical, or fear, reaction; depressive reaction; avoidance of peer interaction; avoidance of teacher interaction; aggressive interaction; and inappropriate behaviors. The scale was normed on a representative sample of 1097 students and yields a Total Behavior Score (a percentile), a Behavior Quotient, and a Behavior Observation Web on which the student's performance is plotted graphically.

Social Skills Rating System (Gresham & Elliott, 1990). The Social Skills Rating System evaluates the social skills of children and youth ages 3 through 18 in both the home and school settings. Forms are available at the preschool, elementary, and secondary levels for teachers, parents, and students. On the parent and teacher versions of the scale across all three levels, social skills and problem behaviors are rated as occurring "Never," "Sometimes," or "Very often." On the student scales, only social skills are assessed. In addition, social skills are also evaluated on parent, teacher, and secondary-level student versions of the scale as to their perceived importance ("Not important," "Important," or "Critical"). Social skills are plotted graphically across five subscales (CARES: Cooperation, Assertion, Responsibility, Empathy, and Self-Control). Problem behaviors are also plotted (as externalizing, internalizing, or hyperactivity) and academic competence is rated by teachers. Skills rated with low frequency and high importance are targeted for intervention and the Intervention Plan Summary facilitates the writing of short-term objectives and instructional planning by the teacher. SSRS ASSIST is also available for IBM and Apple computers for both scoring the scale and planning instruction.

Test of Early Socioemotional Development (Hresko & Brown, 1984). The Test of Early Socioemotional Development is an adaptation of the Behavior Rating Profile-2 for younger children ages 3 through 7. The test includes a 30-item Student Rating Scale orally given to the child, a 34-item Parent Rating Scale, and a 36-item Teacher Rating Scale. Like the Behavior Rating Profile-2, the Test of Early Socioemotional Development permits the identification of children who exhibit problem behaviors, the setting in which these behaviors occur, and the perceptions and tolerances of significant adults in the child's life. In addition, a Sociogram is constructed to examine the child's interactions with his or her peers. The test was standardized on a sample of 1006 children, 1773 parents, and 1006 teachers in 15 states.

Critique of Checklists and Rating Scales. Many rating scales and checklists are available for evaluating behavioral and social-emotional difficulties experienced by students. Many more are constantly being developed; therefore, teachers must select rating scales and checklists cautiously to ensure that they use only those that are appropriate. For example, teachers must examine the items on checklists or rating scales to be sure that these match the intended purpose for the assessment, that the directions are clear, and that the language is comprehensible for the individual who will complete the evaluation. In addition, time to complete and score the instrument must be considered.

Newcomer (1993) cautions teachers to use only those instruments standardized on large, representative sample populations that include children having emotional and behavioral disorders. In addition, she recommends teachers select for use only those instruments that are written clearly and are easy to use and which have high reliability and validity such as those listed previously. Finally, different individuals do demonstrate bias. That is, teachers, parents, and students each may rate the same behavior differently. Teachers must remember, therefore, to use instruments having multiple scales (e.g., teacher, parent, and student versions) or to gather information from all concerned parties before making decisions regarding the behavioral problems of students. Rating scales and checklists may also be used to guide questioning during interviews of parents or teachers.

Interviews and Self-Reports

Interviews and self-report instruments help teachers gather additional relevant information about the perceived behavioral or social-emotional difficulties experienced by their students. Structured interviews are often conducted with parents, teachers, students, or others who are well acquainted with the child to determine the youngster's level of adaptive functioning in the school, home, or community. Structured interviews use a preset format containing a list of questions that guide the conversation to obtain information regarding specific content. For example, parents may be asked questions about their child's developmental history or his or her present behavior. On the other hand, self-reports allow teachers to assess the student's own perceptions regarding self-esteem or self-concept or whether or not children or adolescents are feeling depressed.

AAMR Adaptive Behavior Scales—School (2nd ed.) (Lambert, Nihira, & Leland, 1993). This scale allows systematic questioning during structured interviews with individuals who are familiar with the child's behavior in school. The scale contains two parts. Part 1 assesses personal independence and responsibility across nine behavioral domains: independent functioning, physical development, economic activity, language development, numbers and time, prevocational and vocational activity, self-direction, responsibility, and socialization. Part 2 measures social expectations and maladaptations including social behaviors, conformity, trustworthiness, stereotyped and hyperactive behavior, self-abusive behavior, social engagement, and disturbing interpersonal behavior. Apple and IBM compatible software for scoring and reporting is also available. The scale is well researched and is particularly useful for determining the current functioning and adaptive behaviors of children with mental retardation and emotional and behavioral disorders.

Child Depression Scale (Reynolds, 1985). The Child Depression Scale is a 30-item scale for children ages 8 to 13. Children self-report on a four-point scale on which the items are "Almost never" to "All the time" like themselves, and they record their general well-being on one of five faces depicting emotions from happiness to sadness.

Children's Depression Inventory (Kovacs, 1981). One of the most commonly used instruments to assess child and adolescent depression is the Children's Depression Inventory. For children ages 7 through 17, the student responds to 27 items by choosing one of three statements which best describes him or her during the last 2 weeks. The measure examines both sadness and suicidal ideas, and parent forms are also available.

Coopersmith Self-Esteem Inventories (Coopersmith, 1981). The Coopersmith Self-Esteem Inventories are designed to measure a child's feelings of self-worth in social, academic, and personal contexts. Students respond to 58 items such as "I can usually take care of myself" with one of two choices (i.e., "Like me" or "Unlike me"). Attitudes are assessed toward self and peers, home and parents, and school.

Culture-Free Self-Esteem Inventories (2nd ed.) (Battle, 1992). These self-report scales measure the level of self-esteem in children and youth ages 5 and older. A student's self-esteem is measured using a 60-item scale across five areas including general self-esteem and self-esteem with peers, in school, with parents, and on a lie (i.e., defensiveness) scale. The normative sample for the instrument contains over 5000 individuals with both regular and special students in the sample. A 30-item short version of the scale is also available, as are audio cassette versions in English and Spanish.

Depression and Anxiety in Youth Scale (DAYS) (Newcomer, Barenbaum, & Bryant, 1994). The DAYS contains three rating scales for students ages 6 to 19, their teachers, and their parents. Children and adolescents respond on a four-point scale ("Not at all," "Sometimes," "Often," and "Almost all the time") to indicate the extent to which they experience depression or anxiety. Parent and teacher forms contain 45 and 30 items respectively and use a true-false format on which adults indicate the presence or absence of particular behaviors. The scales were standardized on a norming sample of over 5000 students in 25 states, and norms are also available for students with learning disabilities and with emotional and behavioral disorders.

Multidimensional Self-Concept Scale (Bracken, 1992). The Multidimensional Self-Concept Scale is designed for use with students in grades 5 through 12. Six 25-item scales assess the child or adolescent's self-concept across separate domains of psychosocial functioning including social competence, affect, academic, family, and physical. Together, the 150 items yield an assessment of global self-concept. The scales may be group or individually administered in approximately 20 minutes.

Piers-Harris Children's Self-Concept Scale (Piers & Harris, 1984). The Piers-Harris scale may be used with children and youth in the fourth through the twelfth grades. Using a "Yes"/"No" format, students respond to 80 statements to measure attitudes about themselves. Both positive and negative statements are included across six major areas: behavior, intellectual and school status, physical appearance and attributes, anxiety, popularity, and happiness and satisfaction. These self-report items are written at approximately the third-grade level and the scale requires approximately 20 minutes to administer.

Self-Esteem Index (Brown & Alexander, 1991). This instrument measures the way children and adolescents from ages 7 through 19 perceive and value themselves. A four-point scale ("Always true," "Usually true," "Usually false," "Always false") is used to assess the student's self-perceptions in four areas including academic competence, family acceptance, peer popularity, and personal security (e.g., physical appearance and attributes such as character, conduct, temperament, and emotions). The normative sample for the instrument includes 2455 students from 19 states.

Tennessee Self-Concept Scale (Fitts & Roid, 1988). The Tennessee Self-Concept Scale measures the self-concept and self-esteem of youth ages 12 and above. For each of 90 statements, students respond to a five-point scale from "Completely false" to "Completely true." The measure yields a total self-concept score as well as self-esteem scores in seven areas: self-satisfaction, behavior, physical self, moral-ethical self, personal self, family self, and social self. The scale is easily administered in approximately 20 minutes.

Vineland Adaptive Behavior Scales (Sparrow, Balla, & Cicchetti, 1984). Like the AAMR Adaptive Behavior Scales, the Vineland Adaptive Behavior Scales require the teacher or parent to answer questions concerning a child's appropriate use of functional skills. The Vineland Scales assess skills across several major domains, including communication (e.g., receptive, expressive, and written), daily living skills (e.g., personal, domestic, and community), socialization (e.g., interpersonal relationships, play and leisure time, and coping skills), and gross and fine motor skills. In addition, an optional maladaptive behavior domain may be used for children ages 5 and older. The Vineland Scales are well researched and frequently used to assess the adaptive behaviors of individuals with mental retardation and behavioral disorders.

Critique of Interviews and Self-Reports. The results from interviews and self-reports must, of course, be used carefully. Individuals may, for example, report during interviews varying perceptions of the same behavior, indicating differing degrees of tolerance, bias, or actual situational differences in the child's behavior. In addition, parents may not accurately remember events from their child's past. Self-reports, too, are often criticized because students may choose to lie or distort the information reported. They may answer to please the examiner, or they may simply be unaware of the problems they are experiencing. In addition, feelings may be transitory and situation specific. An adolescent who is administered a self-report scale on one "bad" day may, for example, report herself to be quite unhappy; however, she might have a more positive picture of herself the next day or even in the next class. Again, teachers are cautioned to use only reliable and valid instruments and to gather information for comparison from multiple sources.

Summary of Screening

Checklists, rating scales, interviews, and self-reports are used to identify those students exhibiting behavioral problems beyond those normally expected for a particular age-group. The most important outcome of information gathered at this stage, however, is making an accurate decision regarding which children to refer to special education evaluation and which children to support in the regular classroom without special placement. This decision is critical because research indicates that once a student is referred by his or her teachers for special education evaluation, the probability is high that the student will be placed in a special education program (Algozzine, Christenson, & Ysseldyke, 1982; Sevick & Ysseldyke, 1986). Furthermore, evaluation is an expensive and time-consuming process, and placement of a student in special education results in additional cost to the school and the risk of a possibly stigmatizing label to the young person.

Minor academic difficulties or behavioral problems of a transitory nature are not sufficient for referral for special education evaluation. Children and youth may, for example, exhibit temporary behavioral problems following the birth of a sibling, the separation or divorce of parents, a move to a new home, or the death of a pet or grandparent. Sometimes students and their families experience life events or stressors such as unemployment; accidents resulting in financial or physical losses; or the death of a family wage earner, which may require assistance from social services or other community agencies. For these students, prereferral interventions, adjustments made by teachers to accommodate the needs of children in the classroom, may be sufficient to support these youngsters through temporary setbacks.

Teachers must carefully document the prereferral intervention strategies they have tried and the results of these interventions before referring a child for special education evaluation. Prereferral interventions are an essential step for teachers between the screening and evaluation processes. When several adults in more than one setting suspect that a child has a behavioral problem beyond that normal for the circumstances, and when data collected from prereferral interventions and screening instruments confirm these suspicions, then prompt referral for evaluation for special education must occur.

Classification

Following carefully applied and well-documented efforts to assist students with behavioral problems in the classroom, additional evaluation may be required to determine whether or not some of these students may qualify for special education services. These students may then be further classified to ascertain a primary area of disability, such as emotional or behavioral disorders, to receive appropriate special education services.

The requirements for evaluation and placement into special education programs are specified in IDEA (1990). Among other stipulations, IDEA mandates that the student be evaluated in all areas of suspected disability and in a manner that is not biased against the student's language, culture, or disability. Students must be evaluated by a multidisciplinary team so that no one evaluation procedure is used as the sole criterion for placement, and parents must be fully informed in their native language and must give their consent before their child may be evaluated, labeled, or placed into a special education program. For students with emotional and behavioral disorders, careful assessment and observation of adaptive behaviors and social skills as well as the evaluation of academic performance, health, and cognitive functioning are essential for accurate evaluation and placement.

Classification of children for special education programs, particularly for students with emotional and behavioral disorders, however, remains an inaccurate process (Ysseldyke & Algozzine, 1983; Ysseldyke, Algozzine, & Thurlow, 1992). Making accurate decisions about students with emotional and behavioral disorders who require special education intervention is necessarily a subjective process. Even members of the best multidisciplinary teams ultimately must base their decisions on clinical judgments, which, of course, may be affected by culture, gender, ethnic origin, socioeconomic status, and a host of other variables. As a member of a multidisciplinary team, then, you must make every effort to prevent unnecessary classification of students into special education programs by demonstrating the following professionally responsible behaviors listed by Kauffman (1993, pp. 155–156):

1. Obtain training in appropriate evaluation procedures.
2. Refuse to use evaluation procedures for which you are untrained and refuse to accept data from unqualified personnel.
3. Function as a member of the team to ensure that no lone individual makes the eligibility decision.
4. Insist that many sources of data be made available to the team and that all relevant data are used for decision making.
5. Involve the parents and, if appropriate, the student in the decision-making process.
6. Require documentation of prereferral interventions and their effects prior to evaluation for disability.

7. Document behavior and its effects on the student's educational performance.
8. Consider the interests of all parties affected by the eligibility decision, including the student, peers, parents, and teachers.
9. Estimate the risks and benefits of identifying and not identifying the student for special education services.
10. Remain sensitive to the possibility of bias in the use of procedures and interpretation of data.

Systems of Classification

To facilitate classification of students with emotional and behavioral disorders, professionals have relied on two primary methods: a clinically derived psychiatric system of classification and classification according to statistically derived behavioral dimensions. The *Diagnostic and Statistical Manual of Mental Disorders* (American Psychological Association, 1994) is a widely used psychiatric classification system. The Child Behavior Checklist (Achenbach & Edelbrock, 1991) and the Revised Behavior Problem Checklist (Quay & Peterson, 1987) are two well-researched dimensional classification systems.

Diagnostic and Statistical Manual of Mental Disorders (4th Ed., DSM-IV) (American Psychological Association, 1994). The DSM-IV reflects a traditional psychiatric and medical viewpoint of mental disorders in children and adults. Lists of specific criteria are presented for numerous disorders, and diagnoses are made according to whether or not a child exhibits a predetermined number of these criteria. Multiple axes are used within the DSM-IV to indicate a major category of clinical disorders (e.g., disorders usually first diagnosed in infancy, childhood, or adolescence: attention deficit hyperactivity disorder) as well as personality disorders and mental retardation, general medical conditions, and psychosocial and environmental problems (e.g., problems related to the social environment or educational problems). Although the DSM-IV is a medically oriented classification system, teachers of students with emotional and behavioral disorders are likely to encounter psychiatric reports about their students using DSM-IV terminology.

Child Behavior Checklist (Achenbach & Edelbrock, 1991). The Child Behavior Checklist is a well-researched instrument available in both parent and teacher versions. The teacher rates 112 behaviors on a three-point scale as "Not true," "Somewhat or sometimes true," or "Very true or often true" of the child's behavior. Similarly, the parent rates the child's problem behaviors in the home. Appropriate for children and youth ages 5 through 18, the school version of the Child Behavior Checklist examines broad-band factors such as undercontrolled or externalizing behaviors (e.g., hyperactive, aggressive) and overcontrolled or internalizing behaviors (e.g., socially withdrawn, anxious, immature) as well as the child's adaptive functioning in the school and home. Data from the Child Behavior Checklist Scales appear to identify students with emotional and behavioral disorders who meet the existing federal definition of seriously emotionally disturbed (McConaughy, 1993).

Revised Behavior Problem Checklist (Quay & Peterson, 1987). The Revised Behavior Problem Checklist is another well-researched instrument that allows classification of problem behavior into four major dimensions. Similar to those in the Child Behavior Checklist, these dimensions include conduct disorder (e.g., aggression, negativism, defiance of authority), socialized aggression (e.g., truancy, stealing, gang or delinquent activity), anxiety-withdrawal (e.g., social withdrawal, shy, overanxious), and immaturity (e.g., short attention span, daydreaming). Children with emotional and behavioral disorders consistently score the highest on the conduct disordered dimension with boys typically having higher scores than girls (Cullinan & Epstein, 1985). Two newer scales (motor excesses and psychotic behavior) still require additional research. Teachers and parents can use the checklist to rate behaviors of children and adolescents in Kindergarten through grade 8, although agreements among teachers or parents may not always occur regarding behaviors considered to be deviant (Simpson, 1989 & 1991; Simpson & Halpin, 1986).

Critique of Classification Systems

Although both clinically and statistically derived systems of classification are widely recognized and used by professionals, they are not without criticism. The DSM-IV categories, for example, were developed through a committee process. Clinicians and psychiatrists achieved consensus regarding these categories; however, Walker and Fabre (1987) criticize this system of classification as lacking reliability, validity, and relevance for educational settings.

On the other hand, the Child Behavior Checklist and Revised Behavior Problem Checklist were developed through complex statistical manipulations of behaviors observed and rated by parents and teachers. These behaviors cluster or correlate into broad bands, or dimensions, of problems that reliably occur together. Although these dimensions are empirically determined and reliable, Kauffman (1993) cautions that "clinical" judgment is still applied when using dimensional classification systems. That is, the multidisciplinary team must still use judgment when determining whether or not a student's rating is "high enough" on a particular dimension to be considered disordered.

Informal Assessments

In addition to checklists, rating scales, interviews, and self-reports, teachers may gain valuable information regarding the behavior and social-emotional functioning of their students from informal assessments. Rather than comparing a student's performance to that of peers in a normative group, informal assessments assist teachers to gather information about a child's behavior within a given context and to adjust interventions in the classroom as necessary to produce desireable outcomes. Sociometrics and direct observational procedures

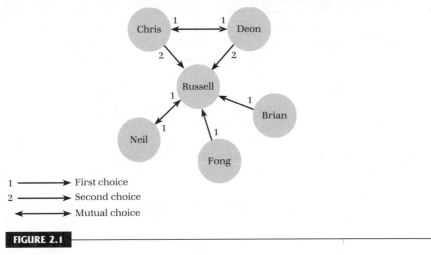

1 ——————▶ First choice
2 ——————▶ Second choice
◀——————▶ Mutual choice

FIGURE 2.1 ————————————————————————————————◆

A Classroom Sociogram for Six Boys

are two commonly used and educationally relevant informal assessments of student behavior.

Sociometrics

Sociometric techniques enable teachers to evaluate the social structure within the classroom as well as to determine a particular child's social status within the classroom group. Sociometric data may be collected through peer nominations, peer ratings, or peer assessments (Maag, 1989). A sociogram is then constructed to provide a visual record of the group's interaction patterns. See Figure 2.1 for a sociogram using the peer nomination method for determining friendship status within a classroom.

You may notice in Figure 2.1 that Deon and Chris and Russell and Neil chose each other as "first picks." In other words, they are "best friends." Although Russell prefers Neil as his best friend, he is quite popular with the other boys and is often chosen as a friend by his peers. On the other hand, notice that no child chooses Brian or Fong as a friend. From the sociogram, however, we do not know if Brian and Fong are simply ignored by their peers or if they are actively rejected by the other boys.

Sociograms are helpful in determining children who are popular as well as those who are isolated, neglected, or rejected by others. Sabornie, Kauffman, and Cullinan (1990) caution that students with mild disabilities may be quite popular, *or* they may be neglected or rejected by their peers. Sociograms, therefore, may assist teachers to form cooperative groups of children who can work well together. Also, sociograms may help teachers group children to ensure that isolated or neglected youngsters are included in classroom activities and that rejected students are placed with those who are likely to be accepting and positive role models. In addition, sociograms may help teachers to determine students in need of social skills instruction within the classroom (Sabornie & Kauffman, 1985).

When using peer nominations, children are asked to nominate secretly by name one or more of their peers who they would most or least prefer for specific work or play activities (e.g., as a "best friend," "play partner," "work partner"). Gresham and Reschly (1988) suggest that both postiive and negative nominations are important because they measure separate dimensions of social status. That is, peer nominations may identify broad social groups including rejected or neglected children, but they are most useful for determining a child's popularity with peers (Coie, Dodge, & Coppotelli, 1982; Dodge, 1983). The major disadvantages of this approach include ethical questions arising from requiring children to make negative nominations and the fact that socially isolated or neglected children may not be nominated by their peers at all.

Whereas peer nominations determine best friendship status, peer ratings indicate a child's overall acceptance by the total peer group. Peer ratings require all students in the classroom to rate all other students in the same classroom, minimizing problems with peer nominations such as children forgetting others or not knowing how to spell another's name. With peer ratings, children are given a roster containing the names of their classmates and are asked to rate their peers according to a Likert-type scale ranging from those "most like" to "least like" certain descriptions. For example, students might rate their peers according to "someone who is always willing to share" or "someone who works hard in the group." To determine the score for a particular child, individual scores are added, and an average score is obtained.

Because a particular student's score is an average determined by the responses of all students in the class, peer ratings may be more reliable than peer nominations. In addition, peer ratings allow the identification of low-status children (i.e., rejected children) without the necessity of asking peers to indicate by name who they would "like to play or work with the least." A child's status within the classroom can be determined simply by adding the number of "1" ratings he or she receives from peers.

Peer ratings, however, have two distinct disadvantages. Students may give many different peers the same rating, or students may rate peers such that most scores fall in the middle of the scale (McConnell & Odom, 1986). Nevertheless, peer ratings may help teachers determine a particular child's general level of acceptance within the classroom group (Gresham & Elliott, 1989). Those students receiving low overall scores are less accepted by their classmates.

Finally, peer assessments require students to rate peers on specific behavioral characteristics or to nominate peers who most closely fit particular behavioral criteria. For example, students might be asked to guess who in your classroom is being described when behavioral descriptors for the most talented, most athletic, or most disruptive child are read (Kauffman, Agard, & Semmel, 1985).

Although sociometric techniques can assist teachers to determine patterns of friendship or social interactions and to form cooperative groups within the classroom, they do not give information regarding specific social skills or behaviors of particular students requiring intervention. Sociometric procedures are best used in combination with checklists, rating scales, and direct observations of behavior.

Direct Observations of Behavior

Direct and frequent measurement of well-defined target behaviors will enable you to make decisions about whether or not a particular student's behavior is in need of change. Direct and frequent observation of behavior will also allow you to determine the effectiveness of a specific behavior change strategy for individual children if you plot the data you have collected on a graph for visual inspection. Systematic techniques for observing behavior and for recording and

Systematic and frequent observation of behavior allows the teacher to determine the effectiveness of specific behavior change strategies implemented with individual children.

graphing data are well documented in the research literature, and a thorough description of these procedures is beyond the scope of this text. You are encouraged, however, to consult Alberto and Troutman (1995); Wolery, Bailey, and Sugai (1988); or Zirpoli and Melloy (1993) for excellent descriptions of these techniques designed for use by teachers. Among the most useful procedures for directly observing and recording behaviors of students in the classroom are anecdotal recording, event recording, duration and latency recording, and time sampling.

Anecdotal Recording. Anecdotal records are objective, written descriptions of a child's behavior within a particular setting (Alberto & Troutman, 1995). Using a standardized format, you write the time of your observation; antecedents, or events, you observe occurring immediately before the student's behavior; the observed behavior of the student; and the consequences that follow the child's behavior. As you write, you must take care to write only what the child, or others, say and do. Following your observation, analyze the antecedents, behavior, and consequences to determine if certain events are contributing to the student's behavior.

For example, after completing the anecdotal record depicted in Table 2.2, you may determine that Fong puts his head down and cries every time another student approaches him or talks to him. When Fong exhibits this behavior, his peers leave Fong alone, thus, negatively reinforcing his withdrawn behavior. You decide to begin a behavior change program so that Fong will become positively reinforced by social interactions with his classmates.

Event Recording. Event recording is a simple method of observing student behavior as it occurs. Sometimes called a *frequency count,* you simply make a tally mark each time you observe a child engaging in a particular behavior

---

Table 2.2 An Anecdotal Record for Fong during Free-Play Time

Time	*Antecedent*	*Behavior*	*Consequence*
2:35 PM	Jay walks to Fong and says "Want to play Monopoly?"	Fong turns head and pulls jacket over himself	Jay walks away
2:40 PM	Children are playing in groups	Fong pulls jacket off and looks out window	Children continue to play
2:45 PM	Checkers roll off table and one rolls near Fong's desk	Fong picks up the checker	Children pick up checkers on floor by play table
2:46 PM	Tomeka says, "Hey Fong, we need that checker, too."	Fong covers his head and puts the checker in his desk	Tomeka walks away

during a specified period. To be most accurate, event recording is used only for behaviors that are discrete (i.e., behaviors that have a distinct beginning and ending and that do not occur continuously over time or at a very rapid rate).

Once the tally marks are counted, the data should be displayed on a chart or a graph to enable you to determine any changes in behavior over time. If the length of your observational sessions remains constant, you may use simple frequency (i.e., the actual number of behaviors counted). If, however, the amount of time you observe varies from one session to the next, you must first convert frequency to rate (i.e., the number of behaviors you counted divided by the length of time you observed equals the number of behaviors per unit of time, or rate) to graph your data.

Suppose, for example, you count the number of obscenities stated by Paul during 30-minute lunch sessions in the school cafeteria. During the first week of daily observation, you count 23, 19, 21, 26, and 22 obscenities. Then, you begin a program to reinforce Paul for using words that are considered acceptable alternatives to obscenities. You notice that Paul's obscenities begin to decrease (e.g., 20, 17, 16, 14, 13), and his use of appropriate alternative words begins to increase. You conclude that this behavior change strategy is effective in changing Paul's behavior during lunchtime; therefore, you continue the procedure until the data indicate an acceptable level of behavior (Figure 2.2).

Duration and Latency Recording. Duration and latency recording are two similar procedures that consider length of time, rather than number, for a targeted behavior. Whereas duration measures the length of time a behavior actually occurs, latency determines the length of time passing *before* a behavior begins to occur. Duration recording is useful in determining how long continuous behaviors last (e.g., "out of seat," "head covering," "crying," or "thumb sucking"). On the other hand, latency recording is helpful to determine, for example, how long it takes a child to comply with your directions.

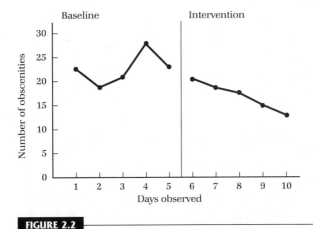

FIGURE 2.2

A Graph of Paul's Use of Obscenities in the Cafeteria

BOX 2.1 **Momentary Time Sampling for Keesha's On-Task Behavior**

Student: _____ Keesha Thomas _____ Date: ____ 11/18 ____
Time: ____ 9:00 AM–9:45 AM ____ Mathematics ____ Interval Length: ____ 3 min ____
Behavior Observed: <u>On task—Writing, reading math book, looking at the teacher,</u>
<u>speaking when recognized by teacher.</u>

Interval Number	+	−
1		−
2		−
3		−
4	+	
5		−
6	/	/
7		−
8		−
9	+	
10	+	
11		−
12		−
13		−
14	+	
15		−

Number of intervals observed: ____ 14* ____
Number of intervals on task: ____ 4 ____
Percent of intervals on task: ____ 29 ____

*Note that during interval 6 the teacher was unable to observe (e.g., a distraction occurred such as a visitor at the classroom door).

If you time each episode of Fong's "head covering behavior" depicted in Table 2.2, you will have a record of the number of times the behavior occurred, the duration of each episode of "head covering," and the total duration for the behavior during the observational session. By converting the total duration to a percentage of time (i.e., total duration divided by length of observation, multiplied by 100), you may graph your data and observe changes in behavior regardless of whether or not the length of your observational sessions varies from one day to the next. Similarly, you may prompt Keesha to sit down and then record the length of time before she begins to respond (i.e., latency). Recording the percentage of latency is helpful both when teachers wish to decrease the time it takes a child to respond and when teachers want to help children "slow down and think before they act" (i.e., to increase latency).

Time Sampling. Time-sampling procedures enable teachers to estimate the frequency and duration of high-rate or continuous behaviors without having to tally or time every single occurrence. The easiest procedure for teachers is momentary time sampling. To use momentary time sampling, divide an observational session (e.g., your 45-minute math class) into intervals of equal length (e.g., fifteen 3-minute intervals). Then, set a kitchen timer or the "beeper" on your watch to go off after the specified interval elapses.

When you hear the beeper or kitchen timer, observe whether or not the student is engaging in the targeted behavior at that exact moment in time. If the child is engaging in the behavior, place a mark in the "Yes" or "+" column next to the appropriate interval on an observation sheet. If the child is not demonstrating the behavior, place a mark in the "No" or "−" column. At the end of your observation session, count the number of intervals after which you observed the behavior to occur and the total number of intervals for which you actually observed. Convert this information to a percentage of intervals for recording on a graph (Box 2.1).

Summary of Informal Assessments ◆

Informal assessments allow teachers to observe behaviors as they occur within a particular context. Both sociometric techniques and direct observation permit teachers to supplement information gathered from standardized assessment instruments and enable professionals to make better decisions regarding behavioral problems and behavior change. Ongoing informal assessments yield valuable information regarding the effectiveness of interventions teachers use in the classroom. ◆

Summary

Effective screening is necessary if children with emotional and behavioral disorders are to be referred accurately for evaluation for special education programs. Early identification and intervention are also essential in maintaining the child in the regular classroom and preventing antisocial behaviors from becoming permanent problems. Accurate screening and classification decisions are made only when multiple sources of information are used by responsible professionals who consider a child's culture and his or her behavior in context.

Numerous standardized assessment instruments are available to assist teachers in detecting the behavioral and social-emotional difficulties of their students. Checklists, rating scales, interviews, and self-reports may help members of a multidisciplinary team identify children whose behavior differs significantly from that of their peers. Both clinically and statistically derived classification systems are used to determine whether or not a student has an emotional or behavioral disorder. Sociometrics and direct observation are informal assessment procedures that allow teachers to evaluate behavior within particular settings and judge the nature of behavior change.

Application Exercises

1. Examine three or four of the standardized assessment instruments listed in Table 2.1. Look carefully at the manual accompanying each test. What information is given regarding the sample population on which the test was standardized? Were students with learning and emotional or behavioral disorders included in the sample?

2. Examine the items included in several of the assessment instruments listed in Table 2.1. Are there any items that might be viewed differently by individuals from cultures varying from your own? Which ones and why?

3. Define a discrete behavior for a friend or a family member (e.g., saying "Please"). Use event recording to count the number of behaviors during set times for 1 week. Plot your data on a graph. Be sure to convert the data to rate if the length of your observation sessions varied from day to day.

4. Interview a member of a multidisciplinary team from your local school district. What types of information are used by the team to assess behavioral or social-emotional difficulties experienced by children and youth in that school? Do professionals in the school require and document prereferral interventions before a child is evaluated for special education?

References

Achenbach, T. M., & Edelbrock, C. S. (1991). *Child Behavior Checklist*. Burlington, VT: University of Vermont.

Alberto, P. A., & Troutman, A. C. (1995). *Applied behavior analysis for teachers* (4th ed.). Columbus, OH: Merrill.

Algozzine, B., Christenson, S., & Ysseldyke, J. (1992). Probabilities associated with referral-to-placement process. *Teacher Education and Special Education, 5*, 19–23.

American Psychological Association. (1994). *Diagnostic and Statistical Manual of Mental Disorders* (4th Ed.). Washington, DC: American Psychological Association.

Battle, J. (1992). *Culture-Free Self-Esteem Inventories* (2nd ed.). Austin, TX: Pro-Ed.

Bracken, B. (1992). *Multidimensional Self Concept Scale*. Austin, TX: Pro-Ed.

Brown, L., & Alexander, J. (1991). *Self-Esteem Index*. Austin, TX: Pro-Ed.

Brown, L., & Hammill, D. D. (1990). *Behavior Rating Profile-2*. Austin, TX: Pro-Ed.

Coie, J., Dodge, K., & Coppotelli, H. (1982). Dimensions and types of social status: A cross-age perspective. *Developmental Psychology, 18*, 557–570.

Coopersmith, S. (1981). *Coopersmith Self-Esteem Inventory*. Monterey, CA: Publishers Test Service.

Council for Children with Behavioral Disorders. (1989). Best assessment practices for students with behavioral disorders: Accommodation to cultural diversity and individual differences. *Behavioral Disorders, 14*(4), 263–278.

Cullinan, D., & Epstein, M. H. (1985). Adjustment problems of mildly handicapped and nonhandicapped students. *Remedial and Special Education, 6*(2), 5–11.

Dodge, K. A. (1982). Behavioral antecedents of peer status. *Child Development, 54,* 1400–1416.

Feil, E. G., & Becker, W. C. (1993). Investigation of a multiple-gated screening system for preschool behavior problems. *Behavioral Disorders, 19*(1), 44–53.

Fitts, W., & Roid, S. (1988). *Tennessee Self-Concept Scale.* Los Angeles: Western Psychological Services.

Gresham, F. M., & Elliott, S. N. (1989). Social skills assessment technology for LD students. *Learning Disability Quarterly, 12,* 141–152.

Gresham, F. M., & Elliott, S. N. (1990). *Social Skills Rating System.* Circle Pines, MN: American Guidance Service.

Gresham, F. M., & Reschly, D. J. (1988). Issues in the conceptualization, classification, and assessment of social skills in the mildly handicapped. In T. Kratochwill (Ed.), *Advances in school psychology* (pp. 203–247). Hillsdale, NJ: Erlbaum.

Hallahan, D. P., Keller, C. E., & Ball, D. W. (1986). A comparison of prevalence rate variability from state to state for each of the categories of special education. *Remedial and Special Education, 7*(2) 8–14.

Hresko, W. P., & Brown, L. (1984). *Test of Early Socioemotional Development.* Austin, TX: Pro-Ed.

Hutton, J. B., & Roberts, T. G. (1986). *Social-Emotional Dimension Scale: A Measure of School Behavior.* Austin, TX: Pro-Ed.

Kauffman, J. M. (1993). *Characteristics of emotional and behavioral disorders of children and youth* (5th ed.). New York: Macmillan.

Kaufman, M., Agard, J., & Semmel, M. (1985). *Mainstreaming: Learners and their environments.* Cambridge, MA: Brookline.

Kovacs, M. (1981). *Children's Depression Inventory.* Pittsburgh: University of Pittsburgh.

Lambert, N., Nihira, K., & Leland, H. (1993). *AAMR Adaptive Behavior Scales—School* (2nd ed.). Austin, TX: Pro-Ed.

Maag, J. W. (1989). Assessment in social skills training: Methodological and conceptual issues for research and practice. *Remedial and Special Education, 10*(4), 6–17.

McConaughy, S. H. (1993). Evaluating behavioral and emotional disorders with the CBCL, TRF, and YSR Cross-Informant Scales. *Journal of Emotional and Behavioral Disorders, 1*(1), 40–52.

McConnell, S., & Odom, S. (1986). Sociometrics: Peer-referenced measures and the assessment of social competence. In P. Strain, M. Guralnick, & H. Walker (Eds.), *Children's social behavior: Development, assessment, and modification* (pp. 215–284). Orlando, FL: Academic Press.

Newcomer, P. L. (1993). *Understanding and teaching emotionally disturbed children and adolescents* (2nd ed.). Austin, TX: Pro-Ed.

Newcomer, P., Barenbaum, E., & Bryant, B. (1994). *Depression and Anxiety in Youth Scale.* Austin, TX: Pro-Ed.

Peacock Hill Working Group. (1991). Problems and promises in special education and related services for children and youth with emotional or behavioral disorders. *Behavioral Disorders, 16,* 299–313.

Piers, E. V., & Harris, D. B. (1984). *Children's Self-Concept Scale (The Way I Feel About Myself) Revised.* Los Angeles: Western Psychological Services.

Quay, H. C., & Peterson, D. R. (1987). *Revised Behavior Problem Checklist.* Coral Gables, FL: University of Miami.

Reilly, T. F. (1991). Cultural Bias: The albatross of assessing behavior-disordered children and youth. *Preventing School Failure, 36*(1), 50–53.

Reynolds, W. (1985). *Child Depression Scale.* Odessa, FL: Psychological Assessment Resources.

Ruiz, N. T. (1989). An optimal learning environment for Rosemary. *Exceptional Children, 56*(2), 130–144.

Sabornie, E. J., & Kauffman, J. M. (1985). Regular classroom sociometric status of behaviorally disordered adolescents. *Behavioral Disorders, 10*(3), 191–197.

Sabornie, E. J., Kauffman, J. M., & Cullinan, D. A. (1990). Extended sociometric status of adolescents with mild handicaps: A cross-categorical perspective. *Exceptionality, 1*(3), 197–209.

Sevick, B., & Ysseldyke, J. (1986). An analysis of teachers prereferral interventions for students exhibiting behavioral problems. *Behavioral Disorders, 11*, 109–117.

Simpson, R. G. (1989). Agreement among teachers in using the Revised Behavior Problem Checklist to identify deviant behavior in children. *Behavioral Disorders, 14*(3), 151–156.

Simpson, R. G. (1991). Agreement among teachers of secondary students in using the Revised Behavior Problem Checklist to identify deviant behavior. *Behavioral Disorders, 17* (1), 66–71.

Simpson, R. G., & Halpin, G. (1986). Agreement between parents and teachers in using the Revised Behavior Problem Checklist to identify deviant behavior in children. *Behavioral Disorders, 12* (1), 54–59.

Sinclair, E., Del'Homme, M., & Gonzalez, M. (1993). Systematic screening for preschool behavioral disorders. *Behavioral Disorders, 18*(3), 177–188.

Sparrow, S., Balla, D. A., & Cicchetti, D. V. (1984). *Vineland Adaptive Behavior Scales.* Circle Pines, MN: American Guidance Service.

Thomas, A., & Chess, S. (1984). Genesis and evolution of behavioral disorders: From infancy to early adult life. *American Journal of Psychiatry, 141* (1), 1–9.

Thomas, A., Chess, S., & Birch, H. G. (1968). *Temperament and behavior disorders in children.* New York: New York University Press.

Walker, H. M., Block-Pedego, A., Todis, B., & Severson, H. (1991). *School Archival Records Search (SARS).* Longmont, CO: Sopris West.

Walker, H. M., & Fabre, T. R. (1987). Assessment of behavior disorders in the school setting: Issues, problems and strategies revisited. In N. Haring (Ed.), *Assessing and managing behavior disorders* (pp. 198–234). Seattle: University of Washington Press.

Walker, H. M., & Severson, H. H. (1990). *Systematic Screening for Behavior Disorders (SSBD): A Multiple Gating Procedure.* Longmont, CO: Sopris West.

Walker, H. M., Severson, H. H., Nicholson, F., Kehle, T., Jenson, W. R., & Clark, E. (1994). Replication of the Systematic Screening for Behavioral Disorders (SSBD) procedure for the identification of at-risk children. *Journal of Emotional and Behavioral Disorders, 2*(2), 66–77.

Walker, H. M., Severson, H., Stiller, B., Williams, G., Haring, N., Shinn, M., & Todis, B. (1988). Systematic screening of pupils in the elementary age range at risk for behavioral disorders: Development and trial testing of a multiple gating model. *Remedial and Special Education, 9*(3), 8–14.

Walker, H. M., Severson, H. H., Todis, B. J., Block-Pedego, A. E., Williams, G. J., Haring, N. G., & Barckley, M. (1990). Systematic Screening for Behavior Disorders (SSBD): Further validation, replication, and normative data. *Remedial and Special Education, 11*(2), 32–46.

Wolery, M., Bailey, D. B., & Sugai, G. M. (1988). *Effective teaching: Principles and procedures of applied behavior analysis with exceptional students.* Boston: Allyn & Bacon.

Ysseldyke, J. E., & Algozzine, B. (1983). LD or not LD: That's not the question! *Journal of Learning Disabilities, 16,* 29–31.

Ysseldyke, J. E., Algozzine, B., & Thurlow, M. L. (1992). *Critical issues in special education (2nd ed.). Boston: Houghton Mifflin.*

Zirpoli, T. J., & Melloy, K. J. (1993). *Behavior management: Applications for teachers and parents.* New York: Merrill.

Main Ideas

♦ *Families operate as complex, dynamic systems with the actions of each member affecting those of all other members.*

♦ *Parents, administrators, teachers, and students from various cultural or ethnic groups may have different expectations for, or interpretations of, behavior.*

♦ *Teachers may have a relatively narrow range of expectations regarding appropriate behaviors and standards of performance in the classroom.*

♦ *Students who deviate from classroom norms, particularly students with academic and behavioral problems, may experience a reduced sense of self-worth and contribute to decreased feelings of teacher self-efficacy or teaching effectiveness.*

♦ *Teachers who attend to the inappropriate behaviors of their troublesome students more often than to appropriate behaviors may find themselves engaged in coercive battles for control.*

♦ *Teachers must provide meaningful learning activities and opportunities for social interaction if students with learning and behavioral problems are to be motivated to learn and taught how to interact.*

Assessing the social-emotional and behavioral needs of students is essential to identify and provide assistance to those children and youth experiencing difficulty. Parents, regular classroom teachers, other school personnel such as the principal or guidance counselor, and peers are excellent sources of information for making decisions about whether or not a student's behavior differs enough from his or her classmates to warrant intervention or referral for special education evaluation. The checklists, rating scales, and other informal procedures for gathering information reviewed in Chapter 2 are valuable for the perspectives they yield; however, they tell us only the *perceptions* of different individuals regarding a particular student's behavior. They do not tell us much about the personal biases, tolerance levels, beliefs, or expectations of these individuals.

In this chapter, then, we will examine an area of importance equal to that of assessing the behaviors and social-emotional development of the individual child. We will consider the expectations of key individuals in the child's environment. Of particular concern are the expectations and beliefs of parents, other family members, and teachers, and how the expectations and needs of these individuals, especially those from differing cultures, interact and influence perceptions about a child's behavior and social-emotional functioning. To that end, we will first consider families as systems. Then, we will explore the expectations and beliefs parents and family members may hold about behavior. Finally, we will examine the expectations and beliefs of teachers that may dramatically affect their interactions with children and youth with emotional and behavioral disorders in the classroom.

Families as Systems

Professionals today view families as complex dynamic systems (Turnbull & Turnbull, 1990). Because the members of a family are in constant interaction, events and circumstances affecting one member of the family have an effect on other family members as well. When teachers consider the interactions among family members and how families must function as smaller units within society, their interventions are more likely to be successful.

Minuchin (1974) suggests that families are structured units with interdependent elements. Within families, interactions are reciprocal, and actions of family members are seen as purposeful attempts to help the family maintain stability. In addition, Shea and Bauer (1994) assert that professionals must consider the family's function across several contexts: (1) The microsystem or events and relationships within the immediate family unit; (2) the exosystem, or external social supports for the family such as church, neighborhood friends, or work; (3) the mesosystem, or the changing interrelationships across time among family members and various agencies such as the school; and (4) the macrosystem, or our societal beliefs about families.

According to Turnbull and Turnbull (1990), family characteristics also play an important role in determining how family members interact both within and outside of the family. Professionals may need to choose, for example, very different approaches for working with one family having two parents, one child, and a moderate income level and another family having only one parent, three children, and a low income. In addition, family cohesion (i.e., the ability of family members to behave independently while still supporting one another) and adaptability (i.e., the degree to which family members are able to change their interactions when under stress) are important considerations for teachers. Families with moderate levels of adaptability and cohesion may be healthier family units than those with higher or lower levels of cohesion and adaptability (Turnbull & Turnbull, 1990).

Simon and Johnston (1987) stress the importance for teachers of understanding the dynamic nature of families when dealing with parents and their children with emotional and behavioral disorders. All too often professionals view one family member, the child, as the "cause" of problems within the family, and interventions are designed to "fix" the youngster rather than address the family as a whole. Yet, a child's or adolescent's behavior is only one small part of the total family system. The youngster's behavior may have meaning or purpose for the family and somehow "fit" when viewed from a family-systems perspective (Paul & Epanchin, 1991).

For example, children, parents, siblings, and other family members form smaller subsystems (i.e., microsystems) within the family unit. Parent and child, child and grandparent, and grandparent and parent each may be microsystems within the total family. Thus, the behavior of a child who fails to complete his or her homework may be better understood if the teacher realizes that (1) grandmother cares for the child in the evening while the parent works, (2) grandmother is unable to help the child with homework and finds it easier to manage the child while watching television in the evening; and (3) the parent is obligated to the grandmother for providing free child care. Although the teacher must still find a way to help the child complete his or her homework, to intervene by addressing only one part of the family system (e.g., calling the parent) may prove futile and place additional stress on the total family.

Professionals are only just beginning to provide comprehensive systems of care to meet the complex needs of children and youth with emotional and behavioral disorders and their families (Epstein, et al., 1993). Parents and family members perceive a need for greater information about available community services and want help in finding recreational activities and alternative programs for their children (Soderlund, Epstein, Quinn, Cumblad, & Petersen, 1995). In addition, inconvenient location, limited hours, high cost, and a long wait to obtain services are barriers to families in need of assistance.

Expectations and Beliefs of Parents and Family Members

Just as children and adolescents have been viewed in the past as the "cause" of problems occurring within families, for many years, teachers and other professionals have also pointed to parents as the "cause" of behavioral and social-emotional difficulties experienced by their offspring. Lax supervision and inconsistent and harsh disciplinary measures used by parents may contribute to antisocial and aggressive behaviors, which become stable over time as the

BOX 3.1 **An Interview with a Family Member: My Sister through My Eyes**

Three years ago my sister was admitted to a psychiatric hospital. She was 16, and I was 13. They gave her all sorts of names such as "behavior disordered." My reaction was anger. "How could a stranger sit down with my sister, whom I had known and loved for 13 years, and pull words out of a book that summed up all her actions and problems?"

I also was angry that my sister was getting so much attention. In my mind, getting away from the chaos at home was more a vacation than a punishment. Family therapy was supposed to help us understand how to deal with my sister, but we didn't learn anything new. It wasn't fair that I had to miss out on things because my sister had problems. She had always had problems.

The 6-foot teenager in her black clothes, pink hair, and half-shaved head is my sister, and I love her this way just as much as I would someone a bit more like me. Although we've always had a good relationship, there were times she hid me in her shadows and embarrassed me. Sometimes she says really mean things to my friends, or "goes off" at them in public places. It's really hard to explain that's just how she is.

While a title for a particular behavior will suffice for doctors and specialists, I choose to think it doesn't come under definition. Rather, it's a part of someone's personality. You may not be able to change it; but given the time and devotion, you can learn to work with them and at times compromise with them. My sister has brought the family challenges, fear, hope, frustration, and, most of all, a love that we're proud to have.

From "My Sister through My Eyes," by J. Obrachter, 1993, *Journal of Emotional and Behavioral Problems*, 2(4), 4, National Educational Service.

child and parent engage in increasingly hostile, punitive, and coercive interactions with each other (Patterson, 1986). The siblings in these coercive families of antisocial children also tend to be more aggressive with each other and more aggressive at school (Stevenson-Hinde, Hinde, & Simpson, 1986). This does not mean, however, that the parents *caused* the behavioral problem. In fact, as we have seen, the behaviors of the parent, child, or other family members may interact in complex ways. That is, the adult lacking parenting skills may be making his or her "best attempt" to control the negative behavior of a difficult child. Even adults with excellent parenting skills may find themselves with offspring having behavioral disorders that produce a tremendous amount of daily stress for the parents and for the family.

The family certainly influences the child's behavior at school, but teachers must not automatically blame the family for all behavioral problems encountered in the classroom. Research has discredited the notion that parents are the primary cause of their children's behavioral difficulties (Kauffman, 1993). As a matter of fact, parents and other family members can be sources for potential solutions to problem behaviors at school (Dean, 1993). In addition, family members can contribute valuable information and insight regarding the strengths of children and youth with behavioral problems and the impact of these problems on the family as a whole (Box 3.1).

You probably noticed after reading Box 3.1 that this young lady poignantly described her sister with compassion, with love, and with an extraordinary degree of insight into her sister's functioning as a member within the family. Family members, particularly parents, have hopes and aspirations for their children. To consider them the cause of behavioral problems exhibited at school is to overlook the strengths of individual family members and to promote an adversarial, rather than a collaborative, approach to problem solving.

Under the Individuals with Disabilities Education Act (1990), parents have a legal right to be informed of and involved in the special education services provided to their children. This requires that parents be treated as active partners in their child's educational process (see Chapter 8 for suggestions on collaborating with parents). Some parents, however, may be unable to participate fully in this process. Caring for younger children at home, irregular or long work schedules, and lack of transportation may prohibit active involvement by some parents in their childrens' education (Lynch & Stein, 1987). Also, some parents may believe that schools and teachers are authorities. To these parents asking questions or offering suggestions to professionals is a sign of disrespect (Salend & Taylor, 1993). Even though the parent is interested in the child's welfare, he or she may refrain from participating as an active partner in meetings, and other

Parents, teachers, and students from diverse cultural or ethnic groups may have different interpretations of behavior.

Cultural Influences on Behavior

Members of cultural or ethnic groups share characteristic behaviors and beliefs. You must take care, however, not to stereotype individuals from particular cultural or ethnic groups. Individuals from the same group may differ from one another as much as they differ from members of other groups. Nevertheless, some social behaviors and beliefs are often shared among people from the same culture (Franklin, 1992; Kuykendall, 1992; Zirpoli & Melloy, 1993).

African Americans

Look away while listening and make constant eye contact while speaking
Stand close to others while speaking
Value family, extended family, the elderly, and religion
Are person-oriented, requiring recognition, affirmation, and positive attention
Come from high-energy, fast-paced home environments where there are simultaneous multiple sources of stimulation (e.g., both television and music playing with people talking and moving about freely)
Prefer active, group-oriented activities
Engage in "stage setting" before beginning work (i.e., behaviors considered to be necessary and important such as sharpening pencil, rearranging desk and posture, and checking directions with neighbors)

Native Americans

Consider eye contact a sign of disrespect or rudeness
Believe that to question or criticize someone in authority is disrespectful; therefore, they may not express differing opinions
Communicate opinions and feelings through subtle gestures and body language
Value sharing, humility, and listening
Believe that verbalizations should not be hurried or interrupted
Value the needs of individuals at the present rather than in the future
Feel they must be able to succeed before beginning a task
Require considerable personal space as a sign of respect
Value cooperation and group attainment over individual success and achievement
Share the responsibility for child rearing with extended family and value the opinions of elders

parents may appear disinterested or apathetic if they mistrust schools and teachers (Harry, 1992).

Moreover, cultural differences may produce barriers to effective communication with parents. For example, if parents have experienced discrimination at schools in the past, they may be unwilling to attend school conferences on behalf of their children (Salend & Taylor, 1993). Cultural differences regarding age, gender, and acceptable roles that various family members may assume also affect who should be invited or who might attend school meetings. In Native American, Latino American, and African American cultures, for example, the

Asian Americans

Consider eye contact or touching of strangers inappropriate

Believe that formality and politeness are essential social behaviors

Smile or laugh rather than express true emotions or feelings

Smile or laugh to avoid conflict

Believe that time is flexible, and one should not hurry

Value learning, high educational standards, and modesty

Value family and extended family

Believe that the behavior of an individual may reflect on the entire family; therefore, problems are not to be shared

Use nonverbal communications such as facial expressions, postures, and gestures to convey meaning

Have strict standards for roles and social behavior according to one's gender

Believe that to make suggestions or to ask questions of someone in authority is a sign of disrespect

Latino Americans

Value loyalty and responsibility to family and religion

Believe that prolonged eye contact is disrespectful

Engage in touching and embracing and gesturing while speaking

Stand close to others while speaking

Value the elderly, children, and helping one another

Express their emotions and feelings freely and openly

Express their opinions assertively

Interrupt one another's conversations and join in group conversations without being considered rude

Demonstrate traditional roles for males and females

Consult parents, extended family, and the elderly for advice regarding important decisions

Prefer to work interdependently within a social context rather than independently

extended family is of great importance, and elders, or grandparents, may be valued in the decision-making process.

Language may be an additional hindrance to communication, and parents from linguistically diverse backgrounds may require the assistance of an interpreter. Even with an interpreter, though, Salend and Taylor (1993) report that many words or concepts may not translate directly from the parent's native language to English (e.g., "Yes" may mean "I heard you" rather than "I agree with you"). In addition, Salend (1994) cautions teachers that Japanese American parents may believe that to discuss personal problems openly in meetings is to cause the family to "lose face" and that Native American families may believe in "holding the future" (i.e., to make negative comments about someone's future may cause that future to happen).

Parents have a responsibility to their children to supervise them carefully at home and to support them in their efforts at school. Certainly parents who express positive attitudes toward school, teachers, and homework and who provide educational stimulation for their children at home contribute to their children's success at school. Parents who voice clear expectations for school achievement, who believe their children can and will learn in school, who demonstrate a warm and encouraging relationship with their children characterized by directive, supportive, and kind but firm discipline, and who talk to their children encourage school success (Hess & Holloway, 1984).

Parents and teachers, however, may not share similar expectations about behaviors "appropriate" for success in school. Teachers often consider listening attentively, following directions promptly, efficiently using time, staying on task, and handling anger or frustration appropriately as behaviors that are essential for success in school (Fad & Ryser, 1993). In contrast, Box 3.2 (pp. 74–75) lists behavioral characteristics common to different cultural groups. Notice that many of these cultural differences may easily be misinterpreted as "inappropriate behavior" by teachers from another culture. For example, the teacher who considers "listening attentively" to be demonstrated by making eye contact and asking questions may believe that a Native American child is "inattentive." Or, the teacher who believes that learning takes place only when children work independently and silently in their seats may perceive the African American child to be "hyperactive" or a "behavioral problem."

In addition, teachers and parents may hold differing beliefs about discipline or about the cause and treatment of behavioral problems. If parents perceive the "cause" of their child's problems to be physical, for example, they may be less accepting of environmentally based behavioral interventions suggested by professionals (Reimers, Wacker, Derby, & Cooper, 1995). Moreover, some Asian and Native American families may use shame and ostracism to punish children, and in many Native American cultures "noninterference" is a form of respect (i.e., a belief that family members and friends must make their own mistakes without the interference of others). Parents from other cultural groups, however, may believe that "to spare the rod is to spoil the child." Salend and Taylor (1993) report that explanations for a child's problems may range from poor educational practices to a belief that problems are caused by spirits, fate, or failure to avoid taboos.

Parents and teachers may not agree on behaviors that are problematic or deviant in school (Simpson & Halpin, 1986). Each has a differing frame of reference for evaluating the child's behavior. Also, parents and teachers have expectations and beliefs about behavior that are firmly rooted in their own cultural values and traditions. Both parents and teachers, however, must take care not to ascribe the same beliefs and behaviors to *all* members of a particular cultural or ethnic group. Teachers must not assume that behaviors are problems caused by parents, that children are "culturally deprived," or that all members of a given group are alike. Rather, teachers must view students as coming to school with a wealth of experiences and then evaluate "behavioral problems" considering the entire family and the sociocultural context for the individual child.

Expectations and Beliefs of Teachers

Teachers are also products of their cultural heritage, and they, like parents, have individual tolerance levels, temperaments, and degrees of skill in managing difficult behaviors. Also like parents, teachers have differing expectations and beliefs regarding which behaviors are, or are not, "appropriate." Despite the growing diversity among children in schools, however, many teachers are likely to be from Caucasian, middle-class backgrounds (Gay, 1989; Gollnick, 1992). These teachers may unknowingly carry stereotypical views of others into their classrooms, which then affect their decisions about behavioral problems (Harry, Torguson, Katkavich, & Guerrero, 1993) (Box 3.3, pp. 78–79).

Although teachers cannot control what goes on in a student's home or community, school personnel can promote appropriate behavior by controlling what takes place during the school day. Kauffman (1993) lists several overlapping school-related factors that might contribute to the development of social-emotional and behavioral problems in the classroom. Expectations and behaviors demonstrated by persons at school that may be problematic for students include the following:

1. School administrators, teachers, and other pupils who are insensitive to a student's individuality
2. Inappropriate expectations held by teachers about their students, including bias and rigid standards for classroom performance
3. The use of inconsistent behavior management practices by some teachers and the incorrect use of reinforcement
4. Instruction that appears irrelevant to a student's life
5. Peers and teachers who are models of undesirable conduct (Kauffman, 1993, p. 251).

Sensitivity to the Needs of Individuals

Schools must promote positive, safe, and orderly climates in which learning can occur. This requires teachers and principals to express their expectations for academic performance clearly and consistently and to set reasonable rules to govern the actions of students (Box 3.4, p. 80). On the other hand, teachers and principals who rigidly adhere to rules that do not make sense to students or who demand the same academic and behavioral performance from all students may set the stage for learning and behavioral problems.

Numerous studies, however, indicate a degree of uniformity among teachers regarding their expectations for appropriate behaviors in the classroom. For example, Center and Wascom (1987) found that teachers perceive children and youth with behavioral disorders, especially boys, to exhibit fewer prosocial behaviors and more antisocial behaviors than peers in the regular classroom at both the elementary and secondary levels. Similarly, teachers view behaviors such as good work habits, academic performance, and

BOX 3.3   Teacher Feature: Finding a Common Ground

Harry and her colleagues (1993) required teachers to conduct interviews with families from cultural or ethnic groups different from their own. The following excerpts are from these interview assignments:

Interview 1.   I would describe my first encounter with Gail Grant's mother as "stepping into another world." I have always considered my life experiences to have been rather varied, but as I approached Gail's neighborhood, I noticed a change that made me a bit apprehensive. It was not a structural change—the stores, the houses, the cars still seemed familiar—but there was something about the people. They were doing normal things like pushing children in strollers, walking from the metro station, and riding bicycles, but they were all different from me—they were all African American.

Some part of my subconscious kept telling me to keep my eyes open, to see whether I could spot another white person, as if such a discovery would somehow reassure me that I was not in the wrong place and that I was safe. I vividly remember having these thoughts while at the same time laughing at myself and thinking, "Man, you're nuts! What are you afraid of?"

As I arrived at the Grant's front door, my thoughts quickly moved to the challenge of the task at hand: I was about to strike up what I expected to be a rather intrusive conversation with a complete stranger about some of her personal family traumas. My heart was racing, and I braced myself.

As I stepped into their home, I saw Mrs. Grant's two young daughters walk past me and run upstairs, the elder carrying a screaming baby, their youngest sibling. They had just been told to put the baby to bed. I said "Hi" as they passed, and they smiled, continuing about their responsibilities. I stood in the dining area and watched as Mrs. Grant wiped the dining table with a cloth, then invited me to sit down. I began to calm down as I realized that this was just a family with young children doing average family things. The things this family had been through, however, were not so "average": The oldest son is a convicted juvenile sex offender who assaulted two young girls and has been incarcerated for two years.

I had tried to condition myself to meet with a family who had suffered this sort of trauma, but I was nervous. How do you talk to a mother whose son has committed such horrible crimes? As I listened to Mrs. Grant talk about her family's concerns, the literature we had read in class began to come alive. Mrs. Grant was experiencing the same concerns all families must face. We spoke of child care, health care, networks of friends, in-laws, religion, and, of course, stress and trauma. I realized that culture, race, and socioeconomic status may

appropriate classroom conduct, including compliance and motivation, to be critical for success in the classroom (Kauffman, Wong, Lloyd, Hung, & Pullen, 1991). Conversely, behaviors that challenge teacher authority or that disrupt classroom order and routine are considered unacceptable by most teachers.

change what a family's activities look like, but they are essentially the same things that every family in every cultural group must do.

As we talked, my petty anxieties dissipated and I saw that she was a mother like any other mother, trying to do the best for her family while coping with some hard realities. I began to admire her for her composure while she wrestled with the mixed feelings of fear, anger, and love she had for her son—her first child—who now faced an uncertain future.

At the end of the interview I felt embarrassed about my irrational concerns, and to some extent I feel embarrassed now to admit them. My work with Mrs. Grant helped me to learn that although we may feel separate and distant from people who are not from our own cultural, ethnic, or racial group, we can readily find things that all people have in common.

Interview 2. Although I looked forward to the interview, it was not until I actually conducted it that I became aware of the numerous negative stereotypes lurking at the back of my brain that influenced my expectations of this meeting. First, Mrs. Evan's personal appearance and manner were impressive, and I was surprised to find myself surprised. She was an attractive, nicely dressed young woman. . . . The information she gave me revealed a strong woman who did not have much formal education but who was clearly intelligent and articulate. Even more surprising than her personal presentation was her intense personal concern for her children. Why should I have been surprised that she was as concerned about her children as I am about mine?

Another clue to my stereotyped expectations was my surprise at Mrs. Evan's skillful and effective handling of her 2-year-old-son. The toddler had gotten hold of a pair of scissors, and his mother convinced him in a calm and positive manner to hand it over to her. I realized that I had expected her to shout at him or even slap him.

Yet another revelation came when Mrs. Evans talked about the many relatives who comprised a strong network of support for her family and about her older son's good relationship with his father, who did not live with them. I was stunned. I had pictured this mother and her children alone and isolated in an awful apartment . . . [rather than living in] one of the newer, more comfortable looking townhouses in the project.

From "Crossing Social Class and Cultural Barriers in Working with Families: Implications for Teacher Training," by B. Harry, C. Torguson, J. Katkavich & M. Guerrero, *Teaching Exceptional Children*, 26(1), 1993, pp. 50–51. Copyright © 1993 by The Council for Exceptional Children. Reprinted with permission.

When students deviate from what is considered acceptable and appropriate by teachers, principals, and peers, they may experience either subtle or blatant pressure to conform. Adults who ignore a student's biological temperament and behavioral style may unwittingly contribute to a cycle of poor self-perception and negative interactions, which facilitates the development of emotional and be-

BOX 3.4 **Characteristics of Reasonable Rules**

Rules are necessary to define expectations for appropriate student behavior and to clarify the consequences of inappropriate behavior. Classroom rules provide stability and consistency in student-student and teacher-student interactions. When developing classroom rules, however, teachers should use the following guidelines:

1. Develop only four or five essential rules.
2. Phrase rules positively (i.e., rules should tell students what to do rather than what not to do).
3. Develop rules with student input whenever possible so that rules "make sense" to students.
4. Clearly state appropriate behaviors that are expected and the positive consequences for following the rules as well as the consequences for breaking the rules.
5. Post the rules for all to see.
6. Review the rules and consequences periodically for practice and to ensure that the rules are still necessary.

havioral disorders (Martin, 1992; Thomas & Chess, 1984). That is, students who enter the classroom with "acceptable" social, behavioral, and academic skills are likely to please their teachers and to produce positive reactions from adults and peers at school. These positive reactions, in turn, may foster additional pleasing behaviors and a positive self-esteem. Students with difficult behavioral styles (e.g., irritability or hyperactivity) who meet with little acceptance or approval at school, however, are likely to react with resentment, hostility, and behaviors such as vandalism, which provoke additional negative and punitive responses from teachers and principals (Kauffman, 1993; Mayer, Nafpaktitis, Butterworth, & Hollingsworth, 1987).

Recently, in an attempt to set clear and consistent rules for student conduct, principals and teachers have begun to adopt school-wide discipline policies and classroom-wide "systems" for behavior management. Clearly written school policies and codes for conduct are essential legal requirements within schools and school systems to inform students and parents regarding behavioral expectations and consequences for noncompliance. A sound school discipline policy is one proactive step schools can take to prevent much student misbehavior and violence. On the other hand, packaged discipline programs are designed to make classroom management systematic and "foolproof" for teachers by providing them with a series of steps or a set of procedures to follow. According to Wolfgang (1995), school administrators often adopt these methods, expect all teachers to follow them after brief workshop training sessions, and then express disappointment when teachers fail to use the methods because they do not "fit" student or teacher needs. For example, two management systems widely adopted in schools, Assertive Discipline (Canter & Canter, 1976) and Positive Classroom Discipline (Jones,

1987), may foster a sense of alienation among some students (Curwin & Mendler, 1988), contributing to discipline problems experienced by teachers in their classrooms.

Assertive Discipline (Canter & Canter, 1976). Assertive Discipline is based on the notion that teachers must (1) Determine the rules and the consequences for compliance and noncompliance with the rules, (2) Explain the discipline plan to all students verbally, (3) Give students a warning so that they may choose to behave or to accept the consequences for their behavior, and (4) Give rewards for complying with the rules and swift and assertive punishment for rule-breaking. Canter and Canter (1976) maintain that teachers have the right to determine and request appropriate behaviors from students that meet the teacher's needs without violating what is in the best interest of the student and that teachers have the right to expect support from parents and principals in disciplining children.

Frequently, in practice, following an explanation and posting of the rules and consequences, the teacher places a marble in a jar or a mark on a chart when students are complying with rules. When students accrue a specified number of marbles or marks, they receive the preset reward (e.g., a "popcorn party" on Friday). When students violate rules, however, the teacher places the student's name on the board as a warning. Each additional rule violation results in a check mark placed beside the student's name with each check carrying an increasing penalty (e.g., one check for 15 minutes detention; two checks for 30 minutes detention and student must call parents; three checks for 30 minutes detention, call parents, and meet with the principal).

Positive Classroom Discipline (Jones, 1987). Jones (1987) instructs teachers to begin the year by teaching *their* rules and consequences. When students comply with rules, they earn incentives called *preferred activity time.* Preferred activities are enjoyable for students, but they are also activities of educational value (e.g., bingo, jeopardy or baseball using math or science facts). When students violate rules, however, teachers are encouraged to set clear limits and to use body language effectively to establish their personal power and control as the teacher. Jones (1987) describes a student's inappropriate behavior in the classroom and the teacher's disciplinary response when setting limits as a poker game with increasing stakes. As Jones (1987) states, "Limit-setting is little more than calmly killing time from a series of predetermined positions. As the students bet, you move in. When they fold, you stop, prompt them back to task if necessary, thank them politely, and slowly move out. Power is control, and control begins with self-control" (p. 102). Jones explicity describes the mechanics of teacher body language:

1. Have eyes in the back of your head.
2. Terminate instruction.
3. Turn, look, and say the student(s) name(s).
4. Walk to the front edge of the student's desk.
5. Prompt (i.e., lean forward and give one or two simple statements telling the student what he or she needs to be doing).

6. Palms (i.e., place both of your palms flat on the far side of the student's desk on either side of his or her work so that you are eyeball to eyeball with the student).
7. Camping out in front (i.e., waiting out the student who is still failing to comply by "oozing" one's weight down onto the elbows).
8. Camping out from behind (i.e., leaning down and between two students who are continuing to misbehave so as to block their view of each other).

Teachers must not assume that there is something inherently wrong in setting rules, providing consistent consequences, and setting limits. To the contrary, these are well-established practices for managing behavior in the classroom, and programs such as Assertive Discipline (Canter & Canter, 1976) can be effective for many students (Mandlebaum, Russell, Krouse, & Gonter, 1983). Moreover, the Canters encourage teachers to involve students in setting rules as the teacher's skill with Assertive Discipline improves. Nevertheless, concerns arise regarding the impact of prepackaged programs such as Assertive Discipline or Positive Classroom Discipline on the needs of *individual* students, particularly when teachers adhere strictly to the procedures outlined in these programs.

For example, Jones (1987) advocates powerful body language to control student misbehavior. His series of steps, however, is designed systematically to invade the student's personal space and this invasion may violate cultural norms for some students. In addition, students who are already anxious may experience increased anxiety when their personal space is violated. Thus, the teacher may actually escalate the child's behavior to increasing levels of aggressiveness or violence (Steiger, 1987). Finally, although teachers cannot teach effectively when students are misbehaving, the series of steps to control behavior described by Jones does detract from the instructional time of other students. This, in turn, may precipitate negative interactions between the student and his or her peers.

In addition, both Assertive Discipline (Canter & Canter, 1976) and Positive Classroom Discipline (Jones, 1987) encourage teachers and school administrators to behave autocratically. Teachers and principals make and enforce the rules and students are expected to obey. Embedded deeply within these models, however, is the implicit assumption that the student is the problem and that his or her reasons for misbehaving are unimportant (Render, Padilla, & Krank, 1989). Students may feel alienated or degraded, for example, when their name is written publicly on the board without any attempt by the teacher to determine the reasons behind the "misbehavior." The student who deviates from the norm quickly learns a lesson about his or her self-worth in the classroom, particularly if peers perceive the student to be responsible for their losing a privilege or missing a marble in the jar (Curwin & Mendler, 1988). Also, students may quickly learn to sabotage the teacher's plan and engage the teacher in coercive interactions to regain control.

Although basic codes for appropriate conduct offer schools a degree of legal protection and are essential for the safe and efficient day-to-day operation of schools, teachers and school administrators may demonstrate insensitivity to the needs of individual students when they rigorously apply the same discipline programs to all students or when they require rigid adherence to the same behaviors and levels of performance for all students. Behaviors occur in complex interactions among teachers and students. Teachers and school administrators who are intolerant, who allow little student participation in determining rules and consequences, and who fail to support the individual needs of students are creating situations in which some students will ultimately fail (Kauffman, 1993).

Yet, students with emotional and behavioral disorders in particular may be more satisfied with their school when they perceive greater levels of involvement, affiliation, and teacher support (Leone, Luttig, Zlotlow, & Trickett, 1990). Teachers may wish to use a standardized instrument such as the Classroom Environment Scale (Moos & Trickett, 1986; Trickett, Leone, Fink, & Braaten, 1993) to measure the perceptions young people with behavioral and learning problems have regarding their classrooms and teachers. The Classroom Environment Scale may give teachers in special education settings a picture of how students view their involvement and level of support in the classroom as well as the students' perceptions of the degree of teacher control, clarity of rules, and overall organization and task orientation within the classroom. Children and youth with behavioral disorders have much to say about the sensitivity, fairness, and respect they hope their teachers will demonstrate toward them (Box 3.5, p. 84).

Appropriate Expectations: Examining Bias and Rigid Standards

Closely related to the notion of insensitivity to individual needs are inappropriate expectations held by teachers. Inappropriate expectations may arise from beliefs teachers hold about a student based on the student's label or from classroom standards that do not match a student's abilities. The concern is that if teachers have preconceived expectations regarding a particular student's behavior then that behavior may become a self-fulfilling prophecy (Rosenthal & Jacobson, 1968).

Teachers do have biases regarding the labels given to children in special education programs. For example, children who are described as aggressive and disruptive are viewed negatively by their teachers (Johnson & Blankenship, 1984). In addition, when given fictitious information about hypothetical students, teachers may perceive those students who are labeled "behaviorally disordered" to be more teachable than those who are labeled "emotionally disturbed" (Lloyd, Kauffman, & Gansneder, 1987). We cannot assume, of course, that biases held by teachers automatically result in the student's demonstrating the expected behavior. We can anticipate, however, that these preconceived notions may set the stage for negative interactions between the teacher and student, or the student and peers, which then may contribute to the student's behavior.

If, for example, you believe that students with behavioral disorders are disruptive, you may direct more effort and attention toward "catching" the disruptive behavior of these students, while overlooking that of other students in the classroom. Similarly, if you do not believe that a particular intervention to manage the behavior of students in your classroom is acceptable or feasible then you may not use it, or you may implement it inappropriately, regardless of its demonstrated effectiveness (Odom, McConnell, & Chandler, 1994; Whinnery,

BOX 3.5 What Students with Behavioral Disorders Believe Their Teachers Should Learn

Students with behavioral disorders, ages 12 to 18, were asked what they believe their teachers should learn or know. Their comments offer excellent suggestions.

Fairness and Respect

Have an open mind and don't be prejudiced against us. Don't go by past history.

Don't pick out one student to be the favorite just because he or she works better.

Don't embarrass students in front of others. Single students out to talk with them rather than in front of the class.

Don't discriminate against students by the way they dress or who they hang around with.

Use books and materials in a way that preserves the dignity of students.

Don't talk down to students, and don't compare kids.

Don't blow things out of proportion or overreact.

Take time to work with all students.

Relationship and Counseling Skills and Personal Qualities

Understand why students get mad, and help them with it instead of punishing them.

Make students feel good about themselves.

Talk more to students. Be willing to take the time to discuss matters of importance to students.

Listen to what students have to say.

Try to feel a student's feelings, and give students a way to express their feelings.

Know that small problems to teachers can be big problems to students.

Be patient, friendly, and open, and have a sense of humor.

Have a positive attitude and be helpful.

Deal with your own anger, and control your emotions so you don't take things out on students at school.

Be nice and be polite.

Behavior Management

Don't be overly strict.

Know how to discipline without hurting.

Know what sets people off so it can be prevented.

Find ways to deal with students other than threatening.

Learn to keep your hands to yourself, and don't push kids around.

Don't rattle the kids.

Adapted from "Don't ratl the kiDs," by E. H. Bacon and L. A. Bloom, *Journal of Emotional and Behavioral Problems*, 3(1), 8–9, National Educational Service.

Fuchs, & Fuchs, 1991). Your beliefs affect your actions and interactions with students in your classroom. These interactions affect the behaviors of your students, which in turn further affect your own beliefs and actions.

Expecting or demanding appropriate behavior does not necessarily result in that behavior occurring, however, particularly if one's expectations are unrealistically high or low. Unfortunately, the expectations of many teachers do not accurately match the abilities of students with emotional and behavioral disorders (Kauffman & Wong, 1991). Regular classroom teachers expect a quiet, orderly atmosphere in which students behave as members of a larger instructional group (Baker & Zigmond, 1990). Behaviors related to work habits (e.g., listens to directions and instructions, completes homework, follows directions, stays on task), to coping skills (e.g., copes appropriately when insulted or when bossed, able to express anger appropriately, avoids argument when provoked, can accept not getting own way), and to peer relationships (e.g., knows how to join group activity, develops and maintains friendships) are considered by teachers as critical for student success in the regular classroom (Fad & Ryser, 1993). Students with learning disabilities or emotional and behavioral disorders, however, may not ask for assistance, answer questions, or otherwise interact with teachers on learning activities at the same rate as their peers (McIntosh, Vaughn, Schumm, Haager, & Lee, 1994).

Regular classroom teachers at both the elementary and secondary levels expect their students to follow classroom rules, listen to teacher instructions, comply with teacher commands, complete assignments, produce work of acceptable quality, ask for assistance appropriately, and respect the property and rights of others (Hersh & Walker, 1983; Kerr & Zigmond, 1986; Walker & Ranking, 1983). Similarly, engaging in inappropriate sexual behavior, stealing, behaving inappropriately in class after being corrected, damaging the property of others, refusing to obey classroom rules, ignoring teacher warnings or reprimands, and making lewd or obscene gestures are behaviors considered intolerable by classroom teachers. In contrast to earlier beliefs (Wickman, 1928), today teachers are considered to be reliable judges of those behaviors that place children at risk for failure in regular classrooms, regardless of whether or not a particular behavior violates the tolerance level or standards of an individual teacher (Garber & Newton, 1989; Kauffman, Wong, Lloyd, Hung, & Pullen, 1991). The range of behaviors necessary for success in school, however, is obviously quite narrow, and, given the aggressive and demanding nature of many students with behavioral disorders, the expectations of classroom teachers may be too high for some of these youngsters.

Individual teachers do, of course, vary on their particular tolerance levels and standards for behavior (Kauffman, Lloyd, & McGee, 1989). Also, regular and special educators may vary somewhat on their perceptions of problem behavior. That is, special education teachers may perceive behaviors to be less deviant or more tolerable than do regular classroom teachers (Landon & Messinger, 1989; Safran & Safran, 1987). In addition, although regular and special educators may agree on the nonacademic, behavioral skills necessary for success in the classroom, they may differ on their perceptions of the extent to which special education students actually possess these skills (Downing, Simpson, & Myles, 1990).

Interestingly, research suggests that the most effective teachers may also have lower tolerance levels and higher standards for behavior (Gersten, Walker, & Darch, 1988; Walker & Rankin, 1983). Effective teachers may actually resist the placement of students into their classrooms who disrupt order and the learning activities of others. Landrum (1992) poses three possible explanations for this resistance: (1) Effective teachers may not believe they are able to handle extreme behavioral or academic deviance; (2) Effective teachers may believe that a particular range of skills contributes to their success as teachers; therefore, children who deviate from the norm may limit their effectiveness; or (3) Effective teachers may believe that special education students require a different type of instruction for which the teacher does not feel either trained or responsible. In addition, the instructional behaviors of more- and less-effective teachers may vary by educational level and setting (Nowacek, McKinney, & Hallahan, 1990). For example, effective elementary-level and special education teachers pose questions and approve of student responses, praise, and call for order more frequently than do secondary-level teachers. On the other hand, effective teachers at the secondary level expect students to focus on content learning and independent assignments, and they transfer responsibility for basic skills and social behaviors to students (Nowacek, McKinney, & Hallahan, 1990).

Students who deviate from the expectations and standards of their teachers, then, may find themselves engaging in increasingly negative interactions with their teachers. Neither teacher nor student experiences a feeling of self-efficacy (i.e., an individual's personal expectations for success, which determine how long and intensely the individual will persist, particularly in the face of problems) (Bandura, 1977). Thus, the motivation and efforts of teacher and student to meet the needs and expectations of the other decrease over time when neither feels successful (Ashton & Webb, 1986; Sachs, 1990). If standards and expectations are too high, students may become frustrated academically and behaviorally and give up, become angry, or demonstrate other "inappropriate" and "intolerable" behaviors. If standards and expectations are too low, however, students are relegated to reduced levels of performance and apathy, and again, they may display "unacceptable" behaviors to gain recognition and success. The teacher who experiences reduced success with the student, in turn, may decrease his or her actions on the student's behalf because he or she feels less competent, less effective, and less successful.

Consistency and the Correct Use of Reinforcement

Teachers who inconsistently or harshly discipline students may, like parents, contribute to the behavioral difficulties of those children and youth in their care (Mayer, Nafpaktitis, Butterworth, & Hollingsworth, 1987). You will recall that one necessary ingredient of a safe, productive classroom is the teacher's consistent enforcement of rules and consequences that students believe to be fair. Teachers who consistently praise and reward the appropriate behaviors and actions of their students, while withholding rewards or attention for inappropriate behaviors, increase desirable student behaviors (Alberto & Troutman, 1995).

Research indicates, though, that teachers may recognize and attend to individuals who *violate* the rules more often than to those who are following the rules (Strain, Lambert, Kerr, Stagg, & Lenkner, 1983). This negative attention may be particularly true of students with behavioral disorders. Students with emotional and behavioral disorders emit more verbal attempts to receive teacher attention and receive more teacher attention for nonacademic behaviors such as being "out of seat" than do their classmates (Slate & Saudargas, 1986). Apparently, teacher-child interactions in classrooms are often characterized by teachers telling students to do or not to do something, with few positive consequences following a student's compliance or demonstration of prosocial behaviors. Additionally, students with behavior disorders, especially aggressive children, are more likely than their peers to receive negative rather than positive consequences from their teachers (Shores et al., 1993).

Unfortunately, as we have seen, appropriate school behaviors and academic tasks may not be particularly rewarding for students with learning and behavioral difficulties. As a matter of fact, these students may perceive academic interactions with their teachers to be unpleasant or aversive stimuli to be avoided (Gunter, Denny, Jack, Shores, & Nelson, 1993). Thus, students with behavioral disorders may engage in noxious behaviors if these behaviors result in the

Students with behavioral disorders may exhibit increasingly troublesome behaviors in the classroom to obtain teacher attention or avoid "unpleasant" academic activities.

removal of the unpleasant task or teacher request. In effect, they coerce their teachers to comply with their demands for attention or for the removal of work by *increasing* their troublesome behaviors.

Similarly, Shores, Gunter, and Jack (1993) suggest that setting rules and arranging consequences may enhance the effects of teacher coercion (i.e., the teacher's attempts to get students to comply with the rules). Teachers, like students, are negatively reinforced when their disapproving statements or reprimands result in the temporary erradication of the student's undesirable behavior. Typical classroom management strategies used by teachers appear, then, to set the events for coercive interactions among teachers and their difficult students. Teachers set the rules and give relatively few positive consequences for compliance. On the other hand, teachers perceive that negative consequences stop inappropriate behavior, at least temporarily. Students with emotional and behavioral disorders, then, escalate their attempts to avoid unpleasant academic activities or the requests of their teachers by engaging in higher levels of troublesome behaviors. When these behaviors result in the desired teacher attention or removal of the activity, the student receives his or her "payoff" for the inappropriate behavior and continues attempts to escape or avoid the aversive task in the future. Landrum (1992) suggests that classroom teachers may actually become the "victims" of students with behavior disorders who are skilled at coercion both at home and at school.

You must not interpret this discussion to mean that teachers should not set rules or enforce the consequences in their classrooms. If teachers set rules that are perceived to be fair by students, and if teachers attend to appropriate student behaviors *more often* than they do to inappropriate behaviors, their students will behave more appropriately. If, on the other hand, teachers ignore misbehavior one day and harshly punish it the next, or if teachers fail to acknowledge students' prosocial behaviors, they will foster behavioral problems.

Relevant Instruction and Acceptable Models of Conduct

To say that students must understand the relevance of instruction to their lives to be motivated to learn sounds simplistic. If, however, students receive daily worksheets and textbook assignments with few "hands-on" experiences, they may not see the relevance of the learning activity to real life. Moreover, if teachers and peers appear unmotivated and unenthusiastic about activities in the classroom, we cannot expect students with academic or behavioral difficulties to become motivated on their own. If teachers or high-status peers are models of rude or cruel behavior, we may expect similar behaviors to spread to others (Bandura, 1986; Kauffman, 1993).

Yet, a climate of control and of limited academic activities and social interactions appears to characterize many programs for students with emotional and behavioral problems (Knitzer, Steinberg, & Fleisch, 1990). Following a "walking tour" of programs considered by school officials to be exemplary, Knitzer, Steinberg, and Fleisch (1990) described the classroom life of students

BOX 3.6   An Example of One Teacher's Classroom: When Nothing Goes Wrong

I had an exceptional day with my class last Monday. It led to an even more exceptional week. The kids were actively involved in the activities; no one told me to do things with my body that were anatomically impossible; and they all turned in their homework.

Let me recap my day. I teach in a junior high school behavioral disordered program and have several different classes in English, social skills, and resource room. For the past eight weeks, we have been reading George Orwell's *Animal Farm* in one of my English classes. This is a large class, about 30 students, many of whom are labeled behaviorally disordered and all of whom are "at risk." We have discussed plot diagrams with rising and falling action, character analysis and comprehension questions in cooperative groups. The groups have stayed together for the entire unit and have become adept at getting work accomplished and at understanding the concepts.

Today's activity involved an interview show, starring Sally Jessy Raphael, a.k.a., Lynne Schroeder, our drama teacher. Each student had the part of an animal from Orwell's book and each was asked questions about their identity, what they did and who they represented in Russian history. These kids knew the material and it showed! We invited an audience, including people from our Central Administration Office . . . and our principal. He sent us a note after the performance, praising the students and their hard work. I copied the note and was amazed at how many of the copies disappeared to show parents, friends, and fellow teachers about our success.

The following week, we developed our own country, much like the pigs did in *Animal Farm.* This was a joint project with Scott Bendler, our social studies teacher, who was teaching a unit on socialism and capitalism. . . . Our classes again rallied to the cause and presented a program on their "new" countries to local newspaper staff.

My next class was studying *Slake's Limbo,* by Felice Holman. This is a book about the homeless and we are creating homes in class much like Slake does in the book. For those not familiar with this work, Slake is a 13-year-old boy who has no home and finds a space under a motel by the New York City subway lines to live. His space is about the size of a refrigerator box, and we have replicated his home in our classroom. We have discussed issues such as free meals, laws for kids under the age of 16, and the art of graffiti, but most importantly, we have learned how difficult life is for people in our own community who are homeless. We are planning to visit areas in our town where homeless people live, such as shelters, missions, and assorted hiding spots. These visits will include reading to kids at a local shelter, serving in a soup line and making beds, etc. As a result of these activities, the class has put together a poetry book with some unbelievable insights into the plight of the homeless.

Adapted from "When Nothing Goes Wrong," by B. Peterson, 1990, *Beyond Behavior,* 2(1), 3–4.

with emotional and behavioral disorders to be at best "dry." Although the class size was usually small, these researchers found, the following:

- ◆ Worksheets and textbooks with teacher directions and questions about these materials were the primary instructional activities.
- ◆ Point systems, classroom arrangements, and teacher instructions frequently prohibited students from interacting with one another, even during social skills lessons.
- ◆ Students were often denied recess, physical education, or other fun activities because of their behavior.
- ◆ Students appeared to be bored and sleepy.
- ◆ Teachers appeared to miss many opportunities to teach important skills and to make connections to their student's daily lives.

Certainly, students with emotional and behavioral disorders may provoke negative reactions from teachers and from one another. These behaviors may precipitate controlling responses from teachers that are designed to limit negative behaviors and reduce opportunities for friction and problematic interactions among their students. We must forgive our students for their unenthusiastic responses to our instruction, however, if we provide them only with activities for which they see no real meaning and if we simultaneously prevent them from engaging in meaningful interactions with each other. If we are models of control and boredom, then we might expect apathetic and controlling responses, rather than excitement and willing participation, from our students. On the other hand, teachers who engage students in real-life instructional activities have less difficulty "motivating" students to learn and keeping students on task (McWhirter & Bloom, 1994). See Box 3.6 (p. 89) for an example of one teacher's classroom that provides numerous opportunities for meaningful learning experiences as well as activities structured to promote interactions among students so that social skills instruction may take place.

Teachers, Schools, and Conflicting Expectations

Schools and teachers must consider the impact of their actions on the behaviors of those students and parents they serve. Certainly, teachers and principals are affected by their own cultural heritage, family pressures, and individual temperaments, or behavioral style. They have personal expectations for behavior, standards for performance, and levels of tolerance that may not always be attuned to the needs of individual children and youth. Teachers and other school personnel are, however, equally impacted by the behavior of those in the school community, including parents, other professionals, and the students in their schools. Teachers receive both subtle and blatant messages from principals, parents, school boards, students, and the media regarding expectations for their performance in the classroom.

Often, the messages teachers receive about their own performance or that of their students is conflicting. The media or parent organizations stress academic achievement levels and standardized test scores and criticize schools for failing to produce students who can compete in a global marketplace. At the same time, local school boards or town, city, or county governments raise "standards" and reduce school budgets, asking schools to do more with less. Parents place blame on teachers for failing to "discipline" children at school, while individual parents threaten to take legal action against the teacher or school when they believe their own child's rights to be violated. State and federal regulations dictate mandates to which school's must comply, although teachers and principals may not believe that these requirements are always in the best interests of *their* students. Committees decree the curricular materials teachers may use, and principals may demand particular behaviors or actions from teachers. Teachers, however, may not perceive these materials or actions to be helping them or their students in the classroom.

Regular classroom teachers and parents, too, may believe that teachers shouldn't do anything different or additional for one child that they aren't doing for others. That is, they may believe that to construct a behavior management plan that is separate or unique for a specific child, for example, is unfair to other children in the classroom. Yet, many professionals and students themselves do believe that a teacher is being most fair when he or she makes adaptations appropriate for the individual child. Important beliefs and conflicting pressures such as these subtly shape our perceptions of our roles and guide our actions.

Understanding the expectations of parents, teachers, and others in your school is a complex, exciting, and demanding task! Before students with emotional and behavioral disorders may be effectively served, however, you must carefully consider your own expectations as well as those of others in the student's environment. We will consider your expectations and philosophy regarding student behavior in Chapter 4; however, to understand the expectations of others, you are encouraged to use the following strategies:

1. Gather information from multiple sources, including the student's files, parents, peers, and other professionals as described in Chapter 2.
2. Conduct interviews with the parents, guardians, or other family members. What strengths do they believe the student has? What behaviors or social skills would they like the student to learn to function better as a member of the family? How do they prefer to handle home-school communications (e.g., by telephone, note home, meetings, home visits)? Do they wish to be informed of problems, or do they expect you to handle school-related problems?
3. Observe the student interacting with his or her peers. How frequently does the student interact with peers? Are these social interactions primarily positive or negative (e.g., name-calling, teasing)? Does the student join in the activities or conversations of others appropriately? Is the student invited by others to join their activities?
4. Observe and interview the regular classroom teacher(s). Pay particular attention to the classroom rules and consequences for following and not following the rules. Observe the interactions between the teacher and the student with emotional and behavioral problems. Use a format to structure your observations and interviews such as the Classroom Ecological Inventory (Fuchs, Fernstrom, Scott, Fuchs, & Vandermeer, 1994) (Figure 3.1, pp. 92–94).

Special education teacher _____ Grade _____ Date _____

Regular education teacher _____ Number of students in regular class _____

Student _____

PART 1: CLASSROOM OBSERVATION

■ Physical Environment

Directions: Please circle or provide the appropriate answer.

1. Is there an area for small groups?   Yes   No

2. Are partitions used in the room?   Yes   No

3. Is there a computer in the classroom?   Yes   No

4. Where is the student's desk located? (for example, front of room, back, middle, away from other students)

_____

■ Teacher/Student Behavior

Directions for #1 to #4: Please circle the appropriate answer.

1. How much movement or activity is tolerated by the teacher?   Much   Average   Little   Unclear

2. How much talking among students is tolerated?   Much   Average   Little   Unclear

3. Does the teacher use praise?   Much   Average   Little   Unclear

4. Was the subject taught to the entire group or to small groups?   Entire   Small

Directions for #5 to #7: Please provide an appropriate answer.

5. During the observation, where did the teacher spend most of the time? (for example, at the board, at teacher's desk, at student's desk) _____

6. What teaching methods did you observe while in the classroom? (for example, teacher modeled the lesson, asked students to work at board, helped small groups, helped individual students) _____

_____

_____

7. How did the teacher interact with students who appeared to be low achieving or slower than their classmates? (for example, helped them individually, talked to them in the large group) _____

_____

_____

■ Posted Classroom Rules

If classroom rules are posted, what are they?

Special Education   **Regular Education**

_____   _____

_____   _____

_____   _____

Is there any other pertinent information you observed about this classroom that would be helpful in reintegrating the student? (for example, crowded classroom)

_____

_____

FIGURE 3.1

The Classroom Ecological Inventory From "A Process for Mainstreaming: Classroom Ecological Inventory," by D. Fuchs, P. Fernstrom, S. Scott, L. Fuchs & L. Vendermeer, *Teaching Exceptional Children,* 26(3), 1994, pp. 14–15. Copyright © 1994 by The Council for Exceptional Children. Reprinted with permission.

■ Classroom Rules

	Special Education	Regular Education

1. During class, are there important rules? (Yes or No) _____ _____

2. If yes, how are they communicated? (for example, written or oral) _____ _____

3. If class rules are *not* posted, what are they? _____ _____
_____ _____
_____ _____
_____ _____

4. If a rule is broken, what is the typical consequence? _____ _____

5. Who enforces the rules? (teacher, aide, students) _____ _____

■ Teacher Behavior

1. a. Is homework assigned? (Yes or No) _____ _____

   b. If so, indicate approximate amount (minutes) of homework, and _____ _____

   c. the frequency with which it is given. _____ _____

Directions for #2 to #4: Using a 3-point scale (1 = Often, 2 = Sometimes, 3 = Never), rate each item according to frequency of occurrence in class. Place an asterisk (*) in the righthand margin to indicate important differences between the special and regular education classrooms.

2. Assignments in class

   a. Students are given assignments:
   - that are the same for all _____ _____
   - that differ in amount or type _____ _____
   - to complete in school at a specified time _____ _____
   - that, if unfinished in school, are assigned as homework _____ _____

   b. Evaluation of assignment is performed by:
   - teacher evaluation _____ _____
   - student self-evaluation _____ _____
   - peer evaluation _____ _____

3. Tests

   a. Tests are:
   - presented orally _____ _____
   - copied from board _____ _____
   - timed _____ _____
   - based on study guides given to students prior to test _____ _____
   - administered by resource teacher _____ _____

   b. Grades are:
   - percentages (for example, 75%) _____ _____
   - letter grades (for example, B+) _____ _____
   - both _____ _____

4. Academic and social rewards

   a. Classroom rewards or reinforcement include:
   - material rewards (for example, stars) _____ _____

   b. Classroom punishment includes:
   - time out
   - loss of activity-related privileges (for example, loss of free time) _____ _____
   - teacher ignoring _____ _____
   - reprimands _____ _____
   - poorer grade, loss of star, and so forth _____ _____
   - extra work _____ _____
   - staying after school
   - physical punishment (for example, paddling) _____ _____

5. To what extent does each of the following contribute to an overall grade? Estimate the percentage for each so that the total sum is 100%.
   - homework _____ _____
   - daily work _____ _____
   - tests _____ _____
   - class participation _____ _____

6. Please list skills that have been taught since the beginning of the school year (Regular Education Teacher Only):

Skill	Will reteach later? (Yes or No)

FIGURE 3.1 ◆

Continued

Directions: Identify one or more discrepancies between special and regular education classrooms. Formulate a plan of action that includes *what* should be accomplished, *when*, and by *whom*; also, explain how the effectiveness of the action will be *evaluated*.

Discrepancy #1:
Plan of action

   a. What:

   b. When:

   c. Who:

   d. Evaluation:

Discrepancy #2:
Plan of action

   a. What:

   b. When:

   c. Who:

   d. Evaluation:

FIGURE 3.1 ◆

Continued

5. For students with behavioral disorders who are to be maintained in the regular classroom, compare the expectations for performance in the regular classroom with those of the special education classroom. Compare the student's behavior in the regular classroom with his or her behavior in the special classroom. Examine expectations for both academic as well as social behavior and performance.

6. Plan to resolve discrepancies between student behavior and classroom expectations by improving the behavior of the student, modifying interactions in the special classroom, the regular classroom, or both, or by changing student behavior as well as classroom interactions.

Summary

Families operate as complex systems with family members in constant interaction. Events affecting one family member will have an affect on all other members of that family. Professionals must remember the dynamic and reciprocal nature of family interactions when planning interventions for children and youth with emotional and behavioral disorders.

Parents and teachers from differing cultural or ethnic groups may perceive behaviors differently. Behaviors that appear to deviate from the norm may be artifacts of culture or ethnicity rather than problematic behaviors. Teachers must not blame parents for causing a student's behavioral problems, although inept parenting skills certainly may contribute to these problems. Rather, teachers must examine behavior within the context of the child's family and cultural group.

Teachers cannot control what takes place outside of the classroom. They can, however, ensure that they do not contribute to social-emotional and behavioral problems among students. Teachers who are sensitive to the needs of individual students, who set realistic standards for behavior and performance, who plan meaningful lessons, and who reward appropriate behaviors consistently have the highest likelihood of fostering positive interactions with their students.

Teacher-student behaviors occur in complex patterns of daily interactions. Expectations and actions of teachers affect the behaviors of students, and beliefs and behaviors of students affect the behaviors of their teachers. Student to student, parent to student, parent to teacher, and teacher to teacher interactions are all reciprocal, each affecting future interactions with others. As teachers, we must understand the reciprocal and dynamic nature of these interactions and strive to match our expectations for behavior and performance in the classroom as closely as possible with the present needs and abilities of our students. The challenge, of course, is to do this without violating the expectations, needs, or rights of others, including ourselves as teachers.

Application Exercises

1. Peruse the local newspapers for 1 week. Find any articles that indicate expectations of the media or of local school boards or state or local governments regarding the performance of teachers and students in your community. Bring these articles to class for discussion. Are any of these expectations conflicting? Are any of these expectations culturally based?

2. List your expectations for student behavior and performance in your classroom. Compare this list to that made by your colleagues. What similarities and what differences do you see? Have you listed any particular expectations that might produce problems for students from ethnic or cultural groups different from your own? If so, what are these, and how might these expectations affect student behavior?

3. Interview a classroom teacher from a cultural or ethnic group other than your own. What expectations for behavior and performance does this teacher hold? What are this teacher's rules and consequences, and how are these rules and consequences enforced? Are these rules or expectations the same or different from your own?

4. Arrange to observe in a classroom for 1 day. What are the rules and consequences in this class that convey the teacher's expectations and standards? Do students readily comply with the rules? Count the number of approving and disapproving statements made by the teacher during the day. Do any particular students receive more approving or more disapproving statements from the teacher than others? Be sure not to use the names of the children, teacher, or school as you collect this information.

5. Describe the microsystems, exosystems, mesosystems, and macrosystems of which you and your family are members.

References

Alberto, P. A., & Troutman, A. C. (1995). *Applied behavior analysis for teachers* (4th ed.). Columbus, OH: Merrill.

Ashton, P. T., & Webb, R. B. (1986). *Making a difference: Teachers' sense of efficacy and student achievement.* New York: Longman.

Bacon, E. H., & Bloom, L. A. (1994). "Don't ratl the kiDs." *Journal of Emotional and Behavioral Problems, 3*(1), 8–10.

Baker, J. M., & Zigmond, N. (1990). Are regular education classes equipped to accommodate students with learning disabilities? *Exceptional Children, 56*(6), 515–526.

Bandura, A. (1977). Self-efficacy: Toward a unifying theory of behavioral change. *Psychological Review, 84,* 191–215.

Bandura, A. (1986). *Social foundations of thought and action: A social cognitive theory.* Englewood Cliffs, NJ: Prentice-Hall.

Canter, L., & Canter, M. (1976). *Assertive discipline: A take-charge approach for today's educator.* Los Angeles: Canter & Associates.

Center, D. B., & Wascom, A. M. (1987). Teacher perceptions of social behavior in behaviorally disordered and socially normal children and youth. *Behavioral Disorders, 12*(3), 200–206.

Curwin, R. L., & Mendler, A. N. (1988). Packaged discipline programs: Let the buyer beware. *Educational Leadership,* (October, 1988), 68–73.

Dean, C. (1993). Strengthening families: From "deficit" to "empowerment." *The Journal of Emotional and Behavioral Problems, 2*(4), 8–11.

Downing, J. A., Simpson, R. L., & Myles, B. S. (1990). Regular and special educator perceptions of nonacademic skills needed by mainstreamed students with behavioral disorders and learning disabilities. *Behavioral Disorders, 15*(4), 217–226.

Epstein, M. H., Nelson, C. M., Polsgrove, L., Coutinho, M., Cumblad, C., & Quinn, K. (1993). A comprehensive community-based approach to serving students with emotional and behavioral disorders. *Journal of Emotional and Behavioral Disorders, 1,* 127–133.

Fad, K. S., & Ryser, G. R. (1993). Social/behavioral variables related to success in general education. *Remedial and Special Education, 14*(1), 25–35.

Franklin, M. E. (1992). Culturally sensitive instructional practices for African-American learners with disabilities. *Exceptional Children, 59*(2), 115–122.

Fuchs, D., Fernstrom, P., Scott, S., Fuchs, L., & Vandermeer, L. (1994). A process for mainstreaming: Classroom Ecological Inventory. *Teaching Exceptional Children, 26*(3), 11–15.

Garber, M., & Newton, S. J. (1989). The influence of instructions on the ratings of problem behaviors. *Behavioral Disorders, 15*(1), 41–49.

Gay, G. (1989). Ethnic minorities and educational equality. In J. A. Banks & C. A. McGee Banks (Eds.), *Multicultural education* (pp. 167–188). Boston: Allyn & Bacon.

Gersten, R., Walker, H., & Darch, C. (1988). Relationship between teachers' effectiveness and their tolerance for handicapped students. *Exceptional Children, 54,* 433–438.

Gollnick, D. M. (1992). Multicultural education: Policies and practices in teacher education. In C. A. Grant (Ed.), *Research and multicultural education* (pp. 218–239). Bristol, PA: Falmer.

Gunter, P. L., Denny, R. K., Jack, S. L., Shores, R. E., & Nelson, C. M. (1993). Aversive stimuli in academic interactions between students with serious emotional disturbance and their teachers. *Behavioral Disorders, 18*(4), 265–274.

Harry, B. (1992). Restructuring the participation of African-American parents in special education. *Exceptional Children, 59*(2), 123–131.

Harry, B., Torguson, C., Katkavich, J., & Guerrero, M. (1993). Crossing social class and cultural barriers in working with families: Implications for teacher training. *Teaching Exceptional Children, 26*(1), 48–51.

Hersch, R. H., & Walker, H. M. (1983). Great expectations: Making schools effective for all students. *Policy Studies Review, 2*(1), 147–188.

Hess, R. D., & Holloway, S. D. (1984). Family and school as educational institutions. In R. D. Parke (Ed.), *Review of child development research (Volume 7).* Chicago: University of Chicago Press.

Johnson, L. J., & Blankenship, C. S. (1984). A comparison of label-induced expectancy bias in two preservice teacher education programs. *Behavioral Disorders, 9*, 167–174.

Jones, F. H. (1987). *Positive classroom discipline.* New York: McGraw-Hill.

Kauffman, J. M. (1993). *Characteristics of emotional and behavioral disorders of children and youth* (5th ed.). New York: Macmillan.

Kauffman, J. M., Lloyd, J. W., & McGee, K. A. (1989). Adaptive and maladaptive behavior: Teachers' attitudes and their technical assistance needs. *Journal of Special Education, 23*, 185–200.

Kauffman, J. M., & Wong, K. L. H. (1991). Effective teachers of students with behavioral disorders: Are generic teaching skills enough? *Behavioral Disorders, 16*(3), 225–237.

Kauffman, J. M., Wong, K. L. H., Lloyd, J. W., Hung, L., & Pullen, P. L. (1991). What puts pupils at risk? An analysis of classroom teachers' judgements of pupils' behavior. *Remedial and Special Education, 12*(5), 7–16.

Kerr, M. M., & Zigmond, N. (1986). What do high school teachers want? A study of expectations and standards. *Education and Treatment of Children, 9*, 239–249.

Knitzer, J., Steinberg, Z., & Fleisch, B. (1990). *At the schoolhouse door: An examination of programs and policies for children with behavioral and emotional problems.* New York: Bank Street College of Education.

Kuykendall, C. (1992). *From rage to hope: Strategies for reclaiming black and hispanic students.* Bloomington, IN: National Educational Service.

Landon, T., & Mesinger, J. F. (1989). Teacher tolerance ratings on problem behaviors. *Behavioral Disorders, 14*(4), 236–249.

Landrum, T. J. (1992). Teachers as victims: An interactional analysis of the teacher's role in educating atypical learners. *Behavioral Disorders, 17*(2), 135–144.

Leone, P. E., Luttig, P. G., Zlotlow, S., & Trickett, E. J. (1990). Understanding the social ecology of classrooms for adolescents with behavioral disorders: A preliminary study of perceived differences in environments. *Behavioral Disorders, 16*(1), 55–65.

Lloyd, J. W., Kauffman, J. M., & Gansneder, B. (1987). Differential teacher response to descriptions of aberrant behavior. In R. B. Rutherford, C. M. Nelson, & S. R. Forness (Eds.), *Severe behavior disorders of children and youth* (pp. 41–52). Boston: College Hill.

Lynch, E. W., & Stein, R. C. (1987). Parent participation by ethnicity: A comparison of hispanic, black, and anglo families. *Exceptional Children, 54*, 105–111.

Mandlebaum, L. H., Russell, S. C., Krouse, J., & Gonter, M. (1983). Assertive discipline: An effective classwide behavior management program. *Behavioral Disorders, 8*(4), 83–93.

Martin, R. P. (1992). Child temperament effects on special education: Process and outcomes. *Exceptionality, 3*(2), 99–115.

Mayer, G. R., Nafpaktitis, M., Butterworth, T., & Hollingsworth, P. (1987). A search for the elusive setting events of school vandalism: A correlational study. *Education and Treatment of Children, 10*, 259–270.

McIntosh, R., Vaughn, S., Schumm, J. S., Haager, D., & Lee, O. (1994). Observations of students with learning disabilities in general education classrooms. *Exceptional Children, 60*(3), 249–261.

McWhirter, C. C., & Bloom, L. A. (1994). The effects of a student-operated business curriculum on the on-task behavior of students with behavioral disorders. *Behavioral Disorders, 19*(2), 136–141.

Minuchin, S. (1974). *Families and family therapy.* Cambridge, MA: Harvard University Press.

Moos, R. H., & Trickett, E. J. (1986). *Classroom Environment Scale Manual* (2nd ed.). Palo Alto, CA: Consulting Psychologists Press.

Nowacek, E. J., McKinney, J. D., & Hallahan, D. P. (1990). Instructional behaviors of more and less effective beginning regular and special educators. *Exceptional Children, 57*(2), 140–149.

Odom, S. L., McConnell, S. R., & Chandler, L. K. (1994). Acceptability and feasibility of classroom-based social interaction interventions for young children with disabilities. *Exceptional Children, 60*(3). 226–236.

Patterson, G. R. (1986). Performance models for antisocial boys. *American Psychologist, 41*, 432–444.

Paul, J. L., & Epanchin, B. C. (1991). *Educating emotionally disturbed children and youth: Theories and practices for teachers.* New York: Macmillan.

Peterson, B. (1990). When nothing goes wrong. *Beyond Behavior, 2*(1), 3–4.

Reimers, T. M., Wacker, D. P., Derby, K. M., & Cooper, L. J. (1995). Relation between parental attributions and the acceptability of behavioral treatments for their child's behavior problems. *Behavioral Disorders, 20*(3), 171–178.

Render, G. F., Padilla, J. N. M., & Krank, H. M. (1989). Assertive discipline: A critical review and analysis. *Teachers College Record, 90*(4), 607–627.

Rosenthal, R., & Jacobson, L. (1968). *Pygmalion in the classroom.* New York: Holt, Rinehart & Winston.

Sachs, J. J. (1990). The self-efficacy interaction between regular educators and special education students: A model for understanding the mainstreaming dilemma: *Teacher Education and Special Education, 13*(3–4), 235–239.

Safran, J. S., & Safran, S. P. (1987). Teacher's judgements of problem behaviors. *Exceptional Children, 54*, 240–244.

Salend, S. J. (1994). *Effective mainstreaming: Creating inclusive classrooms* (2nd ed.). New York: Macmillan.

Salend, S. J., & Taylor, L. (1993). Working with families: A cross-cultural perspective. *Remedial and Special Education, 14*(5), 25–32, 39.

Shea, T. M., & Bauer, A. M. (1994). *Learners with disabilities: A social systems perspective of special education.* Madison, WI: Brown & Benchmark.

Shores, R. E., Gunter, P. L., & Jack, S. L. (1993). Classroom management strategies: Are they setting events for coercion? *Behavioral Disorders, 18*(2), 92–102.

Shores, R. E., Jack, S. L., Gunter, P. L., Ellis, D. N., DeBriere, T. J., & Wehby, J. H. (1993). Classroom interactions of children with behavior disorders. *Journal of Emotional and Behavioral Disorders, 1*(1), 27–39.

Simon, D. J., & Johnston, J. C. (1987). Working with families: The missing link in behavior disorder interventions. In R. B. Rutherford, C. M. Nelson, & S. R. Forness (Eds.), *Severe behavior disorders of children and youth* (pp. 82–92). San Diego: College-Hill Press.

Slate, J. R., & Saudargas, R. A. (1986). Differences in the classroom behaviors of behaviorally disordered and regular class children. *Behavioral Disorders, 12*(1), 45–53.

Soderlund, J., Epstein, M. H., Quinn, K. P., Cumblad, C., & Petersen, S. (1995). Parental perspectives on comprehensive services for children and youth with emotional and behavioral disorders. *Behavioral Disorders, 20*(3), 157–170.

Steiger, L. K. (Ed.). (1987). *Participant workbook: Nonviolent Crisis Intervention.* Brookfield, WI: National Crisis Prevention Institute.

Stevenson-Hinde, J., Hinde, R. A., & Simpson, A. E. (1986). Behavior at home and friendly or hostile behavior in preschool. In D. Olweus, J. Block, & M. Radke-Yarrow (Eds.), *Development of antisocial and prosocial behavior: Research, theories, and issues.* New York: Academic Press.

Strain, P. S., Lambert, D. L., Kerr, M. M., Stagg, V., & Lenkner, D. A. (1983). Naturalistic assessment of children's compliance to teachers' requests and consequences for compliance. *Journal of Applied Behavior Analysis, 16*, 243–249.

Thomas, A., & Chess, S. (1984). Genesis and evolution of behavioral disorders: From infancy to early adult life. *American Journal of Psychiatry, 141*, 1–9.

Trickett, E. J., Leone, P. E., Fink, C. M., & Braaten, S. L. (1993). The perceived environment of special education classrooms for adolescents: A revision of the Classroom Environment Scale. *Exceptional Children, 59*(5), 411–420.

Turnbull, A. P., & Turnbull, H. R. (1990). *Families, professionals, and exceptionality: A special partnership* (2nd ed.). Columbus, OH: Merrill.

Walker, H. M., & Rankin, R. (1983). Assessing the behavioral expectations and demands of less restrictive settings. *School Psychology Review, 12,* 274–284.

Whinnery, K. W., Fuchs, L. S., & Fuchs, D. (1991). General, special, and remedial teachers' acceptance of behavioral and instructional strategies for mainstreaming students with mild handicaps. *Remedial and Special Education, 12*(4), 6–17.

Wickman, E. K. (1928). *Children's behavior and teacher's attitudes.* New York: Commonwealth Fund.

Wolfgang, C. H. (1995). *Solving discipline problems: Methods and models for today's teachers* (3rd Ed.). Boston: Allyn & Bacon.

Zirpoli, T. J., & Melloy, K. J. (1993). *Behavior management: Applications for teachers and parents.* New York: Macmillan.

CHAPTER 4.

MAKING DECISIONS ABOUT STUDENT BEHAVIOR

Main Ideas

◆ *Conceptual models are often used to organize our beliefs about the nature of behavioral disorders and the strategies professionals choose for "treating" behavioral problems.*

◆ *Six major models guide our beliefs about behavior including the biological/biogenic, psychodynamic/humanistic, psychoeducational, behavioral, cognitive-behavioral, and ecological/ sociological schools of thought.*

◆ *Professionals debate the relative strengths and weaknesses of each conceptual model; however, in practice, teachers must be pragmatists, not purists, and sensibly integrate strategies to be effective with all students.*

In Chapter 1, you were challenged to begin examining your own beliefs about students and their behaviors. You probably have some idea about those behaviors you can tolerate and those you consider unacceptable, and you may have generated a list of expectations for student behaviors in your classroom. As we have seen, however, behaviors occur in complex interactions among children and parents and among teachers and students. Your expectations, biases, standards, and tolerance levels are but one piece of the larger puzzle. Students, parents, and colleagues will also have their own expectations and perceptions that will affect what you do in the classroom.

Nevertheless, you must develop a personal philosophy about the behavior of your students to guide you in making wise decisions in your classroom. Expert teachers systematically examine all aspects of a problem before making their decisions, rather than immediately focusing on the problem's solution or using only one method to solve all classroom behavioral problems (DiGangi, 1991). Expert teachers, therefore, must understand and integrate many different strategies to intervene effectively with children and youth having emotional and behavioral disorders (Harris & Graham, 1994).

In this chapter, then, we will introduce the major schools of thought that drive teachers' beliefs about student behavior and their responses to that behavior. We will first present the major conceptual models used to organize beliefs about behavior and an evaluation of these models. Next, we will examine how these models overlap and are interrelated. Finally, we will explore a framework for making decisions about the behaviors of students. Such a framework will help you integrate the conceptual models and select strategies likely to assist children and youth with behavioral disorders in your classroom.

Schools of Thought and Teacher Behaviors

During the 1960s and 1970s, programs for students with emotional and behavioral disorders grew rapidly in the schools. Many of these programs were organized around the major schools of thought, or conceptual models, then used to understand behavioral disorders (Rhodes & Tracy, 1972a, 1972b). According to Cullinan, Epstein, and Lloyd (1983, 1991), conceptual models provide a useful framework for understanding and treating behavior disorders. That is, professionals adhering to a given conceptual model share similar explanations regarding the cause of the child's behavioral problems, and they are likely to use the same types of intervention approaches (Rhodes & Tracy, 1972a, 1972b). The schools of thought most often seen in the literature are listed in Table 4.1 and include the biological/biogenic, psychodynamic/humanistic, psychoeducational, behavioral, cognitive-behavioral, and ecological/sociological models (Cullinan, Epstein, & Lloyd, 1983; Kauffman, 1993; Rhodes & Tracy, 1972a, 1972b). The actual names for the models and intervention techniques grouped within each model, however, vary arbitrarily from source to source in the literature, indicating a degree of overlap among these schools of thought.

Table 4.1 Common Conceptual Models

Model	Philosophy and Interventions
Biological/Biogenic	Behavioral disorders result from neurological and physiological factors.
	Special diets, medication, and physical activity are treatments.
Psychodynamic/ Humanistic	Behavioral disorders result from inner conflicts and an inability to achieve self-fulfillment and self-identity.
	Teacher provides a supportive environment and activities to help children identify, clarify, and express feelings.
Psychoeducational	Behavioral disorders result from inner stress and conflict which produces conflict with others. Feelings affect surface behavior, thus, self-control must come from self-understanding.
	Teacher provides a structured environment to support feelings and teaches academic and coping skills. Self-understanding and self-control are taught through structured dialogues guided by teachers when problems occur.
Behavioral	All behavior is learned. Behavior disorders, therefore, are the result of learned inappropriate behaviors.
	Teachers observe and analyze behavior and structure the environment to produce desired behaviors. Consequences are used to reward appropriate behaviors and decrease behaviors that are inappropriate.
Cognitive-Behavioral	Cognitions affect behavior; therefore, behavioral disorders are related to faulty cognitions.
	Teachers help children to self-monitor and alter their thoughts in order to change their behavior. Self-management strategies are directly taught to children.
Ecological/ Sociological	Behavioral disorders are the result of complex interactions within social systems. Behaviors do not match environmental expectations. Behaviors of parents, children, peers, teachers, and others occur as dynamic and reciprocal actions.
	Comprehensive services must "wrap around" the child and the family. To treat the child the entire family and ecosystem must be assisted by "whatever it takes."

Biological/Biogenic Models

Proponents of the biological/biogenic school of thought maintain that emotional and behavioral disorders are the result of neurological and physiological factors. Thus, the cause of the problem is thought to be, for example, a genetic abnormality, faulty metabolic processes, a biochemical imbalance, or neurological damage. To treat the resulting behavioral disorder, then, drug therapy, diet control, surgery, and exercise are the major interventions suggested.

Although biological factors may account for some severe emotional and behavioral disorders in children and adolescents, they are not useful explanations for most mild to moderate behavioral problems encountered by teachers. Genetic and other biological factors interact in complex ways with the child's social and physical environment; therefore, to state that biogenic explanations account for all behavioral disorders is to oversimplify a complicated problem (Kauffman, 1993). In addition, biological models have little educational relevance for teachers planning interventions in their classrooms.

Teachers must, however, be aware of the medications or special diets prescribed for their students. Also, they should be familiar with the potential side effects of any medications students must take. In addition, teachers can carefully monitor the behaviors of students using medications and let the physician or caregivers know of any unusual observations. Because teachers must understand the many issues surrounding the management of medications for children and youth with emotional and behavioral disorders, the biological/biogenic model will be discussed again in Chapter 11.

Psychodynamic and Humanistic Models

Psychodynamic models, sometimes called *psychoanalytic approaches*, derive from the early work of Sigmund and Anna Freud. Disordered behavior is seen as a symptom of "mental illness" caused by early stressful experiences or faulty passages through critical developmental stages. The primary problem is thought to be within the child, and parents are often viewed as the reason for the disordered behavior. Underlying, hidden "intrapsychic" conflicts are believed to drive the child's behavior; therefore, the behavioral problems will not disappear unless these repressed experiences and conflicts are brought to the surface and understood. Thus, the behavior cannot be treated alone. To treat the emotional or behavioral disorder effectively, the student must experience a "catharsis," or release of pent up emotions and achieve insight into his or her problem (Cullinan, Epstein, & Lloyd, 1983).

Bruno Bettleheim was among the first to use psychodynamic principles to treat behavioral disorders in children. His *therapeutic milieu*, a concept still used at the Sonja Shankman Orthogenic School in Chicago where Bettleheim originated the strategy, emphasized a warm, accepting, permissive environment designed to build a supportive relationship with a trusted adult (Bettleheim, 1950;

Art, music, and play activities may help students identify feelings and express them appropriately.

Bettleheim & Sylvester, 1948). Similarly, Berkowitz and Rothman (1960) employed a permissive educational environment in their school at New York's Bellevue Hospital to enable children to act out their inner conflicts and experience catharsis and insight in an atmosphere of acceptance and support. Carefully selected stories or books and play, music, art, and drama activities are often used within the psychodynamic model to help students identify, understand, and express their feelings.

Usually listed as a separate school of thought, the humanistic model grew as a part of the countercultural and open education movements of the 1960s and 1970s. Humanistic approaches, like the psychodynamic philosophies, view both the problem and its solution as resting within the child. The underlying assumption within the humanistic school of thought is that children can solve their own problems if they are provided with a supportive environment. The teacher's role, then, is to emphasize affective education and to support feelings (Kauffman, 1993; Neill, 1960; Rogers, 1983). The psychodynamic and humanistic models overlap, then, in that they share basic ideas such as the importance of a supportive environment and concern for the acceptance of feelings. Because the strategies offered by these two models differ little in actual classroom practice, we shall consider them together for discussion in Chapter 6.

Psychoeducational Models

According to Cullinan, Epstein, and Lloyd (1991), the psychoeducational model is an educationally oriented outgrowth of the psychodynamic school of thought. Thus, emotional and behavioral disorders are still viewed as symptomatic of underlying conflicts and stressors that must be resolved if behavioral problems are to disappear. The psychoeducational model, however, expanded psychodynamic principles to offer pragmatic strategies for teachers who wished to create a therapeutic milieu in the classroom while still managing the "surface behaviors" of troubled children (i.e., the observable behaviors that are symptomatic of the child's inner stress and conflict) (Long & Newman, 1976). Proponents of the psychoeducational model believe that thoughts and beliefs about stressful environmental events may flood children with intense feelings that drive their behaviors. When youngsters behave inappropriately, they receive negative reactions from others. These negative reactions often increase the level of stress and produce a continuing cycle of conflict for the student and those around him or her (Wood & Long, 1991).

Within the psychoeducational approach, then, children and youth with emotional and behavioral disorders are seen as lacking personal organization, coping skills, and self-control; therefore, the teacher must provide a degree of structure to support students effectively. Simply permitting students to act out their conflicts is insufficient treatment for students with emotional and behavioral disorders in school settings. Rather, teachers must set limits for students and teach them how to cope with problem situations. Teachers confront student misbehavior in a firm but supportive manner, and they often use peer group meetings and structured dialogues to teach better coping and problem-solving skills. Teachers adhering to the psychoeducational model place responsibility for appropriate behavior with the student, even if they must, at first, share this responsibility until the student is able to assume it fully himself or herself.

Based on their work with aggressive youngsters at Pioneer House in Detroit, Redl and Wineman (1951, 1952), for example, described a structured way to talk with young people in crisis called a *Life Space Interview*. The Life Space Interview gave child care workers a technique to use with children at or near the time of a crisis to communicate support while also teaching better self-control and problem-solving skills. Nicholas Long expanded the technique of Life Space Crisis Intervention as a means to interrupt the Conflict Cycle (Wood & Long, 1991). William Glasser (1965, 1969) also describes a structured conversation with children and youth called *reality therapy*, to be conducted individually or in group meetings, to teach students better ways to cope with reality and take responsibility for solving problems in the future (see Chapter 9).

Behavioral Models

Behaviorism originated with the work of psychologist John Watson in the early 1900s. Watson (1913) believed that psychologists should stop focusing on internal and unconscious mental states and focus instead on observable behaviors.

Teachers using behavioral techniques structure the environment to produce and reward appropriate behaviors.

B. F. Skinner, however, was instrumental in prompting professionals operating programs for students with emotional and behavioral disorders to experiment with behavioral techniques (Skinner, 1953; 1968). Essentially, from the behavioral perspective, all behavior is thought to be learned and controlled by events in the environment. Teachers, then, must be directive and structure the environment to promote student learning of appropriate behaviors and social skills (see Chapters 7 and 8).

Behavioral approaches stress analyzing the relationship between specific behaviors and the environmental events affecting them. Antecedent events that trigger behaviors and the consequences that follow are carefully analyzed and arranged so that appropriate behaviors can be prompted and rewarded. Reinforcement is a key behavioral principle for teachers of students with emotional and behavioral disorders. Reinforcement increases the probability that a behavior will occur again; therefore, teachers can increase and maintain appropriate behaviors by structuring the environment to produce a targeted behavior and by reinforcing the behavior immediately, consistently, and frequently. Behavioral techniques also help teachers to shape new behaviors and to decrease undesirable behaviors in their students.

The behavioral model offers many well-researched approaches to the education of children and youth with emotional and behavioral disorders. Moreover, behavioral techniques have more documented evidence of their effectiveness than do strategies within any other school of thought (Cullinan, Epstein, & Lloyd, 1991).

Cognitive-Behavioral Models

Cognitive-behavioral models originated with the early work of Ellis (1962), Mahoney (1974), and Meichenbaum (1977) and merge principles of behavioral theory with those of cognitive psychology. Implicit within cognitive-behavioral models is the notion that our cognitions (i.e., our thoughts and feelings about a situation) affect our behaviors (Dobson & Block, 1988). That is, individuals have different expectancies about an event both before and during its occurrence. Following the event, too, individuals attribute their success or failure to various internal or external factors. These self-evaluations and attributions, then, affect future behaviors because an individual's self-talk influences his or her future feelings and behaviors.

For example, a student beginning to take a test may hold a certain expectancy about his or her likelihood of obtaining an "A" upon completing the test (i.e., a positive outcome). While the student takes the test, he or she may engage in self-talk such as "I know that answer," "I'm bombing this," or "I need to slow down and take my time so I don't make careless errors." Such self-talk, in turn, makes the student feel good and continue his or her efforts to do well on the test or makes the student feel "dumb" and give up rather than persisting. Finally, following the test, the student may attribute his or her success or failure to external factors such as an "easy test" or "a bad teacher" or to internal factors such as "I studied hard and knew the answers." These attributions and expectancies will likely affect the student's future test-taking behaviors in that class.

Dobson and Block (1988) suggest that cognitive activity can be monitored and altered; therefore, behavior change can occur through cognitive change. A child's inner language, then, is viewed as an important part of behavioral change because the child's self-talk mediates his or her behavior (Luria, 1961; Vygotsky, 1962). Helping the student develop positive self-talk or learn an effective self-instructional strategy for taking tests are but two brief examples of cognitive-behavioral interventions based on the notion that inner language guides behavior.

Cognitive-behavioral interventions also employ the structured, direct methods of the behavioral approach. Teachers carefully arrange environmental events and sequence tasks, explicitly model appropriate self-talk and essential self-instructional strategies, and provide numerous opportunities for children to use these cognitions and be rewarded for their use in realistic contexts (Braswell & Kendall, 1988). Many related self-management strategies including self-monitoring, self-evaluation, and self-reinforcement now exist to help learners develop better self-control and self-regulation (Graham, Harris, & Reid, 1992; Harris, 1982; Kanfer & Gaelick-Buys, 1988). Cognitive-behavioral interventions such as these, designed to promote student responsibility, will be discussed in greater detail in Chapter 9.

Ecological/Sociological Models

Ecological and sociological models are relatively recent schools of thought that share the notion that behaviors are products of complex interactions within social systems. To understand a child's behavior, then, one must understand the various ecosystems within which the child must function (Hobbs, 1966, 1978; Rhodes & Paul, 1978). In essence, proponents of ecological approaches believe that there is a mismatch between the child's behavior and the expectations and tolerance levels of those in the child's environment. The child's behavior, then, is disturbing to people around the youngster, and these individuals react in ways that foster additional troublesome behaviors.

From an ecological perspective, to treat the child's behavior alone would be futile. Theoretically, the child and all parts of the child's environment, including the home, school, and community, must collaborate if intervention is to be effective. That is, the child must be taught better ways to behave, but parents, teachers, and peers must also learn new ways to interact with the child while the behavior is changing. It might help for parents, teachers, and community members to tolerate a little more "discordance" (i.e., to adjust their expectations to achieve a better match between the child's behavior and actual environmental requirements) as well as to support behaviors as they change (Lewis, 1974). Most families, however, will require direct assistance if such lasting change is to occur.

During the past 10 years professionals have devoted increasing energy to devising multimodal treatments and comprehensive systems of care for children and youth with behavioral disorders and for their families (Friesen & Wahlers, 1993; The Peacock Hill Working Group, 1991). To attack problems on all possible fronts while limiting the need to remove a child from his or her home, support services are literally "wrapped around" the families of students with emotional and behavioral disorders (Duchnowski, Johnson, Hall, Kutash, & Friedman, 1993; Federation of Families for Children's Mental Health, 1992; Knitzer, 1993). The family of an adolescent experiencing depression, for example, may need information, assistance in working with school officials, help in explaining the problem to other family members or friends, medication, or acute short-term care for their child (Friesen & Wahlers, 1993). Rather than focusing solely on the youngster, then, ecologically based "wrap around" services provide support for the entire family. Thus, this model requires extensive collaboration among teachers, administrators, parents, and community agencies (see Chapter 10).

Evaluating Conceptual Models

Since the initial development of the major conceptual models, professionals have argued and debated the relative merits and weaknesses of each. Cullinan,

Epstein, and Lloyd (1991), for example, state that conceptual models must be judged according to three criteria: (1) How well does the model explain the nature, origins, and continuation of behavior disorders? (2) How replicable, efficient, and broad are the interventions suggested within the model? and (3) What empirical evidence exists for the model that contributes to our scientific understanding of the nature and treatment of behavioral disorders? They used these criteria to evaluate three major conceptual models (i.e., the psychoeducational, behavioral, and ecological models) often discussed in the literature today. According to Cullinan and his colleagues (1991), the behavioral model has the most scientific evidence to support its use, but no one model is sufficient for explaining behavior disorders or for guiding a teacher's choice of interventions.

Proponents of psychodynamic and psychoeducational models assert that their interventions help students identify, label, and express feelings in a non-judgmental environment and that they provide readily available techniques to help teachers and students in crisis situations and to assist professionals when teaching students to problem solve (Heuchert, 1983; Long, 1990). Critics of these models, however, maintain that psychoeducational and psychodynamic approaches lack scientific evidence of their effectiveness, that they are not useful with students having inadequate verbal skills, and that the teacher's attention following a problem may reinforce the student's inappropriate behavior (Gardner, 1990). In addition, because the psychodynamic model assumes the problem to be within the child, teachers must not misinterpret this viewpoint as a license to do nothing. Cullinan, Epstein, and Lloyd (1991) rate interventions within the psychoeducational school of thought as high in breadth (i.e., applicability to a variety of students and problems) and medium in replicability and in empirical support for effectiveness.

Ecological models are gaining in support as professionals are beginning to understand the importance of dynamic social systems and interactions in determining behavior (Kauffman, 1993). Nevertheless, the ecological model is criticized because it is so complex, involving many different interventions across all of the student's many ecosystems. Such complexity makes research regarding the effectiveness of this model extremely difficult to conduct. Yet, collaborative efforts among teachers and other mental health workers to solve the child's behavioral problems across all fronts offer the best potential for successful treatment of children and youth with emotional and behavioral disorders (Morse, 1992).

The cognitive-behavioral model also has received much research support regarding its effectiveness with a wide variety of behaviors (Graham, Harris, & Reid, 1992). Yet, this model, too, has elicited criticism. Cognitive-behavioral interventions are apparently no better at producing generalized behavior change than are the behavioral methods (Abikoff, 1991). Nelson, Smith, Young, and Dodd (1991), for example, concluded that the effects of self-management strategies taught to children will not readily generalize unless teachers specifically and carefully program for this generalization to occur.

According to Cullinan, Epstein, and Lloyd (1991), the behavioral model has the highest level of intervention replicability, efficiency, and breadth.

Although the behavioral model has well-documented evidence of its effectiveness across grade levels and with a variety of troublesome behaviors, this model, too, has received criticism. For example, Knitzer, Steinberg, and Fleisch (1990) observed what they dubbed a "curriculum of control" in many classrooms for students with behavioral disorders. The teachers visited in their study were concerned with maintaining order and quiet, and they often described their behavior management or point systems when asked to talk about their curriculum.

Rewards and point systems, however, may not be the answer for helping all students learn and behave better. For students with developmental delays, for example, even verbal reinforcement or reinforcing gestures like nodding one's head may detract from the learning process (Biederman, Davey, Ryder, & Franchi, 1994). That is, students with severe attentional deficits or delays in processing verbal information may misconstrue the contingencies underlying reinforcement when rewards follow completion of only a small part of the total task requirement.

Similarly, Fisher, Osterhaus, Clothier, and Edwards (1994) suggest avoiding reward systems when working with passive-aggressive children who "won't do anything" in the classroom. For example, they encourage teachers to give children choices and to use natural and logical consequences for poor decisions made by students rather than punishing them. Control and avoidance of unpleasant demands is sought by passive-aggressive and aggressive children; therefore, teachers who use controlling techniques may be setting themselves up for cycles of coercive efforts by students to sabotage the teacher's plans and regain control (Shores, Gunter, & Jack, 1993).

Moreover, Deci asserts that rewards decrease, rather than increase intrinsic motivation for many students (Deci, Nezlek, & Sheinman, 1981). Deci and his colleagues hypothesize that a student's self-esteem and intrinsic motivation are related to the degree of control or autonomy used by a teacher. On the other hand, in classrooms where teachers give children a degree of autonomy and shared responsibility, Deci predicts that children will demonstrate both increased self-esteem and increased intrinsic motivation. Surprisingly, the relationship among self-esteem, intrinsic motivation, and teacher control, or autonomy, is formed during the first 6 weeks of school, and this relationship changes very little during the course of the school year. Teachers, then, must establish a positive classroom environment (see Chapter 5) immediately to maximize the likelihood of healthy self-esteem and personal expectations for students (Nichols, 1992). In addition, when rewards are given in such a way as to emphasize a student's competence, intrinsic motivation may be maintained or enhanced.

One of the most controversial books criticizing the behavioral model (see Nichols, 1993, for an interesting review) is *Punished by Rewards*, written by Alfie Kohn (1993). Kohn reviews research evidence indicating that rewards may be perceived as punitive when they are not received or when the receiver believes he or she is being manipulated. Kohn emphasizes content (i.e., the importance of meaningful rather than pointless work), choice (i.e., individuals do their best when they are offered a degree of autonomy regarding what they are doing and how they can do it), and collaboration (i.e., working with, as opposed to against or apart from, others) in the workplace and in the classroom.

Conversely, Nichols (1992) argues that behavior management systems are not inherently "bad," but rather some teachers may be misusing point and reward systems. This misuse, however, does not mitigate the effectiveness of techniques from the behavioral model when they are properly applied. Further, she suggests that a focus on "control" is understandable from a teacher's perspective. Nichols (1992, p. 6) offers several reasons why professionals are concerned with control and management given the nature of children with emotional and behavioral disorders and the many constraints imposed on teachers:

1. Control is necessary for an orderly, productive existence. Many behaviorally disordered children lack control so teachers make control a central part of their programming.
2. Teachers may believe that enforcing limits teaches a good lesson.
3. Teachers remember their own teachers and believe that controlling is what they are supposed to do.
4. Society and school administrators expect teachers to have excellent classroom control.
5. Published behavior management programs give teachers a prescribed way to deal with behavioral problems. This may help inexperienced or insecure teachers.
6. Teachers may fear their students and fear having to regain control.
7. Being controlling may be a basic personality trait in some teachers.
8. Teachers may be struggling in the classroom, and control may give them the only method they know for dealing with the fear that might otherwise overwhelm them.
9. A curriculum of control works in making some children with behavioral disorders quiet and more appropriate in their behaviors. The teacher is, therefore, reinforced intermittently for using behavioral techniques and is thus likely to continue to use them.

This discussion is not meant to condemn the behavioral model or, for that matter, any other school of thought. Each model has distinct advantages as well as disadvantages and criticisms. As a teacher, you must not automatically "tune out" any particular conceptual model simply because it does not match your beliefs or background. Neither grasping at techniques for which we are not trained in mindless attempts to solve problems nor rigidly adhering to one "right" method in the face of evidence that "our way" is not effective with a particular child will help us become effective teachers of students with emotional and behavioral disorders (Kauffman, 1993). Brendtro (1993) reminds us that there are truths as well as practice pitfalls in each of the major conceptual models when used in the reality of the classroom (Table 4.2).

Interrelationships among Conceptual Models

You must give careful consideration to your own selection of interventions and that, of course, requires you to develop a personal philosophy. Teachers

Table 4.2   Myths and Mistakes in Intervention Models

Brendtro (1993) states that the major conceptual models for working with troubled youth (i.e., the psychodynamic, behavioral, and psychoeducational models) have developed in relative isolation from one another. He also suggests that in the face of raging youth our firmest beliefs seem like flimsy truths. We are subject to many pitfalls when we apply the principles from our philosophical beliefs to actual practice, and we are often surprised with the lack of "goodness of fit" for our best interventions when they are used in the real world. Brendtro offers the following summary of treatment truisms (i.e., our philosophical beliefs based on the conceptual model we choose) and the resulting practice pitfalls.

	Treatment Truisms	*Practice Pitfalls*
Catharsis (Psycho-dynamic)	Vent suppressed anger to foster mental health	Chaos and a loss of control
Consequences (Behavioral)	Apply rewards and punishments to change and control behavior	Conflict and counter-control
Confrontation (Psychoeducational)	Employ teacher and peer influence to create therapeutic changes	Coercion and gang control

Adapted from "Furious Kids and Treatment Myths," by L. K. Brendro, 1993, *Journal of Emotional and Behavioral Problems*, 2(1), 9, National Educational Service.

rate the ability to describe and defend a personal orientation for managing children and youth, which can be translated into educational practices, as one of their most important and most frequently used skills (Bullock, Ellis, & Wilson, 1994). Similarly, Morse, Cutler, and Fink (1964) suggested that programs for students with emotional and behavioral disorders must be built on a solid philosophical base to be effective. Because the teacher is the person responsible for planning and implementing programs and because interactions among teachers and students are critical for a program's success, the conceptual model from which a teacher operates is an important determinant of the teacher's actions and his or her effectiveness in the classroom (Grosenick, George, & George, 1987).

The behavioral model is the school of thought that is the most well-researched and the most often observed in classrooms for children and youth with emotional or behavioral disorders (Grosenick, George, & George, 1987; Knitzer, Steinberg, & Fleisch, 1990). Also, behavioral theory and practice are most often taught prospective teachers in their preservice teacher education programs (Beare, 1991; Kavale & Hirshoren, 1980). Yet, Kauffman (1993) maintains that most educational practices for students with behavioral problems are not governed by any consistent philosophy or any one conceptual framework.

According to Beare (1991) and to Grosenick and her colleagues (Grosenick, George, & George, 1987; Grosenick & Huntze, 1983), teachers actually use a range of models in the classroom. That is, many teachers describe themselves as "eclectic." They combine the major schools of thought within their own belief systems, and they use strategies and interventions from differing conceptual models. The eclectic approach, however, has been criticized. Kauffman (1993) asserts that "there is a limit to the degree to which one can be eclectic, picking and choosing concepts and strategies from various models, without being simple-minded and self-contradictory. Some conceptual models are not complementary; they suggest radically different and incompatible approaches to a problem. Acceptance of one set of assumptions about human behavior sometimes implies rejection of another" (p. 108).

Yet, Kauffman (1993) and others (Beare, 1991; Jones, 1992; The Peacock Hill Working Group, 1991) suggest that teachers may choose interventions, even from different conceptual models, which they believe are likely to be effective in a given situation. Many professionals primarily supporting the behavioral model, for example, now acknowledge the importance of a student's thoughts and feelings, as well as the consequences of behavior, in determining what the student actually does. Morse (1985) calls this blend of developmental psychology and behavioral theory "individual psychology," and Meichenbaum (1977) merges the cognitive psychologist's attention to thoughts and feelings with behavior modification principles in what he first termed *cognitive-behavior modification.* Kauffman (1993) also now leans toward the social-cognitive theory described by Bandura (1986), which proposes that behaviors are the result of reciprocal interactions among one's environment, one's thoughts, feelings, and perceptions, and one's actual behaviors.

More than ever before professionals from differing philosophical perspectives are joining forces to match the treatment to the child's problem and to provide multicomponent treatment efforts (Jones, 1992; The Peacock Hill Working Group, 1991). Indeed, multiple perspectives may be necessary in the classroom to meet the many and varied needs of students with emotional and behavioral disorders, and few professionals in actual practice adhere rigidly to any one conceptual model (Kauffman, 1993). Different strategies may also work better at different age levels (e.g., counseling skills and techniques may be critical for teachers working with adolescents) (Epstein, Foley, & Cullinan, 1992). Finally, teachers rate understanding the major conceptual models and using a variety of behavior management techniques from these models as highly important and useful skills (Bullock, Ellis, & Wilson, 1994).

Interventions from the major conceptual models, then, must be sensibly blended by teachers. Fortunately, strategies within the major schools of thought, particularly the psychodynamic/humanistic, psychoeducational, behavioral, and cognitive-behavioral models, can be viewed as interrelated. For example, teachers of children and youth with emotional and behavioral disorders must provide a safe, supportive classroom environment and establish a positive relationship with their students. The psychodynamic model is a highly supportive model; therefore, many intervention strategies within this approach are useful cornerstones for teachers in building a positive, supportive classroom for their students. *These interventions will never be enough by themselves* in classrooms for students with emotional and behavioral disorders; however, without support, trust, and respect for student feelings, interventions within the other models may become meaningless.

Teachers may, for example, provide students with activities designed to help them identify and label their feelings or express their feelings appropriately. Art, music, and play activities are "safe" ways to express feelings, and they provide avenues through which students may learn important social skills and cooperative behaviors. In addition, interventions within the psychodynamic/humanistic school of thought often stress the importance of empathy in interactions with students, as well as a need for teachers to make "I" statements. For example, a teacher might respond to a child who is upset about another "cutting in line" in front of her with a statement such as, "I understand that you wanted to be line leader, but our duty chart says that today is Alicia's turn to be line leader." Such a statement conveys understanding to the child and gives the teacher an opportunity to conduct a lesson on important social skills as well.

Such supportive or clarifying statements are also the basis for most interventions within the psychoeducational school of thought, and you may recall that psychoeducational interventions grew from earlier psychodynamic theories. Also, nothing prohibits the teacher from following a statement of empathy with a statement of limits or a reminder of the rules and consequences (e.g., "I understand that you want to be line leader. But you need to help Alicia take her turn today," or "If you help Alicia take her turn today, your turn will be on Thursday"). In addition, teachers may still follow supportive statements with a point loss or gain and collect data on a child's "turn-taking" behavior. Thus, interventions typically associated with the behavioral model may be used simultaneously with more psychodynamically oriented strategies.

The behavioral school of thought is also linked to the psychoeducational model. Both of these models share an emphasis on structuring the environment, developing rules and routines, and managing behaviors. As a matter of fact, the psychoeducational strategies of planned ignoring and signal interference (i.e., consistently ignoring minor misbehavior and sending students little signals like frowns or head-shaking to indicate awareness of their behavior) share much similarity in actual practice with behavioral ideas (i.e., extinction and stimulus control respectively). Moreover, both models suggest teachers structure the environment by reducing distractions, giving attention to a predictable daily schedule, and using proximity control (i.e., the teacher's presence near a student). In both schools of thought, the teacher assumes a directive role in the classroom, although a teacher using the psychoeducational model will be likely to direct responsibility increasingly to the student as he or she is able to assume it.

In addition, both psychoeducationally oriented and behaviorally oriented practitioners teach social skills and they both "contract" with students to help them learn more appropriate behaviors. The teacher may still collect data on behaviors targeted for change while using such psychoeducational strategies as peer-group meetings to resolve classroom conflicts or a Life Space Crisis Intervention to help students learn better coping skills.

Finally, techniques from the cognitive-behavioral model such as self-instructional training use explicit procedures derived from the behavioral model. These techniques also acknowledge and harness the child's thoughts and inner language to change his or her behaviors. Interventions within the psychoeducational model such as Reality Therapy and Life Space Crisis Intervention also use the power of language to mediate behavior. Whereas the child's language serves to mediate behavior within the cognitive-behavioral model, psychoeducational interventions use the teacher's language during structured dialogues to mediate student behavior. Thus, the notion of language as a mediator for behavior provides an additional link between the psychoeducational and cognitive-behavioral schools of thought.

An Integrated Framework for Decision Making

Successful strategies can be found within each of the major schools of thought. As a matter of fact, teachers favoring different conceptual models may find themselves simply using different words to describe very similar actions. Teachers do, however, need a theoretical framework around which they can organize their beliefs and determine their "best" course of action. As Pullis (1992) suggests, professionals often ask "Why is this kid doing this?" and "What should I do about it?" The answer often is an unsettling but truthful, "It depends." Theories, then, must be alive and evolving with both actual practice and research. In addition, they must give teachers useful tools for making decisions about interventions in their classrooms (Pullis, 1992).

The integrated framework proposed for this text is merely a starting point for teacher reflection and decision making about student behavior (Figure 4.1). It is intended only to organize information teachers must consider as they make decisions about student behavior and integrate strategies into a unified philosophy and a comprehensive classroom management plan. The framework is also intended to be flexible, modifiable, and grounded in pragmatism (Harris & Graham, 1994). The framework is based on the following assumptions:

1. Conceptual models structure our theories regarding the cause of student behavior; however, children with emotional and behavioral disorders usually do not have a clear-cut "cause" for their problems. For teachers, knowing a cause is less useful than knowing what to do about the child's behavior.
2. Teachers must base their practice on theory, but they also must be pragmatists. Teachers must be concerned with what works in a particular situation for a given child. Conceptual models are, therefore, most useful for teachers in helping them organize intervention strategies.
3. Although some professionals argue that their model is the "only way," in practice there are very few "pure" approaches. Interventions advocated by professionals adhering to different conceptual models share a degree of overlap in the real classroom. The major conceptual models can be integrated into a unified approach to facilitate decision making.

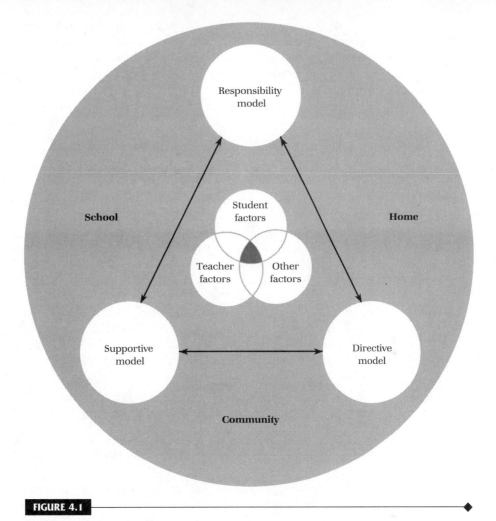

FIGURE 4.1

A Framework for Making Decisions about Student Behavior: Integrating Conceptual Models

4. Some models (e.g., the behavioral model) have more empirical support for their effectiveness than others; however, this does not negate the usefulness of many strategies suggested within the other models. Teachers may find practical and effective interventions within each of the major conceptual models, and they can use systematic, daily, direct measurement (i.e., procedures usually associated with the behavioral model) to determine and document the effectiveness of strategies chosen from the other models.

5. If teachers are unaware of interventions because they are introduced only to a set of techniques within one school of thought, they will be unable to choose from a full range of potentially helpful strategies. Thus, the teacher with a limited repertoire of skills may be limited in his or her effectiveness with some students having emotional and behavioral disorders.

As you examine Figure 4.1, note the larger circle around the figure. Because our behavior is affected by the behavior of others and because the behavior of others is also affected by what we do, teachers must set all decisions within the context of the child's total environment (i.e., teachers must take an ecological perspective). This means that teachers must consider home, school, and community factors that may impact, and be impacted by, their decisions, and teachers must plan to collaborate with others when making important decisions about student behavior. For example, we may need to consider the resources available in the community, the child's cultural or ethnic background, and policies or procedures in place within the school and school district.

Our first key question, then, is what are the expectations and needs of others in the child's environment including parents, peers, other teachers or school administrators, and community members and various professionals involved with the child? The small circle labeled *other factors* in the center of Figure 4.1 reminds us to consider environmental constraints or resources and the expectations of important people surrounding the student as we make our decisions (Table 4.3).

Notice, too, the small circle labeled *teacher factors*. As a teacher, you have your own set of expectations and needs. You feel more comfortable, or better trained, with some ways of handling student behavior than with other ways. Certain interventions may, for example, better "fit" your personality and temperament. In addition, you have particular rules or levels of tolerance that you must honor to reduce your level of stress and to help you feel more effective and competent in your classroom. The key question here is what are your important needs as the child's teacher?

The third important question is what are the student's needs? We must, for example, carefully examine student factors, such as chronological age and developmental level, the child's level of verbal and cognitive ability, and his or her level of academic performance. In addition, we must consider whether or not the young person has learned the behavioral and social skills necessary for success in the school, home, or community. This, of course, entails a critical analysis of the child's behavior in context. Finally, we must give some thought to our own relationship with the child as well as the student's perception about the situation and his or her behavior.

In the integrated framework depicted in Figure 4.1, also notice that four of the major conceptual models (i.e., the psychodynamic/humanistic, psychoeducational, behavioral, and cognitive-behavioral schools of thought) are collapsed within three interrelated philosophies. Psychodynamic and humanistic interventions designed to support, respect, and clarify feelings are included within the label *supportive model*. Behavioral techniques for increasing appropriate behaviors, reducing inappropriate behaviors, and teaching social skills are considered within the directive model. Finally, psychoeducational and cognitive-behavioral interventions are considered together within the responsibility model as children and youth are helped to assume greater responsibility for their own behaviors.

Table 4.3 Questions for Decision Making

Other Factors

What are the expectations of the parents or caregivers?

What are the expectations of other teachers?

What are the expectations of the school principal?

What are the rules, policies, and procedures of the school?

Are prescribed behavior management programs to be followed?

Is there adequate time, space, and privacy for the intervention?

What support is available within the school for the child, the family, and other teachers?

What support is available in the community for the family, for the child, and for the teachers?

What are the cognitive and social-behavioral levels of the other students?

Is the child's behavior violating the rights of other students or interfering with their ability to learn?

Is the child's behavior posing a danger to other students?

Is the child's behavior likely to "spread" to other students?

Teacher Factors

What are your beliefs about teacher control and student autonomy?

What is your level of training and skill with the intervention?

Is the intervention consistent with professionally responsible practice?

Does the intervention fit your personality and temperament?

Does the intervention allow you a margin of comfort given your levels of tolerance?

Does the intervention fit the rules and routines you have established in the classroom?

What support is available to you from the school, home, or community in carrying out the intervention?

How successful have you been in using the intervention with similar students in the past?

Student Factors

Is the child's behavior or your reaction to the child's behavior culturally related or determined?

Does the child have high or low cognitive/verbal ability?

How old is the child chronologically and developmentally?

Will the intervention help the child receive positive feedback from peers, parents, and teachers?

Has the child learned the social or behavioral skills necessary to respond appropriately?

Does the child have adequate self-control?

Does the child appear to be seeking control?

Does the child perceive a need to change?

Is the behavior dangerous to the child?

Many intervention strategies across the conceptual models, then, are compatible; however, the teacher must base decisions regarding a particular intervention on the needs of the child, the needs of others, and his or her own needs as the teacher. Wolfgang and Glickman (1986) and Wolfgang (1995) suggest that teachers consider the seriousness of the child's behavior and the amount of "teacher power" needed (i.e., the more serious or dangerous the child's behavior, the more necessary it becomes for the teacher to assume a greater degree of power and control) when making decisions. Thus, according to Wolfgang and his colleagues (Wolfgang, 1995; Wolfgang & Glickman, 1986), teachers might begin by using the behavioral (i.e., directive) model with very young, immature, or "out-of-control" students and then slowly decrease the teacher's power and control, shifting the responsibility for behavior to the students as they are able to assume it. Conversely, the teacher might begin by giving the students autonomy, increasing his or her power and control if students are unable to handle the responsibility. Strategies based on escalating levels of "teacher control and power," however, may backfire *if* teachers allow themselves to become engaged in coercive exchanges with students (Shores, Gunter, & Jack, 1993).

Similarly, Edwards (1993) suggests that teachers may adhere solely to one model of management, or they may choose to "shift" their philosophy to fit the needs of the situation (i.e., an eclectic orientation). He states that the complexity of behavioral interactions may necessitate an eclectic approach and that teachers may need to use interventions from conceptual models other than their primary philosophical orientation if their interventions, properly used, are not working with a particular student or group of students. He does, however, caution teachers that some interventions may be more appropriate for some students than for others and that teachers and students may become confused if strategies are frequently shifted.

Certainly, you cannot permit inappropriate student behavior one moment in an attempt to be supportive and then be directive and hold students to the rules the next moment. Such teacher behavior would, indeed, appear contradictory, confusing, and "unfair" to students. You can, however, be constantly empathetic and respectful of student feelings while also structuring the classroom environment with reasonable rules, limits, and consequences, and you can simultaneously collect data to monitor the behavior of students. The major decision, then, is not which one of the major models to use. You will always use respect, empathy, support, and activities to help children identify and appropriately express their feelings (i.e., cornerstone interventions from the supportive model), and you will always couch your decisions within the context of the child's ecosystem (i.e., an ecological approach). *The major decision for teachers rests with a choice of directive or responsibility methods for structuring daily interactions designed to change the behaviors of students.* Although there are no "rules" regarding which intervention teachers should choose first, you may wish to consider the following guidelines:

1. Start with examining your own comfort level and degree of familiarity with particular interventions. If you are more familiar or comfortable with one model and its associated interventions, you may wish initially to structure

your classroom accordingly. As you become more experienced and more confident with other approaches, add them one at a time as appropriate to your repertoire of classroom management strategies. Always start with the simplest strategy likely to produce the desired outcome.

2. Constantly use statements of empathy as you begin all interactions with students. Constantly collect and examine data to monitor student behaviors and behavior change. Build a positive learning environment designed to encourage and support learning and appropriate student behavior.

3. Shift your orientation more toward the directive model if your students are very immature. Shift your orientation toward the directive model as well if your students have low cognitive or verbal ability or if they lack self-control and social and behavioral skills.

4. Shift your orientation more toward the responsibility model if students have adequate maturity as well as cognitive and verbal ability. Shift your orientation toward this model, too, if students are adolescents or if they are engaging you in coercive battles for control.

5. Based on the data you collect, adjust your interventions to achieve the desired outcomes. Be sure to consider whether or not your interventions are *teaching* students social skills and more appropriate ways to behave. Also consider whether or not the behavior change is helping the student to have increased self-control, greater responsibility, and more positive interactions with peers, teachers, and family members.

Summary

Teachers are the key ingredients in planning and implementing successful programs. This responsibility entails a knowledge of one's own philosophy regarding student behavior and intervention strategies. The biological/biogenic, psychodynamic/humanistic, psychoeducational, behavioral, cognitive-behavioral, and ecological/sociological models are the major schools of thought used to explain student behavior and to organize intervention strategies. Teachers of students with emotional and behavioral disorders must maintain an ecological position and consider the impact of the environment on their decisions and the impact of their decisions on the child's environment. In addition, the schools of thought can be integrated within three major philosophies, the supportive model, the directive model, and the responsibility model, to form a comprehensive classroom management plan. No one model by itself is likely to meet the many and varied needs of students with emotional and behavioral disorders.

Application Exercises

1. Arrange to observe in a classroom for students with behavior disorders in your local school district. What is the primary conceptual orientation used in the classroom? Interview the teacher following your observation. What factors does the teacher consider important in determining the management plan used in the classroom?

2. Assume you are the teacher of nine boys, ages 6 through 8, in a self-contained classroom for students with behavioral disorders. The boys are all verbally and physically aggressive. What information will you need to consider as you formulate a classroom management plan? How will each piece of information help you to make a better decision?

3. Describe your favorite teacher. What did that teacher do in his or her classroom that made you select this person as your personal favorite? How would you characterize this teacher's management philosophy?

References

Abikoff, H. (1991). Cognitive training in ADHD children: Less to it than meets the eye. *Journal of Learning Disabilities, 24,* 205–209.

Bandura, A. (1986). *Social foundations of thought and action: A social cognitive theory.* Englewood Cliffs, NJ: Prentice-Hall.

Beare, P. L. (1991). Philosophy, instructional methodology, training and goals of teachers of the behaviorally disordered. *Behavioral Disorders, 16,* 211–218.

Berkowitz, P. H., & Rothman, E. P. (1960). *The disturbed child: Recognition and psycho-educational therapy in the classroom.* New York: New York University Press.

Bettleheim, B. (1950). *Love is not enough.* New York: Macmillan.

Bettleheim, B., & Sylvester, E. A. (1948). A therapeutic milieu. *American Journal of Orthopsychiatry, 18,* 191–206.

Biederman, G. B., Davey, V. A., Ryder, C., & Franchi, D. (1994). The negative effects of positive reinforcement in teaching children with developmental delay. *Exceptional Children, 60*(5), 458–465.

Braswell, L., & Kendall, P. C. (1988). Cognitive-behavioral methods with children. In K. S. Dobson (Ed), *Handbook of cognitive-behavioral therapies* (pp. 167–213). New York: Guilford.

Brendtro, L. K. (1993). Furious kids and treatment myths. *Journal of Emotional and Behavioral Problems, 2*(1), 8–12.

Bullock, L. M., Ellis, L. L., & Wilson, M. J. (1994). Knowledge/skills needed by teachers who work with students with severe emotional/behavioral disorders: A revisitation. *Behavioral Disorders, 19*(2), 108–125.

Cullinan, D., Epstein, M. H., & Lloyd, J. W. (1983). *Behavior disorders of children and adolescents.* Englewood Cliffs, NJ: Prentice-Hall.

Cullinan, D., Epstein, M. H., & Lloyd, J. W. (1991). Evaluation of conceptual models of behavior disorders. *Behavioral Disorders, 16*(2), 148–157.

Deci, E. L., Nezlek, J., & Sheinman, L. (1981). Characteristics of the rewarder and intrinsic motivation of the rewarded. *Journal of Personality and Social Psychology, 40,* 1–10.

DiGangi, S. (1991). Expert and novice teachers: Examining decisions in the classroom. *Beyond Behavior, 2*(3), 22–23.

Dobson, K. S., & Block, L. (1988). Historical and philosophical bases of the cognitive-behavioral therapies. In K. S. Dobson (Ed.), *Handbook of cognitive-behavioral therapies* (pp. 3–38). New York: Guilford.

Duchnowski, A. J., Johnson, M. K., Hall, K. S., Kutash, K., & Friedman, R. M. (1993). The alternatives to residential treatment study: Initial findings. *Journal of Emotional and Behavioral Disorders, 1*(1), 17–26.

Edwards, C. H. (1993). *Classroom discipline and management.* New York: Macmillan.

Ellis, A. (1962). *Reason and emotion in psychotherapy.* New York: Stuart.

Epstein, M. H., Foley, R. M., & Cullinan, D. (1992). National survey of educational programs for adolescents with serious emotional disturbance. *Behavioral Disorders, 17*(3), 202–210.

Federation of Families for Children's Mental Health. (1992). *Family support statement.* Alexandria, VA: Federation of Families for Children's Mental Health.

Fisher, D., Osterhaus, N., Clothier, P., & Edwards, L. (1994). Passive-aggressive children in the classroom: The child who won't do anything. *Beyond Behavior, 5*(2), 9–12.

Friesen, B. J., & Wahlers, D. (1993). Respect and real help: Family support and children's mental health. *Journal of Emotional and Behavioral Problems, 2*(4), 12–15.

Gardner, R. (1990). Life space interviewing: It can be effective, but don't . . . *Behavioral Disorders, 15*(2), 111–119.

Glasser, W. (1965). *Reality therapy: A new approach to psychiatry.* New York: Harper & Row.

Glasser, W. (1969). *Schools without failure.* New York: Harper & Row.

Graham, S., Harris, K. R., & Reid, R. (1992). Developing self-regulated learners. *Focus on Exceptional Children, 24*(6), 1–16.

Grosenick, J. K., George, M. P., & George, N. L. (1987). A profile of school programs for the behaviorally disordered: Twenty years after Morse, Cutler, and Fink. *Behavioral Disorders, 12*(3), 159–168.

Grosenick, J. K., & Huntze, S. (1983). *More questions than answers: Review and analysis of programs for behaviorally disordered children and youth.* Columbia, MO: National Needs Analysis Project in Behavior Disorders, University of Missouri-Columbia, Department of Special Education.

Harris, K. R. (1982). Cognitive-behavior modification: Application with exceptional students. *Focus on Exceptional Children, 15*(2), 1–16.

Harris, K. R., & Graham, S. (1994). Constructivism: Principles, paradigms, and integration. *The Journal of Special Education, 28*(3), 233–247.

Heuchert, C. M. (1983). Can teachers change behavior? Try interviews. *Academic Therapy, 18,* 321–328.

Hobbs, N. (1966). Helping the disturbed child: Psychological and ecological strategies. *American Psychologist, 21,* 1105–1115.

Hobbs, N. (1978). Perspectives on re-education. *Behavioral Disorders, 3,* 65–66.

Jones, V. F. (1992). Integrating behavioral and insight-oriented treatment in school based programs for seriously emotionally disturbed children. *Behavioral Disorders, 17*(3), 225–236.

Kanfer, F. H., & Gaelick-Buys, L. (1991). Self-management methods. In F. H. Kanfer & A. P. Goldstein (Eds.), *Helping people change: A textbook of methods* (4th ed.) (pp. 305–360). New York: Pergamon.

Kauffman, J. M. (1993). *Characteristics of emotional and behavioral disorders of children and youth* (5th ed.). New York: Merrill/Macmillan.

Kavale, K., & Hirshoren, A. (1980). Public school and university teacher training programs for behaviorally disordered children: Are they compatible? *Behavioral Disorders, 5,* 151–155.

Kohn, A. (1993). *Punished by rewards: The trouble with gold stars, incentive plans, A's, praise, and other bribes.* Boston: Houghton Mifflin.

Knitzer, J. (1993). Children's mental health policy: Challenging the future. *Journal of Emotional and Behavioral Disorders, 1*(1), 8–16.

Knitzer, J., Steinberg, Z., & Fleisch, B. (1990). *At the schoolhouse door: An examination of programs and policies for children with emotional and behavioral problems.* New York: Bank Street College of Education.

Lewis, W. W. (1974). From Project RE-ED to ecological planning. *Phi Delta Kappan, 55,* 538–540.

Long, N. J. (1990). Comments on Ralph Gardner's article "Life space interviewing: It can be effective, but don't . . ." *Behavioral Disorders, 15*(2), 119–125.

Long, N. J., & Newman, R. G. (1976). Managing surface behavior of children in school. In N. J. Long, W. C. Morse, & R. G. Newman (Eds.), *Conflict in the classroom: The education of emotionally disturbed children* (3rd ed) (pp. 308–317). Belmont, CA: Wadsworth.

Luria, A. R. (1961). *The role of speech in the regulation of normal and abnormal behaviors.* New York: Liveright.

Mahoney, M. J. (1974). *Cognition and behavior modification.* Cambridge, MA: Ballinger.

Meichenbaum, D. (1977). *Cognitive-behavior modification: An integrative approach.* New York: Plenum.

Morse, W. C. (1985). *The education and treatment of socio-emotionally impaired children and youth.* Syracuse, NY: Syracuse University Press.

Morse, W. C. (1992). Mental health professionals and teachers: How do the twain meet? *Beyond Behavior, 3*(2), 12–20.

Morse, W. C., Cutler, R. L., & Fink, A. H. (1964). *Public school classes for the emotionally handicapped: A research analysis.* Washington, DC: Council for Exceptional Children.

Neill, A. S. (1960). *Summerhill.* New York: Hart.

Nelson, J. R., Smith, D. J., Young, R. K., & Dodd, J. (1991). A review of self-management outcome research conducted with students who exhibit behavioral disorders. *Behavioral Disorders, 16,* 169–180.

Nichols, P. (1992). The curriculum of control: Twelve reasons for it, some arguments against it. *Beyond Behavior, 3*(2), 5–11.

Nichols, P. (1993). Some rewards, more punishment: A look at application of behaviorism. *Beyond Behavior, 5*(1), 4–13.

Pullis, M. (1992). Theories and therapies: Evolving themes in thaumaturgy. *Beyond Behavior, 3*(3), 13–18.

Redl, F., & Wineman, D. (1951). *Children who hate.* New York: Free Press.

Redl, F., & Wineman, D. (1952). *Controls from within.* New York: Free Press.

Rhodes, W. C., & Paul, J. L. (1978). *Emotionally disturbed and deviant children: New views and approaches.* Englewood Cliffs, NJ: Prentice-Hall.

Rhodes, W. C., & Tracy, M. L. (Eds.). (1972a). *A study of child variance (Vol.1).* Ann Arbor, MI: University of Michigan Press.

Rhodes, W. C., & Tracy, M. L. (Eds.). (1972b). *A study of child variance (Vol.2).* Ann Arbor, MI: University of Michigan Press.

Rogers, C. (1983). *Freedom to learn for the 80's.* Columbus, OH: Merrill/Macmillan.

Shores, R. E., Gunter, P. L., & Jack, S. L. (1993). Classroom management strategies: Are they setting events for coercion? *Behavioral Disorders, 18*(2), 92–102.

Skinner, B. F. (1953). *Science and human behavior.* New York: Free Press.

Skinner, B. F. (1968). *The technology of teaching.* New York: Appleton-Century-Crofts.

The Peacock Hill Working Group. (1991). Problems and promises in special education and related services for children and youth with emotional or behavioral disorders. *Behavioral Disorders, 16*(4), 299–313.

Vygotsky, L. (1962). *Thought and language.* New York: Wiley.

Watson, J. B. (1913). Psychology as the behaviorist views it. *Psychological Review, 20,* 158–177.

Wolfgang, C. H. (1995). *Solving discipline problems: Methods and models for today's teachers* (3rd Ed.). Boston: Allyn & Bacon.

Wolfgang, C. H., & Glickman, C. D. (1986). *Solving discipline problems: Strategies for classroom teachers* (2nd ed.). Boston: Allyn & Bacon.

Wood, M. M., & Long, N. J. (1991). *Life space intervention: Talking with children and youth in crisis.* Austin, TX: Pro-Ed.

TWO

PRACTICE

By now, you realize that making decisions about students and their behavior involves a complex set of understandings and skills. You have a basic understanding of the major schools of thought regarding the nature of behavior and associated intervention strategies, and you have begun to establish your own personal philosophy for use in your classroom. Now you must begin to develop your skills so that you may implement a range of strategies to meet the many social-emotional needs of your students with behavioral disorders.

In this second section, then, we will discuss the successful practice of interventions from the major conceptual models. In Chapter 5, we will explore ways to build a positive classroom environment and teach students academic skills. In Chapter 6, we will offer many strategies for respecting the feelings of students. In Chapter 7, we will examine behavioral techniques, and in Chapter 8, the teaching of social skills. In Chapter 9, we will discuss the psychoeducational and cognitive-behavioral interventions that focus on teaching students responsibility. Finally, in Chapter 10, we will return to the ecological perspective and explore ways to collaborate with parents, teachers, and others involved with your students.

CHAPTER 5

BUILDING A POSITIVE LEARNING ENVIRONMENT

Main Ideas:

◆ *Effective programs for students with emotional and behavioral disorders are characterized by a safe, supportive classroom environment; by quality instruction and a challenging curriculum; and by collaborative efforts among teachers, parents, and other mental health professionals.*

◆ *Teachers with high self-efficacy believe they are making a positive difference in the lives of children, and they tend to be more effective in the classroom.*

◆ *Effective teachers maximize academic learning time by minimizing disruptions, by grouping students according to skills, and by maintaining an academic focus.*

◆ *Direct instruction and mastery learning are empiricist models of instruction that increase academic learning time.*

◆ *Constructivist models of instruction encourage students to create knowledge that is purposeful and connected to real life.*

◆ *Both empiricist and constructivist models can be sensibly integrated to provide quality instruction and a challenging curriculum to students with emotional and behavioral disorders.*

Teachers have a tremendous impact on the daily lives of the students in their classrooms. The actions of teachers can promote disinterest, apathy, frustration, and a sense of alienation among students. Conversely, a teacher's actions can spark interest, curiosity, learning, and a sense of belonging and satisfaction. When teachers build a positive learning environment, these desirable outcomes are more likely for their students. Teachers of children and youth with emotional and behavioral disorders, in particular, are constantly challenged to provide a positive learning environment for their students.

In this chapter, we will discuss ways to build a positive environment in which children and youth can learn. We will first examine the characteristics of effective programs for students with emotional and behavioral disorders and those factors that promote the development of a positive classroom environment. Then, we will explore effective teacher behaviors designed to encourage student learning and achievement, including a teacher's use of time and choice of instructional model.

Characteristics of Effective Programs for Students with Emotional and Behavioral Disorders

Over three decades ago, Morse, Cutler, and Fink (1964) conducted a classic analysis of programs for students with behavioral disorders and the effects of these programs on those children they served. At that time, of course, the Individuals with Disabilities Education Act (1990) did not exist, and programs for students with behavioral disorders were primarily segregated. Morse and his colleagues found, however, that two important program goals were to free the regular classroom from behavior problems and to expedite changes in student behavior that would enable children to return to the regular class, still important goals for special education programs today (Knitzer, Steinberg, & Fleisch, 1990). The special teacher, though, had the primary responsibility for program planning and implementation, and the actual programs varied greatly. Morse, Cutler, and Fink (1964) suggested that programs having a solid philosophical base are those most likely to be effective.

Grosenick, George, and George (1987) collected similar data 2 decades later and found that although programs for students with behavioral disorders had expanded in both the number of children and the grade levels served, teachers were still the critical element in a program's success. Teachers continue to have responsibility for constructing the curriculum, for determining student goals and documenting progress toward those goals, for maintaining contact with parents and outside service agencies, and for designing appropriate intervention strategies (Grosenick, George, & George, 1987). Unfortunately, very few comprehensive descriptions of programs for students with behavioral disorders are available in the literature (Grosenick, George, & George, 1988).

Despite the lack of adequate program descriptions in the literature, classrooms for students with emotional and behavioral disorders do seem to share a surprising degree of similarity. Knitzer, Steinberg, and Fleisch (1990) describe a lack of educational vitality and imaginative spark in many special education classrooms for children and youth with emotional and behavioral disorders. Worksheets and workbooks, boredom, and little interaction among peers apparently characterize many of these classrooms.

An orderly environment is certainly necessary for learning to occur. As Steinberg and Knitzer (1992) properly remind us, however, students with emotional and behavioral disorders often challenge the patience of their teachers. These students may contribute to a teacher's lowered sense of satisfaction and effectiveness; therefore, teachers may use a "curriculum of control" to reduce their frustration and anger rather than risking peer interactions or teaching students how to take responsibility for their own behaviors.

Steinberg and Knitzer (1992) offer excellent questions to consider when evaluating the effectiveness of programs for students with emotional and behavioral disorders (Box 5.1, pp. 132–133). In addition, promising programs and strategies that appear to be effective with these students share the following overlapping elements (Knitzer, Steinberg, & Fleisch, 1990; The Peacock Hill Working Group, 1991):

♦ A classroom environment that is safe and supportive
♦ Quality instruction and a challenging curriculum
♦ Collaborative efforts among teachers, parents, and other service agencies to address all components of the student's environment and to provide a multifaceted treatment program
♦ Teachers who are committed to sustained interventions and who believe that they are making a positive change in the academic and behavioral performance of the child

A Safe and Supportive Classroom

Children and youth must feel safe, secure, and supported in their attempts to learn. Students with emotional and behavioral disorders, however, often lead what appear to be disorderly and chaotic lives. The teacher, then, must help provide a degree of structure in the classroom so that the child can make sense out of his or her disorderly world. A safe and supportive classroom for students with behavioral disorders entails planning a predictable environment including attention to scheduling, rules and routines, seating arrangements and traffic flow, materials management, and friendly and polite teacher behaviors.

Scheduling. Students with emotional and behavioral disorders often do not handle unlimited choices well. By providing students with a posted, predictable daily schedule, teachers give students an opportunity to learn how to handle time and to make wise choices. Teachers may not be able to control the entire daily schedule for their students; however, in your classroom you can plan for predictability. For example, students may expect to complete a quiet, independent activity such as writing or drawing in their personal journals when they first enter your classroom. This type of activity allows students the opportunity to "settle down" as they begin the school day or class period.

If students are able, give them a choice among two or even three quiet activities (e.g., write in their journal, illustrate a scene from a favorite story, complete a word search puzzle using spelling or vocabulary words). As students are quieted, plan to discuss the posted day's schedule, reviewing each event in order, so students know what to expect. Pay particular attention to any variations in the schedule, explaining what these are, why they are necessary, and answering any questions or concerns students may have about these changes. Be sure to alternate quiet activities with more active ones and independent work with cooperative and group learning arrangements. In addition, by following a focused, academic lesson such as drill and practice using math facts with something "fun" that students prefer to do (e.g., play Jeopardy with vocabulary, facts, and concepts from science or social studies; participate in a physical education, music, or art activity), teachers enhance the likelihood of their students completing the less preferred activities.

Rules, Routines, and Materials Management. Reasonable classroom rules provide consistency and stability by making teacher-student and student-student interactions more predictable. You may recall from Chapter 3

What, If Any, Mental Health Services Do Students Receive and How Are These Integrated into the Daily Life of the Classroom?

Is there a daily time for group sharing of concerns and problems?

Are students provided an acceptable way to express feelings?

Do teachers have access to inservice training and consultation from mental health personnel? What happens when a student has a crisis?

Are crises seen as opportunities for intensive intervention?

Is learning how to socialize seen as a curricular issue?

Is Physical Space Used to Enhance Interpersonal Contact?

Are students expected to work mainly in isolation?

Are they expected to interact, share, and help one another?

Does the teacher teach skills of group process, and are group projects planned and rewarded?

Are social skills integrated into the life of the classroom?

Do children have opportunities for physical activity and for fun?

How Are Parents Involved in the Daily Life of the Classroom?

Are there special staff to reach out to parents so the burden is not all on the teacher?

Are family support services, especially intensive crisis intervention services, linked to school-based services?

From "Classrooms for Emotionally and Behaviorally Disturbed Students: Facing the Challenge," by Z. Steinberg & J. Knitzer, *Behavioral Disorders*, 17(2), 1992, pp. 153–154. Copyright © 1993 by The Council for Exceptional Children. Reprinted with permission.

that a few well-selected and positively phrased rules, which are posted, practiced, and rewarded, contribute to a safe, positive, and supportive classroom environment. Whereas rules are guiding principles governing interpersonal relationships in the classroom, routines are important daily operating procedures for noninstructional activities, which make life in the classroom flow more smoothly. Routines are necessary, for example, for distributing and collecting materials, using the pencil sharpener or the restroom, getting a drink of water, handing in papers, or requesting assistance. Several suggestions for routines are listed in Box 5.2 (pp. 134–135). Placing nonessential or distracting materials out of sight in a closet or cabinet also facilitates structure and predictability for students who can't handle unlimited choices, and hazardous items such as scissors must certainly be secured.

Seating Arrangements and Traffic Flow. Teachers must carefully plan the physical space in the classroom to ensure safety and to promote learning. Arrange furniture so that areas of heavy traffic such as to and from the teacher's desk, the classroom door, the pencil sharpener, or the water fountain are not cluttered. If at all possible, arrange individual student desks away from these

Routines for Noninstructional Activities

Routines guide the day-to-day noninstructional activities in your classroom. These small but important daily operating procedures will enhance the predictability and order in your classroom. Some routines often suggested by experienced teachers include the following:

Routines for Distributing and Collecting Materials

Use table, group, or row monitors to get and distribute materials and to collect materials.

Rotate the job of table, group, or row monitor so that all students have this responsibility.

Provide practice for students in distributing and collecting materials swiftly, and reward them frequently for doing so.

Routines for Handing In Work

Use an "in" basket on your desk or on a nearby shelf in which students may place completed papers.

Use an "out" basket for graded work to be picked up by students at a specified time each day.

Use individual work folders or large manila envelopes at each student's desk for them to place completed work to be handed in at the end of a set period.

Use plastic wall baskets or folders in a box by the door for students to place work in as they leave.

Place work in boxes, color-coded by subject area.

Put work in a class folder at the end of each period using a different folder for each period.

Routines for the Restroom, Pencil Sharpener, and Water Fountain

Post a sign-out sheet at the door for bathroom breaks.

Only one student may leave the classroom to use the restroom or get water at a time.

high-traffic areas. Designate specific areas of the room for particular activities. For example, use a table near the chalkboard for group work or group discussions, a corner of the classroom for a "cooling off" area, and individual student desks for independent work. Be sure to separate individual desks initially so that students are unable to touch one another. As students become more able to work with each other, move the desks closer together to facilitate a peer buddy system for help with seatwork or completing cooperative tasks. Although areas of the classroom are arranged for specific activities, be sure that all parts of the classroom are visible to you at all times and that all areas have appropriate lighting and ventilation.

Friendly and Polite Teacher Behaviors. Teachers must provide appropriate models of friendly, polite behavior. Your attitude toward your students is

Require students to use the water fountain or restroom only at preset times during the day or only during individual work, although you must make allowances for emergencies.

Have students turn over a card hanging near the door as they leave for the restroom and turn it back over as they reenter the classroom.

Give students a "count to three" for speeding up water breaks. Require two pencils to be sharpened as students enter the room.

Keep extra pencils in your desk that may be "purchased" with points earned or collateral held until the pencil's return.

Routines for Requesting Help

Devise an age-appropriate "help sign" for students to place on their desk when they require assistance.

Post and practice a series of steps for requesting help: ask an assigned peer buddy; raise your help sign; try the next item or next assignment.

Student takes a numbered ticket, and when the teacher finishes assisting the student, the teacher replaces the number on a peg and writes the next number on the board.

Student completes work from a folder containing assignments he or she is capable of completing independently for review and maintenance of learning until help is available.

Routines for Finishing Work Early

Post a set of activity choices for things students may do if they finish work early: read a library book or a magazine from the classroom book shelf.

Use the computer when work is completed correctly.

Work on homework.

Complete an activity for extra credit from a prepared set of activity cards (e.g., writing an ending to a story, using the newspaper to answer current events questions).

quickly conveyed to them through what you say, your facial expressions and tone of voice, and body language. To build a positive and supportive relationship with your students, you must take time to listen to what they have to say and be alert to their feelings. Try to spend a little time every day privately speaking to every student. Comment or ask about a nonschool related activity you know to be of interest to the student. Look at students when they speak, and demonstrate interest in what they have to say. Even when students talk about topics at inappropriate times, the teacher might handle the situation by acknowledging the student's interest with a comment like, "I know that's a neat activity for you. Let's get started on this activity first, and then you and I will make a time to sit down and talk about that." Smiles, winks, and your physical presence near students are small ways to reassure them that you are there and rooting for your students and that you value your relationship with them. As the old saying goes,

BOX 5.3   Polite and Friendly Teacher Behaviors

Good teachers of students with social-emotional and behavioral problems demonstrate good human relationship skills. They are warm and friendly and they communicate to all students a sense of acceptance and belonging in the classroom, even when they disagree with a particular student's behavior at the moment. Polite and friendly teachers communicate their respect for students as important human beings by demonstrating the following positive human relationship skills:

◆ A focus on the bright side—Have a positive attitude and stress what the student needs to be doing rather than what he or she is doing that is wrong (e.g., "You need to calm down so we can talk" rather than "You're always yelling, and I'm not going to talk to you if you're yelling.")

◆ Giving regular attention to all students—Say something personal and private to each student every day. Greet students by name as they enter the classroom, and as they leave, let them know you look forward to seeing them again the next day.

◆ Friendliness without being a friend—Be warm and open with students, and share with them some of your own personal interests and hobbies. This does not mean, however, that you become a friend to your students and share with them all your personal secrets. Sooner or later teachers must arbitrate disputes or correct their students, and teachers cannot be both authority figure and friend without confusing students.

◆ Listening empathically—Observe students carefully as they speak. Try to determine what the student is feeling as well as what the student is trying to say. Listening genuinely and acknowledging what the student is saying or feeling communicates interest and caring. Teachers can convey to students that they understand how students feel without condoning or legitimizing their inappropriate actions and without expressing sympathy.

◆ Modeling good manners and courtesy—Be polite and use good manners when addressing students. When students "forget" their manners, you must teach them courtesy through your example. If you insist on good manners from students but you treat them impolitely, students will soon discern the hypocritical nature of your actions, and they may see you as an adult who cannot be trusted.

◆ Conveying enthusiasm and confidence in students—Be enthusiastic about what you are teaching and confident about the ability of students to complete tasks that are appropriately set for them. Give genuine and specific praise to all students as they complete assignments or demonstrate appropriate behaviors, particularly those that are new or difficult for them.

"your students won't care how much you know until they know how much you care" (Box 5.3).

Summary of a Safe and Supportive Classroom ◆

A safe and supportive classroom environment is a personalized environment that signals to students that they belong and are accepted and secure. In addition to giving attention to rules, routines, schedules, seating arrangements, and good manners, teachers may personalize the classroom for students by providing books or posters about topics of interest to individual students or by assisting children to identify their personal space (e.g., label cubbyholes or storage cabinets for young childrens' belongings; personalize desks with student-decorated chair covers, name tags, or overhead posters). Using classroom slogans (e.g., "We are family"), banners, raps, and other rituals can also enhance a sense of belonging and predictable security for students with emotional and behavioral disorders (Redl, 1976). You will find many additional ideas for building a supportive and positive classroom environment in Chapter 6. ◆

Quality Instruction and a Challenging Curriculum

Students must understand the connections between what they are learning and their daily lives. If students see that what they are learning is relevant to their lives, and if students are engaged in real, hands-on experiences, they are more likely to be motivated to participate in instructional activities. A challenging curriculum for students with emotional and behavioral disorders is lively and purposeful, with opportunities for learning behavioral and social skills fully integrated with academic instruction (Knitzer, Steinberg, & Fleisch, 1990).

Quality instruction is also characterized by systematic and data-based interventions, by continuous assessment and monitoring of progress, and by provision for practice of new skills (The Peacock Hill Working Group, 1991). Teachers must use interventions systematically in their classrooms and collect data to ensure that these interventions are achieving the desired outcomes. This means that teachers must frequently observe and directly measure student progress using informal assessment techniques such as those we explored in Chapter 2. Based on direct, daily measurement of student behavior and academic performance, then, teachers can adjust interventions until a desired goal is attained.

Moreover, teachers must provide students with many opportunities to practice critical academic or social skills in context. Teachers may, for example, model appropriate ways for students to handle teasing on the playground and then engage students in structured lessons during which they can rehearse and practice this social skill with the teacher's guidance. Unless students are also given real opportunities to use the new skill (i.e., to handle teasing on the playground) and to evaluate their use of the skill, however, they may not apply the skill when it is actually needed in problem situations. (We will discuss systematic data-based interventions and social skills instruction in Chapters 7 and 8. We will also elaborate on teacher behaviors and instructional models linked to challenging curricula and quality instruction later in this chapter.)

Interestingly, careful teacher attention to important data-based instructional variables may actually reduce problem behaviors. For example, giving students a choice of tasks or a choice of reinforcers and rapidly pacing instruction may decrease even serious behavioral problems such as throwing objects, yelling, and hitting others (Munk & Repp, 1994; West & Sloan, 1986). Moreover, interspersing tasks that a child has mastered or commands the child is likely to follow among tasks the child has yet to master or commands the child is less likely to follow improves performance and compliance (Munk & Repp, 1994). Finally, giving a student one part of a complicated task to complete at a time and minimizing errors made by students on new learning tasks increases student achievement and decreases behavioral problems. Such errorless learning techniques prevent academic tasks from becoming aversive events, which students then attempt to avoid through their misbehaviors (Munk & Repp, 1994).

Collaborative Efforts and Multifaceted Treatment

Successful programs for students with emotional and behavioral disorders are multifaceted and require collaborative efforts among teachers, parents, and other professionals. A single teacher alone cannot assume the entire responsibility for the complex needs of students with behavioral disorders. Successful strategies, then, are often sustained efforts over time to match specific interventions to the student's needs and to address all relevant parts of the student's environment. Parents, for example, may need to learn more effective parenting skills; the regular classroom teacher may require assistance with classroom management; and the bus driver may need procedures for monitoring and rewarding appropriate behaviors to and from school. Family members may require crisis intervention services and teachers working with students having behavioral disorders may need greater support from community mental health personnel (Knitzer, 1993).

The school psychologist, guidance counselors, administrators, teachers, parents, physicians, and community mental health professionals all may need to be involved in successful programs that "wrap around" the student and his or her family. Although legislation and funding patterns often work against such comprehensive systems of care for children with emotional and behavioral disorders and their teachers and their families, these disincentives are slowly changing through federal initiatives designed to link schools and mental health services (Knitzer, 1993). Professionals now realize that without collaborative efforts, any intervention provided in one setting may have only a limited impact on a student's functioning in other settings; therefore, the cumulative, or additive, effects of a multicomponent treatment "package" may be more beneficial than any one element alone (The Peacock Hill Working Group, 1991). We will suggest ideas to foster collaborative efforts to support children, teachers, and families in Chapter 10.

Teacher Self-Efficacy

Teachers must believe that what they are doing is making a difference in the lives of the students they teach. As you can see from reading Box 5.4 (pp. 140–141),

High self-efficacy teachers believe they can make a difference in the performance of their students and tend to be effective in the classroom.

teachers can experience a great deal of stress in their daily lives with students. Unless teachers believe that they can be a positive influence in their students' lives while they are in the classroom, they are unlikely to persist with difficult students in a stress-filled environment.

Bandura (1977, 1982) first suggested that self-efficacy consists of both a general outcome expectancy (i.e., a belief that one's action will lead to a desired outcome) and self-efficacy (i.e., the belief that one possesses the skills to bring about one's desired outcomes). For teachers, then, self-efficacy entails a belief that students can be taught regardless of family, school, or societal difficulties and a belief that we have the ability to affect positive change for our students (Ashton & Webb, 1986; Gibson & Dembo, 1984). Such a belief requires a sense of optimism in our explanatory style (i.e., how we typically explain to ourselves why events happen). Seligman (1991) suggests that people with an optimistic explanatory style view difficult events as temporary, specific, and caused by external circumstances, while they view positive events as permanent, broadly based, and personally caused. Thus, teachers with an optimistic explanatory style may believe that difficulties experienced in the classroom are temporary and not insurmountable. They may persist with their troublesome students having learning and behavioral problems even when the students, themselves, have a very low sense of personal self-efficacy and low expectations for their own performance (Rogers & Saklofske, 1985; Schunk, 1989; Torgeson, 1989; Wells, 1993).

Although we know very little about the relationship among explanatory style, teacher self-efficacy, and teachers of students with emotional and behavioral disorders, we might predict that teachers with an optimistic explanatory style and a high sense of self-efficacy will be more likely to persist with their students than those with a low sense of self-efficacy or a pessimistic explanatory style. We do know, however, that teachers with a high sense of self-efficacy engage in actions

BOX 5.4 Teacher Feature: Beowulf Revisited—Applying What I Really Learned

It was definitely time for spring vacation. I could not even look at my students without feeling overwhelmed and discouraged. How could I put up with their bad language and bad attitudes until June? Why did it seem like I was working harder to earn their credits than they were? Let them all flunk if they wanted to engage in power struggles so often! With this "bad attitude" of my own, I boarded a plane to Boston to spend a few days with my family.

During one of our information-sharing sessions, my mother told me that Mr. Murphy, my high school English teacher, had received an honorary chair for teaching 20 years in the system. I had thought of Mr. Murphy often when I started teaching four years earlier, basing my curriculum on what I remembered learning in his class all those years ago. I decided to visit him and let him know that one of his former students was applying what she had learned.

I noticed that little had changed as I walked in my old school. Indeed, Mr. Murphy's office was where it had been 11 years ago. I was surprised and delighted to find that Mr. Murphy remembered me well. We reminisced a bit, updated each other on professional and family events, and discussed the merits of various curricula. We also talked about the changes we had seen in our students. We shared a sense of concern about how the lives of teenagers have become more complicated and confusing. The meeting was short. He had a class to teach and I had an appointment.

This visit brought back a host of memories about my own teenage years. I had hated high school. The whole experience was miserable and sometimes even terrifying. I am not sure that I had any legitimate reason to be so unhappy. I was lucky to have understanding and kind parents, a safe and happy home, and true, dear friends. Yet, whenever I entered that building, I felt fat, awkward, socially unfit, and academically incapable. In a school full of cliques and groups, I didn't seem to belong anywhere. I can distinctly remember my sense of joy and freedom at graduation. I felt as though my life was just beginning in earnest.

Mr. Murphy was my saving grace in those difficult days. I spent many hours after school with him. I started coming to his office because I was not doing as well as I wanted in his class. I never received higher than a "C+" at a first attempt on an essay. I arrived with drafts before and rewrites after to learn exactly what Mr. Murphy expected in these analytical forays. I don't think I ever mastered these skills to my satisfaction, but by the middle of the year, that was not really why I came. I came because I had found an understanding and gentle adult to help me negotiate the uncertainties and agonies of teenagerhood. I was quiet in my pain: I did not act out, fail classes, or break rules. Mr. Murphy somehow recognized that I needed attention and support. So, in between discussions of Beowulf, The Canterbury Tales, and King Lear, we talked about my hopeless crush on Tommy, my tendency to put myself down and the importance (or not) of fitting in.

I managed to graduate high school intact and went on to college. There, I learned the joys and challenges of working with children, especially "troubled" teens. I decided to pursue a career in special education. Today, I am teaching English to "emotionally disturbed" and "learning disabled" adolescents in an alternative high school program. And I love it, most of the time.

Now I sometimes find that I am sapped of energy and enthusiasm. My colleagues and I battle tremendous odds for the minds and souls of our kids. Some of these odds are in the students' world: drugs, violence, abuse, poverty, poor self-esteem, teen pregnancy, and dysfunctional families. Still, the biggest battles we fight are in our community and society: a lack of funding, resources and support. Education seems to have slipped from its place as a community responsibility to our children to an economic burden we are not sure we want to bear. At the same time, teachers and school personnel are being asked to do more and more to combat the negative forces in our children's lives. I have moments when I am not sure why I am doing this as it seems so unappreciated, not only by my students (which I expect and can understand) but by society in general.

Teenagers can be a prickly bunch. They demand both independence and acceptance. Our troubled and troubling teens are particularly prickly as they can demand these two things in extreme and sometimes unacceptable ways. Still, they need adults who will give them positive attention and accept them for who they are. I don't mean they need us to be their friends. They have friends. They need us to guide, to set expectations and boundaries and to listen. They need us to be mentors. Education is a wonderful way to accomplish this.

My visit with Mr. Murphy brought full circle my understanding of why teachers are important and why I continue to teach, despite the bad attitudes and poor community support. He saw me as worth his time and effort, whether it was to discuss English or growing up. He was a stepping-stone. Though I continued to struggle for awhile after I graduated, this experience stayed with me. And when it came time for me to exit the quagmire of adolescence, I emerged believing that I was capable, bright, and strong.

So, I will return to my students on Monday reminded of why I am there. I will try to be that stepping-stone. I cannot change their world or cure their pain. But I can listen. I can teach them that their feelings matter and that their behaviors have consequences. I can show them they are worth my time and energy. Maybe sometime down the road, they will use this as a foundation to help them make good choices and come to believe in themselves. In the meantime, I may even teach them to appreciate Beowulf.

From "Beowulf Revisited: Applying What I Really Learned," by E. R. Spero, *Beyond Behavior*, 5(2), 1994, pp. 7–8. Copyright © 1994 by The Council for Exceptional Children. Reprinted with permission.

likely to be effective with their problem students. High self-efficacy teachers tend to exhibit the following characteristics:

___ Persist longer with students who are struggling
___ Are less critical of student errors
___ Have greater expectations for student performance and student success
___ Use classroom management strategies characterized by warmth, acceptance, and encouragement
___ Provide individual attention and extra help to individual students
___ Solicit input and help from students and colleagues (Ashton & Webb, 1986; Emmer & Hickman, 1991; Gibson & Dembo, 1984; Woolfolk & Hoy, 1990).

To persist in teaching students with emotional and behavioral disorders, however, requires more than simple motivation or positive beliefs. Teachers must have the knowledge and skills to implement a wide range of strategies likely to help their students. According to Kauffman and Wong (1991), teachers of students with behavioral disorders need not only greater perserverance in the face of failure but also an extensive repertoire of teaching strategies. Let's turn now to an examination of the behaviors that effective teachers use to encourage student learning and achievement.

Effective Teacher Behaviors

Effective teachers assume responsibility for the performance of students in their classroom; they persist with difficult students; and they focus on variables over which they have control. Rather than attributing student success or failure to the child or to his or her family, effective teachers attend to their own skills and behaviors to provide students with quality instruction and a challenging curriculum designed to enhance student achievement. Chief among these skills and behaviors are a teacher's use of time and powerful instructional models likely to promote learning.

The Teacher's Use of Time

The manner in which teachers organize and use their instructional time dramatically affects student performance. Teachers of children and youth with emotional and behavioral disorders have only a limited amount of time with their students, many of whom are already behind academically. This requires teachers to maximize the time children spend engaging in instructional activities rather than clerical and business tasks (e.g., collecting lunch money or papers, distributing materials) or transitions both within and outside of the classroom (e.g., moving to and from recess, physical education, or lunch; changing from one lesson or lesson phase to another).

Teachers, then, must prepare their instructional materials in advance and place them in accessible locations. They must also plan ways to convene instructional groups quickly and to give directions clearly. For example, teachers might place directions for activities on the chalkboard or on the overhead projector, review these orally with students, ask specific questions about the directions to check for student understanding, and then leave the directions posted for all to see throughout the activity. Clear rules and routines also facilitate smooth and organized transitions. In addition, teachers can engage students in review of previous learning during transition times (e.g., students spell a "word of the day" or state a "math fact of the day" as a password to enter or exit the classroom or group; young children recite a nursery rhyme with the teacher or participate in a finger play such as "Itsy Bitsy Spider" or "Open shut them, Open shut them, Give your hands a clap, Open shut them, Open shut them, Put them in your lap").

Berliner (1984) first emphasized the importance of allocating time to instruction in particular academic areas. If a teacher does not systematically set time aside for instruction in content matter such as science or social studies, the academic achievement of his or her students in that area obviously will suffer. Merely allocating instructional time within and across content subjects, however, is not enough to effect student achievement.

During instructional activities, students must be "on task" and "engaged" in learning. That is, students must be *actively engaged in an appropriate task and with a high rate of success.* Berliner (1984) calls this critical time variable *academic learning time.* Children and youth, then, must not merely be "on task." The task itself must be at an appropriate level of difficulty for the student and chosen carefully because it relates directly to important content for which the student will later be held accountable. Furthermore, students must be actively thinking and doing something with the content to learn it. Academic learning time means that students are active participants and that they are achieving a high level of success with the task.

According to Rosenshine (1983) effective teachers maximize academic learning time by reviewing and reteaching previous work to ensure maintenance of learning, by clearly presenting new skills and concepts, by providing supervised practice to check for student understanding, and by giving immediate positive or corrective feedback during practice sessions. In addition, effective teachers reteach skills and concepts when necessary, and they provide structured, independent practice opportunities to promote student mastery of material.

Stevens and Rosenshine (1981) suggest that such effective instruction for students with academic difficulties takes place in teacher-directed, academically focused groups. When children and youth participate in groups, they receive more teacher demonstration and feedback, and they also spend more time "on task" and "engaged" in learning activities than when they work independently. Within groups, students are given many different opportunities to respond to questions and to engage in interactive dialogues with the teacher. Apparently, extensive coverage of important content, engagement in challenging tasks, feedback, and success are key to the academic achievement of children and youth with learning and behavioral difficulties (Englert, 1983, 1984; Sindelar, Smith, Harriman, Hale, & Wilson, 1986). Recent reviews of the research, then, suggest that effective teachers adhere to the following practices (Northwest Regional Educational Laboratory, 1990):

1. Use a preplanned curriculum with goals and objectives carefully sequenced and maintain a brisk pace through the curriculum to introduce new objectives as rapidly as possible (Englert, 1984; Good, Grouws, & Backerman, 1978).
2. Form instructional groups according to student achievement on specific academic skills and adjust group membership frequently as skills improve.
3. Keep time needed for classroom management of disruptive behaviors to a minimum by establishing clear classroom rules and routines and by maintaining awareness of all students in the class, even while working with individuals or small groups, and they communicate this awareness to the students.
4. Set challenging yet attainable standards for all students and hold students accountable for their behavior and achievement.
5. Provide additional and intensive help immediately when students experience difficulty with priority objectives and make comparisons only to a child's own past performance rather than to that of others.

Summary of a Teacher's Use of Time ◆

Effective teachers organize time to promote student learning. They allocate time to essential subject matter, and they design lessons to maximize academic learning time. This requires teachers to assume an active role in selecting and directing the learning activities of their students. In addition, teachers orient students to lesson goals and objectives, they present key skills and concepts clearly, and they use many carefully constructed questions to check for student understanding of material and to focus student attention on critical elements of the lesson content (Brophy & Good, 1986; Stallings, 1985). Effective teachers also pace instruction appropriately to keep students alert and interested and to reduce student errors. ◆

The Teacher's Use of Instructional Models

Teachers must engage in critical instructional behaviors that will profoundly enhance student learning. Instructional models chosen by teachers, however, will also have a dramatic impact on student learning and achievement. Instructional models are paradigms used to describe how teachers teach and learners learn. Many different instructional models exist (Joyce & Weil, 1992); however, most emphasize either empiricist or constructivist philosophies. Empiricist models, such as direct instruction (Becker & Carnine, 1980) and mastery learning (Hunter, 1982), typically emphasize highly teacher-directed and explicit lessons focused on carefully sequenced discrete skills. Within this model, the teacher is seen as the primary provider of knowledge. On the other hand, constructivist models view learning and teaching as holistic enterprises (Harris & Pressley, 1991; Heshusius, 1989; Resnick, 1987). Within holistic models, students are guided to construct and create their own knowledge, and the teacher employs more indirect or "discovery-oriented" teaching approaches. Both paradigms, however, must play a role in providing quality instruction and a challenging curriculum for children and youth with emotional and behavioral disorders (Harris & Graham, 1994).

Empiricist Models: Direct Instruction and Mastery Learning

Both direct instruction and mastery learning encourage rapidly paced, highly sequenced, and explicitly focused lessons (Gersten & Keating, 1987; White, 1988). Teachers present carefully designed lessons to small groups and enthusiastically engage all students in the group in active practice. Teachers also ensure the repetition of key lesson elements and provide abundant feedback to students regarding the accuracy of their responses (Lloyd, 1988).

All lesson plans and lesson activities are congruent with essential lesson objectives and performance outcomes for students. For example, if students must be able to add any two-digit plus two-digit numbers with regrouping involved, then the teacher will write an appropriate instructional objective (e.g., given any two-digit plus two-digit addition problem, Paul will write the sum with 100% accuracy) and design all teaching and practice activities to focus on that objective. To that end, direct instructional and mastery learning lessons typically follow a predictable routine. That is, the teacher opens the lesson, provides a clear demonstration of the skill or concept to be learned, engages the student in supervised practice of the skill, and closes the lesson.

Opening the Lesson. To open a lesson, teachers must obtain student attention and focus them on the purpose for the lesson. They may tell students either orally or in writing the lesson objective, what will be learned, and why that information is important to know. In addition, teachers may relate new learning to information students already know (Englert, 1983; 1984). Box 5.5 (p. 146) lists some behaviors teachers may use when opening lessons.

Demonstrating the New Skill or Concept. When students have been oriented to the lesson, the teacher moves them to a demonstration of the new skill or concept that is short, explicit, repetitive, and focused on the lesson objective (Ysseldyke, Christenson, & Thurlow, 1987). Teachers must phrase well-organized and concise step-by-step explanations and define and repeat critical lesson vocabulary and elements. This entails the teacher task-analyzing the new skill or breaking it down into carefully sequenced and manageable steps. In addition, the teacher must select all examples to be used in the lesson demonstration such that student attention will be consistently focused on the critical features. (See Box 5.6, p. 147, for a sample teacher demonstration.)

Giving Guided Practice. Of more importance than the teacher's demonstration is the student's opportunity to practice the new skill or concept under direct teacher supervision (Ysseldyke, Christenson, & Thurlow, 1987). During guided practice, teachers pose many focused questions to check for student understanding and to "lead" students to correct answers. Narrowly phrased

BOX 5.5 Behaviors of Teachers for Opening Lessons

To open a lesson, teachers might use any combination of the following key behaviors:

1. Obtain student attention. Give a clear signal that the lesson is starting, for example, "Look," "Let's begin," "Eyes on me."
2. Review or summarize previously learned skills or concepts, for example, provide practice on critical preskills, state, "Remember yesterday we . . . ."
3. Remind students of rules to follow during the lesson if necessary, for example, "Remember we speak one at a time."
4. State the purpose of the lesson and write the lesson objective on the chalkboard, for example, "Today we will learn a strategy to help us proofread our papers."
5. State why the new skill or concept is important to learn. Help students understand the relevance or usefulness of the skill or concept in their daily lives, for example, show the students a business letter containing many errors and ask them "Suppose I operated a print shop as a business, and I sent a prospective customer this letter to try to get business. What do you think the customer might believe about my ability to do the job?"

questions also help students focus their attention on the critical features of a task they are just learning. Teachers pose questions, calling on particular students at random or requiring all children in the group to respond in unison. To encourage active participation by all students, teachers must remember to pose the question first and then designate an individual or the group to answer.

When students answer questions, they must be given immediate positive or corrective feedback regarding their answers. In other words, children need to know if they are correct, and they need to know how to correct the answer if an inaccurate one is given. For example, the teacher might restate the child's response so that other students will have an additional opportunity to hear the correct answer (e.g., "Yes, the word is *hope*") or acknowledge accuracy with simple signals such as a nod or a "thumbs-up sign." Praise given for correct answers should be brief and specific so as not to interrupt the flow and pacing of the lesson. When children give incorrect answers, the teacher should first indicate any portion of the answer that was correct and then rephrase questions to lead the child back to the correct answer. Preplanned prompts may also help children respond with greater accuracy. Box 5.7, p. 148, gives examples of guided practice with teacher feedback.

Closing the Lesson. When teachers come to the end of guided practice, they must close the lesson. Sometimes, teachers must move on to new lessons or to a new activity. Thus, the teacher may choose to review or summarize the main points that students learned. Mrs. Nguyen, for example, might choose to have her students complete a "firm-up" trial reading of a list of new CVC-e words.

BOX 5.6 Sample Teacher Demonstration

Let's assume that Mrs. Nguyen is presenting a lesson on reading words following the consonant-vowel-consonant-e (CVCe) rule. She has written the following objective for her lesson: "Given a list of ten words following the CVCe pattern, the student will orally read the words correctly with at least 90% accuracy over three consecutive trials." Furthermore, she has introduced the lesson purpose and reviewed an important preskill with her students (i.e., reading words following the consonant-vowel-consonant pattern such as *cup, mad,* and *pet*). Mrs. Nguyen has carefully chosen the following words as examples for her demonstration and these are printed on the chalkboard before her lesson begins:

made
dime
hope
Pete
cube
hide

Mrs. Nguyen begins her demonstration by pointing to the word *made.* She says, "Look. This is a consonant, vowel, consonant-e word (pointing to each letter in turn, then pointing to the *e* at the end of *made*). When words end in the letter *e,* we say this (pointing to the *a*) letter name. The word is *made.*" She continues by pointing to the word *dime* and saying, "This is a consonant, vowel, consonant-e word". She points to the *e* at the end of the word *dime* and repeats, "Look again. When words end in the letter *e,* we say this (pointing to the *i*) letter name. The word is *dime.*"

Notice that Mrs. Nguyen used explicit language and actions designed to focus student attention on the relevant features of the task. Notice, too, that Mrs. Nguyen chose examples emphasizing the rule rather than using similar examples such as hike, bike, and like. Using these examples, students may have attended to the rhyming pattern rather than to the critical feature of the task, a CVCe word.

She might also reiterate the relevance and usefulness of the information by reminding her students that they will be reading a story containing many CVC-e words later in the day.

At other times, teachers may wish to move students to independent practice of the new skill or concept learned in the lesson. When presenting independent practice, teachers must give directions for the activity that are clear and concise and ask specific questions to check for student understanding of those directions. Having a student rephrase the directions or explain them to other students is often a good way to check for understanding. Teachers are also advised to have everyone's attention *before* giving directions and to work through one or two sample items after giving the directions before allowing students to work independently. Placing a clear reminder of the directions and the task on the chalkboard or overhead projector and circulating around the room to give students feedback are two additional and essential elements of independent practice.

BOX 5.7   **Providing Guided Practice with Specific Feedback**

As Mrs. Nguyen completes her demonstration of the CVC-e rule, (see Box 5.6) she points to the first practice example on her list:

hope

Pete

cube

hide

Mrs. Nguyen asks, "Is this a consonant, vowel, consonant-e word (pointing to each letter in the word *hope* as a prompt while she says this), Paul?" When Paul says, "Yes," Mrs. Nguyen replies, "Yes, this is a consonant, vowel, consonant-e word" (again pointing to each letter in turn). She then asks, "So does this word end in *e*, Keesha?" Keesha says, "Uh-huh," and Mrs. Nguyen responds, "Good, Keesha, the word ends in *e*." So which letter says its name, Paul?" Paul is silent and unsure; therefore, Mrs. Nguyen quickly prompts Paul by referring back to the rule she demonstrated. She states, "Remember that when a word ends in *e*, this letter (pointing to the first vowel, *o*) says its name." Paul then says, "Oh yeah. The *o*." And Mrs. Nguyen gives positive feedback by saying, "Excellent, the *o* says its name. So what's the word, everybody?" When Paul and Keesha and the others say "hope," Mrs. Nguyen responds by restating, "Yes the word is *hope*"!

Notice the sequence of questions Mrs. Nguyen has planned to guide practice. The sequence of questions flows automatically from her demonstration, focuses the children on key features of the task, and is easily used to prompt children when their answers are incorrect:

"Is this a CVC-e word?"

"Does the word end in *e*?"

"So which letter will say its name?"

"What's the word?"

Other prompts Mrs. Nguyen might plan to assist her students in this lesson include the following:

Visual prompts to highlight the correct response:

Pointing to the silent *e* or to the named vowel

Underlining or using color to highlight the named vowel

Verbal prompts to partially supply or describe the answer:

Partially pronouncing the word as in "ho . . . "

Model prompts to show or tell the correct answer:

The word is *hope*. What's the word?

Summary of Direct Instruction and Mastery Learning

Direct instruction and mastery learning entail carefully planned lessons and highly skilled instructional delivery. All phases of the lesson are focused explicitly on the objective and the key features of the skill to be learned. The teacher opens the lesson, provides a demonstration of the new skill or concept, leads the students through guided practice using focused questions and specific feedback, closes the lesson, and supervises independent practice. Direct instruction permits teaching that is highly structured, repetitive, interactive, and successful. As a matter of fact, many professionals believe the direct instructional model to be the most effective method for teaching children and youth with learning and behavioral disorders (Mastropieri & Scruggs, 1994; Meese, 1994; Mercer & Mercer, 1993). ◆

Constructivist Models

Resnick (1987) maintains that true learning must involve the construction and invention of knowledge by the learner rather than the imparting of knowledge by the teacher. In classrooms across the United States today, constructivist methods for teaching are increasingly being used in such content areas as mathematics, science, reading, and language arts. Learning within the constructivist model is viewed as hands-on, activity based, real-life, discovery oriented, and organized around solving interesting and meaningful problems. Holistic teachers also make connections between what students know and what they need to learn, and they build a scaffold or temporary support for students during the learning process to ensure that these important connections are made (Palincsar & Klenk, 1993; Tharp & Gallimore, 1988). Learning occurs continuously as teachers engage in interactive dialogues with their students.

Teachers ascribing to this holistic philosophy, for example, use "whole language" or "literature-based" methods for teaching children to read and write (Goodman, 1989; Graham & Harris, 1994; Smith, 1983). Quality children's literature and purposeful and meaningful writing activities, such as preparing a letter to mail to a relative or writing a story for publication in the classroom library, are used to teach children to read and write and to integrate learning across curricular areas. Students are encouraged in the earlier grades to read and reread favorite stories and books, especially those with predictable and repetitive words and phrases, and to retell stories to one another. They are also encouraged to use invented spellings and to focus on writing as a recursive process consisting of prewriting (i.e., set the audience and purpose for writing and generate ideas), drafting (i.e., get ideas on paper), revising (i.e., review one's writing with others to determine clarity of ideas), and editing activities (Graves, 1983; Graham & Harris, 1988). Because all learning activities must be purposeful and meaningful, children may write stories for "publication" in the school library and read stories they have written to others in an "author's corner."

Later, topics about which children read serve as themes for connecting learning across subject matter. Students may, for example, read a story such as *Tales from Gold Mountain: Stories of the Chinese in the New World* by Paul Yee (1990). These stories may serve to connect lessons in social studies (e.g., westward expansion, exploitation of labor), in history (e.g., the importance of gold to various civilizations), in science (e.g., physical principles regarding the location of gold in deposits, the concentration of gold through sluicing, or the effects on the environment of gold mining), in mathematics (e.g., the weight and density of gold; the current value of gold in our economy), and in language arts (e.g., writing to a gold refinery for information or reading about the gold market in the newspaper and about making gold jewelry in books from the library). Within this unit, students might measure and construct "gold jewelry" from gold-colored paper

Learning within the constructivist model is hands-on, real-life, and integrated across the curricular areas.

or pipe cleaners, visit a gold refinery, write reports and poems about the use of gold in Ancient Egypt, or sluice for gold in a local creek.

Cognitive strategy instruction is also considered by many to be a form of constructivism (Harris & Pressley, 1991). Rather than teaching students content alone, children are also taught *how to learn* the content. Cognitive strategy instruction blends the explicit teaching procedures of the direct instructional and mastery learning models with the notions of interactive dialogue and purposefulness characterizing holistic approaches. The Learning Strategies Intervention Model developed at the University of Kansas (Deshler & Schumaker, 1986; Ellis, Deshler, Lenz, Schumaker, & Clark, 1991) is one excellent example of a curriculum designed to teach adolescents strategies for acquiring, storing, and expressing or demonstrating knowledge in the content areas. Within the Strategies Intervention Model, for example, students learn strategies for paraphrasing passages from textbooks, studying for tests, taking tests, proofreading written work, and writing sensible paragraphs.

Certainly, not all students with emotional and behavioral disorders will require new strategies to be successful in content-area classes. For those students requiring strategy instruction, however, Ellis et al. (1991) offer the following essential procedures for teachers:

Step 1: Pretest the student. Point out strengths and weaknesses on the task for which a new strategy is being considered. Discuss the need for the student to use a more effective strategy, and obtain his or her commitment to try a new approach.

Step 2: Break the strategy into steps and describe each step for the student. Tell the student the importance of each step and where the strategy might be used.

Step 3: Model the strategy by thinking aloud and making all of the thought processes that are a part of the strategy overt and explicit.

Step 4: Have the student verbally rehearse each step in the strategy until he or she can name the steps without error.

Step 5: Require the student to practice using the new strategy with controlled materials close to his or her current performance level. Give positive and corrective feedback until the student can perform to a particular criterion level.

Step 6: Slowly increase the difficulty level of the practice material until it approximates that of the regular classroom.

Step 7: Posttest the student, and share specific information regarding his or her performance improvement.

Step 8: Plan for generalization to occur to the regular classroom by:
Helping the student verbalize where and when the strategy might be used
Encouraging the student to use the strategy in the regular classroom
Giving periodic follow-up and rewards to be sure that the strategy is being used and is still appropriate.

BOX 5.8   **Mr. Ghee Teaches Shelley a Learning Strategy**

Mr. Ghee: Shelley, you know how your teachers are always fussing at you for not paying attention to what you read. You said yesterday that you have trouble staying with the paragraphs that you read in your history text.

Shelley: Yeah, my mind just kind of drifts. I think I know what I've read, but I don't seem to know it to answer the chapter questions or for the tests.

Mr. Ghee: I think I know a way to help you keep yourself more involved when you read your history book or other texts. Would you like to give this method a try?

Shelley: I guess it won't hurt.

Mr. Ghee: Super! Here's how the strategy goes. You remember the word FIST—each letter in the word stands for something you have to remember to do when you are reading each paragraph in a reading assignment. The "F" stands for "First sentence in the paragraph is read" (Mr. Ghee writes the steps for the strategy as he speaks). The "I" stands for "Indicate a question based on the information in the first sentence." "S" means Search for the answer to your question in the paragraph and "T" stands for "Tie your answer to the question with a paraphrase." You just have to remember F-I-S-T.

Shelley: That's not too bad.

Mr. Ghee: No, it isn't. Watch me do an example now. Suppose I read this paragraph (He points to a paragraph in a history text selected at Shelley's current level of performance.) "F" means the first sentence in the paragraph is read and this first sentence reads: As the War of 1812 drew to a close, Tecumseh and William Henry Harrison met again in final battle. The "I", remember, means to indicate a question based on the first sentence. I can think of a couple questions to ask here: Who was Tecumseh? Who was William Henry Harrison? Why was the battle led by these two men important? "S" stands for search for the answer to my question. I'm going to search for the answer to my first question. Let's see, here it is . . .'Tecumseh, the leader of the Shawnee Indian tribe, had sought to unite the Indian nations with the British in order to defeat the new United States and drive back American expansion.' Now, the "T" is tie the answer to the question with a paraphrase. So, I'm going to say, Tecumseh was a leader of the Shawnee Indians who tried to stop the westward expansion of the United States by uniting with the British in the War of 1812.

Shelley: We were just talking about the War of 1812 in history class yesterday. I haven't read that section yet though . . .

Mr. Ghee: I think you could use this FIST strategy to help you remember what you read in history and also in earth science and health. Now, can you tell me the steps to follow when you use the FIST strategy? . . .

Adapted from "A Component Analysis of Effective Learning Strategies for LD Students," by E. S. Ellis and B. K. Lenz, *Learning Disabilities Focus*, 2, 98.

Steps 1 through 3 are particularly critical for student success (Box 5.8). That is, students must be committed to learning a new strategy, and they must see the usefulness in doing so. In addition, they will need abundant controlled practice with teacher feedback and assistance to transfer the strategy to the regular classroom. One final caution is in order: teachers must never teach a learning strategy to students merely for the sake of teaching a "new" or "different" curriculum if there is no clear need to do so. Students should be taught only those strategies that are clearly necessary and helped to devise their own strategies whenever possible. (For additional information about cognitive strategy instruction, contact the Institute for Research in Learning Disabilities, 3061 Dole Building, University of Kansas, Lawrence, Kansas 66045.)

Summary of Constructivist Models

Constructivist models engage students in purposeful activities designed to enable them to discover and create their own knowledge. Whole language and process writing approaches are but two examples of holistic instruction in today's classrooms. Cognitive strategy instruction, too, blends explicit teaching procedures with student construction of meaningful techniques for learning how to learn. ◆

Integrating the Empiricist and Constructivist Models

Although the direct instructional and mastery learning approaches to teaching would appear to be antithetical to a constructivist philosophy, both teaching models can be integrated in the classroom (Harris & Graham, 1994). Teachers can attempt, for example, to excite children and youth with emotional and behavioral disorders to learn by engaging them in real-life and purposeful activities rather than meaningless drill and practice worksheet pages. Reading, writing, and content area instruction can be connected in units and hands-on activities designed to capture interest. When students have difficulty or must learn a particular skill, however, teachers can use direct instructional procedures to ensure skill mastery and to measure student progress.

As Reid (1988, 1993) notes, many teachers in "whole language" classrooms are busily using effective teaching procedures from the direct instructional model to teach students essential phonics or spelling skills. Such instruction is embedded, however, in a meaningful context. Students might learn a particular phonics skill, for example, and then immediately use that skill when reading and writing stories. Or, conversely, when students need to learn a particular rule of grammar to write a story or letter, the teacher may prepare and deliver a direct instructional lesson focused on the skill of interest to the students.

Unless learning is grounded in authentic activities advocated by the constructivist approaches, students with emotional and behavioral disorders are likely to be bored and apathetic in their classrooms. On the other hand, many children and adolescents with learning and behavioral disorders will not learn essential skills without the explicit and focused teaching methods exemplified by direct instruction. Empiricist models such as direct instruction are well researched and hold a highly respected tradition in special education classrooms. Yet, constructivist philosophies may suggest profitable new directions for reaching the diverse needs of students and professionals in today's classrooms (Reid, Robinson, & Bunsen, 1995).

Summary

Quality programs for students with emotional and behavioral disorders are characterized by safe and supportive classroom environments. Such classrooms are organized around reasonable rules and routines and predictable schedules. Quality programs also offer a challenging curriculum and systematic, data-based instruction for students. Exemplary programs emphasize multifaceted and multicomponent treatment efforts that are matched to a child's particular problems.

Professionals engaging in effective teaching behaviors are likely to provide quality programs and a challenging curriculum. Effective teachers minimize transitions and maximize the use of academic learning time. Teachers using empiricist models of instruction such as mastery learning and direct instruction deliver rapidly paced, explicitly focused, and highly sequenced lessons designed around important learning objectives. Constructivist teachers, on the other hand, design lessons around important problems and questions encountered by children so that they may construct their own knowledge. Teachers of students with emotional and behavioral problems must integrate both instructional models within their classrooms to engage their students fully in learning activities.

Application Exercises

1. Arrange to observe a teacher at a chosen grade level in your community. Diagram the teacher's classroom. Are traffic patterns designed to minimize disruptions and facilitate learning? What rules and routines are used to minimize transition times? How does the teacher foster a safe and supportive environment? Ask the teacher how she or he schedules activities across the school day. What factors are important to this teacher when planning the daily and weekly schedule?

2. Design a direct instructional lesson for the following objective: "Given a list of ten consonant-vowel-consonant words, the student will correctly add endings beginning with either a vowel or a consonant with at least 100% accuracy." Consider the following questions as you plan your lesson:
   How will you open the lesson?
   What examples will you use in your demonstration and what will you say to emphasize the key feature of this task (e.g., the doubling rule, which states that when endings beginning with vowels are added to consonant-vowel-consonant words, the final consonant is doubled before adding the ending).
   What questions will you plan to lead students to correct answers and focus their attention on the critical parts of the task? What prompts will you plan to help students having difficulty?

How will you close the lesson, and what independent practice activities will you plan? How will you ensure that students understand what they are to do during independent practice?

3. Observe a teacher presenting a lesson at a chosen grade level. How does the teacher open the lesson? What examples are used in the teacher's demonstration? What examples are used in the guided practice? How does the teacher lead students to the correct answer? What feedback and prompts are used to assist students having difficulty? How does the teacher close the lesson or move students to independent practice of the skill or concept taught?

4. How could the theme "water" be used to integrate lessons across the content areas? What key concepts could be included, for example, in science, mathematics, social studies, music, and reading and the language arts? What hands-on activities could be included within the unit to enhance student learning of these concepts?

References

Ashton, P. A., & Webb, R. B. (1986). *Making a difference: Teachers' sense of efficacy and student achievement.* New York: Longman.

Bandura, A. (1977). Self-efficacy: Toward a unifying theory of behavioral change. *Psychological Review, 84,* 191–215.

Bandura, A., (1982). Self-efficacy mechanism in human agency. *American Psychologist, 37*(2), 122–147.

Becker, W., & Carnine, D. (1980). Direct instruction: An effective approach for educational intervention with the disadvantaged and low performers. In B. Lahey & A. Kazdin (Eds.), *Advances in child clinical psychology* (pp. 429–473). New York: Plenum.

Berliner, D. C. (1984). The half-full glass: A review of research on teaching. In P. L. Hosford (Ed.), *Using what we know about teaching* (pp. 51–77). Alexandria, VA: Association for Supervision and Curriculum Development.

Brophy, J., & Good, T. L. (1986). Teacher behavior and student achievement. In M. C. Wittrock (Ed.), *Handbook of research on teaching.* New York: Macmillan.

Deshler, D. D., & Schumaker, J. B. (1986). Learning strategies: An instructional alternative for low-achieving adolescents. *Exceptional Children, 52,* 583–590.

Ellis, E. S., Deshler, D. D., Schumaker, J. B., Lenz, B. K., & Clark, R. L. (1991). An instructional model for teaching learning strategies. *Focus on Exceptional Children, 23*(1), 1–22.

Ellis, E. S., & Lenz, B. K. (1987). A component analysis of effective learning strategies for LD students. *Learning Disabilities Focus, 2,* 94–107.

Emmer, E. T., & Hickman, J. (1991). Teacher efficacy in classroom management and discipline. *Educational and Psychological Measurement, 51,* 755–765.

Englert, C. S. (1983). Measuring special education teacher effectiveness. *Exceptional Children, 50,* 247–254.

Englert, C. S. (1984). Effective direct instruction practices in special education settings. *Remedial and Special Education, 5*(2), 38–47.

Gersten, R., & Keating, T. (1987). Long-term benefits from direct instruction. *Educational Leadership, 44,* 28–31.

Gibson, S., & Dembo, M. H. (1984). Teacher efficacy: A construct validation. *Journal of Educational Psychology, 76,* 569–582.

Good, T. L., Grouws, D. A., & Backerman, T. (1978). Curriculum pacing: Some empirical data in mathematics. *Journal of Curriculum Studies, 10,* 75–82.

Goodman, Y. M. (1989). Roots of the whole-language movement. *The Elementary School Journal, 90*(2), 113–127.

Graham, S., & Harris, K. R. (1988). Instructional recommendations for teaching writing to exceptional students. *Exceptional Children, 54,* 506–512.

Graham, S., & Harris, K. R. (1994). Implications of constructivism for teaching writing to students with special needs. *The Journal of Special Education, 28*(3), 275–289.

Graves, D. (1983). *Writing: Teachers and children at work.* Exeter, NH: Heinemann.

Grosenick, J. K., George, M. P., & George, N. L. (1987). A profile of school programs for the behaviorally disordered: Twenty years after Morse, Cutler, and Fink. *Behavioral Disorders, 12*(3), 159–168.

Grosenick, J. K., George, N. L., & George, M. P. (1988). The availability of program descriptions among programs for seriously emotionally disturbed students. *Behavioral Disorders, 13*(2), 108–115.

Harris, K. R., & Graham, S. (1994). Constructivism: Principles, paradigms, and integration. *The Journal of Special Education, 28*(3), 233–247.

Harris, K. R., & Pressley, M. (1991). The nature of cognitive strategy instruction: Interactive strategy instruction. *Exceptional Children, 57,* 392–404.

Heshusius, L. (1989). The Newtonian mechanistic paradigm, special education, and contours of alternatives: An overview. *Journal of Learning Disabilities, 22,* 403–415.

Hunter, M. (1982). *Mastery teaching.* El Segundo, CA: TIP Publications.

Joyce, B., & Weil, M. (1992). *Models of teaching* (4th ed.). Boston: Allyn & Bacon.

Kauffman, J. M., & Wong, K. L. H. (1991). Effective teachers of students with behavioral disorders: Are generic teaching skills enough? *Behavioral Disorders, 16*(3), 225–237.

Knitzer, J. (1993). Children's mental health policy: Challenging the future. *Journal of Emotional and Behavioral Disorders, 1*(1), 8–16.

Knitzer, J., Steinberg, A., & Fleisch, B. (1990). *At the schoolhouse door: An examination of programs and policies for children with emotional and behavioral problems.* New York: Bank Street College of Education.

Lloyd, J. W. (1988). Direct academic interventions in learning disabilities. In M. C. Wang, M. C. Reynolds, & H. J. Walberg (Eds.). *Handbook of special education: Research and practice: Volume 2. Mildly handicapped conditions* (pp. 345–366). New York: Pergamon.

Mastropieri, M. A., & Scruggs, T. E. (1994). *Effective instruction for special education* (2nd ed.). Austin, TX: Pro-Ed.

Meese, R. L. (1994). *Teaching learners with mild disabilities: Integrating research and practice.* Pacific Grove, CA: Brooks/Cole.

Mercer, C. D., & Mercer, A. R. (1993). *Teaching students with learning problems* (4th ed.). New York: Macmillan.

Morse, W. C., Cutler, R. L., & Fink, A. H. (1964). *Public school classes for the emotionally handicapped: A research analysis.* Washington, DC: Council for Exceptional Children.

Munk, D. D., & Repp, A. C. (1994). The relationship between instructional variables and problem behavior: A review. *Exceptional Children, 60*(5), 390–401.

Northwest Regional Educational Laboratory. (1990). *Effective schooling practices: A research synthesis 1990 update.* Portland, OR: Author.

Palincsar, A. S., & Klenk, L. (1993). Broader visions emcompassing literacy, learners, and contexts. *Remedial and Special Education, 14*(4), 19–25.

Redl, F. (1976). The concept of a therapeutic milieu. In N. J. Long, W. C. Morse, & R. G. Newman (Eds.), *Conflict in the classroom: The education of children with problems* (3rd ed.) (pp. 217–222). Belmont, CA: Wadsworth.

Reid, D. K. (1988). Reflections on the pragmatics of a paradigm shift. *Journal of Learning Disabilities, 21,* 417–420.

Reid, D. K. (1993). Another vision of "visions and revisions". *Remedial and Special Education, 14*(4), 14–16, 25.

Reid, D. K., Robinson, S. J., & Bunsen, T. D. (1995). Empiricism and beyond: Expanding the boundaries of special education. *Remedial and Special Education, 16*(3), 131–141.

Resnick, L. (1987). Constructing knowledge in school. In L. Liben (Ed.), *Development and learning: Conflict or congruence?* (pp. 19–50). Hillsdale, NJ: Erlbaum.

Rogers, H., & Saklofske, D. H. (1985). Self-concepts, locus of control and performance expectations of learning disabled children. *Journal of Learning Disabilities, 18,* 273–277.

Rosenshine, B. V. (1983). Teaching functions in instructional programs. *Elementary School Journal, 83,* 335–352.

Schunk, D. H. (1989). Self-efficacy and cognitive achievement: Implications for students with learning problems. *Journal of Learning Disabilities, 18,* 261–265.

Seligman, M. E. P. (1991). *Learned Optimism.* New York: A. A. Knopf, Inc.

Sindelar, P. T., Smith, M. A., Harriman, N. E., Hale, R. L., & Wilson, R. J. (1986). Teacher effectiveness in special education programs. *Journal of Special Education, 20,* 195–207.

Smith, F. (1983). *Essays into literacy.* Exeter, NH: Heinemann.

Spero, E. R. (1994). Beowulf revisited: Applying what I really learned. *Beyond Behavior, 5*(2), 7–8.

Stallings, J. A. (1985). A study of implementation of Madeline Hunter's model and its effects on students. *Journal of Educational Research, 78,* 325–337.

Steinberg, Z., & Knitzer, J. (1992). Classrooms for emotionally and behaviorally disturbed students: Facing the challenge. *Behavioral Disorders, 17*(2), 145–156.

Stevens, R., & Rosenshine, B. (1981). Advances in research on teaching. *Exceptional Education Quarterly, 2*(1), 1–9.

Tharp, R. G., & Gallimore, R. (1988). *Rousing minds to life: Teaching, learning, and schooling in social context.* New York: Cambridge University Press.

The Peacock Hill Working Group. (1991). Problems and promises in special education and related services for children and youth with emotional or behavioral disorders. *Behavioral Disorders, 16*(4), 299–313.

Torgeson, J. K. (1989). Cognitive and behavioral characteristics of children with learning disabilities. *Journal of Learning Disabilities, 22,* 166–169.

Wells, P. L. (1993). Optimism: Another factor in the success equation. *Beyond Behavior, 4*(2), 25–29.

West, R. P., & Sloane, H. N. (1986). Teacher presentation rate and point delivery rate. *Behavior Modification, 10,* 267–286.

White, W. A. T. (1988). A meta-analysis of effects of direct instruction in special education. *Education and Treatment of Children, 11,* 364–373.

Woolfolk, A. E., & Hoy, W. K. (1990). Prospective teachers' sense of efficacy and beliefs about control. *Journal of Educational Psychology, 82,* 81–91.

Ysseldyke, J. E., Christenson, S. L., & Thurlow, M. L. (1987). *Instructional factors that influence student achievement: An integrative review* (Monograph No. 7). Minneapolis: University of Minnesota.

CHAPTER 6

RESPECTING FEELINGS

Main Ideas:

◆ *Students with emotional and behavioral disorders require a psychologically safe and supportive classroom environment if they are to learn to express feelings appropriately.*

◆ *Helping students feel that they belong and that they are competent, independent, and responsible for themselves and others requires an empathetic teacher who demonstrates effective listening and communication skills.*

◆ *Active-reflective listening, sending "I" messages, and awareness of body language are important tools for teachers confronted with intense feelings of students, particularly those arising during times of crises.*

◆ *Supportive media such as art, music, play, and bibliotherapy provide outlets for student stress and energy and opportunities to learn social skills.*

Some of the earliest interventions for students with emotional and behavioral disorders were developed by professionals advocating a psychodynamically oriented philosophy. Bruno Bettleheim (1950) and Berkowitz and Rothman (1960), for example, were pioneers in the field of emotional and behavioral disorders who encouraged teachers to provide a warm, permissive classroom atmosphere in which children were free to "act out" their inner conflicts. Behavioral problems were viewed as symptomatic of early stressful experiences repressed by the child. For behavior to improve, then, children had to be helped to express strong feelings like fear or anger to achieve catharsis (i.e., release of bottled-up emotions) and to gain insight into past events and feelings. Originally, from the psychodynamic perspective, awareness and understanding of feelings, as well as a desire to learn more appropriate ways of expressing emotions, occur only when children develop a trusting relationship with an accepting and supportive adult.

Teachers must attend to the mental health needs of children and youth with emotional and behavioral disorders in their classrooms and help them learn better ways to deal with their feelings. As a matter of fact, Nichols (1986) suggests that the teacher must be both a therapist and a counselor to be an effective child helper. In this chapter, then, we will discuss the major interventions that teachers find useful from the psychodynamic and humanistic perspectives. Because both of these schools of thought emphasize support for feelings, we will refer to them together as the *Supportive Model* (Figure 6.1).

Notice in Figure 6.1 that two key ideas for teachers are providing activities designed to help children identify and express their feelings and supporting and clarifying those feelings that children do express. We will begin by presenting a brief overview of psychodynamic and humanistic theories and by exploring ways in which teachers can support and clarify feelings expressed by children and youth. Teachers must, for example, establish a psychologically safe classroom environment so that children can develop a healthy self-esteem and feel

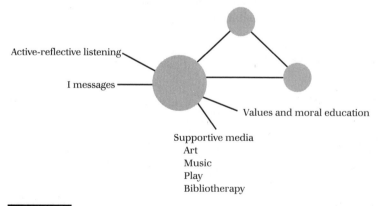

Key ideas
- Support, respect, and clarify feelings
- Provide activities for identification and expression of feelings

Active-reflective listening

I messages

Values and moral education

Supportive media
Art
Music
Play
Bibliotherapy

FIGURE 6.1

Supportive Model

secure enough to express themselves. In addition, teachers also must demonstrate empathy and use effective listening and communication skills to clarify and understand the feelings expressed by students. Teachers also must know how to respond to the intense feelings of students in crisis. Therefore, we will address the teacher's use of verbal techniques to deescalate child behavior when students are losing control of their actions. Finally, we will examine activities designed to help children identify and express their feelings. These activities include the use of supportive media such as art, music, play, and bibliotherapy as well as values, or moral, education.

Psychodynamic and Humanistic Theories

Although forming a trusting relationship with significant adults is crucial for healthy child development, teachers obviously cannot "permit" or "accept" all behaviors in the classroom. We now know, for example, that children learn and continue aggressive behaviors when they are given opportunities to practice aggression and when they receive no aversive consequences for this behavior (Goldstein & Segall, 1983). Thus, early psychodynamic practices, particularly those suggesting a permissive classroom environment, have been criticized for the following reasons (Newcomer, 1993):

1. Psychodynamic theories present a pessimistic view of child behavior controlled by past events and internal states, which may encourage teachers to adopt a passive "I can't do anything about the problem" attitude.
2. Because the child is viewed as "ill" and not responsible for his or her behavior, educators may not teach appropriate behaviors and academic skills in a misguided attempt to provide a "nonrepressive" environment.
3. Psychodynamic theories are largely unsubstantiated and use therapies that are lengthy, expensive, and often considered to be beyond the skill of teachers.

Despite these early criticisms, however, the psychodynamic school of thought has served to focus attention on the significance of a child's feelings of importance, competence, and control for developing a healthy self-concept. Later psychodynamic theories, as a matter of fact, bore little resemblance to the original Freudian concepts of children driven to behave irrationally by hidden instincts, sexual drives, and repressed past experiences. For example, Erik Erikson (1947), a disciple of Anna Freud, maintained that children do not simply respond to id impulses (i.e., innate drives such as those for survival). Rather, children use the conscious capabilities of the ego (i.e., rational cognitive processes such as thinking, reasoning, and remembering) to resolve predictable conflicts occurring across eight different stages of life. The importance of the ego in Erikson's psychosocial theory held immediate appeal for educators, particularly for those working with adolescents who faced the "identity versus identity confusion" stage of personality development.

Alfred Adler (1963) also described human behavior as socially driven, purposeful, and goal oriented. Adler suggested that people possess both conscious and unconscious goals, but that unconscious goals are the real determinants of human behavior. Individuals may repeatedly engage in unrewarding or self-destructive behaviors because these behaviors help them to meet unarticulated psychological needs. The teenage girl may repeatedly date abusive males, for example, despite her stated goals of achieving love and social status with her peers. Thus, the Adlerian therapist helps the individual gain insight into how his or her unconscious goals may be resulting in a self-defeating, rather than rewarding, lifestyle.

More recent expansions of psychodynamic theory emphasize the importance of interpersonal relationships and the fulfillment of one's human potential. Sometimes called *humanists* or *humanistic psychologists*, later theorists focused on the importance of the "self." Maslow (1962), for example, described children as inherently healthy human beings seeking to fulfill basic needs. When lower level needs (i.e., physiological and safety needs, love, and esteem) are met, children are free to pursue the highest level need, that of self-actualization. On the other hand, children who are hungry, who feel in danger, who feel that they do not belong, or who feel that they are not loved will be unable to seek their full human potential.

Carl Rogers (1951, 1961, 1969) is also strongly identified with the concept of self-actualization and with the notion of helping children develop a positive self-concept. Rogers believed that children must receive unconditional positive regard (i.e., adults may disapprove of and criticize *behaviors*, but not the *child*) to foster a healthy self-concept. In addition, Rogers suggested that the individual's self-concept determines his or her perception of events. Thus, a child may behave in a manner that appears to be inappropriate to others but which is consistent with the child's view of reality and his or her self-concept. The counselor's task, therefore, is to clarify the child's perceptions of events and to convey confidence in the child's ultimate ability to solve his or her own difficulties.

Psychodynamic and humanistic schools of thought, then, are closely related. Both emphasize self-awareness and self-esteem as the primary means by which barriers to healthy emotional growth may be removed. In addition, both models advocate a warm, supportive environment as essential for achieving this self-awareness and psychological growth. Both the psychodynamic and humanistic models, too, have been criticized for helping individuals achieve self-awareness with little evidence of lasting change in actual behavior. Although the two models differ in that traditional psychodynamic theories are more pessimistic about human potential than are the humanistic philosophies, the interventions useful for teachers are similar enough in practice that we will consider them together in this chapter.

Interestingly, the psychodynamic and humanistic emphasis on a warm and positive classroom environment is receiving some support from researchers examining the biochemical basis for emotions. Sylwester (1994), for example, reports that an individual's perception of his or her feelings and emotions is determined by peptides (i.e., molecules such as cortisol and endorphins that carry either stressful or positive emotional information, respectively) and by complex interactions between the body and the brain stem and cortex. Sylwester (1994) suggests that a joyful classroom atmosphere and the opportunity to vent negative emotions in a nonjudgmental climate positively affect childrens' ability to relax, concentrate, and learn. On the other hand, he maintains that emotionally stressful school environments do have a physical impact on children and youth counterproductive to their ability to learn.

Today, psychodynamically oriented practitioners are most often found within psychiatric hospitals and mental health clinics. In these facilities, trained professionals may provide group or individual therapy designed to help children gain self-awareness and learn new ways to handle feelings. For older children, therapists may use conversation or conduct psychoanalysis much like that with adults. With younger children, however, play, music, or art activities may become the medium for self-expression and insight. Unfortunately, very few children and youth with emotional and behavioral disorders receive the mental health services of counselors or therapists as provisions on their Individualized Education Plan (Knitzer, Steinberg, & Fleisch, 1990).

Supporting and Clarifying Feelings

Teachers must work hard to establish a trusting and supportive relationship with students having emotional and behavioral disorders. Most of these students do not engage in open, honest, and trusting relationships easily. You must not misinterpret a "supportive relationship" to be one that permits or accepts all forms of student behavior, however. Children and youth with behavioral problems need support from fair rules, predictable schedules and routines, and teachers who are consistent in their actions. A supportive classroom environment, then, is one in which students feel physically and psychologically secure. It is a dependable environment led by a teacher who is proficient in effective listening and communication skills.

Building a Psychologically Safe Classroom

As a teacher, you must carefully consider the psychological or emotional "atmosphere" of your classroom. Although this atmosphere is certainly based on your physical arrangement of the classroom; how you manage materials; and the predictable schedules, rules, and routines that you develop, "atmosphere" is an almost intangible quality that goes well beyond physical and procedural concerns. You may recall a teacher whose classroom was well designed and attractive but who "ran a tight ship." Perhaps you felt afraid to speak or felt powerless in this classroom, or perhaps you felt humiliated or ridiculed by the teacher or your peers whenever you made a mistake. The atmosphere in this classroom was negatively rather than positively charged. The implicit lesson taught in this classroom was "learn and behave or else!"

Most teachers, however, hope their students will learn and even enjoy being in their classrooms. Think about a teacher whose classroom you really enjoyed. This teacher probably presented interesting and challenging lessons that provided you with a sense of success and accomplishment. You knew the rules and routines in the classroom, and you knew the consequences for violating these standards. But even when you made mistakes or broke the rules and received the consequences, you still felt that you were an accepted and valued member of the classroom. The atmosphere was a positive one in which you felt safe to make mistakes and to learn. You felt respect, trust, and a sense of belonging. You felt successful as well as responsible for yourself and for others. Similarly, a personal connection with teachers who are perceived to be clear in their rules, flexible in their attitudes and behaviors, and nonpunitive in their discipline is valued by youth with behavior disorders (Crowley, 1993).

Brendtro, Brokenleg, and Van Bockern (1990) draw upon Native-American philosophies and the teaching of early youth workers to describe how educators might develop such a psychologically safe, or "reclaiming" environment. These authors suggest that today's youth often feel alienated from the four important worlds of childhood (i.e., family, friends, school, and work) described by the developmental psychologist Urie Bronfenbrenner (1986). According to Brendtro, Brokenleg, and Van Bockern (1990), troubled children and youth often:

◆ Engage in destructive relationships. They are hungry for love but are unable to trust. They expect to be hurt again and again because they lack a sense of belonging.
◆ Experience feelings of futility. They feel inadequate, incompetent, and unsuccessful, yet they fear failure.
◆ Learn irresponsibility. Because they are not given any real responsibilities, they defiantly rebel against authority, demonstrate learned helplessness, join negative peer subcultures like gangs, and engage in the narcissistic behaviors of an affluent society.
◆ Lack purpose. They are searching for meaning in a world full of conflicting values. They feel unimportant and unable to develop their own values unless they are given opportunities to be of real value to others (pp. 6–7).

To counteract these feelings of alienation, Brendtro, Brokenleg, and Van Bockern (1990) suggest that classrooms and schools for children and youth with emotional and behavioral disorders must emphasize the positive disciplinary practices used by Native-American cultures. These include a spirit of belonging, mastery, independence, and generosity. These four Native-American values share much in common with the four components of self-esteem (significance, competence, power, and virtue) described by Coopersmith (1967) (Table 6.1). In addition, these ideas overlap tremendously with the 12 key educational principles of Nicholas Hobbs (1982) who believed that schools for troubled children and youth should be places of joy (Box 6.1, p. 166). In stark contrast, however, many children with emotional and behavioral disorders in our Western society today feel unattached, lonely, and distrustful (Brendtro & Brokenleg, 1993).

Curwin (1994) and Mendler (1992) also emphasize the power of positive disciplinary practices. By disciplining students "with dignity," they hope to overcome the many negative feelings experienced by youth today. To generate hopeful attitudes among students at risk, Curwin (1994) suggests that students must accurately believe they are competent in subjects they are learning and that their learning tasks are challenging and personally important ones in which they are actively involved. Teachers, too, must demonstrate a genuine love for their subjects and for teaching. They must, according to Mendler (1992), plan for student motivation and plan lessons that are enjoyable. In addition, Curwin (1994) challenges teachers to make a personal connection to students so that children and youth feel welcome and as if they belong in their school and classroom.

Table 6.1 A Comparison of the Foundations of Self-Esteem with Native American and Western Values

Foundations of Self-Esteem	Native American Values	Western Values
(Coopersmith, 1967)	(Brendtro, Brokenleg, & Van Bockern, 1990	(Brendtro & Brokenleg, 1993)
Significance (Acceptance, Attention, Affection from Others)	**Belonging** (Connectedness, Relationships, Bonds as a Member of a Group)	**Individualism** (Standing on One's Own is Measure of Importance)
Competence (Mastery of the Environment, Success leads to Satisfaction)	**Mastery** (Opportunities and Co-operation for Success at Personal Goals, Achievements Shared By All)	**Winning** (Competition at the Expense of others who must lose)
Power (Feelings of Control over one's Behavior, Gaining Respect of others)	**Independence** (Self-Management, Responsibility, Expectations that People Solve their Own Problems)	**Dominance** (Asserting one's will over others equals power)
Virtue (Feelings of Worthiness as Judged by Others, Spiritual Fulfillment and Meaningfulness in Life)	**Generosity** (Importance is judged by intrinsic rather than extrinsic worth; Giving to others of oneself and one's possessions)	**Affluence** (Worth and status is determined by material possessions and wealth accumulated)

Adapted from "Beyond the Curriculum of Control," by L. K. Brendtro and M. Brokenleg, 1993, *Journal of Emotional and Behavioral Problems, 1*(4), 6, National Educational Service.

Belonging. When we feel that we belong, we experience a sense of acceptance and value. We feel good about ourselves as members of a family, a classroom, or a social group; therefore, these feelings are important to developing a positive self-concept. Teachers can help students feel that they belong as members of the classroom in many different ways. Certainly, all students, for example, should be greeted by name as they enter the classroom. Sometimes this greeting involves a short, personal conversation with individual children (e.g., "Hi, Shelley. That color blue looks lovely on you" or "Good morning, Dante. Did you watch the game on TV last night that you wanted to see?"). At other times, the teacher might simply acknowledge that the student is present (e.g., "Let's see . . . Dante is here, and Shelley . . . "). Regardless, teachers must strive to use students' names positively and daily, as frequently as possible.

A sense of belonging is also fostered when teachers provide personal space for children and youth. If you personalize your desk area in your classroom,

Nicholas Hobbs and Schools of Joy

Although often considered an ecological viewpoint, Hobbs (1982) based his Re-Education schools on psychologically safe and supportive classroom environments. His philosophies are, therefore, included in this chapter because they exemplify the development of a trusting relationship between student and teacher. The twelve key principles of Hobbs' (1982) Re-Ed philosophy are:

1. Life is to be lived now. Teachers must try to make every hour special for children.
2. Trust between child and adult is essential. Teachers must be predictable sources of understanding and support.
3. Competence makes a difference. Teachers must help students feel good about schoolwork so that they will feel accepted by important people in their lives.
4. Time is an ally. Teachers must assume normal emotional functioning.
5. Self-control can be taught. Teachers must help students learn better behaviors.
6. Intelligence can be taught. Teachers must help students learn to make better choices.
7. Feelings should be nurtured. Teachers must provide ways for students to share and express their feelings.
8. The group is very important to young people. Teachers must help children learn to be members of the group.
9. Ceremony and ritual give order, stability and confidence to disorganized lives. Teachers must plan rituals and ceremonies to enhance predictability and belonging.
10. The body is the armature of the self. Teachers must provide physical activity for healthy psychological development.
11. Communities are important for children and youth. Teachers must help students experience a sense of purpose through community service.
12. A child should know some joy in each day and should look forward to some joyous event for the morrow. Teachers must promote joy, laughter, and pleasure for children.

From *The Troubled and Troubling Child: Re-Education in Mental Health, Education and Human Services Programs for Children and Youth*, by N. Hobbs, Jossey-Bass, 1982.

students should receive the same privilege. Some teachers help students personalize covers for their chair backs or make individualized desk nametags. Others help children create personal mobiles to hang above their desks. Young people can personalize their storage cubby area, their lockers, or a section of bulletin board or wall space reserved for their use.

If you have students individualize their space, however, be prepared for some decorations that you may find personally distasteful. Shelley, for example, may choose to decorate her bulletin board with drawings of marijuana leaves and the slogan "Sex, drugs, and rock and roll." How you handle Shelley's choice will communicate to her either support as a valued member of the group or rejection. Rather than demanding that Shelley remove these offensive pictures and "redecorate," the astute teacher will use the drawings to help Shelley learn about her responsibility to the classroom community. For example, the teacher might say privately to Shelley, "Our classroom belongs to everyone in it and everyone who belongs to our classroom has a responsibility to every other class member. I understand that you have chosen things you like to decorate your bulletin board space. But marijuana leaves and "Sex and drug" slogans send messages to people outside our classroom about all of us in this room. Those are the kinds of messages we can talk about in here, but that create public relations problems when students display them openly. Students need to keep these messages more private, in the pages of a notebook for instance. We are all proud of your musical talents though. Maybe you could expand on the rock and roll theme in your space."

Rituals, routines, and ceremonies are also important ways to build a sense of belonging and community. Some teachers, for example, start each day or each class period with a special classroom song, chant, or rap (e.g., "We are the team in Room 114. We are proud. We are strong. We're the best to be seen. If you just stand back and let us do our act, we'll pass the test, above the rest, if you know what we mean!"). Others use special ceremonies (e.g., on birthdays or following difficult accomplishments) to acknowledge and celebrate the achievements of individual children or the entire classroom group. Badges for honor, success, merit, and courage might, for example, be earned and awarded to students who meet specified criteria, or the class might share a common banner, slogan, or T-shirt insignia determined by classmates.

Teachers also build a sense of belonging when they provide opportunities for young people to share their experiences, likes, and dislikes. Teachers, too, must participate in this process of sharing to build rapport and trust and to demonstrate that openness and honesty are valued in the classroom. In the elementary grades, teachers often use "circle time" or provide a daily period during which children "show and tell" things of importance to them. When the teacher participates in a spirit of fun, however, even adolescents and adults can enjoy the good old-fashioned technique of "show and tell."

Many excellent activities to promote a spirit of belonging and to enhance self-esteem can be found in the work of Canfield and Siccone (1993) and Siccone and Canfield (1993). Other activities to foster sharing, connectedness, and a sense of belonging include the following:

- ◆ A "Getting to Know You" bulletin board. Start the year with pictures of yourself at home or doing things that you enjoy outside of school. Then, put up pictures of students and their interests.
- ◆ Randomly select a "Student of the Week" until every child has had a turn. Then, start the process over again. Place a banner over the door or on the wall proclaiming the week to be "Fong's Week." Highlight Fong's interests and activities through pictures and in lessons whenever possible. Have other students state one thing they like about the student of the week. Post these positive qualities on the bulletin board, in the student's personal space, or in the form of leaves decorating a personal-growth tree.

♦ Help young children to make body tracings and older students to make silhouettes. Decorate these with pictures or words describing personal interests, likes, and dislikes (e.g., favorite foods, colors, TV shows, or movies) or have students write, and periodically rewrite, "This is Me" stories to attach to their body tracings.

♦ Develop a "Who's Who in Room *(Number)*" book. Document favorite foods, songs, hobbies, successes, and so forth, in a scrapbook for the entire class.

♦ Have students make and frame a "Me Collage." Children and adolescents can cut pictures and words that best describe them from magazines and then glue them to a tag board. Be sure to make and display a "Me Collage" representing yourself.

♦ Provide a "small smile" for every child every day. Wear a funny pin that you change daily or wear on odd parts of your anatomy. Have a ritual cartoon, joke, or riddle of the day or time period. Arrange a special telephone call, visitor, or privilege for a student.

♦ Arrange a "Success a Day." Have students write down or draw at least one good or successful thing that happens each day. You may need to assist students with finding small successes initially. Save these statements or drawings over time arranged in a booklet or on index cards for the child to review.

♦ Send students home with a personal and special note you wrote just for them sometime during the day. Tell students to open these notes when they leave the classroom. You may also want to include a blank sheet of paper in the note for students to write or draw something of interest to them from their afterschool hours to bring back to you the next day.

Mastery. The key concepts behind mastery are feelings of competence, success, self-efficacy, and self-esteem. Self-esteem and feelings of self-efficacy (Bandura, 1977) are not, however, simply derived from a pleasant, supportive classroom that demands little of students. These feelings are deeply and culturally informed and cannot be taught in an "affective education" time slot or a "feel good" curriculum (Beane, 1991). Mastery assumes that young people are engaged in learning experiences that they perceive to be important, purposeful, and meaningful. When students engage in challenging tasks and meet with success, they learn that they do possess the skills to bring about desirable outcomes. In other words, children experience a sense of self-efficacy and, thus, heightened self-esteem.

Rather than defining mastery as competition with others for grades and teacher recognition, however, Brendtro, Brokenleg, and Van Bockern (1990) encourage teachers of students with emotional and behavioral disorders to use cooperative learning experiences focused on the development of both academic and social skills. Children and youth may, for example, be paired with a peer as a tutor or tutee or assigned a role as a member of a cooperative learning group.

In peer tutoring and cooperative learning arrangements, students help one another learn and demonstrate their mastery of material. Often, cooperative learning groups are formed heterogenously with specific roles and responsibilities assigned to each group member. Slavin (1990, 1991) and Johnson and

Johnson (1986) discuss many different cooperative learning arrangements; however, the ultimate goal of each is for team members to help one another master skills and experience success.

Johnson and Johnson (1986) describe four basic elements necessary for cooperative learning to occur. These include positive interdependence among group members (i.e., all members are responsible for making a contribution to the group, and the final success of the group is dependent on everyone's contribution), individual accountability (i.e., the individual's performance is assessed to determine his or her mastery of the material as well as contributions made to the group), and collaborative and group processing skills (i.e., communication, conflict resolution, and group leadership skills). Obviously, teachers cannot expect students with emotional and behavioral disorders to participate immediately and willingly as skilled members of cooperative learning groups. Roles, responsibilities, and group participation skills must be structured carefully and taught just like academic skills. In addition, using cooperative learning groups does not negate the teacher's responsibility to teach. Teachers must be prepared to supervise groups closely and to intervene whenever appropriate.

Independence. Closely related to feelings of self-efficacy are one's personal feelings of autonomy and power over the environment. As children approach adolescence, they require increasing degrees of responsibility, autonomy, and independence. Yet as Knitzer, Steinberg, and Fleisch (1990) observed, most behavior modification systems used in classrooms for children and youth with behavioral disorders employ virtually identical responsibilities and rewards across the grade levels. Children and adolescents are given very similar levels of responsibility. Decisions are usually made for them, and they are expected to obey.

To learn to manage their own behavior and solve daily problems, young people need opportunities to practice these skills. Giving students a degree of choice in how they will accomplish certain tasks is one example of small responsibilities parents and teachers must give to children. For example, one parent, when repeatedly asked by her daughter if she could have another piece of candy, consistently responded with "What do you think?" On the first three occasions, the child responded "Yes" and took a candy from the bag. By the fourth time, though, the child said "No." Following each decision, the mother said, "Then, that's your decision." The responsibility for a wise decision was placed with the child, giving her a sense of autonomy and control over her world.

Certainly most students with emotional and behavioral disorders will require careful instruction and supervision in self-management. Without being given real responsibility for behavior, however, students are prevented from learning how to be responsible. In addition to small choices throughout the school day, teachers can enhance student autonomy and independence by doing the following:

◆ Involving students in deciding on classroom rules or routines. Students can suggest new rules or routines when necessary, and they can discuss ways to modify old rules that are no longer serving a useful purpose or routines that are hindering, rather than facilitating, classroom life.

- Giving students real responsibility for important roles within the classroom. "Business" or "plant" managers may, for example, monitor the flow of materials or the work accomplished in the classroom. Traffic controllers can monitor lining up for recess, sharpening pencils, and using the restroom. Hallway or safety monitors might look for and report instances of "good behavior" on a daily basis.
- Teaching students to self-monitor behaviors. Students may, for example, self-monitor attention (Hallahan, Lloyd, & Stoller, 1982) or the number of arithmetic problems completed correctly (Reith, Polsgrove, McCleskey, Payne & Anderson, 1978). In addition, they can set their own goals for performance on many different academic and behavioral tasks (e.g., number of spelling words written correctly, words read per minute, or arithmetic problems completed). (See Chapter 9 for a description of these self-monitoring and goal-setting procedures.)
- Encouraging and teaching students to participate as important members of their own Individualized Education Program (IEP) teams (Bacon & Brendtro, 1992).

Generosity. Hedin (1989) contends that students today are bombarded with the trappings of affluence (e.g., money, the "right" clothing, cars, etc.). She maintains that many children are, therefore, growing up self-centered, searching for their values and happiness in material possessions, which leave them still feeling alienated. To counteract these feelings of alienation and worthlessness, Vorrath and Brendtro (1985) emphasize the importance of young people engaging in real and useful community service through which they garner self-respect as well as the respect of others.

Students can make contributions to others, and thus experience a sense of virtue, worthiness, and value, through many community service projects. In many states students are now required to volunteer their time in the community before graduation. Youth who work in homeless shelters, animal shelters, or in homes for the elderly, for example, may experience feelings of usefulness never before encountered (Box 6.2). Young people can also serve as peer helpers, trained to befriend or tutor others (Varenhorst, 1992), or as peer mediators to assist schoolmates with the resolution of conflicts (Evans & Eversole, 1992; Salend, Jantzen, & Giek, 1992; Schrumpf, 1991). Of course, such tasks require careful structure, student training, and teacher monitoring (Box 6.3, pp. 172–173).

Summary

Teachers must strive constantly to help students with emotional and behavioral disorders feel that they belong in the classroom and that they are competent in some area of academic or social functioning. Moreover, teachers must help their students develop a sense of responsibility for self and for others. These are, of course, no easy tasks for teachers of children and youth with behavior problems. To provide a psychologically safe classroom and support the feelings of students requires patience on the part of teachers as well as a genuine respect for children and youth. In addition, the teacher must develop empathy for the student's feelings and proficiency in effective listening and communication skills. ◆

BOX 6.2 **Case Study: Community Service Projects**

To see themselves as caregivers rather than as the recipients of care, adolescent boys with social, emotional, and learning problems at the Pathway School in Philadelphia, Pennsylvania, are given systematic opportunities to participate in community service "clubs." What follows is a description of one project accomplished by Pathway students:

As Halloween approached, the service club decided to raise money for UNICEF. They distributed collection boxes to local businesses and restaurants, dressed in costume to collect at a local grocery store, and organized the younger children to trick or treat for UNICEF while collecting candy. The following morning, everyone gathered to empty the cartons and count the money raised. All the members were amazed and excited to find that their original goal of $30.00 was exceeded by almost $200.00. It was difficult to believe that a handful of people could do so much in so short a period of time. When the coins were converted into a money order for $225.00, the group studied the material sent by UNICEF to learn what that amount could mean to the recipients. When it was discovered that the amount raised by the project was enough to purchase a well for a drought-stricken community in a foreign country, the group realized what a powerful impact they had made.

From "Teaching Courage: Service Learning at Pathway School," by M. D. Ioele and A. L. Dolan, 1992, *Journal of Emotional and Behavioral Problems*, 1(3), 21–22, National Educational Service.

Empathy, Listening, and Communication Skills

Empathy is the ability to take the perspective of someone else, to understand that person's viewpoint or feelings, and to communicate that understanding verbally or nonverbally to the other person. Empathy entails active listening and careful observation of behavior in order to look beyond what the child actually says or does to what the child really means and feels. For example, when Paul throws his paper on the floor and yells, "This class sucks!", the teacher might take offense at his inappropriate language *or* think about what Paul is experiencing. The empathetic teacher might conclude that Paul is frustrated, hurt, and embarrassed because he perceives that the work is difficult for him but easy for his peers. Rather than reacting to Paul's choice of words or to his behavior, then, this teacher might acknowledge his feelings and offer support (e.g., "This math is tough for you, but we'll get through it.").

Empathy does not imply, however, that you must analyze every word or deed of children for hidden conflicts and deep-rooted psychological problems. Nor does empathy mean that you must react sympathetically or feel the hurt or anger of your students. Empathy requires, instead, the ability to "walk in someone else's shoes" and discern the real motivation behind what that person is saying or doing. The empathetic teacher then will calmly communicate this knowledge to the student.

BOX 6.3   Peer Helpers and Peer Mediators

Recently, in response to escalating violence and conflict among youth, many programs have been developed to help students learn to help one another and mediate peer disputes. In one such program, *Teaching Students to Be Peacemakers* (Johnson & Johnson, 1991), students are systematically taught the skills of negotiation and conflict resolution. Then, two students are given the job of official mediators each day. Mediators wear T-shirts and conflicts which students are unable to resolve on their own are to be referred to the class mediators. Within the limits of the school's policies and the law, the decisions of the student mediators are to be respected. Students should not, for example, mediate disputes regarding drugs, weapons, and other illegal activities.

Negotiation

All students are taught to define their conflict, exchange their proposals, view the situation from both sides, explore options for mutual gain, and agree on a decision. Students practice the following steps:

1. State what you want—"I want to use the book now."
2. State how you feel—"I feel frustrated."
3. State the reasons for your wants and feelings—"You have been using the book for the past hour. If I don't get to use the book soon, my report will not be done on time. It's frustrating to have to wait so long."
4. Summarize your understanding of what the other person wants, how the other person feels, and the reasons underlying both.
5. Invent three optional plans to resolve the conflict.
6. Choose one plan and "shake hands" by agreeing to the plan.

Conflict Mediation and Resolution

Students are taught to use the mediation services of others to resolve conflicts peaceably. Mediation involves:

1. An introduction—When mediating a conflict, the class mediator introduces himself/herself as the mediator and asks those in conflict if they wish to resolve their dispute. The mediator will not proceed unless both answer "Yes."
2. An explanation—The mediator explains that mediation is voluntary and that his/her role is simply to help the disputants find a solution to the conflict that is acceptable to all parties. The mediator states that he/she is neutral and will not take sides or decide who is right and who is wrong. The mediator tells each disputant that they will have a chance to present their view of the conflict without interruption.

3. Rules students must follow for mediation—Students agree to the following rules:
   a. Solve the problem.
   b. Do not resort to name calling.
   c. Do not interrupt.
   d. Be as honest as you can.
   e. If you agree to a solution, you must do what you have agreed to do.
   f. Anything said in mediation is strictly confidential.

NOTE: Other excellent references for peer helper, peer mediator, and conflict resolution programs may be obtained from the following resources and organizations:

Benard, B. (1990). *The case for peers.* Portland, OR: Northwest Regional Educational Laboratory.

Community Board Program
1540 Market Street
Suite 490
San Francisco, CA 94102
(415) 552-1250

National Association for Mediation in Education (NAME)
205 Hampshire House
Box 33635
Amherst, MA 01003-3635
(413) 545-2462
(413) 545-4802 (FAX)

National Network of Runaway and Youth Services. (1991). *Youth-Reaching-Youth implementation guide: A peer program for alcohol and other drug use prevention.* Washington, DC: Author.

National Peer Helpers Association
P.O. Box 2684
Greensville, NC 27858
(919) 757-6923

Tindall, J. (1989). *Peer counseling: Indepth look at training peer helpers* (3rd ed.). Muncie, IN: Accelerated Development.

Varenhorst, B. (1983). *Real Friends.* San Francisco: Harper & Row.

The nonverbal behaviors of teachers are particularly important when conveying empathy or when correcting student behavior (Banbury & Hebert, 1992) (Figure 6.2). Nonverbal behaviors such as facial expressions, voice tone, posture, and personal space will convey to the child who is upset either your interest and concern or your lack of time and attention. Students, of course, differ in the amount of personal space they require. A child's position (e.g., seated or standing), physical size, gender, culture, degree of anxiety, and familiarity with the

---

Dante, a student with behavior problems, is sitting in the back of his English class tilted back in his chair with his head resting against the window and his eyes closed. His teacher considers this to be unacceptable behavior and decides to correct Dante. She gives the assertive verbal message, "When you look like you are asleep in my class, I feel frustrated because my time is wasted while I wait for you to participate and I feel like my efforts to plan a good lesson go unnoticed."

Don't

Do

Hostile Body Language. The teacher has clearly invaded Dante's personal space. Her body positioning signals confrontation since she is leaning over the student. The finger pointing is not only a further invasion of Dante's space, but also a threatening and intimidating gesture. These aggressive nonverbal signals defeat the purpose of an assertive message and result in Dante's assuming a tense posture.

Passive Body Language. Equally ineffective is the opposite approach pictured above. Here the teacher appears to be intimidated and fearful of confrontation. Her arms are drawn up over her chest in a protective manner. Her chin is retracted inwardly and her lips are taut. With such submissive body language, it is unlikely that the teacher's message will be taken seriously by Dante.

Assertive Body Language. The teacher gives herself a chance for a successful intervention by considering space, positioning, and body language. In this case, she has approached the student from a nonthreatening angle to the side, near enough to be effective but not invasive. Her facial expression is relaxed, and her eyes are calmly gazing at the student as she makes her point. Since her verbal message is congruent with her nonverbal one, she has increased the likelihood that Dante will participate in the lesson.

FIGURE 6.2 ◆

The Importance of Teacher Body Language From "Do You See What I Mean: Body Language in Classroom Interactions," by M. M. Banbury & C. R. Hebert, *Teaching Exceptional Children,* 24(2), 1992, p. 35. Copyright © 1992 by The Council for Exceptional Children. Reprinted with permission.

teacher may all affect the amount of personal space required. Generally, students who are anxious, seated, or new in your classroom require a greater amount of personal space. Nevertheless, most students will need a personal space of about 3 feet between their body and your own to be comfortable.

Eye contact and body language to some extent are also culturally determined behaviors. Some students and teachers will be uncomfortable with sustained eye contact. Try to look at your students, rather than writing or manipulating papers, books, or other items, while they are talking. Stop what you are doing whenever possible so that your actions convey interest and attention, but don't be afraid to glance away occasionally from the student who is talking. Allow your body posture to be relaxed and calm. If you are seated, lean forward slightly. Whether you are sitting or standing, keep your arms relaxed and your hands visible. Refrain from crossing your arms or placing your hands behind your back or into your pockets.

Your facial expressions and voice tone also must be congruent with your words (Banbury & Hebert, 1992). For example, the teacher who states "I can see that you're upset" with a scowl or a sarcastic tone conveys a clear and belittling message to the student. On the other hand, the same message offered with a look of concern and a soft, caring tone conveys real support and understanding.

According to Carl Rogers, empathy is also the basis for helping relationships between client and therapist and between child and teacher (Rogers, 1951, 1969). Instead of judging children through statements of our approval or our disapproval, Rogers maintains that teachers should speak with children in a manner that enables them to know that they have been listened to and understood. As a matter of fact, Gordon (1974) lists many "natural tendencies" of teachers that he considers to be major barriers to successful communication with children and youth (Box 6.4, pp. 176–177).

Think about a time when your teachers or parents scolded you without hearing your point of view or when a friend dismissed a problem that was important to you. You probably felt hurt, misunderstood, defensive, or resentful. Perhaps you got angry and started an argument. More than likely you were unable to listen to their perspective or to solve your problem because your emotions got in the way.

Instead of relying on Gordon's habitual roadblocks to communication, which may precipitate additional frustration, defensiveness, anxiety, and anger, Rogers (1951) suggests that teachers respond with congruence (i.e., genuineness as demonstrated by a match between what they say and how they are saying it), with unconditional positive regard (i.e., respect for the young person and his or her ability to handle problems), and with real empathy. According to Rogers, "person-centered counselors" use techniques that help them clarify and understand the perceptions and feelings of children and youth. Furthermore, teachers skilled in helping relationships are able to communicate to the student that they hear and understand what the child is saying and feeling. When children believe that they have been heard and understood, they feel accepted, valued, and more open to learning how to solve their own difficulties.

Active or reflective listening skills are communication tools that Rogers (1951) suggests to be helpful when children own (i.e., are experiencing) a problem. On the other hand, Gordon (1974) maintains that teachers must send "I" messages

Major Barriers to Effective Communication

Gordon (1974) asserts that teachers often use statements which serve as road-blocks to building healthy relationships with children and youth. The natural tendency of many teachers to use a "language of unacceptance" slows down or inhibits the two-way process of communication necessary for helping students learn to solve problems.

Telling Students What to Do

(Responses which may temporarily solve a problem for students, but which do not open a dialogue to help students learn to problem solve for themselves):

1. Ordering, Commanding, Directing—"Stop the whining and get your work finished!"
2. Warning, Threatening—"If you don't finish your work, you'll be doing it during recess."
3. Moralizing, Preaching, Giving "Shoulds" and "Oughts"—"Study harder and get your mind off your boyfriend. You need to concentrate on what we're doing and leave your personal problems outside the door."
4. Advising, Offering Solutions or Suggestions—"Work out a time plan for doing your homework and then you won't be turning in so many assignments late."
5. Teaching, Lecturing, Giving Logical Arguments—"You need to do well in this class so you can graduate. If you don't get your high school diploma, you won't be able to get the job that you're hoping for."

Evaluating and Putting Students Down

(Responses which point out student faults and inadequacies. These, like the five responses above, may turn frustrated and anxious children into angry children):

to prevent student defensiveness, yet resolve conflicts when the teacher owns the problem (i.e., when the student's behavior is troubling the teacher).

Active-Reflective Listening Skills. Active listening means that the teacher listens with the heart as well as the head to discover both the content and the feelings contained in a student's message. Reflective listening means that the teacher behaves somewhat like a mirror, summarizing and sharing his or her perceptions of the content and feelings voiced by the child. Through active-reflective listening, the teacher hopes to clarify the child's point of view and reflect it back to the child as a starting point for problem solving. The "basics" of active-reflective listening include the following:

- *Try to understand how the student sees the situation.* Listen for both the content and the feelings. Take the child's perspective as best you can.
- *Use good attending behaviors.* Seek privacy and time for discussion whenever possible. Attend to nonverbal behaviors that encourage rather than discourage conversation.

6. Judging, Criticizing, Disagreeing, Blaming—"You're just being lazy. Why can't you try harder?"

7. Name-calling, Stereotyping, Labeling—"You're behaving like kinder-gartners. No wonder you never get invited to do things with the rest of the fifth graders."

8. Interpreting, Analyzing, Diagnosing—"I know what you're trying to do. You're trying to weasel out of this assignment, but it's not going to work."

Attempting to Make Problems Go Away

(Responses which try to make children feel better or divert attention from the problem. These may produce additional frustration or defensiveness in children):

9. Praising, Agreeing, Giving Positive Evaluations—"I know you'll be able to figure this out. You're really very smart."

10. Reassuring, Sympathizing, Consoling—"I had problems just like this when I was your age. You'll find out that they go away with time. They won't be such a big deal later."

11. Questioning, Probing, Interrogating, Cross-Examining—"What did you say next? Why did you do that?"

12. Withdrawing, Distracting, Being Sarcastic, Humoring, Diverting—"Let's don't worry about that today. You must have gotten up on the wrong side of the bed."

From TEACHER EFFECTIVENESS TRAINING by Thomas Gordon. Copyright © 1974 by Thomas Gordon. Reprinted by permission of David McKay Company, a division of Random House, Inc.

◆ *Use open-ended questions, door openers, and encouragers to facilitate sharing.* Questions such as "Would you like to talk about it?" and state-ments like "Tell me what happened" help students open up and talk. Your verbal and nonverbal behaviors (e.g., "Uh Huh," "Tell me more," head nodding in silence) encourage additional information.

◆ *Paraphrase the content of the student's message to check your understand-ing and to summarize and clarify the child's point of view for him or her.* Use statements such as "So what you're saying is. . . . " or "Let me see if I understand what you said," followed by a concise paraphrase of the stu-dent's message (e.g., "So what you're saying is Mrs. Jones fussed at you for talking in her class, but Keesha said something to you first" or "Let me see if I understood what you said. Mrs. Jones was fussing at you for talking even though Keesha was the one who started talking to you first").

◆ *Look for feelings and emotions underlying the child's message and reflect these back to the student.* Combine your perception of the student's feelings with a paraphrase of what he or she has said. Use a statement such as "You feel *(perceived emotion)* because *(paraphrase of events as child sees them"* (e.g., You felt angry with Mrs. Jones because she accused you of talking even though Keesha asked you a question first").

Active-reflective listening skills are crucial in keeping lines of communication open when children are feeling anxious, frustrated, and angry. They are also critical skills for defusing potentially explosive classroom situations by helping volatile children feel that they have been listened to and understood. For example, when a student issues a rude comment directed toward you, respond with "You sound upset. Take a 2-minute break, and we'll try it again" instead of reprimanding the youngster for his or her comment. Certainly teachers will need to go beyond a paraphrase or a summary of feelings to benignly confront the conflicting statements and emotions of many students with behavioral disorders. Yet, these critical human relations skills are often a necessary first step in helping children and youth calm down, listen, and learn how to solve their problems.

Sending "I" Messages. When the student's behavior is creating a problem for you as the teacher, you are likely to become upset. For example, when Dante saunters into class late, puts his head on his desk while you give directions, and then sneers "What are we supposed to do?", you will probably feel frustrated, embarrassed, and tested in front of the other students. At that point, you might attack Dante with statements like "If you'd get here on time and listen for once, you'd know what you were supposed to do" or "Don't get sarcastic with me young man, or you'll spend the rest of the period in the office."

Rather than responding critically and confronting the student with accusations, demands, or other roadblocks to communication, however, Gordon (1974) suggests that teachers send "I" messages. "I" messages are simple, assertive statements that focus on what the teacher is feeling as a result of the student's behavior. "I" messages clearly describe the child's behavior that is troubling, the effect of the behavior on the teacher, and the teacher's feelings as a result of the behavior. Instead of attacking the student as a "troublesome person," the teacher focuses attention on his or her own needs, thus facilitating a constructive response from the young person. When Dante "tests" you, for example, you might state, "When you came in late and put your head on the desk, I felt you didn't care about today's lesson. Then, I was upset when you asked what to do just as soon as I finished giving directions. That distracted the rest of the class and made me feel like you were trying to embarrass me in front of everyone."

Like active-reflective listening skills, "I" messages alone are not enough to solve all classroom problems. They are, however, effective tools for encouraging open communication and for supporting and clarifying feelings in the classroom. Also like active-reflective listening, sending an "I" message can help to deescalate an explosive situation and help teachers deal with the intense feelings of students during and immediately following times of crises.

Supporting the Feelings of Students in Crisis

William Morse (1976a, 1976b) first suggested the idea of a crisis or helping teacher available to assist students during times of crises. According to Morse, a crisis exists when the child's capacity to cope becomes overloaded. At these moments of crisis, significant opportunities for learning occur. Therefore, rather than waiting for a "specialist" or "therapist" to visit and "treat" the youngster, Morse believed the helping teacher, a person intimately involved in the child's daily life, to be the logical choice for crisis prevention and intervention.

Similarly, Wood and Long (1991) see crises as times during which learning may take place. They maintain that a crisis is a product of a young person's stress. When students do not feel good about themselves and have low self-esteem, even ordinary circumstances may flood them with intense feelings of embarrassment, frustration, self-doubt, confusion, anger, and so forth. These intense feelings then drive a student's behavior, most often in a direction considered unacceptable by teachers or other adults. Thus, when teachers respond with disapproval, criticism, or punishment, the child experiences additional stress, which produces new feelings and behaviors in a spiraling conflict of escalating crisis. As Wood and Long (1991) assert, teachers must interrupt this "conflict cycle" so that their behaviors do not serve to escalate events into an explosive incident. Recognizing stress and feelings experienced by students is a first step in defusing a crisis and putting a stop to the conflict cycle.

According to the National Crisis Prevention Institute (Steiger, 1987), a crisis actually begins when a child is experiencing feelings of anxiety. Usually anxiety is felt as a result of frustration or the presence of some unmet need. When a student exhibits observable changes in his or her normal behaviors (e.g., the quiet child becomes restless or boisterous; the talkative student becomes sullen and withdrawn) or nondirected energy (e.g., pencil tapping, fidgeting, pacing, rocking), that student is showing signs of anxiety. To prevent the crisis from escalating, then, teachers are advised to be supportive. That is, teachers must demonstrate empathy and attempt to find and meet the unmet need whenever possible.

Notice that Morse (1976a, 1976b), Wood and Long (1991), and Steiger (1987) all share an emphasis on preventing a crisis from escalating by recognizing, supporting, and clarifying the student's feelings. This does not mean, of course, that teachers will refrain from setting limits on behavior or from enforcing the consequences of poor behavioral choices. However, if teachers are empathetic and use their active and reflective listening skills early in the crisis, they are more likely to expand the child's "capacity to cope," "interrupt the conflict cycle," and "meet the child's unmet needs."

When a crisis escalates to a level of high verbal behavior (e.g., screaming obscenities; challenging your authority, race, religion, or gender; having a temper tantrum; students provoking one another), children and youth are in the process of losing their self-control. Support for students during these moments entails giving them concise directions regarding the appropriate behavior expected. Responding to their taunts and challenges with defensive statements, threats, or criticisms will only heighten the conflict. Steiger (1987) cautions teachers to isolate the verbally defensive child from his or her peers whenever possible and actively listen for the real problem while the child is shouting. Then, when the child pauses, the teacher must redirect the child back to the task at hand or set a clear and enforceable limit (e.g., "I need you to calm down so we can talk and fix the problem" or "If you abide by the rules, you can continue to play the game. If not, you will have to stop playing"). Of course, the limits you set must be logical responses to the student's behavior, within the guidelines of your school's policies, and they must include options that you are prepared and able to enforce.

During crises, the critical behavior for teachers is to remain calm and convey concern and support. The teacher's body language and tone of voice must project the expectation that the student will regain self-control and be able to solve the problem at hand. In addition, talking with students following a crisis affords an excellent opportunity for teaching better ways to handle similar difficulties in the future. In Chapter 9, we will explore some methods for conducting structured conversations focused on problem solving with children and youth having emotional and behavioral disorders. For now, however, you may wish to review the excellent suggestions for negotiation and conflict resolution, important skills for solving problems following crises, contained in Box 6.3.

Strengths and Limitations of Supporting Feelings

Very few teachers would argue against the need for students to feel that they are comfortable, safe, and secure in the classroom. For a healthy self-concept to develop, students certainly must believe that they are respected, contributing members of the classroom group, that they are competent and able to master important material, and that they have a degree of independence and control over their environment. Empathetic teachers capable of effective listening and communication skills may certainly help children and youth with emotional and behavioral disorders experience these important feelings. Moreover, by using active-reflective listening or by sending "I" messages, teachers serve as powerful models of effective communication and conflict resolution skills for their students.

Both active-reflective listening techniques and the practice of sending "I" messages are not without criticism, however. For example, Ellis (1959) originally disputed Roger's (1951, 1961, 1969) assertion that unconditional positive regard and a nondirective approach are essential for changing behavior. That is, individuals may experience self-awareness yet not know how to change or be unwilling to change their actual behavior. Newcomer (1993) also suggests that intervention strategies that rely on verbal skills, such as active-reflective listening or "I" messages, are not effective for students with low verbal or intellectual ability. Moreover, when students do not know how to behave appropriately or when children are escalating out of control, a more directive approach is necessary (Steiger, 1987). In these circumstances, expecting students to solve their own behavioral difficulties without direction from the teacher may prove not only fruitless but also dangerous. Nevertheless, these skills are an essential component within the repertoire of management strategies necessary for teachers of students with emotional and behavioral disorders.

Activities for Identifying and Expressing Feelings

Up to this point, we have been discussing ways in which teachers can support emotional needs and clarify feelings expressed by their students. Children and youth with emotional and behavioral disorders, however, often are not adept at identifying their feelings or expressing them appropriately. Therefore, teachers may wish to plan activities that give students socially acceptable outlets for examining and releasing feelings. Activities like play and reading, for example, or supportive media such as art and music, provide numerous avenues through which children may learn about feelings. In addition, some authorities advocate that schools reinstate the practice of instructing students in basic values and morals (Lickona, 1993; Ryan, 1993).

Supportive Media

Creative arts and activities (e.g., music, art, play, reading poetry or prose) through the centuries have provided humanity with opportunities to reveal and reflect on the deepest human feelings and emotions. At some point, most of us have reacted strongly to a selection of music or to a particular painting that evoked a certain mood or memory. Moreover, most of us have read at least one book containing a character with whom we could identify. We may have experienced, for example, a sensation that "This character is just like me" or "This song (painting) really tells how I feel." Sometimes called *creative arts therapies*, teachers can use art, music, play, and reading activities in the classroom to help students identify and express their feelings (Box 6.5, pp. 182–184).

Art and Music. Art and music can provide students with emotional and behavioral disorders opportunities to release their emotions safely and to learn appropriate social skills. Teachers, however, are not trained as art or music therapists; therefore, they should not look for hidden meanings in the art or music of their students. For example, the student who decides to color an entire drawing in black may not be exhibiting feelings of hopelessness or despair. He or she may have had only that color crayon available at the time. Also, students who prefer to listen to certain rock music may do so as part of a fad, for peer acceptance, or because they have not yet learned about other forms of music which they may find more enjoyable. Teachers may nevertheless use art and music activities effectively to support feelings in the classroom.

Keyes (1974) and Rubin (1978) assert that art can help the individual reach feelings that words and "talk" sessions cannot touch. Children and youth, for example, may be asked to draw on paper or on the computer or make from other materials pictures of how they see themselves or of how they imagine others see them. Some authorities suggest that the process of creating art such as this *becomes* therapy and facilitates change itself rather than serving merely as a tool for psychotherapy (Kramer, 1979; Robbins & Sibley, 1976; Ulman & Levy, 1980). Others maintain that children who do not have the language skills necessary to express their feelings of anger or frustration verbally may be taught to draw pictures of these emotions to communicate their feelings with an appropriate alternative behavior to that of aggression or noncompliance (Sasso & Riemers, 1988). Uhlin (1992, p. 128) contends that art activities serve many functions for children with special needs including providing:

BOX 6.5   **Teacher Feature: Art and Music Therapy**

These are not the kind of kids whose lives would have been memorialized in Norman Rockwell paintings. In fact, most have childhood canvases with ugly blotches and dark patches. Some have been abused, others neglected. Several have become violent, others suicidal.

Here, though, in a room at the Virginia Treatment Center for Children, the youngsters are given clean slates. Specifically, they are given white drawing paper or mounds of gray clay. These young people—some of whom never have even held a crayon or piece of chalk—become artists. These same kids—some of whom are tone-deaf—can go down the hall and become musicians. They can beat the drums or strum a guitar.

Their drawings don't have to be gallery-quality and their music doesn't have to harmonize. What's important is that the young people have a chance to express themselves.

"Most of these kids didn't have childhoods," said Mary Green, art therapist at the Virginia Treatment Center. "They never got to play."

In this paint-splattered, knickknack-cluttered room, though, creativity is the byword. "Creativity is the essence of a healthy life," Green said. "We'll tell the kids you can dream a new reality for yourself."

And while the young people may consider it fun, at the Virginia Treatment Center for Children, this creativity consciousness falls under the heading of "therapy." Under the auspices of Virginia Commonwealth University's Medical College of Virginia, the center provides intensive psychiatric services for children, adolescents and their families.

If they are in treatment at the center, these young people likely have endangered themselves or others. Most carry heavy emotional baggage. But when the young people are doing things they like to do, therapists often get at deep-seated issues faster than they can using traditional methods. "Stuff comes in the back door," said Rhonda Rinker, the treatment center's music therapist. That's why hospitals, schools and treatment centers are with increasing frequency using creative arts therapy with emotionally disturbed, as well as physically ill, individuals.

As the process is gaining respect, the profession is growing in numbers. There now are about 4000 registered art therapists nationally—1200 more than there were eight years ago. About 90 art therapists work in Virginia. Nationally,

1. A channel for emotional expression through painting, drawing, collage, or clay modeling.
2. An outlet for the release of tensions and expression of emotions through art techniques incorporating subskills such as hammering, squeezing, or bending.
3. A feeling of belonging to a peer-group through sharing of materials and involvement in group activity.

there are about 5,000 music therapists, with about 100 in Virginia. "People tend to think of [creative arts] as entertainment," Rinker said. "But," she added, "a lot of physicians have changed their perspectives."

Barry M. Cohen, a pioneering art therapist at the Psychiatric Institute of Washington, said, "What goes on inside a person is externalized through art." He added, "Drawings become a map to what's going on inside." Also, said Cohen, who serves as program director for the institute's Center for Abuse, Recovery, and Empowerment, the art often can serve as a springboard to "dialogue between the person making the art and the person treating him.". . .

In addition to drawing, young people in art therapy make masks, create puppets and old pottery. Last week, a teen-age boy was putting the finishing touches on what he calls his "Pandora's Box." The covered clay box represented the young man's newfound ability to "keep a lid on his anger." Mask-making—one of the popular art activities for the young people—is particularly powerful, Green said. The kids are asked to design a mask that represents the self they would like to be, the self they feel they must be for others or the self they only show to close friends. In this way, the students have an opportunity to "face themselves."

Many of the young people "are from starved environments," Green said. "The kids get a lot out of coming in here and making something to take home." She added, "The rest of the program is so regimented, this is a nice break for them." Also, she said, "They're so used to being put down." Knowing they're not going to be graded on or criticized for their creativity, "we're seeing the kids become more self-confident," Green said.

"I tell them: 'Art is a thing of beauty. You also are a thing of beauty,'" she added. "They learn to appreciate themselves more." Green said she tries to instill in young people the value of art so they will continue to use creative outlets when they leave the center. "I tell them to go out and buy clay," she said. "When they get mad, they can slam it against the pavement."

Similarly, Rinker said, students in music therapy can "let their anger out on the drums so they don't go out and hit someone." She added, "Empty kids can fill themselves with music." With music, Rinker said, "you sometimes don't have to use words at all." She said she keeps in tune with the musical tastes of young

4. A sense of being part of the school environment through display of one's work in the classroom or hallway.
5. Opportunities for social development when interacting with peers, adults, or persons of authority.
6. Opportunities to develop good work habits such as the use and care of art materials and respect for the rights and property of others.
7. Opportunities for exploring, experimenting, and producing art forms with various media, techniques, and themes.

BOX 6.5 (cont.)

people. However, she said, she analyzes all lyrics before she allows music to be played in the music therapy room and she bars any "disgusting music."

Green, the art therapist, said through all of the center's creative arts programs, young people "learn how to use art to get strong feelings out." She added, "If they can make a volcano and pretend it blows up instead of blowing up themselves, I've been successful." For example, a 13-year-old girl at the center created a painting with one half a dark and gloomy blue, the other a bright translucent orange, entitled "Reaching for the Light." In one corner of the blue section—farthest away from the orange—was a black ball.

"That's where I am," said the creator of the painting. But, she added, pointing to the brighter half, "The more I work at it, the faster I'll be there." During an interview last week, the young artist spoke very calmly about her anger—and her art. A student at the Virginia Treatment Center off and on since last fall, she has used clay, paint, and Styrofoam to unleash a torrent of pent-up emotions. "Art therapy and music therapy help get some of your anger out without fighting, yelling or being destructive," said the young woman who said she's at the treatment center because she has "a problem with anger and how to express it." Her means of expressing it have included destroying her room, shattering mirrors and hitting family members. "Nobody in my family gets along," the young woman said.

Adapted from "Dreaming a New Reality: Psychiatric Services Focus on Creative Arts Therapy," by A. B. Billingsley, 1994, *Richmond Times Dispatch*, Thursday, April 7, E1–E2. Copyright © 1994 Richmond Times Dispatch. Adapted by permission.

NOTE: The interested reader may obtain additional information about Art and Music Therapy by writing to the following organizations:

American Art Therapy Association
1202 Allanson Road
Mundelein, IL 60060
(708) 949-6064

American Association for Music Therapy
P.O. Box 50012
Valley Forge, PA 19484
(215) 265-4006

Similarly, music, especially when combined with rhythm instruments or with dance, can provide students with healthy recreation and an outlet for the release of tension and emotions (Gaston, 1968). According to Nordoff and Robbins (1971) children experience through music a sense of belonging and sharing with others, experiences critical for enhancing self-worth.

Alvin (1966) provides an interesting account of the healing power of music through the ages. Musical activities helpful for identifying and expressing feelings in the classroom include the following:

1. Analyzing or rewriting the lyrics of selected popular songs or composing one's own musical pieces.
2. Identifying the "mood" or "tone" of musical selections or using music to set the classroom climate for particular activities (e.g., quiet contemplation, excitement, and energy).
3. Using instruments, dance, or rhythmic activities to release pent-up emotions and stress.
4. Learning social skills through cooperative activities such as singing together or playing songs on musical instruments.

Play. According to Virginia Axline (1947, 1969), play is a more natural medium for self-expression in children than is talk. Therefore, when play is used to help children act out their feelings of tension, frustration, insecurity, aggression, or fear, play serves a therapeutic purpose. When the adult chooses particular toys or games for play in order to establish a relationship with the student or to develop gross and fine motor, self-help, or communication skills, play therapy assumes a directive form (Schaefer & O'Connor, 1983). In nondirective play therapy, however, children are provided with a selection of toys including dolls, doll houses, toy animals, puppets, sand, water, blocks, and so forth. The child is free to choose his or her toys and to play with them at will, although intentional destruction of play materials, damaging the room, or attacking others is prohibited (Axline, 1969). The task of the play therapist, then, is to observe the child, summarize, and reflect back to the child both the positive and negative feelings expressed by the child during play.

Axline (1969) and Landreth (1991) describe several initial objectives for nondirective play therapy. These include:

◆ Provide a safe environment for the children. Set limits on behavior and be consistent.
◆ Come to an understanding of the children's world and accept it. Have patience until the children express their feelings and then see the children's point of view.
◆ Encourage children to express their emotions but never judge these.
◆ Develop a supportive atmosphere. The children should experience a sense of freedom in making their own choices.
◆ Help the children to make their own decisions. The adult encourages the children to find answers for themselves.
◆ Help the children assume responsibility and a feeling of control. If children think they are in control, they will feel important in their relationship with an adult.
◆ Describe what the children's experiences are. Observe the children's behavior and feelings and communicate these to the children.

Landreth (1991) also maintains that through cooperative play with peers children learn self-control and important social skills. In addition, vigorous play is used to release stress and tension and redirect unacceptable behaviors as well as to help the child develop a positive self-image. Furthermore, play is used to help children who have been victims of abuse, neglect, or sexual abuse "talk about" their experiences and emotions and to assist siblings in coping with homelessness (Gil, 1991; Hunter, 1993). Finally, play is used in hospitals to help children learn about medical procedures to be conducted on themselves or family members, to help youngsters overcome the fear of a hospital stay, to facilitate a child's adjustment to a changed body or to fear of ridicule following treatment, to normalize child growth and development during extended hospital stays, and to provide support for family members before, during, and after hospitalization (Azarnoff & Flegal, 1975).

In classroom settings, of course, teachers will need to be more directive, providing limits on behavior and praising appropriate actions in order to ensure safety. Teachers can, however, effectively use physical activity and play in their classrooms to provide for the release of energy following quiet periods of concentrated work, to teach and reward social skills, to make drill and practice of academic materials exciting and fun, to give children and youth a degree of responsibility, choice, and control over their activities, and to encourage development of healthy recreational behaviors for life.

Bibliotherapy. Reading and sharing poems, stories, or books is a time-honored method for helping young people learn about and cope with normal life experiences as well as life problems (Pardeck & Pardeck, 1984). Through reading, children and young adults may safely confront situations they face in their daily lives such as coping with divorce or separation, changes in family status, failure, group pressure, alcohol and drug abuse, illness and death, sibling relationships, puberty and sexual maturation, or physical disabilities (Ouzts, 1991). Teachers may provide appropriate books for children to read at their own level independently or share stories with an entire group facing similar adjustment problems. After reading a particular selection, teachers can foster additional reflection and decision-making by having children role play the story; rewrite the ending; create murals, illustrations, or puppet shows of chosen scenes; or write poetry to capture their own feelings.

Zaccaria, Moses, and Hollowell (1978) suggest that reading is therapeutic when the reader identifies with a character or situation in a story, experiences a sense of catharsis or release of feelings, and gains insight by sensing that his or her problem is shared by others. To be most beneficial, the character, problem, and solution must be perceived as realistic by the child. That is, if the character in the story is of the same sex, cultural background and approximate age as the reader and if the character solves a real-life problem in a manner that is possible for a child, bibliotherapy is likely to be most effective.

Excellent sources of reading material for all age groups are listed in Box 6.6 (p. 188). In addition, Pardeck and Pardeck (1984) offer the following activities for teachers or librarians to use to help children and youth explore difficulties after reading a story or book:

1. Develop a synopsis of the story, written or tape recorded, using a point of view other than that of the character who told the story.

By reading and sharing stories, poems, and books, students may safely confront life problems.

2. Compose a diary for a book character.
3. Write a letter from one of the book characters to another character.
4. Make a time line or daily schedule for story events or a character's life. Compare it to your own time line or daily schedule.
5. Send a letter or telegram to one of the book characters.
6. Compose a "Dear Abby" letter offering advice about a problem situation in the story, or write a news story concerning an incident from the book.
7. Hold a roundtable, panel discussion, or debate concerning a decision a book character is facing.
8. Hold a mock trial concerning an incident in the book. Role play the character as well as judge, lawyers, and jury.
9. Make a collage or mobile illustrating key events, scenes, or decision points in the story.
10. Using a ballot box, write suggestions or questions directed toward characters in the story.

Strengths and Limitations of Supportive Media

Newcomer (1993) cautions teachers not to "psychoanalyze" or look for hidden meanings in the art, music, play, or reading activities of children. Also, teachers must refrain from forcing children to express their feelings through the creative arts. Expression of one's emotions occurs only when a trusting relationship is established between children and teachers. Finally, most evidence for the ef-fectiveness of these methods comes from case studies and anecdotal accounts in clinical settings. Riordan and Wilson (1989) and Lenkowsky (1987), for example, caution teachers that studies concerning bibliotherapy are fraught with methodological difficulties and conflicting results. Therefore, teachers must not automatically assume that the therapeutic benefits of supportive media will generalize immediately to the classroom setting or that "support" through the creative arts will, in and of itself, be sufficient to change the behavior or self-esteem of children and youth with emotional and behavioral disorders.

In addition, teachers may need to assume a more directive, rather than nondirective, role when using supportive media. Reasonable rules and limits on appropriate behavior must be set and enforced in the classroom; therefore, teachers cannot allow children total permissiveness when engaged in these activities. When considered to be supplementary aids to the ongoing program of academic and behavioral and social skills instruction, however, art, music, play, and reading may provide numerous opportunities for children to release stress and tension, develop self-control and social skills, learn to problem solve, and learn to communicate their feelings safely.

Values and Moral Education

During the "open" climate of the 1960s and 1970s, educators attempted to help young people examine their feelings and determine their own values. The development of values was seen as the result of a three-step process: (1) choosing freely from among alternatives after thoughtful reflection; (2) prizing or cherishing one's choices by affirming these publicly; and (3) acting repeatedly on one's choices consistently in a pattern throughout life (Raths, Harmin, & Simon, 1966). Inappropriate behaviors, then, resulted from the incomplete development of values, from becoming "out of touch" with our values, or from holding values that conflict with the values of those around us.

Teachers were encouraged to provide values clarification activities for children and adolescents to help them explore and determine values for themselves (Raths, Harmin, & Simon, 1966; Simon, 1974, 1976). The teacher's role was to clarify and reflect the values exhibited by students without judging the "rightness" of their decisions. Moralizing and "preaching" about values was strongly discouraged, although teachers and parents were encouraged to think carefully about the "values lessons" taught to young people implicitly through their own daily actions and behaviors as adults (Kirschenbaum & Simon, 1973).

This nondirective approach to teaching values fell out of favor, however, by the mid-1980s. Schools faced growing problems arising from the disintegration of families, from drug and alcohol abuse, and from escalating violence among youth. A values clarification curriculum implying that all values are of equal "moral correctness" and importance simply became incompatible with the realities of daily school life and with the political conservatism of the 1990s.

Today, authorities are suggesting that schools return to the business of moral or character education, one of the earliest goals of schools (Lickona, 1991, 1993). Rather than debating *whose* values schools should teach, proponents of moral education assert that some values are shared by everyone, regardless of cultural or ethnic background, and that these values have been transmitted to others in great art and literature throughout time (Ryan, 1993; Wynne & Ryan, 1992). Core values such as trustworthiness, caring and kindness, courage, loyalty, respect, fairness and justice, responsibility, and citizenship are integrated into the curriculum through the study of history and literature and by adults who model and endorse these values.

In the "new" values education, teachers are expected to state clearly what behaviors are considered morally right and wrong and to establish rules and consequences to reward moral behavior. For example, if a teacher believes that fighting is morally wrong, the teacher must inform students about that belief and about why he or she holds that belief. According to Lickona (1993), moral education in actual classroom practice requires the teacher to do the following:

- ◆ Act as a caregiver, model, and mentor, treating students with respect and fostering moral development by both example and discussion.
- ◆ Create a moral community in which members feel that they belong and are responsible to the group.
- ◆ Practice moral discipline by establishing and enforcing rules.
- ◆ Create a democratic classroom environment in which students are involved in decision making.
- ◆ Incorporate values in the curriculum using the ethical and moral content of literature, history, and science.

BOX 6.7   **Teacher Feature: Actions Speak Louder Than Words—
What Students Think**

What's the most effective way to teach values? According to students, teachers "have to follow the values themselves." They have to be "fair" and "real"—not "phony." Teaching moral values doesn't work, students say, if teachers try to "make it a big deal" or "have a separate class about it."

These are some of the findings from a study I conducted to better understand how moral values and traits of character are taught and learned in classrooms. As a teacher, I was aware of the growing interest in character education across the nation, and I was concerned about the implementation of schoolwide character education programs.

First, I conducted a pilot study to determine how eight of the moral values stated by former Education Secretary William Bennett are learned by students in classrooms. Because "respect for others" had the highest priority for students, it became the focal value in my qualitative/ethnographic study.

To discover how respect was taught to students and learned by them, I surveyed, observed, and interviewed teachers, students (grades 6-8), administrators, and parents in urban and suburban settings, in public and private schools, during one school year. I expected to find that formal lessons about respect produce the best results. Yet, the findings indicate that respect is taught best through the hidden curriculum of modeling and quality teaching that creates a positive moral climate.

Analyzing the data from the perspective of students provides a vantage point that is rarely encountered in classroom research. Had this study been conducted from the teachers' point of view, all of the participants would have been judged effective. They all asserted that it was part of their duty to teach moral values to students, and they all believed that they were successful in teaching character. According to middle school students, however, only some of their teachers ("model teachers") follow through with this stated intention. The other teachers ("poor models") are judged to be insincere and inconsistent.

Students from classrooms with "poor models" report evidence of double standards and differential treatment. For example, these teachers say things like, "You should be kind" and "Respect others." Yet students report that they "choose favorites," "treat us like babies," "don't listen," and "give us busy work." Although these poor models believe they are teaching respect, they are blind to the way their behaviors affect student learning and behavior. As several students put it, "Teachers can't fake it."

When students perceive a teacher as insincere, they talk behind the teacher's back, talk back to the teacher, and exhibit other behaviors generally deemed disrespectful. Students report that they "respect" these teachers only because they "have to."

Character education manifests itself in teacher practice as respect for each student as a responsible, active learner. Model teachers understand that students require an environment of mutual trust and respect. How do model teachers behave? Students say that they:

- ◆ Present clear, consistent, and sincere messages.
- ◆ Do not pull rank—are never authoritarian (e.g., telling students "Because I said so" instead of offering logical reasons).
- ◆ Communicate high expectations.
- ◆ Really listen.
- ◆ Communicate their commitment through their actions.
- ◆ Are hard-working and really care about student learning.
- ◆ Deserve respect.

NOTE: Additional information and materials about moral and character education may be obtained by calling or writing to the following organizations:

Center for the Advancement of Ethics and Character
School of Education
Boston University
605 Commonwealth Avenue
Boston, MA 02215

Center for Applied Ethics
Costello House
861 Bedford Road
Pleasantville, NY 10570

Character Education Institute
8918 Tesoro Drive Suite 575
San Antonio, TX 78217-6253
(800) 284-0499

Ethics Resource Center
1120 G Street, N.W., Suite 200
Washington, D.C. 20005
(202) 737-2258

Jefferson Center for Character Education
2700 East Foothill Blvd. Suite 302
Pasadena, CA 91107
(818) 792-8130

Josephson Institute of Ethics
4640 Admiralty Way Suite 1001
Marina Del Rey, CA 90292-6610
(310) 306-1868
(310) 827-1864 (FAX)

- Use cooperative learning activities to help students share responsibility and learn to work toward common goals.
- Foster the student's appreciation of excellence and hard work as affecting the lives of others.
- Encourage moral reflection through journals, essays, and discussions.
- Teach conflict resolution skills so that students will know how to resolve dilemmas peacefully and fairly.
- Foster caring beyond the classroom through opportunities to perform school and community service.

The return to moral or character education is not without criticism, though. Some educators fear a return to the "judgment free" position of values clarification activities, and others maintain that they already have enough to teach in the curriculum without adding something else. Critics fear that moral education may be misused to promote narrow-minded, intolerant attitudes and that teaching morals will infringe on the student's right to free speech. Still others maintain that values and morals are best taught through the home or church (Berreth & Scherer, 1993).

Those who favor moral and character education, on the other hand, argue that all teaching and curriculum is value laden and that effective schools have always taught morals and values (Lickona, 1991; Wynne & Ryan, 1992). These proponents suggest that one of the central purposes of schooling is to produce responsible citizens. They argue that if students are no longer learning how to be "good people" in the home and in the community, then teachers must actively teach children about "goodness." The teacher's own behaviors and actions, however, may be the most valuable lesson about morals and character that students receive. Teachers serve as important models of prosocial behavior for their students (Box 6.7, pp. 190–191).

Students with emotional and behavioral disorders are often considered to be lower in moral reasoning skills than their nondisabled peers (Schonert & Cantor, 1991). Kohlberg (1975, 1978), for example, theorizes that individuals pass through three stages in their moral development: (1) At the preconventional level children seek to avoid physical punishment and gratify personal needs by deferring to authority and exchanging favors. (2) At the conventional level students seek to please and help others to gain their approval. (3) At the postconventional level, the rights of individuals begin to supersede the need to maintain social order, and decision making is based on universal principles of justice, respect, and trust. Moral discussion groups, then, based on Kohlberg's theories and focused on the debate and resolution of hypothetical situations presenting moral dilemmas, are used to create "disequilibrium" and help students with behavioral problems improve their moral development.

Maag (1989) questions the effectiveness of these moral discussion groups for meeting the needs of students with emotional and behavioral disorders, however. He suggests that the effects of using moral discussion groups are often confounded with other intervention procedures such as teaching, modeling, and rewarding social skills. Furthermore, Maag suggests that training in moral reasoning may not produce lasting and generalizable changes in the student's actual behavior. In addition, Maag (1989) questions the efficacy of using hypothetical situations, rather than genuine dilemmas faced by students, for discussing moral issues.

Blackeney and Blackeney (1991) and Swarthout (1988) offer reasonable guidelines for teachers wishing to improve the moral development of their students with behavioral difficulties. These authors encourage teachers to do the following:

◆ *Determine the logic behind the misbehavior.* Examine what makes the behavior "right" from the child's point of view.
◆ *Examine moral values and issues within the academic curriculum.* Design curricula around the discussion of moral dilemmas from history and literature.
◆ *Encourage discussion of real-life moral dilemmas.* Use the daily occurrences in the classroom as opportunities for discussion about moral issues and for teaching conflict resolution skills.
◆ *Examine the hidden curriculum taught through the behaviors of teachers and administrators and through the policies and "atmosphere" of the school.* Become a model for moral development and reasoning skills.
◆ *Use explicit instruction.* Teach and reward moral behaviors.

Summary

Teachers of students with emotional and behavioral disorders must deal with the intense feelings of these children and youth on a daily basis. Learning to support and clarify the often conflicting emotions of these youngsters is an essential skill for teachers. Support for feelings comes from providing a psychologically safe classroom environment in which students understand the rules, feel secure, and believe that they belong. A sense of mastery, independence, and real responsibility for oneself and others enhances self-esteem and trust in human relationships.

To support and clarify feelings, teachers also must demonstrate empathy and skill in listening and communicating. Active-reflective listening and sending "I" messages are two important ways through which teachers can let their students know that they have been heard and understood. These methods, as well as attending to one's body language, are crucial in defusing potentially explosive classroom situations and preventing and managing crises effectively.

Teachers must take care, however, to seek additional support for their students from psychologists or counselors when a young person's feelings and emotions are overwhelming. Students who are extremely depressed or who are suicidal, for example, require professional care beyond that which teachers can provide in the classroom. When teachers sense that they are getting in "over their head," a referral to a mental health professional is in the student's best interest.

Finally, using supportive media in the classroom provides students with a safe means to identify and express feelings. Art, music, play, and bibliotherapy give children and youth opportunities to release stress and energy, learn social skills, and express difficult emotions. Moral education, the process of teaching children what is right and what is wrong, is also experiencing a recent resurgence of interest in the schools. Activities for identifying and expressing feelings may be valuable supplements to the total instructional program of children and youth with emotional and behavioral disorders.

Application Exercises

1. Think about a "favorite" teacher. List those things this teacher did that made you feel as if you belonged in his or her classroom. How did this teacher help students feel independent and responsible for themselves and others?

2. Keesha says, "He shouldn't have taken my book. I didn't mean to hit him." Paraphrase the content of Keesha's message using a "So what you're saying is. . ." format. What emotions might Keesha be feeling? Phrase a reflective statement (You feel _____ because _____) to check your understanding of Keesha's feelings.

3. Practice the paraphrase and reflective statement from exercise number 2 with a partner. Have a partner check your body language, facial expression, and tone of voice.

4. With a partner or a tape recorder, say, "That sure looks nice on you," changing your tone of voice each time you make the statement. How does your tone of voice change the meaning of the words you say? Describe an instance you recall when someone's words, tone of voice, and body language did not fit together.

5. Paul is talking in class while you are talking. Phrase an "I" message regarding the effect of Paul's behavior on you.

6. Write or call the sources listed in this chapter for information on conflict resolution and negotiation skills (Box 6.3), for the creative arts therapies (Box 6.5), for bibliotherapy (Box 6.6), and for teaching moral and character education (Box 6.7).

7. Select a difficulty of childhood or adolescence (e.g., sibling problems, changing schools, coping with a disability, etc.). Locate three or four books from the sources listed in Box 6.6 that deal with the problem you have selected and that are appropriate for the age range you plan to teach. Read the stories or books. Are the characters and situations realistic? Construct several follow-up activities that you might use to help students think about the problem.

8. Arrange to interview or observe in the classroom of a teacher of students with emotional and behavioral disorders at a chosen grade level. How does this teacher make the classroom "supportive" of student feelings? Does the teacher use art, music, play, or reading activities to help students understand and express feelings? If so, how are these activities used?

References

Adler, A. (1927). *The practice and theory of individual psychology.* New York: Harcourt, Brace & World.

Alvin, J. (1966). *Music therapy.* Chatham, Kent, England: W. & J. Mackay & Co. Ltd.

Axline, V. M. (1947). *Play therapy: The inner dynamics of childhood.* Boston: Houghton Mifflin.

Axline, V. M. (1969). *Play therapy.* New York: Ballantine.

Azarnoff, P., & Flegal, S. (1975). *A pediatric play program: Developing a therapeutic play program for children in medical settings.* Springfield, IL: Charles C. Thomas.

Bacon, J., & Brendtro, L. K. (1992). The missing team member. *Journal of Emotional and Behavioral Problems, 1*(3), 17–20.

Banbury, M. M., & Hebert, C. R. (1992). Do you see what I mean? Body language in classroom interactions. *Teaching Exceptional Children, 24*(2), 34–38.

Bandura, A. (1977). Self-efficacy: Toward a unifying theory of behavioral change. *Psychological Review, 84,* 191–215.

Beane, J. A. (1991). Sorting out the self-esteem controversy. *Educational Leadership, 49*(1), 25–30.

Berkowitz, P. H., & Rothman, E. P. (1960). *The disturbed child: Recognition and psychoeducational therapy in the classroom.* New York: New York University Press.

Berreth, D., & Scherer, M. (1993). On transmitting values: A conversation with Amitai Etzioni. *Educational Leadership, 51*(3), 12–15.

Bettleheim, B. (1950). *Love is not enough.* New York: Macmillan.

Billingsley, A. B. (1994). Dreaming a new reality: Psychiatric services focus on creative arts therapy. *Richmond Times Dispatch,* Thursday, April 7, E1–E2.

Blackeney, C. D., & Blackeney, R. A. (1991). Understanding and reforming moral misbehavior among behaviorally disordered adolescents. *Behavioral Disorders, 16*(2), 120–126.

Brendtro, L. K., Brokenleg, M., & Van Bockern, S. (1990). *Reclaiming youth at risk: Our hope for the future.* Bloomington, IN: National Educational Service.

Brendtro, L. K., & Brokenleg, M. (1993). Beyond the curriculum of control. *Journal of Emotional and Behavioral Problems, 1*(4), 5–11.

Bronfenbrenner, U. (1986). Alienation and the four worlds of childhood. *Phi Delta Kappan, 67,* 430–436.

Canfield, J., & Siccone, F. (1993). *101 ways to develop student self-esteem and responsibility: Volume I: The teacher as coach.* Boston: Allyn & Bacon.

Coopersmith, S. (1967). *The antecedents of self esteem.* San Francisco: W. H. Freeman.

Crowley, E. P. (1993). A qualitative analysis of mainstreamed behaviorally disordered aggressive adolescents' perceptions of helpful and unhelpful teacher attitudes and behaviors. *Exceptionality, 4*(3), 131–151.

Curwin, R. (1994). Helping students rediscover hope. *Journal of Emotional and Behavioral Problems, 3*(1), 27–30.

Ellis, A. (1959). Requisite conditions for basic personality change. *Journal of Consulting Psychology, 23,* 538–549.

Erikson, E. (1947). Ego development and historic change. *Psychoanalytic Study of the Child, 2,* 359–397.

Evans, D., & Eversole, K. (1992). Children as conflict managers. *Journal of Emotional and Behavioral Problems, 1*(2), 39–40.

Gaston, E. T. (Ed.). (1968). *Music in therapy.* New York: Macmillan.

Gil, E. (1991). *The healing power of play: Working with abused children.* New York: The Guilford Press.

Goldstein, A. P., & Segall, M. H. (Eds.). (1983). *Aggression in global perspective.* New York: Pergamon.

Gordon, T. (1974). *Teacher effectiveness training.* New York: Peter H. Wyden.

Hallahan, D. P., Lloyd, J. W., & Stoller, L. (1982). *Improving attention with self-monitoring: A manual for teachers.* Charlottesville, VA: University of Virginia.

Hedin, D. (1989). The power of community service. *Proceedings of the Academy of Political Science, 37*(2), 201–212.

Hobbs, N. (1982). *The troubled and troubling child: Re-education in mental health, education and human services programs for children and youth.* San Francisco: Jossey-Bass.

Hunter, L. B. (1993). Sibling play therapy with homeless children: An opportunity in the crisis. *Child Welfare, 72*(1), 65–74.

Ioele, M. D., & Dolan, A. L. (1992). Teaching courage: Service learning at Pathway School. *Journal of Emotional and Behavioral Problems, 1*(3), 20–23.

Johnson, D. W., & Johnson, R. T. (1986). Mainstreaming and cooperative learning strategies. *Exceptional Children, 52,* 553–562.

Johnson, D. W., & Johnson, R. T. (1991). *Teaching students to be peacemakers.* Edina, MN: Interaction Book Company.

Johnson, D. W., Johnson, R. T., Dudley, B., & Burnett, R. (1992). Teaching students to be peer mediators. *Educational Leadership, 50*(1), 10–13.

Keyes, M. F. (1974). *The inward journey.* Millbrae, CA: Celestial Arts.

Kirschenbaum, H., & Simon, S. B. (Eds.). (1973). *Readings in values clarification.* Minneapolis, MN: Winston Press.

Knitzer, J., Steinberg, Z., & Fleisch, B. (1990). *At the schoolhouse door: An examination of programs and policies for children with behavioral and emotional problems.* New York: Bank Street College of Education.

Kohlberg, L. (1975). The cognitive-developmental approach to moral education. *Phi Delta Kappan, 56,* 670–677.

Kohlberg, L. (1978). The cognitive-developmental approach to behavior disorders: A study of the development of moral reasoning in delinquents. In G. Serban (Ed.), *Cognitive defects in the development of mental illness* (pp. 199–220). New York: Bruner-Mazel.

Kramer, E. (1979). *Childhood and art therapy: Notes on theory and application.* New York: Schocken.

Landreth, G. L. (1991). *Play therapy: The art of the relationship.* Muncie, IN: Accelerated Development, Inc.

Lenkowsky, R. S. (1987). Bibliotherapy: A review and analysis of the literature. *The Journal of Special Education, 21*(2), 123–130.

Lickona, T. (1991). *Educating for character: How our schools can teach respect and responsibility.* New York: Bantam Books.

Lickona, T. (1993). The return of character education. *Educational Leadership, 51*(3), 6–11.

Maag, J. W. (1989). Moral discussion group interventions: Promising technique or wishful thinking? *Behavioral Disorders, 14*(2), 99–106.

Maslow, A. (1962). *Toward a psychology of being.* Princeton, NJ: Van Nostrand.

Mendler, A. N. (1992). *What do I do when? How to achieve discipline with dignity in the classroom.* Bloomington, IN: National Educational Service.

Morse, W. C. (1976a). The crisis or helping teacher. In N. J. Long, W. C. Morse, & R. G. Newman (Eds.), *Conflict in the classroom: The education of emotionally disturbed children* (3rd ed.) (pp. 207–213). Belmont, CA: Wadsworth.

Morse, W. C. (1976b). The helping teacher/crisis teacher concept. *Focus on Exceptional Children, 8*(4), 1–11.

Newcomer, P. L. (1993). *Understanding and teaching emotionally disturbed children and adolescents* (2nd ed.). Austin, TX: Pro-Ed.

Nichols, P. (1986). Down the up staircase: The teacher as therapist. *Teaching Behaviorally Disordered Youth, 2,* 1–13.

Nordoff, P., & Robbins, C. (1971). *Therapy in music for handicapped children.* New York: St. Martin's Press.

Ouzts, D. (1991). The emergence of bibliotherapy as a discipline. *Reading Horizons, 31*(3), 199–206.

Pardeck, J. A., & Pardeck, J. T. (1984). *Young people with problems: A guide to bibliotherapy.* Westport, CN: Greenwood Press.

Raths, L. E., Harmin, M., & Simon, S. B. (1966). *Values and teaching: Working with values in the classroom.* Columbus, OH: Merrill.

Reith, H. J., Polsgrove, L., McCleskey, J., Payne, K., & Anderson, R. (1978). The use of self-recording to increase the arithmetic performance of severely behaviorally disordered students. In R. B. Rutherford & A. G. Prieto (Eds.), *Severe behavior disorders of children and youth* (pp. 50–58). Monograph in behavioral disorders, Arizona State University, Tempe.

Riordan, R. J., & Wilson, L. S. (1989). Bibliotherapy: Does it work? *Journal of Counseling and Development, 67,* 506–508.

Robbins, A., & Sibley, L. B. (1976). *Creative art therapy.* New York: Brunner/Mazel.

Rogers, C. (1951). *Client centered therapy.* Boston: Houghton Mifflin.

Rogers, C. (1961). *On becoming a person.* Boston: Houghton Mifflin.

Rogers, C. (1969). *Freedom to learn.* Columbus, OH: Merrill.

Rubin, J. A. (1978). *Child art therapy: Understanding and helping children grow through art.* New York: Van Nostrand Reinhold.

Ryan, K. (1993). Mining the values in the curriculum. *Educational Leadership, 51*(3), 16–18.

Salend, S. J., Jantzen, N. R., & Giek, K. (1992). Using a peer confrontation system in a group setting. *Behavioral Disorders, 17*(3), 211–218.

Sasso, G., & Reimers, C. (1988). Assessing the functional properties of behavior: Implications and applications for the classroom. *Focus on Autistic Behavior, 3*(4), 1–6.

Schaefer, C., & O'Connor, K. (1983). *Handbook of play therapy.* New York: John Wiley & Sons.

Schonert, K. A., & Cantor, G. N. (1991). Moral reasoning in behaviorally disordered adolescents from alternative and traditional high schools. *Behavioral Disorders, 17*(1), 23–35.

Schrumpf, F. (1991). *Peer mediation: Conflict resolution in schools.* Champaign, IL: Research Press.

Siccone, F., & Canfield, J. (1993). *101 ways to develop student self-esteem and responsibility: Volume II: The power to succeed in school and beyond.* Boston: Allyn & Bacon.

Simon, S. B. (1974). *Meeting yourself halfway: 81 values clarification activities for daily living.* Niles, IL: Argus Communications.

Simon, S. B. (1976). *Caring, feeling, touching.* Niles, IL: Argus Communications.

Slavin, R. E. (1990). *Cooperative learning: Theory, research and practice.* Englewood Cliffs, NJ: Prentice-Hall.

Slavin, R. E. (1991). Synthesis of research on cooperative learning. *Educational Leadership, 48*(6), 71–82.

Steiger, L. K. (Ed.). (1987). *Participant workbook: Nonviolent crisis intervention.* Brookfield, WI: National Crisis Prevention Institute.

Swarthout, D. W. (1988). Enhancing the moral development of behaviorally/emotionally handicapped students. *Behavioral Disorders, 14*(1), 57–68.

Sylwester, S. (1994). How emotions affect learning. *Educational Leadership, 52*(2), 60–65.

Uhlin, D. M. (1992). *Art for exceptional children.* Dubuque, Iowa: William C. Brown.

Ulman, E., & Levy, C. A. (Eds.). (1980). *Art therapy viewpoints.* New York: Schocken.

Varenhorst, B. B. (1992). Developing youth as resources to their peers. *Journal of Emotional and Behavioral Problems, 1*(3), 10–14.

Vorrath, H., & Brendtro, L. (1985). *Positive peer culture* (2nd ed.). New York: Aldine DeGruyter.

Williams, M. M. (1993). Actions speak louder than words: What students think. *Educational Leadership, 51*(3), 22–23.

Wood, M. M., & Long, N. J. (1991). *Life space intervention: Talking with children and youth in crisis.* Austin, TX: Pro-Ed.

Wynne, E. A., & Ryan, K. (1992). *Reclaiming our schools: A handbook for teaching character, academics and discipline.* Columbus, OH: Merrill.

Zaccaria, J. S., Moses, H. A., & Hollowell, J. S. (1978). *Bibliotherapy in rehabilitation, educational, and mental health settings: Theory, research, and practice.* Champaign, IL: Stipes.

IMPROVING BEHAVIORS

Main Ideas:

♦ *The effectiveness of the behavioral model is well documented by research. Methods and procedures developed within this model are extremely powerful; therefore, teachers must consider what is in the best interest of students before implementing any behavior change program.*

♦ *Both positive and negative reinforcement increase and maintain behavior. Understanding and using reinforcement is an essential skill for teachers of students with behavioral disorders.*

♦ *Punishment decreases the behavior of students. Punishment can, however, lead to escalating battles for control and to an aversive classroom environment that students may wish to avoid. Teachers must use nonaversive behavior reduction strategies and the least restrictive or instrusive procedures possible to reduce or eliminate problem behavior.*

♦ *Professionals must always determine and reward appropriate replacement behaviors before considering the reduction of inappropriate behaviors. Teaching appropriate alternative behaviors is the focus of an effective behavior management plan.*

When you provide a positive, safe, and supportive classroom atmosphere where students feel that their opinions are valued and that they belong, and when you present challenging and meaningful academic tasks at which students experience real success, you are likely to help many children and youth with emotional and behavioral disorders improve their self-esteem, behavior, and motivation for learning. Some students, however, will not know *how* to behave. Children like Paul, for example, are distrustful and argumentative, frequently provoking fights with peers and refusing to comply with the requests of teachers. Yet Paul is behaving in the only way he knows how, the only way that makes sense to a youngster who has been physically abused by a stepfather and who has been in and out of numerous foster care homes. Paul has learned these behaviors as survival skills in his hostile and inconsistent world.

Other children will be *unable* to control their behavior. Students like Keesha are immature and distractible or low in cognitive and verbal ability. These students are simply not able to persist at tasks or restrain their impulses for long periods of time. When children are immature or unable to control their behavior or when children have not yet learned how to behave appropriately, teachers must assume a directive role, taking on the responsibility for controlling inappropriate behaviors while simultaneously teaching more appropriate behaviors and social skills.

In Chapter 4, we introduced the behavioral school of thought. This model, you may recall, is based primarily on the work of B.F. Skinner (1953, 1968) who believed that all behavior is learned and controlled by events in the environment. From the behavioral perspective, then, teachers must be directive (Figure 7.1). They must, for example, analyze the relationship between Paul's behaviors and environmental events, structure the environment to produce "on-task behavior" for Keesha, and arrange consequences to increase and maintain appropriate behaviors for both children. Within this model, teachers are not insensitive to the feelings of students such as Paul and Keesha; however, emotions, like

Key ideas
- Observe and analyze behavior
- Structure the environment
- Arrange consequences to reward appropriate behavior

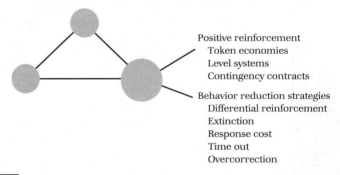

Positive reinforcement
  Token economies
  Level systems
  Contingency contracts
Behavior reduction strategies
  Differential reinforcement
  Extinction
  Response cost
  Time out
  Overcorrection

FIGURE 7.1

Directive Model (Behavioral Approach)

behaviors, are considered to be the result of environmental events and not the cause of our actions (Skinner, 1989). The focus in this school of thought is clearly on observable behaviors, structured environments, and controlled consequences.

Much research is available documenting the efficacy of behavioral interventions. Cullinan, Epstein, and Lloyd (1991) maintain that the behavioral model has a high level of intervention replicability, efficiency, and breadth when compared with other schools of thought. Many effective strategies for improving behaviors and social skills are derived from applications of behavioral theory and these strategies are among those most commonly seen in classrooms for children and youth with emotional and behavioral disorders (Knitzer, Steinberg, & Fleisch, 1990).

The behavioral model is not without its critics, however. Steinberg (1991), for example, reports that in many classrooms for students with behavioral disorders control has become an end in itself rather than a means to an end. Steinberg (1991) maintains that point systems are useful temporary measures for helping students improve behaviors and skills; yet, she asserts that many teachers continue their point systems when they no longer are motivating students to learn or behave. She suggests that the prolonged use of such behavior management techniques stifles real opportunities for children to learn how to be responsible and focuses attention on obeying a teacher who must become the arbiter and reward giver.

Kohn (1993) also believes that a focus on rewards and punishment is counterproductive. He maintains that rewards, contingent on particular behaviors, serve only to motivate children and youth to work for additional rewards. Instead of helping students to be responsible, intrinsically motivated, and proud of themselves, Kohn (1993) contends that rewards and punishments perpetuate external motivation and result in only temporary compliance and a continued need for control.

Nichols (1992), on the other hand, argues that control is necessary for a productive and safe learning environment and that society and school administrators certainly expect teachers to control their classrooms. Teachers who maintain quiet, orderly classrooms are rewarded by their colleagues as well as by supervisors and most parents. She also asserts that when rewards are given in such a way as to signify competence rather than emphasize control students will not suffer a decrease in their intrinsic motivation (Deci, Nezlek, & Sheinman, 1981).

Professionals have long debated the importance of extrinsic motivation (i.e., working for rewards like points, praise, or grades) versus intrinsic motivation (i.e., working for the sake of learning) for improving the academic performance and behavior of students. See Box 7.1 (p. 202) for some opinions of teachers regarding intrinsic and extrinsic motivation. DeCharms (1968, 1976), for example, postulates that intrinsic motivation arises from an individual's need to be in control of his or her own behaviors. Deci and his colleagues also define intrinsic motivation as one's sense of self-determination and competence (Deci, 1975, 1980; Deci & Ryan, 1985; Deci & Chandler, 1986). Harter (1978, 1981), too, hypothesizes that intrinsic motivation in children develops as rewards from adults accompany mastery rather than dependency. That is, when children

Teacher Feature: Responses to Control

In the Winter 1992, issue of *Beyond Behavior,* a professional journal published by the Council for Children with Behavior Disorders, readers were asked to react to several recent articles depicting classrooms for students with emotional/behavioral disorders as entrenched in a curriculum of control. Teachers and teacher educators voiced their opinions, ambivalence, and concerns regarding intrinsic and extrinsic motivation and control in the classroom. Of the 146 respondents, 114 agreed and 16 disagreed with the statement that: "Classrooms of control characterize the school day world of children with emotional or behavioral disabilities and their teachers." Following are some of the teachers' comments:

Until administrators want more than control and stop evaluating BD rooms on that basis, *real* education for these children will not evolve. (Illinois)

As long as *classroom control* is equated with *good teacher,* this will exist. (Pennsylvania)

We as teachers are evaluated on how well we *control* our classes, not on how well we meet the emotional or social needs of our students. (Alabama)

I agree this is the way it is, however not the way it should be. The push in most schools is into the regular classroom. Regular classrooms demand controlled students. (Rhode Island)

Agree—and I have no problem with it. Better for the child to be in a classroom of control than a prison cell of control. (Kansas)

I don't view this as a negative concept. These BD children lack control in their environment, thus until inner control is developed, control (along with order and stability) is needed from the environment. (Florida)

I agree, but how much change can a teacher expect? How do we help others control anger? What else is available besides a token economy? When you're up to your ass in alligators, it's hard to remember your mission was to drain the swamp. (Missouri)

develop feelings of competence and believe they are in control of their success or failure, they engage in additional mastery behaviors and develop a self-reward system. As a matter of fact, Adelman and Taylor (1990) and Switzky and Schultz (1988) maintain that much misbehavior of students with learning and emotional and behavioral disorders derives from their lack of perceived control in their environments. These authorities suggest that although students with behavioral disorders may require a more controlling approach initially their teachers must move beyond external rewards and punishments to focus instead on specific feedback regarding student performance and progress.

Teachers must not assume, however, that a focus on external control or a preference for the behavioral model is "wrong." When students are unable to control their own actions or when students do not know appropriate ways to behave, teachers must exercise control. At the risk of sounding facetious, when you're "hip deep in alligators" you'd better build a structure to stand on, at least until the alligators learn how to do something other than bite! Moreover, if students have experienced only frustration and failure with academic tasks, they will not be intrinsically motivated to pursue learning. Teachers, then, must provide extrinsic rewards to motivate students to work at these "unappealing" tasks.

The behavioral model is well researched and clearly offers the teacher many effective ways to help children learn appropriate behaviors and social skills. The problem of control lies not in the model itself, but rather with an incorrect implementation of the model. Criticism results when teachers are rewarded primarily for "controlling" their classrooms, when they fail to monitor and adjust strategies to meet the needs of individual students, or when they focus on punishment to the exclusion of reinforcement. Problems result, as well, when teachers continue to rely on external reward systems such as points or tokens rather than gradually "weaning" students off the system whenever possible and toward those rewards occurring naturally for most children.

In this chapter, then, we will focus on behavioral interventions effective in classrooms for children and youth with emotional and behavioral disorders. First, we will examine the importance of carefully defining all student behaviors you are considering for change and of analyzing the relationship between those behaviors and environmental events. Next, we will discuss the critical role of reinforcement for increasing and maintaining the appropriate behaviors of students with emotional and behavioral disorders. Finally, we will review the use of nonaversive consequences for reducing the inappropriate behaviors of these students.

Defining, Measuring, and Analyzing Behaviors

As a teacher of children and youth with behavioral disorders, you will be confronted constantly with actions of your students that you, or others, will find unacceptable or troubling. Some students will exhibit behavioral excesses while some will have behavioral deficits. Keesha, for example, is constantly "off task" and "not paying attention." She must learn to stay on task and pay attention for longer periods of time. Paul "argues," "fights," and is "rude to others." He needs to learn alternatives for his aggressive actions. Fong, on the other hand, "never socializes" with his classmates. He must be helped to interact more with his peers.

How will you know when a behavior needs to be changed? Where do you begin when students like Paul have so many troublesome behaviors at once? How will you know when Keesha is "on-task" or that she is "paying attention" more than before? To answer these questions and make wise decisions about a child's behavior, you must first prioritize behaviors you are considering for change and justify why you believe a change is necessary. In addition, you must define and measure the behaviors under consideration for change and analyze the relationship between those behaviors and events occurring in the child's environment.

Teachers must have good justification for targeting behaviors for change. Behavioral methodology is powerful and easily misused; therefore, teachers who behave ethically consider the impact of a behavioral change on the student and important others. Rather than capriciously changing a student's behavior because it is irritating or annoying or because you wish to establish "law and order," as an ethical teacher you must consider whether the change is in the best interests of the student (Alberto & Troutman, 1995). Students have a right to effective treatments designed to change socially significant behaviors (i.e., behaviors that are necessary in order for the child to learn other important skills and behaviors or behaviors that will help the child gain access to reinforcement occurring naturally in the environment) (Van Houten et al., 1988). In addition, when teachers keep the best interests of students in mind, they plan to teach appropriate behaviors instead of simply focusing on eliminating inappropriate ones.

Often, students will have clusters of similar behaviors, all of which are troublesome in the classroom. Paul, for example, demonstrates a cluster of aggressive actions including fighting, arguing, teasing others, and making rude comments to you and to peers. Certainly changing these behaviors will be in Paul's best interest, and each of these behaviors might legitimately be targeted for change. The teacher would do well, however, to prioritize these behaviors first and select only one or two for change initially. Cooper, Heron, and Heward (1987) offer the following guidelines when prioritizing behaviors:

1. Determine if the behavior is of danger to the individual or to others. Generally, we intervene immediately when behaviors are dangerous.
2. Determine the frequency of the present behavior or the child's opportunity to use a new behavior. Behaviors occurring at high frequency or those that will be used often are considered for change first over less frequent behaviors.
3. Determine the duration of the problem. Generally, behaviors that have existed or that have been needed over long periods of time take precedence over problems of shorter duration.
4. Determine which behavior will produce a higher level of reinforcement for the individual.
5. Determine the impact of the behavior on skill development and independence for the student.
6. Determine if learning the new behavior will reduce negative attention the individual receives from others.
7. Determine if learning the behavior will increase reinforcement for others in the student's environment.
8. Determine the time, energy, and cost required to change the behavior.

With Paul's "acting-out" behaviors, then, you might decide that fighting is certainly dangerous to Paul and to others. You must, of course, intervene immediately when Paul is actually fighting; however, you observe that Paul fights only one or two times a week. As you examine Paul's behaviors, you might note that Paul frequently teases other children and makes rude comments to them and that he has done so for a long period. Furthermore, you might notice that Paul's altercations often follow his teasing and rude comments, which provoke other students into fighting. You decide, then, to intervene first with Paul's provocative comments and taunting of others. You believe that replacing Paul's rude and teasing comments with more appropriate behaviors will result in a decrease in fighting and negative attention from others as well as an increase in the amount of reinforcement received by both Paul and his peers.

Once you have justified and prioritized behaviors under consideration for change, your next step is to define the behavior carefully so that you can observe and measure it objectively. When Keesha is paying attention, for example, exactly what is she doing and when is she doing it? Is she paying attention during reading time but not during math time? You might define *paying attention* as writing answers to math problems. Suppose, however, that Keesha is looking at her math book or paper but not actually writing. Is Keesha paying attention or not paying attention in this instance? How you define *paying attention* is important because you must consistently observe the same behavior to measure and record behavioral change.

As a general rule, clear behavioral definitions are stated in observable and measurable terms. Clear behavioral definitions enable teachers to see the behavior as it occurs and count or time it accurately. Furthermore, if a targeted behavior is well defined, someone else should be able to use the definition and "see" the same behavior, counting the same number of occurrences or clocking the behavior for the same amount of time as you do. Keesha's "paying attention during math" behavior, then, might be defined as "Any instance when Keesha is writing answers on her math paper, looking at her math book or math paper, looking at the teacher when the teacher is giving instructions or directions, looking at a student who has been recognized by the teacher to speak, or looking at the chalkboard or other materials when the teacher is pointing to these." Clearly, the teacher can observe these particular behaviors and count or time them. Using this definition, Keesha is paying attention during math when she is engaging in any of these specified behaviors and she is not paying attention if she is demonstrating any other behaviors. If Keesha is looking at her pencil or talking to someone else, for example, she is not paying attention according to this behavioral definition.

When you have defined the target behavior clearly, you can then measure and record occurrences of the behavior and analyze the relationship between the behavior and environmental events. You may recall in Chapter 2 our discussion of anecdotal recording, event recording, duration and latency recording, and momentary time sampling procedures. You may wish to review these methods for counting, timing, and analyzing behaviors targeted for change. Using these techniques, you can easily place the data collected onto a line graph to determine the level of a child's behavior and any increases or decreases in that behavior during intervention. Inspecting data visually presented on a graph such as that depicted in Box 7.2 (pp. 206–207) enables the teacher to make decisions about the effectiveness of a chosen intervention.

At this point, you may also wish to review the characteristics of effective programs for students with emotional and behavioral disorders described in Chapter 5. The teacher must structure the classroom to facilitate learning and provide clear and reasonable rules and consequences for student actions, for example, to promote appropriate behavior (Stainback, Stainback, & Froyen, 1987). To prevent many discipline problems from occurring, teachers must ensure that students understand the rules and consequences, that rules and

BOX 7.2 **Case Study: Increasing Fong's Social Interactions With Peers on the Playground**

Fong often covers his head and refuses to talk when peers approach him in his classroom or on the playground. Consequently, his classmates walk away or often ignore Fong, leaving him alone. Following an anecdotal record of playground antecedents, behaviors, and consequences, you decide to increase Fong's social interactions with his peers on the playground. You justify this target behavior as important to Fong because social interactions are both prerequisite for maintenance in the regular classroom and necessary if Fong is to hold a job or receive reinforcement in the natural environment. You select the playground for the first intervention because of the number of opportunities present for classmates to interact with Fong, and you define social interactions as "Any time Fong responds appropriately to a classmate's statement, request, or question, verbally or physically, without covering his head."

You conduct a frequency count for the first three days during each of two 10-minute playground times, one in the morning and one in the afternoon. You count the following number of social interactions: 0,0,1,0,0,1. You decide to intervene by rewarding Russell, a high-status classmate, for approaching Fong and engaging him in conversation or simple play without walking away. Because Russell is highly regarded by his peers, you believe that others will also interact with Fong as Russell does. As you begin the intervention, you count the following number of social interactions for a one week period: 1,1,2,1,2,3,2,3,3,4.

You plot the data on a line graph depicting baseline (i.e., data recorded during your preintervention phase) and intervention. You note that Fong's social interactions with Russell, as well as with other classmates, are gradually increasing from a level of approximately 0 per observation session to an average

consequences are reviewed frequently, and that students have abundant opportunities to practice and be rewarded for following the rules (Rosenberg, 1986). Moreover, when students are actively involved in meaningful learning tasks inappropriate behavior is minimized and opportunities to reward appropriate behaviors are maximized (Sabatino, 1987).

Increasing Appropriate Behaviors

Notice in Figure 7.2 that the teacher's concern is to *increase* Fong's social interactions instead of to decrease his head covering. All too often, teachers focus on reducing or eliminating inappropriate behaviors rather than considering appropriate alternative behaviors to increase (Alberto & Troutman, 1995). The key to success within the behavioral model is to accentuate the positive to eliminate the negative (Webber & Scheuermann, 1991). That is, teachers must determine ways to reward or reinforce children for their appropriate behaviors instead of chastising them for their poor behaviors.

Reinforcement occurs when a stimulus follows a behavior and increases the likelihood of the behavior occurring again in the future. Positive reinforcement

of 2.2 per session, with an increasing trend. You conclude that for practical purposes the intervention is successful and you decide to continue the intervention on the playground. You also begin a baseline for social interactions in the cafeteria during lunchtime.

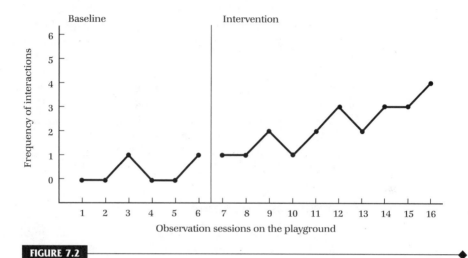

Fong's Social Interactions on the Playground During Twice-Daily Recess Periods

involves the presentation of a stimulus that a student finds pleasant (e.g., earning ten points for coming to class on time) immediately following a behavior. Positive reinforcement is effective because students work to earn something that is rewarding. On the other hand, negative reinforcement means a stimulus, usually something aversive or unpleasant to the student, is removed, or the possibility of it is removed, immediately following a behavior (e.g., If Shelley completes her work during the designated class time, she will not have homework). Therefore, negative reinforcement increases behavior because individuals try to avoid or escape something unpleasant to them. Both positive and negative reinforcement *increase* behavior.

Teachers must certainly understand the effects of negative reinforcement in the classroom. For example, suppose Paul curses and has temper tantrums whenever you request that he completes his math assignments. These temper tantrums are quite unpleasant to you; therefore, you send Paul out of the room and to the office. The aversive stimulus (e.g., Paul's inappropriate language and his loud tantrum) is removed. If in the future you are more likely to send Paul out of the room when he curses and has tantrums, your behavior has been negatively reinforced.

Suppose, too, that Paul dislikes his math assignments. When Paul uses foul language and has a temper tantrum, the unpleasant math assignment is removed. If Paul's tantrums increase in the future as a result of the removal of the math assignment, his behavior is also being negatively reinforced. As a matter of fact, Paul may also experience some quite pleasant consequences in the hall and while sitting in the office.

As a teacher, then, you must understand negative reinforcement to prevent yourself from engaging in negative reinforcement traps and escalating coercive battles for control with students like Paul (Patterson, 1982). Moreover, negative reinforcement may be an important factor in helping students develop adaptive behaviors in the classroom. Teachers can, for example, arrange consequences such that students will behave positively to avoid losing coveted privileges (e.g., Paul must complete his work to avoid losing time on the computer or playground). Because negative reinforcement involves aversive stimuli that may lead to escape and avoidance behaviors, teachers must take care when using this procedure. You will want your students to work and behave because they enjoy being in your classroom, not because they are trying to avoid unpleasant reactions. Overreliance on negative reinforcement may result in a contentious classroom atmosphere; therefore, we will focus our discussions on positive reinforcement instead.

Positive Reinforcement

Positive reinforcement means the contingent presentation of a consequence that increases or maintains a behavior. We say that positive reinforcement has occurred only when a consequence follows a particular behavioral response and that response is maintained or increased as a result of the presentation of the consequence. For example, when Keesha consistently completes all of her math problems correctly in the 20-minute period to receive ten minutes at the computer, we might say that Keesha's math completion behavior is being positively reinforced by earning computer time. Similarly, when Dante makes rude comments to the teacher and these comments are immediately followed by peer laughter, we might say that Dante's rude comment behavior is being reinforced by peer attention.

We can determine that reinforcement is occurring *only by observing the effect of a consequence on a behavior*. When a behavioral response continues or increases when it is immediately followed by the presentation of some stimulus, positive reinforcement is occurring. Thus, you may believe that a particular stimulus is a "positive" one (e.g., You smile and say, "Good job!" each time Keesha raises her hand in class); however, you observe a decrease in Keesha's hand-raising behavior. In this case, smiling and saying "Good job" is not positive reinforcement. Or, conversely, you believe a stimulus is "negative" (e.g., You fuss, "Paul, you know we don't use that sort of language in this class! You stop that this instant!") only to find that Paul's inappropriate language is increasing rather than decreasing. Your fussing may be positive reinforcement for Paul's poor language choices. Consequences are neither inherently good or bad, positive or negative. We can determine that positive reinforcement has occurred only when a stimulus is presented immediately following a behavior and that behavior

**Examples of Primary and Secondary Reinforcers
Appropriate for the Classroom**

Primary Reinforcers: Natural, unlearned, biological

Edibles—food and liquids such as popcorn, raisins, crackers, juice, water.

Sensory experiences—visual, auditory, or kinesthetic activities like listening to music through headphones.

Secondary Reinforcers: Conditioned, learned

Tangible objects—trinkets, toys, pencils, badges, stickers, certificates.

Privileges and activities—first to recess, line leader, opportunity to play a special game or complete a special project.

Social reinforcers—smiles, physical proximity, verbal praise, winks.

Generalized reinforcers—reinforcers allowing access to other primary or secondary reinforcers including points, tokens, money, grades.

continues or increases. Teachers are encouraged to consider the following guidelines when using positive reinforcement:

1. Ensure that students will not have access to the reinforcer unless they earn it.
2. Remember the individual nature of reinforcement (i.e., what you may like, the child may not like).
3. Reinforce approximations of the final target behavior.
4. Reinforce continuously and immediately to build a behavior.
5. Reinforce intermittently after a behavior has been established.

Positive reinforcement describes the relationship between a behavior and a consequence. *Positive reinforcer* is the term for the consequence itself if the consequence immediately follows the behavior, is contingent on the behavior, and increases or maintains the future probability of occurrence of the behavior (Alberto & Troutman, 1995). Positive reinforcers may be either primary (i.e., the reinforcer is natural and of biological importance such as edibles and liquids) or secondary (i.e., the reinforcing properties of these stimuli are learned or conditioned through pairing with primary reinforcers). See Box 7.3 for some examples of primary and secondary reinforcers appropriate for use in the classroom.

Primary and Secondary Reinforcers. Teachers may need to use primary reinforcers when students have not yet learned an appropriate behavior or when students are demonstrating an important behavior at only a very low rate. Primary reinforcers are powerful and quickly increase behaviors; yet teachers must exercise caution with their use. Students may become rapidly satiated when given several pieces of candy in a row, for example. Thus, the candy loses its reinforcing properties. Teachers would do well to vary primary reinforcers like edibles (e.g., a sip of juice, then one piece of popcorn, then a raisin, etc.) and pair a secondary reinforcer such as praise with the presentation of a primary reinforcer. In addition, teachers must ensure that a particular primary reinforcer is not medically contraindicated or forbidden by parents.

Similarly, teachers must exercise caution when choosing secondary reinforcers. Parents, for example, may not appreciate their child coming home with noisemaking toys or rock star trading cards. When selecting potential reinforcers, primary or secondary, teachers are advised to use the following guidelines:

- Consider the age and interests of the student.
- Ask the student what he or she prefers.
- Ask the parents or guardians what the student prefers and what is acceptable.
- Observe the student to determine what he or she selects.
- Choose the most natural reinforcer possible that is acceptable to all involved.
- Observe the effects of the chosen reinforcer on the student's behavior, and adjust the reinforcer as data indicate.

Primary reinforcers must gradually be replaced with secondary reinforcers if students are to succeed in the classroom and in the community. Many trinkets and material objects that might serve as tangible reinforcers are obtainable at little cost from yard sales (e.g., games, books, balls, rock star posters, inexpensive jewelry) or from asking parents for donations through either a class letter or an appeal to the school's parent-teacher organization. In addition, teachers have successfully requested gift certificates from local merchants (e.g., for meals at a local fast food chain) and items from school stores (e.g., school pencils and pens, banners, pins, hats, notebooks, paper, erasers, T-shirts).

Activities and privileges also abound within the school and at home. Students may work to earn many privileges (e.g., exempting themselves from homework or from a quiz, extra time at recess, watching a favorite television show at home) or activities (e.g., a popcorn party, playing a game). Premack (1959) first described the use of activities as reinforcers. The Premack Principle states that a more preferred activity should follow and serve as a reinforcer for less preferred activities. Thus, when Keesha correctly completes her math problems (i.e., a less preferred activity) to earn 10 minutes at the computer (i.e., a more preferred activity), the teacher is applying the premack principle. The activity must, of course, be available immediately and be contingent on the student's demonstration of the appropriate target behavior. That is, if Keesha can obtain time at the computer without completing her math problems, computer time will not be a sensible activity reinforcer.

Similarly, teachers may use many forms of social reinforcers in the classroom including winks, smiles, gestures of approval, positive notes and awards, and proximity to a child. Verbal praise, particularly when it is immediate, varied, and specific, is effective with many students (O'Leary & O'Leary, 1977). For example, instead of repetitively saying "Good job" (i.e., a form of general praise), the teacher using specific praise might state, "Paul, that was a nice job of following my directions. You put your reading book in your desk right away." Box 7.4 provides some examples of activities and privileges and social reinforcers useful for teachers. Of course, teachers must not erroneously assume that the same stimulus will be reinforcing to every student or that the same stimulus will

BOX 7.4 Activities and Privileges and Social Reinforcers Useful in Classrooms

Activities and Privileges	Social Reinforcers
Access to gym or library	Winks
Computer time	Smile
Watch a video	"A-OK" sign with hands
Read a book or magazine	Eat lunch with teacher or special
Draw	person like the principal
Extra recess or playtime	Sit next to teacher
Exemption from homework	Verbal recognition: Super, Excellent,
Exemption from quiz	Outstanding, Looking good, Right
Assume a class role:	on, You've got it, Sensational,
Line leader	Terrific, Awesome, Rock 'n roll,
Pet tender	Hot dog, Fantastic, Perfect, Wow,
Messenger	You made it look easy, That's it,
Clean chalkboards	Good going, Good for you,
Clean erasers	Wonderful, Stupendous, Alright,
Water plants	Nice job, Well done, Marvelous,
Operate audiovisual equipment	Beautiful, Brilliant, That's a
Listen to tapes	winner!
Talk with peer	
Play a game	
Have snack or soda in class	
Choose own seat or work area	
Assist custodian, school secretary,	
lunch room staff	

continue to reinforce a particular student. Having a range of reinforcers available in the classroom increases the likelihood of always finding something for which students will work.

Like social reinforcers, generalized reinforcers are more like those occurring naturally for most children in regular classrooms. Students in the mainstream, for example, may work for grades or hold after school jobs to make money. Other generalized reinforcers, although not as "natural" as money or grades, include points or tokens. Generalized reinforcers are effective because they enable students to obtain other backup reinforcers. That is, Keesha may "trade-in" the points or tokens she earns for tangible rewards, for privileges and activities, or for primary reinforcers such as edibles. Often teachers will arrange token economies, level systems, or contingency contracts as the means through which students systematically earn these reinforcers.

Token Economies. A token economy is much like the use of money as a generalized reinforcer in society (Alberto & Troutman, 1995). Tokens (e.g., poker chips, buttons, stickers, or other durable objects) or points (e.g., holes punched in cards, numbers, check marks) are earned for specified behaviors, just as you might earn a paycheck for your performance at work. These points or tokens, then, may be traded for backup reinforcers having an assigned value like items in a store (e.g., 300 points to purchase a no homework pass, 50 points to buy a soda, 25 tokens to purchase a school pencil). Alberto and Troutman (1995) offer the following guidelines for using token economies:

- Clearly specify and post the behaviors that will earn points and tokens.
- Specify a range of backup reinforcers (e.g., everything from candy and soda, to special privileges, to trinkets), and post pictures of items available.
- Specify how many tokens or points must be earned to purchase each backup reinforcer. Be sure the cost of each item is proportional to its value to the students as well as to the difficulty of the behavioral demands. Students should not be able to purchase highly desirable items, such as games, easily nor should they be required to work extraordinarily hard and made to feel that even the less desired objects are out of their reach.
- Choose tokens that are durable and inexpensive and that students may not easily obtain on their own. If, for example, your students have access to pennies or to paper clips at home, they will quickly figure out how to give themselves the tokens. Consider marking tokens with a predetermined and not easily reproduced symbol to allow verification of all tokens earned.
- Randomly use different colors, stickers, or hole punch patterns for assigning points for student behavior.
- Provide a secure place for individual students to store their earned tokens.
- Arrange a record-keeping system so that students may tally their tokens or points, and make a note of their earnings (Figure 7.3). Some teachers use "bank accounts." Students earn paychecks that are deposited into "bank books," and they must make all purchases by writing checks. Through a record keeping system such as this, students practice addition and subtraction and learn functional skills such as balancing a checkbook.
- Initially, have students tally their points and tokens and exchange these for backup reinforcers frequently. You may, for example, provide time for this once in the morning and once in the afternoon. As student behavior improves, gradually reduce the number of times tokens are exchanged to once a day and then to once a week.
- Prevent students from "hoarding" their tokens by holding periodic sales during which you reduce the price of items not yet purchased. Also, ensure that students are not "in the hole." That is, token systems must be positive and based on earning rewards for appropriate behavior rather than on losing points or tokens for poor behavior.
- Periodically, change the items and prices used for backup reinforcers and adjust the behavioral requirements for students. As a particular behavior becomes easier for Keesha, for example, the point or token value assigned might be reduced and a new, more difficult, behavior with a higher assigned value might be added to Keesha's list.

Token economy systems work well when behaviors are specified for an entire group or when specific behaviors are listed for individual children. In addition, teachers might construct innovative contingency packages to maintain student interest in earning rewards and to motivate students to participate in activities at which they have previously experienced failure (Box 7.5, pp. 214–215). Teachers must, however, plan to move students away from reliance on token economy systems as behavior improves and toward those rewards occurring naturally in the classroom.

Schedules of Reinforcement and Level Systems. Regardless of the form of reinforcement or the token economy system used, teachers of students with emotional and behavioral disorders must enable their students to receive reinforcement in the regular classroom. Student-preferred rewards common to both special and regular education classrooms include grades, free time or special activities and privileges, and verbal praise; however, differences may exist

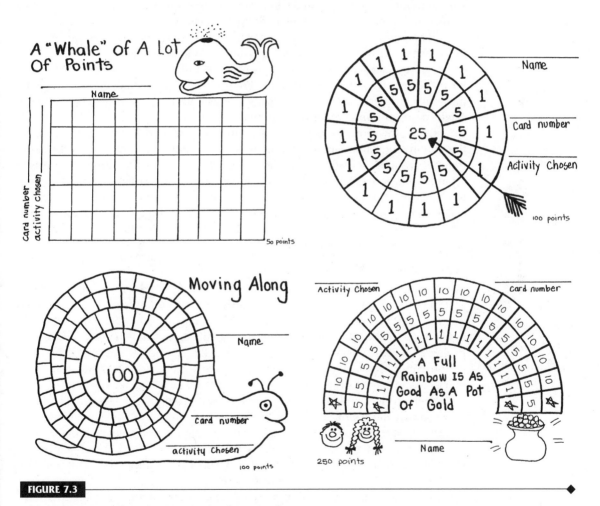

FIGURE 7.3

Cards for Recording Points Earned in a Token Economy   From: *It's Positively Fun: Techniques for Managing Learning Environments*, by P. Kaplan, J. Kohfeldt, and K. Sturla, pp. 31–32. Copyright © 1974 Love Publishing Company. Reprinted by permission.

BOX 7.5 **Contingency Packages for Motivating Students**

Contingency packages are one way to provide reluctant learners with tangible reminders of potential rewards. A contingency package is a three-dimensional structure designed to attractively advertise and display the incentives and rewards that students may earn. As part of the classroom management system, rules are developed that specify the conditions and behaviors for earning rewards. The specified behavioral contingencies may apply to all children within a group or they may be individualized for each child within the group. Periodically reviewing and modifying behavioral contingencies with a group or individual student assures that the operational system is understood.

The contingency package should be displayed in the classroom in such a way that it is in the students' visual range but is physically unattainable (e.g., on top of a high cupboard or in a case with sliding glass doors). In this way it provides students with a concrete visual reminder of the rewards available to them if they display the appropriate predetermined behaviors. . . . A contingency package should be designed so that it contains an element of novelty—presenting of new or unusual stimuli, usually arising from variations on familiar themes. . . . A contingency package theme that is meaningful, relevant, and age-appropriate will have the most appeal for students. For example, a football theme might be particularly appealing to an athletically inclined adolescent, while a robot theme might pique the imagination of younger learners.

Finally, the motivational package should be designed to provide variation in the contingency arrangements. Consistently presenting reinforcers in the same manner frequently leads to satiation. When this happens, a student's desire to continue a task or sustain task completion may be reduced significantly. One way to reduce satiation and enhance motivation is to offer an incentive package that reflects an element of chance in the contingency arrangement. Back-up bonus draws and rewards administered on variable reinforcement schedules provide the opportunity for "double payoff."

Flip-the-Lid Robot

This contingency package is most appropriate for elementary-age learners. Materials for the project include a 15-drawer storage cabinet or other partitioned box (e.g., ketchup or liquor shipping carton), construction paper, colored markers, scissors, and glue. A desirable item such as a small trinket, sticker, or preferred activity pass is placed in each drawer. The lid on the top of the head of the robot is constructed so that it flips open. Inside the head are small construction paper discs with a numeral from 1 to 15 on each.

When students meet the contingency criterion, they are permitted to select a drawer on the robot and keep the drawer's contents. Objects, activities, and stimuli placed in the drawers are based on student preferences. One drawer should contain in addition to the reward a "Lucky You" card, which allows the student to reach into the robot's head and select a free-time disk. The numeral on the disk represents the minutes of free time awarded.

Variations in the "Flip-the-Lid Robot" system can include varying the number of "Lucky You" cards available, the time awarded on the free-time disks, and the types of trinkets, stickers, and preferred activities available in the drawers. For a group contingency, the class can earn points collectively, and when a prespecified number of points has been obtained, each class member is then permitted to select a drawer. Such a group contingency encourages class members to support the efforts of class peers rather than compete against them.

Touchdown Triumph

This contingency package is most appropriate for adolescent learners. Materials to construct the project include a rectangular styrofoam base, pipe cleaners, golf tees, a miniature football, toothpicks, white paint, construction paper, a colored marker, and glue.

A football playing field is designed using a styrofoam base. Goal posts made from pipe cleaners are attached at opposite ends of the field. A golf tee with a football mounted on the top signals the yardage required for a touchdown. Yardage markers are provided on small flags attached to toothpicks, which are inserted on the sides of the playing field. A few of the toothpick bottoms can be colored green with a colored marker. "Special Play" cards and "Touchdown" cards are inserted into slots cut into the side of the football field for quick accessible draws.

The student selects a goal post, and the teacher is assigned the opposite goal post. The football is placed at the 50-yard line. When the student meets the specified contingency criterion, he or she is permitted to move the football 10 yards in the direction of the selected goal post. Upon moving the football, the student checks the yardage marker corresponding to the football placement, and if the yardage marker's tip is colored green, the student is permitted to select a "Special Play" card. These cards list reinforcing events, activities, and stimuli embedded in a rhyming format. Several examples follow:

- ◆ You caught the ball. You need a rest. You're entitled to skip a test.
- ◆ You're working hard to win this game. A school banner is yours for the fame.
- ◆ Even though you fumbled the ball in a clumsy handoff, you've earned film projectionist privileges which is nothing to scoff.
- ◆ The game of football can be rough. You've earned a "no homework pass" for being tough.
- ◆ You've made the team. You've passed the test. You've earned a poster for doing your best.

If the student does not meet the contingency criterion at the end of a prespecified time period, the teacher is permitted to move the football in the direction of his or her goal. Use of the contingency package continues in this manner until the player makes a touchdown and is awarded a "Touchdown" card. Each "Touchdown" card earns 6 minutes of free time for the student during the school day. Together, 10 touchdown cards could earn as much as 60 minutes of free time for the student.

Variations that can be built into "Touchdown Triumph" to maintain student interest include varying the number of bonus yardage markers and changing the awards on the "Special Play" cards. To further modify the contingency, a group of students may play as a team and compete against the teacher.

From "Motivating Reluctant Learners: Innovative Contingency Packages," by D. Raschke, C. Dedrick & M. Thompson, *Teaching Exceptional Children*, 19(2), 1987, pp. 18–20. Copyright © 1987 by The Council for Exceptional Children. Reprinted with permission.

in the amount and type of these reinforcers given students with behavioral disorders in the mainstream (Brady & Taylor, 1989; Martens, Muir, & Meller, 1988). Although students may require a high level of reinforcement initially, teachers must gradually and systematically reduce the amount of reinforcement given so that student behavior is maintained following a schedule of reinforcement similar to that in the regular classroom.

A schedule of reinforcement governs the timing and rate of delivery of rewards to students (Alberto & Troutman, 1995). When every occurrence of a behavior is met with a reward, the student is on a continuous schedule of reinforcement. For example, every time Keesha raises her hand to speak rather than blurting out her question or answer, she receives a piece of popcorn or a point. Obviously, Keesha might soon become tired of earning popcorn or points. Students on a continuous schedule of reinforcement are quite subject to satiation; therefore, this schedule is most appropriately used when teaching students new behaviors or when increasing behaviors that students initially display at very low levels.

Intermittent schedules of reinforcement, on the other hand, are less subject to problems of satiation and produce behaviors that tend to be maintained over time, even with very low rates of reward (Skinner, 1953). An intermittent schedule reinforces some, but not all, occurrences of the targeted behavior, more closely approximating reinforcement available in the natural environment of regular classrooms. You must remember, however, that inappropriate behaviors may also be reinforced intermittently and, therefore, may stubbornly resist change. Suppose, for example, your attention is reinforcing Paul's rude language behavior, and you attempt to ignore him each time he makes rude comments. If you occasionally "goof" and direct your attention to Paul when he makes these comments, you have placed his behavior on an intermittent schedule of reinforcement.

Intermittent schedules may involve a ratio (i.e., a specified number of behaviors are required for the reward) or an interval (i.e., following a specified period, an occurrence of the appropriate behavior is rewarded). In addition, both ratio and interval schedules may be fixed (e.g., every nth behavior is rewarded; or following the passage of x amount of time the appropriate behavior is reinforced) or variable (i.e., on the average every nth behavior is rewarded; or on the average x amount of time passes before an occurrence of the appropriate behavior is reinforced) (Skinner, 1953). When ratio or interval schedules are fixed, students may demonstrate a scalloped pattern of performance (Skinner, 1953). Keesha, for example, may raise her hand repeatedly until she achieves five hand raises to earn her reward. Then, she might pause before another burst of handraising activity. Or, Keesha may become habituated to the passage of time and engage in a flurry of handraising behavior at the end of a 3-minute time interval during which she also yells out many answers. Because students are never quite sure which occurrence of a behavior will result in a reward, variable schedules of reinforcement tend to produce steadier overall rates of appropriate responding (Alberto & Troutman, 1995).

Alberto and Troutman (1995) encourage teachers to begin reinforcement on a dense schedule (e.g., provide continuous reinforcement, a low fixed ratio of reinforcement, or a short fixed interval for reinforcement) and then gradually thin the amount of reinforcement given. Teachers might move, for example, from a continuous schedule, to a fixed ratio five, to a fixed ratio ten, to a variable ratio schedule of reinforcement for Keesha's handraising behavior. Although no hard and fast rules exist for setting behavior to reinforcement ratios, teachers are advised to ensure that students receive a high level of reinforcement initially.

Often, teachers will combine token economies with a systematic thinning of reinforcement in what is now termed a *level system* (Hewett, 1968; Hewett, Taylor, & Artuso, 1968). Within a level system, teachers structure a hierarchy of behavioral expectations and rewards. As students progress through the levels, they are expected to meet increased behavioral demands and demonstrate greater self-management, and in return, they are granted greater freedom, privileges, and rewards. Students advance from one level to the next by exceeding behavioral expectations or by accumulating a prespecified number of points. For major behavioral violations, a student may suffer the consequence of a temporary reduction in his or her level status. As students advance up the levels, they also receive less frequent reinforcement more like that available in the regular classroom.

One well-known example of a level system is that used by the Boys Town Education Model developed at Father Flanagan's Boys' Home in Nebraska (Wells, 1990). This motivational system uses a token economy through which students earn points for specific social skills and attempt to advance across three levels. All students enter at the level of daily points to build social skills. When students attain the progress level, feedback and points are less specific and immediate. Finally, the merit level fosters skill maintenance and generalization providing rewards primarily in the regular classroom.

Bauer, Shea, and Keppler (1986, p. 33) offer excellent guidelines for constructing level systems to individualize behavior management programs for students. These include the following:

1. Determine the usual entry-level behaviors of the students for whom the system is to be designed.
2. Determine the terminal behavior expectations for the students.
3. List at least two, but no more than four, sets of behavioral expectations that seem to be appropriate substeps between those behaviors listed in steps 1 and 2. Write these sets of graduated expectations on paper, labeling them *level 1* through *level 4.*
4. Determine the rewards and privileges appropriate for students beginning the program at Level 1.
5. Determine the rewards and privileges appropriate for students preparing to terminate the program (i.e., students who are at the highest level). These rewards and privileges should closely approximate those in the regular classroom.
6. For each level, list appropriate rewards and privileges, evenly distributed across the levels. Remember to reduce the amount of direct teacher supervision needed as students advance through the levels.
7. Consider the following questions:

◆ How frequently and in what way will a student's status be reviewed (e.g., weekly or biweekly meetings)?

◆ Will a minimum stay be required at each level?

◆ Who will review the student's status (e.g., student himself or herself, peers, teachers, administrators, parents)?

◆ What level of appropriate behavior will be required to remain at a particular level?

◆ What self-monitoring or teacher-monitoring procedures, such as checklists, will be needed?

8. Develop a communication system to share information about student behaviors and privileges at each level with parents, other teachers, and staff.

Although level systems are often described in the literature as an effective means for improving the behavior of students with emotional and behavioral disorders, few studies actually exist to support this claim (Mastropieri, Jenne, & Scruggs, 1988). As a matter of fact, Smith and Farrell (1993) maintain that levels systems in special education are simply classroom interventions having only prima facie appeal rather than research evidence of effectiveness. Others argue that level systems as they are commonly constructed are in violation of the Individuals with Disabilities Education Act of 1990 in that they do the following: (1) restrict access to general education and the least restrictive environment; (2) focus concern on group rather than individual expectations and needs; (3) emphasize arbitrary sequences of behaviors without providing a means for teaching these; (4) emphasize behaviors over academics as appropriate curriculum for students; and (5) mandate entry at the lowest level with no individualized criteria for entry or advancement (Scheuermann, Webber, Partin, & Knies, 1994). Teachers who use level systems should carefully consider these cautions and design ways to individualize behavioral and entry level requirements as well as criteria for advancement to meet the needs of particular students.

Contingency Contracts. One way to provide systematic yet individualized behavioral expectations and rewards is to write a contingency contract (Alberto & Troutman, 1995). A contingency contract is a written agreement stating a specified amount of behavior, to be completed by a particular date, which will result in a predetermined reward for the student. Student and teacher together write, sign, and date the contract (Figure 7.4).

Alberto and Troutman (1995) suggest that contracts serve as an excellent means for documenting and communicating student progress toward individual goals. In addition, contracts help students learn to negotiate, to become active participants in planning for their own education, and to assume greater control over their own learning and classroom environment. Homme (1970) offers several guidelines for contingency contracting in the classroom:

◆ The contract reward must be immediate and frequent. Provide students with the payoff immediately and give frequent small rewards rather than infrequent large ones.

◆ Phrase the contract to call for and reward small approximations (i.e., small steps) of the final behavior. For example, instead of requiring an entire

I've Got An Offer
You Can't Refuse

If_____

_____ by ____

Then_____

_____

_____

———————————————————————————————————
date   student   witness   Teacher

FIGURE 7.4

Sample Contingency Contract Form From *It's Positively Fun: Techniques for Managing Learning Environments*, by P. Kaplan, J. Kohfeldt, and K. Sturla, pp. 37–39. Copyright © 1974 Love Publishing Company. Reprinted by permission.

term paper before reward, the contract might call first for an outline, then a draft of section one, and so on.

◆ Phrase the contract positively to reward accomplishment rather than obedience. Contracts should state what students will do instead of what they will not do.

◆ Reward the performance after it occurs. Require students to demonstrate the behavior *before* they obtain the reward.

◆ The contract must be fair, clear, and honest. The terms of the contract must be written jointly by both the teacher and the student and without any ambiguity. In addition, the behavior required must be perceived by both the student and teacher as fair and proportional to the amount of reward to be given.

Summary of Strategies for Increasing Appropriate Behaviors

The most important tool for teachers in classrooms for students with emotional and behavioral disorders is positive reinforcement. Teachers must set clear rules and consistently reward students for appropriate behavior using either primary or secondary reinforcers. Social reinforcers and generalized reinforcers such as grades may not motivate students initially; however, teachers must plan to move students systematically toward the type and level of reinforcement available in the regular classroom. Token economies, level systems, and contingency contracts are three forms of behavior management systems often used by teachers to provide students with reinforcement sufficient to increase specified appropriate behaviors. ◆

Decreasing Inappropriate Behaviors

Although teachers must focus on increasing appropriate behaviors, they must also plan to reduce or eliminate inappropriate behaviors that are preventing children from learning or from receiving positive attention from peers and adults. Most often, teachers think of punishment when they plan to reduce troublesome behavior. We will return shortly to the concept of punishment; however, for now, consider punishment as your last choice for decreasing inappropriate behavior. Simple and practical alternatives to punishment, such as grouping a disruptive youngster with nondisruptive peers, are readily available for teachers (Stainback, Stainback, Etscheidt, & Doud, 1986). Alberto and Troutman (1995), for example, suggest that teachers first consider using non-punitive behavior reduction strategies such as differential reinforcement or extinction to decrease inappropriate behaviors.

Differential Reinforcement

As we have seen, reinforcement increases behavior. By focusing on appropriate alternatives to the misbehavior of students, reinforcement may be used as well to reduce even highly disruptive inappropriate behavior (Friman, 1990). For example, if Keesha yells out questions and comments in class and this behavior is inappropriate, then you may decide that the appropriate alternative behavior is for Keesha to raise her hand and be recognized by the teacher to speak. Rewarding Keesha for her handraising behavior may result in a simultaneous decrease in her inappropriate "yelling out" behavior. Teachers may consider four differential reinforcement procedures: differential reinforcement of incompatible behavior (DRI), differential reinforcement of alternative behavior (DRA), differential reinforcement of low rates of behavior (DRL), and differential reinforcement of other behavior (DRO).

Differential Reinforcement of Incompatible Behavior and Alternative Behavior. To use these procedures, you must first determine an appropriate behavioral alternative for the inappropriate behavior you are trying to reduce. The strategies are similar except that DRI involves the selection of an appropriate behavior which cannot be exhibited simultaneously with the inappropriate behavior. Keesha cannot, for example, be both in and out of her seat at the same time. If your goal is to reduce Keesha's out-of-seat behavior, then you might plan to reinforce her in-seat behavior heavily and consistently.

On the other hand, if you plan to reduce Keesha's "yelling out" behavior, you might choose DRA and reinforce Keesha for raising her hand. Handraising is certainly an appropriate alternative behavior for blurting out questions and answers in class. Keesha can, however, raise her hand and simultaneously call out a question. The two behaviors are not mutually exclusive. DRI and DRA are positive strategies for behavior reduction because they reward children for exhibiting behaviors that are appropriate alternatives for their inappro-

Table 7.1 Positive Alternatives for Common Classroom Behavior Problems

Undesired Behavior	Positive Alternative Behavior
Talking back	Responses such as "Yes Sir," or "Ok" or "I understand"; or acceptable questions such as "May I ask you a question about that?" or "May I tell you my side?"
Cursing	Exclamations such as "Darn" or "Shucks."
Being off task	Any on-task behavior like looking at a book, writing, or looking at the teacher.
Being out of seat	Sitting in seat with bottom on chair and body in upright position.
Noncompliance	Following directions within _____ seconds with time limit dependent on student age; following directions by second time direction is given.
Talking out	Raising hand and waiting to be called on.
Turning in messy papers	No marks other than answers; no more than _____ erasures; no more than three folds or creases.
Hitting, pinching, kicking, pushing, or shoving	Using verbal expression of anger; pounding fist into own hand; sitting or standing next to other students without touching them.
Tardiness	Being in seat when bell rings or by desired time.

From "Managing Behavior Problems: Accentuate the Positive . . . Eliminate the Negative!" by J. Webber & B. Scheuermann, *Teaching Exceptional Children*, 24(1), 1991, p. 15. Copyright © 1991 by The Council for Exceptional Children. Reprinted with permission.

priate actions. Table 7.1 lists alternatives for many common classroom behavior problems.

Differential Reinforcement of Low Rates of Behavior. You may find that some behaviors of children are desirable, acceptable, or even necessary, when they occur at relatively low rates. However, these same behaviors may become unacceptable or inappropriate when children engage in them at high rates. For example, reporting actions of peers may be acceptable from time to time, but constant tattling is not. Similarly, asking the teacher for help occasionally is desirable and necessary; however, when children depend on the teacher for help instead of independently working on tasks they can do on their own, the same behavior is no longer acceptable.

To use DRL, then, teachers set a certain criterion level for the targeted behavior just below the baseline average. When children exhibit the behavior at or below the preset level, they receive a specified reward and the level of behavior necessary to earn the next reward is lowered once again. Paul might be rewarded for tattling on peers no more than five times per hour, then no more than three times per hour, and so forth, until his behavior is reduced to an acceptable level. Of course, the teacher must be prepared to "accept" five episodes of tattling per hour!

Differential Reinforcement of Other Behavior. DRO involves rewarding children when they refrain from exhibiting a particular behavior for a specified period. For example, if Paul makes no rude comments for a 30-minute class period, he will receive a reward. If an entire 30-minute period is too lengthy, however, the teacher might, of course, break the session into shorter intervals. At first, Paul might be required to make no rude comments for 5 minutes to receive reinforcement. Later, this time period might be extended to 10, 15, 20, then 30 minutes before a reward is given. Setting the first interval length at the average between baseline responses appears to be the most effective starting point (Repp, Felce, & Barton, 1991).

A difficulty with DRO is that Paul may still engage in other inappropriate behaviors during the time interval but not demonstrate the targeted behavior. Webber and Scheuermann (1991) suggest that teachers not reward students if they exhibit a nontargeted but totally inappropriate behavior such as fighting during the interval. In addition, teachers must decide if they will reset the time interval whenever the student engages in the designated inappropriate behavior or simply ignore the behavior and wait for the next interval to begin. Nevertheless, DRO is an effective strategy for reducing many disruptive behaviors of both individual children and groups.

Extinction

Extinction involves the consistent withholding of reinforcement that is maintaining an inappropriate behavior. If, for example, Paul's rude comments are reinforced by your attention (e.g., each time Paul makes a rude comment, you fuss at Paul, reminding him that his remarks are not suitable for the classroom), then you might use extinction by ignoring Paul every time he makes one of these remarks. Extinction is best used, however, in combination with the differential reinforcement procedures. That is, you might ignore Paul's rude comments and also positively reinforce him for appropriate language choices.

Although extinction can be used effectively to reduce many minor misbehaviors, teachers certainly cannot ignore dangerous behaviors like fighting or infractions that are easily imitated and which spread to peers. Teachers who consider using extinction to reduce inappropriate behavior must think carefully before implementing the procedure. Alberto and Troutman (1995) list the following difficulties with the use of extinction:

1. The effect of extinction is not immediate. If an inappropriate behavior has received reinforcement for a lengthy period, particularly intermittent reinforcement, the behavior will be highly resistant to extinction.
2. The behavior will increase in rate or intensity before it begins to decrease; therefore, teachers must be prepared to "live with" a higher level of the poor behavior initially. In addition, students may demonstrate a

pattern of escalating behaviors and aggressive actions to gain reinforcement.

3. Behaviors undergoing extinction often exhibit spontaneous recovery (Skinner, 1953). That is, the behavior may gradually decrease, and then suddenly increase once again. Unless the teacher is prepared for this eventuality, he or she may believe the procedure is no longer working and erroneously attend to the behavior.

4. You must be able to withhold all reinforcement for the behavior. If, for example, peer attention is also maintaining the behavior, and you cannot control peer attention, extinction will not work. Similarly, if you inadvertently attend to the behavior, you have provided intermittent reinforcement for that behavior.

Teachers may use many nonpunitive procedures to decrease inappropriate behaviors of students. They may express clear rules and structure classroom groups so that disruptive children are not placed together. In addition, they might differentially reinforce appropriate behaviors while simultaneously using extinction by ignoring inappropriate behaviors. Teachers of students with emotional and behavioral disorders may also find it necessary, however, to use punishment, albeit carefully, to decrease inappropriate behaviors in the classroom.

Punishment

Whereas reinforcement increases behavior, punishment results in a *decrease* in future occurrence of a behavior. Punishers, then, are consequences that immediately follow a behavior and reduce the likelihood of the behavior occurring again in the future. Telling Keesha to "stop talking" is a punisher only if this consequence decreases her "talking out" behavior in the future. Similarly, smiling and saying "Good job" is also a punisher if this consequence decreases the behavior it follows. Punishers are determined to be such only by observing their effect (i.e., a decrease) on a particular behavior.

Typically, punishers involve either the removal of a reinforcing stimulus or the presentation of an aversive stimulus immediately following an inappropriate behavior. *Because reinforcers are being removed or unpleasant stimuli are being applied, teachers must exercise extreme caution when using punishment in the classroom.* For example, when teachers verbally disapprove of behaviors or reprimand students when they misbehave, the teacher may be negatively reinforced for using punishment as the behavior ceases at least temporarily. Students with emotional and behavioral disorders, however, are often adept at escalating their own attempts to gain reinforcement and teacher compliance with their demands. Also, for children and youth with learning and behavioral problems academic tasks may be aversive stimuli to be avoided (Gunter, Denny, Jack, Shores, & Nelson, 1993). Thus, these students may engage in increasing rates of inappropriate behaviors, which are then met with increasing levels of disapproving comments and reprimands by the teacher. Teacher and student easily become engulfed in coercive interaction patterns instead of positive ones with both teacher and student increasingly employing more aggressive, hostile, and aversive behaviors (Shores, Gunter, & Jack, 1993).

Punishment may have other unintended side effects as well (Newsom, Favell, & Rincover, 1983). Students who are punished, for example, may exhibit additional aggressive behaviors following punishment, or they may fear and seek to avoid the teacher. In addition, students who are physically punished or who observe others being punished may increase their use of aggression to control the behaviors of others. As a matter of fact, harsh and inconsistent punishment is closely linked to aggressive, antisocial behaviors in children (Walker, Colvin, & Ramsey, 1995).

The target behavior may be suppressed in the environment in which it is being punished, yet it may actually increase in other "nonpunishing" settings (Newsom, Favell, & Rincover, 1983). Similarly, other undesirable behaviors may increase as response substitutes for the behavior that is punished. Finally, as a result of punishment, appropriate student behaviors may also be suppressed, or students may fail to use the "punished" behavior in different settings in which that behavior might actually be considered to be adaptive.

Skiba and Deno (1991) argue that the very term *punishment* is emotionally charged because it is often confused with "aversive treatment" and "inhumane" procedures. Most educators do consider interventions that use physical pain, physical discomfort, or social humiliation to be aversive treatments that should be restricted (Tobin & Sugai, 1993), and to be sure, corporal punishment is prohibited in many schools although it is still permitted in many states. Professionals debate, however, the appropriateness of all forms of punishment when used to control the inappropriate actions of students with emotional and behavioral disorders (Zabel, 1985). The Association for Persons with Severe Handicaps (TASH, 1985), for example, published a statement arguing against the use of intrusive behavioral interventions including punishment. Wolery, Bailey, and Sugai (1988), on the other hand, maintain that punishment may be a necessary behavior reduction strategy if professionals carefully evaluate how the strategy will help the individual student.

Numerous cases of liability and alleged violations of student rights have recently received attention in the courts and in the media as a result of interventions used by teachers to reduce the inappropriate behavior of children and youth in special education programs. Singer and Irvin (1987) suggest that schools institute human rights review procedures before implementing any intrusive or restrictive behavioral interventions to guarantee informed consent and right to due process (i.e., parents and students must understand previous treatments attempted, the results of these interventions, the type of proposed intervention and its intended outcome, data collection and monitoring procedures, and their right to withdraw their consent freely at any time). Moreover, the Individualized Education Plan must detail how students are to be taught appropriate behaviors rather than merely describing how students will be disciplined for inappropriate behavior. According to Singer and Irvin (1987), for intrusive or restrictive procedures to be used, precise educational objectives must exist and the intervention must clearly be the least restrictive alternative. See Box 7.6 (pp. 226–227) for the Council for Children with Behavioral Disorder's position statement regarding the use of behavior reduction strategies.

Obviously, teachers must take great care when designing programs to reduce inappropriate student behavior. Environmental modifications, differential reinforcement, and extinction may be effective and least restrictive alternatives for many misbehaviors. Punishment, however, may also be the least restrictive alternative for some inappropriate behaviors of children and youth. Response cost, time-out, and overcorrection are three punishment procedures that may be used in classrooms for students with emotional and behavioral disorders, given the cautions and caveats already mentioned.

Response Cost

Response cost involves the removal of a specific amount of a reinforcer to decrease behavior. For example, if students are given 5 minutes of free time to talk with peers at the end of each class period, they might lose 1 minute of their time for each instance of talking without teacher permission. Similarly, children might be "fined" by losing a minute of recess for disruptive behavior during class time. Teachers are cautioned, however, regarding the ethical and legal ramifications of removing time from a child's participation in entitled activities such as art, music, physical education, lunch or snacks, and bathroom breaks.

Often, response cost is incorporated within a token economy as a penalty or fine for misbehavior. That is, Paul and Keesha earn points or tokens for their appropriate behaviors; however, they may also lose points or tokens if they engage in specific inappropriate behaviors. Obviously, the number of points or tokens lost must be fair and proportional to the "crime."

Teachers must, of course, be able to remove the tokens or points. In addition, students must earn more points or tokens than they lose, or the token economy system and the response cost procedure will rapidly become ineffective. Similarly, if children quickly lose all of their recess time or all of their free time to talk with peers, then they may as well engage in their chosen misbehavior. As a rule, positive reinforcement and response cost might occur in a 4:1 ratio to prevent children from going in the hole. That is, for each occurrence of children losing points, tokens, or minutes of free time, you must quickly try to find four opportunities to reinforce them for appropriate behaviors.

Time-Out

Time-out stands for "time-out from positive reinforcement." Time-out is a punishment, then, because the opportunity to earn positive reinforcement is temporarily removed from students for a specified period to decrease inappropriate behaviors. This procedure implies, therefore, that your classroom environment and the academic activities therein are highly reinforcing for your students, and they will not wish to be removed from these.

Teachers report that they frequently use time-out as a consequence for physical or verbal aggression or destruction of property; however, they also state that their schools often do not have written policies regarding their use of time-out (Zabel, 1986). In addition, numerous court cases have resulted from students being placed into locked or seclusionary time-out rooms, and many states have now developed guidelines for the legal and ethical use of this time-out procedure (Hindman, 1986). Although time-out is sometimes criticized for preventing students from participation in academic tasks, the use of time-out does not adversely affect academic achievement, at least when compared with alternatives such as suspension or truancy (Skiba & Raison, 1990).

Teachers must certainly exercise care when considering any time-out procedure as a behavior reduction strategy. Nevertheless, Alberto and Troutman (1995) describe three time-out procedures, including nonseclusionary time-out, exclusionary time-out, and seclusionary time-out, which may be effective for decreasing the inappropriate behaviors of some students with emotional and behavioral disorders.

Nonseclusionary Time-Out. Nonseclusionary time-out is the least restrictive form of time-out because students are prevented from earning reinforcers

- Behavior reduction programs must include steps to ensure youngsters are protected from violations of their right to due process.
- Provide detailed descriptions of behavior reduction procedures including:
  a. The specific procedure to be used.
  b. The qualifications of the program designers.
  c. The justification for the program with documentation that previous interventions have been unsuccessful.
  d. The length of time the procedures will continue before formal program evaluation.
  e. The potential positive and negative outcomes.
  f. The method used for collecting data to document program effectiveness.
- Make regular contacts with parents, administrators, and other professionals to keep them apprised of the student's progress.

5. Practitioners should develop and subsequently follow a plan detailing the behavior reduction procedure(s) to be used in a particular case (i.e., written as a part of a child's IEP).
6. Once aversive behavior reduction procedures are selected and approved, practitioners should select appropriate procedures for specific situations.
7. Persons responsible for carrying out behavior reduction procedures must be appropriately trained.
8. Practitioners should keep data on the efficacy of the behavior reduction procedures and should communicate these in regularly scheduled staff/parent meetings.

without being removed from the classroom setting. Although not a practice to be advocated, teachers have for many years used nonseclusionary time-out when they have requested that students put their heads down on their desks to remove the social reinforcers given by peers for inappropriate behavior. In this way, reinforcement is temporarily removed from the child while he or she may still observe others participating appropriately in the activity and receiving reinforcement for their participation.

The time-out ribbon (Foxx & Shapiro, 1978), or red card/green card, is an example of a nonseclusionary time-out procedure appropriate for both individuals and groups in classroom settings (Salend & Gordon, 1987; Salend, & Maragulia, 1983). Time-out ribbons having a student's name on one side and "time-out" on the other side, or cards with one green side and one red side, may

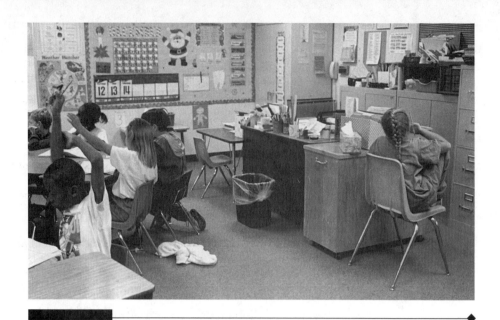

In order for time-out to be effective, the classroom must be a highly reinforcing environment from which students do not wish to be removed.

be placed on an easily visible bulletin board or on the front of a student's desk. When students are engaging in appropriate behaviors, their ribbon shows their name or the card remains on the green side indicating their opportunity to earn reinforcers. If students engage in misbehavior, however, the card is turned to the red side or the ribbon is turned over for a specified period of time-out. At the end of the preset period, if students are behaving appropriately, the ribbon or card is turned back over so that the student may again earn positive reinforcement.

When using nonseclusionary time-out procedures, teachers must exercise caution to minimize potential risks to students. Unless implemented with care, for example, students might suffer a loss of dignity or alienation from peers. Harris (1985) and Cuenin and Harris (1986) offer the following guidelines for teachers using nonseclusionary and other time-out procedures:

1. Carefully define the target behavior resulting in time-out, and collect baseline data.
2. Analyze the situations in which the behavior is occurring.
3. Consider relevant student characteristics to individualize time-out for each child.
4. Choose the least restrictive time-out technique that will allow enforcement and maximize success.
5. Plan the initiation, duration, supervision and termination of the time-out.
6. Plan for reinforcement of desirable alternative behaviors.
7. Make the reason and rules for time-out clear to the student.

8. Monitor and evaluate the time-out intervention to ensure that the target behavior is decreasing and that positive or negative reinforcement are not occurring.
9. Administer the time-out in a matter-of-fact manner; document the effectiveness of the procedures; and switch to a less aversive behavior reduction strategy as rapidly as possible.

Exclusionary Time-Out. When students are removed from an activity to prevent them from earning reinforcement, the teacher is using exclusionary time-out. For example, some teachers place children in a time-out chair in a corner of the classroom for a short period. Other teachers request that students take a time-out behind a screened-off area of the classroom. Although some teachers also send students out into the hall or to the office as a form of exclusionary time-out, this procedure is rarely effective. Children and youth have multiple opportunities to obtain positive reinforcement while in the hall or walking to the office, and some students may run away when sent out of the classroom.

A potential difficulty with exclusionary time-out, then, is the inability of teachers to prevent children from leaving the time-out area or from gaining access to peer reinforcement. When children become the focal point of peer or teacher attention as they sit in time-out, the procedure is clearly ineffective. If students quickly leave the time-out area or play with peers during time-out, choose another procedure.

Seclusionary Time-Out. Seclusionary time-out, also called *isolation time-out,* takes place when students are moved to a time-out room to deny them access to all classroom reinforcers. Because of the potential for abuse or parental misunderstanding arising from the use of seclusionary time-out, teachers must carefully follow the guidelines and recommendations offered by Gast and Nelson (1977a, 1977b), Nelson and Rutherford (1983), and Alberto and Troutman (1995):

1. Use seclusionary time-out only after documenting that other behavior reduction strategies or time-out practices have been tried with no success and only after ensuring that the classroom environment is reinforcing for the student.
2. Use time-out only when the time-out contingency can be enforced by the teacher (i.e., without the student engaging the teacher in a power struggle and without the need to remove the student physically to time-out) and proactively teach students to take a time-out when it is needed.
3. Keep the time-out period short (i.e., no more than 5 minutes), and implement the time-out contingency immediately and consistently.
4. The time-out room should be at least 6 × 6 feet, properly lighted with the light switch outside the room, properly ventilated, and free from objects and fixtures on which children might injure themselves.
5. The time-out room should be fitted with a means by which professionals may visually and auditorially monitor the student (e.g., a high window with an outside covering, a tilted mirror).

6. The time-out room should not be locked. A latch or a self-releasing bolt on the outside of the door might be used only as needed and only with careful monitoring.

7. Before using time-out, be sure the student and parents or guardians understand what behaviors will result in the procedure. Specify these on the IEP. Show the student and parents or guardians the time-out room, and be sure they understand how long the student will be in time-out and the behavior necessary for release from time-out. Obtain consent before using the procedure.

8. When students engage in behaviors resulting in time-out, calmly and specifically tell the student what the behavior is, how long he or she will be in time-out, and what he or she must do to be released from time-out. Refrain from engaging in any other conversation with the student while placing him or her in time-out or during the time-out period.

9. Release the student from time-out at the end of the specified period if the child is behaving calmly and quietly. If the student is still shouting or throwing tantrums, reset the time for 15-second intervals until the student is calm, and then release the student immediately.

10. Refrain from talking to the student during time-out or from commenting on the student's behavior while in the time-out room. Return the student immediately to the activity in which he or she was engaged just before being placed into time-out to avoid negatively reinforcing a student by removing his or her work.

11. Keep careful and accurate records to document each use of time-out. A time-out log might include, for example, the student's name, the behavior of the student that resulted in time-out, the name of the person responsible for placing the student into and monitoring the time-out, the date, the time of day when the student was placed into time-out and the time when the student was released, the total length of time-out, any unusual behaviors or occurrences during time-out, and the form of time-out used.

12. If the duration of time-out may exceed 30 minutes, a supervisor should be consulted. In addition, an advisory committee should be asked to evaluate the time-out if its effects are questionable.

13. Carefully evaluate the effectiveness of time-out for each individual student and switch to a less aversive practice as rapidly as possible.

14. Ensure that students have opportunities to learn academic material missed during time-out and that they are learning and receiving sufficient reinforcement for appropriate alternative behaviors.

Overcorrection

Up to this point, we have been discussing the removal of reinforcers or the opportunity to earn reinforcers to decrease the inappropriate behavior of students. When teachers immediately and contingently present an aversive stimulus to reduce behavior, however, they are using the most intrusive form of punishment. Although the use of aversive stimuli, particularly shouting at students or applying physical force, is not recommended in classroom settings, overcorrection is an acceptable procedure that may punish students while also teaching them more appropriate behavioral alternatives. Two forms of overcorrection, restitutional overcorrection and positive practice overcorrection, are useful for teachers of students with emotional and behavioral disorders.

Azrin and Foxx (1971), for example, developed the procedure called *restitutional overcorrection* in which students are required to restore a classroom or other environment they have disturbed not only to the original condition but also to an even better state. Using this method, the teacher might immediately follow an inappropriate behavior such as Paul tearing papers off of a bulletin board with the request that Paul not only repair and replace the torn paper on that bulletin board but on all other bulletin boards in the classroom as well. Or, when Paul overturns his desk in an angry moment, he might be requested to rearrange his own desk neatly and to straighten the other desks in the classroom too. Similarly, positive practice overcorrection requires the student to repeatedly engage in repetitions of an appropriate behavior following an inappropriate action, although in this case the student has not physically disturbed the environment (Foxx & Azrin, 1973). Teachers use positive practice overcorrection, for example, when they request rowdy students to practice repeatedly lining up calmly and quietly before they go to recess.

Gable, Arllen, and Rutherford (1994, pp. 20–21) offer the following guidelines for teachers wishing to implement overcorrection procedures:

1. Precisely define the problem behavior or behaviors.
2. Record baseline data on the rate, frequency, or percent of intervals of occurrence for the problem behavior. Continue to collect data throughout the program.
3. Select a verbal cue to use when the student engages in the problem behavior (e.g., "No pushing over chairs," or "Line up quietly").
4. Select a restitutional activity or a positive practice activity that is relevant to the problem behavior and of sufficient length and intensity to modify the student's behavior.
5. Decide when the program will be in effect each day, and schedule enough time and assistance to implement it.
6. When the student engages in the problem behavior, give the verbal cue and proceed with the restitutional or positive practice activity. Avoid unnecessary physical contact and conversation during the activity.
7. If during the overcorrection the student reengages in the problem behavior, begin the sequence of activities again.
8. Never use the verbal cue without the overcorrection activities until the behavior is reduced to a low and stable rate.
9. Be sure to provide ample opportunity for the student to receive positive reinforcement and attention for appropriate behaviors during the remainder of the school day.

Summary of Strategies to Decrease Inappropriate Behaviors ◆

The goal of any behavior management program must be to teach students appropriate behaviors rather than merely to eliminate or reduce inappropriate behaviors. When poor behavior must be decreased, teachers should try the least restrictive and least intrusive method of behavior reduction which will result in the necessary change. Differential reinforcement procedures and extinction, when used in combination, are two effective methods for replacing inappropriate behaviors with more appropriate ones. Response cost, time-out, and overcorrection are punishing procedures that may be used with caution when their use is clearly in the best interests of the student. Teachers must never use strategies for decreasing inappropriate behavior without first considering the functional intent behind the behavior and the appropriate alternative behavior to put in its place. ◆

Summary

The behavioral model is well researched, and effective methods and procedures developed within this school of thought are well documented in the literature. Because behavioral methodology is extremely powerful, teachers must demonstrate ethical practice by ensuring that any behavior change under consideration is in the best interest of students. Once behaviors targeted for change are justified and clearly defined, teachers must carefully observe and record behavioral data to determine student performance and intervention effectiveness.

Positive reinforcement increases appropriate behavior; therefore, understanding and effectively using positive reinforcement is a critical skill for teachers. Many primary and secondary reinforcers are available in the classroom. Teachers must move students toward the type and level of reinforcement occurring in the regular classroom if students are to be successful in that environment. Token economies, level systems, and contingency contracts are three special applications of positive reinforcement often used in classrooms for children and youth with behavioral disorders.

Punishment decreases a behavior; thus, teachers must never consider the use of punishment without also first determining the appropriate replacement behavior. Nonpunitive behavior reduction strategies such as the differential reinforcement procedures or extinction are positive alternatives to punishment. When punishment is necessary, teachers must use the least restrictive or intrusive method possible to reduce or eliminate the inappropriate behavior. Response cost, time-out, and overcorrection are three forms of punishment that, when used with caution, are acceptable and effective techniques for the classroom.

Application Exercises

1. Arrange to observe in a classroom for students with behavioral disorders at any grade. Observe one child for a period of 30 minutes of academic instruction with the teacher. How many times does the teacher give the student a form of social reinforcement (e.g., verbal praise, smiles, winks, etc.) during your observation period? Be sure not to use any information that might identify the student or the teacher as you report the results of your observation.

2. Interview a teacher of students with behavioral disorders and a regular classroom teacher from the same school and grade level. What behavior management system is used by each of these teachers? Are there any similarities or differences in the systems used by these teachers?
3. Examine several articles from behaviorally oriented journals such as the *Journal of Applied Behavior Analysis*. What types of behaviors are "treated" in the articles you scanned? What were the results from the studies?

References

Adelman, H. S., & Taylor, L. (1990). Intrinsic motivation and school misbehavior: Some intervention implications. *Journal of Learning Disabilities, 23*(9), 541–550.

Alberto, P. A., & Troutman, A. C. (1995). *Applied behavior analysis for teachers* (4th ed.). Columbus, OH: Merrill.

Azrin, N. H., & Foxx, R. M. (1971). A rapid method of toilet training the institutionalized retarded. *Journal of Applied Behavior Analysis, 4,* 89–99.

Bauer, A. M., Shea, T. M., & Keppler, R. (1986). Levels systems: A framework for the individualization of behavior management. *Behavioral Disorders, 12*(1), 28–35.

Brady, M. P., & Taylor, R. D. (1989). Instructional consequences in mainstreamed middle school classes: Reinforcement and corrections. *Remedial and Special Education, 10*(2), 31–36.

Cooper, J. O., Heron, T. E., & Heward, W. L. (1987). *Applied behavior analysis.* Columbus, OH: Merrill.

Council for Children with Behavioral Disorders. (1990). Position paper on use of behavior reduction strategies with children with behavioral disorders. *Behavioral Disorders, 15*(4), 243–260.

Cuenin, L. H., & Harris, K. R. (1986). Planning, implementing, and evaluating timeout interventions with exceptional students. *Teaching Exceptional Children, 18*(4), 272–276.

Cullinan, D., Epstein, M. H., & Lloyd, J. W. (1991). Evaluation of conceptual models of behavior disorders. *Behavioral Disorders, 16*(2), 148–157.

deCharms, R. (1968). *Personal causation.* New York: Academic Press.

deCharms, R. (1976). *Enhancing motivation: Change in the classroom.* New York: Irvington.

Deci, E. L. (1975). *Intrinsic motivation.* New York: Plenum.

Deci, E. L. (1980). *The psychology of self-determination.* Lexington, MA: D.C. Heath.

Deci, E. L., & Chandler, C. L. (1986). The importance of motivation for the future of the LD field. *Journal of Learning Disabilities, 19,* 587–594.

Deci, E. L., Nezlek, J., & Sheinman, L. (1981). Characteristics of the rewarder and intrinsic motivation of the reward. *Journal of Personality and Social Psychology, 40,* 1–10.

Deci, E. L., & Ryan, R. M. (1985). The general causality orientations scale: Self-determination in personality. *Journal of Research in Personality, 19,* 109–134.

Foxx, R. M., & Azrin, N. H. (1973). The elimination of autistic self-stimulatory behavior by overcorrection. *Journal of Applied Behavior Analysis, 6,* 1–14.

Foxx, R. M., & Shapiro, S. T. (1978). The timeout ribbon: A nonexclusionary timeout procedure. *Journal of Applied Behavior Analysis, 11,* 125–136.

Friman, P. C. (1990). Nonaversive treatment of high-rate disruption: Child and provider effects. *Exceptional Children, 57*(1), 64–69.

Gable, R. A., Arllen, N. L., & Rutherford, R. B. (1994). A note on the use of overcorrection. *Beyond Behavior, 5*(3), 19–21.

Gast, D., & Nelson, C. M. (1977a). Legal and ethical considerations for the use of timeout in special education settings. *The Journal of Special Education, 11,* 457–467.

Gast, D., & Nelson, C. M. (1977b). Time out in the classroom: Implications for special education. *Exceptional Children, 43,* 461–464.

Gunter, P. L., Denny, R. K., Jack, S. L., Shores, R. E., & Nelson, C. M. (1993). Aversive stimuli in academic interactions between students with serious emotional disturbance and their teachers. *Behavioral Disorders, 18*(4), 265–273.

Harris, K. R. (1985). Definitional, parametric, and procedural considerations in timeout interventions and research. *Exceptional Children, 51*(4), 279–288.

Harter, S. (1978). Effectance motivation reconsidered: Toward a developmental model. *Human Development, 45,* 661–669.

Harter, S. (1981). A new self-report scale of intrinsic versus extrinsic orientation in the classroom: Motivation and informational components. *Developmental Psychology, 17,* 300–312.

Hewett, F. M. (1968). *The emotionally disturbed child in the classroom: A developmental strategy for educating children with maladaptive behavior.* Boston: Allyn and Bacon.

Hewett, F. M., Taylor, F. D., & Artuso, A. A. (1968). The Santa Monica project. *Exceptional Children, 34,* 387.

Hindman, S. E. (1986). The law, the courts, and the education of behaviorally disordered students. *Behavioral Disorders, 11*(4), 280–289.

Homme, L. (1970). *How to use contingency contracting in the classroom.* Champaign, IL: Research Press.

Kaplan, P., Kohfeldt, J., & Sturla, K. (1974). *It's positively fun: Techniques for managing learning environments.* Denver, CO: Love.

Knitzer, J., Steinberg, Z., & Fleisch, B. (1990). *At the schoolhouse door: An examination of programs and policies for children with emotional and behavioral problems.* New York: Bank Street College of Education.

Kohn, A. (1993). *Punished by rewards: The trouble with gold stars, incentive plans, A's, praise, and other bribes.* Boston: Houghton Mifflin.

Martens, B. K., Muir, K. A., & Meller, P. J. (1988). Rewards common to the classroom setting: A comparison of regular and self-contained room student ratings. *Behavioral Disorders, 13*(3), 169–174.

Mastropieri, M. A., Jenne, T., & Scruggs, T. E. (1988). A level system for managing problem behaviors in a high school resource program. *Behavioral Disorders, 13*(3), 202–208.

Nelson, C. M., & Rutherford, R. B. (1983). Timeout revisited: Guidelines for its use in special education. *Exceptional Education Quarterly, 3*(4), 56–67.

Newsom, C., Favell, J. E., & Rincover, A. (1983). The side effects of punishment. In S. Axelrod & J. Apsche (Eds.), *The effects of punishment on human behavior* (pp. 285–316). New York: Academic Press.

Nichols, P. (1992). The curriculum of control: Twelve reasons for it, some arguments against it. *Beyond Behavior, 3*(2), 5–11.

O'Leary, K. D., & O'Leary, S. G. (Eds.). (1977). *Classroom management: The successful use of behavior modification* (2nd ed.). New York: Pergamon.

Patterson, G. R. (1982). *Coercive family process.* Eugene, OR: Castalia.

Premack, D. (1959). Toward empirical behavior laws: I. Positive reinforcement. *Psychological Review, 66,* 219–233.

Raschke, D., Dedrick, C., & Thompson, M. (1987). Motivating reluctant learners: Innovative contingency packages. *Teaching Exceptional Children, 19*(2), 18–21.

Repp, A. C., Felce, D., & Barton, L. E. (1991). The effects of initial interval size on the efficacy of DRO schedules of reinforcement. *Exceptional Children, 57*(5), 417–425.

Rosenberg, M. S. (1986). Maximizing the effectiveness of structured classroom management programs: Implementing rule-review procedures with disruptive and distractible students. *Behavioral Disorders, 11*(4), 239–248.

Sabatino, D. A. (1987). Preventive discipline as a practice in special education. *Teaching Exceptional Children, 19*(4), 8–11.

Salend, S., & Gordon, B. (1987). A group-oriented timeout ribbon procedure. *Behavioral Disorders, 12,* 131–137.

Salend, S., & Maragulia, D. (1983). The timeout ribbon: A procedure for the least restrictive environment. *Journal For Special Educators, 20,* 9–15.

Scheuermann, B., Webber, J., Partin, M., & Knies, W. C. (1994). Level systems and the law: Are they compatible? *Behavioral Disorders, 19*(3), 205–220.

Shores, R. E., Gunter, P. L., & Jack, S. L. (1993). Classroom management strategies: Are they setting events for coercion? *Behavioral Disorders, 18*(2), 92–102.

Singer, G., & Irvin, L. K. (1987). Human rights review of intrusive behavioral treatments for students with severe handicaps. *Exceptional Children, 54*(1), 46–52.

Skiba, R. J., & Deno, S. L. (1991). Terminology and behavior reduction: The case against "Punishment". *Exceptional Children, 57*(4), 298–313.

Skiba, R., & Raison, J. (1990). Relationship between the use of timeout and academic achievement. *Exceptional Children, 57*(1), 36–46.

Skinner, B. F. (1953). *Science and human behavior.* New York: Free Press.

Skinner, B. F. (1968). *The technology of teaching.* New York: Appleton-Century-Crofts.

Skinner, B. F. (1989). *Recent issues in the analysis of behavior.* Columbus, OH: Merrill.

Smith, S. W., & Farrell, D. T. (1993). Level system use in special education: Classroom intervention with prima facie appeal. *Behavioral Disorders, 18*(4), 251–264.

Stainback, W., Stainback, S., Etscheidt, S., & Doud, J. (1986). A nonintrusive intervention for acting-out behavior. *Teaching Exceptional Children, 19*(1), 38–41.

Stainback, W., Stainback, S., & Froyen, L. (1987). Structuring the classroom to prevent disruptive behaviors. *Teaching Exceptional Children, 19*(4), 12–16.

Steinberg, Z. (1991). Pandora's children. *Beyond Behavior, 2*(3), 5–14.

Switzky, H. N., & Schultz, G. F. (1988). Intrinsic motivation and learning performance: Implications for educational programming for learners with mild handicaps. *Remedial and Special Education, 9*(4), 7–14.

The Association for Persons with Severe Handicaps. (1985). Resolution on intrusive interventions. *TASH Newsletter, 11,* 3.

Tobin, T. J., & Sugai, G. (1993). Intervention aversiveness: Educators' perceptions of the need for restrictions on aversive interventions. *Behavioral Disorders, 18*(2), 110–117.

Van Houten, R., Axelrod, S., Bailey, J. S., Favell, J. E., Foxx, R. M., Iwata, B. A., & Lovaas, O. I. (1988). The right to effective behavioral treatment. *The behavior analyst, 11,* 111–114.

Walker, H. M., Colvin, G., & Ramsey, E. (1995). *Antisocial behavior in school: Strategies and best practices.* Pacific Grove, CA: Brooks/Cole.

Webber, J., & Scheuermann, B. (1991). Managing behavior problems: Accentuate the positive . . . Eliminate the negative! *Teaching Exceptional Children, 24*(1), 13–19.

Wells, T. (1990). *Boys town education model.* Boys Town, NE: Father Flanagan's Boys' Home.

Wolery, M., Bailey, D. B., & Sugai, G. M. (1988). *Effective teaching principles and procedures of applied behavior analysis with exceptional students.* Boston: Allyn & Bacon.

Zabel, M. K. (1986). Timeout use with behaviorally disordered students. *Behavioral Disorders, 12*(1), 15–21.

Zabel, M. K. (1992). Responses to control. *Beyond Behavior, 4*(1), 3–4.

Zabel, R. H. (1985). Aversives in special education programs for behaviorally disordered students: A debate. *Behavioral Disorders, 10*(4), 295–304.

CHAPTER 8

TEACHING SOCIAL SKILLS

Main Ideas:

◆ *Socially competent students engage in the appropriate social skills for the time and place; therefore, they enjoy greater peer acceptance and popularity than those who are less socially skilled.*

◆ *Teaching socially valid social skills improves the student's quality of life because these skills are judged to be important for success by peers, parents, and teachers.*

◆ *Structured learning approaches use modeling, guided practice in the form of role playing, specific performance feedback, and systematic plans for generalization to teach social skills.*

◆ *Opportunistic approaches to teaching social skills harness the power of the peer group and use situations occurring naturally in the child's environment for instructional purposes.*

◆ *Combining structured learning and opportunistic approaches may enhance the generalization of targeted social skills.*

◆ *Numerous curricula are available for teaching social skills to children and youth with emotional and behavioral disorders.*

Students with emotional and behavioral disorders may spend a substantial portion of each school day in the regular classroom. How teachers and peers view the child's ability to get along with others, then, is crucial to his or her success in the mainstream. Fad (1990), for example, lists numerous coping skills, work habits, and peer relationships frequently identified by regular classroom teachers as crucial for classroom success. These include the following: expressing anger without physical aggression or yelling, avoiding arguments when provoked, listening to teacher directions and instructions, working independently, promptly following teacher requests, initiating conversations, joining group activities, and maintaining friendships.

Teachers, however, consistently rate children with learning and behavioral problems as below their peers in all of these critical social skills (Gresham, Elliott, & Black, 1987). Yet, competence in social skills is essential for long-term adjustment in adulthood as well as for successful employment (Neel, Meadows, Levine, & Edgar, 1988). As a matter of fact, Parker and Asher (1987) assert that dropping out of school and criminal acts committed by juveniles or adults are two outcomes of poor interpersonal relationships for children who are not well accepted by their peers. In addition, Gresham (1984) argues that teaching important social skills is critical if students with learning and behavioral difficulties are to experience a sense of personal competence and self-efficacy in regular classroom settings.

The troublesome and problematic actions of students with learning and behavioral disorders, then, often result from their lack of competence with social skills (Gresham & Elliott, 1989; Schloss, Schloss, Wood, & Kiehl, 1986). Students like Paul may not know, for example, how to obtain teacher or peer attention appropriately or how to disagree without being "disagreeable." Similarly, students with emotional and behavioral disorders may have learned inappropriate ways to accomplish social goals such as these. Other students, like Fong, may not possess the requisite skills for entering a conversation or play group successfully or they may fail to demonstrate the skill in context when it is actually required.

Gresham (1986) differentiates between children and youth who have social skills deficits and those who have performance deficits. For those children who have the necessary social skills, but who fail to perform them at acceptable levels, Gresham suggests that the difficulty is often motivation. Reinforcement and the application of other behavioral techniques discussed in Chapter 7 will be essential to increase the child's appropriate use of social skills. However, when children cannot execute a social skill appropriately, or when they have never demonstrated the skill, they have a skill deficit. In this case, teachers must again use the directive model to directly teach and model social skills. Relevant role plays, specific feedback, and rewarding the use of social skills in context are critical elements of social skills instruction (Figure 8.1).

In this chapter, then, we will discuss the teaching of social skills. First, we will present basic definitions and concepts regarding social skills and social competence. Next, we will explore important components of successful social skills instruction. Finally, we will examine several social skills curricula effective for teaching students with emotional and behavioral disorders to become more socially adept.

Key ideas
- Directly teach and model social skills
- Use relevant role plays with specific feedback
- Reward use of social skills in natural settings

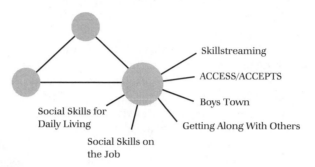

FIGURE 8.1

Directive Model (Social Skills Instruction)

Social Skills and Social Competence

Many definitions of social skills are reported in the literature. Hollinger (1987), for example, defines social skills as those skills necessary for positive interactions with others and for acceptance by peers. Similarly, Walker and colleagues (1983) define social skills as a collection of competencies allowing children to initiate and maintain positive interpersonal relationships and to cope within different social contexts and environments. Regardless of definition, those students who demonstrate appropriate social skills are likely to meet with peer acceptance, while those who do not exhibit these skills are likely to suffer isolation, rejection, and limited friendships (Hollinger, 1987).

McFall (1982) maintains that social skills are specific strategies used by children and youth to accomplish particular social tasks such as greeting others or joining in ongoing activities. Social competence, on the other hand, refers to the judgments of parents, teachers, and peers regarding the effectiveness of the child's strategies for accomplishing desired social outcomes. According to Strain and his colleagues (Strain, Odom, & McConnell, 1984), students demonstrating social competence experience mutually reinforcing interactions, a concept referred to as social reciprocity. When peers, or student and teacher, engage in reciprocal exchanges that are positive for both parties, judgments of social competence and increased interactions in the future are likely. Socially competent students engage in the appropriate social skills at the appropriate time and place. Social skills, therefore, are those skills enabling students to interact effectively and competently with important others at school, at home, and in the community.

Social skills and judgments of social competence, then, are contextually bound. That is, socially competent behaviors may vary by differing cultural, ethnic, or social standards in particular settings. Maag (1992) suggests that students must recognize the relevant aspects of situations that serve as cues for particular social behaviors. For example, Paul must recognize students throwing a ball at a basketball hoop on the playground as a cue for asking them if he may join in their game rather than stealing or kicking the ball away from them. Maag (1990) further asserts that identical social behaviors may be either appropriate or inappropriate, depending on the context. "Hey, Man" might be an appropriate greeting for Dante to give his peers but not to the building principal.

Understanding the social requirements of a situation is an integral part of teaching and learning social skills. Before teaching any given social skill, therefore, teachers must first consider the intended outcome behind a child's behavior (Neel & Cessna, 1990). Even when Paul demonstrates a seemingly inappropriate social behavior, such as stealing the ball from his peers on the basketball court, he may have the intent of joining his peers in the game. Teaching Paul the social skill of "asking to play" or "joining the group" may help him to achieve his intended outcome and become more socially competent.

Relevant social skills that actually improve the child's competence and quality of life in particular social settings are considered to be socially valid (Wolf, 1978). Thus, considering social validity is crucial before teaching any social skill. According to Gresham (1986), desirable social outcomes such as peer acceptance and popularity with peers are closely related to whether or not students demonstrate socially valid social skills. Teaching Paul to raise his hand to get the teacher's attention may be a behavior that will please his classroom teacher. A socially valid behavior more likely to improve Paul's competence with peers, though, is "joining the group," defined as "approaching the group, making eye contact, and politely asking to play." The social validity of a social skill is determined by its importance or significance to others in the child's immediate environment (Gresham, 1986).

To determine the social validity of a particular social skill, teachers might directly ask people in differing settings what students must do to be socially successful. Cafeteria monitors may be asked, for example, what behaviors students must exhibit to be successful in the lunchroom, or bus drivers what behaviors ensure positive outcomes when students are arriving or departing school. Parents and family members, too, might be asked to discuss or rank desirable behaviors required to achieve important social outcomes at home or in the community. Similarly, Carpenter and Apter (1988) maintain that children and youth in small groups may list social behaviors necessary for success in the classroom or during free time. Observation of targeted social skills in these settings may further confirm or disconfirm those skills suggested as essential for positive interactions.

Teaching skills that are socially valid may also improve the generalization of those social skills that are taught. According to Maag (1989), all too often teachers give instruction on social skills that have little relationship to important social outcomes for children. They are then disappointed with the limited effectiveness of their interventions as students fail to use the social skills they are taught. Instead of using "train and hope" methods, teachers must carefully teach socially valid skills and plan systematically for generalization to occur (Stokes & Baer, 1977). Stokes and Osnes (1986) suggest that teachers plan for generalization by doing the following:

- Harnessing naturally occurring reinforcers—socially competent peers may be coached to give other children reinforcement for exhibiting targeted social skills.
- Training diversely—use many different natural settings for training the targeted social skill such as the playground, hallway, or cafeteria.
- Incorporating functional mediators into training—use peers and others in the child's natural environment to prompt the use of those social skills that are taught.

For those students exhibiting social skills deficits, then, systematic instruction in social skills must take place if these children are to become more socially competent and enjoy peer acceptance. Children must receive not only instruction regarding socially valid social skills but also prompting and reinforcement from important others in diverse natural environments if they are to use their new social skills appropriately.

Social Skills Instruction

Over the last decade, numerous approaches have been developed for improving the social skills of students with emotional and behavioral disorders. Most have been criticized, however, as failing to produce behaviors that can be maintained over time and that generalize to other environments (Bellack, 1983; McConnell, 1987). Others have been criticized for teaching skills that are not socially valid for particular children and youth (Maag, 1989; Meadows, Need, Parker, & Timo, 1991). That is, to help students with emotional and behavioral disorders become more socially acceptable, the students and others in the young person's environment must believe that the social skills taught are important and relevant (Nelson, 1988). In addition, both general and special educators must believe that social skills instruction is of equal importance to academic instruction (Maag, 1992). Furthermore, they must be trained to teach essential social skills proactively and to prompt and reward their use in the mainstream (Kauffman & Wong, 1991). Nevertheless, improved social skills that generalize to other settings and that persist over time may be taught using two major approaches, structured learning and opportunistic teaching.

Structured Learning

Structured learning approaches are based primarily on Bandura's (1977) notions of social learning theory. According to social learning theory, children learn behaviors not only through their own experiences but also from vicariously observing the actions of others. When models are viewed positively by children, and when children observe the model performing an appropriate social skill that is rewarded, children will be more likely to imitate the same social skill themselves. Observing a model receiving immediate positive consequences for prosocial behavior is key to social learning theory. So, too, is observing a model receiving appropriate negative consequences for exhibiting a prohibited social behavior.

During a social skills lesson, the teacher first defines the skill, then lists the steps to the skill.

Models who are similar in age, gender, and race, or who have prestige in the eyes of the observer, are more likely to be imitated than are dissimilar models (Bandura, 1977). Models who are seen as having extremely high status, on the other hand, may be rejected by children with low status who see these models as setting unrealistic standards for their own behaviors (Perry & Furukawa, 1986). Using multiple models (e.g., various live models of differing ages, gender, races, and social status; varying symbolic models such as those in videotapes, cartoons, or written stories) may also enhance the generality of presentations for small groups of children.

Students with emotional and behavioral disorders, however, do not learn well indirectly through observation of models alone (Kauffman, 1993). Structured learning approaches, therefore, combine modeling with direct instructional teaching procedures (see Chapter 5) such as a clear demonstration, guided practice in the form of role playing, specific performance feedback, and techniques to encourage generalization (Sasso, Melloy, & Kavale, 1990; Zaragoza, Vaughn, & McIntosh, 1991). When using a structured learning approach, teachers form flexible groups of five to ten children of the same approximate age who have been identified as having similar social skills deficits. Seats are arranged in a small semicircle around a chalkboard or easel to facilitate role playing and active participation by all. Rules for the social skills group are generated and posted and daily or weekly lessons follow a prescribed pattern.

During a social skills lesson, the teacher first defines the social skill, its importance, and the steps in the skill. These steps are displayed on chart paper,

BOX 8.1   **The Structured Learning Teaching Sequence**

Goldstein and his colleagues have conducted extensive research regarding teaching social skills through a structured learning approach (Goldstein, 1983; Goldstein, Sprafkin, Gershaw, & Klein, 1980; McGinnis & Goldstein, 1984, 1989). Modeling, role playing, specific feedback, and "transfer training" are essential elements of this approach. The following sequence for teaching social skills is recommended:

1. Define the skill and the steps in the skill.
2. Model the skill (the teacher and a co-trainer demonstrate the skill while the teacher thinks aloud).
3. Discuss current need for the skill.
4. Set up role playing using real situations students have encountered or are likely to encounter.
5. Select first role player, assign other students in the group specific steps to look for, and conduct the role play.
6. Provide specific feedback starting with students in the group and then proceeding to the teacher.
7. Assign homework to monitor use of the social skill when it is actually needed. Teachers may also assign "red flag" homework assignments in which they tell students they will be "set up" for a particular social skill at some point during the school day.
8. Select the next role player.

the chalkboard, or an overhead projector for all to see. The teacher and an aide, or cotrainer, next provide a realistic portrayal of the targeted social skill with the teacher thinking aloud each step of the skill and receiving reinforcement for its use. Children are encouraged to discuss situations they have faced or will face in which the demonstrated social skill would be helpful. Students are then assisted to practice the social skill through role plays, to receive feedback regarding their performance, and to monitor their use of the social skill through homework assignments. See Box 8.1 for the instructional sequence followed in a structured learning approach to teaching social skills, and see Box 8.2 (pp. 244–245) for a sample lesson.

Opportunistic Teaching

Rather than forming groups for skills lessons, opportunistic approaches, on the other hand, harness the "teachable moment" (Phillips, Phillips, Fixsen, & Wolf, 1974). That is, teachers take advantage of situations that occur naturally in the classroom, cafeteria, and hallway, or on the playground to prompt students to perform particular social skills when they have missed an opportunity to do so. Such opportunities are also seized to praise students specifically for their appropriate use of these skills. Young (1993) also suggests that opportunistic teaching methods allow teachers to give corrective feed-

Teacher Feature: Keesha Learns How to Deal with Pressure from Friends

Keesha is impulsive and often gets into trouble because she is unable to resist pressure from her friends. Her teacher presents the following social skills lesson during daily group time:

Teacher: You know how sometimes friends try to get us to do things we're not sure we want to do. It's hard to tell our friends "no" and do what we want to do instead. Like sometimes our friends might try to get us to go somewhere with them when we've been told we can't go. Has something like that ever happened to you? (Teacher elicits comments from individual students in the group.)

Today, we're going to learn how to deal with pressure from our friends. (Pointing to steps on a chart) Dealing with pressure from our friends means you:

1. Listen to what others want you to do.
2. Think about what might happen.
3. Decide what *you* want to do.
4. If you decide not to do what the group wants, say, "No, I can't because _____" (and give a reason).
5. Suggest something else the group can do.

Now watch me. (The teacher and the aide engage in a role play):

Aide: Hey, Mrs. T., I've got a pass to go down to the bathroom. You wait a minute and then get a pass too. We can hang out in the bathroom and walk around the halls.

back in context when students have incorrectly or inappropriately used a social skill.

Within opportunistic teaching approaches, the child's peer group becomes an important component of instruction. If a critical outcome of teaching social skills is increasing positive interactions with peers, then socially competent peers may be encouraged to engage in social interactions with targeted children and to provide reinforcement to these students when they exhibit prosocial behaviors (Strain, Odom, & McConnell, 1984). Maag (1992) refers to this notion as *promoting entrapment* so that students will be more likely to demonstrate and maintain their newly acquired social skills in context.

Peers might be trained, for example, to initiate bids for play to a withdrawn child such as Fong (Kerr & Nelson, 1989). Kerr and Nelson (1989) suggest that teachers select as peer trainers students of moderately high status who are as similar as possible in age, gender, and race to the targeted child. In addition, materials or activities of interest to the targeted child are given as specific

Teacher: (Thinking Aloud) What is it she wants me to do? She wants me to get a bathroom pass after she leaves and then hang out in the bathroom instead of finishing my math homework. Let me think about what might happen. Well, I could get the pass and go down the hall and we might have lots of fun just like we did yesterday. But then we might get caught and I don't want to get into trouble with the principal again. She said she'd call my mother if I get sent to the office again. Let's see . . . I have to decide what I want to do. I don't want to get in trouble and I don't want math homework to do tonight. So I think I'm going to tell her no I can't go. Okay, I'm going to tell her. (Turning to the Aide) No, I'm going to finish my math because I don't want homework to do tonight. (Suggesting something else to do) Maybe we can play during recess when math time is over.

Aide: Okay. I'll be right back so I can finish my math homework, too!

Following a discussion of the demonstration, the teacher elicits from the children similar situations in which they have had to resist pressure from their friends (e.g., pushing someone, teasing someone, stealing a calculator). She calls on the first child to engage in a role play and asks that child to choose another student in the group to play the role of the friend. She then assigns each child remaining in the group one of the steps in "Dealing with Pressure from Friends" to observe during the role play. During the role play, the teacher assists the student to verbalize each of the steps.

From *Skillstreaming the Elementary School Child: A Guide for Teaching Prosocial Skill* (p. 166) by E. McGinnis and A. P. Goldstein, 1984, Champaign, IL: Research Press. Copyright 1984 by the authors. Reprinted by permission.

examples for the peer trainer to use in initiating social interactions. Peer trainers are explicitly taught what they are to do (e.g., "Try to get Fong to play checkers with you"), and they are also taught to expect some rejection and to be persistent. Teachers must be sure to reward peer trainers for their efforts even when these are unsuccessful at first.

Opportunistic teaching approaches, then, may be particularly well suited to promote the generalization of social skills taught through structured learning groups. Neel (1988) and Maag (1992) also suggest that teachers can arrange their classrooms to foster social interactions and precipitate the use of social skills rather than requiring students with emotional and behavioral disorders to work only in relative quiet and isolation. Cooperative learning groups, for example, may be formed to enhance opportunities for social interaction and for prompting and rewarding essential social skills (Fad, Ross, & Boston, 1995). See Box 8.3 (pp. 246–247) for a description of cooperative learning arrangements and Box 8.4 (p. 248) for specific cooperative learning methods.

BOX 8.3   **Cooperative Learning Arrangements**

Students with emotional and behavioral disorders may have more opportunities to practice social skills when they work in pairs or in small groups. Teachers may wish to begin by pairing students to work together. Later, small cooperative learning groups may be formed to encourage social interaction and mutual assistance and problem solving.

Peer Pairs and Peer Tutoring

Peer pairs may be informal arrangements in which two children are permitted to work together or to share certain materials or activities (e.g., reading a story together, playing a game). Peer pairs may also be formed to enable a socially competent child to prompt another student to exhibit a particular social skill such as handraising to get the teacher's attention. In addition, more formal arrangements such as peer tutoring or peer teaching have been used effectively with peers in the same classroom, with peers in the same grade level but different classrooms, and with older students having behavioral or learning problems tutoring younger peers with or without learning and behavioral disorders. Peer tutoring has most often been used to increase student practice of basic skills such as math facts or sight words; however, pairing students for tutoring also allows them to practice appropriate social skills (Jenkins & Jenkins, 1985). To be most effective teachers must train the tutor in basic instructional procedures for giving reinforcement and feedback, plan the instruction and demonstrate the instructional task for the tutor and tutee, and carefully supervise the tutoring sessions.

Cooperative Learning Groups

Cooperative learning groups are formed so that students help one another master material or complete assignments. Cooperation and mutual assistance are stressed rather than competition. Groups may consist of students having mixed ability levels, the same ability level, or similar interests (Kagan, 1990). Johnson and Johnson (1986) maintain that the following are essential elements of cooperative learning groups:

Summary of Social Skills Instruction ◆

Regardless of the specific social skill targeted for instruction, teachers are encouraged to combine structured learning and opportunistic teaching approaches. In addition, teachers should adhere to the following instructional procedures, which are exemplified in almost all well-accepted social skills programs:

1. Teach only those skills that have been socially validated as necessary for success in a particular situation and for the individual child (Meadows, Neel, Parker, & Timo, 1991).
2. Assess the student's use of the social skill. You may wish to review Chapter 2 for social skills checklists and rating scales, sociometric techniques, and

- Positive interdependence. All students have an important contribution to make to the group and the success of each group member is dependent on the success of the group.
- Individual accountability. The performance of each student is assessed and compared with his or her own past performance.
- Instruction in collaborative and group processing skills. Students will need direct instruction in key group roles and dynamics (e.g., leader, scribe, spokesperson, business manager, managing conflicts, etc.).
- Close teacher supervision and monitoring of performance. Teachers maintain the responsibility for monitoring and managing the instructional environment and performance of all students.

Johnson and Johnson (1986) also offer cautions when using cooperative learning arrangements. They maintain that students with disabilities such as emotional or behavioral disorders may be fearful about participating in groups or they may be passive, withdrawn or disruptive in the group. In addition, students without disabilities may fear their grades will be affected and parents may not understand the nature of cooperative learning groups. To alleviate these difficulties, Johnson and Johnson (1986) recommend that teachers do the following:

- Carefully explain to parents and students in advance the procedures the group will follow.
- Pretrain students in essential social and collaborative skills needed by the group and then prompt or cue the skills as needed during group activities.
- Assign structured roles to students so that they understand their roles and have the skills and ability necessary to be successful in these roles.
- Train other students to prompt and praise the appropriate use of social and collaborative group skills.
- Assign the group an average score and give students improvement points for individual performance so that all students are able to contribute equally to the group's success.

direct observational recording procedures helpful for determining which social skills must be taught. For example, through direct observation and use of a checklist, you might determine that Paul does not greet adults or his peers in an appropriate manner. If students do not have opportunities to demonstrate a particular social skill (e.g., students no longer invite Fong to join in their play activities), the teacher might construct a role play to assess the student's performance using the social skill (Beck, Forehand, Neeper, & Baskin, 1982).

3. Clearly tell students what social skill they are to learn, why it is important that they learn this skill, and the steps necessary for successful performance of the skill. For example, you might say to Paul, "Today we are going to learn how to greet someone politely. When you greet classmates

BOX 8.4 Cooperative Learning Methods

Many cooperative learning methods are described in the literature. Among those methods having extensive use in classrooms are student teams achievement divisions (Slavin, 1990, 1991), teams-games-tournaments (Slavin, 1990, 1991), and numbered heads together (Kagan, 1990; Maheady, Mallette, Harper, & Sacca, 1991).

Student Teams Achievement Divisions

In this cooperative learning method, students are arranged into 4 to 5 member, mixed-ability teams. Following a teacher's lesson, students work together until all students in the group have completed the assignments and mastered the material. Weekly quizzes are administered to all students and each individual's score is compared to his or her previous week's quiz score. Points are given for individual improvement in quiz scores and the improvement points of all team members are combined to determine a team score redeemable for certificates or other rewards.

Teams-Games-Tournaments

Teams-games-tournaments follows the same basic procedure as student teams achievement divisions. Rather than weekly quizzes, however, students of comparable ability from each team compete against each other at tournament tables. The winner of each tournament contributes the same number of points to his or her team regardless of the table at which he or she plays.

Numbered Heads Together

Numbered heads together is an excellent method for increasing active student involvement during a lesson. Before beginning a lesson, students are arranged into mixed-ability, four-member teams seated together. Each member of the team is numbered, "one" through "four." Periodically during the lesson, the teacher pauses and asks a question. The students are then to confer in their groups and be sure that all students in the group know the answer to the question. Following a brief period, the teacher asks, "How many Number _____ (1s, 2s, 3s, or 4s) know the answer?" The teacher calls on one of the students with his or her hand raised to answer the question and then asks for how many students of that number agree with the answer or can expand on the answer. Points or praise may be given for all students who can answer, agree with, or expand on an answer to the question posed.

---

politely, they are more willing to talk or play with you. Greeting someone politely means you look at the person, smile, use a pleasant voice tone, and say 'Hello.'" Post the steps for newly acquired social skills and use picture cues of each step for younger children.

4. Demonstrate the new skill for the student. Modeling of the new skill may be accomplished by using videotapes or through demonstrations by

accomplished peers or teachers. To maximize the likelihood of a successful demonstration, the model must be perceived to be of high or expert status, be of approximately the same age and the same gender as the student, and receive reinforcement for engaging in the social skill. In addition, modeling sequences must be clear and well defined with all thought processes made explicit and overt (Goldstein, 1981).

5. Model many different examples and nonexamples of the new social skill. You might, for example, demonstrate several instances of both polite and impolite greetings and then ask Paul to identify a few additional greetings as either polite or not polite (e.g., ''Who are you?,'' ''Nice to meet you'').

6. Provide role playing and practice opportunities so that the student can receive feedback regarding his or her correct use of the social skill. Constructing real-life and realistic role plays and helping students suggest where they might practice the social skill during the day facilitates generalization of the skill (Goldstein, 1983). Moreover, the teacher must offer specific rather than general feedback regarding the student's use of the social skill. You might tell Paul, for example, ''That was a good job of

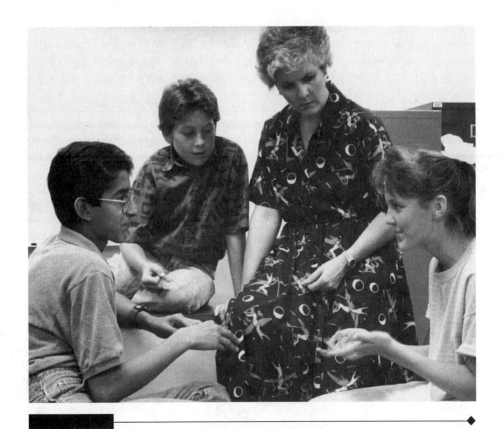

Teachers use realistic role plays to help students practice and receive feedback using relevant social skills.

Name: Paul   Date: February 8, 1996

Skill: Making a Polite Greeting

My homework assignment is to practice: *Making polite greetings*. Each time I make a polite greeting, I will write down when and where it happened, what I did, and what happened next.

Making a polite greeting means:

1. Look at the person.
2. Smile.
3. Use a pleasant tone of voice.
4. Say "Hello," or something similar, like "Hi."

When and where?	*What did I do?*	*What happened next?*

How did I do? ______________________________

____

____

____

FIGURE 8.2

A Social Skills Homework Form for Paul

looking at Keesha and of saying 'Hello' with a pleasant voice tone. Remember to smile when you greet someone, though. Now watch me do it, and we'll practice the greeting again.''

7. Ensure reinforcement following each successful demonstration of the new social skill both during practice sessions and at all natural opportunities occurring throughout the day. To promote generalization, involve parents, teachers, and other professionals in prompting, coaching, and providing reinforcement for appropriate student use of the social skill. In addition, socially competent peers can be participants in role playing sessions, and they may be trained to initiate social interactions and to prompt and reward students for demonstrating social skills in context (Strain & Odom, 1986).
8. Have students complete ''homework assignments'' documenting and evaluating their use of the new social skill (Armstrong & McPherson, 1991). Logs, diaries, journals, checklists, or self-monitoring forms give

students opportunities to assume greater responsibility and control over their use of newly acquired social skills, thus enhancing generalization (Misra, 1992) (Figure 8.2). ◆

Social Skills Curricula

Carter and Sugai (1989), Sabornie and Beard (1990), and Sugai and Fuller (1991) all suggest teachers select social skills programs that incorporate each of the critical steps mentioned previously. Clear and direct instruction, modeling, role playing, specific feedback, and planned activities to promote generalization of skills learned are essential for the success of social skills instruction. In addition to cost and the amount of training required, these authors encourage teachers to examine commercially available social skills curricula to be sure that age-appropriate and relevant social skills are taught, that structured teaching procedures are used, that acceptable assessment procedures and adequate information regarding social validation are included, and that plans for the generalization and maintenance of skills are provided.

Among the social skills curricula available commercially, several meet these criteria. These include *Boys Town Social Skills Curriculum* (Wells, 1990), *Getting Along with Others* (Jackson, Jackson, & Monroe, 1983), *Skillstreaming* (Goldstein, Sprafkin, Gershaw, & Klein, 1980; McGinnis & Goldstein, 1984, 1989), *Social Skills for Daily Living* (Schumaker, Hazel, & Pederson, 1988), *Social Skills on the Job* (Macro Systems, 1988), and *The Walker Social Skills Curriculum* (Walker et al., 1983; Walker, Todis, Holmes, & Horton, 1988).

Boys Town Social Skills Curriculum

The *Boys Town Social Skills Curriculum* (Wells, 1990) consists of a series of 16 specific social skills from how to follow instructions to how to introduce yourself. See Box 8.5 (p. 252) for a list of the social skills included in the Boys Town Curriculum. The first seven social skills are considered critical skills without which students will have difficulty in the regular classroom. Each social skill is broken into a series of discrete steps for direct instruction as well as for instruction and practice through a "teaching interaction" during the school day when the skill is required in context (Downs, Kutsick, & Black, 1985) (For additional information about the Boys Town Social Skills Curriculum or about the Boys Town Education Model contact National Training Center, Father Flanagan's Boys Home, Boys Town Center, Boys Town, NE 68010, (402) 498-1556.)

Getting Along with Others

Getting Along with Others (Jackson, Jackson, & Monroe, 1983) provides a series of scripted social skills lessons, role playing activities, relaxation exercises, and homework assignments for elementary-age students. The material is also easily adaptable for children at the middle school level. Like the *Boys Town Social Skills Curriculum*, *Getting Along with Others* also gives teachers "interactions" for

Boys Town Social Skills Curriculum

1. How to follow instructions.*
2. How to accept criticism or a consequence.*
3. How to accept "No" for an answer.*
4. How to greet someone.*
5. How to get the teacher's attention (asking permission).*
6. How to make a request.*
7. How to disagree appropriately.*
8. How to give negative feedback.
9. How to resist peer pressure (or say "No").
10. How to apologize.
11. How to engage in a conversation.
12. How to give a compliment.
13. How to accept a compliment.
14. How to volunteer.
15. How to report peer behavior.
16. How to introduce yourself.

*Denotes a social skill critical for classroom and adult success.

From *Boys Town Education Model*, by T. Wells, p. 3. Copyright © 1990 Father Flanagan's Boys' Home. Reprinted by permission.

teaching children newly acquired social skills in context throughout the school day.

Effective praise, the first interaction, informs students about correct social behaviors and rewards children for using social skills. Effective praise has two specific components: a statement of affection (e.g., smiling, saying a student's name) and a statement containing specific feedback regarding what the child did correctly (e.g., smiling and saying, "Paul, that was a good job of greeting our guest. You looked at Mr. Meade, you smiled, and you said "Hello" with a pleasant voice tone. Give yourself ten points!").

The teaching interaction is used to interrupt a child's inappropriate behavior and prompt the student to use the correct social skill (Jackson, Jackson, & Monroe, 1983). Again, the teaching interaction starts with a statement of affection or empathy in order to begin the corrective feedback on a positive note. The teaching interaction continues with a specific description of the inappropriate behavior followed by an explanation of the appropriate social skill. Next, the student is asked to practice the skill and he or she is given general praise for doing so.

The teaching interaction offers a positive way to correct student misbehavior and provide instruction on appropriate behavior when this skill is actually required during the day. For example, if Paul were to respond to Mr. Meade's entry into the classroom by yelling, "Hey, who are you?", the teacher might state, "Paul, I understand that you are curious about our guest (e.g., a statement of affection and empathy), but you just forgot how to greet someone (e.g., a description of the inappropriate behavior). What you need to do is smile, look at Mr. Meade and say 'Hello' with a pleasant voice tone (e.g., a description of the appropriate social skill). Please make a polite greeting to Mr. Meade (e.g., a request or prompt to practice the correct social skill)." When Paul complies with this request, the teacher might follow-up the interaction with general praise (e.g., "Thank you, Paul. That was a good job of greeting someone appropriately"). The teacher might also follow the teaching interaction with a point loss and addition (e.g., "Paul, you lost ten points for forgetting to greet someone politely, but you earned five points for following instructions and accepting criticism well").

Whenever a teacher begins an interaction with a student and the student becomes quarrelsome or noncompliant, the teacher enters the third interaction, the direct prompt. The direct prompt is a concise statement telling the student specifically what he or she must do to become correct. To deliver a direct prompt, the teacher calmly and quietly issues a "You need to . . ." statement. If the student complies with the prompt, the teacher follows with a point loss and addition as with the teaching interaction. If the student fails to comply, however, the teacher makes an "If . . . then . . ." statement to set limits for the youngster and follows through with the consequences as necessary. The teacher must, of course, preset these consequences for misbehavior and begin the statement by offering the positive alternative first.

In the previous example, if Paul were to become argumentative during the teaching interaction, you might interrupt his misbehavior by stating, "Paul, you need to greet Mr. Meade politely." If Paul complies, you might follow his behavior with the statement, "Paul, that was a good job of accepting criticism well. You did what you were asked to do without complaining. You lost ten points for forgetting to greet Mr. Meade politely, but you just earned five points for accepting criticism well." If Paul were to continue to display his temper, however, you might respond by saying, "Paul, if you greet Mr. Meade politely, you may earn some points. If you do not greet him politely, you will choose to lose ten points." (The three teaching interactions are described in *Getting Along With Others*, available through Research Press, 2612 N. Mattis Ave., Champaign, IL 61821.)

Skillstreaming

Skillstreaming (Goldstein, Sprafkin, Gershaw, & Klein, 1980; McGinnis, & Goldstein, 1984, 1989) is available for the preschool and kindergarten child, for elementary-level students, and for adolescents. At each level teachers are given a checklist of social skills to facilitate grouping students with similar needs into structured learning groups. Also at each level, the social skills are broken into a series of steps to be taught through modeling, role playing, specific performance feedback, and homework assignments to foster skills generalization. When modeling social skills for children and youth, teachers are encouraged to think aloud, making all of their covert thoughts occurring during the decision-making process overt. (See Chapter 9 for additional information on this self-instructional procedure.)

At the early childhood level, 40 social skills (e.g., dealing with teasing, waiting your turn) are included in six skill groups. For young children, the social skills

Table 8.1 The Skillstreaming Curriculum: Elementary Level

	Student names										
I. Classroom survival skills											
1. Listening											
2. Asking for help											
3. Saying thank you											
4. Bringing materials to class											
5. Following instructions											
6. Completing assignments											
7. Contributing to discussions											
8. Offering help to an adult											
9. Asking a question											
10. Ignoring distractions											
11. Making corrections											
12. Deciding on something to do											
13. Setting a goal											
II. Friendship-making skills											
14. Introducing yourself											
15. Beginning a conversation											
16. Ending a conversation											
17. Joining in											
18. Playing a game											
19. Asking a favor											
20. Offering help to a classmate											
21. Giving a compliment											
22. Accepting a compliment											
23. Suggesting an activity											
24. Sharing											
25. Apologizing											
III. Skills for dealing with feelings											
26. Knowing your feelings											
27. Expressing your feelings											

Table 8.1	The Skillstreaming Curriculum: Elementary Level (cont.)											
	Student names											
III. Skills for dealing with feelings (cont'd)												
28. Recognizing another's feelings												
29. Showing understanding of another's feelings												
30. Expressing concern for another												
31. Dealing with your anger												
32. Dealing with another's anger												
33. Expressing affection												
34. Dealing with fear												
35. Rewarding yourself												
IV. Skill alternatives to aggression												
36. Using self-control												
37. Asking permission												
38. Responding to teasing												
39. Avoiding trouble												
40. Staying out of fights												
41. Problem solving												
42. Accepting consequences												
43. Dealing with an accusation												
44. Negotiating												
V. Skills for dealing with stress												
45. Dealing with boredom												
46. Deciding what caused a problem												
47. Making a complaint												
48. Answering a complaint												
49. Dealing with losing												
50. Showing sportsmanship												
51. Dealing with being left out												
52. Dealing with embarrassment												

Continued.

Table 8.1 The Skillstreaming Curriculum: Elementary Level (cont.)

	Student names									
V. Skills for dealing with stress (cont'd)										
53. Reacting to failure										
54. Accepting no										
55. Saying no										
56. Relaxing										
57. Dealing with group pressure										
58. Dealing with wanting something that isn't mine										
59. Making a decision										
60. Being honest										

From *Skillstreaming the Elementary School Child: A Guide for Teaching Prosocial Skill* (pp. 43–44) by E. McGinnis and A. P. Goldstein, 1984, Champaign, IL: Research Press. Copyright 1984 by the authors. Reprinted by permission.

steps may be taught using picture clues. With students at the elementary level, children are taught any of 60 social skills across five skill clusters. Teachers are encouraged to group children for instruction only for those specific social skills that individual students are lacking. At the adolescent level, 50 prosocial skills, including alternatives to aggression, dealing with feelings and stress, and planning skills, are taught (Tables 8.1 and 8.2). (The entire Skillstreaming program may be obtained from Research Press, 2612 N. Mattis Ave., Champaign, IL 61821.)

Social Skills for Daily Living

Social Skills for Daily Living (Schumaker, Hazel, Pederson, 1988) is a curriculum developed at the University of Kansas Institute for Research in Learning Disabilities. The curriculum is designed for students ages 12 to 21 with learning disabilities, emotional and behavioral disorders, or mild mental retardation. The program consists of 30 social skills arranged in the following four clusters: body basics (e.g., making eye contact, facing the other person, using appropriate voice tones, facial expressions, and body posture), conversation and friendship skills (e.g., active listening, introducing yourself, interrupting), skills for getting along with others (e.g., accepting and saying thanks, apologizing, accepting "no," resisting peer pressure, responding to teasing, accepting criticism), and

Table 8.2 **The Skillstreaming Curriculum: Adolescent Level**		
Group I. Beginning Social Skills		
1. Listening		
2. Starting a conversation		
3. Having a conversation		
4. Asking a question		
5. Saying thank you		
6. Introducing yourself		
7. Introducing other people		
8. Giving a compliment		
Group II. Advanced Social Skills		
9. Asking for help		
10. Joining in		
11. Giving instructions		
12. Following instructions		
13. Apologizing		
14. Convincing others		
Group III. Skills for Dealing with Feelings		
15. Knowing your feelings		
16. Expressing your feelings		
17. Understanding the feelings of others		
18. Dealing with someone else's anger		
19. Expressing affection		
20. Dealing with fear		
21. Rewarding yourself		
Group IV. Skill Alternatives to Aggression		
22. Asking permission		
23. Sharing something		
24. Helping others		
25. Negotiating		
26. Using self-control		
27. Standing up for your rights		
28. Responding to teasing		
29. Avoiding trouble with others		
30. Keeping out of fights		

Continued.

Table 8.2   The Skillstreaming Curriculum: Adolescent Level (cont.)

Group V. Skills for Dealing with Stress		
31. Making a complaint		
32. Answering a complaint		
33. Sportsmanship after the game		
34. Dealing with embarrassment		
35. Dealing with being left out		
36. Standing up for a friend		
37. Responding to persuasion		
38. Responding to failure		
39. Dealing with contradictory messages		
40. Dealing with an accusation		
41. Getting ready for a difficult conversation		
42. Dealing with group pressure		
Group VI. Planning Skills		
43. Deciding on something to do		
44. Deciding what caused a problem		
45. Setting a goal		
46. Deciding on your abilities		
47. Gathering information		
48. Arranging problems by importance		
49. Making a decision		
50. Concentrating on a task		

From *Skillstreaming the Adolescent: A Structured Learning Approach to Teaching Prosocial Skill* (pp. 73–74) by A. P. Goldstein, R. P. Sprafkin, N. J. Gershaw, and P. Klein, 1980, Champaign, IL: Research Press. Copyright 1980 by the authors. Reprinted by permission.

problem-solving skills (e.g., following instructions, getting help, persuasion, negotiation, joining group activities).

A comic book and skill book format is used to present each social skill. Students also use practice cards to role play relevant scenarios with a partner and complete a checklist to monitor their practice of the skill at school, at work, and at home. Surprise Missions and Bonus Missions assist students to apply their newly acquired social skills in varying situations. (Social Skills for Daily Living is available from American Guidance Service, 4201 Woodland Road #1279, Circle Pines, MN 55014.)

Social Skills on the Job

Social Skills on the Job (Macro Systems, 1988) is designed to teach students with mild learning disabilities, emotional and behavioral disorders, and mild mental retardation essential on-the-job behaviors. The 14 critical workplace skills include: wearing appropriate clothing, using good personal hygiene, calling in when sick, getting to work on time, greeting authority figures, using appropriate breaktime behavior, doing one's share of the work, maintaining the work schedule, admitting mistakes, responding to introductions, knowing when to ask for help, knowing who to ask for help, dealing with heckling from a co-worker, and dealing with criticism from an employer. The complete program offers videotaped vignettes of each social skill in actual work settings and teaching suggestions for role playing and practicing the skills. The curriculum is also available on computer software. (Social Skills on the Job may be obtained from American Guidance Service, 4201 Woodland Road #1279, Circle Pines, MN 55014).

The Walker Social Skills Curriculum

The Walker Social Skills Curriculum (Walker, McConnell, Holmes, Todis, Walker, & Golden, 1983; Walker, Todis, Holmes, & Horton, 1988) is available at two different levels. Specific lists of social skills, a pretest, scripted teaching, modeling, and role playing activities, again, are critical instructional elements of the curriculum. The ACCEPTS (i.e., A Curriculum for Children's Effective Peer and Teacher Skills) program is appropriate for students at the elementary level. ACCEPTS contains the following five skill areas: classroom, basic interaction, getting along, making friends, and coping. A behavior management system and optional videotapes are also included.

ACCESS (i.e., Adolescent Curriculum for Communication and Effective Social Skills) gives teachers role playing and structured homework assignments as well as a placement test and student contracts. Thirty-one social skills lessons are contained in the ACCESS program including peer, adult, and self-related skills. (ACCEPTS and ACCESS are both available through Pro-Ed, 8700 Shoal Creek Blvd., Austin, TX 78758.)

Summary of Social Skills Curricula ◆

Although many social skills programs are available commercially, teachers must take care to review these for effective teaching procedures. Direct and explicit instruction, modeling, role playing, specific performance feedback, and homework to promote generalization are essential features of good social skills curricula. In addition, teachers must ensure they are teaching only those socially valid social skills that are necessary for the success of particular students in their individual classroom, home, or community settings. ◆

Summary

Social skills are those skills that enable students to interact effectively with peers and important others. Socially competent students enjoy mutually reinforcing interactions with others because they engage in appropriate social skills acceptable for the time and place. Teaching socially valid social skills improves social competence and peer acceptance.

Structured learning approaches teach social skills through formal lessons presented to small groups of children. Direct instructional teaching procedures, modeling, role playing, specific performance feedback, and homework assignments are key elements of a structured learning approach. Opportunistic teaching approaches harness the power of the peer group and situations occurring in the natural environment. Peer pairs, peer trainers, and cooperative learning groups may be used to foster social interaction and provide opportunities for prompting and rewarding social skills in context. Teachers may use a combination of structured learning and opportunistic teaching to help students generalize newly acquired social skills.

Numerous curricula are available commercially for teaching social skills to students with emotional and behavioral disorders. Well-designed social skills programs provide explicit instruction, modeling, role playing, specific performance feedback, and homework assignments in context to facilitate skill generalization. Teaching only those social skills validated as necessary for the success of individual children in their particular classroom, home, and community environments also helps ensure that students will use the skills appropriately after they are taught.

Application Exercises

1. Examine the social skills curricula used in a local school district. Are the elements of an effective social skills program (e.g., modeling, role playing, specific performance feedback, homework) included in this curriculum? Ask a teacher who uses the social skills curriculum about this program. Is the program taught as a subject during each school day? Are social skills integrated and taught in context throughout the day? How is the program individualized to meet the needs of particular children?

2. With a partner, practice giving effective praise, a teaching interaction, and a direct prompt for the social skill "how to follow instructions." Define this skill as "Look at the person, say 'Okay,' and do what is asked immediately."

3. Ask a bus driver and a cafeteria worker in a local school to describe the social behaviors necessary for success on the bus and in the lunchroom respectively. Arrange to observe in these settings to determine if the behaviors suggested by these individuals are resulting in positive interactions for a particular student.

4. Ask a classroom teacher at a chosen grade level to describe the social skills necessary for success in his or her classroom. Arrange to observe a student in this classroom. If possible, observe the same student you observed in application exercise number 3, and compare your observations of this student's use of social skills across these different settings.

5. Examine the social skills curricula presented in this chapter. In a small group, plan and conduct a structured lesson for a social skill selected from one of these curricular materials.

References

Armstrong, S. W., & McPherson, A. (1991). Homework as a critical component in social skills instruction. *Teaching Exceptional Children, 24*(1), 45–47.

Bandura, A. (1977). *Social learning theory.* Englewood Cliffs, NJ: Prentice-Hall.

Beck, S., Forehand, R., Neeper, R., & Baskin, C. (1982). A comparison of two analogue strategies for assessing children's social skills. *Journal of Consulting and Clinical Psychology, 50,* 596–597.

Bellack, A. S. (1983). Recurrent problems in the behavioral assessment of social skills. *Behavioral Research Therapy, 21*(1), 29–41.

Carpenter, R. L., & Apter, S. J. (1988). Research integration of cognitive-emotional interventions for behaviorally disordered children and youth. In M. C. Wang, M. C. Reynolds, & H. J. Walberg (Eds.), *Handbook of special education research and practice: Volume II* (pp. 155–169). Oxford: Pergamon.

Carter, J., & Sugai, G. (1989). Social skills curriculum analysis. *Teaching Exceptional Children, 22*(1), 36–39.

Downs, J. C., Kutsick, K., & Black, D. D. (1985). The teaching interaction: A systematic approach to developing social skills in disruptive and nondisruptive students. *Techniques, 1,* 304–310.

Fad, K. S. (1990). The fast track to success: Social-behavioral skills. *Intervention in School and Clinic, 26*(1), 39–43.

Fad, K. S., Ross, M., & Boston, J. (1995). Using cooperative learning to teach social skills to young children. *Teaching Exceptional Children, 27*(4), 28–34.

Goldstein, A. P. (1981). Social skills training. In A. P. Goldstein, E. G. Carr, W. S. Davidson, & P. Weher (Eds.), *In response to aggression: Methods of control and prosocial alternatives.* New York: Pergamon.

Goldstein, A. P. (1983). Structured learning: A psychoeducational approach to teaching social competencies. *Behavioral Disorders, 8,* 161–170.

Goldstein, A. P., Sprafkin, R. P., Gershaw, N. J., & Klein, P. (1980). *Skillstreaming the adolescent: A structured learning approach to teaching prosocial skills.* Champaign, IL: Research Press.

Gresham, F. M. (1984). Social skills and self-efficacy for exceptional children. *Exceptional Children, 51*(3), 253–261.

Gresham, F. (1986). Conceptual issues in the assessment of social competence in children. In P. S. Strain, M. J. Guralnick, & H. M. Walker (Eds.), *Children's social behavior: Development, assessment, and modification* (pp. 143–179). Orlando, FL: Academic Press.

Gresham, F. M., & Elliott, S. N. (1989). Social skills deficits as a primary learning disability. *Journal of Learning Disabilities, 22*(2), 120–124.

Gresham, F. M., Elliott, S. N., & Black, F. L. (1987). Teacher-rated social skills of mainstreamed mildly handicapped and nonhandicapped children. *School Psychology Review, 16,* 78–88.

Hollinger, J. D. (1987). Social skills for behaviorally disordered children as preparation for mainstreaming: Theory, practice and new directions. *Remedial and Special Education, 8,* 17–27.

Jackson, N. F., Jackson, D. A., & Monroe, C. (1983). *Getting along with others: Teaching social effectiveness to children.* Champaign, IL: Research Press.

Jenkins, J. J., & Jenkins, L. M. (1985). Peer tutoring in elementary and secondary programs. *Focus on Exceptional Children, 17*(6), 1–12.

Johnson, D. W., & Johnson, R. T. (1986). Mainstreaming and cooperative learning strategies. *Exceptional Children, 52,* 553–562.

Kagan, S. (1990). *Cooperative learning: Resources for teachers.* San Juan Capistrano, CA: Spencer Kagan, Ph.D.

Kauffman, J. M. (1993). *Characteristics of emotional and behavioral disorders of children and youth* (5th Ed.). New York: Merrill/Macmillan.

Kauffman, J. M., & Wong, K. L. H. (1991). Effective teachers of students with behavioral disorders: Are generic teaching skills enough? *Behavioral Disorders, 16,* 225–237.

Kerr, M. M., & Nelson, C. M. (1989). *Strategies for managing behavior problems in the classroom.* Columbus, OH: Merrill/Macmillan.

Maag, J. W. (1989). Assessment in social skills training: Methodological and conceptual issues for research and practice. *Remedial and Special Education, 10*(4), 6–17.

Maag, J. W. (1990). Social skills training in schools. *Special Services in the Schools, 6,* 1–19.

Maag, J. W. (1992). Integrating consultation into social skills training: Implications for practice. *Journal of Educational and Psychological Consultation, 3*(3), 233–258.

Macro Systems, Inc. (1988). *Social Skills on the Job.* Circle Pines, MN: American Guidance Service.

Maheady, L., Mallett, B., Harper, G. F., & Sacca, K. (1991). Heads together: A peer-mediated option for improving the academic achievement of heterogeneous learning groups. *Remedial and Special Education, 12*(2), 25–33.

McConnell, S. R. (1987). Entrapment effects and the generalization and maintenance of social skills training for elementary school students with behavioral disorders. *Behavioral Disorders, 12,* 252–263.

McFall, R. (1982). A review and reformulation of the concept of social skills. *Behavioral Assessment, 4,* 1–33.

McGinnis, E., & Goldstein, A. P. (1984). *Skillstreaming the elementary school child: A guide for teaching prosocial skills.* Champaign, IL: Research Press.

McGinnis, E., & Goldstein, A. P. (1989). *Skillstreaming in early childhood: Teaching prosocial skills to the preschool and kindergarten child.* Champaign, IL: Research Press.

Meadows, N., Neel, R. S., Parker, G., & Timo, K. (1991). A validation of social skills for students with behavioral disorders. *Behavioral Disorders, 16*(3), 200–210.

Misra, A. (1992). Generalization of social skills through self-monitoring by adults with mild mental retardation. *Exceptional Children, 58*(6), 495–507.

Neel, R. S. (1988). Classroom conversion kit: A teacher's guide to teaching social competency. In R. B. Rutherford & J. W. Maag (Eds.), *Severe behavior disorders of children and youth: Volume 11* (pp. 25–31). Reston, VA: Council for Children with Behavioral Disorders.

Neel, R. S., & Cessna, K. K. (1990). Maybe this behavior does make sense. In R. B. Rutherford & S. A. DiGangi (Eds.), *Severe behavior disorders of children and youth: Volume 13* (pp. 18–22). Reston, VA: Council for Children with Behavioral Disorders.

Neel, R. S., Meadows, N. B., Levine, P., & Edgar, E. B. (1988). What happens after special education: A statewide follow-up study of secondary students who have behavioral disorders. *Behavioral Disorders, 13,* 209–216.

Nelson, C. M. (1988). Social skills training for handicapped students. *Teaching Exceptional Children, 20*(4), 19–23.

Parker, J. G., & Asher, S. R. (1987). Peer relations and later personal adjustment: Are low-accepted children at risk? *Psychological Bulletin, 102,* 357–389.

Perry, M. A., & Furukawa, M. J. (1986). Modeling Methods. In F. H. Kanfer & A. P. Goldstein (Eds.), *Helping people change: A textbook of methods* (3rd Ed.) (pp. 66–110). New York, NY: Pergamon.

Philips, E. L., Phillips, E. A., Fixsen, D. L., & Wolf, M. (1974). *The teaching-family handbook.* Lawrence, KS: University Printing Service.

Sabornie, E. J., & Beard, G. H. (1990). Teaching social skills to students with mild handicaps. *Teaching Exceptional Children, 23*(1), 35–38.

Sasso, G. M., Melloy, K. J., & Kavale, K. A. (1990). Generalization, maintenance, and behavioral covariation associated with social skills training through structured learning. *Behavioral Disorders, 16*(1), 9–22.

Schloss, P. J., Schloss, C. N., Wood, C. E., & Kiehl, W. S. (1986). A critical review of social skills research with behaviorally disordered students. *Behavioral Disorders, 12*(1), 1–14.

Schumaker, J. B., Hazel, J. S., & Pederson, C. S. (1988). *Social Skills for Daily Living.* Circle Pines, MN: American Guidance Service.

Slavin, R. E. (1990). *Cooperative learning: Theory, research and practice.* Englewood Cliffs, NJ: Prentice-Hall.

Slavin, R. E. (1991). Synthesis of research on cooperative learning. *Educational Leadership, 48*(6), 71–82.

Stokes, T. F., & Baer, D. M. (1977). An implicit technology of generalization. *Journal of Applied Behavior Analysis, 10,* 349–367.

Stokes, T. F., & Osnes, P. G. (1986). Programming the generalization of children's social behavior. In P. S. Strain, M. Guralnick, & H. M. Walker (Eds.), *Children's social behavior: Development, assessment, and modification* (pp. 407–443). Orlando, FL: Academic Press.

Strain, P. S., & Odom, S. L. (1986). Peer social initiations: Effective intervention for social skills development of exceptional children. *Exceptional Children, 52,* 543–551.

Strain, P. S., Odom, S. L., & McConnell, S. (1984). Promoting social reciprocity of exceptional children: Identification, target behavior selection, and intervention. *Remedial and Special Education, 5*(1), 21–28.

Sugai, G., & Fuller, M. (1991). A decision model for social skills curriculum analysis. *Remedial and Special Education, 12*(4), 33–42.

Walker, H. M., McConnell, S., Holmes, D., Todis, B., Walker, J., & Golden, N. (1983). *The Walker social skills curriculum: The ACCEPTS program.* Austin, TX: Pro-Ed.

Walker, H. M., Todis, B., Holmes, D., & Horton, G. (1988). *The Walker social skills curriculum: The ACCESS program.* Austin, TX: Pro-Ed.

Wells, T. (1990). *Boys town education model.* Boys Town, NE: Father Flanagan's Boys' Home.

Wolf, M. M. (1978). Social validity: The case for subjective measurement or how applied behavior analysis is finding its heart. *Journal of Applied Behavior Analysis, 11,* 203–214.

Young, K. R. (1993). The role of social skills training in the prevention and treatment of behavioral disorders. In B. Smith (Ed.), *Focus '93—Teaching students with learning and behavioral problems* (pp. 341–367). Victoria, British Columbia: Smith and Associates.

Zaragoza, N., Vaughn, S., & McIntosh, R. (1991). Social skills interventions and children with behavior problems: A review. *Behavioral Disorders, 16*(4), 260–275.

TEACHING RESPONSIBILITY

Main Ideas

◆ *Responsibility models acknowledge the influence of beliefs on behavior, thus, an underlying goal of intervention is to change thoughts to modify feelings and behavior.*

◆ *Cognitive behavioral interventions use the child's inner language to mediate behavior.*

◆ *Through structured teaching procedures students become more aware of their actions and learn self-management and cognitive restructuring strategies effective for regulating their behavior in the future.*

◆ *Traditional responsibility models use the language of teachers or peers to mediate between the student's thoughts, feelings, and behaviors and the reactions of others.*

◆ *Life space intervention, reality therapy, and peer-group meetings harness problem situations as opportunities for teaching better coping and problem-solving skills.*

In Chapter 6 you read about how to respect student feelings and in Chapters 7 and 8 you learned how the teacher might structure the classroom environment to produce and reinforce appropriate behaviors and social skills. The teacher cannot realistically, however, permit and support the expression of all feelings or monitor and reward every appropriate behavior for every student. Sooner or later, the teacher must relinquish some control over feelings and behaviors and begin to transfer this responsibility to the students themselves. For the well-being of your students and for your own well-being as the teacher, you must teach your students *how* to behave independently so that they will rely on you less to direct their actions and so that they will be better prepared to function in the regular classroom and in the community.

Teachers and parents have always been concerned with helping children learn how to take charge of themselves, control their own behaviors, and act responsibly. Behaving responsibly entails examining and choosing from competing alternatives, taking action to achieve desired goals, and being accountable for one's decisions and actions. As a beginning teacher, for example, I hung a mobile in my classroom that read "TRY." TRY was an acronym standing for the classroom motto "*Take responsibility yourself*." Although this was certainly an appropriate aim for the young people in my classroom, teaching a group of students with emotional and behavioral disorders, like Paul and Keesha, to assume responsibility can be a daunting and challenging task. Yet, as Brendtro, Brokenleg, and Van Bockern (1990) state, teachers must "discipline" *for* responsibility.

You may recall from reading Chapter 4 that a major goal of the psycho-educational model is to teach children and youth responsibility (Glasser, 1965, 1969). This model, you may also remember, grew from the more traditional psychodynamic perspective. Both schools of thought share an emphasis on accepting and supporting feelings within a warm and trusting adult-child relationship and both share the belief that *inner thoughts influence behavior* (Redl, 1976a). Proponents of the psychoeducational philosophy, however, also believe that students with emotional and behavioral disorders lack coping and problem solving skills. They maintain that behaviors of students must be managed, not merely permitted, to promote self-control and that *support for feelings comes through a structured environment* (Fenichel, 1976; Long & Newman, 1976). Like advocates of the behavioral model, psychoeducational practitioners, then, focus on environmental events. Problem situations that trigger student behavior are used to teach students more effective social and problem-solving skills.

In addition, traditional psychoeducational strategies also share much in common with cognitive behavioral research regarding the influence of beliefs on one's behavior (Meichenbaum, 1977). Cognitive behavioral theorists view covert, internal thought processes as important antecedents and consequences of behavior (Mahoney & Thoresen, 1974). Psychoeducational practitioners, too, contend that children have an "emotional memory bank," a personal storehouse of thoughts and feelings about past experiences that affect behavior whenever a child is faced with stressful events (Wood & Long, 1991). Private speech, our "inner language," then, is a crucial determinant of behavior for both psychoeducational and cognitive behavioral theorists. Thus, if inner language mediates behavior, an important goal of all interventions within the responsibility model is to *change thoughts to modify behaviors* (Figure 9.1).

Key ideas
- Thoughts affect surface behaviors
- Support for feelings is provided through structure
- Use problem situations to teach
- Language mediates behavior

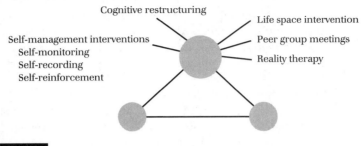

Cognitive restructuring

Life space intervention

Self-management interventions
Self-monitoring
Self-recording
Self-reinforcement

Peer group meetings

Reality therapy

FIGURE 9.1 ◆

Responsibility Model

As you can see, an underlying philosophy behind the responsibility model is that how young people view life events often determines how they behave. Before engaging in a game of tennis with a friend, for example, you have certain beliefs and expectancies about the game. You may evaluate whether or not you can play well against this friend and your likelihood of a positive outcome (i.e., winning the game). Before and during the game, then, you might engage in certain self-talk (e.g., "I can win against her. I've done it before"; "That was a good shot"; "I'm doing well") that further influences your feelings and behaviors during and following the tennis match. If, on the other hand, you believe that you are "not good enough" at tennis to play this friend, you may be likely to avoid playing the game, attribute your lack of success to "the hot weather," or say you "hate tennis because it's a stupid game anyway." What you believe about yourself and a particular situation governs your behavior, and, in turn, your behavior precipitates additional beliefs, feelings, and behavioral reactions within you as well as from those around you.

Children and youth with emotional and behavioral disorders, though, may be unaware of their feelings or of how their thoughts affect their behaviors. In addition, these students often do not realize, or they deny, how their behaviors are responsible for the unfavorable reactions they frequently receive from their peers and from adults (Wood & Long, 1991). Responsibility teachers, therefore, emphasize the importance of thoughts and feelings for guiding the behaviors of students. They may, at least initially, share the responsibility for behavioral control with their students, but ultimately, this responsibility rests with the child.

Within this model, then, teachers attempt to influence behavior by changing what students think or say to themselves about their actions and about particular situations. Some interventions harness the child's own inner language and teach students to control their behaviors by self-monitoring, self-recording, or self-reinforcing what they do (Harris, 1982; Graham, Harris, & Reid, 1992; Williams & Rooney, 1986). Other interventions give students self-instructional techniques for handling frustration or anger so that they may "talk themselves through" problem situations, cope with their feelings, and demonstrate improved self-control (Camp, Blom, Hebert, & Van Doorninck, 1977; Goldstein & Glick, 1987). In still other strategies, the teacher does the talking, and his or her language becomes the mediator between the child's thoughts, feelings, and behaviors and the reactions of others (Glasser, 1965, 1969; Wood & Long, 1991).

In this chapter, then, we will examine several strategies for helping students with emotional and behavioral disorders learn greater responsibility. We will first discuss cognitive-behavioral interventions. These include self-management techniques as well as cognitive restructuring and self-control curricula. Next, we will introduce three more traditional approaches to teaching responsibility, life space intervention, reality therapy, and peer-group meetings. These are important strategies that use structured conversations between teachers and students to lead children and youth to assume greater responsibility for changing their behaviors. Finally, we will explore the major criticisms leveled against each of these methods.

Cognitive-Behavioral Interventions

Since the 1970s, authorities have argued that many students with learning and behavioral problems become passive, rather than active, learners in the classroom (Pearl, Bryan, & Donahue, 1980; Torgesen, 1977). These students may, for example, be more likely than their peers to attribute their successes to external factors (i.e., an external locus of control) and to exhibit learned helplessness (i.e., a belief that failure will always occur no matter how hard one works) (Seligman, 1992). Such beliefs usually result in decreased effort, persistence, and motivation for students in the classroom. Moreover, many students with learning and behavioral difficulties have deficits in social cognition and in metacognitive skills (Pearl, 1992; Short & Weissberg-Benchell, 1989). That is, these students fail to perceive important social clues from others, and they lack an awareness of the strategies available to help them achieve success in particular situations. Thus, many children and youth with emotional and behavioral disorders fail to monitor and regulate their own behaviors to attain a positive outcome.

Recently, authorities have questioned whether or not behaviors produced through traditional external behavior management systems such as token economies will readily generalize to other settings (Kazdin, 1982). In an attempt to overcome this difficulty, as well as student motivational problems and strategy deficits, professionals have begun to investigate cognitive behavioral interventions (Mace, Brown, & West, 1987). Typically, cognitive behavioral interventions combine the explicit instructional techniques of behavioral theory with an interest in the child's cognitions (i.e., a child's thoughts and feelings). The student's inner language, therefore, is viewed as instrumental in governing behavior (Harris, 1990; Luria, 1961; Vygotsky, 1962). Cognitive behavioral interventions, then, attempt systematically to change what children and youth say to themselves as they engage in different activities to help them better self-regulate or self-manage their actions (Meichenbaum & Goodman, 1971). Although many cognitive behavioral interventions are reported in the literature (see, for example, Dobson & Block, 1988), those with the most practical applications for the classroom are frequently self-management strategies or cognitive restructuring approaches. In addition, several self-control and problem-solving curricula are available to help students harness the power of their self-talk and change their own behaviors.

Self-Management Strategies

Self-management strategies are those techniques individuals use to regulate their own behaviors and accomplish specific tasks. You may, for example, set goals for completing coursework in your classes. You might determine the number of pages you need to read or write on a daily basis to finish a term paper on time. Then, you might monitor your progress each day and reward yourself with a special activity for accomplishing your goals. According to Graham, Harris, and Reid (1992), learning to self-regulate is essential in classroom settings if students are to become less disruptive and more independent, on-task, and academically productive. Key self-management strategies, then, are self-monitoring, self-recording, and self-reinforcement.

Self-Monitoring and Self-Recording. Self-monitoring is a simple and effective procedure used to help students become more aware of the presence or absence of certain behaviors. If you are trying to lose or to gain weight, for example, you may use self-monitoring to keep track of the calories you consume or the numbers you read on the bathroom scale. When self-monitoring, students must first observe their own behavior and evaluate or assess whether or not they have performed that behavior. An important component of any self-monitoring procedure, then, is self-assessment or self-evaluation. Students must be able to determine to what extent they have successfully demonstrated a targeted behavior. Self-assessment has been used to improve a wide range of behaviors including reducing disruptions by having a group of students determine whether or not they were following classroom rules (Smith, Young, West, Morgan, & Rhode, 1988), increasing the neatness and accuracy of creative writing homework assignments completed by adolescents (Glomb & West, 1990), and increasing the independent work skills exhibited by preschoolers with disabilities (Sainato, Strain, Lefebvre, & Rapp, 1990).

To construct a visible and permanent reminder to help children monitor performance, students may also self-record their behavior. To self-record, students may place a mark on a self-recording checklist or self-monitoring form, or use a mechanical device such as a wrist counter, to record each time they are engaging in a particular targeted behavior. See Figure 9.2 (p. 270) for a sample self-monitoring form. In addition, self-graphing may be used in conjunction with any given self-monitoring or self-recording system. For example, Keesha might graph the number of arithmetic problems she completes correctly during daily 20-minute math lessons. Similarly, Paul might self-monitor and then self-graph the number of "polite" words he uses at lunch or his number of "talk outs" during quiet class time. Keesha and Paul might also be shown how to set a goal for themselves (e.g., completing at least nine out of ten math problems correctly during the allotted time or using at least ten polite words during lunch) and then encouraged to meet or exceed their goal (Tollefson, Tracy, Johnson, & Chapman, 1985). Plotting information on a graph or placing a mark on a checklist provides

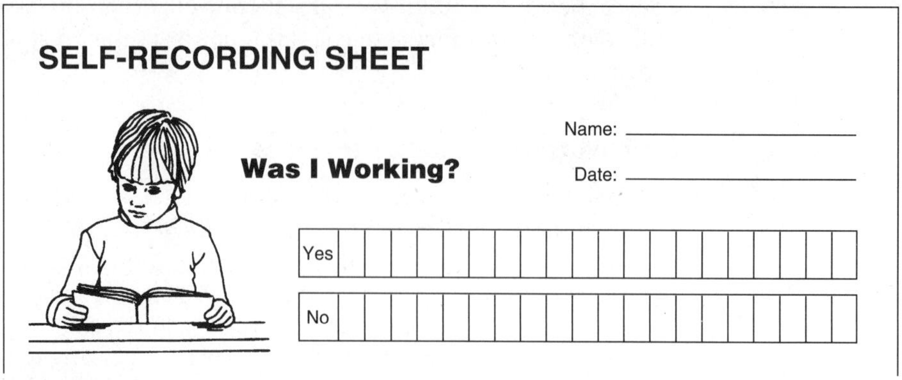

FIGURE 9.2

From "Distractible Students Use Self-Monitoring," by S. S. Osborne, M. M. Kosiewicz, E. B. Crumley & C. Lee, *Teaching Exceptional Children, 19*(2), 1987, p. 66. Copyright © 1987 by The Council for Exceptional Children. Reprinted with permission.

a visual record of behavior for students and seeing one's progress may also serve as a form of self-reinforcement.

Using self-monitoring, teachers have successfully helped children change numerous behaviors, including decreasing the time taken to walk to class (Minner, 1990), reducing disruptive outbursts such as slamming books or pounding the fist (Hogan & Prater, 1993), increasing time spent on task (Hallahan, Lloyd, Kosiewicz, Kauffman, & Graves, 1979), and improving the match between teacher expectancies (e.g., bringing necessary materials to class, being on time, turning in homework, completing classwork, writing homework assignments in an assignment book) and student behavior (Clees, 1995). Although there is no one best way to self-monitor (Reid & Harris, 1993), when this procedure is combined with either self-recording or self-graphing to provide a visual record of performance, self-monitoring appears to improve behavior as well as academic productivity and accuracy (DiGangi, Maag, & Rutherford, 1991; Lloyd, Bateman, Landrum, & Hallahan, 1989; Lloyd & Landrum, 1990). As a matter of fact, Maag, Reid, and DiGangi (1993) maintain that self-monitoring academic productivity and accuracy (e.g., counting and recording how many arithmetic problems have been completed during a specific period or how many of those problems were completed correctly) are generally superior to self-monitoring of on-task behavior alone.

Structured teaching procedures are necessary to ensure that children and youth with emotional and behavioral disorders use self-monitoring and self-recording correctly (Osborne, Kosiewicz, Crumley, & Lee, 1987). The following sequence is recommended for teaching students how to self-monitor (Dunlap, Dunlap, Koegel, & Koegel, 1991; Graham, Harris, & Reid, 1992):

1. Define the target behavior. The behavior must be clearly defined and observable. Demonstrate the behavior for students and be sure they can identify examples and nonexamples of the targeted behavior. Be sure the behavior is one that the student really needs to improve and that is

perceived by the student as important to change. For self-monitoring to be effective, the student must be an involved and contributing party throughout the process.

2. Identify reinforcers for the student. Although external reinforcement usually is not necessary for self-monitoring to be effective, it may initially encourage correct performance of the target behavior and of self-monitoring. However, use external reinforcement only if absolutely necessary, and allow the student to deliver the reinforcement to himself or herself whenever possible (Graham, Harris, & Reid, 1992).

3. Design a self-monitoring method or device. Sticker charts, checklists, and wrist counters are all devices that are effectively used for self-monitoring. Be sure the method chosen is age-appropriate and as unobtrusive as possible to help the student avoid stigmatization. Picture clues may be necessary for the very young child.

4. Teach the child to use the self-monitoring device. Be explicit in your instructions, demonstrating for the child how to self-monitor and self-record the behavior and having the student verbalize the steps in the strategy if necessary. Give many practice opportunities with specific feedback regarding the child's performance.

5. Do not be overly concerned if the student is not totally accurate when self-monitoring. However, if positive effects do not occur, it may be necessary to train or reward accuracy until students are able to assess their own behaviors more precisely (Graham, Harris, & Reid, 1992). Research suggests that students need not be accurate regarding whether they did or did not engage in the targeted behavior for the self-monitoring procedure to be effective in changing the behavior (O'Leary & Dubey, 1979). This does not preclude the teacher evaluating the student's self-records or giving social reinforcement for the child's self-monitoring efforts or performance, however.

6. Fade use of the self-monitoring device and procedure. Systematically reduce the clues provided by the self-monitoring device itself (Box 9.1, p. 272, and Figure 9.3, p. 273).

Self-Reinforcement. Following self-monitoring and self-recording, students must be encouraged to reward themselves for using the appropriate behavior rather than relying solely on external, teacher-controlled reinforcers. In Box 9.1, for example, Keesha is taught to self-reinforce whenever she determines she is paying attention by saying, "Good job, I'm paying attention." Similarly, when you are studying for a class, you probably monitor and assess whether or not you are studying effectively, and you might reward yourself by getting a snack or watching a favorite television show after a specified period of "good studying" behavior. In addition, Paul might be taught to score his daily assignments and determine whether or not he has earned recess (i.e., his selected reward) (Baer, Fowler, & Carden-Smith, 1984). To be most effective, self-reinforcement is best used in combination with explicit self-monitoring procedures (DiGangi & Maag, 1992).

Self-reinforcement, then, involves student selection of reinforcers and student assistance or responsibility for determining standards to be met for earning

BOX 9.1   Teacher Feature: Teaching Keesha to Self-Monitor Attention

Keesha has difficulty paying attention and staying on task. Consequently, she often fails to complete her work in a timely fashion. In order to increase the time Keesha spends paying attention and working, you devise a simple self-monitoring form for Keesha to use at her seat. At the top of the sheet is the question, "Was I paying attention?" and beneath this are two columns with one labeled "Yes" and the other labeled "No." You introduce the self-monitoring of attention procedure to Keesha as follows:

"Keesha, you know how paying attention to your work has always been a problem for you. Your teachers like me tell you things like 'Pay attention' or 'Get to work' or 'What are you supposed to be doing now, Keesha?' Well, today we're going to learn a way to help you help yourself pay attention better. Let's be sure first that you know what paying attention means. This is what I mean by paying attention." (The teacher models several examples of immediate and sustained attention to task such as writing answers on a math sheet and reading a math problem.) "Now this is what I mean by not paying attention." (This time the teacher models nonexamples such as playing with objects or pencils, looking around and out the window, etc.)

"Now, let's see if you can tell me if I was paying attention." (The teacher models several additional examples and nonexamples of paying attention and asks Keesha to categorize each as either paying attention or not paying attention.) "Okay, now let me show you what we are going to do. While you're working, this tape recorder will be turned on and every once in a while you'll hear a little tone like this." (Teacher plays the tone on the tape. Tones are recorded onto the tape so that the time between each tone varies randomly.) "Whenever you hear that sound, quietly ask yourself the question, 'Was I paying attention?' If the answer is 'Yes,' put a check mark in this column (Pointing to the 'Yes' column on the self-recording sheet) and go right back to work. If the answer is 'No,' put a check in this column and go back to work. Now, let me show you how it works." (The teacher demonstrates the entire procedure while asking and answering the questions out loud.) "Now, Keesha, I bet you can do this. Tell me what you're going to do every time you hear a tone. Let's try it. I'll start the tape and you work on this math assignment." (The teacher begins the tape, praises Keesha for using the procedure, and gradually withdraws her presence.)

After a few days of successfully using the procedure, the teacher reduces reliance on the tape recorder as a cue for self-monitoring. The teacher asks Keesha to stop and ask the question "Was I paying attention?" whenever she thinks about it. Later, the self-recording form is also withdrawn and Keesha is asked simply to ask the question, answer it and reward herself by saying "Good job, I'm paying attention" if the answer is "Yes." Keesha is also told to remind herself that "I need to pay attention and get to work" if the answer is "No."

Adapted from Improving Attention with Self-Monitoring: A Manual for Teachers, by D. P. Hallahan, J. W. Lloyd, and L. Stoller, p. 12. Copyright © 1982 University of Virginia Learning Disabilities Research Institute. Reprinted by permission.

Sample Contract

Date _____

**I am responsible for my behavior
and I can work on the following skills:**

I CAN

Independence—I Can work by myself for 15 minutes for 2
weeks in a row when I do seatwork in the resource room.

Completion—I Can finish 8 out of 10 problems on my math
sheet for 5 days in a row.

Accuracy—I Can maintain an 80% average on my math
assignments for 5 days in a row.

Neatness—I Can write the numbers 3, 5, and 9 neatly on my
worksheets for 5 days in a row.

Teacher: _____ will earn the following reward(s)
when he (she) meets his (her) goals:

1. Pick from the Treasure Box.

2. Have a 20-minute free period on Friday.

3. Work on the computer for 15 minutes two times in 1 week.

Parent: _____ will earn the following reward(s)
when he (she) meets his (her) goals:

1. Can stay up 1 hour later on a Friday.

2. Can rent a video of his (her) choice.

_____   _____   _____
Student   *Teacher*   *Parent*

Contract Completed: _____

Contract Revised: _____

FIGURE 9.3

◆

The I CAN Strategy for Self-Reinforcement and Success Swanson (1992)
integrates aspects of self-monitoring, self-reinforcement, and goal setting into the I CAN
strategy for improving the classroom behavior of children and youth with learning and
behavioral problems. Each day students make the self-affirming and encouraging
statement "I am responsible for my behavior and I can work on the following skills."
These skills, important for success in the regular classroom, include independence and
completion, accuracy, and neatness when completing work. Goals are set jointly
between teacher and student and each daily lesson is preceded by a review of student
goals. Following each lesson, students record their results on a progress chart and plan
for changes if goals were not reached. Students may earn rewards at home or at school
or they may self-reinforce. Notice how the I CAN strategy also uses a form of contingency
contracting and encourages home-school communications among parent, teacher, and
child.   From "I CAN: An Acronym for Success," by D. P. Swanson, *Teaching Exceptional
Children, 24*(2), 1992, pp. 23 & 25. Copyright © 1992 by The Council for Exceptional
Children. Reprinted with permission.

a reward (Graham, Harris, & Reid, 1992). Moreover, when self-reinforcing, students evaluate their own performance and self-administer their chosen rewards. Interestingly, research suggests that teacher-determined and student-determined reinforcement demonstrate equal effectiveness (Hayes et al., 1985). Wolery, Bailey, and Sugai (1988) offer several guidelines for teachers using self-reinforcement with their students:

1. Ensure fluency with self-monitoring before teaching the student to self-reinforce.
2. Involve the child in setting criteria for receiving reinforcement and in selecting the reinforcement (i.e., students can help determine the behavior targeted, the reward delivered, and the behavior to reinforcement ratio).
3. Precede student self-reinforcement with teacher administration of reinforcement.
4. Gradually turn responsibility for self-reinforcement to the student by having both the teacher and the student determine whether or not reinforcement should occur. Reward the student's accuracy or match with the teacher's assessment.
5. Fade the teacher's reinforcement over time, but periodically check and reward the student's accuracy.

Cognitive Restructuring

Whereas self-management strategies give students routines for regulating their own behaviors, cognitive restructuring approaches attempt to alter directly what children and youth say to themselves about particular events (Dobson & Block, 1988). An underlying philosophy behind cognitive restructuring interventions is that the student's emotional distress results from his or her maladaptive thoughts. The goal of cognitive restructuring, then, is to replace these maladaptive cognitions with more adaptive ones. Self-instruction (Meichenbaum, 1977) and rational-emotive therapy (Ellis, 1962) are two representative cognitive restructuring interventions used in classrooms for students with emotional and behavioral disorders.

Self-Instructional Training. Meichenbaum (1977) is often credited with developing procedures for helping children "talk themselves through" many different academic and social tasks. Meichenbaum based his work on the research of Luria (1961) and Vygotsky (1962) who first demonstrated the role of language in guiding the behavior of children. That is, these investigators hypothesized that a child's behavior is first under the direction of an adult's overt language. Later, behavior is under the control of the child's own overt language, and, finally, the child regulates his or her behavior through covert or private speech.

You might recall, for example, learning how to dive into a swimming pool. Probably, an instructor "talked you through" the dive step by step, the first time you tried it. Later, perhaps, you repeated these instructions out loud yourself as

BOX 9.2

Teacher Feature: Using a Cognitive-Behavioral Intervention to Reduce Aggressive Classroom Behaviors

Etscheidt (1991) used a cognitive-behavioral training program to reduce the aggressive behaviors of 30 adolescents with behavioral disorders. Aggressive behaviors included such actions as biting, kicking, hitting, throwing, grabbing, teasing, humiliating, threatening, refusing, and destroying or damaging or trying to destroy or damage property. Students participated in 12 structured lessons of 30 to 40 minutes across a period of 3 weeks. The five-step self-instructional strategy taught to students included the following steps:

Step 1: Motor cue and impulse delay. Stop and think before you act; cue yourself (e.g., use covert inhibiting speech such as "Don't say it!" or "Don't do it!" or overt motor responses such as placing a hand over the mouth or tucking the hands under the arms).

Step 2: Problem definition. Say how you feel and exactly what the problem is (e.g., using role playing and stories students identify problems and determine the situations leading to aggression).

Step 3: Generation of alternatives. Think of as many solutions as you can (e.g., students generate different ways to handle the problem such as fight, walk away, talk about it, look at the ceiling, think about something else until you can relax, or move to another predetermined area to escape provocation).

Step 4: Consideration of consequences. Think ahead to what might happen next (e.g., students evaluate their actions in terms of the benefits to them).

Step 5: Implementation. When you have a really good plan, try it (e.g., students try their selected alternative and receive feedback regarding its usage).

From "Reducing Aggressive Behavior and Improving Self-Control: A Cognitive-Behavioral Training Program for Behaviorally-Disordered Adolescents," by S. Etscheidt, *Behavioral Disorders*, 16(2), 1991, p. 111. Copyright © 1991 by The Council for Exceptional Children. Reprinted with permission.

you practiced the dive, and finally, these self-instructions might have become "silent" as you simply thought about the steps during your practice sessions. Both overt language and covert self-talk appear to mediate our behaviors.

Self-instructional training, then, uses an overt to covert language sequence to teach many important behavioral, academic and social skills (see Chapter 8 for methods for teaching social skills that bear a strong resemblance to self-instructional strategies). In particular, self-instructional training may be effective for reducing the impulsivity and hyperactivity of youngsters by getting them to stop and think before they act (Meichenbaum & Goodman, 1971), increasing the interpersonal problem-solving skills of children and youth with

BOX 9.3   **Teacher Feature: Using a Self-Instructional Strategy**
           ZIPPER

ZIPPER is a mnemonic strategy giving youngsters a positive alternative to anger and aggression. The mnemonic stands for:

Z = *Z*ip your mouth.
I = *I*dentify the problem.
P = *P*ause.
P = *P*ut yourself in charge.
E = *E*xplore your choices.
R = *R*eset.

Using the direct instructional procedures effective for teaching social skills combined with the self-instructional teaching sequence advocated by Meichenbaum (1981), the teacher models three or four self-statements and physical self-cues for each step of the ZIPPER strategy. Next, the students are guided through a discussion describing potential outcomes of using the strategy. During the model stage, the teacher distributes a cue sheet with self-statements and physical self-cues appropriate for each step of the strategy. For example, the self-statement and physical self-cues for the Z or zip your mouth step include (a) "Stop," (b) make hand motion for stop, (c) take deep breath, and (d) run fingers across mouth like a zipper. The E or explore choices step include (a) saying, "What can I do?," (b) shrugging shoulders, and (c) selecting an option such as, "I'll try to relax," or "I'll just forget about it."

Role playing activities begin during the modeling stage. An example of an anger-arousing situation is presented (e.g., "Someone teased you"). The teacher and the student then role play the situation using the ZIPPER mnemonic. In the first role play, the teacher plays the student being teased. The teacher models ZIPPER aloud, using the self-statements and physical self-cues. After observing ZIPPER used in a role-play scenario, the student plays the part of the person being teased while under the direction of the teacher who provides the ZIPPER steps. Upon conclusion of the role play, the teacher and student discuss the scenario and the teacher gives corrective feedback. Verbal rehearsal and additional practice opportunities follow the first role playing scenario using other familiar anger-arousing events. Finally, the student's commitment to using the ZIPPER strategy outside the classroom is obtained and situations where ZIPPER might be helpful are listed by the student and teacher.

Adapted from "Effects of Cognitive-Behavioral Training on Angry Behavior and Aggression of Three Elementary-Aged Students," by S. W. Smith, E. M. Siegel, A. M. O'Connor, and S. B. Thomas, 1994, *Behavioral Disorders*, 19(2), 130.

learning and behavior problems (Coleman, Wheeler, & Webber, 1993), reducing aggressive behaviors and teaching prosocial skills (Etscheidt, 1991; Goldstein & Glick, 1987), and teaching acceptance of frustration (Fagen & Hill, 1987) (Box 9.2 and Box 9.3). Meichenbaum (1977) offers the following general steps when conducting self-instructional training:

1. The teacher performs the task while talking aloud (i.e., cognitive modeling). This demonstration of one's overt thought processes should include the following:
   a. The problem definition (e.g., "What is it I have to do? I need to finish this math before recess," or "They want me to go with them, but I know my parents won't let me").
   b. A statement to focus attention and guide the behavioral response (e.g., "I need to work slowly and carefully and keep on working").
   c. A statement of self-reinforcement (e.g., "Good, I just finished another math problem").
   d. Statements modeling coping skills for handling mistakes or problems (e.g., "If I make a mistake, I can erase it and fix it" or "If they tease me, I can tell them to stop").
2. The child performs the task under the direction of the teacher (i.e., overt external guidance).
3. The child performs the task while instructing himself or herself aloud (i.e., overt self-guidance).
4. The child whispers the instructions while performing the task (i.e., faded overt self-guidance).

Students can learn to self-monitor and reward their own behaviors.

5. The child performs the task while guiding his or her own behaviors through private speech (i.e., covert self-instructions).

Meichenbaum (1981) cautions that some children may not need to follow all of the preceding five steps, particularly step number 4. Moreover, allowing students to use their own verbalizations may facilitate both self-instructional learning and generalization. Teachers may use the following ten guidelines when conducting self-instructional training (Meichenbaum, 1981):

1. Analyze the target behavior, including all of the requirements necessary for successful performance (e.g., controlling anger by walking away or by substituting an acceptable physical activity).

2. Listen for ineffective strategies that the student currently uses (e.g., deals with anger by fighting physically).

3. Select instructional tasks that closely approximate the target behavior (e.g., construct role playing scenarios similar to situations occurring on the playground that result in fights).

4. Involve the child in devising the self-instruction (e.g., student suggests what he or she might say or do when angry instead of fighting).

5. Make sure the child has the necessary component skills for using self-instruction (e.g., student has requisite verbal skills or can perform the substitute physical activity).

6. Tell the child how the self-instructions will be useful for performance (e.g., "When you feel like you are getting angry on the playground, you can tell yourself to stop, take a deep breath, and run around the track instead. That way, you won't get into trouble with the principal or the teachers on duty, and your friends will be more likely to want to play with you").

7. Point out specific tasks and settings where the instructions might be used (e.g., "In the lunchroom, you can use this strategy, too. You can stop, take a deep breath, and walk some trash to the garbage bin").

8. Use many different tasks, settings, and trainers to promote generalization (e.g., practice in the lunchroom, bus ramp, playground, etc., with different teachers, staff members, or peers).

9. Include specific coping skills for managing failure (e.g., "When they keep teasing me, I can still handle it. I can tell them firmly to stop teasing me. If I can't handle their teasing, I can always walk away or tell the teacher").

10. Practice until a specific criterion level is reached; then continue to provide follow-up maintenance sessions (e.g., substituting an acceptable physical activity for fighting for five consecutive days on the playground; continue to suggest alternative situations and behaviors where the self-instructions may be useful).

Rational-Emotive Therapy. Ellis (1962) suggests that emotional disturbances are the result of the distorted cognitions (i.e., thoughts and feelings) people have about particular situations. Thoughts and emotions are intertwined, thus, when an individual engages in irrational, absolute thoughts about events in his or her life, intense emotions occur, which then affect that person's behavior. Ellis and Bernard (1983) and Ellis and Harper (1975) list the following irrational beliefs that create difficulty for children and adults in their daily lives:

1. Black holes of approval and love. These are beliefs that we *must* or *should* have love and approval from everyone at all times. If, for example, someone criticizes us, we might believe ourselves to be "lousy," "no good," or unworthy of any respect or love. We think ourselves into feeling miserable, depressed, and unloved (e.g., Keesha says, "Sara doesn't want to play with me. Nobody ever likes me").

2. The superhuman syndrome. This is the belief that we must be absolutely competent at everything all the time and that to make a mistake means we must be incompetent. When we make inevitable errors, we feel guilty and inadequate (e.g., "I missed one problem on my math test, so that must mean I'm a horrible student").

3. Mountains and molehills. We tend to view things as totally negative or totally positive; therefore, we blow things out of proportion and make a small mistake into a catastrophe. We tend to hold onto our viewpoints rigidly and believe we have little control over our lives (e.g., "I can never do this type of test anyway!," "I'm just a bad math student," or "It's raining out, so I know it's going to be a bad day").

4. Rose garden myths. These are beliefs that we ought to be able to solve life's problems easily. When we can't solve a problem, we blame someone else for it (e.g., "I've tried everything, and I just can't get through to him. He won't listen to me. He's driving me crazy!"). See Box 9.4 (p. 280) for some additional irrational beliefs of children, youth, and teachers.

Rational-emotive therapy (RET) is the process used to dispute these irrational beliefs and replace distorted thought patterns with more productive ones (Ellis & Bernard, 1983; Ellis & Harper, 1975). According to Kaplan (1991), children and youth with emotional and behavioral disorders must learn to identify the antecedents (a), or external events that trigger their irrational thoughts and beliefs (b), which then precipitate strong feelings and actions (c). Paul, for example, must learn to identify the following ABC sequence:

> Event (A): I get thrown out during a kickball game at recess.
> Belief (B): Everything must always go my way, and I'm stupid for making a mistake in the kickball game.

Feelings/actions (C): I get angry, cry, and kick the ball hard off the field.

As Paul's teacher, then, you might ask him to tell you what happened at recess (e.g., "I got thrown out during the kickball game") and to state what he thought about (e.g., "I thought I was stupid because I got thrown out") and how he felt when this happened (e.g., "I got angry"). You might also ask him what he did when this happened (e.g., "I cried and kicked the ball off the field, hard!"). The teacher's next task is to get Paul to admit that he holds a faulty belief statement, which made him angry (i.e., "I'm stupid for getting thrown out"). To accomplish this, the teacher might point out other successes Paul achieved during the game of kickball. When Paul admits that being thrown out at kickball does not make him stupid, he may be ready to accept an alternative self-statement (e.g., "If at first I don't succeed, I can try again") to replace his self-defeating one.

BOX 9.4   **Irrational Beliefs of Children, Youth, and Teachers**

Children, youth, and teachers all may experience distorted thoughts about what "should" or "must" happen. These irrational beliefs flood us with intense emotions which then drive our behaviors. Below are some of the common irrational beliefs of children and youth and of their teachers.

Irrational Beliefs of Children and Youth

1. I must be good at everything I do.
2. Everyone must like me.
3. If people do things I don't like, they have to be bad people and they must be punished.
4. Everything must go my way all the time.
5. Everyone must treat me fairly all the time.
6. I never have any control over what happens to me in my life.
7. I should never have to wait for anything I want.
8. When something bad happens to me, I must never forget it and I must think about it all the time.
9. I must be stupid if I make mistakes.
10. I should never have to do anything I don't want to do.

Irrational Beliefs of Teachers

1. If students criticize me, I must have done something wrong.
2. If this student doesn't like me, I must be a lousy teacher.
3. This student should realize how hard I've worked to help him or her.
4. I should be able to reach every single student.
5. I shouldn't get angry or upset with my students.
6. I always get the worst students.
7. I just knew I could never succeed with this type of student.
8. If this child's parents were doing their job at home, I could do my job at school.
9. If the principal were doing her job, I wouldn't be having all these discipline problems.
10. I've tried everything and this student is still driving me crazy.

Adapted from Kaplan, J. S. (1991). *Beyond behavior modification: A cognitive-behavioral approach to behavior management in the schools* (2nd ed.) (p. 167). Austin, TX: PRO-ED, Inc.; and Webber, J., & Coleman, M. (1988). Using rational-emotive therapy to prevent classroom problems. *Teaching Exceptional Children, 21(1),* 33–34.

Although some negative emotions are appropriate and legitimate and help children and youth move toward new goals and better behaviors, the "illegitimate" negative beliefs, which are self-defeating and inappropriate for the actual circumstances, are actively disputed by the teacher and replaced with more productive self-statements. According to Ellis, then, the teacher engaging in RET:

BOX 9.5   **Irrational and Rational Self-Statements**

Kaplan (1991) suggests using the "fair-pair" rule for changing irrational beliefs to rational ones. Teachers give students an appropriate rational statement to replace each self-defeating belief. For example, Kaplan (1991, p. 173) offers the following fair-pair thoughts:

I must be good at everything I do or *I must be stupid if I make mistakes.* Nobody's perfect.

Everyone must like me. You can please some of the people some of the time, but you can't please all the people all of the time.

If people do things I don't like, they are bad people and must be punished. I've done bad things that people don't like, but I'm not a bad person and I don't think I deserve to be punished.

I should never have to wait for anything I want. Waiting sometimes makes the getting more special.

I should never have to do anything I don't want to. Nobody is free to do whatever he or she wants.

Everything must go my way all the time. You can't always get what you want (but if you try, you might find, you get what you need) (Mick Jagger).

1. Makes the student aware of his or her self-defeating remarks and illogical thoughts.
2. Points out to the student how these thoughts are maintaining and creating disturbance.
3. Disputes the student's irrational beliefs by identifying logical and illogical links in his or her internalized sentences.
4. Teaches the student to replace self-defeating thoughts and remarks with more productive ones (Box 9.5).

Zionts (1985) describes the process of disputing irrational beliefs (DIBs) as a key to rational-emotive therapy. Kaplan (1991) also suggests that teachers use the following questions as guidelines for DIBs for kids:

1. What happened? ("I struck out in the game.")
2. What did I think when this happened? ("I'm a real jerk.")
3. How did I feel when this happened? ("Embarassed.")
4. How did I behave when this happened? ("I threw the bat off the side of the field.")
5. How do I know that what I thought about in number 2 is really true? ("Every time I need to make a hit for my team, I strike out. So I must be a jerk.")
6. Is there any reason why my thinking in number 2 might be false? ("I have a high batting average so that must mean I make lots of hits for my team.")
7. If my thinking in number 2 is false, what should I think instead? ("Next time, I'll make the hit," or "Everybody makes mistakes.")

Caputo (1995) combines puppetry, stories containing problem situations, and rational-emotive therapy. Character puppets encounter difficult situations such as a dog puppet finding a fence blocking the way to a prized buried bone. The puppets engage in irrational thinking (e.g., "It's awful, I'll never be able to get to my bone"). The teacher elicits suggestions from children regarding how to solve the problem and handle the situation. The puppets then model adaptive thoughts and behaviors for the students.

Webber and Coleman (1988) also assert that teachers can eliminate statements they make in the classroom that are indicative of irrational beliefs (e.g., phrases containing "always," "never," "should") and model for students more rational and adaptive responses (e.g., "I would prefer that . . ." "It would be better if . . ."). In this way, upsetting and self-defeating emotional responses of students and teachers both may be lessened.

Before engaging in rational-emotive therapy with students, Zionts (1985) believes that teachers must be willing to practice the principles of RET themselves and admit to their own right to make errors. In addition, children and youth must have the ability and willingness to identify and understand their feelings and sufficient awareness to recognize that feelings are a result of one's beliefs about an event. Understanding the individual and unique nature of one's perceptions about events may be particularly difficult for children and adolescents with emotional and behavioral disorders. (Additional information may be obtained by writing the Institute for Rational-Emotive Therapy, 45 East 65th Street, New York, NY 10021.)

Self-Control Curricula

Self-monitoring, self-recording, self-reinforcement, and self-instructional or other cognitive restructuring procedures are frequently combined into treatment programs for children and youth with emotional and behavioral disorders. Several of these programs are now available commercially and offer teachers curricula for helping students learn important social and self-control skills. Among those curricula currently available are *Aggression Replacement Training: A Comprehensive Intervention for Aggressive Youth* (Goldstein & Glick, 1987), *Anger Management for Youth: Stemming Aggression and Violence* (Eggert, 1994), *Second Step: A Violence Prevention Curriculum* (Committee for Children, 1991), *Teaching Acceptance of Frustration/Teaching Self-Control* (Fagen & Hill, 1987; Fagen, Long, & Stevens, 1976), *Think Aloud* (Camp & Bash, 1981), and *The Self-Control Curriculum* (Henley, 1994).

Aggression Replacement Training. *Aggression Replacement Training* (Goldstein & Glick, 1987) is intended for high-risk, delinquent, or behaviorally disordered adolescents (Coleman, Pfeiffer, & Oakland, 1992). The curriculum teaches young people to understand their aggression and to replace their aggressive and antisocial behaviors with more positive alternatives. The same structured learning techniques effective for teaching social skills (i.e., modeling, roleplaying, and specific performance feedback) are also used within this curriculum to teach prosocial skills such as dealing with accusations or group pressure and responding to anger or failure. In addition, students are taught steps for anger control so that they can identify the events and cues that trigger their anger, and they are encouraged to use self-reminders and other anger reducers. Finally, students practice moral reasoning skills through guided discussions of problem situations involving issues like fairness and justice. (Aggression Replacement Training is available from Research Press, 2612 N. Mattis Ave., Champaign, IL 61821.)

Anger Management for Youth. *Anger Management for Youth* (Eggert, 1994) is intended for troubled adolescents in school, juvenile detention, or other mental health settings. The program is based on the concept of cognitive restructuring. That is, by altering their angry thinking, students learn to circumvent their angry feelings and behaviors and also learn specific skills to control their anger. Key instructional features of the program include modeling, verbal rehearsal, self-talk, self-monitoring, and self-evaluation. Also included are scripted lessons and suggestions for supportive activities such as mood diaries. The program is intended for groups of ten or fewer youth; however, it may be adapted for individuals or for use in families. The five specific modules within the curriculum are (1) identifying anger ''triggers'' and typical responses, (2) discovering personal motivators for change, (3) using self-control strategies when anger is triggered, (4) expressing anger constructively when it is aroused, and (5) dealing with crises (Figure 9.4, p. 284). (Anger Management for Youth is available from National Educational Service, P.O. Box 8, 1610 W. 3rd Street, Bloomington, IN 47402-0008.)

Second Step: A Violence Prevention Curriculum. *Second Step* is a school-wide violence prevention curriculum piloted by the Committee for Children between 1988 and 1991. The program is available at four levels: preschool and kindergarten, grades 1 to 3, grades 4 and 5, and grades 6 to 8. The Second Step program gives high-risk and antisocial children and adolescents practice using empathy, problem solving, and anger management skills. The curriculum is designed specifically to teach and reward important prosocial and coping skills to entire, intact classrooms rather than to small groups of ''skill deficient'' students alone. Thus, the curriculum represents an important step in fostering generalization of skills to the regular classroom environment. (Information about *Second Step* may be obtained from the Committee for Children, 172 20th Avenue, Seattle, Washington 98122.)

Teaching Acceptance of Frustration and Teaching Self-Control. *Teaching Acceptance of Frustration* (Fagen & Hill, 1987) is one instructional unit from a larger curriculum, Teaching Self-Control, developed by Fagen, Long, and Stevens (1976). In *Teaching Acceptance of Frustration,* children are taught to manage the negative feelings arising when their efforts or goals are thwarted (Fagen & Hill, 1987). For example, children are first given stories in which characters must deal with frustration. The student's verbalizations about these feelings are analyzed and discussed. Later, children are gradually introduced to frustrating activities and their self-defeating statements (e.g., ''This sucks'') are replaced with more adaptive responses (e.g., ''I can't read what this says'').

8 **Staying Successful**
  • Rewards: internal and external
  • Network support

7 **Monitoring Progress: Daily/Weekly**
  • Check-back activities, diaries
  • Coping with anger: habit checks

6 **Skills Application to Mood Management**
  • Taking control, getting support
  • Using thought refocusing, self-talk scripts
  • Using relaxation and other coping strategies
  • Using problem-solving and negotiation skills

5 **Skills Building: Learning, Practice, More Practice**
  • Inoculations against anger problems, learning, and practice
  • Keeping your cool/QRs, imagery, relaxation practice
  • Coping with arousals, learning, and practice
  • Using play-back analyses, practice, practice, practice

4 **Setting Goals: Deciding to Change**
  • Contemplating change—what would you like to have happen?
  • Setting short-term versus long-term goals for changes

3 **Understanding: Personalizing Data**
  • Discovering what pushes your anger button and why
  • Finding out how you respond in different situations
  • Discovering what the consequences are for you and others

2 **Developing Awareness: Baseline Data**
  • Pre-test, exploring your anger sequence: TTFBC *Triggers, Thoughts, Feelings, Behaviors, Consequences*
  • Linking thoughts, feelings, behaviors

1 **Getting Motivated: Getting Started**
  • Accepting a personal invitation to get involved— *We want you to join and belong*
  • Being persuaded to see that problems are an opportunity for change, growth
  • Having hope and seeing this as a great chance for helping yourself and others

FIGURE 9.4 ━━━◆

The Anger Management for Youth Curriculum From *Anger Management for Youth: Stemming Aggression and Violence,* by L. L. Eggert, p. 12. Copyright © 1994 National Educational Services. Reprinted by permission.

BOX 9.6   **The Self-Control Curriculum**

The Self-Control Curriculum clusters important skills within five broad areas (Henley, 1994, p. 41). Self-control skills important in school settings include:

I. *Controlling Impulses*

Moving in unstructured space
Using instructional materials
Making classroom transitions
Resisting the temptation of off-limit objects

II. *Assessing Social Reality*

Accommodating to classroom rules
Organizing learning materials
Accepting feedback
Appreciating feelings

III. *Managing Group Situations*

Maintaining composure
Appraising peer pressure
Participating in cooperative activities
Evaluating effect of one's own behavior

IV. *Coping With Stress*

Adapting to new situations
Managing competition
Tolerating frustration
Demonstrating patience

V. *Solving Social Problems*

Focusing on present
Learning from past experience
Recalling personal behavior
Resolving conflicts

From Henley, M. (1994). A self-control curriculum for troubled youngsters. *Journal of Emotional and Behavioral Problems*, 3(1), 41.

◆

The Teaching Self-Control Curriculum (Fagen, Long, & Stevens, 1976) contains eight units overall: selection (e.g., focusing, concentrating, and mastering distractions), storage (i.e., visual and auditory memory), sequencing and ordering (e.g., time orientation, sequencing events, planning), anticipating consequences (i.e., developing alternatives and evaluating consequences), appreciating feelings (e.g., identifying and managing feelings, reinterpreting feeling events), managing frustration (i.e., accepting feelings of frustration and tolerating frustration, building coping resources), inhibition and delay (i.e., controlling actions and developing partial goals), and relaxation (i.e., body, thought, and movement relaxation). Each unit contains activities for both groups and individuals focusing on cognitive as well as affective skills considered essential for developing self-control. The entire curriculum is designed to be presented in flexible time patterns to suit the needs of individual students. Edwards and O'Toole (1988) suggest that this curriculum may be effective in helping all students develop greater self-control if teacher resistance to affective education can be overcome.

Think Aloud. *Think Aloud: Increasing Social and Cognitive Skills, A Problem-Solving Program for Children* (Camp & Bash, 1981) uses the technique of verbal mediation to help students learn to talk themselves through difficult situations. Objectives, activities, and teaching scripts are provided for lessons sequenced across several areas such as exercising self-control, realistic goal setting, developing flexibility in planning, predicting consequences, identifying emotions, inferring thoughts of others, and understanding friendship. The lessons are designed for small groups or entire classrooms of children in grades 1 through 6. (*Think Aloud* may be obtained from Research Press, 2612 N. Mattis Ave., Champaign, IL 61821.)

The Self-Control Curriculum. *The Self-Control Curriculum* (Henley, 1994), a part of the Preventive Discipline Project, is divided into five broad skill domains for students at both the elementary and secondary levels (Box 9.6, p. 285). Specific skills within each domain are assessed with an accompanying self-control rating instrument. Self-control is seen as interactive in nature. That is, if skills are to generalize, they must be valid and useful for many different settings outside of the classroom. Each broad curricular domain, therefore, contains skills applicable across a wide array of school and community settings. (Additional information about *The Self-Control Curriculum* or about the Preventive Discipline Project may be obtained by writing Martin Henley, Department of Education, Westfield State College, Westfield, MA 01086).

Summary and Criticisms of Cognitive Behavioral Interventions ◆

Cognitive behavioral interventions are well-researched and offer promise for teaching students with emotional and behavioral disorders to assume greater responsibility for their actions. Although the effects of training for cognitive-behavioral interventions appear to be durable, researchers do still question whether or not students will transfer the strategies they learn in the special education classroom to other settings unless generalization procedures are systematically planned into the teaching program (Clark & McKenzie, 1989; Hughes, Ruhl, & Misra, 1989; Nelson, Smith, Young, & Dodd, 1991). In addition, self-instruction, and self-management strategies appear to be most effective when they are used in combination, although self-instructional training may also be an effective procedure when used separately (DiGangi & Maag, 1992).

An unanswered question, however, is whether or not self-monitoring is more effective than teacher monitoring for controlling behavior (Webber, Scheuermann, McCall, & Colemena, 1993). Moreover, if self-instruction or other cognitive restructuring strategies are to be successful, children and youth must possess the requisite cognitive and verbal skills necessary to use language as a mediator for behavioral change. In addition, Harris (1990) points out that the exact nature and role of private speech in regulating behavior is as yet unknown and that much research remains to be conducted to determine the relative importance of cognitive-behavioral strategies in multicomponent interventions. Finally, teachers, themselves, must be prepared to assume additional responsibility, at least initially, for teaching, monitoring, and rewarding student use of cognitive behavioral interventions as well as for collaborating with parents or other professionals to ensure that generalization occurs (Hughes, Ruhl & Misra, 1989). However, if teachers use the following guidelines when planning and implementing cognitive behavioral interventions, they will increase the potential for student success (Pressley, Symons, Snyder, & Cariglia-Bull, 1989):

1. Ensure that student behavior is first under teacher control.
2. Enlist student assistance and collaboration throughout the process when devising or using cognitive behavioral strategies.
3. Teach only one or two strategies at a time.
4. Teach all procedures thoroughly.
5. Teach children where and when to use the strategies.
6. Maintain student motivation by charting student progress and pointing out how strategies will be of benefit to them.
7. Teach strategies in context and not in isolation.
8. Use explicit teaching procedures, and gradually fade teacher support and directions.
9. Reward use of cognitive strategies over a long period and in as many settings as possible. ◆

Traditional Approaches to Teaching Responsibility

As you began to read this chapter, you were reminded that the psychoeducational model arose from dissatisfaction with early psychodynamic philosophies, particularly when these were applied to group or classroom settings. Fritz Redl and David Wineman (1951, 1952), for example, began their work with aggressive youth at a group home called Pioneer House in Detroit using a "permissive" psychodynamic perspective. They rapidly discovered, however, that these young people required a more structured environment in which coping and problem-solving skills could be learned. Although the overt behaviors of these students were still believed to be symptomatic of hidden, inner conflicts and emotional problems, a youngster's "surface behaviors" had to be managed if children and youth were to become productive members of a group or learn better self-control in school settings (Long & Newman, 1976).

Redl (1976b) thus developed the life space interview, a structured conversation between teacher and student. In the life space interview, the teacher's "talk" serves to mediate between the child, his or her thoughts, feelings and behaviors, and the reactions of others until the student is able to handle stressful circumstances on his or her own. According to Wood and Long (1991), life space intervention interrupts the conflict cycle (i.e., the vicious circle resulting when

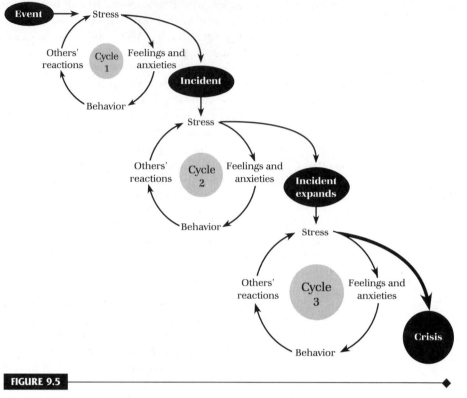

The Conflict Cycle From *Life Space Intervention: Talking with Children and Youth in Crisis* by M. M. Wood and N. J. Long, p. 35. Copyright © 1991 by PRO-ED, Inc. Reprinted by permission.

a child's feelings in stressful situations drive his or her behaviors, which, in turn, produce additional stress, strong emotions, and negative reactions and behaviors from adults (Figure 9.5). Life space intervention, then, uses the daily conflicts and crises encountered by students with emotional and behavioral disorders to teach these youngsters how to handle difficult situations in the future.

Glasser (1965, 1969) also described a similar structured problem-solving interview to be conducted by teachers. Reality therapy is designed to help students learn to take responsibility for their troublesome behaviors and find acceptable solutions to problem situations. In addition, Glasser (1969) and Vorrath and Brendtro (1985) suggest that teachers harness the power of peers and use structured peer-group meetings directed by the teacher or students to promote responsibility in children and youth.

Life Space Intervention

Wood and Long (1991) describe life space intervention (LSI) as a verbal strategy to be used immediately when students are experiencing a crisis. Crises (i.e., the result of a child's unsuccessful attempts to deal with situational stress) are seen as the perfect time for teaching problem-solving and coping skills because emotions are on the surface and motivation to change may be at its highest. To participate successfully in LSI, however, Wood and Long (1991, p. 12) maintain that students must have the following:

◆ Some degree of awareness of self, events, and others.
◆ The ability to attend to verbal and interpersonal stimuli such as the adult talking.
◆ The ability to sustain attention.
◆ Sufficient understanding (i.e., receptive vocabulary) to comprehend the words used by the adult.
◆ The ability to comprehend the stream of content connecting the adult's words.
◆ Sufficient memory to recall a simple sequence of events.
◆ The ability to produce words or signs sufficiently complex to represent the crisis event.
◆ Sufficient trust that the adult cares so that he or she will cooperate and respond to the adult.
◆ Willingness and ability to share at least minimal information with the adult.
◆ Ability to describe simple characteristics of self and others.
◆ Ability to describe personal experiences, even in the simplest form.
◆ Ability to give some reasons why events occur.

For students who meet these criteria, life space intervention occurs in a series of six steps, with three steps directed at examining the problem and three steps directed at finding a solution (Figure 9.6). In step 1, teachers help students to focus on the incident. Here adults use active-reflective listening skills (see Chapter 6) to convey support and understanding, to reduce the emotional intensity of the situation for the child, and to open a dialogue.

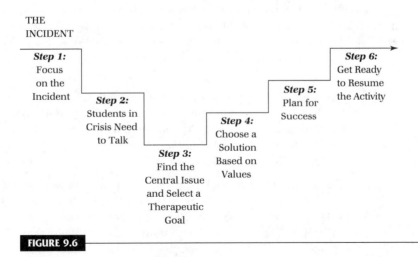

FIGURE 9.6

Steps in Life Space Intervention From *Life Space Intervention: Talking with Children and Youth in Crisis* by M. M. Wood and N. J. Long, p. 8. Copyright © 1991 by PRO-ED, Inc. Reprinted by permission.

If the child has difficulty calming down and is unable to talk about the problem, however, the teacher goes no further with the life space interview. Instead, the teacher gives emotional first aid on the spot (Redl, 1966). Emotional first aid on the spot reduces the emotional intensity of the experience for the child, keeps the lines of communication open between teacher and student, and helps return a crisis situation to a normal one. According to Redl (1966), the five goals of emotional first aid are:

1. Drain off frustration acidity. Defuse strong emotions by conveying support and empathy.
2. Provide support for the management of panic, fury, and guilt. Protect the child and others from the rage and temporary confusion precipitated by the crisis event using empathetic statements or physical intervention if necessary.
3. Maintain communication in moments of relationship decay. Keep the lines of conversation open by discussing neutral topics or ones of mutual interest or by offering a humorous comment.
4. Regulate social and behavioral traffic. Reminding the child of the rules and the consequences of his or her behavior is sometimes enough to provide assistance to the student and allow him or her to return to normal activity.
5. Provide umpire services. Assuming the role of a fair arbitrator of disputes enables students to resolve their differences quickly and peacefully when they are unable to do so on their own.

When students calm down enough that they can talk about the situation, they are ready to enter step 2 of LSI, students in crisis need to talk (Wood & Long, 1991). During step 2, the teacher asks questions or makes reflective comments to clarify the child's perception of events. Long and Pinciotti suggest teachers use the conflict cycle to organize questions asked about the event (note the similarity among these questions and those used in rational-emotive therapy (From "The Snowball Blizzard Incident: A Reality Rub Lifespace Interview," by N. J. Long and D. Pinciotti, 1992, *Journal of Emotional and Behavioral Problems*, 1(3), 28–31, National Educational Service):

1. What happened to you? (stress)
2. How did you feel when that happened to you? (feelings)
3. How did you show that feeling in your behavior? (behaviors)
4. How did others react to your actions? (responses)
5. Did their reactions help you to manage this problem, or did they make things worse? (stress)

When the teacher and student have produced a thorough review of the time, place, and people in the incident, the teacher may move on to step 3, finding the central issue and selecting a therapeutic goal. In step 3, the teacher must analyze the student's perception of the problem as well as the student's insight and motivation to change. The teacher attempts to make a concise statement that summarizes the major issue at hand for the student. Based on the child's perception of events and his or her past patterns of behavior when handling similar situations, then, the teacher selects a therapeutic goal and enters the final three problem-solving steps of life space intervention. This "fixing it" phase of LSI was originally called *clinical exploitation of life events* by Redl (1966) (i.e., using the crisis to explore the habitual patterns of behavior used by the child when he or she is under stress to teach the child better coping skills for the future).

Redl (1966) offered five subtypes of clinical exploitation of life events: reality rub-in, symptom estrangement, massaging numb values, new tools salesmanship, and manipulation of the boundaries of the self. Building on Redl's work, Wood and Long (1991) list five similar therapeutic goals, and Long and Pinciotti (1992) discuss a relatively new goal, the red flag interview:

1. Organize reality. Used with students who are unable to perceive events accurately or who do not see how their behaviors precipitate reactions from others and contribute to the problem. The teacher corrects distortions and interprets events accurately for the students.
2. Confront unacceptable behavior. Used when students are well aware of their behaviors but gain pleasure from their actions or defend their inappropriate behaviors to themselves. The teacher attempts to produce discomfort by confronting the rationalizations students use to justify their behavior.
3. Build values to strengthen self-control. Used when students are overwhelmed by guilt or anxiety following their misbehavior. The teacher points out the students' positive qualities and builds on these to foster self-control.
4. Teach new social skills. Used when students want to gain approval from peers or teachers, but they don't know how to obtain it properly. The teacher shows the students better ways to get the attention that they want.
5. Expose exploitation. Used when students are manipulated by others. The teacher provides insight regarding the behaviors of others and promotes the understanding that friends help rather than hurt one another.
6. Red flag interviews. Often students carry with them to school "baggage" from home or from the school bus. Many difficulties occur within the first 40 minutes of a school day as students act out feelings they bring to school by overreacting to rules, routines, or situations they encounter in the classroom. The red flag interview is used, therefore, to discover the underlying problem carried to school from the home or neighborhood and to teach students to ask adults at school for help or to talk about the problem.

During step 4, then, the teacher helps the student to choose a solution to the problem. To promote ownership, the student is encouraged to develop a solution that is not only suitable for the situation but also is perceived by him or her to be beneficial. As students determine solutions, the teacher guides the student to plan for success in step 5. Both positive and negative outcomes of the chosen problem solution are rehearsed so that students will anticipate the consequences of their actions and seek the potential benefits of using their new strategy. Finally, in step 6, the teacher ends the interview and prepares the student to return to normal activity. Here, the teacher tells the student what is going on in the classroom and closes down discussion of problems and emo-

BOX 9.7   **Case Study: A Sample Life Space Interview with Paul**

Paul was waiting for his group's turn to make kites as an art project during a unit of study on Air. He was unhappy that he drew the number 2, placing him into the second group to work with his teacher; however, she assured him that when the first group finished in about 30 minutes, he would be able to make his kite. Reluctantly, Paul agreed to wait and continued to work in the classroom with his teacher's aide.

After about 30 minutes, Paul made the statement to the aide that "I never get to do the fun stuff." She reassured him that in only a few minutes his group would get to design and build their kites. Unfortunately, the teacher entered the classroom shortly thereafter and announced that a special school assembly had been called, which she had forgotten to tell the children about that morning. The second group would have to postpone their kite making until the following day. Paul's unhappiness escalated into anger as he threw his books on the floor, overturned his desk, and yelled, "Screw you! You never let me do anything!"

Step One (The Drain Off Stage)

As Paul yelled and cried, the teacher asked the aide to take the other students to the assembly. As she listened to Paul, he gradually stopped his tantrums and she asked him to tell her what happened. Paul explained that the teacher had made him wait and do work instead of making his kite and that she had never wanted him to make a kite in the first place. The teacher responded empathetically, "When you had to wait for something you really wanted to do, it was very hard. But when I said you would have to wait again, that made you pretty angry."

Step Two (Establishing an Accurate Time Line)

The teacher said, "Let me see if I understand what you're saying. You drew a number 2, so you had to wait and finish your work and be in the second group to come and make kites. You thought we would start to make our kites in about 30 minutes and you worked hard with Ms. P while group 1 made their kites. But when I came back into the class and told you about the assembly, you thought I wasn't going to let you make a kite." Paul said, "Yeah, you never wanted me

tions. The teacher affirms the student's ability to return to the classroom and cope with the ongoing activities there (see Box 9.7, pp. 292–293, for a sample life space interview). Information about life space intervention and training programs for teachers may be obtained by writing Institute for Psychoeducational Training, 226 Landis Road, Hagerstown, MD 21740.

Reality Therapy

Like Fritz Redl, William Glasser also was trained in the Freudian, psychodynamic tradition. Glasser also quickly discovered that a nondirective, permissive approach was not an effective intervention strategy for working with delinquent

to make a kite!'' That's why I had to wait!'' The teacher then asked Paul, ''Think carefully. Have I ever told you you could do something and then not let you do it?'' Paul reluctantly agreed that she had not.

Steps Three and Four (Select a Goal and Choose a Solution)

At this point, the teacher had an accurate time line of the events. She also understood Paul's faulty belief that she had never intended for him to make a kite. She chose a reality rub interview as a goal to help Paul organize his distorted thinking about the delay in making his kite.

Teacher: ''Paul, when I came back into the classroom and said we had to go to the assembly and save our kite making for tomorrow, what were you thinking?''

Paul: ''You didn't want me to make a kite.''

Teacher: ''Were these thoughts telling you the truth?''

Paul: ''I don't think so.''

Teacher: ''But you believed those thoughts anyway and got upset. So how can you know if what you're thinking is the truth or not?''

Paul: (Pauses for a long moment) ''I guess I could ask you.''

Step Five (Plan for Success)

The teacher then demonstrated for Paul how to ask for more information. Next, she engaged Paul in role playing several situations in which he wasn't sure what was happening and he had to ask her for information instead of overreacting based on his faulty thinking.

Step Six (Prepare to Resume Normal Activity)

The teacher told Paul that the other students would be returning from the assembly in about five minutes. They role played together ways to handle student teasing, if necessary, and she gave Paul a special bathroom pass to use before the students returned.

adolescent girls. Glasser believes that all people have two important basic needs—the need to love and be loved and the need to feel worthwhile to self and others. Well-adjusted individuals, then, are able to meet their own needs without infringing on the right of others to have their needs met. According to Glasser (1965, 1969), as children behave responsibly to meet their needs, they achieve a sense of self-worth, and when basic needs are not met, children begin to deny reality and responsibility.

Glasser (1965, 1969), therefore, believes that emotional problems are the result of students failing to behave responsibly rather than the cause of their irresponsible behaviors. To help children and youth with emotional and behavioral problems, Glasser suggests that teachers must focus these youngsters on the present and on what children are doing to meet their basic needs. Reality therapy (Glasser, 1965), then, is a structured conversation between teacher and student centered around problem situations and solutions chosen by children, which are, or are not, helping them to meet their own needs without violating the rights of others. Reality therapy occurs across the following eight overlapping steps (Glasser, 1965, 1969):

1. Establish a positive relationship. Teacher and student must have developed a trusting relationship in which the student knows that the teacher values and cares for him or her.

2. Review present behavior. The teacher asks "What" questions to ascertain the student's perception of the problem (e.g., "What happened?").

3. Evaluate present behavior. The teacher asks questions to help the student determine how the behavior is helping or hurting in getting what the student wants (e.g., "How is this helping you?" "You got the pencil you wanted but did you also want to get sent to time-out?"). The teacher continues to organize reality for the student, pointing out the child's actions and his or her responsibility in the problem situation that occurred.

4. Generate alternatives. The teacher helps the student list other possible courses of action to get what he or she wanted without also suffering the negative consequences.

5. Select from alternatives and obtain commitment. The teacher helps the student select one alternative to try and then obtains a verbal or written agreement (e.g., a contract) to try the chosen plan.

6. Evaluate outcomes. Teacher and student meet again later to evaluate how well the plan worked. If the plan did not work, the teacher does not express disappointment. Instead, the teacher focuses the student on selecting another alternative and committing to a new plan.

7. Use logical consequences. When students behave irresponsibly or when their plans do not work, children are not relieved of the responsibility for their actions. Rather, students suffer the logical consequences arising naturally from their behaviors (e.g., children destroying or damaging property must replace or repair it).

8. Persist. Teachers use the "rule of threes." That is, the teacher calculates approximately how long it has taken other adults in the past to "give up" on the student and then the teacher triples that length of time. The teacher makes an agreement with herself or himself to work with the student at least that long.

Throughout reality therapy, then, Glasser (1965, 1969) focuses on a student's present, rather than past, behavior and refuses to allow the student to deny responsibility for his or her actions. For example, Glasser helps students to examine questions of right versus wrong by asking children if their actions would still be acceptable if someone else did the same thing to them (i.e., the code of reversibility). Finally, instead of asking "why" questions, the teacher uses "what" questions to help the child focus on what happened and on how these behaviors are helpful or hurtful. The teacher is specific in asking questions and making comments that continue to emphasize the student's responsibility for choosing a particular behavior. (For additional information on reality therapy or for training programs for teachers, contact The Institute for Control Theory, Reality Therapy, and Quality Management, 7301 Medical Center Drive, Suite 104, Canoga Park, California 91307-1904.)

Peer-Group Meetings

Glasser (1969) also suggests that teachers might hold the following three types of meetings in the classroom: open-ended meetings, concerned with academic topics; educational-diagnostic meetings to determine how well students understand concepts presented in the curriculum; and social problem-solving meetings to discuss the students' behavior in school. The teacher conducting the social problem-solving meeting must, according to Glasser (1969), set the following guidelines to ensure a successful outcome.

1. All problems relative to the class as a group and to any individual in the class are eligible for discussion. Thus, the teacher, another professional in the school, or any student may request a group meeting.
2. Discussions must be directed toward solving the problem and not at punishment or fault finding.

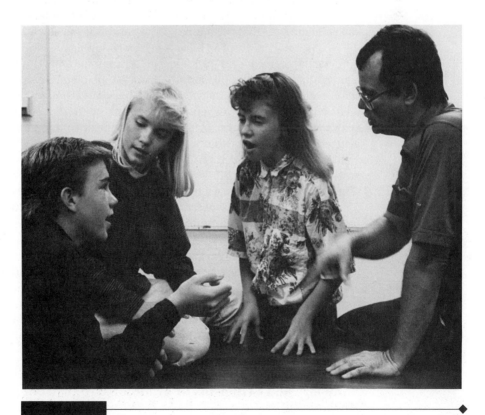

Problem-solving meetings help students resolve conflicts and take responsibility for choosing alternative behaviors.

3. Meetings should be conducted with the teacher and other participants sitting together in a tight circle. The teacher should change his or her position within the circle from one meeting to the next.

4. Students are not corrected for using poor language, and they are not to be interrupted. Usually, students must raise their hands and be recognized to speak, although some groups are able to take turns talking without interrupting one another. Each participant is allowed to speak freely and state his or her opinions and ideas without humiliation or ridicule from others.

Generally, the meetings are focused and short (e.g., 10 to 30 minutes for young children and 30 to 45 minutes for older students). Glasser suggests that meetings be held as long as necessary to solve the problem; however, meetings must not be used as an excuse for students to ignore other responsibilities of the day. Group meetings might be held at a set time every day (e.g., as a first activity or a closing activity each day) and may be called when a problem arises about which discussion cannot be postponed. Glasser (1969) uses the same steps to conduct the problem-solving meeting as he uses for individual reality therapy. That is, the teacher helps students state what happened and how their behavior is or is not helping them, suggest alternatives, and select and make a commitment to an acceptable plan. The teacher serves as both facilitator and moderator for each meeting so that structure, order, and full participation are maintained.

Vorrath and Brendtro (1985) also assert that peers can be a more powerful influence on behavior change than can teachers or other adults. In their positive peer culture model, youth assume leadership roles in helping one another to solve problems. Rather than considering it dangerous to give responsibility to youth who have been irresponsible, Brendtro, Brokenleg, and Van Bockern (1990) state that the real danger is in preventing these young people from assuming leadership and responsibility.

These authorities actively seek to identify natural leaders, including children and youth who have had serious problems, in the elementary and secondary schools. These students are then trained to listen, talk, and assist other students who do not trust the teachers or counseling professionals. Although the teacher frequently monitors and guides the group initially, ultimately within the peer group, students confront one another regarding unacceptable behavior and life choices. According to Brendtro, Brokenleg, and Van Bockern (1990), through the support of peers, students learn real responsibility and build a positive, caring community. Using the positive peer culture model, for example, peer-groups have helped to recover stolen items, effectively and safely confronted peers who were harrassing and attacking students from another school at a basketball game, provided support and tutoring to students who were considering dropping out of school, and reduced school vandalism.

Summary and Criticisms of Traditional Approaches to Teaching Responsibility

Structured conversations and interviews such as life space intervention and reality therapy use the teacher's language to mediate between a child's thoughts and feelings, his or her behaviors, and the actions and reactions of others. By focusing on the present and the problem situations at hand, students learn new ways to solve similar problems in the future. In addition, the students themselves, within structured peer group meetings, may be trained to mediate for one another. Thus, children and youth learn to problem solve and experience enhanced self-worth as they assume real responsibility for helping their peers. Moreover, elements of self-management (e.g., self-monitoring) are now being combined with procedures such as reality therapy to foster student problem solving and responsibility (see, for example, Glasser, 1986 and 1992). According to Gardner (1990), the most often cited advantages for approaches such as life space intervention are that these methods:

1. Enable students to express feelings in a nonjudgmental environment
2. Help students learn to problem solve
3. Provide a technique that is readily available for use by teachers in most crisis situations
4. Help students identify thoughts and resulting feelings that cause the acting out
5. Teach students that they can make changes in their behavior
6. Enable the professional, who is in proximity to the problem, to aid the student as immediately as possible following the problem.

Gardner (1990), however, also outlines several criticisms of methods such as life space intervention. For example, he asserts that focusing on the child's behavior immediately following a crisis situation may reinforce that behavior or, by focusing on feelings, inadvertently give the student an excuse for justifying his or her behavior. He maintains that structured interviews must be conducted proactively (i.e., before an incident occurs) rather than reactively (i.e., following the crisis) in order to prevent reinforcement of inappropriate behaviors. Gardner (1990) also questions the time taken from academic learning to conduct interviews or group meetings. Furthermore, he maintains that it is difficult to train professionals to conduct these interviews and that research regarding the effectiveness of approaches such as life space intervention is dated and primarily based on case study evidence; therefore, the efficacy of these methods is difficult to determine. Finally, students in peer groups meetings must be monitored carefully to prevent children and youth with emotional and behavioral disorders from manipulating one another or from using one individual as a scapegoat for the entire group.

Long (1990), although agreeing that more up-to-date research is needed regarding the effectiveness of life space intervention, disagrees with the concerns expressed by Gardner (1990). For example, according to Long (1990), LSI, and also reality therapy, are designed as reactive, and not proactive, strategies. They are used following problem situations to harness these events as opportunities for instruction. When used by trained teachers and integrated with behavioral technology such as careful observation and data collection procedures, however, both Long and Gardner agree that approaches such as LSI may help students learn and generalize social skills and become more accountable and responsible for their own behaviors.

Teachers must, of course, behave responsibly and ethically themselves when using these interventions. Obtaining adequate training is critical for properly implementing complex strategies such as reality therapy or life space intervention. In addition, some problems experienced by children and youth with emotional and behavioral disorders may be beyond the skill and ability of teachers to address in the classroom. Referring these students to other professionals possessing the requisite training may, in some instances, be the teacher's most responsible course of action. ◆

Summary

Responsibility models acknowledge the influence of a child's thoughts and subsequent feelings on his or her behavior. The student's thoughts, although respected, must be modified if lasting change in behavior is to occur. Structure (i.e., structured environments to manage surface behavior, structured teaching procedures, and structured conversations with students) is a necessary ingredient in the responsibility model classroom to help students learn how to accept greater responsibility and demonstrate increased self-control.

Cognitive behavioral interventions are a recent blend of cognitive philosophy and behavioral theory. Procedures such as self-monitoring, self-recording, and self-reinforcement give students specific methods for regulating their own behaviors. Cognitive restructuring strategies such as self-instruction and rational-emotive therapy use the student's inner language (i.e., his or her thoughts) to guide behavior. These interventions attempt directly to change how students "think and feel" themselves into inappropriate behaviors. More positive self-statements are substituted for the self-defeating ones which drive much student misbehavior. Several self-control curricula are available combining various features of these cognitive behavioral interventions. With these curricula, students are taught how to be more aware of their actions and they are given specific strategies for more effective and acceptable behaviors in the classroom, school, home, or community.

Traditional responsibility approaches use the teacher's, and sometimes the peers', language as the mediator between stressful events, a student's thoughts and feelings about the event, his or her behaviors, and the reactions of others. Structured conversations and interviews such as life space intervention, reality therapy, or peer-group meetings are conducted following problems in the classroom. These daily crises are used as opportunities for teaching students better coping and problem-solving skills so that children will be prepared to handle similar situations in the future. Although these approaches are criticized as lacking research regarding their effectiveness, they do hold promise for helping students learn to accept responsibility for their own actions.

Application Exercises

1. What self-monitoring, self-recording, or self-reinforcement procedures have you or your classmates used in the past (e.g., self-monitoring for weight control, for studying behavior, etc.)? How effective were these in changing your behavior?

2. Think about a time when you were just learning a particular skill. Did your behavior follow the overt to covert language sequence? What self-instructions have you used to guide your behavior? Share your self-instructions with your classmates.

3. Describe for your classmates a time when your thoughts affected your feelings and your behaviors. Did you end up engaged in a self-fulfilling prophecy because you "thought and felt" yourself into a "bad day" or a "bad situation"?

4. Interview a teacher who uses reality therapy or peer group meetings in his or her classroom. How are these interviews or meetings conducted? How does the teacher know that these are helping his or her students to change their behaviors?

5. Write to the addresses included in this chapter for additional information regarding life space intervention, reality therapy, and rational-emotive therapy. Share this information with your classmates.

6. Read and share with classmates examples of life space interviews from *Reclaiming Children and Youth: Journal of Emotional and Behavioral Problems.*

7. Read and share with classmates the debate between Nicholas Long and Ralph Gardner regarding the use of life space intervention. Their respective arguments are found in *Behavioral Disorders, 15*(2), pp. 110–126, February 1990.

8. What similarities and differences do you see between self-instructional strategy training and social skills instruction or among cognitive restructuring approaches, life space intervention, and reality therapy? How can self-management strategies be incorporated within rational-emotive therapy, life space intervention, or reality therapy?

9. Examine the self-control curricula described in this chapter. Which cognitive-behavioral interventions are used in each of these curricula? How are these similar to or different from the structured learning and opportunistic teaching approaches used for teaching social skills?

References

Baer, M., Fowler, S. A., & Cardin-Smith, L. (1984). Using reinforcement and independent-grading to promote and maintain task accuracy in a mainstreamed class. *Analysis and Intervention in Developmental Disabilities, 4,* 157–170.

Brendtro, L. K., Brokenleg, M., & Van Bockern, S. (1990). *Reclaiming youth at risk: Our hope for the future.* Bloomington, IN: National Educational Service.

Camp, B. W., & Bash, M. A. (1981). *Think Aloud.* Champaign, IL: Research Press.

Camp, B. W., Blom, G. E., Hebert, F., & Van Doorninck, W. J. (1977). Think aloud: A program for developing self-control in young aggressive boys. *Journal of Abnormal Child Psychology, 11,* 101–114.

Caputo, R. A. (1995). Puppets, problem-solving, and rational emotive therapy. *Beyond Behavior, 6*(2), 6–12.

Clark, L. A., & McKenzie, H. S. (1989). Effects of self-evaluation training of seriously emotionally disturbed children on the generalization of their classroom following and work behaviors across settings and teachers. *Behavioral Disorders, 14*(2), 89–98.

Clees, T. J. (1995). Self-recording of students' daily schedules of teachers' expectancies: Perspectives on reactivity, stimulus control, and generalization. *Exceptionality, 5*(3), 113–129.

Coleman, M., Pfeiffer, S., & Oakland, T. (1992). Aggression replacement training with behaviorally disordered adolescents. *Behavioral Disorders, 18*(1), 54–66.

Coleman, M., Wheeler, L., & Webber, J. (1993). Research on interpersonal problem-solving training: A review. *Remedial and Special Education, 14*(2), 25–37.

DiGangi, S. A., & Maag, J. W. (1992). A component analysis of self-management training with behaviorally disordered youth. *Behavioral Disorders, 17*(4), 281–290.

DiGangi, S. A., Maag, J. W., & Rutherford, R. B. (1991). Self-graphing of on-task behavior: Enhancing the reactive effects of self-monitoring on on-task behavior and academic performance. *Learning Disability Quarterly, 14*(3), 221–230.

Dobson, K. S., & Block, L. (1988). Historical and philosophical bases of the cognitive-behavioral therapies. In K. S. Dobson (Ed.), *Handbook of cognitive-behavioral therapies* (pp. 3–38). New York: The Guilford Press.

Dunlap, L. K., Dunlap, G., Koegel, L. K., & Koegel, R. L. (1991). Using self-monitoring to increase independence. *Teaching Exceptional Children, 23*(3), 17–22.

Edwards, L. L., & O'Toole, B. (1988). Application of the Self-Control Curriculum with behavior disordered students. In E. L. Meyen, G. A. Vergason, & R. J. Whelan (Eds.), *Effective instructional strategies for exceptional children* (pp. 276–287). Denver, CO: Love.

Eggert, L. L. (1994). *Anger management for youth: Stemming aggression and violence.* Bloomington, IN: National Educational Service.

Ellis, A. (1962). *Reason and emotion in psychotherapy.* New York: Lyle Stuart.

Ellis, A., & Bernard, M. (Eds.). (1983). *Rational-emotive approaches to the problems of childhood.* New York: Plenum.

Ellis, A., & Harper, R. (1975). *A new guide to rational living.* Hollywood, CA: Melvin Powers.

Etscheidt, S. (1991). Reducing aggressive behavior and improving self-control: A cognitive-behavioral training program for behaviorally disordered adolescents. *Behavioral Disorders, 16*(2), 107–115.

Fagen, S. A., & Hill, J. M. (1987). Teaching acceptance of frustration. *Teaching Exceptional Children, 19*(4), 49–51.

Fagen, S., Long, N., & Stevens, D. (1976). A psychoeducational curriculum for the prevention of behavioral and learning problems: Teaching self-control. In N. Long, W. Morse, & R. Newman (Eds.), *Conflict in the classroom: The education of emotionally disturbed children* (3rd ed.) (pp. 272–276). Belmont, CA: Wadsworth.

Fenichel, C. (1976). Psycho-educational approaches for seriously disturbed children in the classroom. In N. J. Long, W. C. Morse, & R. G. Newman (Eds.), *Conflict in the classroom: The education of emotionally disturbed children* (3rd ed.) (pp. 223–229). Belmont, CA: Wadsworth.

Gardner, R. (1990). Life space interviewing: It can be effective, but don't . . . *Behavioral Disorders, 15*(2), 111–119.

Glasser, W. (1965). *Reality therapy: A new approach to psychiatry.* New York: Harper & Row.

Glasser, W. (1969). *Schools without failure.* New York: Harper & Row.

Glasser, W. (1986). *Control theory in the classroom.* New York: Harper & Row.

Glasser, W. (1992). *The quality school: Managing students without coercion* (2nd ed.). New York: HarperCollins.

Glomb, N., & West, R. P. (1990). Teaching behaviorally disordered adolescents to use self-management skills for improving the completeness, accuracy, and neatness of creative writing homework assignments. *Behavioral Disorders, 15*(4), 233–242.

Goldstein, A. P., & Glick, B. (1987). *Aggression replacement training: A comprehensive intervention for aggressive youth.* Champaign, IL: Research Press.

Graham, S., Harris, K. R., & Reid, R. (1992). Developing self-regulated learners. *Focus on Exceptional Children, 24*(6), 1–16.

Hallahan, D. P., Lloyd, J., Kosiewicz, M. M., Kauffman, J. M., & Graves, A. W. (1979). Self-monitoring of attention as a treatment for a learning disabled boy's off-task behavior. *Learning Disability Quarterly, 2*, 24–32.

Hallahan, D. P., Lloyd, J. W., & Stoller, L. (1982). *Improving attention with self-monitoring: A manual for teachers.* Charlottesville, VA: University of Virginia Learning Disabilities Research Institute.

Harris, K. R. (1982). Cognitive-behavior modification: Application with exceptional students. *Focus on Exceptional Children, 15*(2), 1–16.

Harris, K. R. (1990). Developing self-regulated learners: The role of private speech and self-instructions. *Educational Psychologist, 25*(1), 35–49.

Hayes, S. C., Rosenfarb, I., Wulfert, E., Munt, E. D., Korn, Z., & Zettle, R. D. (1985). Self-reinforcement effects: An artifact of social standard setting? *Journal of Applied Behavior Analysis, 18*, 201–214.

Henley, M. (1994). A self-control curriculum for troubled youngsters. *Journal of Emotional and Behavioral Problems, 3*(1), 40–46.

Hogan, S., & Prater, M. A. (1993). The effects of peer tutoring and self-management training on on-task, academic, and disruptive behaviors. *Behavioral Disorders, 18*(2), 118–128.

Hughes, C. A., Ruhl, K. L., & Misra, A. (1989). Self-management with behaviorally disordered students in school settings: A promise unfulfilled? *Behavioral Disorders, 14*(4), 250–262.

Kaplan, J. S. (1991). *Beyond behavior modification: A cognitive-behavioral approach to behavior management in the schools* (2nd ed.). Austin, TX: Pro-Ed.

Kazdin, A. E. (1982). The token economy: A decade later. *Journal of Applied Behavior Analysis, 15*, 431–445.

Lloyd, J. W., Bateman, D. F., Landrum, T. J., & Hallahan, D. P. (1989). Self-recording of attention versus productivity. *Journal of Applied Behavior Analysis, 22*, 315–323.

Lloyd, J. W., & Landrum, T. J. (1990). Self-recording of attending to task: Treatment components and generalization of effects. In T. E. Scruggs & B. Y. L. Wong (Eds.), *Intervention research in learning disabilities* (pp. 235–262). New York: Springer-Verlag.

Long, N. J. (1990). Comments on Ralph Gardner's article "Life space interviewing: It can be effective, but don't . . ." *Behavioral Disorders, 15*(2), 119–125.

Long, N. J., & Newman, R. G. (1976). Managing surface behavior of children in school. In N. J. Long, W. C. Morse, & R. G. Newman (Eds.), *Conflict in the classroom: The education of emotionally disturbed children* (3rd ed.) (pp. 308–316). Belmont, CA: Wadsworth.

Long, N. J., & Pinciotti, D. (1992). The snowball blizzard incident: A reality rub life space interview. *Journal of Emotional and Behavioral Problems, 1*(3), 28–31.

Luria, A. R. (1961). *The role of speech in the regulation of normal and abnormal behaviors.* New York: Liveright.

Maag, J. W., Reid, R., & DiGangi, S. A. (1993). Differential effects of self-monitoring attention, accuracy, and productivity. *Journal of Applied Behavior Analysis, 26*(3), 329–344.

Mace, F. C., Brown, D. K., & West, B. J. (1987). Behavioral self-management in education. In C. A. Maher & J. E. Zins (Eds.), *Psychoeducational interventions in the schools* (pp. 160–176). New York: Pergamon.

Mahoney, M. J., & Thorensen, C. E. (1974). *Self-control: Power to the person.* Monterey, CA: Brooks/Cole.

Meichenbaum, D. (1977). *Cognitive behavior modification: An integrative approach.* New York: Plenum.

Meichenbaum, D. (1981). Cognitive behavior modification with exceptional children: A promise yet unfulfilled. *Exceptional Education Quarterly, 1*, 83–88.

Meichenbaum, D., & Goodman, J. (1971). Training impulsive children to talk to themselves: A means of developing self-control. *Journal of Abnormal Psychology, 77,* 115–126.

Minner, S. (1990). Use of a self-recording procedure to decrease the time taken by behaviorally disordered students to walk to special classes. *Behavioral Disorders, 15*(4), 210–216.

Morse, W. (1993). Fritz Redl for today. *Journal of Emotional and Behavioral Problems, 2*(1), 53–55.

Nelson, J. R., Smith, D. J., Young, R. K., & Dodd, J. M. (1991). A review of self-management outcome research conducted with students who exhibit behavioral disorders. *Behavioral Disorders, 16*(3), 169–179.

O'Leary, S. G., & Dubey, D. R. (1979). Applications of self-control procedures by children: A review. *Journal of Applied Behavior Analysis, 12,* 449–465.

Osborne, S. S., Kosiewicz, M. M., Crumley, E. B., & Lee, C. (1987). Distractible students use self-monitoring. *Teaching Exceptional Children, 19*(2), 66–69.

Pearl, R. (1992). Psychosocial characteristics of learning disabled students. In N. N. Singh & I. L. Beale (Eds.), *Current perspectives in learning disabilities: Nature, theory, and treatment* (pp. 96–125). New York: Springer-Verlag.

Pearl, R., Bryan, T., & Donahue, M. (1980). Learning disabled childrens' attributions for success and failure. *Learning Disability Quarterly, 3,* 3–9.

Pressley, M., Symons, S., Snyder, B. L., & Cariglia-Bull, T. (1989). Strategy instruction comes of age. *Learning Disabilities Quarterly, 12*(1), 16–30.

Redl, F. (1966). *When we deal with children.* New York: Free Press.

Redl, F. (1976a). The concept of a therapeutic milieu. In N. J. Long, W. C. Morse, & R. G. Newman (Eds.), *Conflict in the classroom: The education of emotionally disturbed children* (3rd ed.) (pp. 217–222). Belmont, CA: Wadsworth.

Redl, F. (1976b). The concept of the life space interview. In N. J. Long, W. C. Morse, & R. G. Newman (Eds.), *Conflict in the classroom: The education of emotionally disturbed children* (3rd ed.) (pp. 328–337). Belmont, CA: Wadsworth.

Redl, F., & Wineman, D. (1951). *Children who hate.* New York: Free Press.

Redl, F., & Wineman, D. (1952). *Controls from within.* New York: Free Press.

Reid, R., & Harris, K. R. (1993). Self-monitoring of attention versus self-monitoring of performance: Effects on attention and academic performance. *Exceptional Children, 60*(1), 29–40.

Sainato, D. M., Strain, P. S., Lefebvre, D., & Rapp, N. (1990). Effects of self-evaluation on the independent work skills of preschool children with disabilities. *Exceptional Children, 56*(6), 540–549.

Seligman, M. E. (1992). *Helplessness: On depression, development and death.* San Francisco: W.H. Freeman.

Short, E. J., & Weissberg-Benchell, J. (1989). The triple alliance for learning: Cognition, metacognition, and motivation. In C. B. McCormick, G. E. Miller, & M. Pressley (Eds.), *Cognitive strategy research: From basic research to educational applications* (pp. 33–63). New York: Springer-Verlag.

Smith, D. J., Young, K. R., West, R. P., Morgan, D. P., & Rhode, G. (1988). Reducing the disruptive behavior of junior high school students: A classroom self-management procedure. *Behavioral Disorders, 13*(4), 231–239.

Smith, S. W., Siegel, E. M., O'Connor, A. M., & Thomas, S. B. (1994). Effects of cognitive-behavioral training on angry behavior and aggression of three elementary-aged students. *Behavioral Disorders, 19*(2), 126–135.

Swanson, D. P. (1992). I CAN: An acronym for success. *Teaching Exceptional Children, 24*(2), 22–26.

Tollefson, N., Tracy, D. B., Johnson, E. P., & Chapman, J. (1985). Teaching learning disabled students goal implementation skills. *Psychology in the Schools, 23,* 194–205.

Torgesen, J. K. (1977). The role of nonspecific factors in the task performance of learning disabled children: A theoretical assessment. *Journal of Learning Disabilities, 10,* 27–34.

Vorrath, H., & Brendtro, L. (1985). *Positive peer culture.* New York: Aldine.

Vygotsky, L. (1962). *Thought and language.* New York: Wiley.

Webber, J., & Coleman, M. (1988). Using rational-emotive therapy to prevent classroom problems. *Teaching Exceptional Children, 21*(1), 32–35.

Webber, J., Scheuermann, B., McCall, C., & Coleman, M. (1993). Research on self-monitoring as a behavior management technique in special education classrooms: A descriptive review. *Remedial and Special Education, 14*(2), 38–56.

Williams, R. M., & Rooney, K. J. (1986). *A handbook of cognitive behavior modification procedures for teachers.* Charlottesville, VA: University of Virginia Learning Disabilities Research Institute.

Wolery, M., Bailey, D. B., & Sugai, G. M. (1988). *Effective teaching: Principles and procedures of applied behavior analysis with exceptional students.* Boston: Allyn & Bacon.

Wood, M. M., & Long, N. J. (1991). *Life space intervention: Talking with children and youth in crisis.* Austin, TX: Pro-Ed.

Zionts, P. (1985). *Teaching disturbed and disturbing students: An integrative approach.* Austin, TX: Pro-Ed.

COLLABORATING WITH PARENTS AND PROFESSIONALS

Main Ideas:

◆ *Collaboration implies an equal partnership, rather than an expert-client relationship.*

◆ *Within school settings, special educators must form collaborative partnerships with classroom teachers and other professionals and paraprofessionals. Collaborative partnerships require mutual problem sharing and problem solving.*

◆ *To fully include children with disabilities into regular classrooms, special educators must skillfully form collaborative relationships with general educators.*

◆ *Teachers must respect the needs of parents and families. Rather than viewing parents as adversaries, teachers must help parents build on child and family strengths.*

◆ *Educators must increasingly collaborate with professionals from mental health, social services, and juvenile justice agencies.*

◆ *Children and adolescents with behavioral disorders require total systems of community-based care to prevent unnecessary out-of-home placements and to wrap all necessary services around the child and family.*

Successfully meeting the needs of students with emotional and behavioral disorders requires consistent and honest communication with parents, other teachers, paraprofessionals, and various personnel from community service agencies. Recall from Chapter 3 that parents and other professionals may hold expectations or interpretations of student behavior that differ from your own. Also, the goals and philosophies of agencies within the community may conflict with those of teachers in schools. Understanding the diverse responsibilities of the many professionals with whom our students interact is a first step toward full collaboration to meet the complex needs of children and youth with behavioral disorders (Figure 10.1).

In this chapter, then, we will examine collaborative skills. We will first define what is meant by collaboration and we will discuss collaboration among teachers, other professionals, paraprofessionals and parents within the school environment. In addition, we will discuss the current movement toward full inclu-

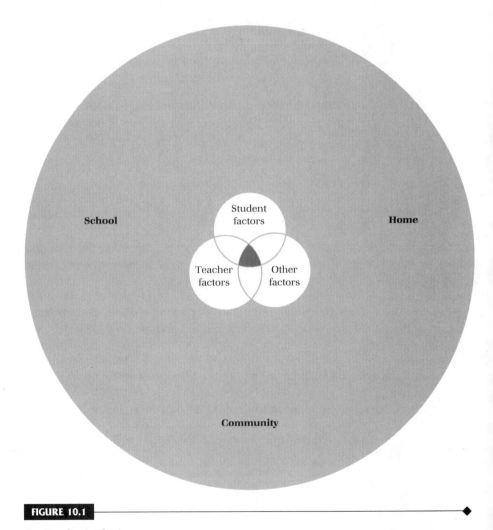

FIGURE 10.1

An Ecological View

sion of children with emotional and behavioral disorders into the regular classroom, a movement requiring teachers to demonstrate expert collaborative skills. Next, we will describe important community agencies often serving the needs of students with emotional and behavioral disorders and their families. These community agencies include mental health services, social services, and law enforcement and juvenile services. We will also examine two major federal initiatives, transitioning and the creation of a Child and Adolescent Service System Program, designed to facilitate collaboration among schools, families, and local community agencies to "wrap" necessary services around the families of children and youth with emotional and behavioral disorders.

Collaboration within Schools

Collaboration implies that all parties involved in an endeavor have equal expertise and equal status. Rather than treating particular individuals as the experts with the answers, teachers who collaborate foster a shared sense of problem solving and decision making. Collaboration is an interactive process enabling those with varied expertise to generate solutions to mutually defined problems (Idol, Paolucci-Whitcomb, & Nevin, 1986). Thus, collaboration necessitates participation by teachers and others as members of interactive teams (Morsink, Thomas, & Correa, 1991).

According to Morsink, Thomas, and Correa (1991), the following dimensions are critical for successful collaboration or interactive teaming:

- ◆ Legitimacy and autonomy—teams must be valued and supported administratively, and members must have the time and resources necessary to plan and reflect together.
- ◆ Purpose and objectives—interactive teams are formed to share information and to make the best possible decisions; therefore, teams must have clearly identified purposes, and members must function interdependently.
- ◆ Competencies of team members and clarity of roles—team members must be competent in their discipline or knowledge and possess excellent collaborative problem-solving, leadership, and communication skills. In addition, teams must clarify the roles of individual members.
- ◆ Role release and role transitions—members of teams must be able to share their information and actively train one another to perform the skills and competencies possessed by each.
- ◆ Awareness of the individuality of team members—team members must value the experiences and perspectives of individuals from various disciplines and from differing stages in their professional development.
- ◆ Process of team building—teams take time to adjust and perform as a unit. Conflicts are inevitable but can be resolved through clear communication and negotiation.
- ◆ Attention to factors that impact on team functioning—team members function as members of a cooperative group and support and acknowledge one another as making valuable contributions to the team's goal. Team members serve positive task and maintenance roles within the group and foster consensus decisions whenever possible.

- ◆ Leadership styles—teams rotate leadership and team leaders encourage contributions from all members in the decision-making process.
- ◆ Commitment to common goals—team members must believe that collaboration and integrating services are effective ways to meet the needs of students.

For collaboration to be successful, then, teachers must develop honest, positive, and trusting relationships with others, and they must have the time, respect, and autonomy necessary to participate as members of teams convened and comprised flexibly of parents and other professionals. Teachers may, for example, collaborate with only one or two other teachers, with parents or other family members, with personnel from community agencies, or with teachers, parents, and other professionals together. Collaboration occurs when interested parties generate viable solutions for problems and engage in interactions characterized by mutual respect, open communication, and consensual decision making (West, 1990).

In addition, if collaborative efforts are to be successful, teachers must be skilled in problem-solving processes (Box 10.1). That is, they must understand how to define and clarify problems, how to explore alternatives and select a strategy acceptable to all parties involved, and how to evaluate the outcomes of strategies chosen for implementation (Gutkin & Curtis, 1990). Phillips and McCullough (1990) also suggest that if collaboration is to be successful within school settings, collaborating professionals must genuinely share responsibility and concern for students and their problems, and they must share joint accountability as well as recognition for problem resolution. They must believe that pooling their talents and resources and conscientiously attending to group processes are mutually advantageous and worth the time, energy, and resources expended.

Pooling talents and resources and collaborating to problem solve does not preclude, however, designating an individual team member to serve as a "case manager" or team leader. The case manager may, for example, locate and coordinate the services and resources necessary to meet the needs of a student and his or her family. In addition, the case manager may delegate particular responsibilities to individual team members. Morsink, Thomas, and Correa (1990) believe that case managers can assist other team members to perform delegated responsibilities successfully by clearly stating the task to be completed, the results expected, and the importance of the task. Although they caution team leaders to tell members *what* to accomplish but not *how* to accomplish the assignment, they also maintain that other team members must know who has the responsibility for particular tasks so that each member will cooperate fully with that individual. Finally, the case manager must ensure systematic follow-up by specifying precisely the date, time, and place for the next meeting in order to evaluate progress and determine new goals.

Collaborating with Teachers and Other Professionals

In many schools, teachers collaborate with other educators and professionals when they participate as members of teacher assistance teams (Chalfant, Pysh,

BOX 10.1	**The Problem-Solving Process**

1. *Define and Clarify the Problem*

- Consider all relevant environmental factors (e.g., teacher-student, parent-student, student-student interactions).
- Phrase a clear, observable, operational definition of the problem that is specific enough to demonstrate that the problem is modifiable.
- State the outcome goals so that all participants understand what the student will be doing when he or she is successful.

2. *Analyze the Problem*

- Determine factors that might prevent or support the student's performance.
- Ask specific questions, observe the student in varying settings, and examine student work samples to gather relevant information about the problem.
- Generate hypotheses about the problem and test the hypotheses through sharing information collected.

3. *Explore Alternatives*

- Brainstorm a list of possible solutions for the problem accepting all ideas as viable.
- Network and link up with all personnel who might have resources for problem-solving.

4. *Select a Strategy*

- Choose a strategy that is acceptable to all members of the group (i.e., can be implemented with minimal time and disruption of individual group members).
- Examine the possible positive and negative side effects of the chosen strategy for all group members.

5. *Clarify the Strategy*

- Ensure that all parties understand individual and shared responsibilities.
- Specify the who, what, when, where, and how of the strategy.

6. *Implement the Strategy and Provide Support*

- Follow-up after implementing the strategy is essential for success.
- Systematic support is offered as team members continue to work together to ensure student success.

7. *Evaluate the Outcome*

- Observe student performance and collect additional data to determine if goals are met.
- Modify the strategy or choose a new alternative if the problem remains unresolved.

BOX 10.2   **Collaborative Teams**

Teacher Assistance Teams

Problem-solving teams are formed by representative classroom teachers who serve as advisors or facilitators for other teachers in the same building.

Intervention Assistance Teams

Teams are formed on an as-needed basis. Because each member has expertise in a particular type of teaching or child management strategy, members may come from both within and outside the school.

School-Based Resource Teams/Mainstream Assistance Teams

Teams are formed within a building, and, like intervention assistance teams, are formed to solve a particular type of problem. Any type of professional may serve on the team including classroom teachers, support staff, and administrators.

Student Support Teams

Teams are formed specifically for a particular student and team members have responsibility for the educational program of that individual student.

Child Study Teams

Teams are formed specifically for a particular student, but the sole purpose of the team is to study the student and his or her presenting problems. These arrangements are often used as placement teams in special education.

Adapted from "Collaborative Consultation in the Education of Mildly Handicapped and At-Risk Students" by J. F. West and L. Idol, 1990, *Remedial and Special Education 11*(1), pp. 22–31. Copyright © 1990 by PRO-ED, Inc. Adapted and reprinted by permission.

& Moultrie, 1979), student support teams (Glickman, 1990; Ramey & Robbins, 1989), or mainstream assistance teams (Fuchs, Fuchs, & Bahr, 1990). Most often, the purpose of each of these teams is to support students with special educational needs within the regular classroom environment. Teams form flexibly, for example, when regular classroom teachers experience difficulty with the academic or behavioral performance of any of their students and subsequently seek assistance from their colleagues. Team members might include other regular or special education teachers, school psychologists, guidance counselors, or principals who meet collaboratively to help the teacher create solutions for such difficulties as student work habits (e.g., following directions, working independently, completing assignments) or classroom behaviors (e.g., disturbing others, staying in one's seat, following rules). Chalfant and Van Dusen Pysh (1989) report that problem-solving teams such as these reduce the number of students referred by classroom teachers for special education evaluation and placement as regular classroom teachers become more confident and competent in handling diverse student behaviors and needs within their own classes. See Box 10.2 for descriptions of various types of collaborative teams.

Enhancing teacher confidence and competence is one important outcome of smoothly operating problem-solving teams. Regular educators are often intimidated by the jargon of special educators and psychologists. Special education teachers, too, may be somewhat "awed" by psychologists, and like classroom teachers, they may be hesitant to contribute in team meetings or to raise disagreements with these professionals. School psychologists can offer far more than assessment results to team problem-solving efforts, however. They can, for example, help teachers to plan effective strategies for managing the behavior of students with emotional and behavioral disorders in the classroom (Rosenfield, 1987). Regular and special educators and psychologists all serve as equal contributing partners on the best collaborative teams.

As teachers form collaborative teams, however, they must be supported in their efforts. Administrative support, time to co-plan, and positive teacher attitudes toward collaboration are essential elements for successful teaming (Karge, McClure, & Patton, 1995; Kruger, Struzziero, Watts, & Vacca, 1995; Voltz, Elliott, & Harris, 1995). Pugach and Johnson (1988) suggest several ways in which teachers can be provided with the time they need to collaborate. Floating substitutes can, for example, be assigned to cover the classes of teachers engaged in collaborative problem-solving meetings or art, music, and physical education periods might be coordinated so that the teachers' planning times coincide. In addition, principals or assistant principals might volunteer themselves to serve as substitute instructors for collaborating teachers. For teachers to collaborate effectively, then, they must:

- ◆ Be given adequate training in collaborative skills
- ◆ Receive administrative-level support for their activities and enjoy the freedom necessary for joint problem solving
- ◆ Be given assistance from student helpers, volunteers, or teacher aides for clerical work and other noninstructional tasks that take time away from team activities
- ◆ Have mutual planning periods or prescheduled time for uninterrupted meetings after school expressly for collaboration (Johnson, Pugach, & Devlin, 1990)

Increasingly, regular teachers and special educators are also engaging in collaborative teaching, or coteaching, within the regular classroom. Collaborative teaching represents an attempt by teachers to improve curriculum coordination and communication between the special education and regular education settings. In addition, cooperative teaching reduces the likelihood that students will be pulled out to the special education class and consequently miss special events (e.g., assemblies or movies) or important concepts taught in the mainstream (Wiedmeyer & Lehman, 1991). According to Self, Benning, Marston, and Magnusson (1991), cooperative teaching enables teachers to infuse specialized instructional strategies or curricular materials into the regular classroom without removing special education students or other at risk learners from the mainstreamed setting.

Collaborative, coteaching arrangements imply equal partnership among teachers in the same classroom. Thus, when collaboratively teaching, regular

BOX 10.3   **Collaborative Teaching Activities**

Wiedmeyer and Lehman (1991) describe collaborative teaching as a cooperative and interactive process between two teachers enabling students with special needs to attain success in the regular education setting. Teachers who coteach, then, engage in many diverse activities on behalf of all learners in the mainstream classroom. Collaborative teaching activities suggested by Wiedmeyer and Lehman include:

1. Sharing in planning, presenting, and checking all assignments in the regular classroom.
2. Adapting curriculum within the regular classroom.
3. Incorporating the regular classroom teachers input into the individualized education program for all shared students.
4. Participating in all parent conferences for shared students.
5. Monitoring of students in any specific classroom (e.g., checking for eye contact and attending behaviors; correcting notes or writing down assignments; using appropriate in-class study time; and understanding, checking for, and rewarding appropriate behaviors and social skills).
6. Developing instructional units with teachers that incorporate social skills or problem-solving skills.
7. Developing materials at a lower level for regular education students who have additional needs or for students with disabilities.
8. Pulling out groups within the regular classroom whenever needed for initial teaching or for additional teaching.
9. Demonstrating or using special techniques and strategies for regular education students who have additional needs or for students with disabilities (e.g., placing notes on board during teacher lecture).
10. Adapting curricular materials for use within the regular classroom (e.g., adapting tests, making study guides or other organizers).

From "The House Plan Approach to Collaborative Teaching and Consultation," by D. Wiedmeyer & J. Lehman, *Teaching Exceptional Children*, 23(3), 1991, pp. 7–8. Copyright © 1991 by The Council for Exceptional Children. Reprinted with permission.

and special educators share the responsibility for planning and delivering instruction to *all* students in a class. Because two professionals teach together as a team, the pupil/teacher ratio in the mainstreamed classroom is reduced and instructional resources are pooled (Thousand & Villa, 1989). Time for coplanning, cooperation among coteachers, and a reduction in work load particularly during training are essential elements for success, however, when implementing any cooperative teaching arrangement (Bauwens, Hourcade, & Friend, 1989). See Box 10.3 for a list of possible collaborative teaching activities. The current movement toward full inclusion of all children with disabilities into the regular classroom, including children and youth with emotional and behavioral disorders, requires more than ever before that special and general educators plan and coteach collaboratively.

Collaborative, coteaching arrangements require time for planning as well as teachers willing to form equal partnerships in the classroom.

Full Inclusion: History and Issues

In 1975, with the passage of Public Law 94-142, students with disabilities were guaranteed a free, appropriate, public education in the least restrictive environment consistent with their needs and to the maximum extent possible alongside peers without disabilities. To provide a least restrictive environment for each child, then, school districts had to form a continuum of placement options, from special residential or day schools for students who required an intensive level of support, to self-contained classrooms within regular school buildings, to resource room support services for students whose needs were less severe, to placement in the mainstream of the regular classroom with assistance given to the teacher and the child. The first wave of effort in special education resulted in increasing numbers of children and youth gaining access to public education programs.

As special education grew, however, critics began to argue that special education programs had become large bureaucratic systems, overly concerned with diagnosing deficits in children and with placing them in expensive "pull-out" programs (Wang, Reynolds, & Walberg, 1988). These critics asserted that special education had focused exclusively on the categorical placement of children rather than on examining the regular classroom to determine how that environment could be changed to enable children to succeed. Furthermore, critics maintained that special education services were not effective because outcomes for children with disabilities were poor (e.g., low achievement gains, high drop-out and low employment rates), that students missed many learning activities while they were out of the regular classroom, and that children with disabilities were unable to learn appropriate social skills when they were isolated from their peers (Stainback & Stainback, 1984; Wang, Reynolds, & Walberg, 1988). These professionals called for a regular education initiative to merge regular and special education and return students with disabilities to the regular main-streamed classroom. Collaborative and coteaching arrangements among regular and special educators were to be used to support students with disabilities in the regular classroom on a permanent basis.

Over the last 5 years, critics of special education, particularly persons advocating for students with severe disabilities, have become increasingly vocal regarding the full inclusion of all students in the regular classroom (The Association for Persons with Severe Handicaps, 1992). Many of these professionals wish to eliminate the continuum of services underlying the system of special education and return *all* students to the regular classroom full-time. In addition, although court interpretations of the least restrictive environment mandate have generally balanced the need for socialization in mainstreamed settings with specialized services necessary for the child to receive an appropriate education, recent court interpretations have placed a greater emphasis on mainstreaming (*Oberti v. Board of Education of the Borough of Clementon School District*, 1993). In the Oberti (1993) decision, for example, the Third Circuit Court of Appeals ruled that a student with Down syndrome and disruptive behavior could not be placed in a segregated setting that would remove him from his fundamental right to associate with his peers without first demonstrating that he could not be educated in the mainstreamed setting with supplementary aids and services (Osborne & Dimattia, 1994).

According to Fuchs and Fuchs (1994), professional associations such as The Association for Persons with Severe Handicaps are advocating for the complete dismantling of special education services and the "radicalization" of special education reform. Apparently, the courts are also demonstrating an increasingly favorable position toward inclusion as the placement of choice, regardless of the severity of a student's disability, unless there is strong evidence that the child will receive no benefit from inclusion.

On the other hand, many other professionals assert that preserving a con-tinuum of services is crucial if all students with disabilities are to receive an appropriate education because general education cannot always meet the needs of students with disabilities (Braaten, Kauffman, Braaten, Polsgrove, & Nelson, 1988; Kauffman, 1989; Kauffman, Gerber, & Semmel, 1988; Walker, & Bullis, 1991). Moreover, several national professional organizations have taken a con-servative stance toward special education reform wishing to preserve the concept of least restrictive environment within a continuum of services (Council for Exceptional Children, 1993; Learning Disabilities Association, 1993; National Joint Committee on Learning Disabilities, 1993).

Organizations representing school administrators have favored full inclu-sion, perhaps prompted by a belief that regulations will be simplified and financial obligations reduced with inclusive classrooms (National Association of State Boards of Education, 1992). Yet, both regular and special education teachers worry that the goal of full inclusion, while perhaps appropriate for some students with physical or severe disabilities, may be inappropriate for other students, particularly those with emotional and behavioral disorders (Council for Children with Behavioral Disorders, 1989, 1993; National Education Association, 1992). As a matter of fact, recent court decisions have indicated that students with emotional and behavioral disorders may be removed from the regular classroom when the child does not benefit educationally and when the child disrupts the learning environment or adversely affects the learning of others (Yell, 1995). Schools must first, however, demonstrate the inappropriateness of the regular classroom by documenting that behavior management plans, training, and consultation for the classroom teacher, and the provision of a behavioral aide are insufficient to maintain the child in an inclusive setting.

Teachers maintain that they have not received the training, curricular and financial resources, or personnel necessary to implement full inclusion; therefore, they fear that learning and behavior will deteriorate for all students. In fact, a major teacher's union, the American Federation of Teachers, has taken the position that a moratorium should be called on inclusion until additional personnel, release time, and money for continuous teacher training to support educators in inclusive settings is guaranteed (Shanker, 1995). (See *Educational Leadership*, January 1995, Volume 52, Number 4, for an entire journal issue devoted to the Inclusive Model.)

Teachers have certain expectations and specific tolerances for behavior which affect their self-efficacy and interactions with students in the classroom (Gersten, Walker, & Darch, 1988). Students with emotional and behavioral disorders, however, are the very students *most likely* to disrupt the behavior and learning of other children and to engage the teacher in negative interactions (Landrum, 1992). These students are also not likely to learn appropriate behaviors from simply observing the social interactions and reinforcement of students without disabilities in the regular classroom (Kauffman, 1993). In addition, students with emotional and behavioral disorders often lack strong advocates and have a history of family problems, abuse, drug use, or juvenile court contacts. These difficulties require intensive and extensive support services for both student and family that may not be available until all personnel in schools accept ownership for all children (Council for Children with Behavioral Disorders, 1993).

At present, schools may have clear policies and procedures for identifying and placing students into programs for children with emotional and behavioral disorders; however, only 37% of the schools participating in a national survey had written procedures for reintegrating these students (Grosenick, George, George, & Lewis, 1991). Unfortunately, regular classroom teachers are all too often not involved in decisions to move students with behavioral disorders back into the mainstreamed setting, nor are they adequately trained and supported in handling challenging behaviors proactively (Lewis, Chard, & Scott, 1994).

Long (1994) reminds educators to "look before they leap" and to examine the previous waves of educational reform, which have come and gone with much fanfare, much expense, and little success. He cautions professionals to think about the following issues before adopting full inclusion for children with emotional and behavioral disorders:

◆ The need to go beyond the rhetoric of inclusion and carefully examine realities (e.g., the current move across the country to slash budgets and reduce the size of governmental agencies).

- Concern for the stress level of regular classroom teachers who must ensure academic excellence and increasing test scores in a decade when student discipline problems and violence are escalating.
- The inadvisability of taking a simplistic, naive view toward the re-education of students with emotional and behavioral disorders (i.e., if special education teachers have difficulty helping these students, will classroom teachers with 30 diverse students have better success?).
- A concern for financial and professional support for teachers (e.g., not making top-down bureaucratic decisions that are implemented before teachers are trained and resources and additional personnel obtained).
- Conflicting goals of having safer, violence free schools and also including more students with emotional and behavioral disorders in the regular classroom. (From "Inclusion: Formula for Failure?" by N. J. Long, 1994, *Journal of Emotional and Behavioral Problems*, 3(3), 19–23, National Educational Service)

According to Long (1994) students with behavioral disorders may demonstrate aggressive and violent behaviors. Yet, their parents may not permit physical restraint or the use of a time-out room. Moreover, school administrators may not unilaterally expel the student or change the student's placement without first demonstrating that the child's behavior cannot be handled in the regular classroom without supplementary aids and services. (See Chapter 11 for a discussion of issues surrounding the suspension and expulsion of children with disabilities.) As Long (1994) points out, the rights of individual students with disabilities, the rights of other students to be protected and to learn in safe schools, and the push for teachers to deliver a curriculum that is academically rigorous and which will increase standardized test scores are competing goals that may soon collide as schools implement inclusion. Neel (1995) reminds us, too, that schools, like families, are complex dynamic systems requiring compromise and that pleas for full inclusion for all children may have surprising, unanticipated results.

Working with Paraprofessionals and Volunteers

Paraprofessionals and volunteers play a crucial role within schools assisting teachers to meet the needs of children and youth with emotional and behavioral disorders in both the special and regular classroom setting. Sometimes called *teacher aides* or *teaching assistants*, paraprofessionals are either full- or part-time paid members of a school's staff. Although paraprofessionals are assigned particular classroom duties, they may not necessarily be licensed to teach (Fimian, Fafard, & Howell, 1994). On the other hand, volunteers receive no pay for their services to schools and their duties may vary on a daily basis. Typically, parents, senior citizens, college students, and members of the local business community volunteer their time in schools.

Paraprofessionals perform a number of duties that can free teachers to engage in collaborative planning and teaching activities. For example, paraprofessionals can locate materials and supplies, type or duplicate instructional materials, make bulletin boards, operate audiovisual equipment, assist students at the computer, take attendance, and supervise students during lunch, recess, or restroom breaks. In addition, paraprofessionals offer instructional support by listening to children read or by reading to them, by supervising independent seatwork, and by grading papers or recording grades when appropriate.

Marozas and May (1988) report that paraprofessionals may even be assuming critical instructional duties such as planning, teaching, and testing students. Such activities, of course, must be carefully supervised by teachers, since little research exists to document the preparation of paraprofessionals to assume these duties or the effectiveness of those paraprofessionals who do perform these tasks (Jones & Bender, 1993). Miramontes (1990), on the other hand, asserts that paraprofessionals may serve as essential members of collaborative teams when they share the same cultural or linguistic background as students. That is, paraprofessionals may assist teachers to communicate with students and parents who are from backgrounds different from that of the teacher's.

Volunteers may perform many of the same instructional and noninstructional duties assumed by paraprofessionals. They may, for example, make materials, games or bulletin boards, read with children, or serve as individual tutors. Importantly, volunteers possess many special talents and skills that they can share, thereby providing enrichment activities related to units under study in the classroom. In addition, volunteers may offer invaluable assistance for classroom parties or for other special events such as field trips or field days.

Boomer (1982) cites numerous advantages of using paraprofessionals in the classroom including mutual or collaborative problem solving, enhanced decision making and instructional creativity, and the ability of paraprofessionals to serve as liasons among teachers and other staff members. McKenzie and Houk (1986a, 1986b) and Blalock (1991) suggest that teachers can help paraprofessionals and volunteers to be successful by following several guidelines:

♦ Orient assistants to the school and the classroom. Give assistants and volunteers maps, handbooks, schedules, and other necessary information. Take them on a tour of the building, and introduce them to important staff members and administrators. Show them where materials are located in your classroom and give them a seating chart, or have students wear name tags, until they become familiar with your students. Provide them with a personal space such as a table or desk and chair as well as a place to secure their belongings.

♦ Plan responsibilities for assistants and post a written and specific schedule of duties daily.

♦ Clearly tell assistants what they need to do and show them how you would like each task accomplished. Ensure that assistants understand your directions and give them the opportunity to ask questions.

♦ Meet daily and regularly with assistants to plan their responsibilities and to evaluate their performance. Give specific feedback and clarify their roles.

◆ Thank volunteers and paraprofessionals for their help and praise them for their accomplishments.

Collaborating with Parents and Families

In addition to serving as volunteers, parents and other family members are considered to be equal participating partners in the best collaborative arrangements. Unfortunately, although IDEA mandates parental involvement in special education planning and decision making, parents are all too often perceived by professionals as adversaries or as apathetic, uncaring, and uninvolved. Finders and Lewis (1994) caution teachers that parental noninvolvement in schools may reflect societal barriers or economic factors rather than apathy, however.

Many professionals, for example, still view parents and families as a mother, a father, and their biological children, who function together within a household as an economically self-sufficient unit. Yet, more than 80% of all children under 18 will spend some of their time in a household headed by a single parent and fewer than 10% of all children today live in a two-parent nuclear family (Norton & Glick, 1986). When parents don't show up for PTA meetings and conferences, help out with homework projects, or volunteer to help in the classroom, then, teachers may complain that parents don't care. These teachers may be overlooking the actual or potential participation of extended family members or of adults who are nonbiological "relatives" or caregivers of children. Administrators, teachers, and other professionals may all too easily speak of families that differ in structure or beliefs from their own as "dysfunctional," forgetting that healthy families today are configured in many diverse ways (Karp, 1993). According to Karp (1993), families of children and youth with emotional and behavioral disorders may believe that the school system unresponsive to their needs is the dysfunctional entity and that the term *dysfunctional family* is simply a way of passing blame from the schools to the home.

Parents, for example, may work evenings or nights or be unable to leave the job site at any time. For many parents, hours spent off the job must be devoted to taking care of the home and meeting family needs with little time left to participate in school-related activities. Moreover, some parents have unhappy memories about their own school experiences, which may, in turn, affect relationships with the teachers of their children. Other parents may have language differences preventing them from participating fully in conferences or from helping children with homework or other projects (Finders & Lewis, 1994). Finally, parents may simply choose not to be involved when they believe that noninvolvement is beneficial for them or for their family members. As a matter of fact, most parents prefer only limited involvement with schools (MacMillan & Turnbull, 1983; Winton & Turnbull, 1981). See Box 10.4 for some concerns voiced by parents.

Parents, family members, teachers, and other professionals must carefully examine their attitudes toward one another if an honest, trusting, and mutually supportive relationship is to be developed for the benefit of the child (Box 10.5, p. 321). One important factor in developing a collaborative partnership with parents, then, is regular and open communication that focuses on child and family strengths. Like the father in Box 10.4, when parents only hear about

BOX 10.4   Voices of Parents

According to Finders and Lewis (1994), parents may not participate in schools for many reasons. When parents are asked what they believe about building positive school and home relationships, they voice many concerns including:

Unhappy School Experiences among Parents

"They expect me to go to school so they can tell me my kid is stupid or crazy. They've been telling me that for three years, so why should I go and hear it again? They don't do anything. They just tell me my kid is bad.

See, I've been there. I know. And it scares me. They called me a boy in trouble but I was a troubled boy. Nobody helped me because they liked it when I didn't show up. If I was gone for the semester, fine with them. I dropped out nine times. They wanted me gone."

Economic and Time Constraints

"Teachers just don't understand that I can't come to school at just any old time. I think Judy told you that we don't have a car right now. . . . Andrew catches a different bus than Dawn. He gets here a half an hour before her, and then I have to make sure Judy is home because I got three kids in three different schools. And I feel like the teachers are under pressure, and they're turning it around and putting the pressure on me cause they want me to check up on Judy and I really can't."

"What most people don't understand about the Hispanic community is that you come home and you take care of your husband and your family first. Then if there's time you can go out to your meetings."

"I don't understand why they assume that everybody has tons of money, and every time I turn around it's more money for this and more money for that. Where do they get the idea that we've got all this money. . . . I just can't send eight more dollars so my daughter can have a yearbook to sign like everyone else."

"It's her education, not mine. I've had to teach her to take care of herself. I work nights, so she's had to get up and get herself ready for school. I'm not going to be there all the time. She's gotta do it. She's a tough cookie. . . . She's almost an adult [12], and I get the impression that they want me to walk her through her work. And it's not that I don't care either. I really do. I think it's important, but I don't think it's my place."

Feelings of Fear, Mistrust, and Little Respect

"Parents feel like the teachers are looking at you, and I know how they feel, because I feel like that here. There are certain things and places where I still feel uncomfortable, so I won't go, and I feel bad, and I think maybe it's just me."

"Whenever I go to school, they want to tell me what to do at home. They want to tell me how to raise my kid. They never ask me what I think. They never ask me anything."

From Finders, M., and Lewis, C. "Why Some Parents Don't Come to School," *Educational Leadership*, *51*, 8: 51–53. Reprinted with permission of the Association for Supervision and Curriculum Development. Copyright © 1994 by ASCD. All rights reserved.

Teachers must develop trusting and mutually supportive relationships with parents.

learning or behavioral problems from their child's teachers, they have little reason to want to continue contact with the school. Shea and Bauer (1991) suggest that instead teachers contact parents frequently to share *positive* comments about students by doing the following:

- ◆ Sending home daily or weekly progress reports
- ◆ Telephoning home to praise children
- ◆ Recording messages on a telephone answering machine so that parents may call at any time for homework assignments, information about special events, or specific suggestions for giving assistance to their children on particular projects
- ◆ Using two-way notebooks in which teachers and parents can write comments or questions for one another
- ◆ Sending home little notes of praise or small behavioral or achievement awards
- ◆ Circulating monthly calendars, newsletters, or notices about student activities and accomplishments or about class events

BOX 10.5 Collaboration Checklists for Professionals and Families

Karp (1993) suggests that professionals and family members often misunderstand what is meant by "partnerships" and "collaboration." She encourages professionals and families to assess their own beliefs and behaviors carefully so that they may enter relationships based on mutual respect. The following questions for self-reflection are offered by Karp:

Collaboration Checklist for Professionals

___ Do I believe that parents are my equal and are experts on their child?

___ Do I show the same respect for the value of families' time as I do for my own time by educating myself about an individual child before appointments or group sessions?

___ Do I speak plainly and avoid professional jargon?

___ Do I actively involve parents in developing a plan of action and then review, evaluate, and revise the plan with the family?

___ Do I make appointments and provide services at times and places convenient for the family?

___ Do I share information with other professionals to ensure that services are not duplicated and that families do not expend unnecessary energy searching for services and providers?

Collaboration Checklist for Families

___ Do I believe I am an equal partner with professionals and do my share of problem solving and planning to help my child?

___ Do I clearly express my own needs and the needs of my family to professionals in an assertive manner?

___ Do I treat each professional as an individual and avoid letting past negative experiences get in the way of a good working relationship?

___ Do I communicate quickly with professionals when significant changes and events occur?

___ When I make a commitment to a professional for a plan of action, do I follow through and complete the commitment?

___ Do I maintain realistic expectations for professionals, myself, and my child?

From "Collaboration with Families: From Myth to Reality," by N. Karp, 1993, *Journal of Emotional and Behavioral Problems*, *1*(4), 21, National Educational Service.

Because parents today are busy people, notes and letters must be concise and to the point. If teachers are requesting a school visit by parents, for example, they should express a clear reason for this request. Letters and newsletters sent home might also welcome parents to the classroom at any time and include the teacher's telephone number with an invitation to call whenever questions arise. Keeping copies of all letters and notes sent home and asking parents to sign and return important letters helps the teacher document his or her continuing communication with parents should problems arise. In addition, asking parents to indicate the best time for teachers to telephone them at home may help set the tone for ongoing and positive communications. E-mail and fax transmissions are two modern methods also suggested by both parents and teachers to promote continuing communication about homework and child progress (Jayanthi, Nelson, Sawyer, Bursuck, & Epstein, 1995; Jayanthi, Sawyer, Newson, Bursuck, & Epstein, 1995).

Certainly teachers will want to call parents at home; however, parents are sometimes threatened by calls from school. To open communication on a positive note, teachers may wish to phone home at the start of the school year to introduce themselves. Periodic phone calls, then, may follow to share good news with parents or to prevent or solve problems should they arise. Some teachers use a calendar to plan and ensure routine phone calls home to all parents. Of course, teachers must be sensitive to the needs of families and refrain from interrupting parents at work, from calling home during suppertime or late in the evening, or from calling home frequently to discuss only a child's misbehavior.

Teachers must remember to be courteous and respectful when talking with parents. Addressing parents as "Mr." or "Mrs." or by another appropriate title conveys respect. Also, avoiding professional jargon communicates a sense of partnership rather than a hierarchical relationship. Teachers must also remember to value the parent's time by keeping phone conversations to the point and relatively brief. Finally, teachers should document all telephone contacts attempted or made with parents. Noting on a contact log or index card the date, time, person contacted, and topic of conversation provides documentation of all parent-teacher communications.

Face-to-face conferences are also essential for continuing communication between parents and teachers. Home visits may be exceedingly helpful in assisting teachers to work collaboratively with the families of students with emotional and behavioral disorders. Meeting parents at home may provide insights regarding the child that are simply not obtainable through telephone calls or meetings held at school. Although parents may be intimidated by teachers visiting at home, they may find home visits more comfortable or convenient than in-school conferences, and parents may view the teacher's effort to visit at home as evidence that the teacher truly cares and is committed to the welfare of their child.

When making home visits, however, teachers must make an appointment in advance and clearly state the purpose for their visit. If the child lives in a neighborhood having an unsafe reputation, teachers should schedule all visits during the daylight hours and arrange to take someone else with them. In addition, teachers should let the school principal know exactly where they plan to be and when they plan to return. Unfortunately, in some school districts, certain neighborhoods are simply off limits for teachers who are told they may not make home visits to families living there. When teachers do visit homes having living conditions or family configurations different from their own, they should avoid showing surprise or disapproval. Rather, teachers can always find something interesting (e.g., photographs on tables or walls) to comment on positively (Howe & Simmons, 1994).

Similarly, when parents are invited to conferences at school, teachers must clarify the purpose for the conference and arrange the conference at a time convenient for the parents. Be sure to arrange a comfortable and private area for the conference. Teachers may wish, for example, to post a "do-not-disturb" sign on their closed classroom door. Be sure to give parents adult-sized chairs in which to sit and refrain from sitting behind the teacher's desk, a position intimidating to some parents. Arrange all materials and work samples in advance, greet parents warmly, take their coats, and provide them with coffee or beverages, if possible, to help them feel comfortable and welcome. Keep in mind, too, that some parents may need assistance with child care or language differences during conferences.

Whether conducting conferences at home or at school, teachers must open the conversation on a positive note by discussing student strengths. Listening to parent concerns, questioning and paraphrasing to check understanding of issues voiced by parents, and clearly and honestly answering all questions parents ask are critical skills for teachers collaborating with families. Empathy, allowing parents to speak without interruption, and reviewing and summarizing points made are additional essential elements of successful conferences. Shea and Bauer (1991) also encourage teachers to stick to the point and to refrain from criticizing parents or arguing with them, gossiping about other children, and belittling the school or school system. On the other hand, teachers who remain professional, who emphasize the positive, who view parents as competent, and who share responsibility with parents foster collaborative partnerships.

Careful planning can minimize anxiety for both parents and teachers whether conferences are conducted at home, at school, or by telephone. Some teachers prefer, for example, to give parents a copy of a conference agenda to be followed. The agenda provides structure for the conversation, assists participants to stay on the topic and keep within time limits, and gives both teacher and parent a ready-made place to jot down notes and questions. The agenda also documents the purpose of each parent-teacher conference. Parents must, of course, be given the time and opportunity to help plan the agenda and they most certainly should receive their own copy of the agenda as the conference begins. Additional suggestions to facilitate collaborative relationships with parents and other family members are listed in Box 10.6 (p. 324).

Summary of Collaboration within Schools ◆

Collaboration implies equal participation and equal responsibility; therefore, successful collaboration requires excellent communication skills and adequate time. Teachers who collaborate with other professionals at school must be supported and rewarded for their efforts. Full inclusion may not be appropriate for all children and youth with emotional and behavioral disorders. Yet, for those children who can be included in the regular classroom, special and regular educators must skillfully collaborate to ensure success. Collaborating with paraprofessionals and volunteers also necessitates attention to time and to individual needs. Finally, teachers must remain sensitive to the demands placed today on parents and other family members. Open, honest, and continuing communication with parents and other caregivers is essential for developing the mutual trust and respect critical for collaboration to occur. ◆

BOX 10.6   **Suggestions to Facilitate Teacher-Family Collaboration**

- ◆ Make school facilities available for many different types of community activities.
- ◆ Invite extended family members to attend all school activities or conferences.
- ◆ Refer to family members by title and greet elder family members first.
- ◆ Help establish carpools or other transportation so that family members may attend school events.
- ◆ Conduct meetings at community-based sites when coming to the school is not convenient or possible for the family (e.g., at a church, day care center, community center, library, etc.).
- ◆ Obtain assistance from other civic organizations in the community to provide child care, transportation, or other necessary services to enable families to attend school conferences.
- ◆ Become acquainted with and solicit help from religious organizations, community or religious leaders, or social agencies in the community that may assist families to attend school events.
- ◆ Involve siblings in discussions or training sessions, when possible, particularly when siblings are serving as primary caregivers to younger brothers or sisters after school.
- ◆ Establish sibling support groups for brothers and sisters of children with emotional and behavioral disorders. The following organizations may be helpful in establishing such sibling or family support groups:

Federation of Families for Children's Mental Health
Barbara Huff, Executive Director
1021 Prince Street
Alexandria, Virginia 22314-2971
(703) 684-7710

Sibling Information Network
A.J. Pappanikov Center
62 Washington Street
Middletown, CT 06457

Siblings of Disabled Children
535 Race Street, Suite 120
San Jose, CA 95126 (408) 288-5010

Collaborating with Community Agencies

Today's families undoubtedly experience tremendous stress. When children or adolescents who are overactive, impulsive, distractible, or aggressive are family members, the level of stress for both parents, as well as for other family members, may be elevated significantly (Baker, 1994; Grotevant, McRoy, & Jenkins, 1988). Hutinger (1988) maintains, however, that stress need not be an inevitable result of having within the family a child at risk for behavioral or learning problems. The amount and type of support offered to families of children and youth with emotional and behavioral disorders may help to preserve that family unit.

Unfortunately, according to Blythe and Kelly (1993), almost 500,000 children in the United States live separately from their families on any particular day in social services, juvenile justice, or mental health facilities. See Box 10.7 (pp. 326–327) for a description of these agencies. These authors assert that many of these children could remain home with the family if effective community-based services were to be provided. They use the term *family preservation* to refer to coordinated efforts to reduce placement of children outside of the home through the following means:

♦ A focus on the entire family
♦ Flexibly delivered services in the home and community available 24 hours a day, 7 days a week, rather than only during office hours
♦ Small caseloads of two families per case manager
♦ Immediate, intensive, but time-limited and goal-oriented, interventions (p. 24)

Family preservation is one effort to decrease expensive, intrusive and restrictive placements outside of the home for children living in stressful family situations. Children and youth with emotional and behavioral disorders, however, often exhibit disruptive behaviors resulting in their removal from the home and placement into residential or psychiatric treatment facilities. For example, Singh, Landrum, Donatelli, Hampton, and Ellis (1994) report that 67% of the students admitted to one child and adolescent psychiatric hospital were voluntary admissions referred by family members or by mental health workers such as therapists, psychologists, or psychiatrists. Aggression and behavioral problems were most often cited as the reason for admission. Students who were admitted involuntarily, though, were most often mandated by the courts to do so because of family instability, risk of abuse and neglect, or aggression to self or others.

Placement in residential, psychiatric facilities is a costly, yet increasingly used, option for students with emotional and behavioral disorders. In one state, for example, psychiatric hospitalization of children and youth increased from 74 beds in 3 facilities at a cost of $4 to $5 million in 1980 to 500 beds in 13 facilities at a cost of $36 million in 1989 (Phillips, Nelson, & McLaughlin, 1993). Behar (1990) asserts that more than 50% of all children and youth placed in these restrictive settings are placed there unnecessarily because no alternative suitable placements are available in the home community.

Knitzer (1993) further maintains that 40% to 60% of all youth in psychiatric hospitals do not belong there. Yet, one third to one half of those children hospitalized are in the custody of state child welfare agencies after being removed from unstable or abusive home environments (Knitzer, 1993). Although hospitalization and residential treatment are components of a comprehensive system of care for children and adolescents with emotional and behavioral disorders, only a small number of youngsters should require such restrictive placements. Unless funding patterns change to encourage the use of limited resources to develop community-based, child- and family-centered alternatives to residential treatment, however, these more restrictive placements will continue to be over-

BOX 10.7 Agencies Serving Children and Youth with Emotional or Behavioral Disorders

Special educators are often unfamiliar with the many community agencies serving children and youth with emotional and behavioral disorders. Families of these students are often impacted by rules and regulations governing these services. Moreover, professionals within these agencies may have goals, definitions, policies, funding criteria, and vocabulary that conflict with those of schools. Teachers must be knowledgeable regarding these community agencies if they are to collaborate fully with other professionals and build school-to-community linkages on behalf of their students.

Mental Health Services

Morse (1992) describes the continuing calls for collaboration to develop mental health and education liasons. Departments of Mental Health and Mental Retardation typically oversee community mental health programs within the states and, historically, departments of mental health have been major service providers for children, adolescents, and adults with emotional disturbance. Although the exact services may vary according to locality, typically these include: (1) 24-hour emergency services for persons experiencing acute mental health or substance abuse problems; (2) out-patient services such as individual, group, or family counseling, psychotherapy, or psychiatric evaluations for children, adolescents, and adults; (3) psychological testing services; and (4) screening for and admission to state mental hospitals or residential treatment facilities, as well as follow-up care on discharge. In addition, most community mental health clinics sponsor speakers for consultation and educational services and operate infant intervention and substance abuse treatment and prevention programs. Professionals within mental health agencies often include psychologists, clinical social workers, and counselors. Mental health services are optional and voluntary rather than mandatory.

Social Services

Child welfare and social services encompass a wide array of human services in a variety of settings. In addition to numerous benefits programs such as food assistance, food stamps, and energy and emergency assistance, departments of social services usually oversee foster care, adoption, and child protection services. Social workers or other personnel in social services often function as case

used (Duchnowski, Johnson, Hall, Kutash, & Friedman, 1993; Knitzer, Steinberg, & Fleisch, 1990).

In addition, many other children and youth with emotional and behavioral disorders find themselves ajudicated delinquent and placed outside the home through the juvenile justice system. Some authorities estimate that most of the incarcerated youth serving time in juvenile detention centers, state training schools, correctional group homes and therapeutic camps, or even in adult jails,

managers to connect families in crisis with necessary resources. The professionals within social services are often the "front line" workers who negotiate total systems of care for children with emotional and behavioral disorders and their families. Unfortunately, these professionals carry large caseloads, which, when combined with limited resources, may make obtaining services frustrating for some families.

Law Enforcement and the Juvenile Justice System

Juveniles may enter the justice system when they have committed a crime or a status offense (i.e., a behavior forbidden to individuals who are not of majority age) and when they have been arrested by police officers. Youth may also enter the justice system through referrals made by school officials, social service agencies, parents, or law enforcement officers for criminal acts, status offenses, or for protective custody in the event of neglect or abuse. An intake officer typically determines whether or not a juvenile's case warrants filing a petition for an adjudicatory hearing, or in the case of older juveniles who have committed numerous or serious offenses, for referral to be tried as an adult. The juvenile court may decide to divert the young person to other agencies or programs or to accept the petition and hold a hearing. If the youth is adjudicated as delinquent, the disposition of the case might include probation, placement in a correctional institution, fines, or removal from the home to foster care or to a special school or treatment facility. (Note, in the juvenile court system, a hearing is conducted, typically without a jury, instead of a trial. Instead of finding a juvenile guilty and sentencing the individual, youth are adjudicated delinquent and the sentence is termed disposition.)

While students are in protective custody or awaiting a hearing, they may be confined to detention centers. Students who are adjudicated delinquent must be provided with education or special education while they are in correctional institutions, training schools, reform schools, diagnostic or learning centers, or in camp or ranch programs located in rural areas. Kauffman (1993) questions whether or not the rights of youth are violated or protected when they are "sheltered" in placements such as these for status offenses or for protective custody by the juvenile courts. (For additional information see: Leone, Rutherford, & Nelson, 1991, or Nelson, Rutherford, & Wolford, 1987.)

are students with behavioral disorders (Eisenmann, 1991; Kauffman, 1993; Murphy, 1986). Although IDEA guarantees special education services for incarcerated youth with disabilities, not all of these students receive appropriate special education programs (McIntyre, 1993). Moreover, behavioral disorders among incarcerated youth may be particularly intractable despite well-designed and structured programs (Kauffman, 1993). Unfortunately, public outrage and fear regarding increases in violent crimes committed by today's youth are fueling

Providing Special Education Services in Correctional Settings: Problems, Issues, and Needs

McIntyre (1993) describes many difficulties associated with providing high-quality special education services for incarcerated youth with disabilities. Among those concerns he lists are the following: (1) Lack of interagency cooperation; (2) Failure of schools to forward IEPs; (3) High turnover rate among incarcerated students; (4) Poor assessment practices; (5) Lack of parental involvement; (6) Lack of preparation for transition back to school or to the world of work; and (7) Difficulty in maintaining treatment gains following intervention. According to McIntyre, these difficulties are attributable to problems with the federal definition of emotional and behavioral disorders and to the inadequate preparation of teachers to serve this population.

Definitional Issues

IDEA excludes socially maladjusted children from receiving special education services unless these students are otherwise seriously emotionally disturbed. Kauffman (1993) discusses the logical inconsistencies in the federal definition of emotional and behavioral disorders, suggesting that most students exhibiting frequent antisocial, aggressive, and delinquent acts must be considered behaviorally disordered. Nevertheless, of the incarcerated youth receiving special education services, most are identified as students with mental retardation or learning disabilities rather than as youth with emotional and behavioral disorders.

Teacher Training

Teachers are often not equipped to teach delinquent youth within the context of a correctional setting. As the correctional system becomes increasingly crowded, only the most violent and manipulative students will be incarcerated.

"get tough" programs such as boot camps for juvenile offenders despite the lack of evidence that these programs are effective (Henggeler & Schoenwalk, 1994). See Box 10.8 for several reasons suggested for the lack of special education services provided in correctional settings and Box 10.9 (pp. 330–331) for what incarcerated youth say about delinquency.

Numerous professionals now decry the alarming increase in the rate and expense of out-of-home placements for children and youth with emotional and behavioral disorders and advocate greater attention to community-based systems of care (Forness, 1988; Knitzer, 1993; The Peacock Hill Working Group, 1991). During the 1980s several problems prohibiting the development of community services for children and adolescents with emotional and behavioral disorders came under scrutiny. These problems included: (1) lack of interaction and collaboration among professionals in state mental health agencies and the other state agencies routinely serving children (e.g., child welfare, juvenile justice, and public schools); (2) Medicaid and other federal or state-level funding patterns that favor hospitalization over community and in-home care; and (3)

Thus, special education teachers must be "street smart" and trained to "earn respect" from these youth. In addition to instructional, counseling, and behavior management skills, then, special educators within correctional settings must be competent in defusing oppositional and violent behaviors and they must be well versed in attending to personal safety.

Teacher Supply and Demand

Steinberg (1991) suggests that a severe shortage exists in the number of teachers prepared to teach students with behavioral disorders in the public schools. The shortage of special educators to teach within correctional facilities, therefore, is even more pronounced. Teachers often do not realize the job opportunities available within correctional facilities, and many are unwilling to teach in these settings. In addition, public attitudes are often unfavorable to providing educational services, rather than "punishment," to juvenile offenders.

Recidivism

Upon release from juvenile correctional facilities or other treatment programs, aggressive youth often fail to maintain the gains made while in custody. Consequently, these youth commit additional crimes and find themselves once again incarcerated. Teachers within correctional facilities assert that juvenile delinquents are well-behaved in small, structured classes; however, improvement in social, academic, and vocational skills are lost when these students are released to unstable, negative home and community environments.

child welfare systems that require parents to give up custody of their children and be declared neglectful by the courts to gain essential services (Knitzer, 1993). Systemic difficulties such as these are only just now beginning to be addressed through federal and state legislation requiring juvenile and family courts to review promptly any decisions to remove children from the home for emergency reasons and to oversee efforts to prevent out-of-home placements and reunify families whenever possible (White, 1993). The courts, of course, must exercise great caution to ensure that children and youth do not remain in dangerous, abusive family situations (Bradley, 1995).

Efforts are beginning to remedy system-wide barriers to comprehensive care. For example, the National Special Education and Mental Health Coalition, an alliance of representatives from various professional associations and agencies concerned with the education and mental health of children and adolescents (e.g., Council for Exceptional Children, National Mental Health Association) formed in 1987, is encouraging collaboration among teachers and mental health professionals to serve the needs of students with behavioral disorders within the

Ask the Experts: Incarcerated Youths' Views on Delinquency

Allen (1992) conducted a study among 110 juvenile male offenders incarcerated at the Youth Center at Topeka, Kansas, the largest juvenile detention center in the state. The boys ranged in age from 14 to 21 and had committed offenses from misdemeanor thefts to first degree murder. These young men were asked to give their thoughts about delinquency on an informal survey with the following results:

1. Have you ever done illegal drugs?
   Yes: 78
   No: 31
2. If you have done illegal drugs, what kind did you do?
   Listed in order of frequency, answers were: marijuana, cocaine, LSD, downers, uppers, PCP, mushrooms, crystal, water (known to most of us as embalming fluid), crack.
3. Are you a parent? If so, how many children do you have?
   Yes: 39
   Number: 52 children listed—range from 1–4 children
4. Have you ever been in other detention centers? How many?
   Yes: 69
   No: 39
   Average of 3.08 other centers
5. Do you have other relatives that are currently locked up or have been in the past?
   Yes: 66
6. What do you think are some of the causes of juvenile delinquency?
   Answers included: family problems, poor parenting, peer pressure,

community (Forness, 1988). In addition, through the National Institute of Mental Health, a Child and Adolescent Service System Program (CASSP) began in 1984. Although relatively small, this program provides grant funds to states to improve mental health services for children by promoting interagency collaboration and developing community-based systems of care including day treatment, therapeutic foster care, case management, and intensive crisis services. Rather than viewing the family as the source of the problem and immediately removing the child, CASSP encourages mental health professionals to build on family strengths and solicit their help as partners when planning, implementing, or evaluating services.

As a matter of fact, two family organizations have also recently formed to lobby for services for their children with emotional and behavioral disorders. The Federation of Families for Children's Mental Health, for example, initially funded through CASSP and established in 1990, is becoming an important national advocacy and parent support group. In addition, the Child and Adolescent Network of the National Alliance for the Mentally Ill (NAMI-CAN) is an organization devoted to improving national policy and mental health services for

gangs, drugs, lack of money, boredom, lack of structure, anger, and mistreatment.

7. What do you think would help prevent juvenile delinquency?
   Answers included: get kids off the street, better drug treatment, more jobs, education, harsher treatment, stricter laws, stop gangs, keep families together, legalize drugs, nothing, and don't know.

8. Do you think the level system (earning your way out like at Youth Center at Topeka) is best, or would you prefer straight time?
   Level System: 33
   Straight Time: 58

9. Do you think juveniles should be tried as adults?
   Yes: 12
   No: 61
   Depends on crime: 31

10. What are your goals?
    Answers included: good job, finish high school, go to college, computer programmer, pro basketball player, rapper, dancer, artist, military, modeling, pro boxer, teacher, policeman, and be in a gang.

11. Where do you think you will be in ten years?
    Answers included: owning a business, being in another state, getting my act together, living peacefully, making better decisions, living a normal life, in a gang, and hauntingly, nine responded dead.

From "Ask the Experts: Students' Views on Delinquency," by R. Allen, *Beyond Behavior*, 3(2), 1992, p. 22. Copyright © 1992 by The Council for Exceptional Children. Reprinted with permission.

both children and families influenced by emotional and behavioral disorders (Friesen & Wahlers, 1993). Family support groups and community-based, family-centered services across the United States are expanding due to the efforts of these two organizations. See Box 10.10 (p. 332) for additional information regarding family support services and organizations.

Increasingly, services within the school and community are literally wrapped around children and youth with emotional and behavioral disorders. Instead of merely providing an appropriate education for the child, today's schools are becoming centers for the provision and coordination of comprehensive systems of care for both child and family so that complex problems may be addressed on many fronts simultaneously (Duchnowski, Johnson, Hall, Kutash, & Friedman, 1993; Federation of Families for Children's Mental Health, 1992). Counseling, medication, and assistance through social services to alleviate family stressors are but a few examples of wrap-around services coordinated by schools in some states. Integrated and multifaceted services such as these, however, require extensive collaboration among many different professionals both within and outside of schools.

BOX 10.10 **Family Support Services**

According to the Federation of Families for Children's Mental Health (1992), family support is described as:

"A constellation of formal and informal services and tangible goods that are defined and determined by families. It is 'whatever it takes' for a family to care for and live with a child or adolescent who has an emotional, behavioral, or mental disorder. It also includes supports needed to assist families to maintain close involvement with their children who are in out-of-home placement and to help families when their children are ready to return home" (p. 1).

Examples of critical family support services identified by the Federation of Families (1992, p. 1) include:

- Self-help, support, and advocacy groups and organizations
- Information and referral assistance
- Education to help families become active and informed decision-makers on behalf of their children
- Advocacy with the family or on behalf of the family when necessary
- Individualized, flexible support services to meet family needs quickly and responsively
- Respite care both in- and out-of-home that emphasizes community participation for the child and support for the entire family
- Cash assistance as needed
- Help with family survival needs such as housing, food, transportation, or home maintenance
- Any other supports as determined necessary by the family

From Family Support Statement, p. 1. Copyright © 1992 Federation of Families for Children's Mental Health. Reprinted by permission.

For additional information on family-support services contact:

National T.A.C. for Children's Mental Health
Technical Assistance Center
Georgetown University
3307 M Street, N.W.
Washington, D.C. 20007
(202) 687-5000

Federation of Families for Children's Mental Health
1021 Prince Street
Alexandria, VA 22314-2971
(703) 684-7710

The Individuals With Disabilities Education Act of 1990 also encourages schools, families, and other community agencies to collaborate. Under IDEA, parents, students, and teachers must plan for adult services that may be needed by students in special education programs after they leave school. For example, IDEA mandates that transition planning begin no later than age 16, and by age

14 or earlier, whenever appropriate. The Individualized Transition Plan (ITP) developed for each student describes the interagency linkages and services needed as adolescents move from school to the adult world. Thus, collaboration among teachers and professionals from adult service agencies such as mental health or vocational rehabilitation is essential for transition planning.

For students with emotional and behavioral disorders, adult outcomes are not particularly positive. Frank, Sitlington, and Carson (1991), for example, suggest that only one third of students with behavior disorders who graduate from high school make a satisfactory adult adjustment. Many of these youth continue to rely on family members for assistance, with one third working less than full-time and one quarter of the graduates "unengaged" (i.e., not involved in any work, homemaking, or vocational training programs). Few graduates or dropouts seek help from adult service agencies such as mental health or vocational rehabilitation in order to solve personal problems or find productive employment. Clearly, increased collaborative efforts are necessary among schools and other agencies if students with behavioral disorders are to become contributing members of families and communities.

Summary of Collaboration among Community Agencies ◆

To maintain children and adolescents with emotional and behavioral disorders in their communities, states are beginning to develop comprehensive systems of care. Increasingly, professionals are being trained as case managers to find and wrap necessary services around children and families (Knitzer, Steinberg, & Fleisch, 1990). Instead of simply providing services that are available or fundable, case managers negotiate for services that are actually needed by individuals and their families. Policies and funding patterns across the state agencies must continue to become more flexible than in the past, however, if professionals in these agencies are to collaborate to provide necessary services within the community and as the child grows into adulthood (Epstein, Cullinan, Quinn, & Cumblad, 1994; Quinn & Cumblad, 1994). See Box 10.11 (pp. 334–335) for some major findings and recommendations from a national study of programs for students with emotional and behavioral disorders. ◆

Summary

Teachers of students with emotional and behavioral disorders must collaborate with other teachers and professionals within schools. Collaboration implies an equal partnership and mutual problem solving rather than a hierarchical, expert-to-client relationship. Team efforts, however, do not preclude one professional being designated as a case manager to assume responsibility for coordinating necessary services.

The full inclusion of children and youth with emotional and behavioral disorders into the regular classroom entails skillful collaboration from both special and general educators. Paraprofessionals and volunteers may provide valuable assistance to teachers in both regular and special education classrooms to help students with emotional and behavioral disorders achieve success.

Some Major Findings and Recommendations from a National Examination of Programs and Policies for Children with Behavioral and Emotional Problems

Knitzer, Steinberg, and Fleish (1990) conducted a national study examining programs for children and adolescents with emotional and behavioral disorders. Among their many concerns and numerous recommendations, the authors listed the following:

Major Findings

◆ Eighteen percent of students with behavioral disorders are removed from the school, with 12% of these students served in either day schools or day treatment programs. Four percent of the students are placed in residential settings, and the remainder, either in correctional facilities, in in-patient hospitals, or on "homebound" instruction." That is, they receive tutoring (sometimes as little as one hour a day) in their own homes.

◆ There are no national data on the number of students identified as having behavioral or emotional disabilities who receive mental health services (i.e., counseling or therapy) as part of their individualized education plans. Whether or not students have access to mental health services varies enormously, and if they do, it is either very short-term or parents pay for it. Children often lack access to therapy and teachers to consultation and support, even in the face of predictable crises.

◆ For many children, emotional and behavioral problems are compounded by family issues. Children with serious emotional or behavioral problems identified by the schools are disproportionately likely to come from single parent homes, and to be poor. Studies suggest that between one quarter and one half of E/BD students live in poverty.

Recent Efforts

◆ Increasingly, schools are making efforts to fine tune "pre-referral" strategies for children manifesting behavioral problems. Pre-referral strategies to ameliorate specific academic or behavioral problems before children are referred for special education evaluation include additional training to classroom teachers and attaching a cadre of aides to the school-based support teams to work with classroom teachers to carry out specialized interventions such as behavior management.

◆ Increasingly, schools are beginning to strengthen their capacity to provide school-based mental health services, including crisis intervention, short-term counseling and teacher consultation to students in regular education. Schools and mental health agencies are beginning to collaborate to provide on-site services.

♦ Efforts to link school-related services more closely to families are growing, especially for the most seriously troubled students. Approaches include more extensive use of family therapies, crisis hotlines for students and families in day treatment programs and formal links between schools and intensive in-home crisis intervention services (also called family preservation services) funded either through child welfare or children's mental health and designed for children at risk of imminent out-of-home placement.

♦ Case management services, for the most seriously troubled children and adolescents who are high users of multiple services, are increasingly recognized as an important intervention and management tool for not only community mental health agencies, but also schools. Most typically (and appropriately) case management initiatives involve collaborations between several systems. Often these are orchestrated by mental health agencies, but sometimes schools are taking the leading role.

♦ Transition programs for older students with identified emotional and behavioral problems are growing. On-site employment coaches, selecting jobs carefully, developing peer support groups for a cohort of students, and developing specialized support services for employers as well are all transition strategies that programs are using.

Major Recommendations

♦ Conduct reviews, both within school districts and on a statewide basis, of the scope and quality of the current mix of educational and mental health services available for children with identified behavioral and emotional disorders.

♦ Strengthen the policy commitment to enhance collaboration between schools and mental health agencies.

♦ Encourage the formation of parent support and advocacy groups and expand opportunities for parents to collaborate in school related efforts to help their children.

♦ Examine current fiscal strategies at all levels of government to ensure that all available dollars for services are being used in the most cost effective ways (e.g., case management services), and to develop strategies to increase resources as appropriate.

The needs of families are often overlooked by teachers who may consider parents to be uninvolved or uncaring adversaries. If teachers are sensitive to the needs of families, they can encourage collaborative partnerships with parents. Increasingly, services for children and youth with emotional and behavioral disorders are becoming family centered and community based. Collaboration across schools and other agencies such as mental health, social services, or the juvenile justice system are essential to prevent expensive, unnecessary, and restrictive out-of-home placements for many students with emotional and behavioral disorders.

Alliances among national organizations, as well as among parents and families, are now forming. These groups continue to advocate on behalf of children and adolescents with emotional and behavioral disorders for more comprehensive and responsive systems of care and for improved interagency collaboration. Schools are increasingly assuming the responsibility for coordinating and integrating all services across state agencies. Such wrap-around programs may ensure more multifaceted and effective treatment of the many complex problems faced by children with emotional and behavioral disorders and their families.

Application Exercises

1. Arrange to interview a teacher of students with behavioral disorders. What helpful suggestions can this teacher give you for collaborating with other teachers and professionals in the school? What tips can he or she give for collaborating with parents?

2. Interview a teacher of students with emotional and behavioral disorders in an "inclusive" classroom. What support does this teacher receive to be successful? Who provides this support?

3. Interview a paraprofessional in a classroom for students with emotional and behavioral disorders. What are the major responsibilities assigned to this individual? What does this paraprofessional most value when interacting with the teachers in his or her school?

4. Interview a parent of a child with emotional and behavioral disorders. Without violating confidentiality, report to the class how this parent feels about his or her child's educational program. Is the parent satisfied with his or her level of involvement, or would he or she like to be more or less involved than at present? What barriers to collaboration with the schools, if any, does the parent perceive?

5. Write to the organizations listed in Boxes 10.6 and 10.10. Share the information you receive with the members of your class.

6. Visit the mental health, social services, or juvenile correction agencies located in your community. What services are provided? What are the criteria for provision of services? Share the information you gather with the members of your class.

7. Interview a teacher in a juvenile correctional facility. What satisfactions and what difficulties are experienced by this teacher? If possible, find out what special education services are provided to students at the facility. Share this information with your classmates.

8. Research and debate the following ethical questions: Are students' rights violated or protected when they are placed involuntarily into residential treatment centers or psychiatric hospitals? Are students' rights violated or protected when they are placed into juvenile correction facilities for "protective custody" or "status offenses"?

References

Allen, R. (1992). Asking the experts: Students' views on delinquency. *Beyond Behavior*, *3*(2), 21–23.

Baker, D. B. (1994). Parenting stress and ADHD: A comparison of mothers and fathers. *Journal of Emotional and Behavioral Disorders*, *2*(1), 46–50.

Bauwens, J., Hourcade, J. J., & Friend, M. (1989). Cooperative teaching: A model for general and special education integration. *Remedial and Special Education*, *10*(2), 17–22.

Behar, L. (1990). Financing mental health services for children and adolescents. *Bulletin of the Menninger Clinic*, *54*, 127–139.

Blalock, G. (1991). Paraprofessionals: Critical team members in our special education programs. *Intervention in school and clinic*, *26*, 200–214.

Blythe, B. J., & Kelly, S. A. (1993). Keeping families and children safe. *Journal of Emotional and Behavioral Problems*, *1*(4), 23–26.

Boomer, L. W. (1982). The paraprofessional: A valued resource for special children and their teachers. *Teaching Exceptional Children*, *14*, 194–197.

Braaten, S., Kauffman, J. M., Braaten, B., Polsgrove, L., & Nelson, C. M. (1988). The Regular Education Initiative: Patent medicine for behavioral disorders. *Exceptional Children*, *55*, 21–27.

Bradley, P. (1995). When to intervene is agonizing question: Reports of mistreatment didn't save child. *Richmond Times-Dispatch*, Sunday, February 5, C1–C2.

Chalfant, J. C., Pysh, M. V., & Moultrie, R. (1979). Teacher assistance teams: A model for within-building problem solving. *Learning Disability Quarterly*, *2*, 85–96.

Chalfant, J. C., & Van Dusen Pysh, M. (1989). Teacher assistance teams: Five descriptive studies on 96 teams. *Remedial and Special Education*, *10*(6), 49–58.

Council for Children with Behavioral Disorders. (1989). Position paper on the regular education initiative. *Behavioral Disorders*, *14*, 201–207.

Council for Children with Behavioral Disorders. (1993). Position statement on full inclusion. *CCBD Newsletter*, August, p. 1.

Council for Exceptional Children. (1993). *Statement on inclusive schools and communities.* Reston, VA: Council for Exceptional Children.

Duchnowski, A. J., Johnson, M. K., Hall, K. S., Kutash, K., & Friedman, R. M. (1993). The alternatives to residential treatment study: Initial findings. *Journal of Emotional and Behavioral Disorders*, *1*(1), 17–26.

Eisenmann, R. (1991). Conduct disordered youth: Insights from a prison treatment program. *Beyond Behavior*, *2*(1), 3–4.

Epstein, M. H., Cullinan, D., Quinn, K. P., & Cumblad, C. (1994). Characteristics of children with emotional and behavioral disorders in community-based programs designed to prevent placement in residential facilities. *Journal of Emotional and Behavioral Disorders*, *2*(1), 51–57.

Federation of Families for Children's Mental Health. (1992). *Family support statement.* Alexandria, VA: Federation of Families for Children's Mental Health.

Fimian, M., Fafard, M. B., & Howell, K. (1984). *A teacher's guide to human resources in special education: Paraprofessionals, volunteers, and peer tutors.* Boston: Allyn & Bacon.

Finders, M., & Lewis, C. (1994). Why some parents don't come to school. *Educational Leadership, 51*(8), 50–54.

Forness, S. R. (1988). Planning for the needs of children with serious emotional disturbance: The National Special Education and Mental Health Coalition. *Behavioral Disorders, 13*(2), 127–139.

Frank, A. R., Sitlilngton, P. L., & Carson, R. (1991). Transition of adolescents with behavioral disorders—Is it successful? *Behavioral Disorders, 16*(3), 180–191.

Friesen, B. J., & Wahlers, D. (1993). Respect and real help: Family support and children's mental health. *Journal of Emotional and Behavioral Problems, 2*(4), 12–15.

Fuchs, D., & Fuchs, L. S. (1994). Inclusive schools movement and the radicalization of special education reform. *Exceptional Children, 60*(4), 294–309.

Fuchs, D., Fuchs, L. S., & Bahr, M. W. (1990). Mainstream assistance teams: A scientific basis for the art of consultation. *Exceptional Children, 57*, 128–139.

Gersten, R., Walker, H., & Darch, C. (1988). Relationship between teachers' effectiveness and their tolerance for handicapped students. *Exceptional Children, 54*, 433–438.

Glickman, C. D. (1990). *Supervision of instruction: A developmental approach* (3rd ed.). Boston: Allyn & Bacon.

Grosenick, J. K., George, N. L., George, M. P., & Lewis, T. J. (1991). Public school services for behaviorally disordered students: Program practices in the 1980's. *Behavioral Disorders, 16*, 87–96.

Grotevant, H. D., McRoy, R. G., & Jenkins, V. Y. (1988). Emotionally disturbed, adopted adolescents: Early patterns of family adaptation. *Family Process, 27*, 439–457.

Gutkin, T. B., & Curtis, J. M. (1990). School-based consultation: Theory, techniques and research. In T. B. Gutkin & C. R. Reynolds (Eds.), *The handbook of school psychology* (2nd ed.) (pp. 577–611). New York: Wiley.

Henggeler, S. W., & Schoenwald, S. K. (1994). Boot camps for juvenile offenders: Just say no. *Journal of Child and Family Studies, 3*(3), 243–248.

Howe, F., & Simmons, B. J. (1994). *Nurturing the parent-teacher alliance: A guide to forming a facilitative relationship.* (Unpublished manuscript). Longwood College, Farmville, VA.

Hutinger, P. (1988). Stress: Is it an inevitable condition for families of children at risk? *Teaching Exceptional Children, 20*(4), 36–39.

Idol, L., Paolucci-Whitcomb, P., & Nevin, A. (1986). *Collaborative consultation.* Rockville, MD: Aspen.

Jayanthi, M., Nelson, J. S., Sawyer, V., Bursuck, W. D., & Epstein, M. H. (1995). Homework-communication problems among parents, classroom teachers, and special education teachers: An exploratory study. *Remedial and Special Education, 16*(2), 102–116.

Jayanthi, M., Sawyer, V., Nelson, J. S., Bursuck, W. D., & Epstein, M. H. (1995). Recommendations for homework-communication problems: From parents, classroom teachers, and special education teachers. *Remedial and Special Education, 16*(4), 212–225.

Johnson, L. J., Pugach, M. C., & Devlin, S. (1990). Professional collaboration. *Teaching Exceptional Children, 22*, 9–11.

Jones, K. H., & Bender, W. N. (1993). Utilization of paraprofessionals in special education: A review of the literature. *Remedial and Special Education, 14*(1), 7–14.

Karge, B. D., McClure, M., & Patton, P. L. (1995). The success of collaboration resource programs for students with disabilities in grades 6 through 8. *Remedial and Special Education, 16*(2), 79–89.

Karp, N. (1993). Collaboration with families: From myth to reality. *Journal of Emotional and Behavioral Problems, 1*(4), 21–23.

Kauffman, J. M. (1993). *Characteristics of emotional and behavioral disorders of children and youth* (5th ed.). New York: Merrill/MacMillan.

Kauffman, J. M. (1989). The Regular Education Initiative as Reagan-Bush education policy: A trickle-down theory of education of the hard to teach. *The Journal of Special Education, 23,* 256–278.

Kauffman, J. M., Gerber, M. M., & Semmel, M. I. (1988). Arguable assumptions underlying the Regular Education Initiative. *Journal of Learning Disabilities, 21,* 6–11.

Knitzer, J. (1993). Children's mental health policy: Challenging the future. *Journal of Emotional and Behavioral Disorders, 1*(1), 8–16.

Knitzer, J., Steinberg, Z., & Fleisch, B. (1990). *At the schoolhouse door: An examination of programs and policies for children with behavioral and emotional problems.* New York: Bank Street College of Education.

Kruger, L. J., Struzziero, J., Watts, R., & Vacca, D. (1995). The relationship between organizational support and satisfaction with teacher assistance teams. *Remedial and Special Education, 16*(4), 203–211.

Landrum, T. J. (1992). Teachers as victims: An interactional analysis of the teacher's role in educating atypical learners. *Behavioral Disorders, 17*(2), 134–144.

Learning Disabilities Association. (1993). *Position paper on full inclusion of all students with learning disabilities in the regular education classroom.* Pittsburgh, PA: LDA.

Leone, P. E., Rutherford, R. B., & Nelson, C. M. (1991). *Special education in juvenile corrections.* Reston, VA: Council for Exceptional Children.

Lewis, T. J., Chard, D., & Scott, T. M. (1994). Full inclusion and the education of children and youth with emotional and behavioral disorders. *Behavioral Disorders, 19*(4), 277–293.

Long, N. J. (1994). Inclusion: Formula for failure? *Journal of Emotional and Behavioral Problems, 3*(3), 19–23.

MacMillan, D. L., & Turnbull, A. P. (1983). Parent involvement with special education: Respecting individual preferences. *Education and Training of the Mentally Retarded, 18*(1), 4–9.

Marozas, D. S., & May, D. C. (1986). *Issues and practices in special education.* New York: Longman.

McIntyre, T. (1993). Behaviorally disordered youth in correctional settings: Prevalence, programing, and teacher training. *Behavioral Disorders, 18*(3), 167–176.

McKenzie, R. G., & Houk, C. S. (1986a). The paraprofessional in special education. *Teaching Exceptional Children, 19,* 246–252.

McKenzie, R. G., & Houk, C. S. (1986b). Use of paraprofessionals in the resource room. *Exceptional Children, 53*(1), 41–45.

Miramontes, O. B. (1990). Organizing for effective paraprofessional services in special education: A multilingual/multiethnic instructional service team model. *Remedial and Special Education, 12*(1), 29–36.

Morse, W. (1992). Mental health professionals and teachers: How do the twain meet? *Beyond Behavior, 3*(2), 12–20.

Morsink, C. V., Thomas, C. C., & Correa, V. I. (1991). *Interactive teaming: Consultation and collaboration in special programs.* New York: Merrill-Macmillan.

Murphy, D. (1986). The prevalence of handicapping conditions among juvenile delinquents. *Remedial and Special Education, 7*(3), 7–16.

National Association of State Boards of Education. (1992). *Winners all: A call for inclusive schools.* Washington, DC: NASBA.

National Education Association. (1992). *Integrating students with special needs: Policies and practices that work.* Washington, DC: NEA. (ERIC Document Reproduction Service No. ED 301 739).

National Joint Committee on Learning Disabilities. (1993). *A reaction to "full inclusion": A reaffirmation of the right of students with learning disabilities to a continuum of services.* NJCLD.

Neel, R. S. (1995). The land of new languages. *Beyond Behavior, 6*(2), 13–22.

Nelson, C. M., Rutherford, R. B., & Wolford, B. I. (Eds.). (1987). *Special education in the criminal justice system.* Columbus, OH: Merrill.

Norton, A. J., & Glick, P. C. (1986). One-parent families: A social and economic profile. *Family relations, 35,* 9–17.

Oberti v. Boards of Education of the Borough of Clementon School District. (1993). 995 F.2nd 1204 (3dCir.).

Osborne, A. G., & Dimattia, P. (1994). The IDEA's least restrictive environment mandate: Legal implications. *Exceptional Children, 61*(1), 6–14.

Phillips, V., & McCullough, L. (1990). Consultation-based programming: Instituting the collaborative ethic in schools. *Exceptional Children, 56,* 291–304.

Phillips, V., Nelson, C. M., & McLaughlin, J. R. (1993). Systems change and services for students with emotional/behavioral disabilities in Kentucky. *Journal of Emotional and Behavioral Disorders, 1*(3), 155–164.

Pugach, M. C., & Johnson, L. J. (1989). The challenge of implementing collaboration between general and special education. *Exceptional Children, 56,* 232–235.

Quinn, K., & Cumblad, C. (1994). Service providers' perceptions of interagency collaboration in their communities. *Journal of Emotional and Behavioral Disorders, 2*(2), 109–116.

Ramey, P., & Robbins, P. (1989). Professional growth and support through peer coaching. *Educational Leadership, 46*(8), 35–38.

Rosenfield, S. A. (1987). *Instructional consultation.* Hillsdale, NJ: Erlbaum.

Self, H., Benning, A., Marston, D., & Magnusson, D. (1991). Cooperative teaching project: A model for students at risk. *Exceptional Children, 58*(1), 26–34.

Shanker, A. (1995). Full inclusion is neither free nor appropriate. *Educational Leadership, 52*(4), 18–21.

Shea, T. M., & Bauer, A. M. (1991). *Parents and teachers of children with exceptionalities.* Boston: Allyn & Bacon.

Singh, N. N., Landrum, T. J., Donatelli, L. S., Hampton, C., & Ellis, C. R. (1994). Characteristics of children and adolescents with serious emotional disturbance in systems of care. Part I: Partial hospitalization and inpatient psychiatric services. *Journal of Emotional and Behavioral Disorders, 2*(1), 13–20.

Stainback, W., & Stainback, S. (1984). A rationale for the merger of special and regular education. *Exceptional Children, 51,* 102–111.

The Association for Persons with Severe Handicaps. (1992). CEC slips back; ASCD steps forward. *TASH Newsletter, 18,* 1.

The Peacock Hill Working Group. (1991). Problems and promises in special education and related services for children and youth with emotional or behavioral disorders. *Behavioral Disorders, 16*(4), 299–313.

Thousand, J. S., & Villa, R. A. (1989). Enhancing success in heterogeneous schools. In S. Stainback, W. Stainback, & M. Forest (Eds.), *Educating all students in the mainstream of regular education* (pp. 89–103). Baltimore, MD: Paul Brookes.

Voltz, D. L., Elliott, R. N., Jr., & Harris, W. B. (1995). Promising practices in facilitating collaboration between resource room teachers and general education teachers. *Learning Disabilities Research and Practice, 10*(2), 129–136.

Walker, H. M., & Bullis, M. (1991). Behavior disorders and the social context of regular class integration: A conceptual dilemma? In J. W. Lloyd, A. C. Repp, & N. N. Singh (Eds.), *The Regular Education Initiative: Alternative perspectives on concepts, issues, and models* (pp. 75–93). Sycamore, IL: Sycamore.

Wang, M. C., Reynolds, M. C., & Walberg, H. J. (1988). Integrating the children of the second system. *Phi Delta Kappan, 70*, 248–251.

West, J. F. (1990). Educational collaboration in the restructuring of schools. *Journal of Educational and Psychological Consultation, 1*(1), 23–40.

West, J. F., & Idol, L. (1990). Collaborative consultation in the education of mildly handicapped and at-risk students. *Remedial and Special Education, 11*(1), 22–31.

White, P. J. (1993). Abused and neglected children in the juvenile and family courts. *Journal of Emotional and Behavioral Problems, 2*(4), 20–23.

Wiedmeyer, D., & Lehman, J. (1991). The house plan approach to collaborative teaching and consultation. *Teaching Exceptional Children, 23*(3), 6–10.

Winton, P. J., & Turnbull, A. P. (1981). Parent involvement as viewed by parents of preschool handicapped children. *Topics in Early Childhood Special Education, 1*(3), 11–19.

Yell, M. L. (1995). *Clyde K. and Sheila K. v. Puyallup School District:* The courts, inclusion, and students with behavioral disorders. *Behavioral Disorders, 20*(3), 179–189.

PART THREE

REFLECTIONS

As you have probably discovered, teaching children and youth with emotional and behavioral disorders is an exciting endeavor. Many effective intervention strategies are available for teachers, but with each promise of potential success comes many questions that are not easily answered. In the remaining two chapters, then, we will reflect on some of the questions and concerns encountered by teachers as they interact daily with their students. In Chapter 11, for example, we will consider several ethical and legal issues arising from the practice of special education for students with behavioral disorders. Then, in Chapter 12, we will return to the question of teacher self-efficacy and reflect on our own responsibility when teaching to reduce our level of stress and increase our effectiveness and professionalism in the classroom.

Main Ideas:

◆ *Teachers and students experience increased levels of violence in schools today necessitating proactive strategies for violence prevention and plans for crisis management.*

◆ *Search and seizure, suspension and expulsion, and transfer of records for violent offenders are three controversial methods currently used by school officials to eliminate gangs, drugs, and weapons from school grounds.*

◆ *Physical interventions are highly controversial and potentially dangerous procedures that should be used only by well-trained teachers as a last option when confronted by assaultive students.*

◆ *Teachers must recognize the warning signs of potential student suicides and take these signals seriously.*

◆ *Assisting in the management of medications is an important responsibility of teachers within a wrap-around program providing a multicomponent treatment package for students and their families.*

◆ *Students with emotional and behavioral problems not eligible for special education under the Individuals With Disabilities Education Act may still qualify for services under Section 504 of the Vocational Rehabilitation Act.*

BOX 11.1   **Exclusion of Children Who Are Socially Maladjusted**

Under IDEA, the definition of serious emotional disturbance specifically excludes from receiving services students "who are socially maladjusted unless it is determined that they are seriously emotionally disturbed." Critics of this exclusion argue that it violates the research base and inclusive intent of the definition's originator (Bower, 1982). Too, many states and school districts interpret "social maladjustment" to mean "conduct disordered" and exclude from receiving services many antisocial children and youth who most need assistance if they are to complete school and become productive citizens (Wood, Cheney, Cline, Sampson, Smith, & Guetzloe, 1991). According to Pullis (1991), children with conduct disorders represent a significant number of those students receiving special education programs for behavioral disorders; therefore, to exclude those children and youth would result in a large reduction in an already underserved group. Conduct disordered students could then be suspended, expelled, or "pushed out" of school for their troublesome behaviors, solving the problem for teachers and administrators but not for the student whose prognosis becomes even worse. Similarly, Maag and Howell (1992) argue that the terms *social maladjustment* and *juvenile delinquency* are socially contrived concepts that evoke images of gangs and violence and produce little tolerance for individuals so labeled. To exclude students who are "socially maladjusted" is to engender support from teachers and parents as schools strive to reduce conflicts and budgets.

On the other hand, proponents of this exclusion argue that including children with social maladjustments will open the door for juvenile delinquents and other children with conduct disorders to receive expensive special education programing. These critics assert that conduct disordered, socially maladjusted students exercise choice when engaging in antisocial behaviors, whereas children who are seriously emotionally disturbed have no control over their behaviors and feelings (Clarizio, 1987). Students who deviate in their beliefs and behaviors from cultural norms are not necessarily considered by these professionals to be emotionally disturbed (Weinberg, 1992).

In 1990, the Council for Children with Behavioral Disorders devoted an entire issue of *Behavioral Disorders* (See Volume 15, Number 3, May, 1990) to the topic of excluding socially maladjusted children from special education services. Chief among the concerns expressed by CCBD (1990a) in their position paper were the following:

Teachers of students with emotional and behavioral disorders face many challenges on a daily basis. The behaviors of these students are governed by many complex and interacting factors, necessitating thoughtful and sometimes difficult decisions to be made by teachers. Each decision, however, may carry with it important consequences for both teacher and student affecting the quality of future interactions within the classroom, school, family, and community. Teachers, family members, and other professionals must collaborate and reflect on

- Historical and legal precedent supports the inclusion of children with conduct disorders. Students may qualify for services under Section 504 of the Rehabilitation Act of 1973, although they may not qualify under IDEA.
- Arbitrary exclusion violates both the letter and the spirit of IDEA.
- There is no widely accepted definition of social maladjustment and no evidence that children who are socially maladjusted and those who are emotionally disturbed represent two different populations.
- No assessment devices or techniques exist that can distinguish social maladjustment from other conditions.
- There is no history of providing separate services to children with emotional disturbance and social maladjustment, nor do we have differentially valid treatments.
- The rationales typically provided for excluding students with conduct disorders reflect financial or administrative convenience and are irrelevant to educational considerations.
- The exclusion of children in need represents a human tragedy more costly in the long term (pp. 181–184).

The following four recommendations were proposed by the Council for Children with Behavioral Disorders based on the concerns previously listed: (1) Oppose efforts on the part of some states to exclude or decertify children with conduct disorders from special education; (2) Remove from both federal and state definitions any clause excluding children who are socially maladjusted from special education services; (3) Refine assessment methodology for identifying students disabled by their behaviors; and (4) Revise the federal definition to emphasize functional and educationally relevant aspects of behavioral disorders reflecting collective knowledge of professionals in the field. Although the definition proposed by the National Mental Health and Special Education Coalition in 1990 addresses many of these concerns (Forness & Knitzer, 1992), the definition has not yet been adopted into IDEA by Congress (see Chapter 1). Moreover, some professionals maintain that the emphasis on cultural norms within the proposed definition may actually result in the exclusion of students from urban areas, low-income families, and other minority groups (McIntyre, 1993).

all sides of each issue to make the decision that will best meet the needs of the student as well as the needs of peers and adults who must live with the youngster.

In the preceding chapters, we examined several issues arising from identifying and teaching students with emotional and behavioral disorders. For example, according to recent reports to Congress, students with behavioral disorders continue to be an underserved special education population (U.S. Department of Education, 1994). Youth with emotional and behavioral disorders

BOX 11.2   **Use of Punishment and Level Systems**

As observed by Knitzer, Steinberg, and Fleisch (1990), teachers of students with emotional and behavioral disorders are quite concerned about controlling behaviors. Although behavior management and point systems may provide the initial structure and safety essential for students to learn appropriate behaviors and problem solving skills, such systems may also unwittingly encourage escalating "bids" for power and control, precipitating increasingly aggressive behaviors from students and punitive responses by professionals (Shores, Gunter, & Jack, 1993). Positive and mild punishment may sometimes be necessary to manage the behavior of students; however, inconsistent and harsh or punitive behavior management may contribute to antisocial and difficult behavior (Mayer, Nafpaktitis, Butterworth, & Hollingsworth, 1987; Walker, Colvin, & Ramsey, 1995).

Generally, teachers view certain punishments as aversive practices in need of restriction. Interventions using physical pain or discomfort and those involving social humiliation, for example, are considered quite aversive by most teachers (Tobin & Sugai, 1993). To be sure, corporal punishment has been abolished in 27 states, either by law or by state regulations, and 46 professional associations including the Council for Exceptional Children have passed resolutions denouncing the use of corporal punishment (Evans & Richardson, 1995). The U.S. Supreme Court, however, maintains that corporal punishment does not violate the Eighth Amendment protection against cruel and unusual punishment or the Fourteenth Amendment guarantee of due process, and parents and teachers vary in their opinions regarding its use and effectiveness. Slate, Waldrop, and Justem (1991), for example, report that minority youth and those from low income families are more likely than peers to receive physical punishment at school. Yet, Hanna (1988) asserts that the "supportive" and "mild" behavior management practices accepted by the middle class culture may be confusing signs of weakness and disinterest to parents and children accustomed to a more physical style of interaction.

In addition, teachers frequently use increasingly restrictive placements to manage students with behavioral disorders. Teachers routinely use time-out (Hindman, 1986), for example, and many teachers consider the level system to be an acceptable practice for motivating their students. Level systems, however, may contain arbitrary criteria for advancement and the expectation that all

drop out of school at higher rates than do any other students with disabilities, and they are more likely than other youth to be served in special education programs outside of the regular school environment. In addition, programs for students with behavioral disorders are often characterized by behavior management systems designed to control behavior rather than by quality curriculum and instruction likely to engage children in learning and to teach them more appropriate behaviors and social problem-solving skills (Knitzer, Steinberg, & Fleisch, 1990). Other important issues suggested in the previous chapters include the exclusion of children and youth who are socially maladjusted from the

students will begin at the lowest level of the system. Scheuermann, Webber, Partin, and Knies (1994) caution that arbitrary considerations such as these violate mandates contained within IDEA for an individualized educational program in the least restrictive environment to be provided for all students in special education.

Although professionals disagree regarding the use of aversive and restrictive practices to manage students with emotional and behavioral disorders (Zabel, 1985), the Council for Children with Behavioral Disorders has published a position paper concerning the use of such behavior reduction strategies. The CCBD (1990b) position paper calls for involvement and consent from human rights committees and parents and guardians, the use of less aversive and restrictive procedures first whenever possible, appropriate training for all relevant staff in the proper use of any strategies determined to be necessary, and careful documentation as to the effectiveness of any aversive interventions used. Furthermore, Evans and Richardson (1995, p. 35) list ten questions to help teachers and principals formulate alternatives to aversive behavior management techniques:

- Are you familiar with the various conceptual models of behavior management?
- Do you hold class discussions on conflict resolution?
- Do you involve students in developing discipline codes?
- Are you consistent in enforcing school and classroom rules?
- Are you flexible, and do you consider individual situations when enforcing discipline?
- Do you use positive reinforcement and teach self-regulation?
- Do you teach prosocial skills to develop character and moral reasoning?
- Do you seek professional help when all your efforts are unsuccessful?
- Do you involve parents in planning and implementing a behavior management program?
- Do you encourage cooperative learning and teach students to mediate and to solve their problems?

federal definition of serious emotional disturbance and the use of punishment and restrictive level systems in behavior management programs for students with behavioral disorders (Box 11.1, pp. 346–347, and Box 11.2).

Which children to include in special education programs for students with emotional and behavioral disorders and how best to manage the difficult behaviors of these youngsters continue to be important areas for professional discussion. Other more far-reaching concerns, however, now face all teachers in schools today. In this chapter, then, we shall turn our attention to those issues currently challenging America's teachers. We will first examine how teachers cope with crises and violence in schools. We will discuss how schools must develop proactive strategies for crisis prevention and management, including plans for handling school emergencies; breaking up fights or intervening physically to protect student safety; and eliminating gangs, drugs, and weapons from school grounds. We will also discuss the difficult task of supporting the feelings of staff, students, and parents following a suicide or other school crisis. Finally, we will explore two additional issues currently affecting both classroom teachers and special educators—the management of medications prescribed for students and the provision of Section 504 services to children and youth with disabilities who are not eligible for special education programs.

Coping with Crises and Violence in Schools

Although the overall rate of violent crimes committed in the United States has remained stable over the last 15 years, the rate of violent juvenile crime has escalated dramatically (Furlong, 1994; Wilson & Howell, 1993). Aggravated assaults, robbery, and murder among youth have risen substantially in our nation. According to national reports, more than 135,000 students carry guns to school each day, and in Chicago alone, 26% of elementary school children report they have witnessed a shooting and 29% say they have seen a stabbing (Children's Defense Fund, 1991). Similarly, in a poll conducted by the National School Boards Association, 82% of the schools surveyed reported increasing violence over the past 5 years, and 60% reported weapons incidents (Amundson, 1994).

Walker, Colvin, and Ramsey (1995) assert that violence among our nation's youth arises from several conditions, including a family history of abuse or neglect, poverty, alcohol, or drug abuse, exposure to demonstrations of violent acts, and depression, frustration, and hopelessness. These authorities also note that children who engage in severe antisocial behavior from an early age are at serious risk for delinquency, later violence, and poor developmental outcomes. As a matter of fact, lack of parental supervision, parental rejection, and lack of parent involvement are powerful predictors of conduct problems and delinquency among youth (Loeber & Stouthamer-Loeber, 1986). With increasing age, running away from home, or sibling incarceration, come increased risk of major offending for youth with emotional and behavioral disorders (Bryant et al., 1995).

Elevated levels of violence among children and youth dictate strong actions across many fronts. In some states, for example, parents are now fined, sent to parenting classes, or even jailed for the crimes of their children (Leo, 1995). Yet merely increasing the harshness of punishment and adopting more and more stringent "get tough" policies are not likely to be effective. As Kauffman (1994) suggests, to reduce violence we must do the following:

1. Provide consequences for aggression that are immediate, certain, and nonviolent.
2. Teach nonaggressive alternatives and responses to problems.
3. Stop aggression early by intervening from the first occurrences of violence in very young children.
4. Restrict public access to weapons.

5. Reduce and reform public displays of aggression such as those at sporting events, on television, or in movies.
6. Correct societal conditions that foster aggression.

Clearly, today's children experience levels of violence unprecedented in the history of our nation. School districts routinely prepare students and personnel for handling emergencies such as fires; yet, only recently have they faced the difficult task of helping teachers prevent violence and manage school crises effectively. During crises, student and staff confusion may be fueled by rumors, and television, radio, and newspaper reporters may heighten anxiety and fear among students, teachers, parents, and community members (Long, 1992). Schools must have plans for managing on- and off-campus emergencies. Attention to the physical structure of schools, to student and staff records, to training of personnel, to communication and management of factual information, and to involvement of parents and community agencies are essential elements of school crisis prevention and management (Box 11.3, pp. 352–353).

So, too, are concerted efforts by schools and community leaders to plan for student safety and teach alternatives to gang membership and aggression. In some school districts (e.g., Baltimore, Maryland), business and home owners are joining forces with schools to provide children with safe havens to enter if they become suspicious or fearful on their way to and from school (Crouch & Williams, 1995). In other cities, law enforcement officers are helping educators across the grade levels to teach alternatives to gang membership (see, for example, *The Paramount Plan: Alternatives to Gang Membership,* 16400 Colorado Avenue, Paramount, CA 90723 (310) 220-2140). In still other school districts, entire student bodies or small cadres of students are taught conflict resolution skills including defining what each disputant wants, describing feelings, explaining reasons underlying one's wants and feelings, generating three options with maximum benefits for both parties, and agreeing on a course of action (Johnson & Johnson, 1995). (For additional training and information on Conflict Resolution, contact the Association for Supervision and Curriculum Development at (708) 830-8770 or the Resolving Conflict Creatively Program, 163 Third Avenue #103, New York, NY 10003.)

Despite the best efforts of teachers, administrators, and community leaders, however, student safety cannot always be guaranteed at school. Unfortunately, explosive fights and student assaults, weapons in the hands of children or intruders, gang activities, and suicides are but a few of the crises with which today's teachers and youth must cope.

Preventing and Breaking Up Fights

You may recall from Chapter 6 that professionals often describe crises as occurring in a series of escalating events (Stieger, 1987; Wood & Long, 1991). When a youngster is experiencing anxiety and frustration, teachers are advised to be empathetic, observing the student and listening to determine the source of the child's agitation. Using a calm body posture, remaining outside of the student's personal space, and making nonjudgmental statements that offer support to the student during this early stage of a crisis are often enough to

BOX 11.3   Elements of School Crisis Prevention and Management

School personnel cannot foresee all emergency situations. They can, however, prevent many crises from occurring and minimize the negative affects of a crisis situation by careful planning in the following four major areas:

Building Security

- ◆ Lock doors from the outside that are not routinely used after school begins. Be sure all doors have panic bars to allow them to be opened easily from the inside.
- ◆ Build lockers flush with the walls so that hallways are completely visible.
- ◆ Place trained adult monitors throughout hallways.
- ◆ Provide two-way communication devices for every classroom.
- ◆ Ensure that all classroom doors are easily locked from the inside.
- ◆ Clearly post notices requiring all visitors to report to the school office and to wear the identification badge given them by office staff.
- ◆ Provide hall monitors and teachers on playgrounds with walkie-talkies or cellular telephones.
- ◆ Where necessary, install weapons detection devices or employ school security guards.
- ◆ Install in the school office at least one private telephone line with an unpublished number in order to keep lines of communication open to appropriate community agencies during emergencies when public lines to the school become jammed with calls from parents and media.

Student and Staff Records Management

- ◆ Ensure that records for students and staff members are updated frequently and contain relevant information regarding medical conditions as well as addresses and telephone numbers for persons to be contacted if an emergency arises. Be sure all information is readily visible in each file.
- ◆ Clearly list persons authorized to pick up students and refuse to release the student to anyone who is not authorized to do so in writing by the parent or guardian.
- ◆ Computerized databases may make student and staff records more accessible and manageable during emergency situations.

defuse the situation. If the student enters a level of high verbal activity, however, he or she is beginning to lose self-control. At this point, the teacher must remain calm, objective, and outside of the child's personal space. Isolating the student from peers, setting clear, logical, and enforceable limits, and refraining from responding to verbal challenges or taunts are essential at this point in the conflict.

Fights among students also follow similar patterns of escalation. For example, you might observe students sending notes, using eye contact and facial

Teacher and Staff Training

- ◆ Appoint and train within each school a crisis management team.
- ◆ Ensure that all staff have appropriate training for handling different emergency situations. Be sure all staff understand what they can reasonably be expected to do and not do.
- ◆ Remember to include all professionals, paraprofessionals, clerical and custodial staff in the training.
- ◆ Train staff in the use of communications devices as well as in the correct emergency procedures to follow.
- ◆ Train all staff to monitor visitors in the school and to ask all unidentified visitors to report to the office for an identification badge.
- ◆ Be sure to keep *all* staff members, particularly those answering the telephones, fully informed during a school emergency.
- ◆ Brief all teachers and staff following an emergency before allowing them to return home.

Involvement of Parents and Community Agencies

- ◆ Use e-mail systems or fax machines to notify school district offices or other schools immediately regarding the status of emergency situations.
- ◆ Assign one person to handle all contacts with the media.
- ◆ Release the facts immediately to the media to dispel rumors.
- ◆ Fear and anger are normal reactions from parents and citizens following an emergency. Holding public meetings and providing details and important facts regarding school emergencies are essential for rebuilding public support.
- ◆ Provide counseling for teachers, staff, students, and parents when needed following a school crisis.

Note: Schools should be open and available to parents and community members throughout the school day. They should not become fortresses locked against intruders. Prudent measures such as those listed previously, however, can help to make schools safe and secure for children and teachers so that the business of schools, student learning, can occur.

Adapted from *Containing Crisis: A Guide to Maintaining School Emergencies*, by R. S. Watson, J. H. Poda, C. T. Miller, E. S. Rice and G. West. Copyright © 1990 National Educational Services. Reprinted by permission.

expressions indicating hostility, gesturing to one another, or moving about the classroom or halls without purpose during the earliest stage of a crisis. When students are shouting at or taunting one another, though, they are beginning to lose rational thought and self-control. Verbal teacher direction at this stage of crisis escalation again is essential. Calmly but assertively approaching students, remaining outside of their personal space, and redirecting them to the task at hand or setting appropriate limits for their behavior are critical teacher skills at this time.

Early intervention by the teacher may prevent many student fights from escalating to physical confrontations.

Students may fight one another for many reasons including fear, to save face, to defend real or imagined threats to their property or territory, or to "test the pecking order," (Rokoske & Wyka, 1990). Regardless of the reason for the fight, however, the teacher's best alternative is to stop a physical confrontation *before* it occurs. By intervening as early as possible, calling for assistance from other teachers or from school administrators, and separating students to allow them to cool down and solve their differences peacefully teachers can prevent many acts of student violence.

Sometimes, despite the efforts of observant teachers, however, fights erupt quickly in the halls or classroom. Fights among students are frightening events for the participants as well as for both teachers and onlookers. Therefore, astute teachers immediately seek out the school and school district policies and procedures regarding their role and responsibilities for students who are fighting when they join any instructional staff. The National Crisis Prevention Institute recommends the following guidelines for teachers who must break up student fights (Rekoske & Wyka, 1990):

◆ Ensure that there are adequate school policies and procedures regarding how to handle student fights.
◆ Respond to early warning signs to prevent physical confrontations whenever possible.
◆ Call or send for assistance from administrators, other teachers, or school security personnel.

- Remove peers by ordering them to leave the area or by quickly asking another teacher to assist.
- Remove obstacles and objects that might be used as weapons.
- Approach the students who are fighting calmly and confidently, but remain outside of their personal space, and use a supportive body posture.
- Use a distraction such as blinking the lights or making a loud noise to try to interrupt the fight.
- If the distraction stops the fight, set limits using an assertive tone, and then remove the participants to separate rooms to cool down.
- Never intervene in a fight alone.
- Never step into a fight to separate the combatants unless you know you are able to manage their strength and size.
- If you can manage the participants, and you have the appropriate training and assistance, do not step in until you can determine who is the aggressor and you observe a lull in the combatants' energy expenditure.
- If necessary, restrain the students, and transport them to separate areas so that they may calm down.
- Talk with students individually, and later together, to help them plan how to resolve their differences in the future.

Physical Intervention

Crises can escalate very rapidly. When you are working with other children or speaking briefly with a visitor at your classroom door, for example, you may not have observed the signs of anxiety preceding the crisis. If a crisis involves physical actions on the part of the student (e.g., two students engage in a fight, a student becomes physically aggressive toward you), you will need to know how to protect your safety, that of other students, and the safety of the child who is now out-of-control. You may need to use physical intervention to restrain the child who is acting out physically or to separate students who are in a fist fight. Steiger (1987) and Wood and Long (1991) assert that physical restraint, properly used, can be therapeutic, communicating safety, concern, and support to students until they are able to regain control of their emotions and talk about the problem.

Before using any form of physical intervention in response to a crisis, however, teachers must be well-trained in safe physical intervention techniques and must follow the policies and procedures of their school and school district. Because of the tremendous potential for injury to the student or to yourself, as well as the possibility of litigation, you are advised to be familiar with the policies regarding the use of physical intervention offered by the Council for Exceptional Children (Box 11.4, pp. 356–357) and to consider the following guidelines:

1. Use physical intervention techniques only as a last resort, when a clear danger is present, when other interventions have been tried and have failed, and only until the student is able to regain his or her self-control.
2. Use physical intervention techniques only when you have been well trained in their use and when your school and school district clearly permit the proper use of these methods. If your school has no written policy regarding physical intervention, seek to have one developed. (Note:

BOX 11.4 The Council for Exceptional Children Policy Regarding the Use of Physical Intervention

The Council recognizes the right to the most effective educational strategies to be the basic educational right of each special education child. Furthermore, the Council believes that the least restrictive positive educational strategies should be used, as they relate to physical intervention, to respect the child's dignity and personal privacy. Additionally, the Council believes that such interventions shall assure the child's physical freedom, social interaction, and individual choice. The intervention must not include procedures that cause pain or trauma. Intervention techniques must focus not only on eliminating a certain undesirable behavior, but also upon a determination of the purpose of that behavior, and the provision/instruction of a more appropriate behavior. Lastly, behavior intervention plans must be specifically described in the child's written educational plan with agreement from the education staff, the parents, and when appropriate, the child.

The Council recommends that physical intervention be used only if all the following requirements are met:

a. The child's behavior is dangerous to herself/himself or others, or the behavior is extremely detrimental to or interferes with the education or development of the child.

b. Various positive reinforcement techniques have been implemented appropriately and the child has repeatedly failed to respond as documented in the child's records.

c. It is evident that withholding physical intervention would significantly impede the child's educational progress as explicitly defined in his or her written educational plan.

d. The physical intervention plan specifically will describe the intervention to be implemented, the staff to be responsible for the implementation, the process for documentation, the required training of staff and supervision of staff as it relates to the intervention and when the intervention will be replaced.

e. The physical intervention plan will become a part of the written educational plan.

f. The physical intervention plan shall encompass the following provisions:

   1. A comprehensive analysis of the child's environment including variables contributing to the inappropriate behavior.

   2. The plan to be developed by a team including professionals and parents/guardians, as designated by state/provincial and federal law.

   3. The personnel implementing the plan shall receive specific training congruent with the contents of the plan and receive ongoing supervision

from individuals who are trained and skilled in the techniques identified in the plan.

4. The health and medical records of the child must be reviewed to ensure that there are no physical conditions present that would contraindicate the use of the physical intervention proposed.

5. The impact of the plan on the child's behavior must be consistently evaluated, the results documented, and the plan modified when indicated.

The Council supports the following prohibitions:

a. Any intervention that is designed to, or likely to, cause physical pain.

b. Releasing noxious, toxic or otherwise unpleasant sprays, mists, or substances in proximity to the child's face.

c. Any intervention that denies adequate sleep, food, water, shelter, bedding, physical comfort, or access to bathroom facilities.

d. Any intervention that is designed to subject, used to subject, or likely to subject the individual to verbal abuse, ridicule or humiliation, or which can be expected to cause excessive emotional trauma.

e. Restrictive interventions that employ a device or material or objects that simultaneously immobilize all four extremities including the procedure known as prone containment, except that prone containment may be used by trained personnel as a limited emergency intervention.

f. Locked seclusion, unless under constant surveillance and observation.

g. Any intervention that precludes adequate supervision of the child.

h. Any intervention that deprives the individual of one or more of his or her senses.

The Council recognizes that emergency physical intervention may be implemented if the child's behavior poses an imminent and significant threat to his or her physical well-being or to the safety of others. The intervention must be documented and parents/guardians must be notified of the incident.

However, emergency physical intervention shall not be used as a substitute for systematic behavioral intervention plans that are designed to change, replace, modify, or eliminate a targeted behavior.

Furthermore, the Council expects school districts and other educational agencies to establish policies and comply with state/provincial and federal law and regulations to ensure protection of the rights of the child, the parent/guardian, the education staff, and the school and local educational agency when physical intervention is applied.

From "Professional Policies: Physical Intervention," by The Council for Exceptional Children *CEC Today, 1*(3), 1994, pp. 20–21. Copyright © 1994 by The Council for Exceptional Children. Reprinted with permission.

Training in managing aggressive behavior safely may be obtained for a fee from the National Crisis Prevention Institute, 3315-K North 124th Street, Brookfield, Wisconsin 53005 (800) 558-8976 or from David Mandt and Associates, P.O. Box 831921, Richardson, Texas 75083-1921 (214) 495-0755.)

3. Document the types of behaviors that might result in the use of physical intervention. Include on the student's IEP the interventions to be used with these behaviors. If possible, demonstrate the physical interventions for parents and guardians so they will understand when and how you will use these procedures.

4. Carefully document any use of physical intervention, including in your incident report the behavior of the student, your actions, and all unusual occurrences. Report these incidents to the parents or guardians.

5. Establish a team within your school and a simple method for enlisting the aid of this team as early as possible during a crisis. When you have the support of other trained team members, you are more likely to resolve a crisis safely, swiftly, and productively.

6. Plan to talk with students when they have regained control to help them learn how to cope with similar difficulties in the future.

Obviously, physical restraint carries with it the potential for abuse, injury, and litigation. The relationship between teacher and student may all too easily be damaged by professionals who restrain unnecessarily or improperly. Physical restraint is a highly restrictive behavior reduction strategy that must be used by teachers *only as a last resort when a clear danger is present, only with appropriate training, only in conjunction with positive and proactive behavior change methods, and only in compliance with professional guidelines* (CEC, 1994). Teachers should use physical restraint only when children and parents are informed in advance that school policy allows such measures to be used if students are assaultive, behaving dangerously, or engaging in fights. Unfortunately, although today's educator must frequently deal with fights, few schools have clear policies or training for teachers regarding procedures such as physical restraint.

Gangs, Drugs, and Weapons in Schools

One major source for student conflict is that of gang activity within schools. You may recall from Chapter 1 that gangs offer members social contact, support, status, protection, and a sense of acceptance and affiliation that many youth no longer receive from the family or community. Unfortunately, gang members also commit violent acts three times more often than their peers not in gangs. This increased likelihood of violent crime may be due to an escalating use of weapons by gang members as well as to their involvement in drug activities (National School Safety Center, 1988). Schools represent to gangs a fertile ground for recruiting new members and for distributing drugs. As a matter of fact, in a survey of 3324 schools nationwide, most reported a present and increasing problem of gang violence (Cognosys Corporation, 1993).

To improve our nation's schools, professionals are now focusing attention on the National Education Goals. Goal Number Seven, entitled the "Safe Schools"

Security guards, metal detectors, and strict dress codes are common measures used in schools to reduce youth violence.

goal, states that by the year 2000 each school in the United States will be free of drugs, violence, and the unauthorized presence of firearms and alcohol, and that schools will offer a disciplined environment in which learning can occur. To accomplish this goal, professionals must collaborate with law enforcement and other community agencies.

Many schools are installing metal detectors at entrance ways and many others are employing security guards, both unarmed and armed. Restrooms are being renovated to increase visibility and decrease drug trafficking and locker searches are routine requirements in many schools. In addition, other schools prohibit students from carrying book bags or from wearing jackets in school as these items may be used for concealing weapons and carrying beepers or other communications devices associated with drugs and other illegal activities. Still others discourage students from wearing particular colors, color combinations, or articles of clothing associated with gang membership. With each of these procedures designed to protect students, however, come important considerations regarding student freedoms and rights.

Students have a right, for example, to due process in school disciplinary procedures including notice and hearing (*Goss v. Lopez*, 419 U.S. 565, 1975) and the right to privacy from unreasonable searches of one's person or property (*New Jersey v. T.L.O.*, 469 U.W. 325, 1985). On the other hand, all students have a right to a safe environment in which they can reasonably be expected to learn. Although schools are not automatically responsible for all injuries that may occur at school, courts have ruled that schools have a duty to take reasonable precautions to protect students from foreseeable criminal acts (Clontz, 1987; Underwood & Mead, 1995). In public schools, therefore, the constitutional rights of students are often balanced by state interests in maintaining order and discipline (Valente, 1994). To protect students from drugs, weapons, and violent acts in school, school administrators may use search and seizure, suspension and expulsion, and notification when records are transferred for violent juvenile offenders.

Search and Seizure. The Fourth Amendment protects students against unwarranted and unreasonable searches and seizures. School administrators may search students and their property (e.g., book bags, purses) at school, however, when they have "reasonable suspicion" to justify a search. Reasonable suspicion may include information provided by other students, police tips, anonymous tips or phone calls, and unusual student conduct (e.g., flight, in a suspicious location, furtive movement) indicating that drugs or weapons may be carried by an individual (Valente, 1994). Certainly strip searches conducted by an administrator of the same sex as the student or drug dogs "sniffing" the person of a particular student would require clear evidence of a serious need and of individualized suspicion of wrongdoing by that student (Valente, 1994). Regular inspections of lockers and use of metal detectors to discourage weapons from entering a school are usually not considered intrusive measures when they are applied routinely and equally to all students. Some authorities do worry, however, that a disproportionate number of students who are searched are students with disabilities (Boomer, 1992).

Suspension and Expulsion. A suspension refers to a short-term exclusion from school of 10 days or less, whereas expulsion means denying a student school attendance for an extended period, usually longer than 10 days. Although laws vary from state to state, typically schools suspend or expel students for repeated noncompliance with school rules or reasonable requests of school personnel, for stealing or vandalizing school or personal property, and for violence, noise, coercion, or force that disrupts school purposes (Hindman, 1986). In *Goss v. Lopez* (419 U.S. 565, 1975), the U.S. Supreme Court held that students have a constitutional right to due process in school disciplinary procedures resulting in suspension or expulsion. Students must have some form of notice and hearing, whether formal or informal, so that they are notified of the "charge" against them and so that they have full opportunity to respond to that charge, even when the student has engaged in violent or illegal behavior involving weapons or drugs. In the Goss decision, however, the Court ruled that students whose presence would present a continuing danger to person or to property or a constant disruption to the academic process could be removed immediately as long as a postsuspension hearing was given the student as soon as possible (Valente, 1994).

The suspension and expulsion of students with disabilities presents an even more difficult situation. In *Honig v. Doe* (484 U.S. 305, 1988) the U.S. Supreme Court dealt for the first time with the discipline of special education students with behavioral disorders. Although the Court concluded that it did not intend to preclude schools from using disciplinary procedures normally used with all students (e.g., time-out, detention, restriction of privileges, short-term suspensions of up to 10 days), the court did rule that school administrators may not suspend a student with a disability for more than 10 days or expel that student without first determining whether or not the student's behavior is related to his or her disability.

Long-term suspensions of more than 10 days and expulsions were determined by the Court to constitute a change in the student's educational placement and program in violation of the due process requirements of IDEA. Therefore, schools must first convene hearings to determine if the student is receiving appropriate individualized services in the least restrictive environment consistent with his or her needs and to discern if the behavior in question is related to the disability before long-term suspension or expulsion may occur (Bartlett, 1989; Yell, 1989). If a student's behavior is related to his or her disability, a multidisciplinary committee must reconsider the student's educational program. If the misbehavior is not related to the disability, the school may use normal suspension and expulsion procedures. Regardless of whether or not the misbehavior is related to the disability, however, schools must continue to provide educational programs (e.g., in homebound or alternative placements) to students receiving services under IDEA during the period of suspension or expulsion (Underwood & Mead, 1995). Yell (1989) summarizes many court cases and lists the following principles pertaining to students with disabilities:

- ◆ Temporary suspensions may be used to discipline students with disabilities. Suspensions of fewer than 10 days do not constitute a change in placement; however, serial suspensions or suspensions of more than 10 days may be considered an expulsion by the courts.
- ◆ Expulsions and long-term suspensions are changes in educational placement, thus, the procedural safeguards of IDEA must be followed.
- ◆ A trained and knowledgeable committee must determine whether the misbehavior is causally related to the student's disability. If a relationship exists, the student may not be expelled.
- ◆ Due process procedures must be followed when suspending or expelling a student with a disability. All students, with or without disabilities, must be afforded the opportunity for a hearing in which evidence from all sides may be considered.

♦ School districts may opt to move a disruptive or violent student to a more restrictive setting, although due process procedures must be followed.

In *Honig v. Doe* (1988), the Court ruled that it did not intend for schools to be "hamstrung" in their ability to deal with dangerous students, but it stated that Congress intended for schools to be unable to exclude unilaterally disabled students, particularly students with emotional disturbances (Crawford & Crawford, 1994). Schools may, however, obtain preliminary injunctive relief by providing the courts with evidence and documentation that a student should be removed to a more restrictive setting to receive an appropriate education and to reduce the potential for harm to others (Crawford & Crawford, 1994). Furthermore, the courts have typically favored removal of students with disabilities to short periods of in-school suspension when students have received adequate notice regarding the reasons for placement in such a suspension and when they receive appropriate classwork to complete during the placement (Yell, 1990). According to Center and McKittrick (1987), in-school suspension programs should follow the "10-day" rule with policies also established for multiple suspensions or failure to complete the in-school suspension period.

Some professionals worry that schools may be reluctant to identify students with emotional and behavioral disorders, particularly those whose behaviors are antisocial and aggressive, if they believe their disciplinary options will be restricted (Nelson, Rutherford, Center, & Walker, 1991). In addition, IDEA was recently amended to provide that a student with a disability who brings a gun to school may be placed in an interim alternative setting, in accordance with state laws, for not more than 45 days. The child would remain in that setting throughout any due process hearings initiated by parents or guardians (CCBD, 1994). Thomason (1994) suggests that teachers use the IEP as a vehicle for listing the standards and limits of appropriate behavior as well as the interventions and consequences to be used in order to smooth transitions to alternative placements if students with behavioral disorders engage in acts of violence.

Alternative schools are increasingly being used by school districts throughout the country to remove dangerous and volatile students, with and without disabilities, from the mainstream of education. Behavior management and curricular approaches vary greatly within these alternative schools; however, Gold (1995) suggests two criteria for success: (1) Preventing failure through a curriculum individualized according to student interests and abilities and (2) Providing students with warm, personal, and supportive relationships with caring staff members. Troublesome, delinquent youth, then, must be "expelled to friendlier places" if their antisocial behavior is to be changed (Gold & Mann, 1984). Such alternative programs may not be effective in all cultural settings, though, or with youth who are extremely anxious or depressed (Gold, 1995). In addition, the long-term effects (e.g., reducing delinquent acts or adult crime) of placement in the "best" alternative programs is as yet unknown.

Transfer of Records. State laws and policies regarding privacy of student records vary greatly. The Family Educational Rights and Privacy Act of 1974 guarantees record access to students and their parents and prevents the disclosure of personally identifying student information to unprivileged parties without the consent of the affected student and guardian (Underwood & Mead, 1995; Valente, 1994). Although school personnel have an obligation to protect confidential student information, they also have the responsibility to protect the public interest and safety. Therefore, in many states laws are being proposed allowing for the disclosure and interagency sharing of information regarding juveniles who have committed violent offenses.

Information systems to share the records of violent juvenile offenders are being developed in many school districts. Juvenile justice officials are rightfully concerned with protecting the privacy of youth and with protecting sensitive information that might be easily abused or that might unnecessarily stigmatize a young person. Nevertheless, teachers and school administrators also have a right to know relevant information about violent young persons to prevent risks to their safety and that of other students. Computerized records transfers among juvenile courts, law enforcement agencies, and school districts across the country are essential if teachers are to be prepared adequately to handle students who are volatile and easily agitated.

Summary of Gangs, Drugs, and Weapons in Schools ◆

To protect rule-abiding students from the effects of gangs, drugs, and weapons on school grounds, school personnel are resorting to many different measures to detect drugs and weapons and to discourage gang activity (see also Chapter 1). Attention to building security including the controversial use of armed guards, reasonable searches, suspension and expulsion, and access to student records are but a few of the methods now being employed by schools to cope with increasing violence. Although student rights are to be protected, this need must always be balanced by protecting the rights of potential victims of violent youth (Box 11.5, p. 364, and Box 11.6, p. 365). ◆

To make schools safe, teachers and other school personnel must be knowledgeable about drugs and about gang indicators in their local area. Working carefully with law enforcement agencies will help teachers stay attuned to changes in their students. Implementing curricula to teach children about the hazards of drug use or to help them learn peaceful conflict resolution skills are two additional keys to reducing school violence (see Chapter 6). Finally, teachers must treat all students with respect and confront issues of school safety. Youth rarely assult teachers who they perceive to be firm, fair, or appropriately assertive and academically rigorous, yet gang members may exploit teachers who they perceive to be weak and easily intimidated (Huff, 1989).

Suicide

Suicide is another tragedy increasingly observed by teachers. According to Guetzloe (1991, 1993), more than 5000 young people commit suicide each year in the United States. Moreover, Guetzloe suggests that for every completed suicide there are between 100 and 350 suicide attempts, and even preschoolers have been hospitalized for attempting suicide. Unfortunately, adolescents with emotional and behavioral disorders, particularly females, may

BOX 11.5   Weapons in Schools

Despite school precautions, guns and knives still may occasionally surface within the school. When the teacher suspects a student possesses a weapon, he or she should notify school authorities immediately and discreetly. In many school districts, teachers are given training for how to assess a situation calmly and then send for the help of school administrators or security guards. Moreover, in some schools, students are taught how to exit a classroom, when given a signal, either through the door or through windows if someone has a weapon. If a student brandishes a weapon, however, teachers must remain calm and refrain from attempting to take the weapon away from the individual. Some guidelines for teachers who may be faced with weapons include the following:

- Plan the classroom so that obstacles are not blocking the door or windows.
- Remain aware of unusual student behavior.
- If you suspect that a student has a weapon, send for help immediately.
- Do not confront the student about the suspected weapon in the presence of other students.
- If threatened with a weapon, do not try to wrestle it away from the student.
- Remain calm.
- Evacuate the classroom according to a preestablished plan if at all possible.
- Do not approach the student. Remain outside of his or her personal space, and stay immobile with your arms and hands visible.
- Scan the classroom for nearby places to duck if necessary.
- Avoid confrontational language (e.g., "Give me that gun right now") and use a nonthreatening tone of voice.
- Engage the student in conversation using his or her name and obtaining a series of little "yesses" to questions (e.g., "Is it okay if I take a little breath?" "Is it okay if I back up just one step?" "May the students in the front row leave the classroom?").
- If the student exhibits signs of drug use, he or she may not respond to your attempts to engage him or her in rational conversation.

Never attempt to be a hero when faced with a weapon. You can obtain additional information and training regarding weapons in schools by contacting the National Crisis Prevention Institute in Brookfield, Wisconsin.

be more likely than their peers to have suicidal ideas and to commit suicide (Miller, 1994).

Teachers, especially teachers of students with emotional and behavioral disorders, must recognize that children and adolescents may be thinking about suicide. Those youth who have a family history of mental illness, drug or alcohol abuse, and suicide, or a personal history of foster care placement, absent parents, aggressive behavior, psychiatric disorders, and hopelessness may be at increased

Teacher Feature: Teachers See Signs of Discipline Crisis

Brazen acts of violence, fortunately, are not common in the Richmond (Virginia) public schools. But poor discipline is high on the list of problems plaguing the nearly 28,000-student district. And even though arrests are being made when most violent acts occur, central office is not doing enough, according to officers of the Richmond Education Association. The association, which represents 80 percent of the district's teachers, contends the situation may soon reach crisis proportions.

Consider this three-day string of incidents that occurred just last week:

◆ On Wednesday, a 14-year-old middle school student pushed a substitute teacher. She fell to the floor of the cafeteria, where he struck her. He was arrested and charged with assault and battery.

◆ After being told to sit down, a 14-year-old student at a middle school struck a substitute teacher three times Thursday. That student also was arrested and charged with assault and battery.

◆ On Friday, school officials spotted a bulge under the shirt of a 15-year-old student. . . . They soon discovered a loaded revolver. The student was arrested and charged with possession of a weapon.

Teachers say a few troublemakers cause most of the unruliness. "We have a small core of students who blatantly disregard the school board's discipline policies and they are not dealt with in an effective manner," said a math and science teacher at one high school. "So they become repeat offenders and they pull other children into doing things because they see they can get away with it."

"The administrators at each school also fail to consistently enforce rules of student conduct," said a teacher of students with emotional problems at another high school. "The kids are running the building. . . . They're not attending classes. They are hiding out and hanging out in the halls. Fights are constantly occurring."

This teacher believes the problem goes beyond lack of respect. And the solution requires involvement from the entire community, he added. "Until we find a way for the community and the school system to come together and address the problem, it will only get worse."

From "Teachers Fear Crisis in Discipline, Public Discussion Set in May," by Robin Farmer, 1995, *Richmond Times Dispatch*, April 16, pp. B1–B6. Copyright © 1995 Richmond Times Dispatch. Reprinted by permission.

risk for suicide (Guetzloe, 1991). In addition, certain life crises may be important warning signals of impending suicide attempts among adolescents (e.g., the loss of a boyfriend or girlfriend, family conflicts, problems in school) and among younger children (e.g., the wish to join a deceased relative or pet, feelings of guilt following parental divorce, severe punishment or fear of such punishment) (Guetzloe, 1993). Finally, adolescents who abuse alcohol are more likely than their peers to be depressed and depressed adolescents often abuse alcohol, placing these young people in a cycle of worsening depression and increased risk for suicide (King, 1993). Regardless of these risk factors, however, common warning signs of a possible suicide include the following:

- Extreme changes in the child's normal behavior
- Signs of depression (see Chapter 1)
- Making final arrangements such as giving away favorite possessions and saying good-bye to friends, family, and teachers
- Having the means and a plan for committing suicide
- A history of previous suicide attempts

When teachers observe these signs or believe a child or adolescent may commit suicide, they should make referrals to counselors, school psychologists, or other mental health professionals immediately. Having prearranged agreements with the child's family to contact appropriate professionals may be an essential ingredient of a suicide prevention plan. Moreover, parents must be made aware of the problem and encouraged to seek appropriate support and assistance for their child. Because child and adolescent suicides are more likely to occur between 3:00 PM and midnight and in the late spring and early summer (i.e., times when the child is not in school and is likely to be upset about grades or lonely), parents must understand the importance of taking suicidal behavior seriously (Guetzloe, 1993; Morgan, 1994).

In addition, teachers must take seriously any warning signs or any statements made by the child regarding thoughts of suicide. Teachers must never ignore or belittle the student by making statements such as "Oh, you don't really mean that." Morgan (1994) asserts that more than 80% of suicidal adolescents have indicated their thoughts to their parents, and 15% have expressed suicidal intentions to their teachers, counselors, or doctors. Providing assistance to help students overcome their immediate problems (e.g., a special tutor, dropping a class, removing the threat of a punishment) and experience some sense of increased control and decreased hopelessness may help the youngster through the crisis stage (Guetzloe, 1988).

If a young person attempts suicide, he or she will require extended assistance. Professionals suggest that the student will need immediate and positive changes at home, in school, or in the community, and the provision of continuing therapy, counseling, supervision, and support (Guetzloe, 1993). Teaching alternative coping and problem-solving skills may also help young people face difficult situations in the future with an increased sense of control (Miller, 1994). Peer support programs, crisis centers and hotlines, and general suicide education to alert all students to the warning signs of suicide are also elements of schoolwide plans for the prevention of suicide. (For additional information on suicide prevention programs write for a free copy of the guide "Youth Suicide Prevention Programs: A Resource guide," The Centers for Disease Control, National Center for Injury Prevention and Control, MS K60, 4770 Buford Highway N.E., Atlanta, GA 30341-3724.)

When a student has completed a suicide, teachers and other school professionals must be prepared to help the survivors deal with feelings of guilt, grief, and anger. Teachers must be fully informed and honest if they are to help peers cope with the suicide of a friend. Private discussions with classmates are healthy; however, teachers must take care not to glorify suicide as a solution to problems.

Permitting students and teachers to attend the memorial service at a funeral home and to voice their feelings of anger and guilt can be therapeutic. School schedules should not be changed, and memorial services should not be held at school, though, since these may tend to focus other students on the deceased young person as a role model to "copy" (National School Safety Center, 1992).

In today's society, school professionals must also be prepared to cope with publicity and litigation following the suicide of a student, whether on or off the school grounds. According to the National School Safety Center (1992), school personnel should check state and local laws to determine their responsibilities and potential liabilities for suicides committed by students. In several states, for example, school officials have been held liable if personnel failed to report to parents suicidal statements made by a child to teachers or even to other students, and in other states suicide prevention is a prescribed course of study. Additional recommendations made by the National School Safety Center (1992) for dealing with the media following a suicide include the following:

- ◆ Identify an information source who can be forthcoming with reporters and advise all school personnel of the name of this contact person.
- ◆ Advise teachers that they may make positive comments about the student but that they should exercise care not to comment on confidential information such as the young person's emotional state.
- ◆ Be sure that the parent's are advised of the school or school district information policy; offer them assistance in dealing with the media through the school contact person; and assure them that confidential records are protected.

Other Issues

Violence and crises in schools have received much attention from the media and from professionals. Although these are certainly important issues, classroom teachers today face an increasingly diverse student population. Two additional areas of concern to teachers, therefore, are the management of medications prescribed by physicians to students for a variety of conditions and the mandate to provide services for children and youth with disabilities under Section 504 of the Vocational Rehabilitation Act Amendments of 1973.

Student Medications and Side Effects

Obviously teachers play a supportive role in the management of medications prescribed for students. Teachers must be aware of medications taken by students, however, and they must carefully observe the behavior of any student taking a prescription medicine. Most commonly, children take medications such as antihistamines (e.g., Benadryl) to control the effects of allergies or antibiotics to fight infections following an illness. Other students must use anticonvulsant medications such as Dilantin to prevent seizures.

Medications are also commonly used to improve the behaviors of students. As a matter of fact, approximately 11% of students with emotional and behavioral disorders use psychotropic medications to help them control their behaviors

(Singh, Epstein, Luebke, & Singh, 1990). Stimulant medications, for example, such as Ritalin, Dexedrine, and Cylert are often prescribed by physicians for children who are hyperactive, have attention deficit disorder, are aggressive, or are conduct disordered. These stimulants help children calm down, control physical activity, decrease impulsivity, distractibility, and disruptive behaviors, and increase attention. In addition, antianxiety or antipsychotic drugs such as Thorazine and Mellaril are sometimes prescribed to calm children and improve their social functioning, and increasingly, children are prescribed Prozac to counteract the effects of depression.

Although prescription drugs do help many students control their overt behaviors and pay attention, they do not by themselves help students learn (Swanson, Cantwell, Lerner, McBurnett, Pfiffner, & Kotkin, 1992). As a matter of fact, dosage levels high enough to control a child's behavior may actually impair the child's cognitive performance. Drugs are only one part of an overall intervention plan, and they are certainly no substitute for good teaching. Some professionals worry that medications are too often prescribed for children without attention given to long-term educational interventions in the home and classroom. In addition, most drugs have side effects that must be weighed against the seriousness of the child's behavior (Table 11.1), and the long-term effects of many medications prescribed for children are not yet known. Nevertheless, medication may be one important component of a multifaceted treatment plan for children and youth with emotional and behavioral disorders.

The teacher's primary responsibility for children taking prescription medications, then, is to observe the behavior of the child, particularly changes in behavior or side effects, and report these observations through the appropriate channels to the child's physician. In addition, the teacher can help by modifying the classroom structure or lessons to help the child adjust to his or her new behavior, and the teacher can check to be sure that the child takes his or her medicine while at school. Through careful observa-

---

Table 11.1 Common Student Medications and Side Effects

Medications	Side Effects
Stimulants	
Ritalin	Nausea, loss of appetite, weight loss, insomnia, impaired
Dexedrine	growth, nervousness, depression, crying, irritability
Cylert	
Antipsychotics	
Thorazine	Nausea, drowsiness, dry mouth, lethargy, weight gain, rashes,
Mellaril	nervousness, impaired cognition, motor tics, and disorders—
Haldol	either permanent or temporary
Anticonvulsants	
Dilantin	Softening of gums, nutritional deficits, drowsiness
Valproic acid	

tion and communication teachers can fulfill their responsibilities within a multicomponent treatment plan involving the home as well as professionals in the school and community. The teacher's role thus becomes one of integrating the use of medications at school with other interventions and services provided to the child and his or her family in a wrap-around program. Teachers are concerned, however, that they have too little involvement in decisions about a child's use of medication and not enough knowledge about their school's policy regarding children taking medications (Singh, Epstein, Luebke, & Singh, 1990).

Professionals must have policies in line with state laws and regulations for dispensing medications to children in school. Typically, the school nurse or a professional other than the teacher is designated to dispense medications. Walker and Shea (1995, pp. 275–276) list the following guidelines to help schools develop comprehensive policies for dispensing student medications where state law permits:

- ◆ Have parents and physicians complete permission forms, and place these in the student's records.
- ◆ Store all medications in a central location that is secure, clean, well ventilated, and well lighted. Be sure that medications are properly refrigerated when needed and that water is available.
- ◆ Medications must be properly labeled with both the child's and the physician's name and with directions for use clearly written on the label.
- ◆ Log all medications in and out of the school, inventory all medications frequently, and appoint one individual in the school to be a contact person with parents and physicians regarding student medications.
- ◆ Be sure a responsible and properly designated adult is present when students take their medications.
- ◆ Complete a log each time the child takes his or her medication including the name of the child, the name of the person administering the medication, the name and exact dosage of the medication given, the date and time, and unusual comments or behaviors of the child.

Section 504

Section 504 of the Vocational Rehabilitation Act Amendments of 1973 states that "No otherwise qualified individual with a disability . . . shall solely by reason of her or his disability, be excluded from the participation in, be denied the benefits of, or be subjected to discrimination under any program or activity receiving federal financial assistance." Thus, in schools, as agencies of state and local governments, employees, parents, and children and youth of school-age are protected from discrimination on the basis of disabilities. Qualified individuals with disabilities must be provided with "reasonable accommodations" to meet their needs "as adequately as the needs of nondisabled persons are met." Under Section 504, then, students with physical disabilities or orthopedic impairments, for example, may, require accommodations designed to make their classrooms accessible for a wheelchair or differing assignments enabling them to use alternative forms of communication.

Although its requirements are not as specific as those of IDEA, a group knowledgeable about a student, evaluation, and placement options must examine all relevant data from a variety of sources to determine whether or not a child qualifies for services under Section 504. If the child is determined to qualify for Section 504, a plan, with evidence of parental participation, must be written to detail the accommodations to be provided. The process of referral, determining eligibility, and writing an educational plan are similar for both Section 504 and IDEA; therefore, in actual practice, schools often begin with a consideration of IDEA. If the child does not meet the eligibility requirements of IDEA, the school then proceeds to a determination of whether or not the student qualifies for services under Section 504.

Under Section 504, an individual may qualify for protection if that individual "(i) has a physical or mental impairment which substantially limits one or more of such person's major life activities, (ii) has a record of such an impairment, or (iii) is regarded as having such an impairment." Major life activities include "caring for one's self, performing manual tasks, walking, seeing, hearing, speaking, breathing, learning, and working." The definition of disability contained within Section 504 is much broader than that stated in IDEA; therefore, students eligible for special education services through IDEA would always fall under Section 504 protection as well. Not all students qualifying for Section 504 protection would be eligible for services under IDEA's more restrictive definitions, however. Students with AIDS or attention deficit disorder are two examples of children and youth who may not be eligible for programs under IDEA but who may be considered disabled under Section 504.

Of particular concern to teachers, then, are students with hyperactivity and behavioral problems associated with attentional deficits. Such students may be eligible for special education as students with learning disabilities, with emotional and behavioral disorders, or with other health impairments. If students with attention deficit disorders are not determined to be disabled according to the definitions of these categories contained in IDEA, however, they may still require Section 504 accommodations in the regular classroom, including the following:

- Repeating and simplifying instructions about classwork and homework assignments
- Supplementing verbal instructions with visuals
- Using effective behavior management techniques
- Adjusting class schedules to decrease attentional difficulties
- Modifying test delivery or assignment requirements
- Using audiovisual equipment and computer-assisted instruction
- Modifying textbooks and workbooks
- Reducing class size
- Providing a tutor or mentor

Otherwise qualified students with disabilities, such as those with attention deficit disorders, are also protected under Section 504 from suspension and expulsion without the benefits of due process in much the same way as are students served under IDEA. With the more recent passage of the Americans With Disabilities Act of 1990, however, "local educational agencies may take disciplinary action pertaining to the use or possession of illegal drugs or alcohol against any handicapped student who currently is engaging in the illegal use of drugs or in the use of alcohol to the same extent that such disciplinary action is taken against non-handicapped students" (Underwood & Mead, 1995).

Schools are only now beginning to wrestle fully with the provision of reasonable accommodations and protection for students with disabilities under Section 504. In many states, school districts follow the more comprehensive and detailed procedures of IDEA to ensure full compliance with Section 504 requirements. School personnel should consider the existence of a disability and the possibility of Section 504 protection, then, whenever the following occur:

- Suspension or expulsion, particularly for repeated behavioral problems, is being considered.
- Retention is a consideration for a student.
- Students demonstrate a pattern of little benefit from instruction being provided.
- Students are referred for evaluation, but a decision is made not to evaluate under IDEA.
- Students are evaluated and found not to qualify for special education services under IDEA.
- Students have chronic health conditions.
- Students are identified as "at risk" or exhibit the potential for dropping out of school.
- A new building or remodeling is being considered (Douglas, 1995).

Summary

As teachers attempt to accommodate an increasingly diverse student population, they face many difficult and unresolved issues. The safety of all students in an age of escalating discipline problems and student violence has necessitated efforts by school personnel to develop proactive plans and strategies for managing crisis situations. Today's teacher requires training in preventing and breaking up fights and in eliminating gangs, drugs, and weapons from school grounds. School administrators and teachers must also be knowledgeable regarding recent court decisions and state laws to conduct legal searches for weapons or drugs, suspend or expel students with due process, and transfer records of violent juveniles without violating a student's rights to privacy and confidentiality of information.

Teachers must also be alert to the warning signals of potential suicidal behavior in both young children and adolescents. Suicide prevention programs are now required in some localities, and teachers must be prepared to cope with the anger, grief, and guilt experienced by peers, parents, and fellow teachers. In addition, today's teacher must observe the behavior of students taking a wide range of prescription medications and ensure that medications are taken properly, following the directions provided by the physician and in accordance with state laws and school policies governing the dispensing of medications within schools.

Schools also must provide services for students with disabilities who are not eligible for special education programs under IDEA. Section 504 of the Vocational

Rehabilitation Act of 1973 mandates that schools and teachers make reasonable accommodations to meet the needs of qualified students with disabilities. Students with disabilities are protected from long-term suspensions and expulsions without the benefits of due process under both the Individuals with Disabilities Education Act and Section 504.

Application Exercises

1. Interview an official from a local school. Does the school have a plan for handling emergencies such as fights or weapons? Describe the plan for your classmates including provisions for building security, staff training, and information management. How does this plan relate to the school's overall plan for student conduct and discipline?

2. Examine the state laws and regulations in your area regarding search and seizure, suspension and expulsion, and transfer of records. What are the local school district's procedures for handling the suspension or expulsion of students with behavioral disorders?

3. Interview a teacher from a local school. Does this teacher perceive violence or student discipline to be a problem in his or her school? Has this teacher ever had to intervene in a student fight? If so, what training has he or she received? Does the teacher perceive gangs, drugs or weapons to be a problem in the local schools? What preparation was the teacher given to handle these potential crisis situations?

4. Locate articles from local newspapers or magazines indicating any gang or drug activities in your area. Share this information with your classmates.

5. Invite local law enforcement or juvenile justice authorities to speak with your class regarding gang or drug activity in your area and prevention programs they sponsor in collaboration with the schools.

6. Invite a school nurse to talk with your class about common medications prescribed for students, the side effects of these medications, and the procedures used for managing medications in his or her school.

7. Conduct a debate regarding the pros and cons of providing services to students with emotional and behavioral problems under Section 504. Summarize the major points arising from the debate.

8. Talk with an administrator from a local school. How is this school providing for the needs of Section 504 students?

References

Amundson, K. J. (1994). *Violence in the schools: How America's school boards are safeguarding your children.* Alexandria, VA: National School Boards Association.

Bartlett, L. (1989). Disciplining handicapped students: Legal issues in light of *Honig v. Doe. Exceptional Children, 55*(4), 357–366.

Boomer, L. W. (1992). The law and school searches. *Journal of Emotional and Behavioral Problems, 1*(1), 27–30.

Bower, E. (1982). Defining emotional disturbance: Public policy and research. *Psychology in the Schools, 19,* 55–60.

Bryant, E. S., Rivard, J. C., Addy, C. L., Hinkle, K. T., Cowan, T. M., & Wright, G. (1995). Correlates of major and minor offending among youth with severe emotional disturbance. *Journal of Emotional and Behavioral Disorders, 3*(2), 76–84.

Center, D. B., & McKittrick, S. (1987). Disciplinary removal of special education students. *Focus on Exceptional Children, 20*(2), 1–10.

Children's Defense Fund. (1991). *The state of America's children.* Washington, DC: Children's Defense Fund.

Clarizio, H. F. (1987). Differentiating emotionally impaired from socially maladjusted students. *Psychology in the Schools, 24,* 237–243.

Clontz, D. (1987). Victims can sue bullies, schools. *National School Safety Center Newsjournal,* Fall, 32.

Cognosys Corporation. (1993). *School-based violence: Growing problem in all schools, not just inner-city.* Philadelphia: Cognosys Corporation.

Council for Children with Behavioral Disorders. (1990a). Position paper on the provision of service to children with conduct disorders. *Behavioral Disorders, 15*(3), 180–189.

Council for Children with Behavioral Disorders. (1990b). Position paper on use of behavior reduction strategies with children with behavioral disorders. *Behavioral Disorders, 15*(4), 243–260.

Council for Children with Behavioral Disorders. (1994). IDEA's "stay-put" provision amended. *Council for Children with Behavioral Disorders Newsletter, 8*(3), 1.

Council for Exceptional Children. (1994). Professional policies: Physical intervention. *CEC Today, 1*(3), 20–21.

Crawford, C. A., & Crawford, J. G. (1994). Relief is just a motion away. *Teaching Exceptional Children, 26*(2), 26–29.

Crouch, E., & Williams, D. (1995). What cities are doing to protect kids. *Educational Leadership, 52*(5), 60–62.

Douglas, J. (1995, March 22). *Section 504 implementation in the classroom.* Paper presented to administrators and staff of the Lunenberg County Public Schools, Lunenberg, VA.

Evans, E. D., & Richardson, R. C. (1995). Corporal punishment: What teachers should know. *Teaching Exceptional Children, 27*(2), 33–36.

Farmer, R. (1995). Teachers fear crisis in discipline: Public discussion set in May. *Richmond Times Dispatch,* April 16, B-1.

Forness, S. R., & Knitzer, J. (1992). A new proposed definition and terminology to replace "serious emotional disturbance" in Individuals with Disabilities Act. *School Psychology Review, 21,* 12–20.

Furlong, M. (1994). Evaluating school violence trends. *National School Safety Center News Journal, 3,* 23–27.

Gold, M. (1995). Charting a course: Promise and prospects for alternative schools. *Journal of Emotional and Behavioral Problems, 3*(4), 8–11.

Gold, M. & Mann, D. W. (1984). *Expelled to a friendlier place: A study of effective alternative schools.* Ann Arbor: University of Michigan Press.

Goss v. Lopez, 419 U.S. 565 (1975).

Guetzloe, E. (1988). Suicide and depression: Special education's responsibility. *Teaching Exceptional Children, 20*(4), 25–28.

Guetzloe, E. C. (1991). *Depression and suicide: Special education students at risk.* Reston, VA: Council for Exceptional Children.

Guetzloe, E. C. (1993). Answering the cry for help—Suicidal thoughts and actions. *Journal of Emotional and Behavioral Problems, 2*(2), 34–38.

Hanna, J. (1988). *Disruptive school behavior: Class, race, and culture.* New York: Homes & Meier.

Hindman, S. E. (1986). The law, the courts, and the education of behaviorally disordered students. *Behavioral Disorders, 11*(4), 280–289.

Honig v. Doe, 484 U.S. 305, 1988.

Huff, C. R. (1989). Youth gangs and public policy. *Crime and delinquency, 35*(4), 524–537.

Johnson, D. W., & Johnson, R. T. (1995). Why violence prevention programs don't work—And what does. *Educational Leadership, 52*(5), 63–68.

Kauffman, J. M. (1994). Violent children and youth: A call for attention. *Journal of Behavioral Education, 4*(2), 153–155.

King, C. A. (1993). Alcohol abuse and depression in teenagers. *Journal of Emotional and Behavioral Problems, 2*(3), 16–18.

Knitzer, J., Steinberg, Z., & Fleisch, B. (1990). *At the schoolhouse door: An examination of programs and policies for children with behavioral and emotional problems.* New York: Bank Street College of Education.

Leo, J. (1995). Punished for the sins of the children. *U.S. News & World Report, 118*(23), June, 12, 18.

Loeber, R., & Stouthamer-Loeber, M. (1986). Family factors as correlates and predictors of juvenile conduct problems and delinquency. In M. Tonry & N. Morris (Eds.), *Crime and justice: An annual review of research* (pp. 29–150). Chicago: University of Chicago Press.

Long, N. J. (1992). Managing a shooting incident. *Journal of Emotional and Behavioral Problems, 1*(1), 23–26.

Maag, J. W., & Howell, K. W. (1992). Special education and the exclusion of youth with social maladjustments: A cultural-organizational perspective. *Remedial and Special Education, 13*(1), 47–54.

Mayer, G. R., Nafpaktitis, M., Butterworth, T., & Hollingsworth, P. (1987). A search for the elusive settings events of school vandalism: A correlational study. *Education and Treatment of Children, 10,* 259–270.

McIntyre, T. (1993). Reflections on the new definition for emotional or behavioral disorders: Who still falls through the cracks and why. *Behavioral Disorders, 18*(2), 148–160.

Miller, D. (1994). Suicidal behavior of adolescents with behavior disorders and their peers without disabilities. *Behavioral Disorders, 20*(1), 61–68.

Morgan, S. R. (1994). *At-risk youth in crises: A team approach in the schools* (2nd ed.). Austin, TX: Pro-Ed.

National School Safety Center. (1988). *Gangs in schools: Breaking up is hard to do.* Malibu, CA: National School Safety Center.

National School Safety Center. (1992). *Update: Teen suicide—Developing a plan for prevention.* Westlake Village, CA: National School Safety Center.

Nelson, C. M., Rutherford, R. B., Center, D. B., & Walker, H. M. (1991). Do public schools have an obligation to serve troubled children and youth? *Exceptional Children, 57*(5), 406–415.

New Jersey v. T. L. O., 469 U.S. 325 (1985).

Pullis, M. (1991). Practical considerations of excluding conduct disordered students: An empirical analysis. *Behavioral Disorders, 17*(1), 9–22.

Rekoske, D., & Wyka, G. T. (1990). *Breaking up fights: How to safely defuse explosive conflicts.* Brookfield, WI: National Crisis Prevention Institute.

Scheuermann, B., Webber, J., Partin, M., & Knies, W. C. (1994). Level systems and the law: Are they compatible? *Behavioral Disorders, 19*(3), 205–220.

Shores, R. E., Gunter, P. L., & Jack, S. L. (1993). Classroom management strategies: Are they setting events for coercion? *Behavioral Disorders, 18*(2), 92–102.

Singh, N. N., Epstein, M. H., Luebke, J., & Singh, Y. N. (1990). Psychopharmacological intervention. I: Teacher perceptions of psychotropic medication for students with serious emotional disturbance. *The Journal of Special Education, 24*(3), 283–295.

Slate, J., Waldrop, P., & Justen, J. (1991). Corporal punishment used in a discriminatory manner. *The Clearing House, 64*(6), 361–364.

Steiger, L. K. (Ed.). (1987). *Participant workbook: Nonviolent crisis intervention.* Brookfield, WI: National Crisis Prevention Institute.

Swanson, J. M., Cantwell, D., Lerner, M., McBurnett, K., Pfiffner, L., & Kotkin, R. (1992). Treatment of ADHD: Beyond medication. *Beyond Behavior, 4*(1), 13–21.

Thomason, J. (1994). The IEP—Our first line of defense against student violence. *CEC Today, 1*(5), 2.

Tobin, T. J., & Sugai, G. (1993). Intervention aversiveness: Educators' perceptions of the need for restrictions on aversive interventions. *Behavioral Disorders, 18*(2), 110–117.

Underwood, J. K., & Mead, J. F. (1995). *Legal aspects of special education and pupil services.* Boston: Allyn & Bacon.

U.S. Department of Education. (1994). *16th Annual report to Congress on the implementation of IDEA.* Washington, DC: U.S.D.O.E., Office of Special Education Programs.

Valente, W. D. (1994). *Law in the schools* (3rd Ed.). New York: Macmillan.

Walker, H. M., Colvin, G., & Ramsey, E. (1995). *Antisocial behavior in school: Strategies and best practices.* Pacific Grove, CA: Brooks/Cole.

Walker, J. E., & Shea, T. M. (1995). *Behavior management: A practical approach for educators* (6th ed.). Englewood Cliffs, NJ: Merrill/Prentice Hall.

Watson, R. S., Poda, J. H., Miller, C. T., Rice, E. S., & West, G. (1990). *Containing crisis: A guide to managing school emergencies.* Bloomington, IN: National Educational Service.

Weinberg, L. A. (1992). The relevance of choice in distinguishing seriously emotionally disturbed from socially maladjusted students. *Behavioral Disorders, 17*(2), 99–106.

Wilson, J., & Howell, J. (1993). *A comprehensive strategy for serious, violent, and chronic juvenile offenders.* Washington, DC: U.S. Department of Justice, Office of Juvenile Justice and Delinquency Prevention.

Wood, F. H., Cheney, C. O., Cline, D. H., Sampson, K., Smith, C. R., & Guetzloe, E. C. (1991). *Conduct disorders and social maladjustments: Policies, politics, and programming.* Reston, VA: Council for Exceptional Children.

Wood, M. M., & Long, N. J. (1991). *Life space intervention: Talking with children and youth in crisis.* Austin, TX: Pro-Ed.

Yell, M. L. (1989). *Honig v. Doe:* the suspension and expulsion of handicapped students. *Exceptional Children, 56*(1), 60–69.

Yell, M. L. (1990). The use of corporal punishment, suspension, expulsion, and timeout with behaviorally disordered students in public schools: Legal considerations. *Behavioral Disorders, 15*(2), 100–109.

Zabel, R. H. (1985). Aversives in special education programs for behaviorally disordered students: A debate. *Behavioral Disorders, 10*(4), 295–304.

Main Ideas:

♦ *Teaching, particularly teaching students with emotional and behavioral disorders, can be a stressful occupation.*

♦ *Although teachers cannot control all of the sources of stress in their school, they can develop healthy strategies for coping with stress on a daily basis.*

♦ *Using "best" practices enhances the teacher's sense of effectiveness and self-efficacy in the classroom and contributes to reduced stress and burnout.*

♦ *Teachers have a professional responsibility to abide by the CEC code of ethics, to demonstrate the competencies outlined in the CEC Common Core of Knowledge and Skills Essential for All Beginning Special Educators, and to develop the additional skills necessary to increase their effectiveness with children and youth having behavioral disorders.*

♦ *Membership in professional associations and participation on school-based committees enables the teacher to stay current with developments in the field and to influence decisions that impact programs for students within the local school.*

♦ *Developing a personal philosophy regarding student behavior is a starting point for decision making in the classroom and a topic for reflection throughout a teacher's professional career.*

BOX 12.1   Teacher Feature: Do I Really Want to Teach These Kids?

Below are a few of the experiences and emotions highlighting one teacher's first year with behavior disordered inner city teenagers. Her trials and tribulations are not much different from others who teach in our urban educational fortresses.

During the first week of September, I enthusiastically stepped onto my new career path, a bit apprehensive, but fairly confident that my personality and skills would guarantee a positive experience. Besides, how different and difficult could behavior disordered children be? Wow! Was I in for a surprise!

The first few weeks of the semester were relaxed and uneventful. I concentrated my efforts on the small group of students that attended each day. Finally, toward the end of September, the rest of my students began showing up. Holy Cow!!! From the get-go, I was continually challenged, degraded as an authority figure, and insulted as a woman. My "sharks" glared hungrily at me each time I stepped into the classroom, ready to devour me. Before entering, I would take a deep breath and try to create a stern and confident facade. That projected image did not play as I had hoped. I often felt that I was the student and they were my instructors. But what was the lesson to be learned here? I felt confused and overwhelmed. This was not the type of school or student that I had read about in my textbooks. I followed my textbook's advice to plan interesting lessons and be enthusiastic, but contrary to expectations, my pupils did not sit still with their hands folded, or thrust them into the air accompanied by sounds of "Ooh! Ooh! I know! I know! Call on me!"

Let me introduce my class. Eight of my twelve students had "done time" (been incarcerated). They and others frequently fell into the classroom smelling like breweries, or with their eyes glazed over from smoking dope in the bathroom. It broke my heart to see them this way. No matter how much I spoke to them in concern (not nagging), these kids vented their frustrations in ways that made classroom life very difficult.

On one typical day, I was working hard to settle my active students. Just as they began responding to my lesson, one drugged student, in an effort to refocus the attention of the group back onto him, began to call out obscenities that would have made a longshoreman blush. Other students became outraged. A behavioral chain reaction occurred. Garbage cans were kicked, binders were propelled from desks, and the ritual insulting of mothers ensued. My lesson was shot for that day.

By now, you have discovered that teaching students with emotional and behavioral disorders can be a challenging and exciting task. You know, for example, that professionals have many different ways to view student behavior and to intervene when that behavior is considered inappropriate. In addition, you know that many decisions you make in your classroom have profound legal and ethical implications and that each decision, no matter how small, has an immediate impact on you and your students. You realize, as well, that behavior is a function

Drugs and alcohol were major influences upon the actions and performance of my kids. I was so concerned about these students being impaired, that not only did I speak with their counselors, but also the head of a group that counsels and works with streetwise youth. When summoned to see their assigned counselors, the psychological merry-go-round started again. The kids felt betrayed. They were cutting classes trying to discover the identity of the "snitch" who reported them. Aware of the adage that "Snitches get stitches," I wondered how to approach my disgruntled charges. . . . I wasn't allowed much time to mull this over. My paraprofessional . . . told the students that I was the squealer.

The kids came into my class angry as hell. Once again, instead of conducting a lesson, I spent that time explaining to them why I was so concerned about their welfare. We took the time to reconnect and bond. It was time well spent. Although I often felt that I coddled them too much, sometimes this seemed to be what they (and I) needed in order to continue.

Violence was a normal part of our school day. Fights frequently ensued during passing to classes, and even during classes. Knives and guns were commonly used to threaten or injure students and teachers. Local gangs periodically came to "visit." I remember that for weeks, "the Deceps" were a constant concern with the frightened pupils in my class. "Who the heck are the Deceps?" I asked the students. Apparently, the Decepticons were a very violent group of youth who thought nothing of robbing people and even killing their victims if necessary to get what they desired. I dismissed this talk as mass hysteria until one day I came face-to-face with these creatures from hell.

We were in the middle of an intense review for an exam. The room was so hot that I decided to open the door for ventilation. Shortly thereafter, three disheveled and demonic-looking boys wearing lavender and blue headbands entered my room. They began to make sexually suggestive forays toward my female students. . . . I decided to approach the boys, and held out my hand to them indicating that I wanted to make peace rather than promote conflict. They looked at each other and snickered. One said, "Yo, the bitch wants to be friends." I sighed with relief until I felt my hand being crushed by the handshake. Then this punk pulled the rings off my fingers. The other creep stole my coat. . . . After they sashayed from the area, I quickly reported the incident to the administration, but was told that there was nothing they could (or would) do.

of complex interactions among students, their peers, and their teachers. Beliefs and expectations, cultural background, home and community environments, and daily life in the classroom reciprocally influence one another to produce complicated patterns of behavior and chains of events.

You may recall that in Chapter 1 you were asked to examine your own philosophy about teaching, learning, and student behavior so that you might develop a framework to guide your actions in the classroom. According to

BOX 12.1 (cont.)

One day, I was working my tail off trying to keep my students enthused about the lesson on the human body. Suddenly, an administrator entered my class to conduct a surprise observation. Up to the time he entered the room, my kids were devouring the work (instead of me) and enthusiastically volunteering answers and making funny, yet related comments. I was proud of the progress of my students and was glad that my supervisor would see them in action. However, once they spotted him, they put their heads down on their desks and wouldn't respond. I was confused and embarrassed. Two of the students kept the lesson moving, but all-in-all it was not a lesson representative of the midyear progress we had made. I did receive a "satisfactory" on my observation, but it bothered me that the administrator never saw these kids in action. Later, I asked my students why they had clammed up. They told me that they didn't like or trust our visitor. Therefore, they would not work in his presence. In the interest of self-preservation, I told them how important it was for my career that they behave and respond in class. They didn't let me down the second time around.

Recently, some of my students from last year came by to talk with me on a parent-teacher night. Three generations often arrive together. I couldn't believe that five of the students from the previous year had children of their own. While my former students were in other rooms finding out how they are doing grade-wise this year, I ended up with balloons tied to my chair, bottles on my desk, knick-knacks on the floor, and wet babies on my lap. My room looked more like a nursery than a classroom. I didn't mind having the babies in my room, but feared an administrator would have something to say about its unprofessional appearance. It certainly was a strange evening; just another one of those situations they don't tell you about in college.

In closing I have mixed feelings on being a teacher of behavior disordered youth. On one hand, I adore working with teenagers. They can be such joy, and I gain great pride in guiding them toward adulthood. . . . On the other hand, there are students who only know violence as a way of life. Because of them, I have lost five friends and colleagues.

From "Do I Really Want to Teach These Kids? An Analysis of One Teacher's First Year with Behavior Disordered Adolescents," by T. McIntyre & M. Stefanides, *Beyond Behavior*, 5(1), 1993, pp. 17–21. Copyright © 1993 by The Council for Exceptional Children. Reprinted with permission.

Grosenick, George, and George (1987), the teacher is still the most important determinant of the quality of educational programs for children and youth with emotional and behavioral disorders. As a teacher, then, your job is heavily charged with responsibility. Like the beginning teacher whose experiences are described in Box 12.1, you may face challenging behaviors, violence, and unexpected reactions from students on a daily basis. You may feel dismayed, perplexed, and frustrated, and you may wonder why "they never taught us about this in college." You may, however, also experience joy, deep satisfaction, and pride in the progress of your students and in your development as a professional.

The information you gain from college or university classes or from reading textbooks such as this one is only the beginning. Textbooks and professors can provide you with a solid foundation for beginning your teaching career, but they cannot tell you exactly how to handle every situation you will encounter. As you become a teacher, you have the responsibility for asking questions and pursuing answers, for carefully examining the effects of your decisions and actions, and for staying abreast of new information. You also have a responsibility to care for yourself so that you may better serve those students in your charge.

In these final pages, then, we will consider your growth and development as a teacher. We will return to the question of self-efficacy and examine ways in which you might reduce your stress and minimize your risk of burnout in the classroom. In addition, we will reflect on several factors related to professional practice, including adherence to a code of ethics, the use of teaching competencies and behaviors known to be effective, and the empowerment of teachers so that they may become responsible professionals. Finally, we will reconsider your philosophy regarding student behavior as a critical starting point for your teaching career.

Self-Efficacy, Stress, and Burnout in Teaching

Like the teacher in Box 12.1, you probably entered the teaching profession enthusiastically and confidently. Perhaps you had some healthy nervousness regarding your skills or your ability to handle students with emotional and behavioral disorders; however, you most likely also had a sincere desire to help these students learn more appropriate behaviors and social skills. You want your students to be successful in their lives and to respect you, themselves, and others. You hope your students will come to enjoy learning and being in your classroom. Beliefs such as these, about yourself and about your students, profoundly influence your actions as a teacher.

Teachers must believe they are making a difference in the lives of their students. Self-efficacy for teachers means the belief that our students can be taught regardless of family, community, school, or societal difficulties (Ashton & Webb, 1986; Bandura, 1982). Furthermore, teachers with high efficacy believe they have the skills and the ability to produce student learning. This belief, in turn, influences the teacher's level of motivation, effort, and persistence as well as teacher-student interactions and student achievement (McDaniel & DiBella-McCarthy, 1989). According to Allinder (1993), high-efficacy teachers not only believe they *can* teach, they *do* teach more effectively than their low-efficacy colleagues, who tend to view student failure as a result of poor home environments or low ability levels. High-efficacy teachers also tend to create classrooms characterized by "warmth" and "positive" behavior management strategies in which students feel accepted and encouraged (Allinder, 1993).

Although researchers have only begun to examine teacher efficacy in special education, considering the beliefs and expectations of teachers serving students with emotional and behavioral disorders is of particular importance. As a teacher of students with behavioral problems, you are expected to be patient and in control and to provide interesting, motivating, and challenging lessons. Yet, your students may make very slow progress and exhibit behaviors that are extreme and unpredictable. Over time, the unmotivated and confrontational behaviors of your students, combined with their slow progress, may produce stress and a diminished sense of competence in your teaching ability, unless you are able to set realistic expectations for yourself and your students.

For teachers, particularly special educators, the sources of stress are numerous. See Box 12.2 for some signs of stress in teachers. The pupil/teacher ratio for teachers of students with behavioral disorders ranges from 3.1 to 35 students per teacher, and as the caseload increases, student achievement decreases (Algozzine, Hendrickson, Gable, & White, 1993). Similarly, McManus and Kauffman (1991) report that teachers of students with behavioral problems work in highly demanding settings and in relative isolation from their colleagues.

Teachers of students with emotional and behavioral disorders report that they work an average of over 56 hours per week and that they feel relatively unprepared to collaborate with other professionals (Gable, Hendrickson, Young, & Shokoohi-Yekta, 1992). These teachers encounter substantial levels of both verbal and physical aggression (Ruhl & Hughes, 1985), and they report that dealing with disruptive student behavior and irate or unresponsive parents are significant sources of stress (Pullis, 1992). In addition, a perceived lack of support from colleagues, principals, or from other supervisors contributes to low morale and stress for teachers (Cherniss, 1988; Zabel & Zabel, 1982). As a matter of fact, teachers who are "potential leavers" do not leave education because of personal characteristics such as experience, training, or competence (George, George, Gersten, & Grosenick, 1995). Rather, they are differentiated from the "stayers" by variables such as the school's organizational structure, the adequacy of support they receive, the type of service delivery model in which they teach, and the time they have available for developing curricula and completing paperwork.

Finally, perceptions regarding the inadequacy of resources within a program or setting are correlated with feelings of emotional exhaustion and depersonalization (Schmid et al., 1990). Job satisfaction directly affects the teacher's decision to remain in teaching, yet job satisfaction is also highly correlated with previously mentioned work-related variables such as principal support and classroom stress (Cross & Billingsley, 1994; Littrell, Billingsley, & Cross, 1994).

Suppose, then, that like the teacher in Box 12.1, you begin teaching students with emotional and behavioral disorders enthusiastically and confidently. Day after day, however, you face highly disruptive and belligerent student behavior, few resources, and little administrative or parental support. Your expectations about teaching do not match the realities of daily life in the classroom, and you being to experience stress, emotional and physical exhaustion, and increased negative interactions with students, parents, and colleagues (Zabel, Boomer, & King, 1984). You experience a diminished sense of competence and self-efficacy, and you become more likely to attribute student failure and misbehavior to external factors (e.g., unsupportive parents, violent communities, low ability) beyond your control. In effect, you give up on your students to protect your own sense of ability as a teacher. You experience a slow increase in emotional exhaustion, and you begin to distance yourself from your students and from

BOX 12.2   **Signs of Stress in Teachers**

Some level of stress is healthy in any occupation. Stress helps the individual to make necessary changes and to set and accomplish worthy goals (Miller, 1979; Seyle, 1984). When stress is excessive, however, it may affect perceptions we hold regarding our work, our colleagues, and our own performance. Although we may not be able to control all of the organizational (e.g., work schedules, negative colleagues or supervisors) or societal (e.g., community violence) sources of stress in our daily lives, we must recognize the signs of stress so that we can make positive changes in those factors we can control. Rosenberg, O'Shea, and O'Shea (1991) list the following signs of stress in teachers:

◆ Avoidance of school through absences, tardiness, and a desire to leave school early
◆ Apathy toward parents, students, and other teachers
◆ Lowered productivity in one's teaching, especially for teachers who have been highly productive in the past
◆ Constant negative self-statements regarding one's effectiveness as a teacher
◆ Physical symptoms, including headaches, stomach pains, and voice problems
◆ Real or imagined fatigue and mental fatigue over time
◆ Refusal to comply with school rules and policies
◆ Crying and depression
◆ Feelings of a loss of control over one's career, business matters, or personal life
◆ Constant complaints to loved ones or friends

others in the workplace (Frank & McKenzie, 1993). As an apathetic and burned out teacher, you may decide to leave teaching or to remain in the classroom, seriously impacting the educational achievement and quality of life of your students.

The preceding paragraphs are not meant to discourage you from entering the teaching profession or from teaching students with emotional and behavioral disorders. Although the reasons for teachers leaving the classroom are still unclear (Brownell & Smith, 1992), many former teachers do return to teaching (Singer, 1993). Teachers are most likely to leave the classroom during their first few years, and those who survive this period often remain in the profession for many years (Singer, 1992). The key is to recognize those factors that may contribute to your stress and to set realistic expectations for yourself and your students. If you are aware of your beliefs and expectations as a teacher, of sources of stress, and of healthy ways to cope with daily stressors, you will be more likely to experience enhanced self-efficacy and job satisfaction in the classroom (Greer & Greer, 1992). You will also be more likely to influence student achievement and behavior positively, contributing to a continuing sense of competence, efficacy, pride, and longevity in teaching.

Although you cannot control all of the sources of stress in your life, you can change many factors, which will effectively reduce your stress and likelihood of burning out in the classroom. For example, you might improve your organization in the classroom and your time-management skills so that you do not feel overwhelmed with paperwork or rushed to meet deadlines. In addition, you might adopt some healthy strategies to help yourself cope with those stressors you cannot change. Keep in mind, however, the word "healthy." Obviously, some strategies for coping with stress (e.g., excessive smoking; overeating; using alcohol, drugs, or prescription medications) may hurt rather than help you. Some healthy ways to reduce or cope with stress include the following:

Organize Your Time and Activities

1. Set realistic and flexible professional goals and objectives. If your expectations are too low, you may feel lethargic and unmotivated. If your expectations are too high, you may experience frustration, guilt, failure, and additional pressure (CEC, 1989).

2. Establish priorities. Each day, do those things that must be done rather than procrastinating. Cohen and Hart-Hester (1987) have identified five keys to effective time management:

   Make a List. Make a list of items needing attention, and rank them according to importance and deadlines. As an item is accomplished, check it off your "to do by" list.

   Design a Work Area. Design a work area in the classroom that is isolated from others. A partitioned-off area facing two walls rather than doors or windows is ideal. When teaching, face away from the door, or post a "do not disturb" sign to reduce distracting visitors.

   Develop Forms. Develop forms to speed up notes on conferences, meetings, observations, and teaching suggestions. With premade formats, you need only fill in the established blanks.

   Perform Similar Tasks. Perform tasks that require similar materials or resources during the same work session (e.g., make calls at a specified time, do all the filing or copying at the same time, etc.) to reduce time wasted traveling around the building or gathering supplies.

   Reduce Wasted Time. Reduce the time wasted in meetings by raising questions to redirect sidetracked discussions back to the task at hand.

3. Leave your work at school. Going into school early or staying a little later may help you complete paperwork, grading, and planning without needing to take work home (CEC, 1989). Compartmentalizing your job and personal life enables you to turn off thoughts about school so that you can relax at home.

4. Pace yourself. Rather than trying to get everything done at once, show steady progress toward your goals (CEC, 1989). Learn how to say "No" to those unnecessary demands or activities that take up your time.
5. Use available human resources. Take the time to train parent or student volunteers or paraprofessionals to do many of the clerical tasks that take up your time (CEC, 1989).

Teachers must engage in healthy self-reflection to identify sources of stress and satisfaction in the school and classroom.

Teacher Feature: Teaching and Stress—A Personal View

How do you spell stress? T-E-A-C-H-I-N-G. Stress may be a one-word definition of teaching. Even the traditional three-month summer vacation may be insufficient time for some teachers to recover from the wear and tear of the past school year and to regroup for the year ahead. I have been a classroom teacher for fifteen years, and in that time I have noticed that the stresses associated with managing a roomful of students or dealing with just one difficult student can have powerful effects on a teacher. My teaching career's longevity and success is owed in large part to my responses to stress.

There are things and people I try to avoid. I avoid the wait at the xerox machine during certain busy times, delay making telephone calls at lunch hour when people are less likely to be available, and go around negative people whenever possible. When negative people cannot be evaded, I work hard at not getting defensive about their critical comments and make a special effort not to fall in the trap of being critical myself. I avoid saying yes to requests I should not take on and monitor my urge to spontaneously volunteer my time, energy, and resources to every good cause.

I get to my classroom early so that I have time to work without interruptions. Occasionally, I may even have to close my door. I promote humor by making puns, laughing at and learning from my mistakes, and sharing and posting cartoons. My students like the poster of . . . Charlie Brown, his head on his desk, with the statement, "It's never to late to learn, but sometimes, it's too early." I purchase things that enhance my classroom (decorations, novelty erasers, pencils, the posters) or are necessary to run my program (software, videos, workbooks, student reinforcers). My students are often surprised when I ask them, "Is it fun, yet?" While learning new concepts may be hard, the effort and accomplishment may be simultaneous with feeling pleasure and pride.

I write grants for items not in the school materials and supplies budget. . . . I go to conferences to get renewed, refreshed, and rejuvenated. My active participation in a professional organization provides the benefits of an informational network on issues, research regarding effective teaching methods, and peer support. Bringing in baked goods occurs less frequently these days, but

6. Organize your classroom. Catalogue materials and place similar items together. Develop a filing system for student information, work completed, memos, etc. (CEC, 1989).

Be Open to Change, Innovation, and New Opportunities

1. Change your environment. If stress is increasing, you may want to try changing roles (e.g., from resource to self-contained teacher, or from elementary to middle school level) to reduce your stress or to rejuvenate your interest (CEC, 1989).

it is one way I can show appreciation to support personnel and colleagues. It is hard to be grouchy and tense while munching on tasty brownies. Sharing and exchanging articles from journals and newspapers occurs regularly.... Periodically a group of us take an after school field trip to a local restaurant to socialize, ventilate, and support each other. Enrollment in graduate school has provided the opportunity to learn ways to be a more effective and therapeutic teacher. Learning to use computers in the classroom has given both me and my students new skills and the power of mastery over technology.

Have I mentioned that I am an enthusiastic consumer of chocolate and coffee? I am also working on the skill of juggling and on developing control over a pair of roller blades. These activities are an outlet for me. Although I am not always successful, I try to maintain an upbeat attitude and make consistent use of the kind of positive reinforcement that provides feedback and expectations to help my students regulate their behavior. I may look like a teacher with my long skirts, sensible shoes, and book bag, but you will not hear me refer to myself as "just" a teacher nor will you see me wearing the T-shirt stating "The 3 best things about teaching are June, July, and August." I work at being organized and goal-oriented. I continue to reorganize, consult with peers and administration, and maintain humor and flexibility in the face of a challenge. Teaching, for me, is an intellectual adventure with daily rewards.

While developing personal habits that include eating right, sleeping enough, and tending to one's physical and mental condition may improve the ability to tolerate stress, it does not necessarily change the stress to be tolerated. Some stressors in the teaching profession are not in our personal control and may be a source of chronic irritation anxiety. The media is critical of education and the government is aiming for national reforms. Financial cutbacks are the norm. Using knowledge of one's own patterns of response will better enable teachers to enjoy their profession to retirement with added benefits to their students, colleagues, family, and friends.

From "Teaching and Stress: A Personal View," by F. Mueller, *Beyond Behavior,* 5(1), 1993, p. 3. Copyright © 1993 by The Council for Exceptional Children. Reprinted with permission.

2. Keep yourself motivated. Attend professional meetings and conventions, or take classes to prevent stagnation. Try a new strategy in the classroom, or develop new materials (CEC, 1989).
3. Look for personal learning experiences. Take a class or workshop purely for interest (e.g., car maintenance, pottery, quilting, etc.) (CEC, 1989).

Take Care of Yourself

1. Eat a well-balanced diet, and get plenty of rest and exercise (Raschke, Dedrick, & DeVries, 1988).

2. Apply GTMs (good-to-myselfs) (Raschke, Dedrick, & DeVries, 1988). Take a hot soak; make a long-distance telephone call; see a new movie; participate in your favorite hobby; relax with soothing music; or give yourself some other reminder that you are an important and valuable human being.

Be Positive about Yourself and Your Profession

1. Allow moments of glory (CEC, 1989). Recognize your own accomplishments as well as those of colleagues rather than exhibiting false modesty. Give credit and praise where it is due. Catch students and colleagues being good and deliver praise with enthusiasm (Raschke, Dedrick, & DeVries, 1988).
2. Look for the silver lining (CEC, 1989). Focus on the positive aspects of even frustrating situations. Make positive self-statements rather than self-defeating, irrational ones to change the effects of your self-talk on your behavior (Kaplan, 1991; Webber & Coleman, 1988). Adopt an optimistic explanatory style in which you "own" your successes and view your failures as only temporary setbacks (Wells, 1993).
3. Become involved. Seek out professional support services, build networks, and become active in professional associations (CEC, 1989). Continue with the committees and classes that are productive, and resign or say "No" to those that are unproductive.

4. Remember the children you serve. Focus on the needs of your students rather than blaming them or their parents for difficulties (CEC, 1989). Don't be afraid to ask for help and support from colleagues.

Also see Box 12.3, pp. 386–387, and Box 12.4, p. 388, for a personal view on teaching and stress and for some survival tips for first year teachers.

Professional Responsibility

You can do many things to alleviate your stress and prevent burnout in your classroom. As you know, however, the academic and behavioral performance of your students is highly related to your sense of self-efficacy as a teacher. You must, therefore, ensure that you are using the best instructional and classroom management practices possible, those that are known to be effective for most students with emotional and behavioral disorders. In addition, as a teacher you must behave in an ethical and professional manner with the interests and welfare of your students and colleagues constantly in mind.

The Council for Exceptional Children offers a set of statements guiding the professional conduct of all special educators. These statements, which make up the CEC code of ethics, are listed in Box 12.5 (pp. 390–396). In addition, in 1992, the Council for Exceptional Children adopted a set of statements indicating a Common Core of Knowledge and Skills Essential for All Beginning Special Education Teachers (Swan & Sirvis, 1992) (see Box 12.5). These skills are considered to be the minimal teaching competencies necessary for beginning special educators. Additional skills and personal characteristics may be necessary, however, for effective teachers of students with emotional and behavioral disorders, including a more extensive repertoire of instructional and management procedures and greater perseverance in the face of failure (Kauffman & Wong, 1991).

You may recall in Chapter 5 that we listed elements of successful strategies and programs for students with behavioral disorders. These included systematic, data-based interventions, continuous assessment and monitoring of progress, provision for practice of new skills, treatment matched to problem, multicomponent treatments, programing for transfer and maintenance, and commitment to sustained interventions. This set of knowledge and skills is certainly contained within the CEC common core. Yet, professionals still debate which competencies are most essential for effective teaching of students with emotional and behavioral disorders (The Peacock Hill Working Group, 1991).

Bullock, Ellis, and Wilson (1994) compared the knowledge and skills often reported to be taught by programs preparing teachers of students with emotional and behavioral disorders, including those contained in the CEC common core, with the perceived importance and actual frequency of use by teachers. Behavior management and collaboration with other professionals were the knowledge and skills categories rated highest in both importance and frequency of use by teachers of students with behavioral disorders. Not surprisingly, these teachers report that their ability to understand the ethical and legal responsibilities associated with behavioral interventions and

(Text continued on p. 397)

BOX 12.5

The Council for Exceptional Children Code of Ethics and Common Core of Knowledge and Skills Essential for all Beginning Special Education Teachers

In 1983, the Delegate Assembly of the Council for Exceptional Children adopted the CEC Code of Ethics. The Council maintains that, as professionals, we must uphold our obligations to the exceptional students we teach, to our employers, and to the special education profession itself. Ethical responsibilities in each of these three areas have been translated into the eight principles comprising the Code of Ethics which form the basis for professional conduct. These eight principles have also been translated into a set of minimum standards called the Standards for Professional Practice. In addition, in 1992, the Council for Exceptional Children Professional Standards and Practice Standing Committee adopted a Common Core of Knowledge and Skills Essential for All Beginning Special Education Teachers. A subcommittee comprised of 36 members including representatives from each of CEC's divisions, student CEC members, colleges and universities, CEC teachers of the year, and local school districts, worked to develop the Common Core. The divisions within CEC, such as the Council for Children with Behavioral Disorders (CCBD), are working as well to develop a list of additional knowledge and skills essential for beginning teachers in particular areas of special education (Bullock, Ellis, & Wilson, 1994).

CEC Common Core of Knowledge and Skills Essential for All Beginning Special Education Teachers

Preamble

The standards of the profession of special education are a formally codified set of beliefs. These belief statements represent the special educator's principles of appropriate ethical behavior and are based on several assumptions. One assumption of this common core of knowledge and skills is that the professional conduct of entry level special educators is foremost governed by the *CEC Code of Ethics:*

Special Education Professionals

- ◆ Are committed to developing the highest educational and quality of life potential for exceptional individuals.
- ◆ Promote and maintain a high level of competence and integrity in practicing their profession.
- ◆ Engage in professional activities which benefit individuals with exceptionalities, their families, other colleagues, students, or research subjects.
- ◆ Exercise objective professional judgement in the practice of their profession.
- ◆ Strive to advance their knowledge and skills regarding the education of individuals with exceptionalities.
- ◆ Work within the standards and policies of their profession.
- ◆ Seek to uphold and improve where necessary the laws, regulations, and policies governing the delivery of special education and related services and the practice of their profession.

◆ Do not condone or participate in unethical or illegal acts, nor violate professional standards adopted by the Delegate Assembly of CEC.

Second, special education has within its heritage the perspective of embracing individual differences. These differences include the traditional consideration of the nature and effect of exceptionalities. Special education professionals must continue to broaden their perspective to ensure vigilant attention to the issues of diversity such as culture, language, gender, religion, and sexuality. Diversity is such a pervasive concern that statements involving diversity were infused throughout the model.

Third, this common core of knowledge and skills may change over time. As with the adoption of the CEC Code of Ethics, time should provide for continuing examination, debate, and further articulation of these knowledge and skills for entry level special educators.

Knowledge and Skills Statements

I. Philosophical, Historical, and Legal Foundations of Special Education.

Knowledge

1. Models, theories, and philosophies that provide the basis for special education practice.
2. Variations in beliefs, traditions, and values across cultures within society and the effect of the relationships between child, family, and schooling.
3. Issues in definition and identification procedures for individuals with exceptional learning needs.
4. Assurances and due process rights related to assessment, eligibility, and placement for students who are culturally and/or linguistically diverse.
5. "Rights and responsibilities" of parents, students, teachers, and schools as they relate to individuals with exceptional learning needs.

Skills

6. Articulate personal philosophy of special education including its relationship to/with regular education.
7. Conduct instruction and other professional activities consistent with the requirements of law, rules and regulations, and local district policies and procedures.

II. Characteristics of Learners

Knowledge

8. Similarities and differences between the cognitive, physical, cultural, social, and emotional needs of typical and exceptional individuals.
9. Differential characteristics of children and youth with exceptionalities (including levels of severity where applicable).
10. Characteristics of normal, delayed and disordered communication patterns of exceptional individuals.

BOX 12.5 (cont.)

11. Effects an exceptional condition may have on an individual's life.
12. Characteristics and effects of the cultural and environmental milieu of the child and the family (e.g., cultural diversity, socioeconomic level, abuse/neglect, substance abuse, etc.).
13. Effects of various medications on the educational, cognitive, physical, social, and emotional behavior of individuals with exceptionalities.
14. Educational implications of characteristics of various exceptionalities.

Skills

15. Access information on various cognitive, physical, cultural, social, and emotional conditions of exceptional individuals.

III. Assessment, Diagnosis, and Evaluation

Knowledge

16. Basic terminology used in assessment.
17. Ethical concerns related to assessment.
18. Legal provisions, regulations, and guidelines regarding student assessment.
19. Typical procedures used for screening, prereferral, referral, and classification.
20. Appropriate application and interpretation of scores (e.g., grade score vs. standard score, percentile ranks, age/grade equivalents, and stanines).
21. Appropriate use and limitations of each type of assessment instrument.
22. Influence of diversity on assessment, eligibility, programming, and placement of exceptional learners.
23. The relationship between assessment and placement decisions.
24. Methods for monitoring student progress.

Skills

25. Collaborate with parents and other professionals involved in the assessment of students with individual learning needs.
26. Create and maintain student records.
27. Gather background information regarding academic, medical, and family history.
28. Use various types of assessment procedures (e.g., norm-referenced, curriculum-based, work samples, observations, task analysis) appropriately.
29. Interpret formal and informal assessment instruments and procedures.
30. Report assessment results to students, parents, administrators, and other professionals using appropriate communication skills.
31. Use performance data and teacher/student/parent input to make or suggest appropriate modification in learning environments.

32. Develop individualized assessment strategies for instruction.
33. Use assessment information in making instructional decisions and planning individual student programs.
34. Evaluate the results of instruction.
35. Evaluate readiness for integration into various program placements.

IV. Instructional Content and Practice

Knowledge

36. Differing learning styles of students and how to adapt teaching to these styles.
37. Demands of various learning environments (e.g., individualized instruction in general education classes).
38. Curricula for the development of motor, cognitive, academic, social, language, affective, and functional life skills for individuals with exceptional learning needs.
39. Instructional and remedial methods, techniques, and curriculum materials.
40. Techniques for modifying instructional methods and materials.
41. Life skills instruction relevant to independent, community, and personal living and employment.
42. Diversity and dynamics of families, schools, and communities as related to effective instruction for individuals with exceptional learning needs.

Skills

43. Interpret and use assessment data for instructional planning.
44. Develop and/or select assessment measures and instructional programs and practices which respond to cultural, linguistic, and gender differences.
45. Develop comprehensive, longitudinal individualized student programs.
46. Choose and use appropriate technologies to accomplish instructional objectives and to integrate them appropriately into the instructional process.
47. Prepare appropriate lesson plans.
48. Involve the student in setting instructional goals and charting progress.
49. Conduct and use task analysis.
50. Select, adapt, and use instructional strategies and materials according to characteristics of learner.
51. Sequence, implement, and evaluate individual student learning objectives.
52. Integrate affective, social, and career/vocational skills with academic curricula.
53. Use strategies for facilitating maintenance and generalization of skills across learning environments.

BOX 12.5 (cont.)

54. Use instructional time properly.
55. Teach students to use thinking, problem-solving, and other cognitive strategies to meet their individual needs.
56. Choose and implement instructional techniques and strategies that promote successful transitions for persons with exceptional learning needs.
57. Establish and maintain rapport with learner.
58. Use verbal and nonverbal communication techniques.
59. Conduct self-evaluation of instruction.

V. Planning and Managing the Teaching and Learning Environment

Knowledge

60. Basic classroom management theories, methods, and techniques for students with exceptional learning needs.
61. Research based best practices for effective management of teaching and learning.
62. Ways in which technology can assist with planning and managing the teaching and learning environment.

Skills

63. Create a safe, positive, and supportive learning environment in which diversities are valued.
64. Use strategies and techniques for facilitating the functional integration of exceptional individuals in various settings.
65. Prepare and organize materials in order to implement daily lesson plans.
66. Incorporate evaluation, planning, and management procedures which match learner needs with the instructional environment.
67. Design a learning environment that encourages active participation by learners in a variety of individual and group learning activities.
68. Design, structure, and manage daily classroom routines, including transition time, effectively for students, other staff, and the general classroom.
69. Direct the activities of a classroom paraprofessional, aide, volunteer, or peer tutor.
70. Create an environment which encourages self-advocacy and increased independence.

VI. Managing Student Behavior and Social Interaction Skills

Knowledge

71. Applicable laws, rules and regulations, and procedural safeguards regarding the planning and implementation of management of student behaviors.

72. Ethical considerations inherent in classroom behavior management.
73. Teacher attitudes and behaviors that positively or negatively influence student behavior.
74. Social skills needed for educational and functional living environments and effective instruction in the development of social skills.
75. Strategies for crisis prevention/intervention.
76. Strategies for preparing students to live harmoniously and productively in a multiclass, multiethnic, multicultural, and multinational world.

Skills

77. Demonstrate a variety of effective behavior management techniques appropriate to the needs of exceptional individuals.
78. Implement the least intensive intervention consistent with the needs of the exceptional individual.
79. Modify the learning environment (schedule and physical arrangement) to manage inappropriate behaviors.
80. Identify realistic expectations for personal and social behavior in various settings.
81. Integrate social skills into the curriculum.
82. Use effective teaching procedures in social skills instruction.
83. Demonstrate procedures to increase student self-awareness, self-control, self-reliance, and self-esteem.
84. Prepare students to exhibit self-enhancing behavior in response to societal attitudes and actions.

VII. Communication and Collaborative Partnerships

Knowledge

85. Importance and benefits of communication and collaboration which promote interaction with students, parents, and school and community personnel.
86. Typical concerns of parents of individuals with exceptional learning needs and appropriate strategies to help parents deal with these concerns.
87. Developing individual student programs working in collaboration with team members.
88. Roles of students, parents, teachers, other school and community personnel in planning a student's individualized program.
89. Ethical practices for confidential communication to others about individuals with exceptional learning needs.

Skills

90. Use collaborative strategies in working with students, parents, and school and community personnel in various learning environments.

91. Communicate and consult with students, parents, teachers, and other school and community personnel.
92. Foster respectful and beneficial relationships between families and professionals.
93. Encourage and assist families to become active participants in the educational team.
94. Plan and conduct collaborative conferences with parents or primary care givers.
95. Collaborate with regular classroom teachers and other school and community personnel in integrating students into various learning environments.
96. Communicate with regular teachers, administrators, and other school personnel about characteristics and needs of students with specific exceptional learning needs.

VIII. Professionalism and Ethical Practices

Knowledge

97. One's own cultural biases and differences that affect one's teaching.
98. Importance of the teacher serving as a model for students.

Skills

99. Demonstrate commitment to developing the highest educational and quality of life potential of individuals with exceptional learning needs.
100. Demonstrate positive regard for the cultures, religion, gender, and sexuality of students.
101. Promote and maintain a high level of competence and integrity in the practice of the profession.
102. Exercise objective professional judgement in the practice of the profession.
103. Demonstrate proficiency in oral and written communication.
104. Engage in professional activities which may benefit exceptional individuals, their families and/or colleagues.
105. Comply with local, state, provincial, and federal monitoring and evaluation requirements.
106. Use of copyrighted educational materials in an ethical manner.
107. Practice within the CEC Code of Ethics and other standards and policies of the profession.

From "The CEC Common Core of Knowledge and Skills Essential for all Beginning Special Education Teachers," by W. W. Swan & B. Sirvas, *Teaching for Exceptional Children, 25*(1), 1992, pp. 16–20. Copyright © 1992 by The Council for Exceptional Children. Reprinted with permission.

their use of varied behavior management plans are essential and frequently used skills. Moreover, they rate the ability to develop collaborative relationships with regular educators and with parents as essential. Critical behavior management skills are ranked by these teachers, in order of importance, as follows:

1. Use a variety of nonaversive behavior management techniques (e.g., planned ignoring, proximity control).
2. Establish and maintain pupil attention and present reinforcement or correct pupil responses.
3. Develop and implement appropriate classroom rules and a means for enforcing these rules.
4. Develop and implement consistent classroom routines.
5. Use varied behavior management plans (e.g., behavior modification, life space interviews, logical and natural consequences) in a classroom setting.
6. Plan and implement a variety of crisis management procedures (e.g., time-out, physical intervention) to control or contain severe behavior.
7. Use various techniques (e.g., modeling, rehearsal, prompting, feedback, discussion, lecture) in isolation or in combination for providing appropriate instruction for students.
8. Develop and implement a positive reinforcement plan to change and maintain behavior.
9. Select target behaviors to be changed, and identify the critical variables affecting the target behavior.
10. Self-evaluate your own teaching and classroom management skills, and use the results constructively.

Although teachers might perceive these and other skills to be essential, they may also face organizational and system obstacles interfering with their use of or success with these skills. You may, for example, set clear and positive rules and consistently enforce the consequences of following, or not following, these rules. You may be in charge of your classroom, yet you maintain a focus on teaching appropriate social skills and behaviors as an ongoing and essential part of your total curriculum throughout the school day. The atmosphere in your classroom is positive and respectful of children and their feelings, and you treat each problem as an opportunity for teaching coping skills and responsibility. When a child seriously violates a rule, however, you might find that the principal removes the child from your class or suspends him or her without consulting you. You may feel that your control and authority in the classroom are undermined when you are not included in important decisions.

Given financial and legal constraints, criticisms from the media, and state and federal laws regulating schools, teachers often feel powerless. They may hope to be creative in their lessons; however, they are told they must use a certain curriculum with all children, that all children must achieve a certain level of performance by a particular time of the year, or that all children in a school must improve their performance on a standardized test. The school and school district atmosphere encourages control of students and control of teachers (McLaughlin, 1992). As a result, teachers often end up feeling confused. They have tremendous responsibilities but no real voice and no real power over what they may do in the classroom.

At the very heart of this role confusion is the question of whether or not teachers are truly professionals. Professionals share a well-defined body of knowledge, set of skills, and mode of inquiry that can be transmitted to those entering the profession. In addition, professionals govern both the criteria by which new members are admitted to the profession (i.e., licensing) and the standards according to which all members must perform. Teachers, then, might be seen as only quasiprofessionals. Although we have taken steps toward professionalization by adopting statements regarding our ethics and standards, such as the CEC Code of Ethics and Common Core of Knowledge and Skills, we still have no real control over how members are admitted to our profession. Teaching is governed by the law of supply and demand. When the need goes up for a particular type of teacher (e.g., a special education teacher for students with emotional and behavioral disorders), state departments of education and local school districts often relax the qualifications necessary to enter the classroom to fill vacant positions and meet state and federal regulations for pupil/teacher ratios. Thus, teachers and teacher educators lose control over who enters the profession.

In addition, as Skrtic maintains (Thousand, 1990), professions and bureaucracies do not mix well. Bureaucracies such as schools emphasize standardization. They are organized to provide the same services and programs over and over again to serve the majority of students as efficiently as possible. Teachers, particularly special educators, on the other hand, are taught to think individually to meet the needs of specific children in the classroom. When the work to be performed must be innovative, creative, and personalized for individuals (i.e., teaching diverse children in real classrooms), yet teachers and schools cannot control many of the requirements and mandates imposed on them (Hargreaves, 1995; Odden & Wohlstetter, 1955), confusion, frustration, and conflict may result as teachers clash with a bureaucratic system (Thousand, 1990).

In response to criticisms from the media and to address concerns raised in a series of reports from national committees (National Commission on Excellence in Education, 1983; National Governor's Association, 1986), schools have begun a wave of educational "reform," "restructuring," and "renewal" efforts. As a part of this reform, many large school districts are "decentralizing" and "empowering" teachers. That is, the control that has been largely based in a central office is being returned to the local schools and to the teachers in those schools. Through site-based management, reformers hope that schools will be able to make decisions that make sense for individual children and youth in the particular community served by the school (Glickman, 1992).

Teachers are slowly assuming greater power in making important decisions surrounding curriculum, assessment, scheduling, staffing, school goals, and the allocation of financial and other resources through participation on committees within their school. In addition to teachers, these committees are composed of other professionals, parents, leaders from local business and industry, and other

Professional responsibility includes attending workshops or conferences and participating in site-based decision-making teams.

community members. To participate on such a committee one must have excellent listening and communication skills and an ability to be honest about and open to new ideas and perspectives. According to Russell, Cooper, and Greenblatt (1992, p. 39), however, working with others to share decision making requires careful attention to several factors including the degree to which teachers do the following:

- ◆ Are involved in framing the vision, mission, and goals of the school
- ◆ Have adequate time, reduced teaching loads, waivers from contracts and regulations, and changed schedules to permit collegial work to occur
- ◆ Participate in determining the school program, curriculum goals, textbook selection, educational materials, and classroom pedagogy
- ◆ Participate in matters related to designing and implementing the school budget
- ◆ Can design and implement staff development activities that meet their own needs
- ◆ Are involved in managing the building, including its use, maintenance, and improvement
- ◆ Share in setting standards for their own performance and for student performance and discipline

As a teacher, then, you must be prepared to behave ethically, to use those practices that you know to be successful, and to participate fully as a member of a school-based team. You will have a responsibility not only to your students and your profession but also to all students and colleagues in your school. Your task will be to share information and share in the decision-making process so that each student with emotional and behavioral problems can participate in daily school life with his or her peers, as fully as is possible. As Eleanor Guetzloe (1993) recently and eloquently remarked, "We have considerable knowledge of things that work. We have time-honored traditions of meeting children's basic needs; working with parents, community agencies, and treatment providers; providing a full continuum of educational placements; providing a safe and positive school environment; modifying curriculum to meet individual needs; providing appropriate structure and rewards; teaching academic and social skills; documenting results; and sharing information with our colleagues. We cannot claim to be doing everything right with every child in every setting, but . . . we have the knowledge and skills necessary to provide appropriate programs for the children for whom we accept responsibility. Our restructuring movement should be in the direction of remembering, recalling, reviewing, refining, renegotiating, repossessing, and rebuilding our programs" (p. 305).

Obviously, the decade of the 1990s is an exciting and challenging time to assume the responsibility of teaching. As some professionals advocate for full inclusion of all students in the regular classroom regardless of the severity of their needs (Stainback & Stainback, 1990; 1992), others like Guetzloe (1993) and Kauffman (1993) assert that we must not forget the lessons learned in our professional past, when the education of students with disabilities was not regulated by a law mandating a full continuum of services and a free, appropriate public education. In the coming years, you will face difficult questions regarding how best to serve your students as your school faces financial cutbacks, restructuring, and reform. To demonstrate professional responsibility in your teaching, then, you must do the following:

◆ Behave in accordance with the Code of Ethics of the Council for Exceptional Children.
◆ Use what are known to be "best" practices in classrooms for children and youth with emotional and behavioral disorders.
◆ Collect data, and base decisions on these data to ensure that interventions are effective for individual students.
◆ Choose the most positive behavior change strategies possible so that students have the opportunity to learn appropriate behavior, social and problem-solving skills, and responsibility for themselves.
◆ Advocate for your students within your school and your community, and share information about your program.
◆ Collaborate with parents, colleagues, and other professionals to form multidimensional solutions to the problems students face.
◆ Seek out support and new ideas, and renew and refresh yourself through taking classes or through membership and participation in professional associations and conferences.
◆ Reflect daily about your expectations, attitudes, and behaviors and how these might affect the students in your classroom.

Developing a Personal Philosophy

I began this text by stating that how you view students and their behavior profoundly affects how you go about responding to student misbehavior in your classroom. We examined the importance of your expectations and attitudes and how these influence your decisions and interactions with students in your classroom. We described the interrelated nature of your behavior toward the student and the student's behavior toward you. We also explored the impact of those expectations and attitudes held by a student's peers, parents, teachers, and other professionals on your behavior, as well as those of your students, and the reciprocal influence of your behavior on these individuals. We discussed many ways to respect student feelings, improve behaviors and social skills, teach responsibility, and collaborate with parents and other professionals. We reflected on legal and ethical concerns arising from the decisions you make in the classroom, and we outlined your professional and personal responsibilities as a teacher.

Needless to say, making decisions about behavior in the classroom is a complex matter. You must, however, have some notion regarding how you will organize your classroom, what behaviors you will expect, what behaviors you can and cannot tolerate, and how you will respond to those behaviors that you find unacceptable. *By articulating your beliefs, you will be better able to behave proactively to foster appropriate student behavior and to react consistently when students exhibit inappropriate behavior.* (See Box 12.6, pp. 402–403, for one teacher's developing beliefs about behavior management in her special education classroom.) You will also be better prepared to determine whether your beliefs are or are not in congruence with those of important others who interact with your students.

To help you begin to phrase your personal philosophy regarding student behavior, you may wish to answer the questions listed in Box 12.7 (p. 404). Although at first glance these questions appear to be relatively easy to answer, you will find, upon reflection, that clearly articulating your ideas may be difficult. Keep in mind that your answers to these questions represent simply a starting point for the development of your philosophy. The dilemmas and complexities you will face in your teaching career will demand that you continually examine multiple perspectives regarding how children learn and behave and how teachers teach (Phelan & McLaughlin, 1995). Moreover, professionals must continue, as they have only recently begun, to work across arbitrary philosophical boundaries to find effective interventions for students (Wood, 1995). Returning to these questions continually throughout your teaching career, then, may help you adjust your philosophy as your needs and those of your students and others around them change.

The professional challenges and responsibilities you will face as a teacher of students with emotional and behavioral disorders are tremendous. Yet, the joy and pride in your professional accomplishments and in the individual growth of your students can be extremely rewarding. The bottom line is that the learning and behavior of your students will be dramatically affected by your actions and decisions as a teacher. I hope you will enjoy your professional journey and that you will be successful in leading your students to a better quality of life!

BOX 12.6 **Teacher Feature: Jane's Story**

The following account describes one teacher's development of her personal philosophy for managing the behavior of students. Jane Woolard has taught students with emotional/behavioral disorders and learning disabilities for four years. She is about to begin her fifth year as a special education teacher in Virginia:

Since before day one of my teaching career, I have been searching for strategies to help me be more effective in managing students whose behavior is challenging. I have selected and/or designed and implemented intervention strategies that I hoped would change both academic and social behaviors. I have frequently formed a partnership with another teacher, school administrator, guidance counselor, secretary, and/or janitor to help increase positive behavior of my students and promote generalization of the behavior.

My very first class was a self-contained class for seriously emotionally disturbed students in grades five through eight. As a psychology major, I came to the classroom with knowledge of various theories and counseling practices. I used an "eclectic" approach to behavior management, pulling whatever I could from that knowledge base and incorporating counseling and behavior strategies based on the works of Skinner, Bandura, Rogers, Ellis, and others. When possible, I used the techniques of the supportive model (e.g., active-reflective listening, questioning, paraphrasing). However, I quickly learned that while those skills were useful and therapeutic and helped build rapport and closeness, they did not provide the structure, teaching, and limit setting my students needed. I decided to incorporate strategies from both the directive model and the responsibility model. We had a level system and a token economy. I did a baseline for target behaviors and my students graphed weekly behavior results on a bulletin board to keep track of progress. We had a class meeting at the end of each day and problem-solving meetings whenever a situation arose that needed to be dealt with immediately. I taught the class the ABC model of rational emotive thinking. We worked on monitoring and changing our self-talk, and practiced self-monitoring and self-recording many behaviors.

My second year I again taught E/BD students, this time from grades four through eight, as well as sixth grade students with learning disabilities. That year, I used basically the same strategies as the year before. However, I did drop the level system, although I continued to use a token economy. I had had nonviolent crisis intervention training over the summer so I added those skills to my repertoire. They worked well when I was called on to use them. That year I also introduced social skills into our daily schedule. These strategies were helpful and we experienced some success. However, given that I had 14 preparations each night and a very difficult mix of children I never felt really on top of either academics or behavior.

My third and fourth years I taught mainly sixth grade students with learning disabilities. My one E/BD student and several of the LD students had major behavior problems. The LD students were what I would describe as "socially maladjusted." The behavior of these students was very similar to my former ED students.

The third and fourth years I made a few changes in my behavior management program. I decreased the use of primary reinforcers and increased the use of secondary reinforcers. The third year was my first year without an aide and I had 15 students in each of my classes. It was difficult to feel competent and consistent. . . . I have just finished my fourth year. I used the same strategies this year, but I was much more relaxed and comfortable with them. I gave lots of positive reinforcement and I was much more consistent in all my practices than in past years. I was able to build close relationships with most of my students. They received a lot more personal attention from me and I was able to help several of them gain some much-needed self-control.

My goal for the coming school year is to develop a positive, warm, inviting classroom in which all of my students will feel accepted and encouraged, receive personal attention, develop realistic expectations for themselves, take increasing responsibility for their behavior, and be successful in meeting their academic and behavioral goals and objectives. . . . I believe that the best way to handle discipline problems is to prevent them from occurring in the first place. Establishing and maintaining a warm, positive atmosphere and classroom rules and routines, paying close attention to the arrangement of classroom furniture and equipment, using my time effectively, developing assignments that are related to the interests of students, and adopting a friendly professional manner with students can help reduce the number of behavioral problems.

I also believe different children need different strategies and interventions to find success in the classroom. What works for one student won't work for another. What works for a student at a given time, like the start of the year, will not always work at other times. The teacher must know her students in order to choose the appropriate strategy for that child. She must have a broad repertoire of possibilities to choose from. I have also learned that I must own my classroom management style. I cannot adopt someone else's methods and use them successfully if I am not comfortable with them. That comfort comes from a good fit with my own personality and repeated practice of the skills. I am comfortable with the supportive model, but at times it's too "touchy-feely" for me. I have to use directive strategies because that's what works best for some of my students, but I get tired of rules and consequences, rewards and punishers. I am most comfortable with the responsibility model because it provides the structure and opportunities for real teaching that I feel are most important in the classroom. But it isn't for all of my students. . . . In looking back on the past four years, I sometimes wonder if the successes I've had don't really have more to do with simple things like the love and concern I have for my kids and the way we have learned to enjoy being together.

Adapted from Woolard, J. (1995). The fifth year: A history of and plan for discipline in the classroom. Unpublished manuscript, Longwood College, Farmville, VA. Adapted by permission.

BOX 12.7 Developing a Personal Philosophy Regarding Students and Behavior

Questions for Reflection:

- ◆ What behaviors bother me and why?
- ◆ How much control do I need in the classroom, and how much control is expected of me by others? Do I view control as power over students or as teaching students how to assume responsibility for themselves?
- ◆ What are my expectations for appropriate classroom behavior? Can I state exactly how I would like students to behave in my classroom?
- ◆ Are my expectations reasonable, and can I clearly convey my expectations to my students, their parents, and my colleagues?
- ◆ Are my expectations based on my cultural background or biased against those from cultures or groups different from my own?
- ◆ Which conceptual models for explaining student behavior do I accept? Which interventions from each conceptual model do I feel comfortable with, and which ones am I trained to implement?

Articulating Your Personal Philosophy:

1. List the behaviors you find bothersome. Eliminate those that are minor annoyances and those for which you cannot easily give a reason as to why they bother you.
2. Write a sentence stating the level of control you find necessary to be comfortable in your personal and professional life. Indicate in your statement whether you need a high, moderate, or low level of control (i.e., whether you see control as your responsibility, as a shared responsibility with students, or as the students' responsibility).
3. Describe the behaviors you expect of students in your classroom. Be sure you can specify exactly what students who behave appropriately are doing. Eliminate any behavioral expectations for which you cannot convey a clear justification.
4. List the conceptual models for explaining student behavior which you can accept and list the interventions which you feel comfortable implementing.
5. Based on your responses to items 1 through 4, write a paragraph stating your philosophy regarding how you will manage student behavior in your classroom. Include the following sentence stems in your paragraph:

- ◆ Students in my classroom will demonstrate the following behaviors:
- ◆ These behaviors are important because . . . .
- ◆ When students engage in these behaviors, I plan to . . . .
- ◆ When students engage in inappropriate behaviors, I plan to . . . .
- ◆ Behavioral control in my classroom is best described as . . . because . . . .

6. Examine your philosophy statement carefully. Is it consistent with professionally responsible practice?
7. Reexamine your philosophy statement at least once every month. Are you behaving consistently according to your statement? Do you need to revise any part of your philosophy statement?

Summary

Teachers face many stressors in the classroom and school environment. Teachers of students with emotional and behavioral disorders face higher levels of occupational stress than their colleagues. Although teachers cannot control every source of stress in their classroom or school, they can develop healthy strategies for coping with daily stress. To prevent stress and burnout, teachers must ensure that they are using effective practices. When teachers sense that they are effective in the classroom, they experience increased self-efficacy, greater persistence, and reduced levels of stress.

Teachers have the professional responsibility to abide by the code of ethics adopted by the Council for Exceptional Children. In addition, teachers must demonstrate those competencies listed in the Common Core of Essential Knowledge and Skills Essential for All Beginning Special Education Teachers. Although these may not be the only essential skills for effective teaching of students with emotional and behavioral disorders, they represent the minimum "best practices" to be demonstrated by special educators.

As schools restructure and reform, teachers are increasingly participating on site-based management committees. Teachers of students with emotional and behavioral problems must collaborate fully as members of these school-based teams to ensure that the needs of their students are communicated clearly and are being adequately met.

Making decisions about students and their behavior is a complex process. Teachers must engage in careful daily self-reflection to examine their teaching practices and the effects of their decisions and actions on others. In addition, teachers must continually evaluate and revise their personal philosophy regarding the management of student behavior. One's personal philosophy is simply a starting point for growth and development in a professional teaching career.

Application Exercises

1. Compare the experiences of the teacher in Box 12.1 with those of the teacher in Box 12.3. What stressors are similar for both teachers? What stressors are different? How does the level of support from administrators and colleagues differ for these two teachers? How does this difference contribute to decreased stress for the teacher in Box 12.3? What healthy means for coping with stress are used by the teacher in Box 12.3?

2. Interview a teacher of children with emotional and behavioral disorders at any grade level in your local school district. What are the stressors perceived by this teacher (e.g., disruptive student behavior, gang activity, paperwork, parents, insufficient resources, lack of support from administrators or colleagues)? Share these with your classmates. Look for similarities among teachers, and generate a list of the four or five biggest stressors among teachers.

3. Ask the teacher you interviewed in question 2 to tell you what healthy strategies he or she uses for coping with stress. Discuss these with your classmates, and generate a list of ways to handle stress in the classroom (e.g., time management tips).

4. Examine the CEC Common Core of Knowledge and Skills for Beginning Special Education Teachers. Share this list of competencies with a practicing teacher. Which skills does this teacher perceive to be most important?
5. Interview a teacher of students with behavioral problems or invite this teacher to come speak to your class. How does the overall organization and structure of his or her school help or hinder performance in the classroom? How does this teacher participate in educational reform efforts, if any, in his or her school district?
6. Make a list of the stressors in your daily life. Develop a strategy for coping with these stressors (e.g. keep a "to do today" list of prioritized items, organize your time, learn to say "no," etc.), and keep a personal journal of your efforts.
7. Describe your personal philosophy regarding students and their behavior to your classmates. How is your philosophy similar to or different from those developed by your colleagues? How might differing philosophies impact your ability to collaborate with one another successfully in your future careers?

References

Algozzine, B., Henrickson, J. M., Gable, R. A., & White, R. (1993). Caseloads of teachers of students with behavioral disorders. *Behavioral Disorders*, *18*(2), 103–109.

Allinder, R. M. (1993). I think I can, I think I can: The effect of self-efficacy on teacher effectiveness. *Beyond Behavior*, *4*(2), 29.

Ashton, P. A., & Webb, R. B. (1986). *Making a difference: Teachers' sense of efficacy and student achievement.* New York: Longman.

Bandura, A. (1982). Self-efficacy mechanism in human agency. *American Psychologist*, *37*(2), 122–147.

Best, G. A. (1990). Survival hints for the new teacher. *Teaching Exceptional Children*, *23*(1), 54–55.

Brownell, M. T., & Smith, S. W. (1992). Attrition/retention of special education teachers: Critique of current research and recommendations for retention efforts. *Teacher Education and Special Education*, *15*(4), 229–248.

Bullock, L. M., Ellis, L. L., & Wilson, M. J. (1994). Knowledge/skills needed by teachers who work with students with severe emotional/behavioral disorders: A revisitation. *Behavioral Disorders*, *19*(2), 108–125.

Cherniss, C. (1988). Observed supervisory behavior and teacher burnout in special education. *Exceptional Children*, *54*(5), 449–454.

Cohen, S. B., & Hart-Hester, S. (1987). Time management strategies. *Teaching Exceptional Children*, *20*, 56–57.

Council for Exceptional Children. (1989). *Fourteen tips to help special educators deal with stress* (ERIC Digest #E467). Reston, VA: The Council for Exceptional Children.

Cross, L. H., & Billingsley, B. S. (1994). Testing a model of special educators' intent to stay in teaching. *Exceptional Children*, *60*(5), 411–421.

Frank, A. R., & McKenzie, R. (1993). The development of burnout among special educators. *Teacher Education and Special Education*, *16*(2), 161–170.

Gable, R. A., Hendrickson, J. M., Young, C. C., & Shokoohi-Yekta, M. (1992). Preservice preparation and classroom practices of teachers of students with emotional/behavioral disorders. *Behavioral Disorders*, *17*(2), 126–134.

George, N. L., George, M. P., Gersten, R., & Grosenick, J. K. (1995). To leave or to stay? An exploratory study of teachers of students with emotional and behavioral disorders. *Remedial and Special Education*, *16*(4), 227–236.

Glickman, C. D. (1992). The essence of school renewal: The prose has begun. *Educational Leadership, 50*(1), 24–27.

Greer, J. G., & Greer, B. B. (1992). Stopping burnout before it starts: Prevention measures at the preservice level. *Teacher Education and Special Education, 15*(3), 168–174.

Grosenick, J. K., George, M. P., & George, N. L. (1987). A profile of school programs for the behaviorally disordered: Twenty years after Morse, Cutler, and Fink. *Behavioral Disorders, 12*(3), 159–168.

Guetzloe, E. C. (1993). The special education initiative: Responding to changing problems, populations, and paradigms. *Behavioral Disorders, 18*(4), 303–307.

Hargreaves, A. (1995). Renewal in the age of paradox. *Educational Leadership, 52*(7), 14–19.

Kaplan, J. S. (1991). *Beyond behavior modification: A cognitive-behavioral approach to behavior management in the schools* (2nd ed.). Austin, TX: Pro-Ed.

Kauffman, J. M. (1993). How we might achieve the radical reform of special education. *Exceptional Children, 60*, 6–16.

Kauffman, J. M., & Wong, K. L. H. (1991). Effective teachers of students with behavioral disorders: Are generic teaching skills enough? *Behavioral Disorders, 16*(3), 225–237.

Littrell, P. C., Billingsley, B. S., & Cross, L. H. (1994). The effects of principal support on special and general educators' stress, job satisfaction, school commitment, health, and intent to stay in teaching. *Remedial and Special Education, 15*(5), 297–310.

McDaniel, E. A., & DiBella-McCarthy, H. (1989). Enhancing teacher efficacy in special education. *Teaching Exceptional Children, 21*(4), 34–38.

McIntyre, T., & Stefanides, M. (1993). Do I really want to teach these kids? An analysis of one teacher's first year with behavior disordered adolescents. *Beyond Behavior, 5*(1), 16–23.

McLaughlin, M. W. (1992). How district communities do and do not foster teacher pride. *Educational Leadership, 50*(1), 33–35.

McManus, M. E., & Kauffman, J. M. (1991). Working conditions of teachers of students with behavioral disorders: A national survey. *Behavioral Disorders, 16*(4), 247–259.

Miller, C. (1979). *Dealing with stress: A challenge for educators.* Bloomington, IN: Phi Delta Kappa.

Mueller, F. (1993). Teaching and stress: A personal view. *Beyond Behavior, 5*(1), 3.

National Commission on Excellence in Education. (1983). *A nation at risk: The imperative for educational reform.* Washington, DC: U.S. Government Printing Office.

National Governors' Association. (1986). *Time for results.* Washington, DC: Author.

Odden, E. R. (1995). Making school-based management work. *Educational Leadership, 52*(5), 32–36.

Phelan, A. M., & McLaughlin, H. J. (1995). Educational discourses, the nature of the child, and the practice of new teachers. *Journal of Teacher Education, 46*(3), 165–174.

Pullis, M. (1992). An analysis of the occupational stress of teachers of the behaviorally disordered: Sources, effects, and strategies for coping. *Behavioral Disorders, 17*(3), 191–201.

Raschke, D., Dedrick, C., & DeVries, A. (1988). Coping with stress: The special educator's perspective. *Teaching Exceptional Children, 21*(1), 10–14.

Rosenberg, M. S., O'Shea, L., & O'Shea, D. J. (1991). *Student teacher to master teacher.* New York: Macmillan.

Ruhl, K. L., & Hughes, C. A. (1985). The nature and extent of aggression in special education settings serving behaviorally disordered students. *Behavioral Disorders, 10*(2), 95–104.

Russell, J. J., Cooper, B. S., & Greenblatt, R. B. (1992). How do you measure shared decision making? *Educational Leadership, 50*(1), 39–40.

Schmid, K. D., Schatz, C. J., Walter, M. B., Shidla, M. C., Leone, P. E., & Trickett, E. J. (1990). Providing help: Characteristics and correlates of stress, burnout, and accomplishment across three groups of teachers. In R. B. Rutherford, & S. A. DiGangi (Eds.),

Severe behavior disorders of children and youth, Volume 13 (pp. 115–127). Reston, VA: Council for Children with Behavioral Disorders.

Selye, H. (1984). *The stress of life* (Rev. Ed.). New York: McGraw-Hill.

Singer, J. D. (1992). Are special educators' career paths special? Results from a 13-year longitudinal study. *Exceptional Children, 59*(3), 262–279.

Singer, J. D. (1993). Once is not enough: Former special educators who return to teaching. *Exceptional Children, 60*(1), 58–72.

Stainback, S., & Stainback, W. (1992). *Curriculum considerations in inclusive classrooms: Facilitating learning for all students.* Baltimore, MD: Brookes.

Stainback, W., & Stainback, S. (1990). A rationale for integration and restructuring: A synopsis. In J. W. Lloyd, A. C. Repp, & N. N. Singh (Eds.), *The regular education initiative: Alternative perspectives on concepts, issues, and models* (pp. 225–239). Sycamore, IL: Sycamore Press.

Swan, W. W., & Sirvis, B. (1992). The CEC Common Core of Knowledge and Skills Essential for All Beginning Special Education Teachers. *Teaching Exceptional Children, 25*(1), 16–20.

The Peacock Hill Working Group (1991). Problems and promises in special education and related services for children and youth with emotional or behavioral disorders. *Behavioral Disorders, 16*(4), 299–313.

Thousand, J. S. (1990). Organizational perspectives on teacher education and renewal: A conversation with Tom Skrtic. *Teacher Education and Special Education, 13*(1), 30–35.

Webber, J., & Coleman, M. (1988). Using rational-emotive therapy to prevent classroom problems. *Teaching Exceptional Children, 21*(1), 32–35.

Wells, P. L. (1993). Optimism: Another factor in the success equation. *Beyond Behavior, 4*(2), 25–29.

Wood, F. H. (1995). Positive responses to student resistance to programs of behavior change. *Reclaiming Children and Youth: Journal of Emotional and Behavioral Problems, 4*(1), 30–33.

Woolard, J. (1995). *The fifth year: A history of and plan for discipline in the classroom.* Unpublished manuscript, Longwood College, Farmville, Virginia.

Zabel, R. H., Boomer, L. W., & King, T. R. (1984). A model of stress and burnout among teachers of behaviorally disordered students. *Behavioral Disorders, 9*(3), 215–221.

Zabel, R. H., & Zabel, M. K. (1982). Factors in burnout among teachers of exceptional children. *Exceptional Children, 49*(3), 261–263.

ORGANIZATIONS AND RESOURCES

Organizations and Resources by Topic

AIDS/HIV

CEC National AIDS Clearinghouse
P.O. Box 6003
Rockville, MD 20849-6003
(800)458-5231

CDC National AIDS Hotline
(800)342-AIDS (English Service) 24 hours
(800)344-7432 (Spanish Service) 7 days 8 AM-2 AM
(800)243-7889 (TTY/TDD Service) M-F, 10 AM-10 PM

CDC National Sexually Transmitted Disease Hotline
(800)227-8922

National Education Association
1201 16th St. N.W.
Washington, DC 20036
(202)833-4000

Sex Information and Education Council of the U.S. (SIECUS)
130 West 42nd Street, Suite 350
New York, NY 10036
(212)819-9770

Alcohol and Other Substance Abuse

Al-Anon/Alateen
Box 862
Midtown Station
New York, NY 10018-0862
(800)356-9996

Children of Alcoholics Foundation
P.O. Box 4185
Grand Central Station
New York, NY 10163-4185
(800)359-COAF

National Association for Children of Alcoholics
11426 Rockville Pike, Suite 100
Rockville, MD 20852
(301)468-0985
(301)468-0987(FAX)
*This association has several curriculum packages available including:

The General Education Package with a video "Poor Jennifer She's Always Losing Her Hat." This comes with a teaching guide and lesson plans and a pamphlet entitled "It's Elementary: Meeting the Needs of High Risk Youth in the School Setting" as well as two audio cassettes, a comic book Alcoholism and Marvel comic book posters.

The Elementary School Package with a Resource Folder, posters, comic books and two booklets: "COAs Meeting the Needs of the Young COA in the School Setting" and "It's Elementary Meeting the Needs of High Risk Youth in the School Setting." These come with a guidebook for the elementary school principal, the teacher, and the school counselor.

National Association for Native American Children of Alcoholics
1402 3rd Avenue, Suite 1110
Seattle, WA 98101
(800)322-5601

National Black Alcoholism/Addictions Council
1629 K Street, NW Suite 802
Washington, D.C. 20006
(202)296-2696

National Clearinghouse for Alcohol and Drug Information
P.O. Box 2345
Rockville, MD 20852
(800)729-6686
(301)468-2600
(301)230-2867 TDD
*Has available the "Discovery Kit, Positive Connections for Kids" designed for use with 10 to 15 year olds. Includes video and audio cassettes, books, posters, activity work sheets, and leader support materials *(free)*.

National Council on Alcoholism & Drug Dependence Hopeline
12 West 21st Street
New York, NY 10010
(800)NCA-CALL

National Drug Abuse Treatment Hotline
(800)662-4357 (English Service)
(800)662-YUDA (Spanish Service)
(800)288-0427 (TTY/TDD Service)

Child Abuse and Neglect

Action for Child Protection
4724 C Park Road
Charlotte, NC 28209
(704)529-1080 (professional and institutional inquiries only)

American Academy of Pediatrics
Publications Department
141 Northwest Point Boulevard
P.O. 927
Elk Grove Village, IL 60007
(800)433-9016

American Bar Association Center on Children and the Law
740 15th St. N.W. 9th Floor
Washington, DC 20005-1109
(202)662-1720 (professionals and institutional inquiries only)

American Humane Association
American Association for Protecting Children
63 Iverness Drive East
Englewood, CO 80112-5117
(800)227-5242

American Public Welfare Association
810 First Street, N.E.
Suite 500
Washington, DC 20002-4267
(202)682-0100

C. Henry Kempe Center for Prevention and Treatment of Child Abuse and Neglect
1205 Oneida Street
Denver, CO 80220
(303)321-3963

Child Welfare League of America
440 First Street, N.W.
Suite 310
Washington, DC 20001
(202)638-2952 (professional and institutional inquiries only)

Childhelp USA
6463 Independence Avenue
Woodland Hills, CA 91367
Hotline: (800)4-A-CHILD or (800)422-4453

Committee for Children
172 20th Avenue
Seattle, WA 98122
(206)322-5050
(800)634-4449

National Association of Social Workers
750 1st St. NE.
Washington, DC 20002
(202)408-8600 (professional and institutional inquiries only)

National Association of State VOCAL Organizations (NASVO)
P.O. Box 1314
Orangeville, CA 95662
(919)863-7470
(800)745-8778

National Center for Child Abuse and Neglect
Clearinghouse on Child Abuse and Neglect Information
P.O. Box 1182
Washington, DC 20013
(800)394-3366
(703)385-7565

National Center for Missing and Exploited Children
2101 Wilson Boulevard
Suite 550
Arlington, VA 22201
(800)843-5678 (to report cases and for general information)

National Committee for Prevention of Child Abuse
332 South Michigan Avenue, Suite 1600
Chicago, IL 60604-4357
(312)663-3520
(312)939-8962 (FAX)

National Council of Juvenile and Family Court Judges
1041 N. Virginia St. 3rd Floor
Reno, NV 89507
(702)784-6012 (8 AM-5 PM, M–F)
*Has available informational packets and materials:
   Keeping Families Together: Facts on Family Preservation Services (1987)
   Making Reasonable Efforts: Steps for Keeping Families Together (1987)
   Reasonable Efforts Training Video Notebook (1991)

National Council on Child Abuse and Family Violence
1155 Connecticut Avenue, N.W., Suite 400
Washington, DC 20036
(800)222-2000
(800)422-4453, information and referral
(800)537-2238, spouse abuse
(800)879-6682, elder abuse
(800)221-2681, counseling

National Crime Prevention Council
1700 K Street, N.W., 2nd Floor
Washington, DC 20006-3817
(202)466-6272

National Network of Runaway and Youth Services
1319 F St. N.W., Suite 401
Washington, DC 20004
(202)783-7949
(202)783-7955 (FAX)
(800)878-2437, AIDS hotline for youth serving agencies

National Organization for Victim Assistance
1757 Park Road, N.W.
Washington, DC 20010
(202)232-6682

National Resource Center on Child Sexual Abuse Information Service
2204 Whitesburg Drive, Suite 200
Huntsville, AL 35801
(205)533-KIDS
(800)KIDS-006

National Runaway Switchboard Metro-Help, Inc.
3080 North Lincoln
Chicago, IL 60657
(312)880-9860 (business)
(800)621-4000 (also serves as a National Youth Suicide Hotline)

Parents Anonymous
675 West Foothill Blvd. Suite 220
Claremont, CA 91711
(909)621-6184

Parents United/Daughters and Sons United/Adults Molested As Children United
232 East Gish Road
San Jose, CA 95112
(408)453-7616
(408)279-1957 24-Hour Hotline

Victims of Child Abuse Laws (VOCAL)
12 North Broadway, Suite 133
Santa Ana, CA 92701
(714)558-0200 (10 AM–5:30 PM, M–F)

Depression and Suicide

American Academy of Child and Adolescent Psychiatry
Public Information Office
3615 Wisconsin Avenue, N.W.
Washington, DC 20016
(202)966-7300

American Association of Suicidology
4201 Connecticut Ave. Suite 310
Washington, DC 20008
(202)237-2280

National Depressive and Manic Depressive Association
730 North Franklin, Suite 501
Chicago, IL 60610
(312)642-0049
(312)908-8100 (crisis hotline)

National Institute of Mental Health
5600 Fishers Lane
Rockville, MD 20857
(301)443-4513

Youth Suicide National Center (YSNC)
445 Virginia Ave.
San Manteo, CA 94402
(415)342-5755

Youth Suicide Prevention (YSP)
65 Essex Rd.
Chestnut Hill, MA 02167
(617)738-0700

Gangs, Cults, and Violence

Center to Prevent Handgun Violence
1225 I Street, NW., Suite 1100
Washington, DC 20005
(202)298-8008

Chicago Police Department Bureau of Community Services
Preventive Programs
1121 South State Street
Chicago, IL 60605
(312)744-5490

Cult Awareness Network
2421 West Pratt Boulevard, Suite 1173
Chicago, IL 60645
(312)267-7777

Gang Awareness Resource Program
Substance Abuse and Narcotics Education
Los Angeles County Sheriff's Office
11515 S. Colima Road
Whittier, CA 90604
(310)946-SANE

National School Safety Center
4165 Thousand Oaks Boulevard, Suite 290
Westlake Village, CA 91362
(805)373-9977
(805)373-9277 (FAX)

Task Force on Violent Crime
614 Superior Avenue West, Suite 300
Cleveland, OH 44113-1306
(216)523-1128

The International Cult Education Program
P.O. Box 1232 Gracie Station
New York, NY 10028
(212)533-5420
(212)533-0538 (FAX)

The Paramount Plan: Alternatives to Gang Membership
16400 Colorado Avenue
Paramount, CA 90723
(310)220-2140
(310)630-2713 (FAX)

The Prepare Curriculum (edited by Arnold Goldstein)
Research Press
2612 North Mattis Avenue
Champaign, IL 61821
(217)352-3273

Homelessness

Children's Defense Fund
25 E Street, N.W.
Washington, DC 20001
(202)628-8787

Interagency Council on the Homeless
451 Seventh Street, SW., Room 7274
Washington, DC 20410
(202)708-1480

Metro-Help/National Runaway Switchboard
3080 N. Lincoln
Chicago, IL 60657
(312)880-9860
(800)621-4000

National Coalition for the Homeless
1621 K Street, N.W. Suite 1004
Washington, DC 20006
(202)775-1322
(202)775-1372 (recorded hotline)

National Network of Runaway and Youth Services, Inc.
1319 F Street, N.W. Suite 401
Washington, DC 20004
(202)783-7949

National Volunteer Clearinghouse for the Homeless
425 2nd Street, N.W.
Washington, DC 20001
(202)393-1909

U.S. Department of Education
Education of Homeless Children and Youth
400 Maryland Avenue, S.W.
Washington, DC 20202
(202)401-1692

Organizations and Resources: General

American Association on Mental Retardation
444 N. Capitol Street, N.W., Suite 846
Washington, DC 20001
(202)387-1968

American Guidance Service
4210 Woodland Road #1279
Circle Pines, MN 55014
(800)328-2560

American Psychological Association
750 1st. Street, N.E.
Washington, DC 20002-4242
(202)336-5500

Association for Retarded Citizens
500 E. Border Street
Arlington, TX 76010
(800)433-5255

Association for Supervision and Curriculum Development
1250 N. Pitt Street
Alexandria, VA 22314
(703)549-9110

Association of Birth Defect Children (ABDC)
Orlando Executive Park
5400 Diplomat Circle, Suite 270
Orlando, FL 32810
(407)629-1466

Bruner/Mazel Publishers
19 Union Square West
New York, NY 10003
(800)825-3089

Center for Applied Linguistics (bilingual education)
1118 22nd Street, N.W.
Washington, DC 20037
(202)429-9292

Center for Applied Psychology, Inc.
Childswork/Childsplay
P.O. Box 61586
King of Prussia, PA 19406
(800)962-1141
(610)277-4546 (FAX)

Childrens' Defense Fund
25 E Street, N.W.
Washington, DC 20001
(202)628-8787

Children with Attention Deficit Disorders (CHADD)
499 70th Avenue, N.W., Suite 109
Plantation, FL 33317
(305)587-3700

Clearinghouse on Disability Information
Office of Special Education and Rehabilitative Services
U.S. Department of Education
Switzer Building, Room 3132
Washington, D.C. 20202-2524
(202)205-8241

Council for Exceptional Children (and divisions including: Council for Children with
    Behavior Disorders, Division of Learning Disabilities, and Mental Retardation Division)
1920 Association Drive
Reston, VA 22091
(703)620-3660

Council for Learning Disabilities
P.O. Box 40303
Overland Park, KS 66204
(913)492-8755

Father Flanagan's Boy's Home
Boys Town, Nebraska 68010
(402)498-1596
Boys's Town Hotline (800)448-3000

Federation for Students with Special Needs
95 Berkely, Suite 104
Boston, MA 02116
(617)482-2915

Institute for Control Theory, Reality Therapy, and Quality Management,
  Dr. William Glasser
7301 Medical Center Drive, Suite 104
Canoga Park, CA 91307-1904
(818)700-8000

Institute for Psychoeducational Training, Dr. Nicholas Long
226 Landis Road
Hagerstown, MD 21740
(301)733-2751

Interstate Migrant Education Council
707 17th Street, Suite 2700
Denver, CO 80202-3427
(303)299-3680

Judge David L. Brazelton Center for Mental Health Law
1101 15th Street, N.W., Suite 1212
Washington, DC 20005
(202)467-5730

Learning Disabilities Association of America
4156 Library Road
Pittsburgh, PA 15234
(412)341-1515

National Association for Bilingual Education
Room 407, 1201 16th Street, NW
Washington, DC 20036
(202)822-7870

National Association for the Education of Young Children
1834 Connecticut Avenue, NW
Washington, DC 20009
(202)232-8777
(800)424-2460

National Association of Protection and Advocacy Systems
900 Second Street, N.E., Suite 211
Washington, DC 20002
(202)408-9514

National Center for Learning Disabilities
381 Park Avenue South, Suite 1420
New York, NY 10016
(212)545-7510

National Crisis Prevention Institute
3313-K North 124th Street
Brookfield, WI 53005
(800)558-8976

National Down Syndrome Society
666 Broadway
New York, NY 10012
(800)221-4602

National Education Association
1210 16th Street, N.W.
Washington, DC 20036
(202)833-4000

National Educational Service
1610 W. 3rd Street
P.O. Box 8
Bloomington, IN 47402
(800)733-6786

National Information Center for Children and Youth with Disabilities (NICHCY)
P.O. Box 1492
Washington, D.C. 20013-1492
(800)695-0285

National Legal Resource Center for Child Advocacy
1800 M Street NW
Washington, DC 20036
(202)331-2250

National Mental Health Association
Federation of Families for Children's Mental Health
1021 Prince Street
Alexandria, VA 22314-2971
(703)684-7710

Orton Dyslexia Society
Chester Bldg., Suite 382
8600 LaSalle Rd.
Baltimore, MD 21286-2044
(410)296-0232

Paperbacks for Educators
426 West Front Street
Washington, MO 63090
(800)227-2591
*Excellent books for bibliotherapy (see Chapter 6)

Parent Information Center
P.O. Box 1422
Concord, NH 03301
(603)224-7005

Parents Helping Parents, Inc.
3041 Olcott Street
Santa Clara, CA 95054-3222
(408)727-5775

Pro-ED
8700 Shoal Creek Boulevard
Austin, TX 78757-6897
(512)451-3246

Research Press
2612 North Mattis Avenue
Champaign, IL 61821
(217)352-3273

Sibling Information Network
A.J. Pappanikov Center
62 Washington Street
Middletown, CT 06457
(203)344-7500

Sonja Shankman Orthogenic School
1365 East 60th Street
Chicago, IL 60637
(312)702-1203

Sunburst Communications
39 Washington Avenue
P.O. Box 40
Pleasantville, NY 10570-0040
(800)431-1934

Tourette Syndrome Association
42-40 Bell Boulevard
Bayside, NY 11361
(718)224-2999

Very Special Arts
1331 F Street, N.W.
Education Office
John F. Kennedy Center for the Performing Arts
Washington, DC 20566
(202)662-2800
(800)933-8721
(202)737-0645 (TDD)

William Gladden Foundation
7 Bridge Street
Cameron, WV 26033
(304)686-3247
To Order information from the Gladden Foundation contact:
Continental Press Publisher
520 East Bainbridge Street
Elizabethtown, PA 17022
(800)795-7475

SOCIAL REINFORCERS: BUTTONS, CERTIFICATES, AND NOTES

Reinforcement Buttons

Hard Work Award

_____ has worked very hard today.

This award is given because of _____

hard work and effort.

_____
Teacher

Neatness Award

This award is given to

_____

for outstanding neatness.

_____
Teacher

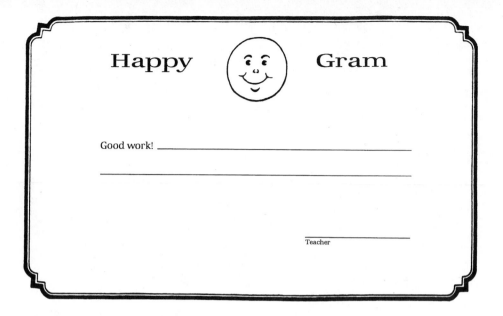

Happy Gram

Good work! _____

_____

_____
Teacher

I'm not lion!

_____ did a fantastic job of

_____

_____
Teacher

CERTIFICATE OF MERIT

This certifies that

_____

has done excellent work.

_____ *has* _____

_____.

_____
Teacher

Certificate of Improvement

_____ has improved performance on

_____

Keep up the good work!

Seal of
approval

_____
Teacher

Cooperation Award

_____

has been cooperative and helpful in the classroom.

_____
Date

_____
Teacher

_____

worked like a dog today to finish the work.

_____
Teacher

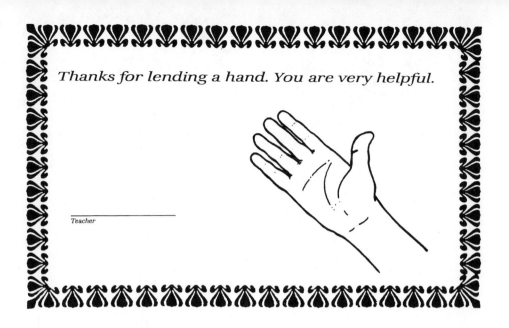

Thanks for lending a hand. You are very helpful.

_____
Teacher

_____

has had terrific bee-havior today.

_____
Date

_____
Teacher

_____

has earned _____ minutes of free time.

Congratulations!

Teacher

Top Secret Note

_____

has been doing very well at school.

_____

has worked hard, cooperated, and
followed the rules.

Teacher

Keep this note secret!

Thank You!

Your efforts at improving _____

_____ have been greatly appreciated.

Keep up the good work!

_____
Teacher

Daily Report Card

_____ had a fantastic day when it came to:

☐ Reading
☐ Arithmetic
☐ Handwriting
☐ Science
☐ English
☐ _____
☐ _____

☐ Cooperating
☐ Working hard
☐ Being helpful
☐ Getting along with others
☐ Finishing work
☐ _____

Date _____

_____
Teacher

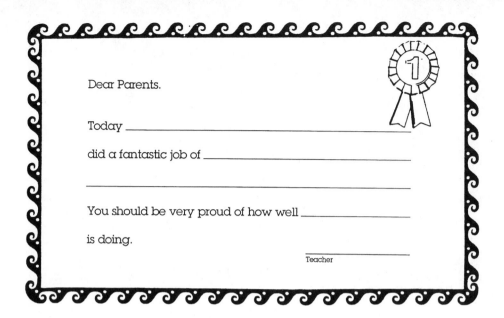

Dear Parents,

Today _____

did a fantastic job of _____

_____

You should be very proud of how well _____

is doing.

_____
Teacher

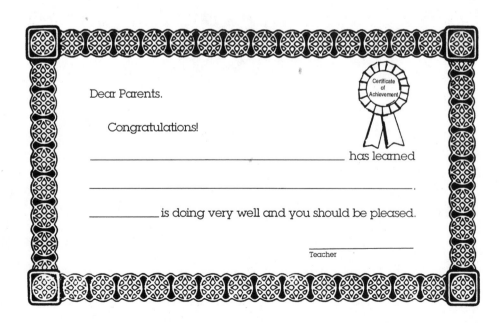

Dear Parents,

Congratulations!

_____ has learned

_____.

_____ is doing very well and you should be pleased.

_____
Teacher

Foley, R. M., 28
Forehand, R., 247
Forness, S. R., 8, 13, 14, 15, 328, 330, 347
Fortmeyer, D. J., 11
Fowler, S. A., 271
Foxx, R. M., 204, 231
Franchi, D., 111
Frank, A. R., 333, 383
Franklin, M. E., 74
Frick, P. J., 11
Friedman, R. M., 109, 326, 331
Friend, M., 312
Friesen, B. J., 109, 331
Friman, P. C., 220
Fuchs, D., 83, 91, 92, 310, 314
Fuchs, L., 83, 91, 92, 310, 314
Furlong, M., 350
Furukawa, M. J., 242

G

Gabel, R. A., 231, 382
Gadow, K. D., 29
Gaelick-Buys, L., 108
Gansneder, B., 83
Garber, M., 85
Gardner, R., 110, 297
Gast, D., 229
Gaston, E. T., 184
Gay, G., 77
George, M. P., 113, 130, 315, 380, 382
George, N. L., 113, 130, 315, 380, 382
Gersten, R., 86, 145, 315, 382
Gibson, S., 139
Giek, K., 170
Gil, E., 186
Glasser, W., 106, 266, 268, 288, 293, 294, 295, 296
Glick, P. C., 16, 318
Glickman, C. D., 120, 310, 398
Glomb, N., 269
Goerge, R. M., 22
Gold, M., 362
Golden, N., 239, 251, 259
Goldstein, A. P., 161, 243, 245, 249, 251, 253, 256, 258, 268, 276, 282
Gollnick, D. M., 77
Gonter, M., 82
Gonzalez, J. J., 9
Gonzalez, M., 46
Good, T. L., 144
Goodman, J., 268, 275
Goodman, Y. M., 149
Gordon, T., 175, 176

Graden, J. L., 309
Graham, S., 102, 108, 110, 116, 145, 149, 153
Grant, S., 22
Graves, A. W., 270
Graves, D., 149
Green, S. M., 11
Greenblatt, R. B., 399
Greer, B. B., 383
Greer, J. G., 383
Gresham, F. M., 49, 58, 238, 240
Griffith, D. R., 25
Grosenick, J. K., 113, 130, 315, 380, 382
Grotevant, H. D., 324
Grouws, D. A., 144
Guerrero, M., 77, 78, 79
Guetzloe, E. C., 15, 346, 363, 365, 366, 400
Guevremont, D. C., 9
Gunter, P. L., 87, 88, 111, 120, 223, 348
Gutkin, T. B., 308

H

Haager, D., 85
Hale, R. L., 143
Hall, K. S., 109, 326, 331
Hallahan, D. P., 16, 86, 170, 270, 272
Halpin, G., 56
Hammill, D. D., 47
Hampton, C., 325
Hanna, J., 20, 348
Hargreaves, A., 398
Haring, N., 46
Harmin, M., 189
Harper, R., 278, 279
Harriman, N. E., 143
Harris, D. B., 52
Harris, F. C., 15
Harris, I. D., 13
Harris, K. R., 102, 108, 110, 116, 144, 145, 149, 151, 153, 228, 267, 268, 269, 270, 271, 274, 287
Harris, W. B., 311
Harry, B., 74, 77, 78, 79
Harper, G. F., 248
Harter, S., 201
Hayes, S. C., 274
Hazel, J. S., 251, 256
Hebert, C. R., 174, 175
Hebert, G., 268
Hecimovic, A., 28
Hedin, D., 170
Heflin, L. J., 23, 24
Henggler, S. W., 328
Henley, M., 282, 285, 286

Wood, M. M., 106, 179, 266, 267, 268, 287, 288, 289, 290, 291, 350, 355
Woodruff, G., 25
Woolard, J., 403
Wright, G., 9, 29, 350
Wright, J. D., 23
Wulfert, E., 274
Wyka, G. T., 354
Wynne, E. A., 189, 192

Y

Yee, P., 149
Yell, M. L., 315, 361, 362
Young, C. C., 382

Young, K. R., 243, 269
Young, R. K., 110, 286
Ysseldyke, J., 53, 54, 145

Z

Zabel, M. K., 202, 225, 382
Zabel, R. H., 224, 349, 382
Zaccaria, J. S., 186
Zaragoza, N., 242
Zettle, R. D., 274
Zigmond, N., 84, 85
Zionts, P., 281, 282
Zirpoli, T. J., 19, 20, 60, 74
Zlotlow, S., 83

F

Facial expressions, 175
Families
  collaborating with parents and, 318–324
  expectations and beliefs of, 71–77
  preservation of, 325
  as systems, 70–77
  support services for, 332
Family Educational Rights and Privacy Act (1974),
    362–363
Family therapy, 72
Federation of Families for Children's Mental Health,
    330
Feelings, 160–193
  activities for identifying and expressing, 180–193
  psychodynamic and humanistic theories, 161–163
  strengths and limitations of supporting, 180
  supporting, of students in crisis, 178–179
  supporting and clarifying, 163–180
Fetal alcohol effect, 24
Fetal alcohol syndrome, 24
Fights, preventing and breaking up, 351–355
Foster care, children and youth living in, 21–23
Fourth Amendment, 360
Frequency count, 60–61
Freud, Anna, 104, 161
Freud, Sigmund, 104
Frustration, teaching acceptance, 283

G

Gangs, 358–363
  membership in, 28–33
  and search and seizure, 360
  slogans and terminology for, 34
  and suspension and expulsion, 360–362
  and transfer of records, 362–363
Generosity, 170
Goss v. Lopez, 360
Guided practice, 145–146

H

HIV infection and children with AIDS, 26–28
Honig v. Doe, 361, 362
Humanistic models, 104–105, 162

I

I CAN Strategy for Self-Reinforcement and Success,
    273
"I" messages, sending, 175–176, 178, 180
Id impulses, child responses to, 161
Inattention, 9
Inclusion, full, 313–316

Independence, 169–170
Individuals, sensitivity of teachers to needs of, 77–83
Individuals with Disabilities Education Act (IDEA)
    (1990), 9, 44, 130
  definition of serious emotional disturbance, 346
  and guarantee of appropriate special eduction pro-
    grams under, 327
  and level systems, 218
  rights of parents under, 73
  and transition planning, 332–333
Informal assessments of students with emotional and
    behavioral problems, 56–63
  anecdotal recording in, 60
  direct observation of behavior in, 59–60
  duration and latency recording in, 61–63
  event recording in, 60–61
  sociometrics in, 57–59
  time sampling in, 63
Instruction
  quality, 137–138
  relevant, and acceptable models of conduct, 88, 90
  teacher's use of models for, 144–145
Intermittent schedules of reinforcement, 216
Interviews in assessing students with emotional and
    behavioral disorders, 50–53
Invented spellings, 149

J

Job, social skills on, 259
Juvenile delinquency, 28–33, 346
Juvenile justice system and law enforcement, 327

L

Latency recording, 61–63
Law enforcement, and the juvenile justice system, 327
Learning, structured, 241–243
Learning Strategies Intervention Model, 151
Life Space Crisis Intervention, 116
Life Space Interview, 106
Listening skills, active-reflective, 175, 176–178, 180
Literature-based methods, 149

M

Mastery, 168–169
Mastery learning, empiricist models for, 145–149
McKinney, Stewart B., Homeless Assistance Act in
    1987, 23
Media, supportive
  strengths and limitations of, 187–188
  use of, in identifying and expressing feelings,
    181–187
Medications, side effects of, 367–368

I'd like to ask you a small favor. I have worked very hard to make this book readable and stimulating and would like to know if I have succeeded. Would you take a few minutes to fill out this form and tell me your reactions to this textbook? I will use your comments, suggestions, and criticisms to improve the next edition of *Strategies for Teaching Students with Emotional and Behavioral Disorders.*

School:_____

Instructor's name:_____

1. What did you like most about the book? _____

_____

_____

_____

2. What did you like least about the book? _____

_____

_____

_____

3. Were all the chapters assigned for you to read?   Yes _____   No_____

   If not, which ones were omitted?_____

4. Did you use the Application Exercises?   Yes_____   No _____

   Did you find them useful?   Yes _____   No_____

5. Do you own a computer? Yes_____   No _____

   If so, what type?_____

6. Do you use the Internet?   Yes _____   No _____

   If so, do you use it at school _____ , at home _____ , or both _____ ?

7. Will you keep this book or will you sell it? _____

8. In the space below (or in a separate letter) please make any other comments that you have about the book. I would really like to hear from you.

_____

_____

_____

Many thanks for taking the time to fill out this request.

Best wishes,
Ruth Lyn Meese

Brooks/Cole is dedicated to publishing quality books for special education. If you would like to learn more about our publications, please use this mailer to request our catalogue.

Name: _____

Street Address: _____

City, State, and Zip: _____

FOLD HERE

BUSINESS REPLY MAIL

FIRST CLASS   PERMIT NO. 358   PACIFIC GROVE, CA

POSTAGE WILL BE PAID BY ADDRESSEE

ATT: *Special Education* _____

**Brooks/Cole Publishing Company
511 Forest Lodge Road
Pacific Grove, California 93950-9968**

FOLD HERE